York Medieval Texts, second series

General Editors: Elizabeth Salter and Derek Pearsall
University of York

The Poems of the Pearl Manuscript

Pearl, Cleanness, Patience,
Sir Gawain and the Green Knight

Edited by Malcolm Andrew
and Ronald Waldron

University of California Press
Berkeley and Los Angeles
1979

© 1978 M. Andrew and R. A. Waldron

University of California Press
Berkeley and Los Angeles

ISBN 0-520-03794-4

Library of Congress Catalog Card Number: 78-64464

Printed in Great Britain

Contents

Preface

We are indebted to the British Library and the Council of the Early English Text Society for permission to base this edition on the manuscript and on the Society's facsimile edition (*Pearl, Cleanness, Patience and Sir Gawain, reproduced in facsimile from the unique MS. Cotton Nero A.x. in the British Museum,* with introduction by Sir I. Gollancz, London 1923).

The edition is presented as a fresh critical examination of the poems themselves and of their associated scholarship, and is designed to enable the modern reader, and particularly the university student, to reach a sensitive first-hand understanding of the text. An enterprise involving literature which has been as fully studied as these poems have in recent years could nevertheless not be carried out satisfactorily without a continuous critical use of the work of other scholars. Foremost among this previous work we must put the major editions of the separate poems (especially those of Gollancz, Tolkien, Gordon, Davis, Menner, and Anderson) which have served as constant mentors and guides; while we have tried to reach an independent judgement on every issue, we are gratefully aware that this is only possible in relation to the opinions of other scholars who have worked in the same field. The editions of the four poems by Cawley and Anderson, 1976, and by Moorman, 1977, and also the separate edition of *Cleanness* by Anderson, 1977, were published too late to be taken into account in the preparation of our own text and notes. We are happy, however, to have the opportunity of including a brief discussion of a number of points from the latter edition in the Additional Notes.

We gratefully acknowledge the help of the many colleagues who have answered queries or offered suggestions and also that of numerous groups of students with whom we have studied these poems over the years. Responsibility for the result, whatever its errors and deficiencies, can only be ours.

We owe a special debt of gratitude for secretarial help to Pat Nightingale and we also wish to thank our respective academic institutions, the University of East Anglia, Norwich, and University of London King's College for the generous provision of time and facilities for research.

Abbreviations

AV	Authorized Version
ChR	*Chaucer Review*
Cl	*Cleanness*
CT	*The Canterbury Tales*, ed. F. N. Robinson, in *The Complete Works of Geoffrey Chaucer* (2nd edn., London, 1957)
EDD	*English Dialect Dictionary*
EETS	Early English Text Society (OS: Ordinary Series; ES: Extra Series)
ELH	*ELH: A Journal of English Literary History*
ELN	*English Language Notes*
EME	Early Middle English
ES	*English Studies*
Fr	French
FMLS	*Forum for Modern Language Studies*
G	*Sir Gawain and the Green Knight*
Heb	Hebrew
JEGP	*Journal of English and Germanic Philology*
L	Latin
MÆ	*Medium Ævum*
ME	Middle English
MED	*Middle English Dictionary*
MLN	*Modern Language Notes*
MLQ	*Modern Language Quarterly*
MLR	*Modern Language Review*
ModE	Modern English
ModFr	Modern French
MP	*Modern Philology*
MS	Manuscript
Neophil.	*Neophilologus*
Neu.Mitt.	*Neuphilologische Mitteilungen*
NQ	*Notes and Queries*
NT	New Testament
OE	Old English
OED	*Oxford English Dictionary*
OF	Old French
OIcel	Old Icelandic
om.	*omits*
ON	Old Norse
OT	Old Testament
Pat	*Patience*
Pe	*Pearl*

PL	*Patrologiae Cursus Completus* . . . Series Latina, ed. J.-P. Migne (Paris, 1878–90)
PMLA	*Publications of the Modern Language Association*
PPl	*Piers Plowman*
PQ	*Philological Quarterly*
RES	*Review of English Studies* (ns: new series)
SOED	*Shorter Oxford English Dictionary*
SP	*Studies in Philology*
Spec.	*Speculum*
Stud.Neo.	*Studia Neophilologica*
TG, TG-Davis	see Bibliography, section **2d**
Trevisa	*On the Properties of Things: John Trevisa's translation of 'Bartholomæus Anglicus De Proprietatibus Rerum'*, 2 vols. (Oxford, 1975)
UTQ	*University of Toronto Quarterly*
Whiting	Bartlett J. Whiting and Helen W. Whiting, *Proverbs, Sentences, and Proverbial Phrases from English Writings mainly before 1500* (Cambridge, Mass. and London, 1968)

Select Bibliography

1 *Facsimile*

Pearl, Cleanness, Patience and Sir Gawain, reproduced in facsimile from the unique MS. Cotton Nero A.x. in the British Museum, intro. Sir I. Gollancz (London, EETS OS 162, 1923)

2 *Editions of Individual Poems*

a *Pearl*

Pearl, ed. and tr. Sir Israel Gollancz (London, 1891; rev. edn., 1897; 2nd edn., with Boccaccio's *Olympia*, 1921)
The Pearl, ed. Charles G. Osgood (Boston and London, 1906)
The Pearl, ed. Stanley P. Chase and others (Boston, 1932)
Pearl, ed. E. V. Gordon (Oxford, 1953)
The Pearl, ed. and tr. Sister Mary V. Hillmann (New York, 1961; 2nd edn., with intro. by Edward Vasta, 1967)
Anonymous: The Pearl, ed. Sara deFord, tr. Sara deFord and others (Northbrook, Ill., 1967)

b *Cleanness*

Purity, ed. Robert J. Menner (New Haven, Conn. and London, 1920; repr., Hamden, Conn., 1970)
Cleanness, ed. Sir Israel Gollancz (London, Part I, 1921, Part II, 1933; repr. in one vol., with tr. by D. S. Brewer, Cambridge and Totowa, N.J., 1974)
Cleanness, ed. J. J. Anderson (Manchester and New York, 1977)

c *Patience*

Patience, ed. Hartley Bateson (Manchester, 1912; 2nd edn., 1918)
Patience, ed. Sir Israel Gollancz (London, 1913; 2nd edn., 1924)
Patience, ed. J. J. Anderson (Manchester and New York, 1969)

d *Sir Gawain and the Green Knight*

Syr Gawayne, ed. Sir Frederic Madden (London, 1839)
Sir Gawayne and the Green Knight, ed. R. Morris (London, EETS OS 4, 1864; rev. Sir Israel Gollancz 1897 and 1912)
Sir Gawain and the Green Knight, ed. J. R. R. Tolkien and E. V. Gordon (Oxford, 1925) [referred to in notes as TG]
Sir Gawain and the Green Knight, ed. Sir Israel Gollancz, with intro. by Mabel Day and Mary S. Serjeantson (London, EETS OS 210, 1940)

6   *Bibliography*

Sir Gawain and the Green Knight, ed. J. R. R. Tolkien and E. V. Gordon, 2nd edn., rev. Norman Davis (Oxford, 1967) [referred to in notes as TG-Davis]
Sir Gawain and the Green Knight, ed. R. A. Waldron (London, 1970)
Sir Gawain and the Green Knight, ed. J. A. Burrow (Harmondsworth, 1972)
Sir Gawain and the Green Knight, ed. and tr. W. R. J. Barron (Manchester and New York, 1974)

3   *Editions of more than one Poem*

Early English Alliterative Poems, ed. Richard Morris (EETS OS 1, 1864) [contains *Pearl, Cleanness* and *Patience*]
Pearl; Sir Gawain and the Green Knight, ed. A. C. Cawley (London and New York, 1962)
Pearl, Cleanness, Patience and Sir Gawain and the Green Knight, ed. A. C. Cawley and J. J. Anderson (London and New York, 1976)
The Works of the 'Gawain'-Poet, ed. Charles Moorman (Jackson, Miss., 1977)

4   *Translations (see also* 2a, b, d)

Sir Gawain and the Green Knight, tr. Gwyn Jones (London, 1952)
Sir Gawain and the Green Knight, tr. Brian Stone (Harmondsworth, 1959)
Medieval English Verse, tr. Brian Stone (Harmondsworth, 1964) [contains translations of *Patience* and *Pearl*]
The Complete Works of the Gawain Poet, tr. John Gardner (Chicago, London and Amsterdam, 1965)
Sir Gawain and the Green Knight, tr. Marie Borroff (New York, 1967)
The Owl and the Nightingale; Cleanness; St Erkenwald, tr. Brian Stone (Harmondsworth, 1971)

5   *Textual Notes*

[discussions of textual matters, other than those listed under critical studies]

a   *Pearl*

Oliver F. Emerson, *PMLA*, 37 (1922), 52–93, 42 (1927), 807–31
Wilhelm Fick, *Zum mittelenglischen Gedicht von der Perle: Eine Lautuntersuchung* (Kiel, 1885)
David C. Fowler, *MLN*, 74 (1959), 581–4; *MLQ*, 21 (1960), 27–9
E. V. Gordon and C. T. Onions, *MÆ*, 1 (1932), 126–36, 2 (1933), 165–88
Marie P. Hamilton, *JEGP*, 57 (1958), 177–91
F. Holthausen, *Archiv*, 90 (1893), 143–8
E. Kölbing, *Englische Studien*, 16 (1892), 268–73
Elizabeth M. Wright, *JEGP*, 38 (1939), 1–22, 39 (1940), 315–18

b   *Cleanness*

Hartley Bateson, *MLR*, 13 (1918), 377–86, 19 (1924), 95–101
Bülbring, quoted by Karl Schumacher, *Studien über den Stabreim in der mittelenglischen Alliterationsdichtung* (Bonn, 1914)

Oliver F. Emerson, *MLR*, 10 (1915), 373–5; *PMLA*, 34 (1919), 494–522
David C. Fowler, *MP*, 70 (1972–3), 331–6
C. A. Luttrell, *NQ*, 197 (1952), 23–4
P. G. Thomas, *MLR*, 17 (1922), 64–6

c *Patience*

Eilert Ekwall, *Englische Studien*, 47 (1913–14), 313–16, 49 (1915–16), 144–6,
   483–4; *Anglia Beiblatt*, 24 (1913), 133–6
Oliver F. Emerson, *MLN*, 28 (1913), 171–80, 29 (1914), 85–6, 31 (1916), 1–
   10; *Englische Studien*, 47 (1913–14), 125–31
J. H. G. Grattan, *MLR*, 9 (1914), 403–5
C. T. Onions, *Englische Studien*, 47 (1913–14), 316–17
Julius Zupitza, *Alt- und mittelenglisches Übungsbuch* (5th edn., Vienna, 1897)

d *Sir Gawain and the Green Knight*

J. A. W. Bennett, *Supplementary Notes on G*, 1–4 (Cambridge, 1972–6)
Ralph W. V. Elliott, 'Some Northern Landscape Features in *G*', in *Iceland
   and the Mediaeval World: Studies in Honour of Ian Maxwell*, ed. Gabriel
   Turville-Petre and John S. Martin (Melbourne, 1974)
Thomas A. Knott, *MLN*, 30 (1915), 102–8
C. T. Onions, *NQ*, 146 (1924), 203–4, 244–5, 285–6
Elizabeth M. Wright, *JEGP*, 34 (1935), 157–79, 339–50

6 *Textual Notes on more than one Poem*

Oliver F. Emerson, *MP*, 19 (1921–2), 131–41
Joseph Fischer, *Die Stabende Langzeile in den Werken des Gawain-Dichters*
   (Bonn, 1901)
C. A. Luttrell, *Neophil.*, 39 (1955), 207–17, 40 (1956), 290–301; *NQ*, 207
   (1962), 447–50
Charles Moorman, *Southern Quarterly*, 4 (1965–6), 67–73

7 *Criticism on individual Poems*

a *Pearl*

Robert W. Ackerman, 'The Pearl-Maiden and the Penny', *Romance
   Philology*, 17 (1964), 615–23 [*see* Conley, 1970]
Ian Bishop, *Pearl in its Setting: A Critical Study of the Structure and Meaning of
   the Middle English Poem* (Oxford, 1968)
Louis Blenkner, 'The Pattern of Traditional Images in *Pearl*', *SP*, 68 (1971),
   26–49
———, 'The Theological Structure of Pearl', *Traditio*, 24 (1968), 43–75 [*see*
   Conley, 1970]
John Conley, ed., *The Middle English 'Pearl': Critical Essays* (Notre Dame
   and London, 1970) [contains, with other reprints, Ackerman, 1964;
   Blenkner, 1968; Conley, 1955; Davis, 1966; Hoffman, 1960; Johnson,
   1953; Kellogg, 1956; Luttrell, 1965; Macrae-Gibson, 1968; Moorman,

1955; Pilch, 1964; Robertson, 1955a,b, Spearing, 1962; Stern, 1955; Tristman, 1955; Vasta, 1967; Visser, 1958]

James W. Earl, 'Saint Margaret and the Pearl Maiden', *MP*, 70 (1972–3), 1–8

Dorothy Everett and Naomi D. Hurnard, 'Legal phraseology in a passage in *Pearl*', *MÆ*, 16 (1947), 9–15

John Finlayson, '*Pearl*: Landscape and Vision', *SP*, 71 (1974), 314–43

Jefferson B. Fletcher, 'The Allegory of the Pearl', *JEGP*, 20 (1921), 1–21 [*see* Blanch, 1966]

John Gatta, Jr., 'Transformation Symbolism and the Liturgy of the Mass in *Pearl*', *MP*, 71 (1973–4), 243–56

Marie P. Hamilton, 'The Meaning of the Middle English *Pearl*', *PMLA*, 70 (1955), 805–24 [*see* Blanch, 1966]

Elizabeth Hart, 'The Heaven of Virgins', *MLN*, 42 (1927), 113–16

A. R. Heiserman, 'The Plot of *Pearl*', *PMLA*, 80 (1965), 164–71

Constance Hieatt, '*Pearl* and the Dream-Vision Tradition', *Stud.Neo.*, 37 (1965), 139–45

Elton D. Higgs, 'The Progress of the Dreamer in *Pearl*', *Studies in Medieval Culture*, 4 (1974), 388–400

Stanton de V. Hoffman, 'The *Pearl*: Notes for an Interpretation', *MP*, 58 (1960–61), 73–80 [*see* Conley, 1970]

Wendell S. Johnson, 'The Imagery and Diction of *The Pearl*: Toward an Interpretation', *ELH*, 20 (1953), 161–80 [*see* Conley, 1970]

P. M. Kean, *The Pearl: An Interpretation* (London, 1967)

C. A. Luttrell, 'The Mediæval Tradition of the Pearl Virginity', *MÆ*, 31 (1962), 194–200

——, '*Pearl*: Symbolism in a Garden Setting', *Neophil.*, 49 (1965), 160–76 [*see* Blanch, 1966; Conley, 1970]

John C. McGalliard, 'Links, Language and Style in *The Pearl*', in *Studies in Language, Literature and Culture of the Middle Ages and Later: Studies in Honor of Rudolph Willard*, ed. E. Bagby Atwood and Archibald A. Hill (Austin, Texas, 1969)

O. D. Macrae-Gibson, '*Pearl*: The Link-Words and the Thematic Structure', *Neophil.*, 52 (1968), 54–64 [*see* Conley, 1970]

Michael H. Means, 'The "Pure" Consolatio: *Pearl*', in *The Consolatio Genre in Medieval English Literature* (Gainesville, Fla., 1972)

James Milroy, '*Pearl*: The Verbal Texture and the Linguistic Theme', *Neophil.*, 55 (1971), 195–208

Charles Moorman, 'The Role of the Narrator in *Pearl*', *MP*, 53 (1955–6), 73–81

James P. Oakden, 'The Liturgical Influence in *Pearl*', in *Chaucer und seine Zeit: Symposium für Walter F. Schirmer*, ed. Arno Esch (Tübingen, 1968)

Howard R. Patch, *The Other World, According to Descriptions in Medieval Literature* (Cambridge, Mass., 1950)

Paul Piehler, '*Pearl*', in *The Visionary Landscape: A Study in Medieval Allegory* (London, 1971)

Herbert Pilch, 'Das mittelenglische Perlegedicht: Sein Verhältnis zum Rosenroman', *Neu.Mitt.*, 65 (1964), 427–46 [appears in Conley, 1970, tr.

Heide Hyprath, as 'The Middle English *Pearl*: Its Relation to the *Roman de la Rose*']

Thomas A. Reisner, 'The "Cortaysye" Sequence in *Pearl*: A Legal Interpretation', *MP*, 72 (1974–5), 400–403

F. E. Richardson, 'The Pearl: A Poem and Its Audience', *Neophil.*, 46 (1962), 308–16

D. W. Robertson, Jr. 'The Doctrine of Charity in Mediaeval Literary Gardens', *Spec.*, 26 (1951), 24–49

——, 'The "Heresy" of *The Pearl*', *MLN*, 65 (1950a), 152–5 [*see* Conley, 1970]

——, 'The Pearl as a Symbol', *MLN*, 65 (1950b), 155–61 [*see* Conley, 1970]

Maren-Sofie Røstvig, 'Numerical Composition in *Pearl*: a Theory', *ES*, 48 (1967), 326–32

Larry M. Sklute, 'Expectation and Fulfillment in *Pearl*', *PQ*, 52 (1973), 663–79

A. C. Spearing, 'The Alliterative Tradition: *Pearl*', *Medieval Dream Poetry* (Cambridge, 1976)

——, 'Symbolic and Dramatic Development in *Pearl*', *MP*, 60 (1962–3), 1–12 [*see* Blanch, 1966; Conley, 1970]

Milton R. Stern, 'An Approach to *The Pearl*', *JEGP*, 54 (1955), 684–92 [*see* Conley, 1970]

Richard Tristman, 'Some Consolatory Strategies in *Pearl*', [*see* Conley, 1970]

V. E. Watts, '*Pearl* as a Consolatio', *MÆ*, 32 (1963), 34–6

René Wellek, '*The Pearl*', *Studies in English by Members of the English Seminar of the Charles University, Prague*, 4 (1933), 5–33

Edward Wilson, 'Word Play and the Interpretation of *Pearl*', *MÆ*, 40 (1971), 116–34

Ann D. Wood, 'The Pearl-Dreamer and the "Hyne" in the Vineyard Parable', *PQ*, 52 (1973), 9–19

b *Cleanness*

Penelope B. R. Doob, 'Nebuchadnezzar and the conventions of Madness', in *Nebuchadnezzar's Children: Conventions of Madness in Middle English Literature* (New Haven, Conn. and London, 1974)

Michael M. Foley, 'A Bibliography of *Purity* (*Cleanness*), 1864–1972', *ChR*, 8 (1973–4), 324–34

T. D. Kelly and J. T. Irwin, 'The meaning of *Cleanness*: parable as effective sign', *Mediaeval Studies*, 35 (1973), 232–60

C. A. Luttrell, '*Cleanness* and the Knight of La Tour Landry', *MÆ*, 29 (1960), 187–9

Charlotte C. Morse, 'The Image of the Vessel in *Cleanness*', *UTQ*, 40 (1970–71), 202–16

——, *The Pattern of Judgment in the 'Queste' and 'Cleanness'* (Columbia, Mo. and London, 1978)

c *Patience*

J. J. Anderson, 'The Prologue of *Patience*', *MP*, 63 (1965–6), 283–7

Malcolm Andrew, 'Jonah and Christ in *Patience*', *MP*, 70 (1972–3), 230–33
——, '*Patience*: the "Munster Dor" ', *ELN*, 14 (1976–7), 164–7
Normand Berlin, '*Patience:* A Study in Poetic Elaboration', *Stud.Neo.*, 33 (1961), 80–85
F. N. M. Diekstra, 'Jonah and *Patience*: The Psychology of a Prophet', *ES*, 55 (1974), 205–17
Ordelle G. Hill, 'The Audience of *Patience*', *MP*, 66 (1968–9), 103–9
——, 'The Late-Latin *De Jona* as a Source for *Patience*', *JEGP*, 66 (1967), 21–5
Ellin M. Kelly, 'Parallels between the Middle English *Patience* and *Hymnus Ieiunantium* of Prudentius', *ELN*, 4 (1966–7), 244–7
Charles Moorman, 'The Role of the Narrator in *Patience*', *MP*, 61 (1963–4), 90–95
Jay Schleusener, 'History and Action in *Patience*', *PMLA*, 86 (1971), 959–65
A. C. Spearing, '*Patience* and the *Gawain*-Poet', *Anglia*, 84 (1966), 305–29
William Vantuono, 'The Question of Quatrains in *Patience*', *Manuscripta*, 16 (1972), 24–30
David Williams, 'The Point of *Patience*', *MP*, 68 (1970–71), 127–36

d   *Sir Gawain and the Green Knight*

Robert W. Ackerman, 'Gawain's Shield: Penitential Doctrine in *G*', *Anglia*, 76 (1958), 254–65
Larry D. Benson, *Art and Tradition in 'Sir Gawain and the Green Knight'* (New Brunswick, N.J., 1965) [*see* Fox, 1968; Howard and Zacher, 1968]
Sacvan Bercovitch, 'Romance and Anti-Romance in *G*', *PQ,* 44 (1965), 30–37 [*see* Howard and Zacher, 1968]
Morton W. Bloomfield, '*G*: An Appraisal', *PMLA*, 76 (1961), 7–19 [*see* Howard and Zacher, 1968]
Marie Borroff, '*Sir Gawain and the Green Knight': A Stylistic and Metrical Study* (New Haven, Conn. and London, 1962) [*see* Fox, 1968; Howard and Zacher, 1968]
R. H. Bowers, '*G* as Entertainment', *MLQ,* 24 (1963), 333–41 [*see* Howard and Zacher, 1968]
John Burrow, *A Reading of 'Sir Gawain and the Green Knight'* (London, 1965) [*see* Fox, 1968]
——, reply to Hills, 1963, in *RES*, ns 15 (1964), 56 [*see* Howard and Zacher, 1968]
——, 'The Two Confession Scenes in *G*', *MP*, 57 (1959–60), 73–9 [*see* Blanch, 1966]
Cecily Clark, '*G*: Characterization by Syntax', *Essays in Criticism*, 16 (1966), 361–74 [*see* Fox, 1968]
——, '*G*: Its Artistry and Its Audience', *MÆ*, 40 (1971), 10–20
Paul Delany, 'The Role of the Guide in *G*', *Neophil.*, 49 (1965), 250–55 [*see* Howard and Zacher, 1968]
George J. Engelhardt, 'The Predicament of Gawain', *MLQ* , 16 (1955), 218–25 [repr. in *Middle English Survey*, ed. Edward Vasta (Notre Dame, 1965)]

W. O. Evans, 'The Case for Sir Gawain Re-opened', *MLR* 68 (1973), 721–33

P. J. C. Field, 'A Rereading of *G*', *SP*, 68 (1971), 255–69

M.M.Foley,'Gawain's Two Confessions Reconsidered',*ChR*,9(1974),73–9

Denton Fox, ed., *Twentieth Century Interpretations of 'Sir Gawain and the Green Knight'* (Englewood Cliffs, N.J., 1968) [contains an introductory essay and edited extracts from Benson, 1965; Borroff, 1962; Burrow, 1965; Clark, 1966; Everett, 1955; Howard, 1964; Spearing, 1966; Speirs, 1949; and others]

Albert B. Friedman, 'Morgan le Fay in *G*', *Spec.*, 35 (1960), 260–74 [*see* Blanch, 1966]

Richard H. Green, 'Gawain's Shield and the Quest for Perfection', *ELH*, 29 (1962), 121–39 [*see* Blanch, 1966; also repr. in *Middle English Survey*, ed. Edward Vasta (Notre Dame, 1965)]

Avril Henry, 'Temptation and Hunt in *G*', *MÆ*, 45 (1976), 187–99

David F. Hills, 'Gawain's Fault in *G*', *RES*, ns 14 (1963), 124–31 [*see* Howard and Zacher, 1968]

Donald R. Howard, 'Structure and Symmetry in *G*', *Spec.*, 39 (1964), 425–33 [*see* Blanch, 1966; Fox, 1968; Howard and Zacher, 1968]

—— and Christian K. Zacher, ed., *Critical Studies of 'Sir Gawain and the Green Knight'* (Notre Dame and London, 1968) [contains, with other reprints, Bercovitch, 1965; Bloomfield, 1961; Bowers, 1963; Burrow, 1964; Delany, 1965; Hills, 1963; Howard, 1964; Loomis, 1959; M. Mills, 1965; and extracts from Benson, 1965; Borroff, 1962; Spearing, 1964]

S. S. Hussey, 'Sir Gawain and Romance Writing', *Stud.Neo.*, 40 (1968), 161–74

R. C. Johnstone and D. D. R. Owen, ed., *Two Old French Gauvain Romances: 'Le Chevalier à L'Epée' and 'La Mule sans Frein'* (Edinburgh, 1972)

George Kane, *Middle English Literature: A Critical Study of the Romances, the Religious Lyrics and Piers Plowman* (London, 1951)

J. F. Kiteley, 'The *De Arte Honeste Amandi* of Andreas Capellanus and the Concept of Courtesy in *G*', *Anglia*, 79 (1961), 7–16

John Leyerle, 'The Game and Play of Hero', in *Concepts of the Hero in the Middle Ages and the Renaissance*, ed. Norman T. Burns and Christopher Reagan (New York, 1975)

Laura H. Loomis, '*Gawain and the Green Knight*', *Arthurian Literature in the Middle Ages: A Collaborative History*, ed. Roger S. Loomis (Oxford, 1959) [*see* Howard and Zacher, 1968]

T. McAlindon, 'Magic, Fate, and Providence in Medieval Narrative and *G*', *RES*, ns 16 (1965), 121–39

Alan M. Markman, 'The Meaning of *G*', *PMLA*, 72 (1957), 574–86 [*see* Blanch, 1966]

Dieter Mehl, ' "Point of View" in mittelenglischen Romanzen', *Germanisch-romanisch Monatsschrift*, 45 (1964), 35–45

David Mills, 'An Analysis of the Temptation Scenes in *G*', *JEGP*, 67 (1968), 612–30

M. Mills, 'Christian Significance and Romance Tradition in *G*', *MLR*, 60 (1965), 483–93 [*see* Howard and Zacher, 1968]

D. D. R. Owen, 'Burlesque Tradition and *G*', *FMLS*, 4 (1968), 125–45

D. A. Pearsall, 'Rhetorical "Descriptio" in *G*', *MLR*, 50 (1955), 129–34

Alain Renoir, 'Descriptive Technique in *G*', *Orbis Litterarum*, 13 (1958), 126–32

Henry L. Savage, *The Gawain Poet: Studies in his Personality and Background* (Chapel Hill, N.C., 1956)

——, 'The Significance of the Hunting Scenes in *G*', *JEGP*, 27 (1928), 1–15

Hans Schnyder, *'Sir Gawain and the Green Knight': An Essay in Interpretation* (Berne, 1961)

Gordon M. Shedd, 'Knight in Tarnished Armour: The Meaning of *G*', *MLR*, 62 (1967), 3–13

Theodore Silverstein, 'The Art of *G*', *UTQ*, 33 (1963–4), 258–78 [*see* Howard and Zacher, 1968]

——, '*Sir Gawain*, Dear Brutus, and Britain's Fortunate Founding: A Study in Comedy and Convention', *MP*, 62 (1964–5), 189–206

G. V. Smithers, 'What *G* is About', *MÆ*, 32 (1963), 171–89

A. C. Spearing, *Criticism and Medieval Poetry* (London, 1964) [*see* Howard and Zacher, 1968]

John Speirs, '*G*', *Scrutiny*, 16 (1949), 274–300 [*see* Fox, 1968]

Martin Stevens, 'Laughter and Game in *G*', *Spec.*, 47 (1972), 65–78

P. B. Taylor, 'Commerce and Comedy in *G*', *PQ*, 50 (1971), 1–15

Joan Turville-Petre, 'The Metre of *G*,' *ES*, 57 (1976), 310–28

Rüdiger Zimmerman, 'Verbal Syntax and Style in *G*', *ES*, 54 (1973), 533–43

8   *Criticism on more than one Poem, or of more general interest*

Albert C. Baugh, 'The Alliterative Revival', in *A Literary History of England* (New York, 1948)

Robert J. Blanch, ed., *'Sir Gawain' and 'Pearl': Critical Essays* (Bloomington, Indiana and London, 1966) [contains: on *Pe*: Blanch, 1965; Hamilton, 1955; Luttrell, 1965; Spearing, 1962; Wellek, 1933; on *G*: Burrow, 1959; Friedman, 1960; Green, 1962; Howard, 1964; Markman, 1957; Moorman, 1956]

D. S. Brewer, 'Courtesy and the *Gawain*-Poet', in *Patterns of Love and Courtesy: Essays in Memory of C. S. Lewis*, ed. John Lawlor (London, 1966)

J. A. Burrow, *Ricardian Poetry: Chaucer, Gower, Langland and the 'Gawain' Poet* (London, 1971)

W. A. Davenport, *The Art of the Gawain-Poet* (London, 1978)

Dorothy Everett, 'The Alliterative Revival', *Essays on Middle English Literature*, ed. Patricia Kean (Oxford, 1955)

Barnet Kottler and Alan M. Markman, *A Concordance to Five Middle English Poems: Cleanness, St Erkenwald, Sir Gawain and the Green Knight, Patience, Pearl* (Pittsburg, 1966)

Charles Moorman, *The Pearl-Poet* (New York, 1968)

Charles Muscatine, 'The *Pearl* Poet: Style as Defense', in *Poetry and Crisis in the Age of Chaucer* (Notre Dame and London, 1972)

J. P. Oakden, *Alliterative Poetry in Middle English*, 2 vols. (Manchester, 1930, 1935)

D. D. R. Owen, 'The Gawain-Poet', *FMLS*, 8 (1972), 79–84

Derek Pearsall and Elizabeth Salter, *Landscapes and Seasons of the Medieval World* (London and Toronto, 1973)

Elizabeth Salter, 'The Alliterative Revival', *MP*, 64 (1966–7), 146–50 and 233–7

A. C. Spearing, *The Gawain-Poet: A Critical Study* (Cambridge, 1970)

John Speirs, *Medieval English Poetry: the Non-Chaucerian Tradition* (London, 1957)

Thorlac Turville-Petre, *The Alliterative Revival* (Cambridge and Totowa, N.J., 1977)

William Vantuono, '*Patience, Cleanness, Pearl*, and *Gawain*: the case for common authorship', *Annuale Medievale*, 12 (1971), 37–69

D. J. Williams, 'Alliterative Poetry in the Fourteenth and Fifteenth Centuries', in *History of Literature in the English Language*, vol. 1, *The Middle Ages*, ed. W. F. Bolton (London, 1970)

Edward Wilson, *The Gawain-Poet* (Leiden, 1976)

Introduction

The four poems here edited are extant in one manuscript only—MS Cotton Nero A.x, Art. 3, in the British Library—written in the late fourteenth century. *Pearl*, *Cleanness* and *Patience* were first edited for print by Morris as late as 1864, though *Sir Gawain* had been published earlier in a separate edition for the Bannatyne Club (*Syr Gawayne*, ed. Sir Frederic Madden). They have since won an assured place of esteem among readers of Middle English literature, though limits have been set to their popularity by their difficult language and the overtly religious subject-matter of three of them.

The poems belong to the native tradition of alliterative composition, which was maintained in the West and North, rather than to the newer continental modes of verse practised by Chaucer and Gower in the court circles of the South-east. Chaucer probably expects his readers to smile in sympathy when he has the Parson say

> But trusteth wel, I am a Southren man,
> I kan nat geeste 'rum, ram, ruf,' by lettre,
>
> > (*CT* X.42f)

but we would surely be wrong to assume that Chaucer's poems and these belong to two entirely different cultures. Medieval patrons of letters like John of Gaunt (who owned estates and castles in many parts of the midlands and the north, as well as in London) were both courtiers and provincial magnates, and their taste in literature was undoubtedly more catholic than that of Chaucer's Parson (Salter, **8**[1] 1966–7). Langland, though a western man who chose the alliterative long line for his poem, nevertheless spent much of his life in London, and *Piers Plowman* was read in the fourteenth century well beyond the confines of the areas where alliterative composition was actually practised. Furthermore, within these four alliterative poems—to look no further into the works of the 'Alliterative Revival'—there is evidence of familiarity with court life and courtly romance, with the niceties of legal terminology and rhetorical precept, as well as a good deal of miscellaneous learning. The poems are provincial only in the sense that it was still possible for a writer in the fourteenth century—before the development of an exclusive 'standard English'—to use a provincial dialect, without affectation, as a literary vehicle for any subject-matter whatever.

The poems are almost universally regarded as the works of a single author

---

[1] The bold numbers in references indicate the section of the Bibliography in which the work can be found.

(variously designated 'the *Gawain*-poet' and 'the *Pearl*-poet') but there is no external evidence of this[2] and much of what has been claimed or assumed as evidence in the past can be challenged if taken piecemeal. The facts that the poems survive in the same manuscript and are written in one hand in a consistent dialect which must be very close to that of the originals may, of themselves, point no farther than to the scribe. Arguments based on similarities of expression are rendered unreliable by the common nature of alliterative phraseology; and judgements of similarity of thought and attitude necessarily have a large subjective element.

Nevertheless it has been the experience of many readers who have approached the poems without preconceptions as to authorship that with familiarity the conviction of an individual poetic personality grows: we recognize an unbroken consistency of thought throughout; a group of favoured themes (e.g. patience and humility set against pride, earthly and heavenly courtesy, purity, perfection) is woven into a variety of patterns, often in language which is immediately reminiscent of other contexts. The resemblances extend from those of structural thought-pattern (e.g. in all four poems a human—the Dreamer, Jonah, Abraham, Gawain—is in intellectual conflict with an 'other-world' being, and echoes of characterization and 'tone' break through the different stories) to similarities of imagery, diction and figures of speech. The persuasiveness of these similarities as evidence that the hand of one man was responsible for the poems is enhanced by their range and variety, by the complete absence of any counter-evidence of multiple authorship, and by the sheer number of instances.[3]

Quite apart from the hypothesis of common authorship, it is the reader's sense of common areas of thought and expression in these poems that justifies (over and above the mere fact of their occurrence in a single manuscript) their publication as a unified body of poetic works. The poems do, of course, make sense individually and can be read as separate works; read together, they also insistently illuminate one another and create a sense of articulated unity which is initially surprising, perhaps, in view of the very apparent differences between them in structure and genre.

The most cohesive force in the four poems is the body of intellectual and moral beliefs assumed and analysed within them. These beliefs are in essence those of orthodox medieval Christianity together with those of the chivalric social morality of the high Middle Ages, here held in a specially close relationship, so that (for instance) God's grace towards Nineveh is an example of

---

[2] Attempts to reveal the name Masse (Massey), by the use of numerological keys, have not been entirely convincing (see B. Nolan and D. F. Hills, *RES*, ns 22 [1971], 295–302; C. J. Peterson, *RES*, ns 25 [1974], 49–53, 257–66).

[3] See Spearing, **7c** 1966, **8** 1970; Vantuono, **8** 1971. Göran Kjellmer, in *Did The "Pearl Poet" Write 'Pearl'?*, Gothenburg Studies in English 30, 1975, gives a useful bibliography of the authorship question. His own contribution, however, which examines the degree of deviation from a 'norm' in the poems' use of eight linguistic variables, is vitiated by his failure to recognize that most (if not all) of the chosen variables might be affected by formal characteristics of the poems—especially stanza-form, length and rhythm of the line, dream-vision convention, and genre.

cortaysye or *debonerté* (*Pat* 417f) and Gawain's virtues, as symbolized in the pentangle, are simultaneously the virtues of perfect knighthood and perfect Christian conduct. At lowest estimate we have in these poems a number of very skilful exercises in the translation of moral didacticism into distinct forms of art: literary homily, dream vision, romance. However, this is far from implying that the poetry is something superadded to the theology and morality. For the sacramental view of the things of earth which we meet in these poems—the urge to link and merge the earthly with the heavenly—makes the use of literary vehicles such as character, action, metaphor, allegory, ambiguity, and symbolism not merely illustrative and persuasive, but also analytical and exploratory.

Literary Homily: Patience and Cleanness

Two of the poems—*Patience* and *Cleanness*—are in an overt and unambiguous way didactic and provide us with the simplest pattern of the relation between art and morality. Superficially, the art most in evidence here is the direct persuasive art of the sermon, with its explicit moral exhortation, its affective *exempla* and its warnings of the consequences of sin. The poem's audience, whether this is conceived as a group of listeners or a solitary reader, is cast in the role of recipient of instruction, a role akin to that of a congregation hearing a sermon. This relationship between poet and audience, implicit for the most part in *Cleanness*, presented more explicitly in *Patience*, creates a didactic context for the purely aesthetic qualities in both poems and defines the poet's ruling concern as that of pointing out Christian principles and encouraging his audience to follow them.

In the medieval sermon a Christian precept is presented and defined in abstract terms, often in relation to a scriptural text, and is then demonstrated in an *exemplum*, a story designed to illustrate or exemplify the precept in practice. It is this method which underlies the structure of *Patience* and *Cleanness*; but this is not to say that the poems are only sermons in verse. In both poems the narrative element (a single biblical story in *Patience*, three main episodes and a number of subsidiary ones in *Cleanness*) is much greater than it would be in a sermon and carries much of the persuasive force; the biblical material is retold with vivid realistic detail and the reader is drawn in emotionally, in a pattern of identification with and aversion to the characters in the stories. The method is demonstrated particularly clearly in *Patience*; the fact that we are here presented with a single story about one central character makes it possible for the audience to feel much more familiar with Jonah and to identify far more closely with his motives and emotions than is the case with any of the characters in *Cleanness*.

At the centre of *Patience* is the story of the relationship between a man and God. The story of Jonah opens with the first encounter between them; God, explaining that the sins of the Ninevites have become more than he can tolerate, instructs Jonah to become a prophet, to go to Nineveh and preach to the people. Jonah's response is anger and a determination not to obey. This is expressed in two brief monologues of attempted self-justification (75–88, 93–6), which actually have the effect of exposing Jonah's self-deception: while he claims that it is reasonable to refuse to carry out such an unreasonable errand, it becomes apparent that his real motive is simple fear for his own safety (Spearing, **7c** 1966). Another prominent characteristic of his refusal to obey God is its folly. The reluctant prophet is confident that if he runs away to Tarshish, God will be unable to do anything about it, a view that the poet ridicules at some length (109–28): it would be odd indeed if the creator of the world had such limited power, or if the creator of all sight had such restricted vision (cf. *Cl* 581ff). As Jonah flees, with false confidence and desperate haste (his anxiety to escape reflected in the urgent description of the dockside bustle of Joppa [97–108]), he is a mildly ludicrous figure. In rejecting his duty to God and his fellow men, he is refusing to accept the part he has been chosen to play in the divinely ordered world; later in the poem he again rebels against the will of God, when he takes umbrage over the pardoning of the Ninevites. Appropriately, on both occasions God puts pressure on Jonah through the forces of nature—properly functioning components of the divinely ordered world. The promptness with which the winds, the sun, the woodbine, and the worm obey divine commands is in striking contrast to Jonah's refusal to do so, while the devastating effectiveness of their actions demonstrates God's total control over nature, and his inexorable power.

But the poet is not content with demonstrating God's power over man and nature: he also wishes to show the justice and mercy which inform God's actions, and to contrast with this the unstable, and often selfish and irrational, conduct of Jonah. For this reason it is important for God's decisions to be explained and for his motives to be specified. From the beginning of the story, when Jonah is first ordered to Nineveh, God's motives are made clear (69–72), and later in the poem God gives Jonah a long and detailed account of his reasons for wishing to pardon the repentant Ninevites (495–523). Similar explanations are found in *Cleanness*, for instance in the accounts God gives both Noah and Abraham of why he intends to take revenge on the sinful (303–8, 682–712). The effect of these divine apologies (which have an expository function in relation to the audience of the poem) is that God becomes somewhat humanized, for his reactions to experience are described entirely in terms of human emotional response. This tendency is very much at odds with the tradition of medieval Christian commentators, who took care to preserve the mysterious and unknowable quality of God's ways. Similar humanizing of the motives and actions of God can be observed in the best-known popular didactic form current in the Middle Ages, the Mystery Plays. The poet of *Patience* and *Cleanness* is also willing to sacrifice something of divine mystery and dignity for the sake of didactic and poetic effectiveness, for the God of these two poems (like the *gentyl Cheuentayn* of *Pearl*—cf. especially 601–12) is imagined on the analogy of the ideal earthly ruler, dominated alike by the qualities of *ryȝt, mesure,* and *fraunchyse,* and is thus brought closer to medieval human experience.

The major source for the narrative section of *Patience*, the Old Testament Book of Jonah, is a work whose strength lies in its economy and restraint, its lack of embellishment or explanation. The poet transforms this into something quite different: a lively, vigorous story, by turns serious, terrifying, and comic, in which human emotions and motives are not merely specified, but explored, and in which every opportunity is taken to flesh out the bare bones of the Vulgate narrative and bring it to life for a contemporary audience. To read these two versions of the story of Jonah side by side is to observe the poet of *Patience* translating, expanding episodes, modifying emphases, altering or supplying motives, and adding new passages, short and long. His technique is remarkably varied. At one extreme, he will expand the merest suggestion in the Book of Jonah into a whole episode: thus a single verse (Jonah 2:1) is all that exists by way of source for the marvellously entertaining and original account of Jonah in the whale's belly—an episode fully sixty lines long (245–304). At the other, as in the prayer from the belly, he stays fairly close to the Vulgate—thirty-two lines (305–36) being based on eight biblical verses (2:3–10). But even here, where the poet stays closest to the Old Testament original, *Patience* is never mere translation: the ideas and images of the Vulgate are entirely recreated in the language and imagery of fourteenth-century alliterative poetry. The poet also modifies the biblical story by the addition of specific motives. For instance, in the biblical narrative there is no explanation for Jonah's refusal to obey the divine command to go to Nineveh (1:3); the poet, in marked contrast, dramatizes the process of decision, presenting Jonah's thoughts and revealing his motives in the two little monologues already discussed above (75–88, 93–6). The poet's creative and original modification of his source endows *Patience* with an imaginative clarity and concreteness which make the poem not only highly entertaining but also very effective didactically.

The didacticism which is thus served in the recreation of the biblical story is mediated more directly to the audience in the prologue (1–60) and epilogue (524–31) of the poem. The prologue discusses at some length the nature of the virtue which the poet wants to recommend, and relates it, by setting *pacience* in the context of the Beatitudes (9–40), to the highest and most relevant authority, Christ in his role as preacher.

Although we are thus very close to homily in this opening section, there is nevertheless a fictional element present even here, in the poet's characterization of himself in the *persona* of a preacher and a man among men; and even this most overtly moral part of his discourse contains imaginative and non-rational embellishments. Out of the Beatitudes, for instance, he creates a group of ladies with whom the reader can imagine himself in love (29–36); unobtrusively he keeps the metaphor alive in the lines that follow (see notes to 31–3, 35f, 37–9) and even allows himself a little wry humour in alluding to poverty (the companion of patience) as a rather importunate dame who *nyl be put vtter*: 'won't be sent packing'. Since I am saddled with two of them together, he says, I may as well put up with it and compliment them on their manners (*her lotes prayse*) rather than try to argue, because I'd surely get the worst of it! In the epilogue, the final warning on the self-destructive folly of anger is reinforced by another homely little parable (526f).

Many of the poem's verbal devices also illustrate the use of literary means to enforce the moral lesson. For instance, both medieval rhetorical precept and alliterative practice encouraged the use of synonymous expressions and variation. In the opening exposition the virtue is referred to by a number of different nouns and verbs: *pacience, suffraunce, suffer, abyde, pole,* and there are almost as many variant expressions for the feelings which need to be repressed: *heuy herttes, swelme, malyce, pro.* The repetition of ideas in different words not only imitates the preacher's emphatic pulpit style, but also develops the double idea which the poet finds in the virtue of *pacience*: that of waiting, holding back, and that of submitting to pain or anguish of mind. The pun, then, on the word *suffer* (5 and 6), and also perhaps the double meaning in *pole*, draws attention to the complexity of the concept of *pacience*. Insofar as it is the enduring of pain and anguish (in the dominant modern sense of *suffer*) it is a passive thing; but there is also an allusion to the active side of the virtue which we can glimpse through the other sense of suffer: 'consent, allow, put up with'. The meaning of *pacience,* as the poet uses it, is, in fact, very different from the meaning which the word normally has today. We quickly see that it does not simply mean 'waiting without fretfulness for something to happen', for Jonah is commanded to *Rys radly . . . and rayke forth euen* (65). Something of what *pacience* means emerges from Jonah's negative reaction to this command: *Al he wrathed in his wyt, and wyperly he pozt* (74). Anger is a prime constituent of Jonah's character (409f, 433, 480f). From medieval confessional manuals (of which Chaucer's 'The Parson's Tale' is a handy example) we learn that

> The remedie agayns Ire is a vertu that men clepen Mansuetude ['meekness'], that is Debonairetee; and eek another vertu that men callen Pacience or Suffrance . . . of pacience comth obedience, thurgh which a man is obedient to Crist and to alle hem to whiche he oghte to been obedient in Crist . . . (*CT* X.654, 673)

This traditional opposition between the deadly sin of Wrath and the virtue of Patience explains how the angry and disobedient Jonah can function as an apt antithesis of patience. Christ, of course, was the exemplar of supreme meekness and obedience. In the medieval biblical commentaries, Jonah figures as a type and subfulfilment of Christ, and therefore both as a pattern and a warning (see note to 95f).

There is thus a good deal more consistency than one might suppose: a story which may seem to have been used as an illustration chiefly for its dramatic features, its compact narrative structure, and its human interest, turns out to be exactly right in relation to the contemporary understanding of *pacience*, and verbal devices which seem trivial actually broaden one's insight into the concept. A similar exploration of the meaning and implications of key moral and spiritual terms—*clannesse, cortaysye, trawpe, deme, ryzt*—is a recurrent feature of the four poems.

The story of Jonah is conceived primarily as a negative *exemplum*; he is an example of angry rebellion to be avoided, and at the same time, in the cosmic scale of the poem, of the folly of all sin. In view of the contrast between God's infinite power and man's feebleness, sin must be not only perverse but also foolish. The choice between wise and fruitful conformity to God's will and foolish and futile rebellion is a choice that the poet keeps constantly before us in *Patience* and *Cleanness*. Jonah's expedients for escaping from an unwelcome burden of duty are understandable in the context of his own interests. In the context of the universal divine power, they are ludicrous. This is especially relevant to the particular sin dealt with in this poem, but there is a similar flavour in the dual presentation of the human beings in all four poems: as a human being himself, the reader can feel for the human character engaged in a contest with superhuman power or wisdom; at the same time the reader is forced to view the human character with wry pity for the futility of his attempts to oppose, evade, or outwit.

*

When we turn to the other poetic homily, *Cleanness*, it is even more necessary than in the case of *Patience* to look to the unity-in-diversity of the central concept for an understanding of the poem's design; for the various stories and expository links make a pattern of connections between the diverse senses and metaphorical associations of the ME word *clene* (with its derivatives *clannesse*, *clanly*). In appropriate contexts of use, the adjective can connote, for instance: free from admixture, not dirty, healthy, wholesome, morally righteous, morally pure, innocent, decent, proper, ceremonially pure, clear, transparent, bright, shining, splendid, elegant, excellent, complete, perfect, discerning, skilful. Some of the apparent farfetchedness in the poet's attempts to blend such disparate senses into a single complex entity may be the result of our unfamiliarity with the balance of senses in the medieval word. For instance, when the poet is talking about Christ's courtesy, he cites the tradition that though Christ always broke bread with his hands it parted more cleanly than any knife could have cut it (1103–8). It is only with difficulty that we now associate the notion of a *clean* break with other senses of the word. Then again, the sense 'complete, perfect' (or as an adverb 'completely, perfectly') is a common one in these poems: all the Green Knight's *vesture uerayly watz clene verdure* (161), for example. It is a sense which survives vigorously until the nineteenth century, though now obsolescent, and which contributes an important element to the meaning of this group of words in this poem, where *clannesse* is identified as a quality of the court of Heaven. Essentially the approach to meaning is a poetic one, which delights in hidden connections and unexpected similarities.

Into the pattern created by the different meanings of *clene* and *clannesse* the poet weaves other, partly synonymous terms: *schyre, pure, honest*, etc., which enrich the central concept by their own connotations, and he also links associated conceptual systems, notably that of *trawþe* and that of *cortaysye*. The latter concept is coupled with *clannesse* throughout the poem—see, e.g., 12f, 1089, and the many juxtapositions of *clene* and *cort*, e.g. 17, 1109. The word has its own semantic complexity which is explored separately in *Sir Gawain*. There *clannes* is an element in the hero's *cortaysye*; here the relationship between the two is more difficult to pin down because there is an indeterminate metaphorical factor in almost every use of the two terms. On a purely mundane level cleanness and courtliness go together because aristocratic people are noticeably cleaner than the non-courtly; in *Sir Gawain* they wash before meals, wear clean linen, put white surcoats with brightly embroidered badges over shining armour. In addition, this freshness and fairness is ideally an attribute of conduct and morals. Words like *honest, haʒer(lich), clene, pure, fayre* are equally at home in both the material and the moral world of courtesy. In *Cleanness* (as in *Pearl*) *clannesse* and *cortaysye* are closely associated in the spiritual realm, where there is just as much affinity between them, because of the purity and brightness of heaven, on the one hand, and its hierarchical nobility, on the other:

> He is so clene in His courte, þe Kyng þat al weldez (17).

We should perhaps think not so much of metaphorical substitution as of a continuum between *cortaysye* as a set of social values (among them *clannesse*) and as an attribute of heaven and the Godhead. Thus in the parable of the Wedding Feast the clean *festiual frok* symbolizes the *menske* (courtesy, consideration, good manners) necessary to a dinner-guest at the great house, as well as the *werkez* which are to be *clene, honest,* if you are to

> se þy Sauior and His sete ryche (176).

The long homiletic interlude which follows the destruction of the cities develops the association in terms of the perfect *clannesse* and *cortaysye* of the birth and life of Christ; then at the end of the poem, the uncleanness at the court of Belshazzar is made almost synonymous with its distorted and perverted courtesy.

The noun *trawþe* (with its related and synonymous terms, positive and negative—*trwe, lel(ly), vntrwe, mistrauþe, false*) also signifies a concept with wide-ranging significance, essentially loyalty to God and faith to one's God-given nature and proper role in the world. It is a concept we encounter again near the moral centre of *Sir Gawain*, where also it appears in close relation to *clannesse* and a highly spiritualized *cortaysye* (see especially G 625ff, 653). There are thus very firm links, in the philosophical system of the poems, between *clannesse* and *trawþe*, through *cortaysye*. In its own right, moreover, *trawþe* may signify 'righteousness' (e.g. 723) and thus comes close to some of the senses of *clannesse*. A further link is forged through the concept of *kynde* 'nature' with which both *clannesse* and *trawþe* must conform: of the first race of men before the Flood we are told:

> Þer watz no law to hem layd bot loke to kynde,
> And kepe to hit, and alle hit cors clanly fulfylle (263f);

and the exceptions to the unnatural way of Sodom and Gomorrah, for whom Abraham makes his hypothetical plea, would be those

> Þat neuer lakked Þy laue, bot loued ay trauþe,
> And reʒtful wern and resounable and redy Þe to serue (723f);

(cf. also Gawain's association of *vntrawþe* with the abandonment of his *kynde*—his true nature as a knight—in G 2374-83).

The meaning of *clannesse* is made specifically sexual in the first two main *exempla.* The sin which provoked God's wrath in the Flood was 'unnatural' sex (265f). This, it is implied, produces complete disorder in nature; devils couple with human beings and produce giants, and simultaneously violence and tyranny spread. (The swift progression from *contraré werkez agayn kynde* in 266 through *men meþelez and maȝty* in 273 to the *feȝt* and *bale* of 275f may be intended as an explanation of the violence of God's wrath against sins of the flesh, which were considered less serious than those of the spirit.)

The poet is at some pains to exempt heterosexual behaviour from the stigma of *fylþe,* which is the term he uses systematically as an antonym to *clannesse.* This he does beyond any possibility of misunderstanding by putting into the mouth of God a vindication of sexual pleasure which is strikingly at variance with the tortuous distinctions of many contemporary moralists (697–708). In a poem which harshly denounces physical impurity, written in an age in which most Christian moralists regarded sexuality even within marriage with the gravest suspicion, such sentiments—particularly attributed, as they are, to God —are totally unexpected. God claims to have *portrayed* (designed) the *play of paramorez* himself and to be thoroughly appreciative of its joys. The poet's intention in introducing this speech just before the story of the destruction of Sodom and Gomorrah, a punishment motivated by God's anger at the perversion of his natural order, is evidently to distinguish between the Sodomites' deviant conduct and the natural and joyful heterosexual love ordained by God.[4]

He is also concerned to portray the virtue of *clannesse* as something more positive and less narrow than absence of *fylþe.* It is surely significant that the poet nowhere uses the terms *chaste* and *chastitee* as synonyms for *clene* and *clannesse* (although he has the precedent of traditional phrases like *chaste cleannesse,* which had long been in use in such contexts); presumably they would be too limiting for his purpose. In the passages of direct moral exhortation, as also in the Belshazzar episode, there is very clearly a wish to see *clannesse* (without minimizing its traditional associations) in a context of wider morality and spirituality. The extended treatment of the sacred vessels of the Temple in the latter part of the poem makes them particularly apt vehicles of a broadened concept of *clannesse* as 'reverence for what is sacred to God' (see especially 1274–80, 1313f., 1447f.). The adjectives which the poet uses (*aþel, bryȝt, schyre, fayre, vertuous*) do more than describe the physical brilliance of the vessels; they carry some of the metaphorical meaning which they have acquired as synonyms for spiritual *clannesse* earlier in the poem. Through their physical

---

[4] The destruction of the cities was often cited (e.g. in 'The Parson's Tale') as a punishment for *lecherie;* in spite of this, the poet refers no more specifically to *marriage* than the qualification *when two true togeder had tyȝed hemseluen* (702). The same desire to draw a sharp distinction between sex as such and the *fylþe* of Sodom may lie behind the introduction (from Genesis 19) of the story of Lot's offer of his daughters to the crowd outside his house: it underlines Lot's horror at the Sodomites' wish to molest the angels (see 861–72n), though it is difficult to regard the addition as a moral or artistic success. It is striking that Lot's words in 865 echo those of God in 697.

splendour, the significance of the vessels as objects dedicated to God impresses itself on Nebuchadnezzar:

> He sesed hem with solemneté, þe Souerayn he praysed
> Þat watz aþel ouer alle, Israel Dryʒtyn (1313f)

When the vessels are next described, as they are unpacked from *kystes ful mony* (1438) for the profane delight of Belshazzar, we are once again reminded of their true office

> In þe solempne sacrefyce þat goud sauor hade
> Bifore þe Lorde of þe lyfte in louyng Hymseluen (1447f)

but we also see them through the astonished gaze of the revellers, simply as ornate and costly objects of art *þat wyth so curious a crafte coruen watz wyly* (1452). The description of 1451ff. is accordingly made up of somewhat naïve technical detail.

It has been pointed out (see Morse, **7b** 1970–1) that medieval theologians saw man as a vessel consecrated to God and that this would enrich the symbolism of the vessels in the poem. There are specific strands of allusion within the poem itself which connect the vessels of the Jewish Temple with the *renkez of relygioun* of 7–16—priests who should *in clannes be clos* because they *aprochen to Hys presens, teen vnto His temmple, Reken with reuerence þay rychen His auter* (cf. 1262, 1276, 1318, 1496). Above all, the vessels acquire their spiritual *clannesse* from their service in the presence of God, and thus echo the theme of the beatitude and the parable of the Wedding Feast.

The structure of *Cleanness* has generally been found less satisfactory than that of *Patience*. However, while there may be disproportion in the treatment of Nebuchadnezzar and Belshazzar, the laxity in the choice of material which some critics have found is in reality only a reflection of the complexity of the expository task which the poet has set himself. The exemplification of the virtue again proceeds by opposites, but in the longer poem the poet has illustrated his argument, as he says himself at the end, *vpon þrynne wyses* (1805). He means the three main *exempla* which dominate the poem and account for about two-thirds of its length: the Flood, the Destruction of Sodom and Gomorrah, and Belshazzar's Feast. In addition, *Cleanness* also contains a number of other shorter stories, such as those of the Falls of Lucifer and of Adam; the main *exempla* themselves, moreover, are treated with an expansiveness which allows the narration of contiguous episodes, especially those of Abraham and Lot as an introduction to Sodom and Gomorrah, and of Nebuchadnezzar as an introduction to Belshazzar's Feast. All this gives independent interest and momentum to the separate narrative episodes and contributes to a sense of a more circuitous approach to the major moral themes than is the case in the shorter poem. *Cleanness* is, however, by no means the loose collection of heterogeneous stories yoked clumsily together that it has often been thought. The main narrative sweep is a chronological one, from the fall of Lucifer down to the end of the Babylonian domination of Israel; the realization that the main biblical stories were interpreted by medieval Christian commentators as types of the Last Judgement (Morse, **7b** 1970–1) blends with the pervasive consciousness of the throne and court of God in heaven, to impart a grand design to the poem which is reminiscent of a Corpus Christi play in miniature. Moreover, the striking similarity, in tone and content, between *Cleanness* and 2 Peter 2:4–13 makes it possible that both the theme of the poem and its association with some of these biblical stories were suggested by this passage.[5] Far from being arbitrarily chosen, therefore, the stories fit into the pattern of association laid down by their use in other contexts. Further, the poet adapts and moulds the stories, while never losing touch with the biblical originals, so that their latent relevance to his complex theme is made explicit. The minor stories are not only historically contiguous but also given thematic relevance as subsidiary *exempla* (often in illustration of the supporting notions of *trawþe* and *cortaysye*). The overall coherence of the poem derives from factors which give shape to *Patience* too: the poet's stance as a moral instructor, his method of alternating theoretical statement with illustrative stories, and the unifying influence of his theme.

The structure may be set out in the following form:

Introduction:
  Praise of *clannesse* (1–22)
  The Beatitude, Blessed are the pure in heart (23–48)
  The parable of the Wedding Feast and its application (49–192)
Introduction to the three exempla (193–204)
First Exemplary Sequence (205–544)
  Minor *exemplum* (1): The fall of Lucifer (205–234)
  Minor *exemplum* (2): The fall of Adam (235–248)
  Major *exemplum*: The flood (249–544)
Link passage (545–600)
Second Exemplary Sequence (601–1048)
  Minor *exemplum* (1): God visits Abraham and Sarah (601–676)
  Minor *exemplum* (2): The fate of Lot and his family (677–890, 973–1000)
  Major *exemplum*: The destruction of the cities (890–972, 1001–1048)
Link passage (1049–1148)
Third Exemplary Sequence (1149–1804)
  Minor *exemplum* (1): Nebuchadnezzar's seizure of the vessels, conversion and death (1157–1332)
  Major *exemplum*: Belshazzar's feast and end (1333–1650, 1709–1804)
  Minor *exemplum* (2): Daniel's account of Nebuchadnezzar's conversion (1651–1708)
Conclusion (1805–1812)

The poem begins with an encomium of the virtue of *clannesse*, supported by the sixth Beatitude (Matt. 5:8): God cannot abide uncleanness and we should not try to go to heaven in an unclean state, any more than we would go in torn and filthy clothes to a banquet given by an earthly lord. This serves as an introduction to the parable of the Wedding Feast (49–160). The parable

[5] There is also a less striking parallel in the apocryphal Book of Wisdom (10:1–7).

presented in this way in a commanding position at the beginning of the poem serves a function rather different from the short Old Testament stories which support the main *exempla*. As a parable of Jesus it already has authoritative allegorical significance in the New Testament, and the poet's retelling of it both provides justification for the value placed on *clannesse* in the poem and creates an overall context for the theme. It is noteworthy that each reversion from narrative to direct moral comment (545ff, 1049ff, 1805ff) brings the reader back to the picture of God as king in his court; the Wedding Feast parable, therefore, stands in a special explanatory relationship to the Beatitude which is the text of the whole poem, and particularly to its promise: 'they shall see God'.

The two subsidiary *exempla* which follow, those of the Fall of Lucifer and the Fall of Adam (205–48), are relevant to the central theme in a number of ways. They provide a context for the story of the Flood, in that they represent the first and second occasions on which God takes revenge for evil, while the Flood is the third. They also provide a contrast: God's wrath was aroused in the vengeance against fleshly filth in the Flood, while his punishment for disobedience in the two Falls was administered more in sorrow than in anger. Nevertheless, the stories do illustrate failure in that portion of moral duty to God which is designated *trawþe* (Lucifer is *þe falce fende*, who is a traitor to God—205ff—and Adam is *a freke þat fayled in trawþe* and *inobedyent*—236f).

The Flood (249–544), the first of the main *exempla*, is presented specifically in terms of punishment for uncleanness: God takes revenge because man persists in his *fylþe in fleschlych dedez* (265). Here is established the essential pattern for all three main *exempla*: the reader is encouraged to pursue *clannesse* by being told a negative *exemplum*, a story of the evil conduct of the unclean and the terrible fate they suffer. At the same time, a series of positive characters—those who are exceptions to the depraved norm, and are chosen by God to survive, or defy and oppose the unclean—begins with Noah. Unlike some of the authors of the Mystery Plays, the poet resists the accretions which had formed round the Noah story—the comedy of the verbal and physical strife between Noah and his wife, with its rich opportunities for anti-feminism—and keeps to what is relevant to his purpose. The poet also touches again on his supporting theme of truth, describing the raven, who selfishly gorges on rotting flesh rather than doing his duty to others and returning with news to the ark, as *corbyal vntrwe* (456). The story of the Flood is followed by a linking passage of moral commentary (545–600) in which the audience is directly exhorted to realize how loathsome to God is *fylþe*, and not to be so foolish as to think that any evil deed can be hidden from the all-seeing God. Although God has repented, says the poet (557–80) of the wholesale destruction of mankind and has mercifully undertaken not to repeat it, nevertheless, groups of particularly unclean people later suffered a similar terrible vengeance. From this observation the story of the destruction of Sodom and Gomorrah, the second exemplary sequence (601–1048), follows naturally.

Its relevance to the poem as a whole is clear: it is a story of the punishment of sexual uncleanness, and thus conforms to the pattern of negative *exempla* of cleanness. Within this sequence there are two episodes—those concerning

Abraham and Sarah, and Lot and his family—which are tangential to the actual destruction of the cities. The first of these, that of Abraham and Sarah, serves a number of functions. It provides an introduction to the main story and presents the poem's second major positive character in Abraham, whose considerate conduct in serving the Trinity as honoured guests in his house demonstrated his courtesy and his truth—his faith in God—and whose bold pleading with God demonstrates God's patience and forbearance even in anger; Sarah's doubting and mocking God's word with regard to her future childbearing, on the other hand, demonstrates her failure to understand that God is all-powerful and (as has just been pointed out in 581–99) all-seeing. The second subsidiary *exemplum* is that of Lot and his wife; while Lot is primarily presented as an exception to the *fylþe* of Sodom, the story of his wife (813–28 and 978–84) is essentially a story of disobedience (*mistrauþe*) and punishment, as the poet suggests in 996; it thus echoes the stories of Lucifer and Adam.

Between the second and third sequences of *exempla* comes another passage of moral commentary in the poet-homilist's own voice (1049–1148). This is a renewed exhortation to be clean, if we wish to see the face of God, and a lyrical eulogy of the exemplary cleanness of Christ and the Virgin, followed by a passage in praise of the pearl (in which the symbol is used with the same range of association that is developed so comprehensively in *Pearl*). Finally he warns us that those who have become clean through shrift must avoid backsliding, for God's wrath is aroused by the loss of anything that was once consecrated to him, even if it is only a basin or a dish, and this serves as an entry to the third and longest *exemplum*, the story of Belshazzar's Feast, which has as its focus the crime of Belshazzar in defiling the sacred vessels of the Temple.

Like the second sequence, this contains two subsidiary *exempla*, one as an introduction to the story of the vessels and one inserted in the middle of the major *exemplum*. At the outset we are told how the Jews were *founden vntrwe* (1161) in their faith, and how they and their king, Zedechiah, were punished for their faithlessness by being overthrown by Nebuchadnezzar. Thus the theme of this subsidiary *exemplum* is again 'untruth', a theme which is taken up once more in the final subsidiary *exemplum*, that of the rise, fall, and reinstatement of Nebuchadnezzar (1651–1708), which is related by Daniel directly to Belshazzar. Nebuchadnezzar's pride had led him to set himself up as a God on earth and Belshazzar's vainglory and blasphemy are similar but unregenerate. The poem ends with a brief peroration (1805–12) in which the poet once more touches on the theme of God's love of *clannes* and *coyntyse*, and the importance of the garment of pure deeds for those who wish to serve in his sight.

By comparison with *Patience*, where human weakness is explored more gently and the main emphasis is on God's infinite capacity for forgiveness, the tone and sentiment of *Cleanness* are predominantly severe, even harsh. Though the didactic purpose in the two poems is not radically dissimilar—the encouragement of virtue through negative *exempla*—the emotive effects are fundamentally different, and intentionally so. The sinners of *Patience*—the

Ninevites and Jonah—are pardoned. Those of *Cleanness* are destroyed, and their destruction is in every case brought about with appalling violence and suddenness. For the aim in *Cleanness* is to use these illustrations of God's destructive anger as a deterrent to sin.

The poet's skill and subtlety are nowhere more evident than in his treatment of this grim subject-matter, for he excels in the alliterative tradition's characteristic facility in describing scenes of violent action and high drama. His account of the destruction of Sodom and Gomorrah (947–72) is a case in point. Every element in this splendid alliterative set piece has clear thematic relevance. The violent turmoil in the sky, the roasting of the cities in fire, brimstone and rain, the terrifying opening of the earth, and the vain cries from the doomed people, are all described in poetry which has compelling power, but in no way distracts from the didactic intent. The scene begins with God's instructions to the winds, demonstrating his total control over the world, and ends with the evildoers tipped into a hell visualized in familiar, traditional terms, demonstrating the fate of the sinful. Even so fine and original a poetic effect as the simile:

> . . . clouen alle in lyttel cloutes þe clyffez aywhere,
> As lauce leuez of þe boke þat lepes in twynne (965f)

serves a thematic—and thus didactic—purpose. The startling shift of perspective, by which great rocks become like fluttering leaves of parchment, provides a powerful imaginative impression of the vast and irresistible power of God, by comparison to which man is puny indeed.[6]

The connection between sin and folly, which is so prominent a theme in *Patience*, is kept constantly before us in *Cleanness* as well, but again the outlook is characteristically harsher here. In addition to the folly of the sinful, the poet stresses their pride. Pride—traditionally regarded as Lucifer's sin, and thus the original and exemplar of all sin—is seen as essentially foolish, in that it is derived from the self-delusion that man is greater and more powerful than he actually is, or than he proves to be: for rebellion against God always fails. It is, then, not surprising to find the poet pointing out the folly of certain sinful characters like the Sodomites (696) and Lot's wife (996), or even the folly of sin itself: *fylþe of þe flesch þat foles han vsed* (202). Similarly, folly is implicit in the pride of Lucifer (217–20) and that of Belshazzar (1356–60). At times, the point is suggested through the use of a wry, sardonic humour, as in the description of Belshazzar with his false gods (1340–48). The humour derives from our awareness of the absurdity and inappropriateness of Belshazzar's actions, an awareness established by reference to a universal order governed by God.

---

[6] An instance very similar (except that the perspective shift operates in the opposite direction) is used to precisely the same end in *Patience*. Jonah, about to be swallowed by the whale, is visualized *As mote in at a munster dor, so mukel wern his chawlez* (268)—and the comparison of the proud man to a speck of dust has a telling effect. The difference between the two events is representative of the difference between the two poems. That in *Cleanness* describes terrible and final destruction; that in *Patience* an occurrence admittedly terrifying and undoubtedly salutary but one the final outcome of which is forgiveness and deliverance.

The ostensibly negative tone of *Cleanness*—an uncompromisingly didactic work which encourages virtue by showing the bitter fruits of sin, and in which good is most often suggested by the exposure of its opposite—makes it necessary to emphasize the elements which contribute to a more positive and celebratory picture of virtue. Though the God of *Cleanness* appears primarily as the irresistible destroyer, he is also, paradoxically, portrayed as creator. It is constantly emphasized that the world is God's creation, that he has ordained a right and proper order, innately and ultimately good, and that sin consists in the contravention or perversion of natural order (see, for instance, God's words on the good and evil use of sex—697–708—discussed above, p. 24f). The major virtuous characters—Noah, Abraham, Lot (to a lesser extent), and Daniel—also play a positive and instructive role in opposing evil, providing continuity of human virtue, prophesying the truth, and serving God. And there is one other characteristic of the poet's attitude towards his narrative world which connects the harsh moralist and unswerving denouncer of sin with the humane and gentle mind behind the other poems. In these the central human being, though imperfect, is a mixed character and (for this reason) one with whom the reader can readily identify. Jonah suffers and repents, and during much of the action he is obedient to God; the *Pearl* Dreamer emerges from his vision in a more resigned and enlightened frame of mind; and Sir Gawain remains, in spite of his fault, by human standards a splendidly moral knight. In *Cleanness* too, from time to time, the suffering, even of admittedly evil characters, clearly engages the poet's sympathy—an instance being his account of the victims of the Flood (373–402). The sense of sympathy is evoked by his technique of imaginatively creating exemplary situations in a series of brief but vivid scenes and describing within each exactly how people in that situation would have felt. Most medieval homilists would have shown little sympathy for the plight of sinners such as these. But the poet's vision is sufficiently subtle and generous for him to be able to portray the victims of the Flood as human beings whose sufferings the audience can identify with and pity, without prejudicing the central principle of God's justice. Through all four works (even, intermittently, in *Cleanness*) there breathes a spirit of sympathetic identification with human frailty besides a zealous dedication to ideal virtue.

Dream Vision: Pearl

The formal differences between the literary homilies we have just discussed and *Pearl* are considerable, but we shall also find some deep similarities. The poem belongs to the dream-vision genre, a type which had both secular and religious antecedents (in, for example, *Le Roman de la Rose*, on the one hand, and Dante's *Divine Comedy* on the other) and which was discovered by other fourteenth-century English poets—notably Langland and Chaucer—and used by them as a didactic and philosophical medium.

It is noteworthy that in their works in the genre, as in *Pearl*, the focus of attention is the dreamer's mental and spiritual life and the effect upon it of his revelation. The ornate metrical form, as will be seen below, is in keeping with

the apocalyptic subject-matter, and the complexity of its formal design ans-
wers to the intricacy of its thought and imagery. Passages from the Bible
(notably the parables of the Vineyard and the Pearl of Price, and the descrip-
tion of the New Jerusalem) are again important constituents but they are now
incorporated in a narrative and dramatic frame; and although we are engaged
with doctrinal matters which cannot fail to remind the reader of the central
concerns of *Patience* and *Cleanness*—resignation to the will of God, the beauty of
purity and perfection—there is no direct admonition to the reader. Instead,
instruction and persuasion are conveyed indirectly through the Dreamer's
first-person narrative, which consists of a progressive (and in a subtle way
retrospective) account of his experience from his own point of view, and itself
includes the words of his sublime teacher.

Pearl is a poem about transformation. Central to its meaning is the transfor-
mation of the Dreamer's state of mind from anguished and rebellious mourn-
ing at the beginning to mourning no less intense, but tempered by the ordering
of a new metaphysic at the end. Juxtaposition of these two states of mind is
encouraged by the poem's form. In dramatic setting, as well as in poetic
pattern, its end is a return to its beginning: the Dreamer wakes in the *erber
wlonk* (1171) where he had previously lost the pearl (9) and gone to mourn its
loss (38), his head on the mound (1172) where the pearl first *trendeled doun* (41).
His initial response on waking—*I raxled, and fel in gret affray* (1174)—is a
return to the intense mourning of the beginning (e.g. 49–56). But the possib-
ility of a structure of values which could place loss in a philosophical context
and thus render it acceptable and comprehensible has been suggested from the
very first through the retrospective point of view of the dreamer-narrator: he
was obsessed with sorrow

> Þaȝ resoun sette myseluen saȝt (52)

and his mind was a turmoil of conflicting emotions

> Þaȝ kynde of Kryst me comfort kenned (55).

When at the end he turns from restating his sorrow (1174) to an affirmation of
acceptance of his lot and obedience to God (1176), what we are seeing is the
realization of this potential source of order and comfort. The end of the poem
thus both echoes its beginning and presents a change of major importance.
This transformation, its nature, its significance, and how it is brought about, is
the subject of the main body of *Pearl*.

In a way which is consistent with the metaphorical mode of the other poems
of the group, the central images of *Pearl* reflect this process of transformation.
The pearl is put forward in the first stanza in terms of its great earthly value: it
is

> to prynces paye
> To clanly clos in golde so clere:

—'suitable for a (human) prince to set radiantly in pure gold'; by the time we
reach the last stanza, his concern is with pleasing the Prince (1201) of
heaven—that he should become one of the *precious perlez vnto His pay*. A

similar development may be seen in the image of the rose. When it is first used, in resonant lines of telling finality:

> For þat þou lestez watz bot a rose
> Þat flowred and fayled as kynde hyt gef (269f),

it draws its effect from the traditional association of the rose with mutable beauty and its use in love poetry to symbolize the woman as an object of love. The Maiden argues that such desire is earthly, and therefore—touching on the mutability at the heart of the secular image—impermanent and of less value than the everlasting *perle of prys*. This is early in the Maiden's debate with the Dreamer, at which point the central issue is the distinction between earthly and heavenly values. Towards the end of their encounter, by which stage the Dreamer has been brought to a state of acquiescence with God's will, and the central concern has become the explication and celebration of the life of the saved in heaven, the rose reappears as a transformed image (906). It now stands for the beauty of the blessed, again drawing on tradition, this time on the Christian concept of the *rosa caritatis* (rose of heavenly love).

Not all the images which reflect this vitally important transformation do so through the straightforward dualistic division between earthly and heavenly values. The image of the garden is a case in point. The first garden is presented not only as a place of great natural beauty, but also as one of growth juxtaposed with decay (25–48); this setting, through the vision, is transformed into the garden of the Terrestrial Paradise, a place whose beauty is emphatically supernatural—with the crystal cliffs (74), the trees adorned with silver leaves (77), the gravel of pearls (81)—and which is clearly beyond growth and decay. But if the natural garden is a shadow of the Terrestrial Paradise, this in its turn is a shadow of the full glory of heaven. Three locations, not two, are recognized, and along with them, a threefold order of perfection. Even in his vision, the Dreamer is inexorably excluded from the third and it is noteworthy that, though the sight of it is for him the most ravishing part of his dream, he is all the time aware how remote it is from ordinary human experience (1081–92). The simple dualism of earthly values set against their heavenly counterparts is also modified, though in a different way, in the handling of the metaphor of the jeweller. At the outset, though the word itself is not used, the *idea* of valuing jewels and making judgements about their value is presented in the first stanza (particularly 7), in the context of the Dreamer's original estimation of the pearl as worthy of providing pleasure for a prince of this world. (The past tense here gives us, by implication, the attitude of mind of the first-person narrator before his vision.) This idea is picked up in the fifth section (241–300), where it is encapsulated in the word *jueler*, used by the Maiden to address the Dreamer. During this section, the Dreamer's values are exposed to a searching analysis conducted by the Maiden from a non-worldly viewpoint; in the process their essential worldliness is established, and the term *jueler* is used almost ironically (e.g. in 265, 289) of someone who judges values by the impoverished criteria of this world alone. As with the image of the rose, it is the development of the debate which generates the transformation. By the time the argument has reached the stage where the Maiden has expounded the essentials of Christian doctrine and is encouraging the Dreamer to change the values by which he lives, she can refer to the merchant in the parable of the Pearl of Price (Matt. 13:45–6) as *joueler* (733–5), with the clear implication that this involves a transformed structure of values. This image is given a further dimension when the Maiden by implication characterizes herself as a 'jeweller' by referring to Christ as her *Juelle* (795, 1124). Thus, in the varied and sometimes allusive use of the concept of the jeweller, we see something considerably more subtle and complex than the overt contrast between earthly and heavenly values, which nonetheless informs the metaphor in every application.

The developing implications of the term *jueler* draw constantly on our understanding of the meaning of *perle*. This is, of course, the central image—at once the most complex and the most fundamental to an understanding of the poem—the idea with which it begins and ends, and which, in an unbroken scholarly and editorial tradition, has provided its name. In approaching the problem of defining the meaning or meanings of the pearl, we should start from the one unequivocally definitive statement in the poem. At that vital point in the argument where the Maiden finally advises the Dreamer to follow the example of the merchant of the parable, we find:

'This makellez perle þat boȝt is dere,
Þe joueler gef fore alle hys god,
Is lyke þe reme of heuenesse clere' (733–5).

Here, at least, we can say with confidence that the pearl symbolizes heaven. In the first description of the Maiden (161–240), great emphasis is put upon the fact that her clothes and crown are adorned with pearls at every point, and that

... a wonder perle withouten wemme
Inmyddez hyr breste watz sette so sure (221f)

Clearly enough, the dominant symbolic significance of the pearls is that the Maiden is an inmate of heaven; the great pearl is probably intended to be identified with the pearl of price—alluded to in the other passage (733–5)—and thus with salvation. Beyond this, the central image of the pearl is a poetic rather than an allegorical symbol. Its significance cannot be unlocked in any mechanical way; it functions, rather, with a wide range of metaphorical suggestions and connotations, yielding rich and many-faceted significance and representing many different things and concepts in relation to different strands in the total meaning of the poem.[7] In the opening stanzas it is the material

---

[7] The ramifications of the pearl symbolism, and in particular the significance of the lost pearl introduced in the first stanza, have been matters of bitter and protracted controversy in the past. The polarizing stages are conveniently summarized in Wellek, **7a** 1933 and in the Introduction to Gordon, **2a** 1953. Critics have tended to divide into those who see *Pearl* as a total and consistent allegory and those who recognize a significant elegiac element. The former would interpret the lost pearl at the beginning of the poem as an allegorical representation of some spiritual quality, while the latter would interpret it as a symbolic representation of a dead child. The tide of critical

gem; used metaphorically by the narrator for his dead child it suggests her preciousness to him (and—by an anticipatory current running counter to the earth-bound grief described at this point—her immortality); in contrast to the earth of the garden and to the fading earthly rose, it suggests everlastingness; through its whiteness and perfect roundness (as well as through its use in the biblical parable) it comes to stand for innocence and perfection, the immortal soul, the Pearl of Price, the Kingdom of Heaven, and the company of the saved. Through these various connotations it participates as well in a number of related metaphorical systems: for instance, as a valued things itself, it comes to act as a symbol for value in general (and thus to link up with the concept of reward), and its connection with princes and courts in the first lines, and at the end of the poem, helps to unite the *cortaysye* which is an attribute of noble manners and conduct with the *cortaysye*, or grace, of the court of heaven.

If the pearl is the symbolic heart of what the Dreamer learns, his instruction is made possible and given authority through the medium of the dream. The authority of dreams as vehicles for communicating a revelation of divine truth derives from the scriptures, where there are many instances, and was reinforced by such medieval works as Macrobius's commentary on *The Dream of Scipio* and Boethius's *The Consolation of Philosophy*. The dream vision is a medium peculiarly well suited for revelation, in that through it the protagonist may be simultaneously in touch with the actual world and (in some sense) out of it. In *Pearl*, the idea of an intermediate plane of existence between earth and heaven is embodied in the Terrestrial Paradise. While it is clearly an image of heavenly perfection, it is unequivocally separate from, and inferior to, heaven; indeed, in the Middle Ages it was also believed to be an actual, if remote, location on earth (see note to 65ff). Its more abstract associations, of paradise lost, and conversely, of man's ultimate perfectibility through Christ, could hardly be more relevant to the situation in *Pearl*. The Dreamer tells us that, while his body remains below, his spirit goes, through the grace of God, *in auenture per meruaylez meuen* (64)—a characteristic application of words normally associated with romance and the quest for human love and personal fulfilment (cf. *Pat* 35-9, *Cl* 1057-9, and notes), to a quest for spiritual truth; and one paralleled in the similarity between the description of the Terrestrial Paradise and the conventional gardens of the literature of love. However, the Dreamer is always aware that the special significance of this marvellous land is spiritual. Beautiful as they are in purely decorative terms, the main function of

---

opinion has, during the past two or three decades, been flowing against the allegorists, which may be partly due to the fact that though they agree that the poem is a total allegory, they signally fail to agree on what it is a total allegory of. The majority of readers find it hard to accept the allegorists' denial of any reference to a dead person in the narrator's early allusions to the pearl. Most feel that the poem resists the straitjacket of total allegorical interpretation, that the central image suggests many layers of meaning—some dominant, others secondary, some mere hints—and so functions mainly in a symbolic rather than an allegorical manner. It is furthermore now widely acknowledged that the recognition of an allusion in the poem to the death of a child, the daughter of the Dreamer, by no means commits the reader to taking the poem as literal autobiography, or even as elegy in the strict sense.

the descriptive passages is to communicate the effect of the Terrestrial Paradise on the Dreamer—his great sense of wonder, and the revision which takes place in his feeling for worldly beauty when he sees that beauty transformed by the 'artifice of eternity'. It is in this setting that the Dreamer is educated in Christian values, here that he experiences his glimpse of the New Jerusalem— and from here that he must return to the world where the lessons are to be applied.

The return at the end of *Pearl* to the setting and situation with which it opened will draw the reader's attention to its symmetry and balance. Indeed, the words in which the Maiden, speaking of the Pearl of Price, compares its perfection of form to heaven:

> For hit is wemlez, clene, and clere,
> And endelez rounde, and blyþe of mode (737f)

could well be applied to the poem itself. This quality is not, however, some-thing of which the reader is only conscious retrospectively. Throughout *Pearl*, one is aware of the controlled artistry with which the work unfolds, the poet gradually developing and interweaving events, ideas, and symbols until a design of superb symmetry and astonishing intricacy is complete. The key structural unit is the stanza. Each contains twelve four-stress lines, which create an impression of intricate balance through their combination of allitera-tion and a complex rhyme-scheme (ababababbcbc) which uses only three rhymes. The stanzas also relate to each other in a precisely controlled pattern of interdependence. They are arranged in groups of five,[8] each stanza within the group ending with a refrain which is echoed in the first line of the follow-ing stanza, thus producing the effect of *concatenatio* ('concatenation' or 'link-ing'). The first line of each stanza group or section of the poem also echoes the concatenation words of the preceding section. The concatenation words of the final section of the poem *His* (i.e. *Prynsez*) *pay* echo the first line, thus complet-ing a structure which effectively links and binds the physical components of the poem in a continuous chain.

Form is closely related to meaning. The precise ordering of the form reflects a similarly conscious artistry in the presentation of subject-matter—the con-catenation words marking, summarizing, and encapsulating each stage of an argument which is articulated with meticulous precision. Sections I and XX are set in the garden, for (as was observed earlier) the end of the poem returns to the setting—physical and psychological—of its beginning, though a setting the significance of which has been fundamentally transformed. Within this framework of garden sections we find two passages of matching size balancing each other at either end of the poem—the vision of the Terrestrial Paradise in sections II to IV and the vision of the New Jerusalem in sections XVII to XIX. And within this second 'frame' is the central debate between the Dreamer and the Maiden, which dominates the poem and occupies sections V to XVI. In this too the formal ordering is significant. The argument may be seen as falling into three groups of four sections, the first group (V–VIII) presenting the Dreamer's misconceptions about Christian doctrine and the

[8] Except for section XV, which contains six stanzas: see note to 841–912.

Maiden's rebuttal of his views, the second (IX–XII) containing the Maiden's narration of the parable of the Vineyard and her summary of essential Christian doctrine on grace, and the third (XIII–XVI) applying these ideas directly to the Dreamer and going on to elaborate on the state of the saved in heaven. Thus at the heart of *Pearl* we find the parable of the Vineyard and the doctrine of grace: the first eight sections of the poem develop from the opening situation towards this, while the last eight build on it, towards the final resolution.

The encounter between the Dreamer and the Maiden is presented in the form of a debate. Though this was a literary type widely used in the Middle Ages, the poet's adoption of it here is far from uncritical conventionality, for it enables him to invest the process by which the Dreamer is instructed in Christian doctrine and morality with a remarkable degree of dramatic intensity, psychological insight, and human sympathy. The process is portrayed as something akin to a conversion; for, though the Dreamer is nominally a Christian from the outset, his response to loss (as is made clear in the opening section of the poem) is not informed by an understanding of the full implications of Christian values. He is aware of the existence of patterns of Christian consolation, but is unable at this stage to derive comfort or enlightenment from them (49–56). It is through his encounter with the Maiden that the Dreamer comes to a full and active awareness of the meaning of Christian faith, and learns to apply doctrine to the understanding of his own experience and the evaluation of his own conduct. The tendency for most medieval writers would have been to characterize this debate as a confrontation between the proud and ignorant man on the one hand and the humble but authoritative spokesman of divine truth on the other. With characteristic subtlety of vision the poet avoids this simple dichotomy. Though the Dreamer is sometimes obstinate and self-opinionated, sometimes outspoken or self-pitying, and repeatedly fails to understand the full implications of heavenly values, the reader sympathizes with his responses and identifies with him. The failure to understand derives partly from the difficulty of the concepts involved, but mainly from the intensity with which the Dreamer grieves for his loss and desires its restoration. The immediate effectiveness of logical argument when set against the intensity of deep feeling is limited, even when the logic has divine authority. We sympathize with the Dreamer because his grief and his difficulties with doctrine are recognizable as fundamental human responses, and, conversely, may find the Maiden's unshakeable righteousness and complete clarity somewhat disconcerting—as he does. Nevertheless, the Maiden is explicating the divine order, and so in the end her authority must prevail. A series of queries, objections, and misunderstandings of Christian doctrine are posed by the Dreamer; each in turn is answered by the Maiden, thus providing a growing enlightenment. In this manner the debate progresses. Its turning-point is marked by the Maiden's long doctrinal speech (601–744) in which she explains the central Christian concept of redemption; after this the Dreamer still has questions, but objects no more.

Thus the debate at the centre of *Pearl* dramatizes the processes by which a human being, ignorant and headstrong perhaps, but certainly portrayed with sympathy and compassion, is brought to a state of Christian understanding and humble acquiescence to the will of God. The use of the Dreamer as first-person narrator creates a close relationship with the audience, who are thus tacitly encouraged to relate his experience directly to their own lives. This narrative technique also identifies the Dreamer-narrator with the poet himself, and presents the loss and the vision as elements from his actual experience. The effect of this identification (whether fictional or not) on the tone and feeling of the poem as a whole is crucial. *Pearl* is neither harsh in its didacticism nor smug in its optimism. The poet's world view is sufficiently subtle and humane for him to recognize that, while it is natural for fallen man to err, it is more fruitful to explore the nature and implications of his inevitable weaknesses than merely to denounce them. As in *Patience*, *Cleanness*, and *Sir Gawain*, Christian doctrine is not propounded in abstraction, but is discussed with close reference to the realities of the human condition. Nonetheless, *Pearl* remains a didactic poem. At its physical centre lies the narration of a parable and the exposition of key doctrine, while at its imaginative core is the conversion of the Dreamer from ignorance and resentment to understanding and acceptance of divine order. At the end of her long and crucial speech on doctrine, the Maiden exhorts the Dreamer:

> 'I rede þe forsake þe worlde wode
> And porchace þy perle maskelles.' (743f)

The mode and form of *Pearl* make it clear that this advice is intended to be as relevant to the audience as it is to the Dreamer.

Romance: Sir Gawain and the Green Knight

Sir Gawain is an example of a radically different type of didacticism from either the biblical homilies of *Patience* and *Cleanness* or the more indirectly instructive dream-vision of *Pearl*. In itself, it is a very accomplished example of medieval chivalric romance; yet at the same time it is again a poem of rich psychological and moral interest in which we encounter many of the themes which have become familiar from the other three poems: in particular the mutual implications of *trawþe*, *clannesse* and *cortaysye*, the relation between perfection and earthly endeavour, and the nature of true penitence and humility. If there is a new factor at the level of moral significance it is that the fuller commitment to fictional 'objectivity', particularly in characterization, introduces an element of indeterminacy which is absent from the other poems; or possibly we should say that, because moral *questions* rather than moral certainties form the essential subject-matter of the poem, the appropriate mode is the more independently fictional romance.

Sir Gawain has many of the principal characteristics of the medieval genre: a glittering and idealized chivalric background (in this case an Arthurian one), a quest in unknown country, a trial of courage, the attempted seduction of a Christian knight by a mysterious enchantress, elements of the marvellous and supernatural. Yet this material is used with light ironic humour and a detachment which is by no means typical of medieval romance in general and, although the poet sweeps us into his world on a wave of romance superlatives

(44–59), it soon becomes apparent that within the poem ideal chivalry is being tested in situations which approximate, in complexity and unexpectedness, to those of real life.

The poem has the twofold quality of all fiction which induces a high degree of imaginative realization in the mind of the reader—descriptive and dramatic power. The poet's descriptive art is many sided and varied in this poem, ranging from the exhaustive picture, like that of the Green Knight and his horse, to the enlarged detail, like that of the lady's face, when Gawain opens his eyes to find his whole field of vision filled by her chin and cheek, her slender laughing lips (1204–7). He can at times saturate the text with particulars. When he writes of clothing and armour, architecture, feasting, hunting or any other aspects of aristocratic life, he is particularly lavish, for he shares with other writers of courtly romance an unashamed delight in heightened descriptions of contemporary court life for their own sake. At the same time, the style exemplified in these descriptions is an attribute of the medieval concept of courtesy itself; the wealth of minute descriptive detail helps to establish a sense of the civilized life of the two courts, with all its material adjuncts: *all þe wele of þe worlde* (50). In the description of movement and action—for instance, when Gawain lifts the axe (421–6) or when the lady quietly enters his room for the first time (1182ff)—the technique is different but no less effective. Here there is a selective particularity (*þe kay fot*—the *left* foot [422], *a corner of þe cortyn* [1185])which gives the reader a sense of an actual scene and of shared experience. When we turn to the 'dramatic' aspects of literary composition—depth and consistency of characterization, the creation of episodes involving people in conversation and conflict—we find a comparable skill and subtlety. A major element in the poet's success here is his command of life-like speech (a facility abundantly demonstrated in the other poems as well—for instance, in Jonah's inner monologue in *Pat* 75–88, the words of the sailors in *Pat* 196–204, and in the Dreamer's conversations with the Maiden in *Pearl*). To a remarkable degree the characters are individualized and differentiated through their linguistic mannerisms, while at the same time there is conveyed a sense of the appropriate register for the occasion. Gawain's courtly deference is expressed in an involuted syntax, an exquisite deviousness of phrasing, which is noticeable as much in his public address to the king (343–61) as in his exchanges with the lady of the castle (e.g. 1218–21, 1263–7, 1535–48, 1801–12). The Green Knight, by contrast, consistently uses a brusque direct manner of speech, full of sharp statements and exclamations, and lacking in periphrasis (e.g. 448–56, 2239–49), though in Fitt IV his speech, appropriately, is somewhat modified by traits borrowed from that of his courtly other-self, while Gawain finds it impossible to sustain *his* elaborate politeness of address under the strain to which he is subjected.

In the long run the most significant factor in the poet's narrative technique is his adoption of a point of view within the action, which is no doubt related both to the ability to enter sympathetically into the predicament of his characters which we have observed in the other three poems and also to the use there of a projected first-person narrator (homilist or dreamer). In *Sir Gawain*, the initial long description of the Green Knight and his horse puts the reader in the position of King Arthur's courtiers, inasmuch as it is organized to follow their perceptions and their reactions to what they see. This point-of-view technique, which involves the reader emotionally in this way at the beginning, becomes even more important in the second, third, and fourth fitts, where Gawain's is the dominating consciousness in the poem. Just as the Round Table's corporate reputation for bravery and honour is now entrusted to Gawain, to stand or fall by his achievement as an individual, so from the beginning of Fitt II the reader's hopes and fears are identified with the hero's; and so to some extent is his view of what happens. Certainly the reader's awareness of what is taking place must be presumed to be a little more comprehensive than that of Gawain; but on the whole the evidence offered to us is limited to what he might have been able to observe. With the exception of the hunting episodes (which have no causal relation to his fate, though they may contain indirect poetic allusions to it), scarcely anything is recorded that does not take place in his presence, and at every important juncture we are aware of sharing in his perceptions and his emotional attitude towards the events and scenes described.

That the poet intends to use his considerable narrative powers in the exploration of a moral theme first becomes unmistakable at the beginning of Fitt II, where the sense of the inexorable drawing on of time is conveyed superbly in the kaleidoscopic picture of the sequence of the seasons. It is here that the more serious implications of what had seemed (in the context of Christmas gaiety) only a macabre joke receive graver emphasis (495–9). Gawain's performance in the return bout of the beheading game is all at once the focus of attention and it is apparent that the first fitt has merely been the dramatic prelude to a prolonged test of character.

This test is first and foremost one of honour in the face of death. Gawain must rise and go of his own volition and seek out his own destruction simply because he has given his word to do so. In preventing him from binding himself to any religious oath (402–4) the Green Knight has ensured that he will be acting purely from motives of honour and not to avoid divine punishment. The term used by both participants in the agreement (*bi þi trawþe* [394], *by my seker trawþe* [403]) is one that has been discussed earlier (see above, p. 24) as an important concept in *Cleanness*. There it was defined as 'loyalty to God and faith to one's God-given nature and proper role in the world'. Here initially in *Sir Gawain* it is more specifically 'truth to one's given word' and in this sense it is repeated constantly in relation to beheading agreement and the exchange bargains which Gawain makes with the host in Fitts II and III (1108, 1638, 2287, 2348, 2470). But with its synonyms and antonyms *trwe*, *lel(ly)*, *leuté*, *falce*, *falssyng*, *vntrawþe* it comes to denote, in relation to its various contexts of use in the poem, the religious and moral virtues of knighthood; in his own eyes, Gawain's fault has been

> my *kynde* to forsake:
> Þat is larges and lewté, þat longez to knyȝtez.
> Now am I fawty and falce, and ferde haf ben euer
> Of trecherye and *vntrawþe* (2380–3).

For despite the semi-exemplary nature of the poem, the poet has no wish to hold an isolated virtue up for admiration in an otherwise rather inhuman character. On the contrary he is concerned with a variety of virtues in interaction and competition. Whether he himself or some earlier writer was responsible for joining the various plots of the Beheading Game, Temptation, and Exchange of Winnings in their present form (the story patterns appear separately in other, French and Latin, works), their interlacement is cleverly exploited to show the difficulties which beset moral choice—and also moral judgement—in the complexities of real life. The poet knew that in life any genuine test of character comes unexpected, and as if in demonstration of this truth he faces Gawain—and the reader—with a series of deceptive situations which always catch him on the wrong foot:

Þe forme to þe fynisment foldez ful selden (499).

At a time when little courage appears to be demanded of him (358), when social tact and rhetoric are all that is required to secure him the opportunity of ridding the court of the troublesome intruder, he finds that he has taken on a real trial of nerve; after bracing himself for the return blow a year later, he finds that he has already been tested, on other conditions, in the social warmth and security of Bertilak's castle.

Furthermore, the moral danger to Gawain is complicated by the very mixture of demands made upon him by his own code of conduct. The ideal of *cheualry* to which he adheres is a composite code of behaviour which the later Middle Ages forged together from a number of disparate elements. The old Germanic attitudes of martial prowess, loyalty to one's lord, and generosity to one's followers formed the basis. Christianity contributed its moral absolutes— faith, charity, humility, chastity, etc.—and an emphasis on the use of power for the benefit of the weak; at the same time, the symbolism and ritual of the Church set formal precedents which were followed in the investiture rites of the orders of chivalry. Finally, the various social accomplishments which flowered among the feudal nobility of the high Middle Ages—the arts of music, poetry and elegant conversation, as much as horsemanship, jousting, and hunting—all made their contribution to the complex idea of the perfect knight. Medieval social theorists tend to stress the martial and religious side of chivalry. A somewhat different, and perhaps more generally influential, conception of knighthood—one in which social arts and refined manners are particularly prominent—was disseminated by the aristocratic literature of entertainment, the romances; and in the romance conception of knighthood, love between the sexes (as an adjunct of social manners) plays a part of such importance that it can be regarded as the *sine qua non* of courtesy.

The pentangle device which Gawain wears (*þat Salamon set sumquyle In bytoknyng of trawþe* [625f]) is the symbol of his whole character as a knight, and the poet's discussion of this symbolism, with its blending of Christian and courtly terminology, draws attention to the mixture of religious and secular virtues in the chivalric code. Through his somewhat strained allegory of the five lines and five points, the poet declares Gawain's senses (*fyue wyttez*) and his actions (*fyue fyngres*) to have been pure because of his trust in the salvation (*fyue woundez*) of Christ; his supreme martial virtue of fortitude (*forsnes*) also has a religious source in his devotion to the Five Joys of the Virgin. The fifth pentad consists of moral virtues particularly associated with knighthood, though each of these terms had both secular and religious connotations. Two of them, *clannes* and *cortaysye*, are important in other poems of the group and it is these that are also most relevant to the story of Gawain. We have seen from the treatment of the term in *Cleanness* that *clannes* can be viewed as a single concept with a broad range of meaning extending from physical cleanliness to moral purity and spiritual perfection. *Cortaysye* has a similar mobility of reference, embracing the superficial graces of behaviour at one end of the spectrum and theological Grace at the other (cf. *Pe* 432, etc., 457f, 467f, 480). In this poem, the terms *cortaysye*, *cortays(ly)* sometimes take on the wider meanings of *cheualry* and *cheualrous* (in 263, for instance, the Green Knight equates *cortaysye* with 'knightly conduct, daring') while continuing to designate the narrower set of social qualities exemplified, for instance, in Gawain's address to the king or his behaviour towards the lady of Hautdesert.

Also of importance for the significance of *cortaysye* (and by implication *trawþe*) in the poem is its juxtaposition with *clannes* in the pentangle passage: whatever other people might mean by the word, the author wishes to portray the perfect knight as free from the taint of sinful love, though he will not reject anything from the traditional concept of *cortaysye* which can possibly be reconciled with Christian morality; his knight cannot be a prig or a prude. Thus, though Gawain does of course defend his chastity in the course of the action, he never once bases an argument on religious conviction or abstract morality. In order to tempt Gawain to have intercourse with her, the lady insists on discussing and acting out the conventional tenets of *fin' amour* and, for fear of discourtesy, even the knight of Mary cannot refuse point-blank to take part in this elegant game. The lady's idea of the obligations of courtesy is obviously not the same as Gawain's, but he will parry her assaults on his virtue only by pretending to misunderstand her, or by protesting his own unworthiness—anything rather than openly criticize her conduct. The poet's intention is to place his knight in a situation in which the sides of the pentangle rub a little uncomfortably against one another. In this way the question of the compatibility of one element with another in this blend of manners, social obligation, and high religious ideals is delicately explored. The author of *Sir Gawain* shows an awareness of the latent contradictions in the idea of chivalry, and of the difficulty of behaving with *trawþe* to all its ideals; his insistence on the integrity of the pentangle figure, as the pattern of a well-integrated man, is the ironical prelude to a test in which circumstances make conflicting demands upon the hero and in which his system of virtue is somewhat divided against itself.

It is entirely consistent with the view of human nature which we meet in the other three poems that Gawain comes out of his test flawed—if only slightly. The poet devotes almost the whole of the description of the three long interviews with the lady to demonstrating Gawain's success in balancing the demands of courtesy with those of chastity and *trawþe* to his host— in showing that he is indeed *on þe fautlest freke þat euer on fote 3ede* (2363). If it is true that his chastity is attacked through his courtesy, it is also true that he achieves his victory through that attribute of courtesy for which he is most famous, his skill in *þe teccheles termes of talkyng noble* (917); to that extent his courtesy vindicates itself.

His single error of judgement occurs at the end of the third conversation, when he agrees to conceal from the host his acceptance of the girdle, thus violating the agreement made between them on the night of the first hunt and renewed on the two subsequent evenings. This temptation cannot, of course, be considered in complete isolation from the others, though it is of a different kind. There is an element of cunning in its placement just before the lady's final departure from his room, for his sustained success in resisting one type of inducement to sin over three days would make him especially vulnerable to a superficially casual suggestion which contained no threat to his chastity. Nor can we discount the possible effect on his resolution of the all-pervading atmosphere of intimate gaiety, luxury, and ease in the castle (note the emphasis, for instance, in 1310ff, 1468ff, 1560ff, 1729ff). However, we can be sure (with the Green Knight—cf. 2367) that 'wooing' plays no direct part in his action, for he has previously had little difficulty in refusing the offer of a ring as a keepsake. Politeness, again, can be only a minor factor. It is true that the lady extracts from him the promise of concealment only after he has accepted the gift but we cannot infer (after his displays of skill in extricating himself from similar social traps) that he had no choice but to agree. He agrees to the deception principally because he sees in the belt the possibility of saving his life.

It is by no means self-evident that we are to see this as an unworthy motive (or even contrary to the beheading agreement). On the face of it, as long as Gawain keeps his word by presenting himself at the appointed time and takes the return blow *withoute dabate* (2041), his moral duty in regard to his compact with the Green Knight is fulfilled; and he can hardly be blamed for taking the chance of magical protection against an adversary who so obviously has magic at his disposal. This appears to be the view which the Green Knight himself takes of the matter when, at the end of Fitt IV, he drops his terrifying pose and merges in character once more with the genial Sir Bertilak. Gawain is gently reproved for breaking his word in neglecting to yield up the whole of his winnings of the third day, but to Sir Bertilak (2368), as to the narrator (2037ff), it is a mitigating factor that his motive was one of self-preservation. Sir Bertilak, in other words, appears to take into account the gap in importance between the matter of life and death to which Gawain is committed at the Green Chapel and the exchange of winnings agreement. The levity with which the latter is proposed, and which accompanies its performance and reaffirmation each time, might indeed suggest to the reader (and presumably to Gawain too) that this agreement belongs to the realm of burlesque; the pledges are mock-solemn ones, made always *in bourde* 'in jest' (1409; cf. 1404, 1112f, 1680–85) and the incongruous 'winnings' are exchanged amid laughter and jokes (1392–9, 1623, 1644–7, 1932ff).

In retrospect, however, Gawain's breach of the exchange-agreement becomes a grave moral fault for him. In fact, his bitter self-condemnation when he knows he has been found out is in marked contrast to the 'plain man's' view taken of his fault by the narrator, by Sir Bertilak, and later by the knights of the Round Table (2513ff). He accuses himself repeatedly of *cowardyse* and *couetyse* (2374, 2379f, 2508), the first principally an offence against courage (the major virtue of chivalry), the second primarily a vice in the Christian code, the root of all evil and the antithesis of charity, but also in the poem the antithesis of *larges and lewté, þat longez to knyȝtez* (2381). (The deliberate crossing of the two terminologies is as noticeable in these passages as in the description of the pentangle, and serves a similar purpose.)

The mixture of evidence and attitude which is built into the poem presents the reader with a group of interconnected moral problems to contemplate, rather than a simple moral verdict on the nature and degree of Gawain's fault. There is perhaps no indubitably correct view of Gawain's culpability, only a series of further questions. In condemning himself so severely, Gawain might be accused of making *ernest of game*. But it is a recurring theme of the poem that game and earnest are in continual alternation, the two faces of a single destiny (cf. 16–19, 495ff, 564f, 1681f), and that it is often impossible to foresee the consequences of trivial action (495–9). The beheading agreement itself begins as a *Crystemas gomen* (283)—and a foolish one at that (323f, 358). We are led to wonder to what extent circumstances *do* alter cases, or whether to have any meaning at all a principle like *trawþe* is not absolute and unqualified. Again, if Gawain's remorse appears excessive (it appears, in the sentiments expressed in 2511f, to go counter to any teaching a priest might have given him on forgiveness), it nevertheless exposes as superficial the cheerful readiness of the Arthurian courtiers to identify with his triumph rather than his shame.

Two factors account for the greater openness of the didacticism in *Sir Gawain*, as compared with that of the other poems. One of these is the part played by the fictional element in the poem. A third-person narrator is by implication an observer merely (though he may at times assume a superhuman knowledge of his characters' motives), the characters in fiction are in a sense 'historical' persons and therefore debatable on the evidence given, and situations presented as fact continually exercise the reader's moral judgement. Secondly, we are never allowed to forget that what is under examination in *Sir Gawain* is a code of practical morality in secular society. There can, of course, at this date be no ultimate division between the religious and the secular outlook on conduct, and the touchstone of Christian doctrine is never far in the background. It is significant that all the major passages of rhetorical amplification (prologues to Fitt I and Fitt II, pentangle passage, description of the ladies) have a universality that contributes to the moral gravity of the poem. Through them the actions of Gawain are placed in a context successively of world history, the natural order, moral law, and the mutability of human life and beauty. No precedent for these passages exists in any of the known analogues; they are evidently designed by the author to direct the reader's attention to the significance he wishes the story material to bear. Even in these passages, however, he prefers in general to avoid direct moralizing and to rely on the resonance of traditional religious language (cf. notes to 528ff, 497, 943–69, 2208–10) to bring home to the reader the more serious implications of the tale.

The poet's aim may be specified as a loving critique of courtesy. He perhaps wished to show that as the exemplar of a refined chivalry Gawain was also as nearly perfect a Christian as can ordinarily be expected in this imperfect world, and to demonstrate this without distorting the concept of true knighthood which he had learned from the most courtly romances. It is precisely his lightness of touch, his avoidance of overt didacticism, and his preference for irony, suggestion and implication, that enabled him to make his romance the vehicle of a wise morality without in the least disfiguring it as a romance.

Note on Language and Metre

The English of the poems is that of the north-west midland area in the late fourteenth century. Essential grammatical information (irregular past forms of verbs and plurals of nouns, etc.) will be found in the glossary and notes. The following additional features of language and style should be noticed:

1   The present infinitive of the verb may have *-en*, *-e*, or no ending.

2   In the present indicative, the first person singular inflexion is regularly *-e* or no ending; the second and third person singular form ends in *-(e)s/z* (*-tz* in a few common monosyllabic verbs, e.g. *gotz* 'goes', *hatz* 'has') and thus contrasts with the subjunctive form in *-e* or without ending: *þou leue Pe* 865, *hit displese Pat* 1. In the present indicative plural the usual ending is *-e* or *-en* (occasionally *-(e)s/z*, especially where the verb is separated from its subject, e.g. in a subordinate clause), though inflexion is absent in a number of instances. The present subjunctive plural ending is no longer strictly distinctive in this dialect.

3   The (polite) plural imperative of the verb usually ends in *-(e)s/z*: *Dysplesez Pe* 422, *Tas yow G* 1390 (reflex.). The imperative (singular and plural) is sometimes reinforced by *do*: *Do gyf Pat* 204, *Dos techez G* 1533.

4   The present participle ends in *-and(e)*: *dawande Pat* 445, *Meuande Cl* 783; the *-yng* forms are mostly verbal nouns: *lokyng* 'gaze' *Pe* 1049, *talkyng* 'conversation' *G* 917 (apparent exceptions, like *sykyng Pe* 1175, *G* 753 and *gruchyng G* 2126, are probably re-interpreted prepositional phrases: [*with*] *sykyng*, etc.).

5   The past participle ends in *-e*, *-(e)n* (strong verbs) or *-d(e)*, *-t* (weak verbs); the prefix *i-* is found only in *ichose* 'chosen' *Pe* 904.

6   The present tense can be used with future sense: *We byde* 'we will wait' *Cl* 622, *take* 'will receive' *G* 383.

7   The verb *be* is used regularly to make the perfect and pluperfect of intransitive verbs (where modern English has *have*): *watz passed, departed* 'had passed, departed' *Cl* 395f, *watz fayled* 'had finished' *Cl* 658, *wern woned* 'had subsided' *Cl* 496, *watz sesed* 'had ceased' *G* 1.

8   Impersonal constructions are common: *hym moʒt haf lumpen worse* 'something worse might have happened to him' *Cl* 1320, *hym wondered* 'it was a puzzle to him' *G* 1201.

9   Double negatives (e.g. *Pe* 4, 225f, *Cl* 21, 513, *Pat* 223, 346, *G* 706f, 1809) are equivalent to single negatives (also in indirect prohibitions, e.g. *Cl* 45, *G* 1156f).

10   A main verb of motion is often omitted after an auxiliary or modal, e.g. *Pat* 346, *G* 1959, 2132.

11   Relative clauses are often separated from their antecedents, e.g. *Cl* 388, *Pat* 233, *G* 331, and see note to *G* 145f.

12   Prepositions often follow their nouns (pronouns): *me ouer Pat* 312, *þe brymme bysyde G* 2172.

13 Poetic inversion is frequent, e.g. *Pe* 170 ('when I had noticed her noble form'), *Pat* 270 ('which seemed like a road to him'), *G* 389 ('that you are to strike this blow').

14 An adverbial adjunct may anticipate the clause to which it belongs: *Pe* 287 ('If I were now'), *Pe* 709, *Cl* 1703f ('that it was in truth none other'), *G* 1182f ('heard a little noise [made] stealthily at his door').

15 Adjectives sometimes function as nouns: *þat schene* 'that beautiful one' *Pe* 166, 965, *þo wery forwroȝt* 'those (men) exhausted with toil' *Pat* 163, *þe naked* 'the bare flesh' *G* 423, *þis wyly* (i.e. the fox) *G* 1905.

16 In description, a 'catalogue' style (nominal, prepositional, and participial phrases where finite verbs might be expected) is sometimes used, e.g. *Cl* 1401–16, *G* 568–89.

17 Phrases like *in erde, þat tyde, in londe* (e.g. *Cl* 122, 601, *G* 585) are sometimes metrical expletives of very little (or only intensive) meaning; they can be used aptly on occasions, however, and allowance should always be made for the possibility of special significance; see *G* 196n.

18 The alliterative poet needed synonyms of varying phonetic form for at least the most common concepts; one result of this is that words of specialized meaning are used in alliteration in a generalized sense: *cleche Cl* 12 (normally 'seize, grasp', here 'obtain'), *wale G* 398 (normally 'choose', here 'find'); cf. *G* 154n, 288n. The tendency can be a poetic asset, in that it often imparts greater immediacy and concreteness to the language.

19 Alliterating pairs of words within the line may be used with little precise difference of sense but mainly for alliteration, emphasis, and variety of expression: *þryuen and þro Pe* 868, *þe sege and þe assaut G* 1, *spyed and spured G* 901; see also the note to *a berfray on basteles wyse Cl* 1186f.

The long lines of *Cl*, *Pat*, and *G* are composed in the alliterative metre which was inherited, through Old English poetry, from the prehistoric Germanic period. Since no treatise on this kind of versification survives we can only attempt to deduce its principles from the poetry itself.[1] Although there was evidently some continuity in the practice of alliterative versification between the Old English period and the fourteenth century, it should not be assumed that the principles were unchanged. Indeed some modifications—an overall increase in the number of syllables in the line, changed alliterative rules, and perhaps the use of the full line (rather than the half-line) as a syntactical unit—appear to have emerged as natural consequences of developments in the language itself. Another factor which must be allowed for is the existence of an alternative form of verse in the late medieval period—the accentual metres which came to dominate English poetry in subsequent centuries. The alliterative verse of the fourteenth century kept its separate identity by differentiation from these newer metres, though a compromise is already appearing in various combinations of alliteration and stanza form (as the verse-structures of *Pe* and—in part—*G* illustrate). When in the early sixteenth century it ceased to exist as a distinct mode, this was because it had merged with a line of accentual triple time (called by James I 'tumbling verse').

[1] For fuller discussion of alliterative metre in these poems see Borroff, **7d** 1962; Turville-Petre, **7d** 1976.

All these factors make it legitimate to regard the alliterative versification of the fourteenth century as a form of verse in its own right with the following characteristics:

1 An underlying regularity of pace, marked by four chief stresses to the line.

2 A central caesura—i.e. a greater syntactical break between second and third stresses than between first and second or third and fourth.

3 Repetition of the initial sounds (alliteration) of some of the stressed syllables (in principle the first three), which gives extra prominence to these syllables and bridges the caesura.

4 Variation in the number of unstressed syllables between the stresses.

The system thus outlined parallels that of accentual verse in the general sense that it provides for a *ground-pattern* with *variation*. In accentual verse the ground-pattern is that of a regular alternation of stressed syllables with a determined number of unstressed syllables. This is, of course, a purely notional pattern, merely suggested to the mind of the reader by the actual stress and intonation pattern of the lines of spoken English and in turn imposed by the mind of the reader on lines which deviate from the pattern more than a little. Variation may be said to be a necessary part of the system: not only is the actual intonation of spoken English more complex than such an abstract pattern recognizes (in using, for instance, more than two degrees of relative stress) but a great deal of the variety of English verse is achieved through deliberate flexibility in approximation to and deviation from the conceptual 'norm'.

In fourteenth-century alliterative verse the notional ground-pattern is set up by lines such as

$$\overset{\times}{\text{Þurȝ}} \ \overset{\times}{\text{þe}} \ \overset{/}{\text{faut}} \ \text{of} \ \overset{\times}{\text{a}} \ \overset{\times}{\text{}} \ \overset{/\,(\times)}{\text{freke}} \ \| \ \overset{\times}{\text{þat}} \ \overset{/}{\text{fayled}} \ \overset{\times}{\text{in}} \ \overset{\times}{\text{}} \ \overset{/}{\text{traw}} \overset{(\times)}{\text{þe}} \quad Cl\ 236$$

$$\overset{\times}{\text{Bot}} \ \overset{\times}{\text{he}} \ \overset{/}{\text{dredes}} \ \overset{\times}{\text{no}} \ \overset{/}{\text{dynt}} \ \| \ \overset{\times}{\text{þat}} \ \overset{/}{\text{dotes}} \ \overset{\times}{\text{for}} \ \overset{/\,(\times)}{\text{elde}} \quad Pat\ 125$$

in which the caesura is present, alliterative prominence coincides with the first three stresses (a a a x), and the spoken intonation has marked regularity of pace. The special rhythmical variety of alliterative verse is achieved in a number of ways, but principally by the use of phrase patterns with varying numbers of unstressed syllables between the stresses. In particular in the first half-line (which is on average a syllable or two longer than the second) there may be three or more unstressed syllables between the stresses:[2]

$$\overset{\times}{\text{And}} \ \overset{\times}{\text{he}} \ \overset{/}{\text{luflyly}} \ \overset{\times\ \times\ \times}{\text{hit hym}} \ \overset{/}{\text{laft}} \quad G\ 369a$$

while in both first and second half-lines the two stresses may come together with no intervening unstressed syllable:

$$\overset{\times}{\text{Þe}} \ \overset{\times}{\text{most}} \ \overset{/}{\text{kyd}} \ \overset{/}{\text{knyȝtez}} \ \| \quad G\ 51a$$

$$\| \overset{\times}{\text{}} \ \overset{\times}{\text{and}} \ \overset{/}{\text{þe}} \ \overset{/\,(\times)}{\text{wers haue}} \quad Pat\ 48b$$

[2] R. F. Lawrence, *ES*, 51 (1970), established that in the *Wars of Alexander* a single unstressed syllable between the two stresses is sometimes avoided by formulaic variation, the poet preferring x/xx/x or x/ /x.

Other methods of achieving rhythmical variety are quite common. The first half-line often contains more than two alliterating words, and here we may assume, with Borroff, **7d** 1962, that the extra alliterative prominence can coincide with an intermediate degree of stress (\) on that syllable but that it does not disturb the underlying regularity of two chief stresses per half-line:

$$\overset{/}{\textbf{Br}}\overset{\times}{a}\overset{\times}{y}\overset{\times}{de}\overset{\times}{z} \text{ out a } \overset{\setminus}{\textbf{br}}\overset{/}{y}\overset{}{}\text{3t } \textbf{br}\text{ont}\quad G \text{ 1584a}$$

The rhythmical and syntactical patterns of these extended half-lines occur also without the extra alliteration:

$$\overset{/}{\textbf{G}}\overset{(\times)\times}{ederez} \overset{\times}{vp} \text{ hys } \overset{\times}{\textbf{g}}\text{rymme} \overset{\setminus}{to}\text{le}^3\quad G \text{ 2260a}$$
$$\overset{/}{\textbf{F}}\overset{\times}{yn}\text{des} \overset{\times\times}{he a} \overset{\setminus}{\textbf{f}}\overset{/}{a}\text{yr schyp}\quad Pat \text{ 98a}$$

In some lines, on the other hand, alliteration may occur on only two stresses, just enough to link the two half-lines:

$$\text{For me þink hit not } \textbf{s}\text{emly—as hit is } \textbf{s}\text{oþ knawen}\quad G \text{ 348}$$

In others there is alliteration on consonant groups rather than single consonants:

And **sp**are **sp**akly of **sp**yt, in **sp**ace of My þewez   *Cl* 755
Þe **pr**uddest of þe **pr**ouince, and **pr**ophetes childer   *Cl* 1300

or a double alliterative pattern:

Schaued wyth a **sch**arp **kn**yf, and þe **sch**yre **kn**itten   G 1331

Alliteration sometimes introduces an unstressed word or syllable, instead of coinciding with one of the chief stresses:

$$\text{Þenne a}\textbf{scr}\text{yed þay hym } \textbf{sck}\text{ete} \quad \text{and a}\textbf{sk}\text{ed ful loude}\quad Pat \text{ 195}$$
$$\text{Be þay } \textbf{f}\text{ers, be þay } \textbf{f}\text{eble, } \textbf{f}\text{orlotez none}\quad Cl \text{ 101}$$
$$\text{'And } \textbf{f}\text{yue wont of } \textbf{f}\text{yfty,' quoþ God, 'I schal for3ete alle'}\quad Cl \text{ 739}$$
$$\text{Er me } \textbf{w}\text{ont þe } \textbf{w}\text{ede, } \textbf{w}\text{ith help of my frendez}\quad G \text{ 987}$$
$$\text{And þat is þe } \textbf{b}\text{est, } \textbf{b}\text{e my dome, for me } \textbf{b}\text{yhouez nede } (\textit{or } \textbf{b}\text{e my dome})\quad G \text{ 1216}$$

The device of separating alliteration from stress often seems to be used to level out prominences for the more prosaic uses of the metre. Vocalic alliteration—the recognition of any vowel as alliterating with any other vowel or with *h*—can have a similar effect:

---

³ It is not always possible to say with certainty whether a final unaccented -*e* was still pronounced in the area of these poems at the time at which they were written. Some, however, like that of *tole* (direct object) were merely spelling conventions (here indicating long medial -*o*-) and were never pronounced. Elision (a feature of accentual verse at this time) can be assumed where a final -*e* is followed by a vowel in the next word.

Þaȝ I be not now he þat ȝe of speken   *G* 1242

And als, in myn vpynyoun, hit arn of on kynde   *Pat* 40

The caesura also, though in general a feature of this type of verse, can be overridden in individual lines:

Þat schal schewe hem so schene schrowde of þe best   *Cl* 170

He telles me þose traytoures   arn typped schrewes   *Pat* 77

Þe gome glyȝt on þe grene   graciouse leues   *Pat* 453

In each of these lines grammatical analysis would reveal a more fundamental break between first and second or third and fourth stress than between second and third.

The alliterative metre can thus serve the skilled practitioner as an instrument of wide-ranging style. Its variety enables it to contribute to many kinds of emphasis, antithesis, and irony. What is more surprising is that (far from being a crude matter of 'rum, ram, ruf') in passages of quiet conversation or discourse it can seem quite unobtrusive and natural (as for instance in *G* 1208–36).

A double oblique stroke in the left-hand margin of the MS (similar to that marking the beginning of the stanza in *Pe* and *G*) occurs in the text of *Cl* and *Pat* at the beginning of every fourth line. On the strength of these marks some editors have printed these poems in four-line 'stanzas' or 'quatrains'. There is little doubt that a basic four-line syntax underlies the two poems: major syntactical breaks (indicated by a semi-colon or full stop in modern punctuation) occur too often for coincidence at the ends of lines which are multiples of four. (Some of the disturbances to this system of verse-paragraphing may be the result of scribal interference—see, e.g., *Pat* 509–15n; others are undoubtedly cases of temporary suspension by the poet.)

In view of the fact, however, that no strictly metrical criteria are involved we consider the terms 'stanza' and 'quatrain', and the visual division of the poems into groups of four lines, inappropriate; we accordingly print them as continuous blank verse.[4]

In *G* blocks of long lines are used to form stanzas of varying length, each of which is rounded off by a line of one stress (the 'bob') followed by a rhyming quatrain (the 'wheel') of three-stressed lines, the second and fourth of which rhyme with the bob. Although alliteration is used in these rhymed lines, there is a noticeable shift in rhythm towards the accentual type of verse used in *Pe*.

An account of the stanzaic structure of *Pe*, its rhyme scheme, its system of stanza-grouping by refrain word, and its concatenation, has been given on p. 35f above. Alliteration is here used less systematically than in the long lines of the other three poems, stylistically rather than structurally. While there may

---

[4] For fuller discussion see Mabel Day, *Englische Studien*, 66 (1931–2), 245–8, J. R. Hulbert, *MP*, 48 (1950–51), 73–81, and Vantuono, **7c** 1972.

be four, three, or two alliterating words in the line, about one line in four, on average, has no alliteration at all. The governing principle of rhythm here is that of four-stressed accentual verse of an iambic pattern. Gordon (**2a** 1953, pp. 89ff) may well be right in discerning some influence from the rhythm of the unrhymed alliterative line in the tendency of the *Pe* line to fall into two halves and in its freedom in the use of unstressed syllables, though this observation would apply to much of the rhymed verse of the period, non-alliterative as well as alliterative.

Note to the Text

This edition is based on the EETS facsimile of the MS (on the MS itself in cases of doubt) and the text has been compared throughout with that of the principal earlier editions of the individual poems. Except in cases of uncertainty or special interest, the abbreviations of the MS and contemporary corrections are interpreted without notice. Substantive emendations (credited in parentheses) are recorded in the textual notes beneath the text, with further discussion, if necessary, in the explanatory notes. The spelling of the MS is followed exactly, with the proviso that the functions of letter forms with a double use are distinguished: that is to say, a distinction is made between *i/j* as a vowel (printed *i*) and as a consonant (printed *j*), and also between the symbol *ȝ* as representing the velar and alveolar spirant (printed *ȝ*) and as representing the voiced sibilant (printed *z*); *-tȝ* (probably the sound of unvoiced *-s*) is printed *-tz*. In about 15 cases throughout the MS we have supplied a word-final or -initial consonant, though we suspect that the omission may reflect elision in speech (e.g. *Pe* 142, 185, 286, *Cl* 1429, *Pat* 523, *G* 113, 773, 1069). Emendation is not resorted to solely for the sake of restoring rhyme; in one or two cases, however, we have been guided by alliterative pattern or rhythm.

Stanzaic division in *Pe* and *G* are dictated by formal metrical criteria. On the question of stanzaic division in *Pat* and *Cl*, see p. 49. In *Pe*, a large decorated initial marks the beginning of each group of stanzas (misplaced in line 961—see note); in the other three poems, large initials occur at the following lines: *Cl* 1, 125, 193, 249, 345, 485, 557, 601, 689, 781, 893, 1157, and 1357; *Pat* 1, 61, 245, 305, and 409; *G* 1, 491, 619, 763, 1126, 1421, 1893, 1998, and 2259. While these often occur at important transitions in the poems, they are located unevenly and sometimes arbitrarily, apparently by scribal rather than authorial choice. They are here taken as marking distinct divisions in the text only in the case of the four extra large and prominent initials at *G* 1, 491, 1126, and 1998, which have traditionally been accepted by editors as marking the beginnings of four narrative fitts.

Pearl

I

Perle plesaunte, to prynces paye   [f39ʳ]
To clanly clos in golde so clere:
Oute of oryent, I hardyly saye,
Ne proued I neuer her precios pere.
So rounde, so reken in vche araye,   5
So smal, so smoþe her sydez were;
Queresoeuer I jugged gemmez gaye
I sette hyr sengeley in synglure.
Allas! I leste hyr in on erbere;

1f. 'Lovely pearl, which it pleases a prince to set radiantly (*or* chastely) in gold so
bright'. The first line of the poem is echoed in the last, by which stage the *prynce*, here
an earthly ruler, has come to signify Christ. The opening echoes a formula common
in medieval verse lapidaries (see W. H. Schofield, *PMLA*, 24 [1909], 585–675). This
suggests the earthly appreciation of the pearl as an object of value—a view which,
like the significance of *prynce*, is to be transformed during the course of the poem.
3f. 'I declare assuredly that I never found her equal in value among those of the
orient.' The emphatic use of the first-person pron. sets a pattern, maintained
throughout the poem, of ideas presented through the experience and reflections of a
created and fully realized *persona*. *Oryent*: pearls from the orient were highly valued
(cf. 82, 255, and [e.g.] Chaucer, *The Legend of Good Women* [F] 221), and *orient pearl*
came to mean 'brilliant or precious pearl' (see Marlowe, *The Jew of Malta* IV.1.66f,
V.4.28). Here the word derives further resonance from the medieval association of
paradise with the orient: see note to 65ff. *Her*: in *Cl* 1117ff the pearl is referred to as
both *ho* and *hyt* (MS *hym*): the usage, therefore, appears to be variable. Here, how-
ever, the feminine pronouns (cf. 6, 8, 9, etc.) prepare for the later identification of
the pearl with the Maiden, while the neuter pronouns of 10, 13, etc. keep in mind
the symbol-object.
5f. These lines clearly anticipate the identification of the pearl with the Maiden (see
189ff, 241ff, 411f, and notes). The poet draws on stock epithets used in courtly
literature to describe beautiful women (cf., for instance, Chaucer, *Troilus* III.1248).
9. *erbere*: 'garden'. This word is derived from OF *erbier* ('garden', and also 'grass plot'
and 'vegetation'), and in the late 14th c. had a range of meaning which could have
included 'garden', 'herb garden', 'pleasure garden', and 'grass plot': see *MED* and
Luttrell, **7a** 1965. In medieval literature, gardens are usually associated with
seclusion and delight, sacred (as in the terrestrial paradise) or profane (as in the
gardens of love in romance). This tradition, both verbal and iconographic, shows the
absorption of the classical idea of the *locus amoenus* ('delightful place'): see Ernst R.
Curtius, *European Literature and the Latin Middle Ages*, tr. Willard R. Trask (London,
1953), 192–200, and Pearsall and Salter, **8** 1973, 56–118. In its sacred applications,
the garden is associated with the *hortus conclusus* ('enclosed [pleasure-] garden') from

Þur₃ gresse to grounde hit fro me yot.   10
I dewyne, fordolked of luf-daungere
Of þat pryuy perle withouten spot.

Syþen in þat spote hit fro me sprange,
Ofte haf I wayted, wyschande þat wele
Þat wont watz whyle deuoyde my wrange   15
And heuen my happe and al my hele—
Þat dotz bot þrych my hert þrange,
My breste in bale bot bolne and bele.
₃et þo₃t me neuer so swete a sange
As stylle stounde let to me stele.   20
Forsoþe þer fleten to me fele.
To þenke hir color so clad in clot!

the Song of Songs 4:12: this was variously interpreted as allegorically representing the Virgin Mary, Christ's human nature, Christ's resurrection, and the Church (see Hamilton, **7a** 1955). At this point, however, the garden is primarily to be understood literally, the sacred and symbolic associations emerging in the transfigured landscape of the vision.

10. *yot:* 'ran, fell'. This is probably a pa.t. of *yette* 'pour' (OE ₃*eotan*, see *OED yet*), which can be used both transitively and intransitively. The word is applied in ME to tears, blood, etc.; here it is transferred to the round, tear-like pearl, perhaps to suggest the Dreamer's grief as well as the tenuousness of his hold on his treasure. The *OED*'s identification with ₃*ode* 'went' is less convincing.

11. *luf-daungere:* The compound may be the poet's own, but the word *daungere* ('feudal power') signifies the power of the mistress over her suitor, specifically her power to keep him at a distance, and is so personified in the *Roman de la Rose* (cf. also the usage in 250 below). *Luf-daungere* is here used metaphorically to suggest longing for, and separation from, any loved object, and the whole line is perhaps reminiscent of the phrase *quia amore langueo* ('for I am sick for love'). The Song of Songs, from which this phrase comes (2:5, 5:7–8), was interpreted spiritually as the soul's longing for Christ (cf. *luf-longyng*, 1152, and 1149–52n). See W. R. J. Barron, ' "Luf-daungere", ' in *A Medieval Miscellany presented to Eugène Vinaver*, ed. F. Whitehead, A. H. Diverres, and F. E. Sutcliffe (Manchester and New York, 1965).

12–60. On the function of concatenation in *Pe*, see Introduction, p. 35f. In this section, the concatenation word *spot(e)* is used in two senses, 'blemish' and 'place', between which wordplay is maintained throughout, one sense occurring in the last line of each stanza, the other in the first line of the next. The words *withouten spot* (12, 24, etc.) translate the Vulgate *sine macula*, a phrase applied to the Brides of the Lamb in Rev. 14:5—thus suggesting some anticipation of the heavenly vision near the end of the poem. See D. W. Robertson, Jr., **7a** 1950b.

14. *wyschande þat wele:* 'longing for that precious thing'.

17. *þat:* i.e. keeping watch.

19–22. 'Never yet did a song seem to me to have such sweetness as a moment of peace let steal over me. In truth there used to come fleetingly to me many (such moments). To think of her colour clad, as now, in mud!' This interpretation, which follows W. A. Davenport, 'Desolation, not Consolation: *Pearl* 19–22', *ES*, 55 (1974), 421–3, takes ₃*et* (19) as temporal and makes the sense of the lines retrospective. Previous

O moul, þou marrez a myry juele,
My priuy perle withouten spotte.

Þat spot of spysez mot nedez sprede,   25
Þer such rychez to rot is runne,
Blomez blayke and blwe and rede
Þer schyne ful schyr agayn þe sunne.
Flor and fryte may not be fede
Þer hit doun drof in moldez dunne,   30
For vch gresse mot grow of graynez dede;
No whete were ellez to wonez wonne.
Of goud vche goude is ay bygonne:
So semly a sede moȝt fayly not,
Þat spryngande spycez vp ne sponne   35
Of þat precios perle wythouten spotte.

25. mot] MS . . . t (*blotted*)
26. runne (Gollancz)] MS runnen
28. schyne (Luttrell)] MS schynez
35. spryngande] MS sprygande

editors have taken *ȝet* in the sense 'however', understanding the lines to refer in anticipation to the consolation of the heavenly vision, or even (so Gordon) to the poem (*sange*) in which the vision is embodied.

22f. The description of the burial of the pearl suggests human burial (a theme returned to in 320, 857, and 957f), and is retrospectively identified with the burial of the Maiden. Since there was a traditional belief that the pearl survived untarnished its burial in mire, the Dreamer is here unconsciously betraying his earthbound view (cf. *Cl* 1111–48n).

25. *mot:* Morris and Gollancz read *myȝt*, Osgood and Gordon *mot.* In the MS, the first letter appears to be *m*, but only the final *t* is entirely clear. Immediately before *t*, the tail of another letter, probably *ȝ*, is faintly visible. However, since there is room for only one letter between *m* and *t*, it seems likely that this faint tail is the remnant of an erased letter.

27. *blayke:* 'pale, white'.

27f. Gollancz compares the Chaucerian *The Romaunt of the Rose* 1577f.

28. *schyne:* The emendation of MS *schynez* to the infinitive *schyne*, suggested by Luttrell, **7a** 1965, makes this word dependent, like *sprede* (25), on *mot.* Thus the break in the continuity of grammar and argument is eliminated.

29f. 'Flower and fruit cannot be faded where it (the pearl) sank down into dun clods'. *Fede:* probably from OF *fade* 'faded', modified for rhyme. (Cf. OIcel *feyja* 'decay').

31f. Cf. John 12:24–5, 1 Cor. 15:35–8. This is a familiar Christian formula of *solacium* ('consolation, solace') for the inevitable fact of death: see Bishop, **7a** 1968, 14ff.

32. 'otherwise no wheat would be brought to the homes (i.e. brought in, harvested).'

34–6. 'so lovely a seed could not fail to be productive, so that flourishing spice plants would not shoot up from that precious spotless pearl.'

To þat spot þat I in speche expoun   [f39ᵛ]
I entred in þat erber grene,
In Augoste in a hyȝ seysoun,
Quen corne is coruen wyth crokez kene.   40
On huyle þer perle hit trendeled doun
Schadowed þis wortez ful schyre and schene:
Gilofre, gyngure, and gromylyoun,
And pyonys powdered ay bytwene.
Ȝif hit watz semly on to sene,   45
A fayrre flayr ȝet fro hit flot,
Þer wonys þat worþyly, I wot and wene,
My precious perle wythouten spot.

Bifore þat spot my honde I spennd
For care ful colde þat to me caȝt;   50
A deuely dele in my hert denned,
Þaȝ resoun sette myseluen saȝt.

46. fayrre flayr (Gollancz)] MS fayr reflayr

39f. Various identifications for the *hyȝ seysoun* have been suggested: the Transfiguration of Christ (Sister Mary Madeleva, *'Pearl': A Study in Spiritual Dryness* [New York, 1925], supported by William J. Knightley, *MLN*, 76 [1961], 97–102), the Assumption of the Virgin (Osgood), and Lammas (Gollancz and Gordon). Of these, the Feast of Lammas (August 1), with its associations of harvest, seems the most appropriate. Harvesting is represented as the occupation of the month for August (and/or July) in medieval calendars (e.g. in the Très Riches Heures of the Duc de Berri, and the Peterborough Psalter)—and this is reflected in encyclopedic literature (see, e.g., Trevisa IX.16), and ecclesiastical carving (e.g. in the schemes at Chartres, Amiens, and Paris), as well as in poetry. The tradition of the occupations of the months is discussed by Rosemund Tuve, *Seasons and Months: Studies in a Tradition of Middle English Poetry* (Paris, 1933, repr. Cambridge and Totowa, N. J., 1974), 122–70, and Pearsall and Salter, **8** 1973, 128–60. In the light of the reminiscences of St John and St Paul (see note to 31f) the harvesting imagery clearly symbolizes the possibility of resurrection, which the Dreamer does not yet understand. The St John text is used to make the same point in *PPl* C.XIII.179ff.

45f. 'If it was lovely to look at, still fairer was the scent that floated from it'. *Fayrre flayr* (46): the word division of the MS (here *fayr reflayr*) is not always a reliable guide to the poet's intention. Both *flayr* and *reflayr* (cf. *Cl* 1079) occur in ME with similar meaning, but the syntax (*ȝif* [45] and *ȝet* [46] reinforcing the expectation of a comparative) favours the reading adopted. This interpretation derives further support from the syntax of 147f.

47. 'where that precious one lives, I believe and know'.

51. *deuely:* 'desolating', probably from late OE **deaflic*, cf. OIcel *daufligr* 'lonely, dismal'.

51–6. The contrast between the responses prompted by reason and those prompted by passion anticipates the theme of the central debate between the Dreamer and the Maiden, through which he is brought by reason to an understanding of Christian doctrine and acceptance of God's will.

I playned my perle þat þer watz penned,
Wyth fyrce skyllez þat faste faȝt.
Þaȝ kynde of Kryst me comfort kenned,   55
My wreched wylle in wo ay wraȝte.
I felle vpon þat floury flaȝt,
Suche odour to my hernez schot;
I slode vpon a slepyng-slaȝte
On þat precios perle withouten spot.   60

II

Fro spot my spyryt þer sprang in space;
My body on balke þer bod. In sweuen
My goste is gon in Godez grace,
In auenture þer meruaylez meuen.
I ne wyste in þis worlde quere þat hit wace,   65

53. penned (Holthausen)] MS spenned
54. fyrce] MS fyrte
60. precios] MS precos

53. *penned:* As the poet usually avoids identical rhyme, it is likely that this was the original reading; cf. 702n.

57–60. Hamilton, **7a** 1955, points out that a special perfume associated with divine grace occurs frequently in such works as Grail legends and Saints' Lives. *Slepyng-slaȝte* (59) signifies a sudden heavy sleep. *Slaȝte* is derived from OE *slæht*, which has a range of meaning including 'slaughter', 'death by violence' on the one hand, and 'stroke', 'blow' on the other. In *Pat* 192 the ME word clearly has a metaphorical development of the latter meaning. Here, the metaphor could suggest either a sleep like death, or else sleep which descends with the suddenness of a blow. Kean, **7a** 1967, 27, compares similar sudden onsets of sleep in the Bible (e.g. Gen. 2:21 and 15:12, and 1 Kgs. [AV 1 Sam.] 26:12), and observes that in these cases, as in *Pe*, the sleep is a source of revelation.

61–120. The concatenation word *adubbement(e)* focuses attention on the supernatural splendour of the terrestrial paradise, which is presented as a transformed garden, the concept of artifice being used metaphorically to set off the transitoriness of the natural world.

61–4. 'From that place my spirit ascended after a time; my body remained there on the mound. In sleep, through God's grace, my spirit went on a quest where marvels occur.'

65ff. Line 65 may be idiomatic ('I had no idea at all where it was'); alternatively, it may allude to the medieval notion of the actual existence of paradise in a remote part of the world. Pearsall and Salter, **8** 1973, 56, quote Honorius of Autun's *Elucidarium: Quid est paradisus? . . . locus amoenissimus in Oriente* ('What is paradise? . . . a most delightful place in the Orient' [*PL* 172:1117]). On the presentation of the paradisal garden in medieval literature, see 9n and Patch, **7a** 1950.

Bot I knew me keste þer klyfez cleuen.
Towarde a foreste I bere þe face,
Where rych rokkez wer to dyscreuen.
Þe ly3t of hem my3t no mon leuen,
Þe glemande glory þat of hem glent,   70
For wern neuer webbez þat wy3ez weuen
Of half so dere adubbemente.

Dubbed wern alle þo downez sydez   [f40ʳ]
With crystal klyffez so cler of kynde.
Holtewodez bry3t aboute hem bydez   75
Of bollez as blwe as ble of Ynde;
As bornyst syluer þe lef on slydez,
Þat þike con trylle on vch a tynde;
Quen glem of glodez agaynz hem glydez,
Wyth schymeryng schene ful schrylle þay schynde.   80
Þe grauayl þat on grounde con grynde
Wern precious perlez of oryente;
Þe sunne bemez bot blo and blynde
In respecte of þat adubbement.

The adubbemente of þo downez dere   85
Garten my goste al greffe for3ete.
So frech flauorez of frytez were,
As fode hit con me fayre refete.
Fowlez þer flowen in fryth in fere,
Of flaumbande hwez, boþe smale and grete;   90

72.   adubbemente (Gollancz)] MS adubmente

71.   The later Middle Ages produced particularly splendid tapestries. Cf. *Cl* 91f, 749ff: the other world can only be described through earthly comparisons, but the poet keeps the ultimate inadequacy of such images before us.
77–80.   'the leaves, which quivered densely on every branch, slid over each other like burnished silver. When the gleam from clear patches of sky glided over them, they shone most brightly with a lovely shimmering.' (The sense seems to be that the clear patches of sky appear to be moving because of the movement of the clouds.) *Con trylle:* This is a periphrastic verbal construction developed from *gan* ('began to') + infinitive. It is most often used as a metrical past tense in these poems (here 'did quiver'), e.g. *Pe* 81, 149, 313, *Cl* 301, 344, 1362, *Pat* 10, 138, 445, *G* 230, 275, 340. In *Pe* the construction is also used with present meaning, e.g. *Pe* 271, 495, 509. Its function as a syllabic expletive is shown by the fact that in *G* it occurs most frequently in the concluding quatrain; it can also supply an alliterative stave in the long line, e.g. *Cl* 768, *G* 2212. See M. Tajima, *Neu. Mitt.*, 76 (1975), 429–38.
83.   *þe sunne bemez:* 'beams of the sun'. Cf. 1045ff.
87f.   'The scents from the fruits (fruit trees?) were so fresh that it nourished me delightfully like food.'

Bot sytole-stryng and gyternere
Her reken myrþe moȝt not retrete,
For quen þose bryddez her wyngez bete,
Þay songen wyth a swete asent.
So gracios gle couþe no mon gete   95
As here and se her adubbement.

So al watz dubbet on dere asyse
Þat fryth þer Fortwne forth me ferez
Þe derþe þerof for to deuyse
Nis no wyȝ worþé þat tonge berez.   100
I welke ay forth in wely wyse,
No bonk so byg þat did me derez.
Þe fyrre in þe fryth, þe feier con ryse
Þe playn, þe plonttez, þe spyse, þe perez;
And rawez and randez and rych reuerez,   105
As fyldor fyn her bonkes brent.
I wan to a water by schore þat scherez;
Lorde, dere watz hit adubbement!

The dubbemente of þo derworth depe   [f40ᵛ]
Wern bonkez bene of beryl bryȝt.   110
Swangeande swete þe water con swepe,
Wyth a rownande rourde raykande aryȝt;
In þe founce þer stoden stonez stepe,

95. gracios] MS gracos
106. bonkes] MS b nkes (o *incomplete*)
113. stoden] MS stonden

97–100. 'The wood where Fortune was taking me forward was arrayed in so entirely splendid a fashion (that) no one capable of speech is able to describe the glory of it.' Though at this stage the Dreamer thinks he is led by haphazard fortune, retrospectively the power guiding him is seen to be divinely ordained: cf. 129–32n, 241–52n.

103–6. 'The further in the wood, the fairer rose the meadow, the shrubs, the spice-plants, the pear-trees, and hedgerows, and water-meadows, and splendid riverbanks, their steep slopes like fine gold thread.'

107. *a water:* As Gordon points out, this is identified with the river of the water of life, which flows from beneath the throne of God, as is described later (in 974 and 1055–60). Cf. Rev. 22:1–2.

113–16. 'there shone on the bottom brilliant stones, which glowed and glinted like a beam of light through glass—as stars streaming with light shine in the winter sky while earth-men sleep'. The exotic river with jewels on its bed is found frequently in medieval literature—not only in mystical visions (see Dante, *Paradiso* XXX.61–9), but also in travel books like Mandeville, and romances such as *Floire et Blancheflor*: for further references see Patch, **7a** 1950; Kean, **7a** 1967, 105–8, and Pearsall and

As glente þurȝ glas þat glowed and glyȝt—
As stremande sternez, quen stroþe-men slepe,   115
Staren in welkyn in wynter nyȝt;
For vche a pobbel in pole þer pyȝt
Watz emerad, saffer, oþer gemme gente,
Þat alle þe loȝe lemed of lyȝt,
So dere watz hit adubbement.   120

III

The dubbement dere of doun and dalez,
Of wod and water and wlonk playnez,
Bylde in me blys, abated my balez,
Fordidden my stresse, dystryed my paynez.
Doun after a strem þat dryȝly halez   125
I bowed in blys, bredful my braynez;
Þe fyrre I folȝed þose floty valez,
Þe more strenghþe of joye myn herte straynez.
As Fortune fares þeras ho fraynez,
Wheþer solace ho sende oþer ellez sore,   130
Þe wyȝ to wham his wylle ho waynez
Hyttez to haue ay more and more.

115. As] MS a
131. his] MS her

Salter, **8** 1973, 58. *Stoden* (113): in writing *stonden*, the scribe may have been attracted
by the form of the following *stonez*; this portion of the narrative is consistently in the
pa.t. *Stroþe-men* (115): the precise meaning of *stroþe* (here and in *G* 1710) is uncer-
tain. Gordon argues from place-name evidence for the existence of an OE **stroð*
'marshy land overgrown with brushwood' (related to OIcel *storð* 'stalks of herbage',
and suggests that *stroþe-men* is a generalized usage meaning 'men of this world'). It
would thus give a sense of the lowness and darkness of the world in comparison to the
stars, and perhaps also of the inevitably 'soiled' nature of the inhabitants (cf. the
phrase *man fenny* in *Cl* 1113, and also *Pat* 342n). Elliott (**5d** 1974, 140f) also points to
OIcel *storð* but in the sense 'a young wood, plantation' (Snorri) and to OE *stroð*
'marshy land covered with bushes or trees' and proposes, for *stroþe-men*, 'country-folk,
woodlanders'.

121–80. The concatenation words of this section, *more and more*, mark a climax in
tension leading to the recognition of the Maiden.

125f. 'Down along a stream that continually flows I went in bliss, my brains brimful
(with joy)'.

129–32. 'As Fortune goes just where she wishes, whether she sends pleasure or else
pain, the man to whom she sends his desire seeks to have more and more (of it) all
the time.' The overall sense of the passage, which is that a man in the position of the
Dreamer, who is achieving his desire, will wish for more and more, appears to
demand *his* rather than MS *her* (131). The MS reading is easily explained by the
scribe's having been attracted by the repeated feminine *ho* in 129, 130, and 131.

More of wele watz in þat wyse
Þen I cowþe telle þaȝ I tom hade,
For vrþely herte myȝt not suffyse   135
To þe tenþe dole of þo gladnez glade.
Forþy I þoȝt þat paradyse
Watz þer ouer gayn þo bonkez brade;
I hoped þe water were a deuyse
Bytwene myrþez by merez made;   140
Byȝonde þe broke, by slente oþer slade,
I hoped þat mote merked wore.
Bot þe water watz depe, I dorst not wade,
And euer me longed ay more and more.

More and more, and ȝet wel mare,   [f41ʳ] 145
Me lyste to se þe broke byȝonde,
For if hit watz fayr þer I con fare,
Wel loueloker watz þe fyrre londe.
Abowte me con I stote and stare;
To fynde a forþe faste con I fonde,   150
Bot woþez mo iwysse þer ware,
Þe fyrre I stalked by þe stronde;
And euer me þoȝt I schulde not wonde
For wo þer welez so wynne wore.
Þenne nwe note me com on honde   155
Þat meued my mynde ay more and more.

More meruayle con my dom adaunt.
I seȝ byȝonde þat myry mere

---

138. ouer (Gollancz)] MS oþer
142. hoped (Morris)] MS hope
144. ay (Gollancz)] MS a

133–6. This theme, of the inadequacy of the human body and mind to perceive and comprehend paradisal and heavenly experience, has already been touched on (99f) and is picked up later in the poem, e.g. at 223–6 and 1189ff.

139f. 'I supposed that the water was a division between pleasure-gardens laid out beside pools'. The Dreamer assumes that such an ordered estate must be that of a great house: thus the emphasis of 141f.

149–54. 'I stopped and stared about me; I tried hard to find a ford, but indeed there were more perils the further I walked along the shore. And all the time it seemed to me that I should not hesitate for (fear of) harm, where there were such delightful joys.' *Woþez* (151) and *wo* (154) appear to connote the risk of discovery, rather than physical danger. The Dreamer's state of mind is that of a social inferior trespassing in the grounds of a castle. Later the Maiden finds him *vncortoyse* (303) and criticizes his manners (313ff); the same metaphor of social class (cf. 264n) is implicit or explicit in many of the exchanges of Dreamer and Maiden (e.g. 381f, 389–94, 489–92).

A crystal clyffe ful relusaunt:
Mony ryal ray con fro hit rere.   160
At þe fote þerof þer sete a faunt,
A mayden of menske, ful debonere;
Blysnande whyt watz hyr bleaunt;
I knew hyr wel, I hade sen hyr ere.
As glysnande golde þat man con schere,   165
So schon þat schene anvnder schore.
On lenghe I loked to hyr þere;
Þe lenger, I knew hyr more and more.

The more I frayste hyr fayre face,
Her fygure fyn quen I had fonte,   170
Suche gladande glory con to me glace
As lyttel byfore þerto watz wonte.
To calle hyr lyste con me enchace,
Bot baysment gef myn hert a brunt.
I seȝ hyr in so strange a place—   175
Such a burre myȝt make myn herte blunt.
Þenne verez ho vp her fayre frount,
Hyr vysayge whyt as playn yuore:
Þat stonge myn hert ful stray astount,
And euer þe lenger, þe more and more.   180

IV

More þen me lyste my drede aros: [f41ᵛ]
I stod ful stylle and dorste not calle;

---

179.   astount (Gollancz)] MS atount

160–94. It has been suggested that this passage may show the influence of Dante, in particular his account of the meeting with Beatrice in *Purgatorio* XXX.31–99.
163. Cf. Rev. 19:8.
165f. 'Like glistening gold which has been cut, so shone that fair maiden below the cliff.' *Schene anvnder schore* (166): see note to 775–80.
169–74. 'The more I scrutinized her fair face, when I had noticed her noble form, such gladdening exultation swept to me as had been but little wont to do so before. Desire urged me to call her, but confusion dealt my heart a blow.'
178. Similar comparisons occur in the Harley Lyric 'A Wayle whyt ase whalles bon' 1, and Chaucer, *The Book of the Duchess* 946.
179. 'that stung my heart into bewildered amazement'. Gordon retains MS *atount* (OF *ato(u)ner*); the alliteration would appear to support the emendation.
181–240. The concatenation gives emphasis to the connection between the newly-discovered Maiden and pearls, both as objects and symbols.
181. 'My fear grew greater than my longing (*lit.* I longed)'.

Wyth yȝen open and mouth ful clos
I stod as hende as hawk in halle.
I hoped þat gostly watz þat porpose;   185
I dred onende quat schulde byfalle,
Lest ho me eschaped þat I þer chos,
Er I at steuen hir moȝt stalle.
Þat gracios gay withouten galle,
So smoþe, so smal, so seme slyȝt,   190
Rysez vp in hir araye ryalle,
A precios pyece in perlez pyȝt.

Perlez pyȝte of ryal prys
Þere moȝt mon by grace haf sene,
Quen þat frech as flor-de-lys   195
Doun þe bonke con boȝe bydene.
Al blysnande whyt watz hir beau biys,
Vpon at sydez, and bounden bene
Wyth þe myryeste margarys, at my deuyse,
Þat euer I seȝ ȝet with myn yȝen;   200

185. hoped (Gollancz)] MS hope
192. precios] MS precos
197. biys (Osgood)] MS uiys

185. None of the usual interpretations of *porpose*—'significance' (Gordon), 'import' (Hillmann), 'intention' (Gollancz), 'intended meaning' (Osgood)—fit easily in this context. It is more likely that the word means 'aim, quarry' (*OED* sense 1), and continues the hunting metaphor implicit from 183. This metaphor is further developed in *eschaped* (187), and *stalle* (188), which *OED* glosses 'bring (a hunted animal) to a stand'. Translate: 'I thought that that quarry was spiritual.'

186–8. 'I was afraid about what might happen, in case she whom I beheld there eluded me before I could stop her for a meeting.'

190. The striking echo of 6 reinforces the growing sense of the identification of the pearl Maiden with the lost pearl described at the beginning of the poem—though this is not made explicit until 241–52.

193–6. 'There by good fortune one might see pearls of royal worth set, when that (one) fresh as a fleur-de-lys directly came down the slope.'

197. Cf. Rev. 19:8.

197–228. This passage provides a detailed picture of the Maiden's costume, which is essentially that of an aristocratic young woman in the second half of the 14th c. The long sleeves (201) fashionable during the period are also mentioned in *Winner and Waster* 410–12. Gordon (who provides further comment on costume in his note to 228) points out that while maidens and brides wore their hair unbound (as in 213f) matrons wore theirs coifed. Cf. *G* 1738n.

199f. By returning to the theme of judging gems, the poet reinforces the connection between this passage and the beginning of the poem (cf. 7f, 190n).

Wyth lappez large, I wot and I wene,
Dubbed with double perle and dyʒte;
Her cortel of self sute schene,
With precios perlez al vmbepyʒte.

A pyʒt coroune ʒet wer þat gyrle   205
Of marjorys and non oþer ston,
Hiʒe pynakled of cler quyt perle,
Wyth flurted flowrez perfet vpon.
To hed hade ho non oþer werle;
Her lere-leke al hyr vmbegon;   210
Her semblaunt sade for doc oþer erle,
Her ble more blaʒt þen whallez bon.
As schorne golde schyr her fax þenne schon,
On schylderez þat leghe vnlapped lyʒte.
Her depe colour ʒet wonted non   215
Of precios perle in porfyl pyʒte.

Pyʒt watz poyned and vche a hemme—   [f42ʳ]
At honde, at sydez, at ouerture—
Wyth whyte perle and non oþer gemme,
And bornyste quyte watz hyr uesture.   220
Bot a wonder perle withouten wemme

205–8. 'That girl also wore a decorated crown of pearls and no other stone, with high
pinnacles of clear white pearl, with perfect flowers figured on (it).'
209. *werle*: The exact sense is uncertain, but 'circlet' seems probable: cf. OE *hwirfel*
'whirlpool', *hwirfling* 'orb, something round', and *hwerfan* 'to revolve'; and OIcel
hvirfill 'ring'.
210–16. 'her wimple entirely encompassing her; her face grave enough for a duke or
earl, her complexion purer white than ivory. Her hair, that lay lightly on her
shoulders, unbound, then shone like bright cut gold. The intense whiteness of her
complexion was not inferior even to that of a precious pearl set in an embroidered
border.' The difficult MS *lere leke* (210) has been variously treated. Most editors
emend *lere* to *here* ('hair'), which involves the awkward reading of *leke* as a pa.t. It
also weakens the logical development of the poet's description, for the Maiden's hair
is dealt with in 213f, and it would be clumsy for the subject to be anticipated here.
Hillman retains the MS reading, taking *lere* to mean 'face' (derived from OIcel *hleor*
'cheek'), and *leke* 'radiance' (connected with OE *lacan* 'to flash'). *MED* suggests,
more convincingly, that *leke* is a form of ME *lake* 'fine linen' (*MED lake*, n²), and that
lere-leke means 'face-linen, wimple'.
221. The Maiden later (729–44) associates this great pearl with the Pearl of Price
(Matt. 13:45–6), and also refers to it as a symbol of salvation. This latter significance
is reinforced in the vision of the New Jerusalem, when the Dreamer observes that
similar pearls are worn by all the saved (1103f).

Inmyddez hyr breste watz sette so sure;
A mannez dom moȝt dryȝly demme
Er mynde moȝt malte in hit mesure.
I hope no tong moȝt endure   225
No sauerly saghe say of þat syȝt,
So watz hit clene and cler and pure,
Þat precios perle þer hit watz pyȝt.

Pyȝt in perle, þat precios pyse
On wyþer half water com doun þe schore.   230
No gladder gome heþen into Grece
Þen I quen ho on brymme wore;
Ho watz me nerre þen aunte or nece:
My joy forþy watz much þe more.
Ho profered me speche, þat special spyce,   235
Enclynande lowe in wommon lore,
Caȝte of her coroun of grete tresore
And haylsed me wyth a lote lyȝte.
Wel watz me þat euer I watz bore
To sware þat swete in perlez pyȝte!   240

V

'O perle,' quoþ I, 'in perlez pyȝt,
Art þou my perle þat I haf playned,

223–6. 'a man's judgement might be utterly baffled before his mind could conceive its magnitude. I think no tongue could have power to describe that sight in adequate speech'. Cf. 133–6n. The magnitude of the pearl symbolizes its value and significance. Cf. *Cl* 117n.

231f. '(There was) no gladder man from here to Greece than I, when she was on the bank'. Cf. the similar idiom in *G* 2023.

233. On the basis of this line many critics have seen the relationship between the Dreamer and the Maiden as that of father and daughter, and this view is indeed consistent with the varying tone of their speeches to each other. However, it is probably significant that an explicit statement of their relationship is not made; the reader is thereby encouraged to see the theme of loss in a more general light.

235. *þat special spyce:* Spice is a traditional metaphor for an admired woman, probably as a reminiscence of the Song of Songs 4:12–16.

236. *in wommon lore:* 'in womanly fashion' (*wommon* is an uninflected gen. pl. 'of women').

237. The removal of the crown should probably be seen as a gesture of humility—as in *The Awntyrs off Arthure* 626—signifying the Maiden's willingness to set aside her heavenly authority and meet the Dreamer as an equal. It is striking that in 255 she replaces her crown before rebuking him for his erroneous views.

241–300. The concatenation word *jueler(e)* is rich in potential significance. In 7 the

Regretted by myn one on nyȝte?
Much longeyng haf I for þe layned,
Syþen into gresse þou me aglyȝte.   245
Pensyf, payred, I am forpayned,
And þou in a lyf of lykyng lyȝte,
In paradys erde, of stryf vnstrayned.
What Wyrde hatz hyder my juel vayned,
And don me in þys del and gret daunger?   250
Fro we in twynne wern towen and twayned,
I haf ben a joylez juelere.'

That juel þenne in gemmez gente   [f42ᵛ]
Vered vp her vyse with yȝen graye,
Set on hyr coroun of perle orient,   255
And soberly after þenne con ho say:
'Sir, ȝe haf your tale mysetente,
To say your perle is al awaye,
Þat is in cofer so comly clente
As in þis gardyn gracios gaye,   260
Hereinne to lenge for euer and play,
Þer mys nee mornyng com neuer nere.

262. nere] MS here

Dreamer has presented himself as a judge of gems; the varied use of the word in the present section, however, draws attention to the contrast between earthly and heavenly values—a distinction which he has yet to learn. The use of the word in 730 and 734 further identifies the true 'jeweller' with the merchant of the parable of the Pearl of Price (Matt. 13:45–6).

241–52. With its echoes of the beginning of the poem, the first part of this speech identifies the Maiden with the lost pearl (cf. 190n). The injured, self-pitying tone of the second half establishes the Dreamer's partial blindness at this stage of his experience and complicates the reader's sympathy for him. *Wyrde* (249, 273) is, from the Dreamer's point of view, random fate, but from that of the Maiden, which comes increasingly to dominate the poem, it suggests rather the power of Providence. Cf. 97f, 129–32, 411f, and notes; cf. also *Pat* 247n and *G* 2134.

245. 'since you slipped away from me into the grass'.

250. *daunger:* cf. 11n.

254. *graye:* Heroines of medieval romance often have grey eyes: cf. *G* 82, and (e.g.) Chaucer, 'General Prologue' *CT* I. 152, and *The Awntyrs off Arthure* 599. It is, however, possible that ME *gray(e)* (and OF *vaire*) when applied to eyes designated a colour which we would call blue, or that it referred to brilliance rather than hue, and hence meant 'bright, shining' (see Muriel Kinney, *Romanic Review*, 10 [1919], 322–63).

255. Cf. 237n.

257–60. 'Sir, you have spoken heedlessly, to say that your pearl is entirely lost, that is so beautifully enclosed in a coffer as in this charmingly fair garden'. Paul Piehler, **7a** 1971 (145) points out the rich ambiguity between the senses 'treasure chest' and 'coffin'; in *Cl, cofer* is employed metaphorically to describe the ark (310, etc.).

Her were a forser for þe, in faye,
If þou were a gentyl jueler.

'Bot, jueler gente, if þou schal lose 265
Þy joy for a gemme þat þe watz lef,
Me þynk þe put in a mad porpose,
And busyez þe aboute a raysoun bref;
For þat þou lestez watz bot a rose
Þat flowred and fayled as kynde hyt gef; 270
Now þurȝ kynde of þe kyste þat hyt con close
To a perle of prys hit is put in pref.
And þou hatz called þy Wyrde a þef,
Þat oȝt of noȝt hatz mad þe cler;
Þou blamez þe bote of þy meschef; 275
Þou art no kynde jueler.'

A juel to me þen watz þys geste,
And juelez wern hyr gentyl sawez.
'Iwyse,' quoþ I, 'my blysfol beste,
My grete dystresse þou al todrawez. 280
To be excused I make requeste.

263. 'Here would be a casket for you, indeed'.
264. *gentyl:* 'courteous, noble'. The courtly term is used to imply metaphorically the
equivalent spiritual value: see note to 421–80. *Kynde* (276) belongs to the same
metaphorical system by virtue of its use in the sense 'proper, courtly' (e.g. in *G* 473,
and cf. *kyndely, G* 135, *vnkyndely, Cl* 208).
267–72. 'it seems to me that you are set on a mad purpose, and concern yourself on
account of a transitory cause; for what you lost was only a rose that flowered and
withered as nature allowed it; now through the nature of the chest which encloses it,
it is shown to be a precious pearl.' An ancient tradition associates the rose with
mutable beauty. In courtly poetry, it is frequently used to symbolize the woman as
an object of love, most strikingly as the central image of the *Roman de la Rose*, while in
religious writings it becomes the *rosa caritatis* ('rose of divine love')—a transformation
which takes place between the two occurrences of the symbol in *Pe*: cf. 906, and see
Introduction, p. 32.
274. The Maiden's point is usually understood to be that God has made the Dreamer
something eternal out of something ephemeral—the pearl out of the rose. An inter-
esting alternative view is offered by Alfred L. Kellogg, *Traditio*, 12 (1956), 406–7
(and Conley, 7a 1970, 335–7), who suggests that this is an allusion to the
Augustinian concept of *creatio ex nihilo* ('creation out of nothing'), and that the
Maiden is advising the Dreamer that he should be grateful to God for his very
existence. (There is an unambiguous reference to this theological concept in
Chaucer's 'Truth' 24f).
275. *of:* to be construed with *blamez* rather than *bote:* 'you blame the remedy for your
misfortune.'
277–88. The stanza functions ironically, since the Dreamer's blithe optimism is based
on a misunderstanding of the true import of the Maiden's *gentyl sawez.*

I trawed my perle don out of dawez;
Now haf I fonde hyt, I schal ma feste,
And wony with hyt in schyr wod-schawez,
And loue my Lorde and al His lawez   285
Þat hatz me broʒt þys blys ner.
Now were I at yow byʒonde þise wawez,
I were a joyfol jueler.'

'Jueler,' sayde þat gemme clene,   [f43ʳ]
'Wy borde ʒe men? So madde ʒe be!   290
Þre wordez hatz þou spoken at ene:
Vnavysed, forsoþe, wern alle þre.
Þou ne woste in worlde quat on dotz mene;
Þy worde byfore þy wytte con fle.
Þou says þou trawez me in þis dene   295
Bycawse þou may with yʒen me se;
Anoþer, þou says in þys countré
Þyself schal won with me ryʒt here;
Þe þrydde, to passe þys water fre:
Þat may no joyfol jueler.   300

VI

'I halde þat jueler lyttel to prayse
Þat leuez wel þat he sez wyth yʒe,

---

286. broʒt] MS broʒ
302, 308. leuez (Gollancz)] MS louez

282f. 'I believed that my pearl was annihilated; now I have found it I shall rejoice'.
Hyt (283f): the neuter pron. is reminiscent of the usage in the first section (see note to 3f).
287. 'If I were now beside you beyond these waves (i.e. this water)'.
291. *wordez:* 'statements'.
293f. 'You do not know at all what one (of them) means; your speech escaped before you thought (*lit.* before your understanding).'
301–60. The different meanings of the concatenation word *deme* (variously 'allow', 'consider', 'judge', condemn', 'ordain': see Glossary) draw attention to the gap between the Dreamer's fallible will and judgement and the power of God to ordain what will be.
301–8. Cf. the ironical use made by Chaucer of this argument in *The Legend of Good Women*, Prologue 1–16.
302, 308. *leuez:* Gollancz's emendation restores the sense, and derives support from *leuez* in 304.

And much to blame and vncortoyse
Þat leuez oure Lorde wolde make a lyȝe,
Þat lelly hyȝte your lyf to rayse,   305
Þaȝ Fortune dyd your flesch to dyȝe.
Ȝe setten Hys wordez ful westernays
Þat leuez noþynk bot ȝe hit syȝe;
And þat is a poynt o sorquydryȝe,
Þat vche god mon may euel byseme,   310
To leue no tale be true to tryȝe
Bot þat hys one skyl may dem.

'Deme now þyself if þou con dayly
As man to God wordez schulde heue.
Þou saytz þou schal won in þis bayly;   315
Me þynk þe burde fyrst aske leue—
And ȝet of graunt þou myȝtez fayle.
Þou wylnez ouer þys water to weue;
Er moste þou ceuer to oþer counsayl.
Þy corse in clot mot calder keue,   320
For hit watz forgarte at paradys greue;
Oure ȝorefader hit con misseȝeme.
Þurȝ drwry deth boȝ vch man dreue,
Er ouer þys dam hym Dryȝtyn deme.'

---

309. is] MS ins (īs)
323. man] MS ma

303–6. 'and (I consider) very blameworthy and discourteous one who believes our Lord, who faithfully promised to raise your life though Fortune caused your flesh to die, would tell a lie.'

307–12. 'You, who believe nothing unless you have seen it, set His words completely awry. And it is an instance of pride, which ill befits every good man, to believe no account to be true when put to the test except what his judgement alone can understand.' Some interplay between courtly and Christian ethical vocabulary is evident in phrases like *poynt o sorquydryȝe* (309)—cf. *G* 311, 2457, and *þat vche god mon may euel byseme* (310)—cf. in particular the account of the pentangle in *G* 640ff. *Westernays* (307) has been much debated. Osgood emends to *besternays* (OF *bestorneis*), which provides a suitable meaning, 'awry', but destroys the alliteration. Following Bradley (*A Middle English Dictionary*, ed. F. H. Stratmann, revised and enlarged by Henry Bradley [Oxford, 1891], p. 708), Gollancz and Gordon retain the MS reading, on the assumption that *westernays* is a form of the OF word modified as a result of its application to churches facing west instead of east. Hillman's reading *west ernays* 'empty pledge' (derived respectively from OE *weste*, and *ernes = ernest* 'pledge') is less convincing.

313–15. 'Now judge yourself whether you have spoken in the way in which man ought to address words to God. You say you will live in this realm'.

318–24. 'You wish to pass over this water; you must first attain to another course of action. Your corpse must sink, colder, into the earth, for it was forfeited at the grove

'Demez þou me,' quoþ I, 'my swete,   [f43ᵛ]   325
To dol agayn? Þenne I dowyne.
Now haf I fonte þat I forlete,
Schal I efte forgo hit er euer I fyne?
Why schal I hit boþe mysse and mete?
My precios perle dotz me gret pyne.   330
What seruez tresor bot garez men grete,
When he hit schal efte with tenez tyne?
Now rech I neuer for to declyne,
Ne how fer of folde þat man me fleme.
When I am partlez of perle myne,   335
Bot durande doel what may men deme?'

'Thow demez noȝt bot doel-dystresse,'
Þenne sayde þat wyȝt; 'why dotz þou so?
For dyne of doel of lurez lesse
Ofte mony mon forgos þe mo.   340
Þe oȝte better þyseluen blesse,
And loue ay God, in wele and wo,
For anger gaynez þe not a cresse.
Who nedez schal þole, be not so þro;
For þoȝ þou daunce as any do,   345

335.   perle (Osgood)] MS perlez
342.   in (Morris)] MS and (ꞇ)

of paradise (i.e. the Garden of Eden). Our ancestor (Adam) failed to guard it. Every man must make his way through cruel death before God allows him over this water.' As in the best of the religious lyrics, these physical details reinforce the hope of immortality.

326. Cf. 11.

327–9. 'Now I have found what I lost, shall I give it up again before I end my life? Why must I lose it as well as find it (i.e. both find and lose it)?'

331. 'What does treasure avail, but cause one to weep?'

333f. 'Now I do not care if I fall from prosperity, nor how far away I am driven.' This may contain an allusion to the theme of exile, common in OE poetry, and associated in ME poetry with unrequited love.

335. *perle:* It is likely that the proximity of *partlez* caused a scribe to write *perlez* instead of *perle*.

336. 'what can one expect but lasting sorrow?' Cf. the tone of Jonah's outbursts against God in *Pat* 425ff, 482ff, and 493ff.

339f. 'Through the tumult of grief for lesser sorrows many a man often loses the greater (thing)': i.e. excessive indulgence in mourning an earthly loss can lead to sin, which may reduce a man's chances of salvation.

341–8. 'You ought rather to cross yourself (*or* pray for blessing), and always praise God, in prosperity and suffering, for anger does not profit you a jot. Whoever must necessarily suffer, let him not be so stubborn; for though you writhe like a doe,

Braundysch and bray þy braþez breme,
When þou no fyrre may, to ne fro,
Þou moste abyde þat He schal deme.

'Deme Dryȝtyn, euer Hym adyte;
Of þe way a fote ne wyl He wryþe.   350
Þy mendez mountez not a myte,
Þaȝ þou for sorȝe be neuer blyþe.
Stynt of þy strot and fyne to flyte,
And sech Hys blyþe ful swefte and swyþe;
Þy prayer may Hys pyté byte,   355
Þat mercy schal hyr craftez kyþe.
Hys comforte may þy langour lyþe,
And þy lurez of lyȝtly fleme;
For, marre oþer madde, morne and myþe,
Al lys in Hym to dyȝt and deme.'   360

VII

Thenne demed I to þat damyselle: [f44ʳ]
'Ne worþe no wrathþe vnto my Lorde,
If rapely I raue, spornande in spelle:
My herte watz al with mysse remorde,

353. Stynt (Gollancz)] MS stynst
358. fleme (Gordon)] MS leme
363. I (Gollancz)] MS *om.*

struggle and bray out your wild agonies, when you can (go) no further, this way or that, you must endure what He will ordain.' Cf. the earlier use of a hunting metaphor: see 185n. These lines are very close to the moral of *Pat* (specifically, cf. 342 with *Pat* 525, and 344 with *Pat* 5–8).

349–52. 'Censure the Lord, arraign Him for ever; He will not turn aside a foot from the path. Your recompense is increased not a jot, even if in your misery you should never be happy.'

353. *Stynt:* Cf. the MS error in *Cl* 359.

355f. 'your prayer can penetrate His pity, so that mercy will make known her skills.' *Mercy* is a quasi-personification: cf. *Pat* 31–3n.

357f. 'His comfort can assuage your anguish and easily banish your griefs'. *Fleme* (358): no convincing interpretation has been offered for MS *leme*. A scribal error appears to have been caused by false expectation of alliteration.

361–420. The concatenation phrase emphasizes the central concern of section VII: the understanding of the difference between true and false felicity. This is the theme of Boethius's *De Consolatione Philosophiae* ('The Consolation of Philosophy').

362f. 'Let there be no offence to my Lord if I rashly rave, stumbling in discourse'. *I* (363): a similar emendation is needed in 977.

As wallande water gotz out of welle.   365
I do me ay in Hys myserecorde.
Rebuke me neuer with wordez felle,
Þaʒ I forloyne, my dere endorde,
Bot kyþez me kyndely your coumforde,
Pytosly þenkande vpon þysse: 370
Of care and me ʒe made acorde,
Þat er watz grounde of alle my blysse.

'My blysse, my bale, ʒe han ben boþe,
Bot much þe bygger ʒet watz my mon;
Fro þou watz wroken fro vch a woþe,   375
I wyste neuer quere my perle watz gon.
Now I hit se, now leþez my loþe.
And quen we departed we wern at on;
God forbede we be now wroþe;
We meten so selden by stok oþer ston.   380
Þaʒ cortaysly ʒe carp con,
I am bot mol and manerez mysse;
Bot Crystes mersy and Mary and Jon,
Þise arn þe grounde of alle my blysse.

'In blysse I se þe blyþely blent,   385
And I a man al mornyf mate.
Ʒe take þeron ful lyttel tente,
Þaʒ I hente ofte harmez hate.
Bot now I am here in your presente,
I wolde bysech, wythouten debate,   390

---

369. kyþez (Holthausen)] MS lyþez
382. manerez (Holthausen)] MS marerez

---

365. Cf. Ps. 21:15 (Vulgate), 22:14 (AV). This simile, here used of uncontrolled human emotion bursting forth, later recurs as an image of God's limitless bounty (607f), thus conforming to the pattern of transformation from earthly to heavenly values: see Introduction, pp. 31ff.

366. 'I put myself at His mercy always.'

368. *forloyne:* Cf. *Cl* 750n. *Endorde:* this word was taken by earlier editors as a form of 'adored', but it is convincingly argued by Gert Rønberg (*ES* 57 [1976], 198) that it is from OF *endorer* 'to invest with gold or a gold-like quality', and thus here means 'gold-adorned'.

375f. 'after you were removed from every peril, and I had no idea at all where my pearl was gone.'

378. 'And when we parted we were in harmony'.

380. *by stok oþer ston:* 'anywhere'.

388. 'though I often suffer burning sorrows.' In OE poetry the pangs of suffering are often described as hot, as in *The Seafarer* 11, *Beowulf* 282.

3e wolde me say in sobre asente
What lyf 3e lede erly and late,
For I am ful fayn þat your astate
Is worþen to worschyp and wele, iwysse;
Of alle my joy þe hy3e gate,   395
Hit is in grounde of alle my blysse.'

'Now blysse, burne, mot þe bytyde,'   [f44ᵛ]
Þen sayde þat lufsoum of lyth and lere,
'And welcum here to walk and byde,
For now þy speche is to me dere.   400
Maysterful mod and hy3e pryde,
I hete þe, arn heterly hated here.
My Lorde ne louez not for to chyde,
For meke arn alle þat wonez Hym nere;
And when in Hys place þou schal apere,   405
Be dep deuote in hol mekenesse.
My Lorde þe Lamb louez ay such chere,
Þat is þe grounde of alle my blysse.

'A blysful lyf þou says I lede;
Þou woldez knaw þerof þe stage.   410
Þow wost wel when þy perle con schede
I watz ful 3ong and tender of age;
Bot my Lorde þe Lombe þur3 Hys godhede,
He toke myself to Hys maryage,
Corounde me quene in blysse to brede   415
In lenghe of dayez þat euer schal wage;
And sesed in alle Hys herytage
Hys lef is. I am holy Hysse.

395f. 'the highway of all my joy, it is in the foundation of all my bliss.'

407f. 'My Lord, the Lamb, who is the foundation of all my bliss, always loves such demeanour.'

411f. The Maiden herself here echoes the usage of the opening stanzas, where the pearl is a symbol for the dead child: see 241–52n.

413. *godhede:* 'godhead, divinity'. The form is also current in the 14th c. in the sense 'goodness': possibly both meanings are intended here.

414. 'He took me in marriage to Him'. The mystical marriage is a traditional symbol for the state of salvation.

417f. 'and His dear one is made possessor of all His heritage. I am wholly His.' Kean, **7a** 1967, 187f, points out that the language has legal associations, *sesed in* meaning 'to possess legally', and *herytage* 'something given or received as a legal possession'. These lines thus anticipate the distinction between the innocent who are saved by right and those who, stained by the sin inevitably attendant upon living in the world, need the mercy of God: see section XII.

Hys prese, Hys prys, and Hys parage
Is rote and grounde of alle my blysse.'   420

VIII

'Blysful,' quoþ I, 'may þys be trwe?—
Dysplesez not if I speke errour—
Art þou þe quene of heuenez blwe,
Þat al þys worlde schal do honour?
We leuen on Marye þat grace of grewe,   425
Þat ber a barne of vyrgyn flour.
Þe croune fro hyr quo moȝt remwe
Bot ho hir passed in sum fauour?
Now, for synglerty o hyr dousour,
We calle hyr Fenyx of Arraby,   430
Þat fereles fleȝe of hyr Fasor—
Lyk to þe quen of cortaysye.'

'Cortayse quen,' þenne sayde þat gaye,   [f45^r]
Knelande to grounde, folde vp hyr face,
'Makelez moder and myryest may,
Blessed bygynner of vch a grace!'   435

> **431.** fereles (Hamilton)] MS freles
> **433.** sayde (Morris)] MS syde
> **436.** bygynner] MS byngyner

421–80. The poet's use of the concatenation word *cortaysye* and the terminology of an
earthly court is typical of his willingness to use courtly language metaphorically to
express the values and relationships of heaven. Thus *cortaysye*, a word which suggests
the attributes of courtly graciousness, comes to suggest those of divine grace when
applied to the Virgin Mary (432, etc.). Cf. *Cl* 1069ff.

425–32. 'We believe in Mary, from whom grace grew, who bore a child in virginity;
who could remove the crown from her unless she surpassed her in some noble
quality? Now, because of the uniqueness of her sweetness, we call her Phoenix of
Arabia, which flew unique from her Creator—as did the queen of courtesy.' *Synglerty*
(429): cf. 8. *Fenyx of Arraby* (430): it is more common for the phoenix to symbolize
Christ than the Virgin. However, Fletcher, **7a** 1921, points out that in Albertus
Magnus's treatise *De Laudibus Beatae Mariae* ('In praise of the blessed Mary'), V.1.1,
VII.3.1, the Virgin's uniqueness is related to that of the phoenix. Chaucer uses the
comparison in a secular context to praise the uniqueness of Blanche in *The Book of the
Duchess* 982. *Fereles* (431): MS *freles* has usually been interpreted as 'flawless' (cf.
OIcel *frjīulaust*). However the emphasis in this passage is on the uniqueness of the
Phoenix (cf. 429), and Hamilton's emendation to *fereles* (*lit.* 'without equal') is
therefore adopted (see also Luttrell, **6** 1962).

436–40. '"blessed originator of every grace!" Then she rose and paused, and then
spoke to me: "Sir, here many strive for and win a prize, but there are no usurpers
within this domain" '.

Þenne ros ho vp and con restay,
And speke me towarde in þat space:
'Sir, fele here porchasez and fongez pray,
Bot supplantorez none withinne þys place;   440
Þat emperise al heuenz hatz—
And vrþe and helle—in her bayly;
Of erytage ȝet non wyl ho chace,
For ho is quen of cortaysye.

'The court of þe kyndom of God alyue   445
Hatz a property in hytself beyng:
Alle þat may þerinne aryue
Of alle þe reme is quen oþer kyng,
And neuer oþer ȝet schal depryue,
Bot vchon fayn of oþerez hafyng,   450
And wolde her corounez wern worþe þo fyue,
If possyble were her mendyng.
Bot my lady of quom Jesu con spryng,
Ho haldez þe empyre ouer vus ful hyȝe,
And þat dysplesez non of oure gyng,   455
For ho is quene of cortaysye.

'Of courtaysye, as saytz Saynt Poule,
Al arn we membrez of Jesu Kryst:
As heued and arme and legg and naule

---

443. 'yet she will oust none from their heritage'.

445f. 'The court of the kingdom of the living God has an attribute in its own nature'.

449–52. 'and yet one shall never dispossess another, but each one (be) glad of the others' possession, and wish their crowns were five times as precious, if any improvement of them were possible.' The use of the figure five in such phrases is idiomatic: cf. 849, *Troilus* II.126. A similar emphasis on the shared nature of heavenly joy occurs in the EME *Sawles Warde* (included in Richard Morris's collection of homilies, EETS OS 34 [263]).

453. *of quom Jesu con spryng:* 'from whom Jesus grew' (perhaps in allusion to Isa. 11:1).

455. *gyng:* 'company'.

459–66. 'just as head and arm and leg and navel belong to their body very firmly and faithfully, in just the same way each Christian soul is a limb belonging to the Master of spiritual mysteries. Then consider: what hatred or bitterness is implanted or fixed between your limbs? Your head has neither resentment nor spite if you wear a ring on arm or finger.' This argument is derived from 1 Cor. 12:14ff.; cf. its use in John of Salisbury, *Policratus* VI.24 and in Shakespeare, *Coriolanus* I.1.94ff. *Mayster of myste* (462): an alternative interpretation, suggested by Daniel M. Murtaugh (*Neophil.*, 55 [1971], 295–302), is that *myste* is a form of ME *mystery*, used here in the sense 'service, office, ministry' (medieval Latin *misterium*), and that *Mayster of myste* therefore means 'Master of ministries'.

Temen to hys body ful trwe and tryste,   460
Ryȝt so is vch a Krysten sawle
A longande lym to þe Mayster of myste.
Þenne loke: what hate oþer any gawle
Is tached oþer tyȝed þy lymmez bytwyste?
Þy heued hatz nauþer greme ne gryste   465
On arme oþer fynger þaȝ þou ber byȝe.
So fare we alle wyth luf and lyste
To kyng and quene by cortaysye.'

'Cortaysé,' quoþ I, 'I leue,   [f45ᵛ]
And charyté grete, be yow among;   470
Bot my speche þat yow ne greue,
·   ·   ·   ·   ·   ·
Þyself in heuen ouer hyȝ þou heue,
To make þe quen þat watz so ȝonge.
What more honour moȝte he acheue   475
Þat hade endured in worlde stronge,
And lyued in penaunce hys lyuez longe
With bodyly bale hym blysse to byye?
What more worschyp moȝt he fonge
Þen corounde be kyng by cortaysé?   480

IX

'That Cortayse is to fre of dede,
Ȝyf hyt be soth þat þou conez saye.

460. tryste (Morris)] MS tyste
461. sawle] MS sawhe
472. *Line missing in MS*
479. he (Osgood)] MS ho

469–92. The debate between the Maiden and the Dreamer centres upon the confrontation between the Old Law of justification by works and the New Law of grace (see Hamilton, 7a 1955).
471. 'but provided that my speech does not offend you (i.e. if you do not mind my saying so)'.
473f. 'You raise yourself over-high in heaven, to make yourself, who were so young, a queen.'
481–540. *Date*, the concatenation word in this section, is used by the poet with great dexterity to suggest a range of meanings associated with time, measurement, and degree. The Dreamer's scale of values is thus kept in mind, as the central agent of its modification—the telling of the parable of the Vineyard, with its teaching about heavenly rewards—is introduced.
481f. 'That Courteous One is too liberal in action, if what you say is true.' Cf. Jonah's complaint about God's prodigal 'courtesy' in *Pat* 417ff. *That Cortayse*: cf. *Cl* 1097.

Þou lyfed not two ȝer in oure þede;
Þou cowþez neuer God nauþer plese ne pray,
Ne neuer nawþer Pater ne Crede—   485
And quen mad on þe fyrst day!
I may not traw, so God me spede,
Þat God wolde wryþe so wrange away.
Of countes, damysel, par ma fay,
Wer fayr in heuen to halde asstate,   490
Oþer ellez a lady of lasse aray;
Bot a quene!—hit is to dere a date.'

'Þer is no date of Hys godnesse,'
Þen sayde to me þat worþy wyȝte,
'For al is trawþe þat He con dresse,   495
And He may do noþynk bot ryȝt.
As Mathew melez in your messe
In sothfol gospel of God almyȝt:
In sample He can ful grayþely gesse
And lyknez hit to heuen lyȝte.   500
"My regne," He saytz, "is lyk on hyȝt
To a lorde þat hade a uyne, I wate.
Of tyme of ȝere þe terme watz tyȝt,
To labor vyne watz dere þe date.

'"Þat date of ȝere wel knawe þys hyne.   [f46ʳ]   505
Þe lorde ful erly vp he ros
To hyre werkmen to hys vyne,
And fyndez þer summe to hys porpos.

484–6. 'you never knew how either to please or to pray to God, nor (did you) ever (know) either Paternoster or Creed—and made a queen on the first day!' The Pater and Creed were the first prayers a child would have learned.

489f. 'On my word (*lit.* by my faith), young lady, it would be fine to hold the rank of countess in heaven'.

492. *to dere a date:* 'too exalted a rank'.

493–8. In her exposition of the nature of heavenly reward, the Maiden uses the same sermon technique as is used by the narrator in *Pat* (cf. especially *Pat* 57–60)—a moral statement supported by scriptural illustration. As in *Pat* 9 and *Cl* 51, the biblical text is seen from the layman's point of view, in the context of the *messe* (which appears to be used in *Cl* 51 as a synonym of *gospel*).

497–500. 'As Matthew relates in the true gospel in your mass, about almighty God, in a parable He discerns very aptly and likens it to bright heaven.'

501–72. The parable of the Vineyard is based on Matt. 20:1–16.

501. *on hyȝt:* this qualifies *regne:* 'My kingdom on high'.

503f. 'The beginning of the season had come, the time was right to work (in) the vineyard.'

505. *þys hyne:* cf. *G* 1139n.

Into acorde þay con declyne
For a pené on a day, and forth þay gotz,   510
Wryþen and worchen and don gret pyne,
Keruen and caggen and man hit clos.
Aboute vnder þe lorde to marked totz,
And ydel men stande he fyndez þerate.
'Why stande ȝe ydel?,' he sayde to þos;   515
'Ne knawe ȝe of þis day no date?'

' " 'Er date of daye hider arn we wonne:'
So watz al samen her answar soȝt.
'We haf standen her syn ros þe sunne,
And no mon byddez vus do ryȝt noȝt.'   520
'Gos into my vyne, dotz þat ȝe conne:'
So sayde þe lorde, and made hit toȝt;
'What resonabele hyre be naȝt be runne
I yow pay in dede and þoȝte.'
Þay wente into þe vyne and wroȝte,   525
And al day þe lorde þus ȝede his gate,
And nw men to hys vyne he broȝte
Welneȝ wyl day watz passed date.

' "At þe date of day of euensonge,
On oure byfore þe sonne go doun,   530
He seȝ þer ydel men ful stronge
And sade to hem with sobre soun:
'Wy stonde ȝe ydel þise dayez longe?'
Þay sayden her hyre watz nawhere boun.
'Gotz to my vyne, ȝemen ȝonge,   535
And wyrkez and dotz þat at ȝe moun.'
Sone þe worlde bycom wel broun;

---

524.   pay (Gollancz)] MS pray
529.   date of day (Osgood)] MS day of date
532.   hem] MS hen

509–14.   'They came to an agreement for a penny a day, and then went out (*or* on their way), (they) labour and work and take great pains, cut and tie and make it (the crop) secure. About the third hour the master goes to the market, and there he finds men standing unemployed.'
516.   'don't you recognize any beginning to this day?'
524.   *in dede and þoȝte:* i.e. 'fully, absolutely'—a legalistic formula.
526–8.   'and all day the master went on his way like this, and he brought new men into his vineyard until the day was almost past its end.'
536.   'and work and do what you can.' *Þat at* is probably an elision of *þat þat*, though *at* exists as a conjunction in its own right.

Þe sunne watz doun, and hit wex late.
To take her hyre he mad sumoun;
Þe day watz al apassed date. 540

X

'"The date of þe daye þe lorde con knaw, [f46ᵛ]
Called to þe reue: 'Lede, pay þe meyny;
Gyf hem þe hyre þat I hem owe,
And fyrre, þat non me may reprené,
Set hem alle vpon a rawe 545
And gyf vchon inlyche a peny.
Bygyn at þe laste þat standez lowe,
Tyl to þe fyrste þat þou atteny.'
And þenne þe fyrst bygonne to pleny
And sayden þat þay hade trauayled sore: 550
'Þese bot on oure hem con streny;
Vus þynk vus oȝe to take more.

'"'More haf we serued, vus þynk so,
Þat suffred han þe dayez hete,
Þenn þyse þat wroȝt not hourez two, 555
And þou dotz hem vus to counterfete.'
Þenne sayde þe lorde to on of þo:
'Frende, no waning I wyl þe ȝete;
Take þat is þyn owne, and go.
And I hyred þe for a peny agrete, 560

538. and] MS and and
558. waning (Gollancz)] MS wanig

541–600. This section concentrates on the question of the quantitative evaluation of reward—emphasized by the concatenation word *more*—and ends, at the poem's halfway point, with a direct confrontation between earthly and heavenly values.

541f. 'The master perceived the end of day and called to his reeve: "Sir, pay the workers"'.

544. 'and, moreover, so that no one may reproach me'.

553–9. '"We who have suffered the day's heat have deserved more, it seems to us, than these who worked not two hours, and you liken them to us." Then the master said to one of them: "Friend, I do not wish to make any reduction (of what is due) to you; take what is your own and go."' An alternative interpretation of 558 is offered by Fowler, 5a 1959: '"Friend, I will allow thee no lamentation"—that is, the master of the vineyard will not recognize the validity of (OIcel *játa* 'to say "yes" to') any complaint on the part of the labourer.' As Fowler admits, the first explanation is closer to the sense of the Vulgate.

Quy bygynnez þou now to þrete?
Watz not a pené þy couenaunt þore?
Fyrre þen couenaunde is noʒt to plete;
Wy schalte þou þenne ask more?

‘"'More, weþer louyly is me my gyfte—   565
To do wyth myn quatso me lykez?
Oþer ellez þyn yʒe to lyþer is lyfte
For I am goude and non byswykez?'
Þus schal I," quoþ Kryste, "hit skyfte:
Þe laste schal be þe fyrst þat strykez,   570
And þe fyrst þe laste, be he neuer so swyft,
For mony ben called, þaʒ fewe be mykez."
Þus pore men her part ay pykez,
Þaʒ þay com late and lyttel wore,
And þaʒ her sweng wyth lyttel atslykez,   575
Þe merci of God is much þe more.

'More haf I of joye and blysse hereinne,   [f47ʳ]
Of ladyschyp gret and lyuez blom,
Þen alle þe wyʒez in þe worlde myʒt wynne
By þe way of ryʒt to aske dome.   580

---

572.   called] MS calle

---

563.   'One can by no means claim more than is agreed on'.

565–8.   'Moreover, is not my giving lawful to me—doing whatever it pleases me (to do) with my own? Or else is your eye turned to evil because I am righteous and cheat no one?' The idiom *yʒe to lyþer is lyfte* (567) is explained by a Hebrew figure of speech connoting malice, envy, and greed (cf. Prov. 23:6–7, 28:22; Deut. 15:9; Matt. 6:22–3).

569–88.   Here it is stated explicitly that the penny symbolizes salvation, and that the Maiden has received her 'penny' (cf. 614). The identification between the penny in this parable and salvation is traditional: see *Glossa Ordinaria, PL* 114:876, and Ackerman, **7a** 1964.

570–72.   'the last shall be the first who comes, and the first shall be last, however swift he be, for many are called, though few are chosen.' These lines translate Matt. 20:16, *mykez* (572) rendering Vulgate *electi* 'the chosen'. *Myke* is probably an apheptic form of *amike* 'friend' (from Latin *amicus* 'friend') here with the extended sense 'chosen one'.

573–5.   'Thus poor men always gather their share, though they came late and were insignificant (on earth), and though their labour is soon (*or* with small result) spent'. *Lyttel* (574) perhaps carries overtones of the literal sense 'small' in allusion to the Maiden as a child on earth.

579f.   'than all the people in the world could win if they were to ask for a reward according to justice.' This is the central theme of section XII.

Wheþer welnygh now I con bygynne—
In euentyde into þe vyne I come—
Fyrst of my hyre my Lorde con mynne:
I watz payed anon of al and sum.
Зet oþer þer werne þat toke more tom,   585
Þat swange and swat for long зore,
Þat зet of hyre noþynk þay nom,
Paraunter noзt schal to-зere more.'

Then more I meled and sayde apert:
'Me þynk þy tale vnresounable;   590
Goddez ryзt is redy and euermore rert,
Oþer holy wryt is bot a fable.
In sauter is sayd a verce ouerte
Þat spekez a poynt determynable:
"Þou quytez vchon as hys desserte,   595
Þou hyзe Kyng ay pertermynable."
Now he þat stod þe long day stable,
And þou to payment com hym byfore,
Þenne þe lasse in werke to take more able,
And euer þe lenger þe lasse þe more.'   600

581. 'Although I began just now'.

581–8. This interpretation of the parable has been much discussed. The labourers in the vineyard are traditionally seen as virtuous Christians, and their varying times of entry as the different times of life at which they were converted (see St Augustine, Sermon 87 [*PL* 58:530–39]). In the poet's interpretation, entry into the vineyard at the eleventh hour is taken to represent the death of a baptized Christian in childhood. Many critics have felt that this is at odds with the traditional reading. However, Robertson, **7a** 1950a, points out that there were variations on the Augustinian view which did not actually contradict it; he quotes the interpretation of the 12th c. commentator Bruno Astensis, who, without contradicting Augustine's reading, adds that the eleventh hour may also refer to any, including children, converted shortly before death.

585–8. 'Yet there were others who took more time, who laboured and sweated for a long time, who still received nothing (in the way) of pay, and perhaps will (receive) nothing more this year (i.e. for a long time).'

593–6. The reference is to Ps. 61:12–13 (AV 62:11–12).

596. 'You high King ever supreme in judgement' (see Kean, **7a** 1967, 191). The usual editorial emendation to *pretermynable*, with its inappropriate meaning 'who pre-ordains', is unnecessary.

597–600. 'Now if you came to payment before him who remained steadfast all day long, then those who have done less work are entitled to take more, and however much less so much the more.' The last line is more emphatic than logical. St Augustine provides the answer to the Dreamer's point: *Non murmuret ergo qui post multum tempus accepit, contra eum qui post modicum tempus accepit* 'therefore let him who has received (the reward) after a long time not complain against him who has received it after a short time' (*PL* 38:533).

XI

'Of more and lasse in Godez ryche,'
Þat gentyl sayde, 'lys no joparde,
For þer is vch mon payed inlyche,
Wheþer lyttel oþer much be hys rewarde.
For þe gentyl Cheuentayn is no chyche,   605
Queþersoeuer He dele—nesch oþer harde:
He lauez Hys gyftez as water of dyche,
Oþer gotez of golf þat neuer charde.
Hys fraunchyse is large: þat euer dard
To Hym þat matz in synne rescoghe—   610
No blysse betz fro hem reparde,
For þe grace of God is gret inoghe.

'Bot now þou motez, me for to mate,   [f47ᵛ]
Þat I my peny haf wrang tan here;

601–4. ' "No risk of more or less exists in God's kingdom," said that gentle being, "for there every man is paid the same, whether his dessert be great or small." ' It is standard Christian doctrine that the reward of heavenly life will be given to all the saved, but that there will be variations in the degree and kind of the joys in heaven. This is emphasized by St Augustine (*op. cit., PL* 38:533), and in *PPl* C.XV.136–53.

605–8. 'For the noble Ruler is no niggard, whichever He metes out—what is pleasant or what is hard: He pours out His gifts like water from a ditch or streams from a deep source that has never ceased to flow.'

609–12. 'His (God's) generosity is great (*or* abundant): those who at any time in their lives submitted to Him who rescues sinners—from them no bliss will be withheld, for the grace of God is great enough.' These difficult lines have been much debated: see especially Gordon n, F. Th. Visser, *ES*, 39 (1958), 20–23, R. E. Kaske, *Traditio*, 15 (1959), 418–28, and Bruce Mitchell, *NQ*, 209 (1964), 47. The main problems are as follows. *Dard* (*to*) (OE *darian* 'lurk in dread') appears to be used here in an extended sense 'stand in awe of, submit to'. This is not a great leap of sense, however, for a poet who habitually stretches the meanings of words in rhyme, alliteration, and concatenation. The use of *dare* in a hawking allusion in Skelton's *Magnificence*—'I haue an hoby (i.e. falcon) can make larkys to dare' (ed. Robert L. Ramsay [EETS ES 98], 1342)—suggests that there may be another buried hawking metaphor here (cf. 184ff and especially 1085). It is less likely, on grounds of grammatical form, that *dard* could be a pa.t. of *durren* 'dare' at this date. *Euer* may be 'always' or 'at any time'; in view of the application of the parable, Visser's view that it here means 'at any time of life' is convincing (cf. note to 581–8). *Fraunchyse* may be either 'generosity' or 'privilege', depending on whether the determiner *hys* is taken as referring to God or the sinner. Here it is understood to mean 'God's generosity', and the lines punctuated accordingly. This interpretation eliminates what would be a clash between sing. *hys* and pl. *hem* (611).

613f. 'But now you argue, in order to shame me (*or* overcome me in argument) that I have unjustly received my penny here'. Emerson (**5a** 1927) proposed that *now* (613) be emended to *inow* (a form of *inoghe*) for the sake of concatenation. However, *now* makes better sense; moreover this may be a case of punning concatenation, as in 732f, 756f, and 865; see also 913–72n.

Þou sayz þat I þat com to late 615
Am not worþy so gret fere.
Where wystez þou euer any bourne abate
Euer so holy in hys prayere
Þat he ne forfeted by sumkyn gate
Þe mede sumtyme of heuenez clere? 620
And ay þe ofter þe alder þay were,
Þay laften ryȝt and wroȝten woghe.
Mercy and grace moste hem þen stere,
For þe grace of God is gret innoȝe.

'Bot innoghe of grace hatz innocent: 625
As sone as þay arn borne, by lyne
In þe water of babtem þay dyssente.
Þen arne þay boroȝt into þe vyne.
Anon þe day with derk endente
Þe niyȝt of deth dotz to enclyne. 630
Þat wroȝt neuer wrang er þenne þay wente
Þe gentyle Lorde þenne payez Hys hyne.
Þay dyden Hys heste; þay wern þereine;
Why schulde He not her labour alow?
Ȝys, and pay hym at þe fyrst fyne? 635
For þe grace of God is gret innoghe.

'Inoȝe is knawen þat mankyn grete
Fyrste watz wroȝt to blysse parfyt.

616.   fere (Gordon)] MS lere

616.   *fere:* 'dignity, reward'. The MS reading *lere* is incomprehensible; Gordon's emendation *fere* is more convincing than that adopted by Gollancz and Osgood, *here* 'wages'.

617–20.   'Did you ever know any man (who) remained all the time so holy in his prayers that he did not in some kind of way, at some time, forfeit the reward of bright heaven?' *Where* (617) is here interpreted as a contraction of *Wheþer* introducing a direct question.

625–7.   'But an innocent has grace enough: as soon as they are born they descend in due course into the water of baptism.' Cf. *Cl* 163f.

629–32.   'Soon the night of death causes the day to sink, inlaid with darkness. Those who never worked amiss before they departed the noble Lord then pays (as) His labourers.' *Niyȝt* (630): the MS reads either *myȝt* or *niyȝt*, of which the latter fits better into the metaphorical scheme. Some editors emend to *nyȝt*—unnecessarily, as similar forms occur in *G* 929 and *Cl* 359 and 1779.

633.   *þereine:* i.e. in the vineyard.

634f.   'why should He not recognize their labour? Yes, and pay them first and in full?'

637–48.   The Maiden expounds the central Christian doctrine of atonement, with particular emphasis on innocence and baptism.

637f.   'It is very well known that mankind in general was first created for perfect bliss.'

Oure forme fader hit con forfete
Þurȝ an apple þat he vpon con byte; 640
Al wer we dampned for þat mete
To dyȝe in doel out of delyt
And syþen wende to helle hete,
Þerinne to won withoute respyt.
Bot þeron com a bote astyt; 645
Ryche blod ran on rode so roghe,
And wynne water; þen, at þat plyt,
Þe grace of God wex gret innoghe.

'Innoghe þer wax out of þat welle, [f 48ᵛ]
Blod and water of brode wounde. 650
Þe blod vus boȝt fro bale of helle,
And delyuered vus of þe deth secounde;
Þe water is baptem, þe soþe to telle,
Þat folȝed þe glayue so grymly grounde,
Þat waschez away þe gyltez felle 655
Þat Adam wyth inne deth vus drounde.
Now is þer noȝt in þe worlde rounde
Bytwene vus and blysse bot þat He withdroȝ,
And þat is restored in sely stounde;
And þe grace of God is gret innogh. 660

XII

'Grace innogh þe mon may haue
Þat synnez þenne new, ȝif hym repente,

---

649. out] MS out out

641f. 'we were all condemned because of that food to die in grief, deprived of joy'.
645. 'But soon there came a remedy for it'.
649–56. St John's Gospel (19:34) describes how a soldier (not named in St John, but called Longinus in the apocryphal Gospel of Nicodemus) pierces the side of the crucified Christ with a spear, and how blood and water pour forth. The poet draws on the traditional symbolic identification of this outpouring of blood and water with the grace made available to man through Christ's sacrifice. This motif is also linked with the image of the well or fountain of grace (649; cf. 607f, 1058ff).
653–9. 'to tell the truth, the water that followed the spear so cruelly sharpened is baptism, which washes away the deadly guilts through which Adam drowned us in death. Now there is nothing in the round world between us and bliss but what He removed, and that (i.e. bliss) is restored in a blessed hour'.
661–720. In this section a whole line is used for concatenation, with only slight variation. The theme, the right of the innocent to salvation, is of central significance both dramatically (because the Maiden is one of the innocent) and thematically (because the point is essential to her exposition of Christian doctrine).
661–4. The poems share a general concern with penance; see, for instance, *Cl* 1111ff, *Pat* 305ff, and *G* 2385ff.

Bot with sorȝ and syt he mot hit craue,
And byde þe payne þerto is bent.
Bot Resoun, of ryȝt þat con not raue,   665
Sauez euermore þe innossent;
Hit is a dom þat neuer God gaue
Þat euer þe gyltlez schulde be schente.
Þe gyltyf may contryssyoun hente
And be þurȝ mercy to grace þryȝt;   670
Bot he to gyle þat neuer glente
As inoscente is saf and ryȝte.

'Ryȝt þus I knaw wel in þis cas
Two men to saue is God—by skylle:
Þe ryȝtwys man schal se Hys face,   675
Þe harmlez haþel schal com Hym tylle.
Þe sauter hyt satz þus in a pace:
"Lorde, quo schal klymbe Þy hyȝ hylle,
Oþer rest withinne Þy holy place?"
Hymself to onsware he is not dylle: 680
"Hondelyngez harme þat dyt not ille,
Þat is of hert boþe clene and lyȝt,
Þer schal hys step stable stylle":
Þe innosent is ay saf by ryȝt.

672. As (Holthausen)] MS at
673. þus] MS þus þus
675. face] MS fate
678. hylle] MS hyllez

665f. 'But Reason, which cannot stray from justice, always saves the innocent person'. God is here portrayed as a quasi-personification of reason (cf. *Koyntyse*, 690); for the confrontation between *ryȝt* (665) and *mercy* (670) cf. note to *Pat* 323f.
671f. 'but he who never deviated towards treachery as an innocent person is redeemed and justified (by divine grace).' The Maiden is here applying the logic of 665f. *As* (672): Holthausen's **5a** emendation is preferred to Gordon's (*And*). Despite its awkwardness, MS *at* is retained by other editors, though Gollancz emends *and* (later in 672) to *by*.
673f. 'This is how I know for sure that God is to save two (kinds of) men—for this reason'. The final *by skylle* (cf. *G* 1296) re-emphasizes the opening *Ryȝt þus*. *God* has usually been taken as an adj. 'good', but this gives a weak sense.
675–84. This passage echoes the Beatitudes (also used in *Pat* 13–28 and *Cl* 23–8): see Matt. 5:3–10. Cf. also Rev. 22:4, 1 Cor. 13:12, and 677n.
677. 'The psalter says it in this way in one passage'. The reference is probably to Ps. 14 (AV 15):1–3 or Ps. 23 (AV 24):3–6.
680–83. 'He (the Psalmist) is not slow to answer himself: "He who did no evil with his hands, who is pure and unsullied at heart, shall there set his foot (i.e. stand) at rest"'.

'The ryȝtwys man also, sertayn,   [f48ᵛ] 685
Aproche he schal þat proper pyle—
Þat takez not her lyf in vayne
Ne glauerez her nieȝbor wyth no gyle—
Of þys ryȝtwys sayz Salamon playn,
Hym Koyntyse oure con aquyle;   690
By wayez ful streȝt He con hym strayn,
And scheued hym þe rengne of God awhyle,
As quo says, "Lo, ȝon louely yle:
Þou may hit wynne if þou be wyȝte."
Bot hardyly, withoute peryle,   695
Þe innosent is ay saue by ryȝte.

'Anende ryȝtwys men ȝet saytz a gome,
Dauid, in sauter, if euer ȝe seȝ hit:
"Lorde, Þy seruaunt draȝ neuer to dome,
For non lyuyande to Þe is justyfyet."   700

689.   sayz] MS saȝ *or* saz
690.   Hym] MS how
       Koyntyse (Bradley)] MS kyntly
700.   For] MS sor

685–8. 'The righteous man shall also, certainly, come to that fair stronghold—those who do not spend their life in folly or deceive their neighbour with guile'.
689–94. 'Solomon tells us plainly about this righteous man, (that) our Wisdom received him; He made him go along most narrow ways and showed him the kingdom of God for a time, like one who says, "Behold yonder beautiful domain: you may win it if you are valiant."' This passage is based partly on Wisd. 10:10: *Haec profugum irae fratris iustum deduxit per vias rectas, et ostendit illi regnum Dei dedit illi scientiam sanctorum, honestavit illum in laboris et complevit labores illius* 'She [Wisdom] conducted the just, when he fled from his brother's wrath, through the right ways, and shewed him the kingdom of God, and gave him the knowledge of the holy things, and made him honourable in his labours, and accomplished his labours.' The poet changes the gender of the personification *Wisdom* (*He*, 691), possibly to conform to the common medieval identification of Wisdom with Christ (an association best illustrated in late medieval literature by the morality play *Wisdom*: cf. *Pat* 37ff and note). *Sayz* (689): whereas the MS form can hardly be anything but the pa.t. of *se*, the context demands the sense 'says', and *saȝ* (or *saz*) is therefore emended to *sayz*. Line 690, clearly defective in the MS, has been emended variously: Bradley (*Academy*, 38 [1890], 201f), followed by Gordon, reads *Koyntise onoure* for MS *kyntly oure*; Hillmann simply emends *oure* to *onoure*; in his first edition, followed by Osgood, Gollancz retains *kyntly oure* and adds *kyng hym*; in his second, he changes *kyng* to *Koyntise*. It is reasonable to assume that MS *kyntly* derives from an original *Koyntyse* 'Wisdom', and MS *how* could easily be a corruption of *hym*, the original direct object for *aquyle*. Emendation of *oure* is unnecessary in view of the identification of Wisdom with Christ.
697–700. 'Also, concerning just men, a certain man, David, says in the Psalter, if you have ever seen it: "Lord, never bring Your servant to judgement, for no living man is justified before You."' Cf. Ps. 142 (AV 143):2.

Forþy to corte quen þou schal com
Þer alle oure causez schal be cryed,
Alegge þe ryȝt, þou may be innome,
By þys ilke spech I haue asspyed.
Bot He on rode þat blody dyed,   705
Delfully þurȝ hondez þryȝt,
Gyue þe to passe, when þou arte tryed,
By innocens and not by ryȝte.

'Ryȝtwysly quo con rede,
He loke on bok and be awayed   710
How Jesus Hym welke in areþede,
And burnez her barnez vnto Hym brayde.
For happe and hele þat fro Hym ȝede
To touch her chylder þay fayr Hym prayed.
His dessypelez with blame "Let be!" hym bede   715
And wyth her resounez ful fele restayed.
Jesus þenne hem swetely sayde:
"Do way, let chylder vnto Me tyȝt;
To suche is heuenryche arayed":
Þe innocent is ay saf by ryȝt.   720

XIII

'Ryȝt con calle to Hym Hys mylde,   [f49ʳ]
And sayde Hys ryche no wyȝ myȝt wynne

702.   cryed (Gollancz)] MS tryed
714.   touch] MS touth
721.   Ryȝt] MS Jesus

701f.   The Maiden is, of course, speaking of the Last Judgement.
702.   *cryed:* 'called'. Gollancz's emendation derives support from alliteration and from the recurrence of *tryed* at 707.
703f.   'if you plead right you may be refuted in argument by this same speech that I have noticed': i.e. that no man can claim salvation by right. This use of legal terminology is discussed by Dorothy Everett and Naomi P. Hurnard, **7a** 1947.
707.   *Gyue þe to passe:* 'grant you to go free'.
709–15.   'He who can read correctly, let him look at the book and be instructed how Jesus walked among the people in old times, and people brought their children to Him; they humbly begged Him to touch their children for the happiness and healing that went from Him. His disciples commanded them with reproof "Leave off!"'
711–24.   This passage is mainly based on Luke 18:15–17, but also reflects the influence of the accounts of Matthew (19:13–15) and Mark (10:13–16).
721–80.   In the thirteenth section, the concatenation is supplied by *mascellez* (or *makellez*) *perle*. There is some play between the similar but distinct meanings of *mascellez* 'spotless' and *makellez* 'matchless': a distinction picked up by the Maiden in 781–4. In the final line of the section the two words are used together.
721–3.   'Justice summoned His gentle ones (i.e. the disciples) to Him, and said no one

Bot he com þyder ryȝt as a chylde,
Oþer ellez neuermore com þerinne.
Harmlez, trwe, and vndefylde,   725
Withouten mote oþer mascle of sulpande synne:
Quen such þer cnoken on þe bylde,
Tyt schal hem men þe ȝate vnpynne.
Þer is þe blys þat con not blynne
Þat þe jueler soȝte þurȝ perré pres,   730
And solde alle hys goud, boþe wolen and lynne,
To bye hym a perle watz mascellez.

'This makellez perle þat boȝt is dere,
Þe joueler gef fore alle hys god,
Is lyke þe reme of heuenesse clere—   735
So sayde þe Fader of folde and flode—
For hit is wemlez, clene, and clere,
And endelez rounde, and blyþe of mode,

could win His kingdom unless he came to it absolutely like a child'. *Ryȝt* (721): in
the MS, the only break in the pattern of concatenation occurs at this point, where
one would expect the line to start with *ryȝt*. Emerson (**5a** 1927) suggests adding *Ryȝt*
before MS *Jesus*, but this is unacceptable both syntactically and metrically. The
conviction seems unavoidable, in view of the formal regularity of the poem, that the
poet wrote *Ryȝt con calle*, personifying Jesus as 'Justice', and that MS *Jesus* is a scribal
substitution for the sake of greater explicitness. Similar personifications, in which the
deity is equated with a single virtue, have occurred at 665 (*Resoun*) and 690 (*Koyntise*,
most edd.). Moreover, the name *Jesus* has been used twice in the preceding stanza;
the poet could therefore reasonably expect the reader to make the identification.

725f.   The idea of sin soiling the purity of the soul recurs throughout the poems: see
1060, *Pat* 342, *Cl* 12, 134, 169–76, 1111ff, *G* 2436, and notes.

728.   'the gate will be opened to them at once.'

729–39.   The Maiden associates the great pearl she wears with that in the parable of
the Pearl of Price (Matt. 13:45–6)—an association already suggested in 221. She
interprets the pearl of the parable as signifying salvation, and thus heaven. In this
she does not depart from the accepted medieval exegetical viewpoint (though there
are considerable differences in emphasis between the various commentators: see
Osgood's note to 735–43, and D. W. Robertson, Jr., **7a** 1950b).

733.   *makellez:* Here and in 757 Osgood and Gollancz emend this word to *maskellez*,
but this can hardly be justified: see 721–80n.

734.   'for which the jeweller gave all his goods'.

735.   *heuenesse clere:* 'bright heavens'.

738.   *endelez rounde:* The pearl's shape is thus seen to symbolize the perfection and
infiniteness of heaven. It may be argued that the poem itself, with its meticulously
proportioned construction, imitates this formal perfection. In particular, the end of
Pe echoes its beginning, thus providing the sense of circular form. This is a character-
istic shared, in varying degrees, by the other three poems.

And commune to alle þat ryȝtwys were.
Lo, euen inmyddez my breste hit stode: 740
My Lorde þe Lombe, þat schede Hys blode,
He pyȝt hit þere in token of pes.
I rede þe forsake þe worlde wode
And porchace þy perle maskelles.'

'O maskelez perle in perlez pure,   745
Þat berez,' quoþ I, 'þe perle of prys,
Quo formed þe þy fayre fygure?
Þat wroȝt þy wede he watz ful wys;
Þy beauté com neuer of nature—
Pymalyon paynted neuer þy vys,   750
Ne Arystotel nawþer by hys lettrure
Of carped þe kynde þese propertéz;
Þy colour passez þe flour-de-lys,
Þyn angel-hauyng so clene cortez.
Breue me, bryȝt, quat kyn offys   755
Berez þe perle so maskellez?'

'My makelez Lambe þat al may bete,'   [f49ᵛ]
Quoþ scho, 'my dere Destyné,

739. ryȝtwys] MS ryȝtywys
752. carped (Gollancz)] MS carpe

740. *stode:* This is interpreted 'shone' rather than 'stood' (cf. 113n).

747f. 'who formed your fair figure? Whoever made your clothing was most skilful'.

749–52. The usual view, that in this passage the poet is drawing directly on the *Roman de la Rose* (Chaucerian version, 3205–16), is questioned by Herbert Pilch (Conley, **7a** 1970, 165ff), who argues that the comparison is traditional.

750–52. 'Pygmalion never painted your face, nor did Aristotle through his learning speak of the nature of these special virtues'.

753. Cf. 195.

755. *offys:* Though there is a gap between pen-strokes at the top of the second *f*, we (like Osgood) see no reason to read the word as anything but *offys*. Most edd. have interpreted the small vertical pen-stroke as a superscript *i* and have read *oftriys*. Bradley's (unpublished) suggestion that this is *ostriys* 'oysters' (connecting it with the pearl-metaphor) has recently been supported by E. Talbot Donaldson, *Neu.Mitt.*, 73 (1972), 75–82. Gollancz reads *of triys* and glosses 'of peace'. Gordon, reading *oftriys*, emends to *offys*. In the following passage (757–68) the Maiden goes on to describe her *offys* 'office, position' in heaven.

757–60. '"My peerless Lamb," she said, "my beloved Destiny who can amend everything, chose me for His bride, although at one time such a union seemed unfitting."'

Me ches to Hys make, alþaȝ vnmete
Sumtyme semed þat assemblé.   760
When I wente fro yor worlde wete
He calde me to Hys bonerté:
"Cum hyder to Me, My lemman swete,
For mote ne spot is non in þe."
He gef me myȝt and als bewté;   765
In Hys blod He wesch my wede on dese,
And coronde clene in vergynté,
And pyȝt me in perlez maskellez.'

'Why, maskellez bryd þat bryȝt con flambe,
Þat reiatéz hatz so ryche and ryf,   770
Quat kyn þyng may be þat Lambe
Þat þe wolde wedde vnto Hys vyf?
Ouer alle oþer so hyȝ þou clambe
To lede with Hym so ladyly lyf.
So mony a comly onvunder cambe   775
For Kryst han lyued in much stryf,
And þou con alle þo dere outdryf,
And fro þat maryag al oþer depres,
Al only þyself so stout and styf,
A makelez may and maskellez.'   780

XIV

'Maskelles,' quoþ þat myry quene,
'Vnblemyst I am, wythouten blot,

761. *wete:* The adjective is perhaps intended to emphasize the contrast between the
natural world of flower and flesh, as described in the opening section, and the world
of eternity, as embodied poetically in the jewelled, urban imagery of the New
Jerusalem, 985ff (cf. also 269–72); or it may refer to the contrast between the harsh
climate of the fallen world and the eternal spring of paradise.

763f. This is based on the Song of Songs (4:7–8)—from which the metaphor of the
mystical marriage is derived.

766f. 'on the dais He washed my clothing in His blood, and crowned me pure in
virginity'. The clothes symbolize the state of the soul: cf. *Pat* 342, and *Cl* 12, 134, and
169–76, and notes.

768. As Hillmann observes, the soul is represented in scripture as a bride adorned
with jewels: see Isa. 61:10.

773–80. The Dreamer's incredulity is similar to that in 421–32, where the claims of
the Maiden appear to him to challenge the position of the Virgin Mary.

775–80. 'So many (beautiful) ladies have lived in hard struggle for Christ, and you
have thrust out all those noble ones, driving away all others from that marriage, you
alone (being) strong and firm enough, a peerless and flawless maiden.' *Comly onvunder
cambe* (775) is a periphrasis for '(beautiful) lady'. For extensions of this type of
construction, see 166, 1100.

781–840. Once again concatenation is thematically significant. *Jerusalem* emphasizes

And þat may I with mensk menteene,
Bot "makelez quene" þenne sade I not.
Þe Lambes vyuez in blysse we bene,   785
A hondred and forty þowsande flot,
As in þe Apocalyppez hit is sene:
Sant John hem syȝ al in a knot.
On þe hyl of Syon, þat semly clot,
Þe apostel hem segh in gostly drem,   790
Arayed to þe weddyng in þat hyl-coppe,
Þe nwe cyté o Jerusalem.

'Of Jerusalem I in speche spelle.   [f 50ʳ]
If þou wyl knaw what kyn He be—
My Lombe, my Lorde, my dere Juelle,   795
My Joy, my Blys, my Lemman fre—
Þe profete Ysaye of Hym con melle

that the Maiden is speaking from the viewpoint of an inmate of the City of God; its association with the earthly Jerusalem continues the contrast and juxtaposition of earthly values with their heavenly counterparts; and the references to the Apocalypse remind us that the knowledge expounded there was shown to John (see 788n) in a mystical vision and made available to man through scripture. This discussion of John's vision also anticipates the Dreamer's (977ff), and perhaps reminds us of the dream vision medium through which the Dreamer is instructed, and the poem presented to the audience.

783–6. 'and that I may maintain with honour, but I did not say "matchless queen". We are the brides of the Lamb in happiness, a company of a hundred and forty thousand'. In 786, Gollancz adds *fowre* after *forty*—comparing 870 and Rev. 14 : 3; Gordon follows him. Though *fowre* might easily have been omitted by a scribe after the similar word *forty*, the emendation assumes a literal consistency which the poet by no means always maintains. Moreover, the line is metrically more regular as it stands.

788. 'St John saw them all in a group.' The author of Revelation was usually identified with the apostle St John.

790. *gostly drem:* Medieval writers commonly divide mystical visions into three categories—corporeal, spiritual, and intellectual. In the first, a man physically sees an object invisible to others; in the second, a man in sleep or in prayer sees images through divine revelation; in the third, the soul is 'ravished' inwardly. As the poet's terminology suggests, John's Apocalyptic vision was normally assigned to the second category. See David Knowles, *The English Mystical Tradition* (London, 1961), 125, and Edward Wilson, *Neu. Mitt.*, 69 (1968), 90–101.

791f. See Rev. 19 : 7–8, 21 : 2.

794. 'If you want to know what He is like'.

795. *Juelle:* The use of this word to designate Christ gains force and meaning from the cumulative associations surrounding the ideas of pearls and jewels on the one hand and the role of the 'jeweller' or judge of gems on the other (see Introduction, pp. 32–4).

797–802. 'the prophet Isaiah speaks compassionately of His meekness: "That glorious Innocent One who was put to death without any charge of crime, was led like a sheep to the slaughter, and, like a lamb that the shearer has taken in hand". The

Pitously of Hys debonerté:
"Þat gloryous Gyltlez þat mon con quelle
Withouten any sake of felonye,   800
As a schep to þe slaȝt þer lad watz He,
And, as lombe þat clypper in hande nem,
So closed He Hys mouth fro vch query,
Quen Juez Hym jugged in Jerusalem."

'In Jerusalem watz my Lemman slayn   805
And rent on rode with boyez bolde,
Al oure balez to bere ful bayn
He toke on Hymself oure carez colde;
With boffetez watz Hys face flayn
Þat watz so fayr on to byholde.   810
For synne He set Hymself in vayn,
Þat neuer hade non Hymself to wolde;
For vus He lette Hym flyȝe and folde,
And brede vpon a bostwys bem;
As meke as lomp þat no playnt tolde   815
For vus He swalt in Jerusalem.

799.   Gyltlez] MS gystlez
802.   hande] MS lande
       nem (Morris)] MS men

reference is to Isa. 53, a key Messianic prophecy in the Christian interpretation of
the Old Testament.
799.   *Gyltlez:* MS *gystlez* is meaningless. There are faint signs that the scribe may have
tried to alter *s* to *l*.
802.   *hande:* As in 799, it seems that the scribe attempted to correct the error (in this
case, to *hande*). *Lande* may have originated from false scribal expectation of allitera-
tion.
803.   Christ's silence is prophesied in Isa. 53:7, and dramatized with great effec-
tiveness in some of the mystery plays (e.g. York No. 35).
805–16.   Osgood justly points out that the language of these lines is similar to that
used in some meditations on the Passion.
806.   *with boyez bolde:* 'by wicked ruffians'. The uncouthness as well as the ruthlessness
of those responsible for putting Christ on the Cross becomes a commonplace in the
Middle Ages; this is illustrated in the mystery plays (e.g. York No. 35 and Chester
No. 16). There is also an interesting parallel in *Pat* 95f: when Jonah expresses his fear
of possible crucifixion, he characterizes his imagined persecutors as merciless ruffians.
809f.   Cf. Matt. 26:67, Mark 14:65, and Luke 22:64.
811–14.   'He who Himself never had any (sin) about Him set Himself at nought for
sin. For us He let Himself be scourged and bowed, and stretched on a crude beam'.
To wolde (812): literally 'in (His) possession' (*OED wield*, noun). *Folde* (813): i.e.
under the weight of the cross. These lines are also reminiscent of Isa. 53; cf. 2 Cor.
5:21 and 797–802n.
815.   *lomp:* 'lamb'.

'In Jerusalem, Jordan, and Galalye,
Þeras baptysed þe goude Saynt Jon,
His wordez acorded to Ysaye.
When Jesus con to hym warde gon, 820
He sayde of Hym þys professye:
"Lo, Godez Lombe as trwe as ston,
Þat dotz away þe synnez dryȝe
Þat alle þys worlde hatz wroȝt vpon.
Hymself ne wroȝt neuer ȝet non, 825
Wheþer on Hymself He con al clem.
Hys generacyoun quo recen con,
Þat dyȝed for vus in Jerusalem?"

'In Jerusalem þus my Lemman swete [f50ᵛ]
Twyez for lombe watz taken þare, 830
By trw recorde of ayþer prophete,
For mode so meke and al Hys fare.
Þe þryde tyme is þerto ful mete,

817. In (Gollancz)] MS *om.*
829. swete (Gollancz)] MS swatte

817. *In:* The emendation is clearly demanded by the sense. *In* could easily have been omitted as a result of the similarity of the following word in its abbreviated form, *Irm̄.*
817f. In the Gospels John is described as baptizing in Jordan (see Matt. 3:13, Mark 1:4–9, Luke 3:3, John 1:28), and some of these accounts imply proximity to Jerusalem. Various explanations for the inclusion of *Galalye* have been offered— Osgood that it is through association with Herod being Tetrarch of Galilee, Gordon that it indicates a lack of familiarity with the geography of the region, and Gollancz that it is the result of a particular interpretation of John 1:28.
818. *Þeras:* 'where'.
819–24. The Maiden cites the words of John the Baptist from John 1:29 as a direct allusion to the prophecy of Isa. 53.
820. 'When Jesus came towards him'.
822. *as trwe as ston:* 'as firm as rock'. This is a familiar simile in ME. Interestingly enough, it occurs in the MS, in a couplet (the origin of which is not known) written above the picture of Lady Bercilak visiting Sir Gawain (f125ʳ): 'Mi minde is mukel on on þat wil me noȝt amende/Sum time was trewe as ston and fro schame couþe hir defende.'
823–6. 'who puts an end to the heavy sins that all this world has committed. He never yet committed one Himself, yet He claimed them all for Himself.' Cf. Isa. 53:6, 9, 11.
827f. Cf. Isa. 53:8.
829–1152. The Book of Revelation is the main source for this part of the poem.
829. *swete:* MS *swatte* probably reflects scribal misapprehension of the word as a verb ('bled, died').
831. *ayþer prophete:* that is, both Isaiah and John the Baptist (see note to 819–24).
833f. 'The third time, written clearly in the Apocalypse, agrees well with the others'. Cf. Rev. 5:6.

In Apokalypez wryten ful ȝare:
Inmydez þe trone, þere sayntez sete,
Þe apostel John Hym saȝ as bare,
Lesande þe boke with leuez sware
Þere seuen syngnettez wern sette in seme.
And at þat syȝt vche douth con dare,
In helle, in erþe, and Jerusalem.

835

840

XV
'Thys Jerusalem Lombe hade neuer pechche
Of oþer huee bot quyt jolyf
Þat mot ne masklle moȝt on streche,
For wolle quyte so ronk and ryf.
Forþy vche saule þat hade neuer teche
Is to þat Lombe a worthyly wyf.
And þaȝ vch day a store He feche,
Among vus commez nouþer strot ne stryf,
Bot vchon enlé we wolde were fyf—
Þe mo þe myryer, so God me blesse!

845

850

836. saȝ (Gollancz)] MS saytz
848. nouþer (Gordon)] MS non oþer

835–40. Cf. Rev. 5:1, 3, 6–8, 13.

836–9. 'the apostle John saw Him as plainly as possible, opening the book with square leaves where the seven seals were attached to the border. And at that sight every host bowed down'. The poet visualizes the scroll of Revelation as a book. *Saȝ* (836): for the reverse scribal error see 689. *Con dare* (839): cf. 609n.

841–912. This section is unique in that it contains six stanzas instead of the usual five. Osgood (xlvi) argues that a stanza should probably be rejected—his candidate for expulsion is the second (853–64). Gollancz is in partial agreement, saying that *if* a stanza should be rejected it is this, while Gordon (88) suggests that 901–12 is otiose. Against their arguments should be weighed the interesting fact that (*including* this extra stanza) *Pe* contains 101 stanzas, the same number as *G*—a parallel hard to credit as coincidence. The concatenation words *neuer þe les(se)* emphasize the limitless quality of heavenly bounty.

841–4. 'This Lamb of Jerusalem never had any contamination of any colour but lovely white that no spot or stain could cling to, so luxuriant and abundant was the white wool.' See 1 Pet. 1:19, Rev. 1:14. Cf. Dan. 7:9, Exod. 12:5.

845f. See Rev. 14:4–5; cf. Rev. 19:7–8.

847–50. The Maiden provides a final answer to the Dreamer's earlier objection that her elevation involved the displacement of other candidates for the marriage (773–80). It is interesting that the metaphorical use of *fyf* (849) echoes that in the similar context of 451.

849. 'but we would wish that every single one were five'.

In compayny gret our luf con þryf,
In honour more and neuer þe lesse.

'Lasse of blysse may non vus bryng
Þat beren þys perle vpon oure bereste,
For þay of mote couþe neuer mynge   855
Of spotlez perlez þat beren þe creste.
Alþaȝ oure corses in clottez clynge,
And ȝe remen for rauþe wythouten reste,
We þurȝoutly hauen cnawyng;
Of on dethe ful oure hope is drest.   860
Þe Lombe vus gladez, oure care is kest;
He myrþez vus alle at vch a mes.
Vchonez blysse is breme and beste,
And neuer onez honour ȝet neuer þe les.

'Lest les þou leue my talle farande,   [f51ʳ]   865
In Appocalyppece is wryten in wro:
"I seghe," says John, "þe Loumbe Hym stande
On þe mount of Syon ful þryuen and þro,
And wyth Hym maydennez an hundreþe þowsande,
And fowre and forty þowsande mo.   870
On alle her forhedez wryten I fande
Þe Lombez nome, Hys Faderez also.

---

856. þat (Osgood)] MS þa
861. Lombe] MS lonbe

853–64. See note to 841–912.
855. *mote:* 'quarrel, dispute' (OE *mōt*).
857f. Cf. 320 and note to 318–24.
859. 'we have understanding completely'—i.e. complete understanding. As Gordon points out, complete knowledge in heaven is promised in 1 Cor. 13:11–12.
860. 'our hope is entirely derived from one death.' The death is, of course, that of Christ, through which salvation is made possible. Cf. Heb. 10:14.
865. 'In case you should think my wonderful story false'. The Maiden once more uses scripture to authorize her words. *Les:* if this is the adjective ('false'), which yields best sense, we have here another instance of punning concatenation; cf. note to 613f.
866–900. This account is based on Rev. 14:1–5.
869. *maydennez:* This word is probably intended to include both men and women (it could be used in ME without reference to gender). In the Homilies on the Apocalypse attributed to St Augustine it is emphasized that the 144,000 are those, regardless of their sex, who were pure Christians and thus made themselves fit to be brides of Christ: see Robertson, 1950b.

A hue fro heuen I herde þoo,
Lyk flodez fele laden runnen on resse;
And as þunder þrowez in torrez blo—   875
Þat lote, I leue, watz neuer þe les.

'"Nauþeles, þaȝ hit schowted scharpe,
And ledden loude alþaȝ hit were,
A note ful nwe I herde hem warpe,
To lysten þat watz ful lufly dere.   880
As harporez harpen in her harpe,
Þat nwe songe þay songen ful cler,
In sounande notez a gentyl carpe;
Ful fayre þe modez þay fonge in fere.
Ryȝt byfore Godez chayere   885
And þe fowre bestez þat Hym obes
And þe aldermen so sadde of chere,
Her songe þay songen, neuer þe les.

'"Nowþelese non watz neuer so quoynt,
For alle þe craftez þat euer þay knewe,   890
Þat of þat songe myȝt synge a poynt,
Bot þat meyny þe Lombe þat swe;
For þay arn boȝt, fro þe vrþe aloynte,
As newe fryt to God ful due,

892.   Lombe þat (Kölbing)] MS lombe þay

873–6. 'Then I heard a shout from heaven, like the voices of many waters gathered in
a rushing torrent; and as thunder rolls among dark thunder clouds—that sound I
believe was never the less (i.e. was just as loud).' *Torrez* (875): Gordon identifies
this with OE *torr* 'hill' (from Celtic); but it is more likely that it is from OF *tur*
'tower', used metaphorically here, as in *Cl* 951, to mean 'towering clouds', perhaps
specifically 'thunder clouds'.

878–80. 'and though they were loud voices, I heard them utter quite a new sound,
that it was most pleasant to hear.'

886f. Cf. Ezek. 1:10 and Rev. 4:4, 6–8. As Hillmann points out, the *aldermen* are
the four and twenty elders, identified by commentators with the holy men of the Old
and New Testaments, and the *fowre bestez* represent the four orders of nature—man,
cattle, birds, and wild animals. It is worth adding that it was from this account of the
four orders of nature that the symbols of the Evangelists, so familiar in medieval
iconography, developed—the man standing for Matthew, the lion for Mark, the ox
for Luke, and the eagle for John.

889–94. 'Nevertheless, no one was ever so skilful, for all the arts they ever knew, as to
be able to sing a strain of that song, except for the company that follow the Lamb;
for they have been redeemed, far removed from the earth, as first fruits due to God'.
The harvest metaphor, which at the beginning of the poem (25ff) conveys predomin-
antly the sense of loss, is here reintroduced in more overt reference to the hope of
resurrection.

And to þe gentyl Lombe hit arn anjoynt,   895
As lyk to Hymself of lote and hwe;
For neuer lesyng ne tale vntrwe
Ne towched her tonge for no dysstresse.
Þat moteles meyny may neuer remwe
Fro þat maskelez mayster, neuer þe les." '   900

'Neuer þe les let be my þonc,'   [f51ᵛ]
Quoþ I, 'my perle þaȝ I appose;
I schulde not tempte þy wyt so wlonc,
To Krystez chambre þat art ichose.
I am bot mokke and mul among,   905
And þou so ryche a reken rose,
And bydez here by þys blysful bonc
Þer lyuez lyste may neuer lose.
Now, hynde, þat sympelnesse conez enclose,
I wolde þe aske a þynge expresse,   910
And þaȝ I be bustwys as a bose,
Let my bone vayl neuerþelese.

XVI

'Neuerþelese, cler, I yow bycalle,
If ȝe con se hyt be to done;

---

911. bose] MS blose

901–4. ' "Let my thanks be no less (i.e. do not think I am any the less grateful)," I said, "if I interrogate my pearl; I should not so presumptuously test the wisdom of you who are chosen for Christ's bridal-chamber." ' Here the Dreamer speaks for the first time since 780; it is apparent that, in the interim, the transformation of his frame of mind from rebellious pride to obedient humility has been completed.

905–8. 'I am only filth and dust mingled together, and you are so exquisite a fresh rose, and live here by this pleasant bank where delight in life can never fade.' The Dreamer's words in 905 are reminiscent of his earlier statement in 381f, and of Abraham's similarly self-deprecatory attitude in *Cl* 736. The significance of the rose image (906) has been transformed from that of mutable earthly beauty to that of heavenly perfection: see note to 267–72 and Introduction, p. 32.

909–12. 'Now, gracious lady, in whom sincerity dwells (*lit.* [you] who contain simplicity), I want to ask you something explicitly, and though I am rough as a peasant, let my request prevail.' *Sympelnesse* (909): as Gollancz suggests, this is probably intended to imply a contrast with pride. *Bose* (911): MS *blose* is unknown in ME. It is therefore emended to *bose*, taken as a form of *boce* 'boss', *MED* sense 3(d) 'a "lump of a man" used disparagingly'. The usage in the alliterative poem *Mum and the Soothsayer* III.98 and the evidence provided in the note on this line in the edition of Day and Steele (EETS OS 199) suggest that *Bosse* was used as a nickname, emphasizing roughness and clumsiness, for the bear.

913–72. In this section the concatenation form *mote* (sometimes *motelez*) involves play

As þou art gloryous withouten galle,   915
Withnay þou neuer my ruful bone.
Haf ȝe no wonez in castel-walle,
Ne maner þer ȝe may mete and won?
Þou tellez me of Jerusalem þe ryche ryalle,
Þer Dauid dere watz dyȝt on trone,   920
Bot by þyse holtez hit con not hone,
Bot in Judée hit is, þat noble note.
As ȝe ar maskelez vnder mone,
Your wonez schulde be wythouten mote.

'Þys motelez meyny þou conez of mele,   925
Of þousandez þryȝt so gret a route;
A gret ceté, for ȝe arn fele,
Yow byhod haue, withouten doute.
So cumly a pakke of joly juele
Wer euel don schulde lyȝ þeroute,   930
And by þyse bonkez þer I con gele
I se no bygyng nawhere aboute.
I trowe alone ȝe lenge and loute
To loke on þe glory of þys gracious gote.
If þou hatz oþer bygyngez stoute,   935
Now tech me to þat myry mote.'

932.   I] MS and I
934.   gracious] MS gracous
935.   bygyngez (Gordon)] MS lygyngez

between two words, meaning 'blemish' and 'city', and thus continues the juxtaposition of earthly and heavenly values.

913–18. 'Nevertheless, beautiful one, I call on you, if you can see that it may be possible: as you are glorious and without impurity, do not reject my piteous prayer. Have you no dwelling-place with castle-wall, no manor where you may meet and live?' *Cler* (913): in other editions this is interpreted as an adv. meaning 'clearly' or 'with a clear voice'. For other instances of the vocative use of complimentary adjectives, see 755 and *G* 1794. As Gordon observes, the Dreamer visualizes the heavenly city in terms of a medieval town, with a castle and houses within a perimeter wall. Cf. the presentation of Babylon in *Cl* 1385ff.

919. *þe ryche ryalle:* 'the royal kingdom'. Alternatively, *ryche* may be interpreted as an adj., 'rich, magnificent'.

923. *vnder mone: lit.* 'under moon', here 'completely'—a development of the sense 'on earth, everywhere'. Cf. 1068, 1081, 1092.

925–36. 'You tell me of this spotless company, such a great company of thousands in a throng; there are so many of you that you must have a great city, without doubt. It would be a bad thing if so beautiful a gathering of lovely jewels had to sleep out of doors, but by these slopes where I have lingered I see no building anywhere about. I think you come here and stay only to look on the splendour of this lovely stream. If you have strong buildings elsewhere, direct me to that fair walled city.'

'That mote þou menez in Judy londe,' [f52ʳ]
Þat specyal spyce þen to me spakk,
'Þat is þe cyté þat þe Lombe con fonde
To soffer inne sor for manez sake, 940
Þe olde Jerusalem to vnderstonde,
For þere þe olde gulte watz don to slake.
Bot þe nwe, þat lyȝt of Godez sonde,
Þe apostel in Apocalyppce in theme con take.
Þe Lompe þer withouten spottez blake 945
Hatz feryed þyder Hys fayre flote;
And as Hys flok is withouten flake,
So is Hys mote withouten moote.

'Of motez two to carpe clene,
And Jerusalem hyȝt boþe nawþeles— 950
Þat nys to yow no more to mene
Bot "ceté of God" oþer "syȝt of pes"—
In þat on oure pes watz mad at ene;
With payne to suffer þe Lombe hit chese;
In þat oþer is noȝt bot pes to glene 955
Þat ay schal laste withouten reles.
Þat is þe borȝ þat we to pres
Fro þat oure flesch be layd to rote,
Þer glory and blysse schal euer encres
To þe meyny þat is withouten mote.' 960

---

958. flesch (Morris)] MS fresth

938. *spyce:* See 235n.
939–43. 'that is the city that the Lamb visited in which to suffer pain for man's sake, that is to say the old Jerusalem, for there the old guilt was brought to an end. But the new, that descended by God's embassy'. *Þe olde gulte* (942): the sin of Adam, from which man is redeemed by Christ's sacrifice.
944. *in theme con take:* 'gave an account of'. Cf. *Pat* 37.
947f. The emphatic wordplay is similar to that between *Lombe* and *lompe* in 1045ff. There would have been no impropriety for a contemporary audience, despite the solemnity of the subject.
949–56. 'To speak plainly of two cities, both nevertheless called Jerusalem—that means no more to you than "city of God" or "vision of peace". In one our peace was made certain: the Lamb chose to suffer pain in it. In the other there is only peace to be gleaned, which will last for ever without end.' The first interpretation of the significance of *Jerusalem* is based on Heb. 12:22 and Rev. 3:12, while the second is found frequently in medieval literature, from Cynewulf's *Christ* (*sibbe gesihð* [49]) onwards.

'Motelez may so meke and mylde,'
Þen sayde I to þat lufly flor,
'Bryng me to þat bygly bylde
And let me se þy blysful bor.'
Þat schene sayde: 'Þat God wyl schylde;   965
Þou may not enter withinne Hys tor;
Bot of þe Lombe I haue þe aquylde
For a syȝt þerof þurȝ gret fauor.
Vtwyth to se þat clene cloystor
Þou may, bot inwyth not a fote;   970
To strech in þe strete þou hatz no vygour,
Bot þou wer clene, withouten mote.

XVII

'If I þis mote þe schal vnhyde,   [f52ᵛ]
Bow vp towarde þys bornez heued,
And I anendez þe on þis syde   975
Schal sve, tyl þou to a hil be veued.'
Þen wolde I no lenger byde,
Bot lurked by launcez so lufly leued,
Tyl on a hyl þat I asspyed
And blusched on þe burghe, as I forth dreued,   980
Byȝonde þe brok, fro me warde keued,
Þat schyrrer þen sunne with schaftez schon.
In þe Apokalypce is þe fasoun preued,
As deuysez hit þe apostel John.

977.   I (Morris)] MS *om.*

961.   In the MS *Motelez* is given a decorated initial. Presumably a scribe mistook this for the beginning of a new section as a result of the extra stanza in section XV (see note to 841–912).

967f.   'but I have obtained permission from the Lamb, through (His) great favour, for (you to have) a sight of it.'

971f.   'you have no power to make your way into the street, unless you were pure, without stain.'

973–1032.   In section XVII, the concatenation words *þe apostel John* (see note to 788) serve to emphasize the scriptural authority for the vision. The major source is Rev. 21:10–21. Kean, **7a** 1967, 207–9, compares the vision in *Purgatorio* XXIX.4–18.

975f.   'and I shall follow opposite you on this side, until you are brought to a hill.'

979–82.   'until on a hill I caught sight of the city and gazed at it as I made my way onwards, situated beyond the brook, at some distance from me, shining brighter than the sun with beams of light.' The New Jerusalem is brought down from heaven to the terrestrial paradise so that the Dreamer may see it: the Maiden has spoken (967f) of the special dispensation by which this happens.

As John þe apostel hit syȝ with syȝt,   985
I syȝe þat cyty of gret renoun,
Jerusalem so nwe and ryally dyȝt,
As hit watz lyȝt fro þe heuen adoun.
Þe borȝ watz al of brende golde bryȝt,
As glemande glas burnist broun,   990
With gentyl gemmez anvnder pyȝt,
With bantelez twelue on basyng boun,
Þe foundementez twelue of riche tenoun;
Vch tabelment watz a serlypez ston,
As derely deuysez þis ilk toun   995
In Apocalyppez þe apostel John.

As John þise stonez in writ con nemme,
I knew þe name after his tale.
Jasper hyȝt þe fyrst gemme
Þat I on þe fyrst basse con wale—   1000
He glente grene in þe lowest hemme.
Saffer helde þe secounde stale;
Þe calsydoyne þenne withouten wemme
In þe þryd table con purly pale;
Þe emerade þe furþe so grene of scale;   1005
Þe sardonyse þe fyfþe ston;

997. John (Gollancz)] MS *om.*

988. See note to 979–82.

991–4. 'set beneath with noble gems, with twelve tiers fixed on the base, the twelve layers of the foundation admirably joined; each tier was a different stone'. *Bantelez* (992): the word *bantel* means a tier or coursing of a building. Here, the context and the account in Rev. (21:14, 19) indicate that the poet is referring to layers of the foundation, whereas in *Cl* 1459 (see note) the reference is clearly to projecting coursings high up on a wall.

998. *name:* i.e. the name of each stone. Gollancz's emendation to *namez* is unnecessary; as Gordon points out, the distributive singular is common in OE and ME.

999. *Jasper:* This is not the same as the modern jasper. *OED* states that in ME this name is applied to any chalcedony except carnelian, but particularly to green stones. See also Trevisa XVI.52.

1003. *calsydoyne:* This word has a complex history, which is reviewed in *OED*. However, it is clear enough that the poet here intends 'a cryptocrystalline sub-species of quartz ... having the lustre nearly of wax, and being either transparent or translucent' (*OED*). According to Trevisa it 'is a pale stone and schewiþ a dym colour' (XVI.27).

1006. *sardonyse:* 'A variety of onyx or stratified chalcedony having white layers alternating with one or more strata of sard' (*OED*).

Þe sexte þe rybé. He con hit wale
In þe Apocalyppce, þe apostel John.

Ʒet joyned John þe crysolyt,   [f53ʳ]
Þe seuenþe gemme in fundament;   1010
Þe aʒtþe þe beryl cler and quyt;
Þe topasye twynne-hew þe nente endent;
Þe crysopase þe tenþe is tyʒt;
Þe jacynght þe enleuenþe gent;
Þe twelfþe, þe tryeste in vch a plyt,   1015
Þe amatyst purpre with ynde blente.
Þe wal abof þe bantels bent
O jasporye, as glas þat glysnande schon.
I knew hit by his deuysement
In þe Apocalyppez, þe apostel John.   1020

As John deuysed ʒet saʒ I þare:
Þise twelue degrés wern brode and stayre;
Þe cyté stod abof ful sware,

1012.   twynne-hew (Gordon)] MS twynne how
1014.   jacynght (Gollancz)] MS jacyngh
1015.   tryeste (Gollancz)] MS gentyleste
1018.   O] MS Of (f *added in later hand*)

1007.   *rybé:* In the Vulgate this gem is *sardinus* or *sardius* (Rev. 21:20). Gollancz therefore emends to *sarde*, suggesting that *rybé* is the result of scribal interference, motivated by the desire to differentiate this gem from the preceding *sardonyse*. Gordon's argument, that *rybé* is probably what the poet intended, as *sardius* in Exod. 28:17 is sometimes interpreted as 'ruby', is more convincing, particularly in view of the allusion to the Exodus text in 1041.

1011.   Beryl comes in a variety of shades; Trevisa (XVI.20) suggests that the palest beryl was the most highly valued.

1012.   As Trevisa says, the topaz 'haþ tweye colours' (XVI.95). Gordon's emendation clarifies the sense and is based on the assumption of a simple scribal error.

1014.   *jacynght:* This always has final *t* in ME.

1015.   Its efficacy against many complaints is a virtue traditionally associated with the amethyst: according to Trevisa (XVI.9) '. . . þe vertu þerof helpeþ aʒeines dronkenesse, and makeþ whachelle, and putteþ away ydil þouʒtes, and makeþ good vnderstondyng.' As it is probable that MS *gentyleste* is a scribal repetition of *gent* (1014), Gollancz's conjecture *tryeste* is adopted.

1017f.   'The wall set above the tiers was of jasper, that shone glistening like glass.' *Bent* is interpreted 'attached', as in *G* 2224.

1023–32.   'above stood the city, perfectly square, most beautiful, and equal in length, breadth, and height. The streets of gold were as clear as glass, and the wall of jasper shone like egg-white. The walls inside were adorned with all kinds of precious stones that could be present. Each square side of this manor contained twelve furlongs' distance in height, width, and length to traverse, for the apostle John saw the measurement of it.' Cf. *Cl* 1385f. *Twelue forlonge space* (1030): the biblical account has

As longe as brode as hyȝe ful fayre.
Þe stretez of golde as glasse al bare,   1025
Þe wal of jasper þat glent as glayre.
Þe wonez withinne enurned ware
Wyth alle kynnez perré þat moȝt repayre.
Þenne helde vch sware of þis manayre
Twelue forlonge space, er euer hit fon,   1030
Of heȝt, of brede, of lenþe to cayre,
For meten hit syȝ þe apostel John.

XVIII

As John hym wrytez ȝet more I syȝe:
Vch pane of þat place had þre ȝatez,
So twelue in poursent I con asspye,   1035
Þe portalez pyked of rych platez,
And vch ȝate of a margyrye,
A parfyt perle þat neuer fatez.
Vchon in scrypture a name con plye
Of Israel barnez, folewande her datez,   1040
Þat is to say, as her byrþ-whatez;
Þe aldest ay fyrst þeron watz done.
Such lyȝt þer lemed in alle þe stratez
Hem nedde nawþer sunne ne mone.

Of sunne ne mone had þay no nede;   [f53ᵛ] 1045
Þe Self God watz her lombe-lyȝt,

12,000 furlongs (Rev. 21 : 16), and it is not clear why the poet altered this figure: but cf. 786n. Gollancz omits *space* and adds *þowsande* after *Twelue*, implausibly arguing that *space* was originally a marginal gloss on *sware* (1029), which later found its way into the line, causing *þowsande* to be dropped subsequently on metrical grounds.

1033–92. The concatenation word (*mone*) again serves as a focus for the contrast between heaven and earth (see note to 1069f). This section draws heavily on Rev. 21 and 22.

1033f. 'I saw more of what John describes. Each side of that palace had three gates'.

1039–41. 'To each one in written characters was joined a name of the children of Israel, following their dates, that is to say, according to their dates of birth'. These lines draw on the description of the High Priest's ephod in Exod. 28 as well as on Rev. 21. As Gordon observes, these two texts were often related in Christian commentary; cf. 1007n.

1046. 'God Himself was their lamp light'. Note the pun on *lamp* and *lamb*, continued in 1047, and cf. note to 947f.

Þe Lombe her lantyrne, withouten drede;
Þurȝ Hym blysned þe borȝ al bryȝt.
Þurȝ woȝe and won my lokyng ȝede;
For sotyle cler noȝt lette no syȝt.   1050
Þe hyȝe trone þer moȝt ȝe hede
With alle þe apparaylmente vmbepyȝte,
As John þe appostel in termez tyȝte.
Þe hyȝe Godez Self hit set vpone.
A reuer of þe trone þer ran outryȝte   1055
Watz bryȝter þen boþe þe sunne and mone.

Sunne ne mone schon neuer so swete
As þat foysoun flode out of þat flet;
Swyþe hit swange þurȝ vch a strete
Withouten fylþe oþer galle oþer glet.   1060
Kyrk þerinne watz non ȝete,
Chapel ne temple þat euer watz set;
Þe Almyȝty watz her mynster mete,
Þe Lombe þe sakerfyse þer to refet.
Þe ȝatez stoken watz neuer ȝet,   1065
Bot euermore vpen at vche a lone;
Þer entrez non to take reset
Þat berez any spot anvnder mone.

The mone may þerof acroche no myȝte;
To spotty ho is, of body to grym,   1070
And also þer ne is neuer nyȝt.

1050. syȝt (Gollancz)] MS lyȝt
1058. As (Gollancz)] MS a
1063. mynster] MS mynyster
1064. refet (Wright)] MS reget
1068. anvnder] MS an vndez

1050. *syȝt:* As the poet appears to avoid identical rhyme (cf. 1046) and as the sense of 1049f requires *syȝt* here, MS *lyȝt* is probably scribal. A scribe would easily have made this error, first because of the similarity of the forms of *l* and *s*, and second through the expectation of a word alliterating with *lette*.
1055f. 'Directly out of the throne ran a river brighter than both the sun and moon.' The river symbolizes the outpouring of the holy spirit: cf. 605ff.
1060. This alludes to the familiar symbolic association of filth with sin: see note to 725f.
1065-8. 'The gates were never yet shut, but were always open at every roadway; no one enters there to take refuge who bears any blemish under the moon.' Cf. Rev. 21:27.
1069f. The description derives relevance from the position of the sphere of the moon in medieval cosmology, in which it forms the border between the unchanging aetherial regions above and changeable nature below (hence 'sublunary'). See C. S. Lewis, *The Discarded Image* (Cambridge, 1964), 92ff and Milton, *Paradise Lost* I.291.

What schulde þe mone þer compas clym
And to euen wyth þat worþly ly3t
Þat schynez vpon þe brokez brym?
Þe planetez arn in to pouer a ply3t,   1075
And þe self sunne ful fer to dym.
Aboute þat water arn tres ful schym,
Þat twelue frytez of lyf con bere ful sone;
Twelue syþez on 3er þay beren ful frym,
And renowlez nwe in vche a mone.   1080

Anvnder mone so gret merwayle   [f54ʳ]
No fleschly hert ne my3t endeure
As quen I blusched vpon þat baly,
So ferly þerof watz þe fasure.
I stod as stylle as dased quayle   1085
For ferly of þat frech fygure,
Þat felde I nawþer reste ne trauayle,
So watz I rauyste wyth glymme pure.
For I dar say with conciens sure,
Hade bodyly burne abiden þat bone,   1090
Þa3 alle clerkez hym hade in cure,
His lyf wer loste anvnder mone.

XIX

Ry3t as þe maynful mone con rys
Er þenne þe day-glem dryue al doun,

1086.   frech] MS freuch

1072-4.   'Why should the moon climb a circuit there and vie with that glorious light that shines on the surface of the brook?'
1077-80.   See Rev. 22:2.
1085.   Again the poet expresses the Dreamer's feelings of shock in terms of a hunting metaphor: cf. notes to 185 and 344-8.
1086.   *frech:* MS *freuch* is an attested form of *frough* 'weak, loose, fickle'. *MED* suggests that here we have a modification of this sense, and glosses 'delicate; ? delightful', but offers no other citations to support this interpretation. It seems more likely that *freuch* represents scribal miswriting of *fre(s)ch*—an adj. applied to the Maiden in 195. Gordon, following Morris's suggestion, reads *frelich* 'noble', but this is metrically inferior.
1093-1152.   The concatenation word *delyt*, with its overlapping senses of 'delight' and 'desire', suggests the function of this section—to emphasize both the bliss of salvation and the Dreamer's growing desire to cross the water and join the saved. Once more the poet draws extensively on Rev., particularly 5:6-13.
1093f.   'Just as the powerful moon rises before the sun (*lit.* light of day) quite sinks away'.

So sodanly on a wonder wyse   1095
I watz war of a prosessyoun.
Þis noble cité of ryche enpresse
Watz sodanly ful, withouten sommoun,
Of such vergynez in þe same gyse
Þat watz my blysful anvnder croun.   1100
And coronde wern alle of þe same fasoun,
Depaynt in perlez and wedez qwyte;
In vchonez breste watz bounden boun
Þe blysful perle with gret delyt.

With gret delyt þay glod in fere   1105
On golden gatez þat glent as glasse;
Hundreth þowsandez I wot þer were,
And alle in sute her liuréz wasse.
Tor to knaw þe gladdest chere.
Þe Lombe byfore con proudly passe   1110
Wyth hornez seuen of red golde cler;
As praysed perlez His wedez wasse.
Towarde þe throne þay trone a tras.
Þaȝ þay wern fele, no pres in plyt,
Bot mylde as maydenez seme at mas,   1115
So droȝ þay forth with gret delyt.

Delyt þat Hys come encroched   [f 54ᵛ]
To much hit were of for to melle.
Þise aldermen, quen He aproched,
Grouelyng to His fete þay felle.   1120
Legyounes of aungelez togeder uoched
Þer kesten ensens of swete smelle;
Þen glory and gle watz nwe abroched;
Al songe to loue þat gay Juelle.

1104. with gret (Morris)] MS withouten
1111. golde] MS glode

1098–1100. 'was suddenly, without summons, full of similar virgins in the same dress as my blissful crowned one.' *Blysful anvnder croun* (1100): see note to 775–80. Cf. Rev. 14:4.
1104. *with gret:* Morris's emendation is supported by 1105.
1106. See Rev. 21:21.
1107. See Rev. 5:11, 7:9.
1108f. 'and their garments all matched. It was hard to know (which was) the happiest face.'
1114f. 'Though they were many, there was no crowding in their array (i.e. grouping), but mild as modest maidens at mass'.
1117f. 'It would be impossible to describe the delight His coming brought.'

Þe steuen moȝt stryke þurȝ þe vrþe to helle   1125
Þat þe vertues of heuen of joye endyte.
To loue þe Lombe His meyny inmelle
Iwysse I laȝt a gret delyt.

Delit þe Lombe for to deuise
With much meruayle in mynde went.   1130
Best watz He, blyþest, and moste to pryse,
Þat euer I herde of speche spent;
So worþly whyt wern wedez Hys,
His lokez symple, Hymself so gent.
Bot a wounde ful wyde and weete con wyse   1135
Anende Hys hert, þurȝ hyde torente.
Of His quyte syde His blod outsprent.
Alas, þoȝt I, who did þat spyt?
Ani breste for bale aȝt haf forbrent
Er he þerto hade had delyt.   1140

The Lombe delyt non lyste to wene;
Þaȝ He were hurt and wounde hade,
In His sembelaunt watz neuer sene,
So wern His glentez gloryous glade.
I loked among His meyny schene   1145
How þay wyth lyf wern laste and lade;
Þen saȝ I þer my lyttel quene
Þat I wende had standen by me in sclade.
Lorde, much of mirþe watz þat ho made
Among her ferez þat watz so quyt!   1150
Þat syȝt me gart to þenk to wade
For luf-longyng in gret delyt.

1126. *vertues:* one of the nine orders of angels. A brief review of this subject is provided by C. S. Lewis (*op. cit.* in note to 1069f), 71–4.
1127f. 'Indeed I conceived a great desire to praise the Lamb amongst His followers.'
1135. This is, of course, the wound inflicted at the Crucifixion. Cf. note to 649–56.
1139f. 'Any heart ought to have burned up for sorrow before it had any desire for that.'
1141. 'No one would see fit to doubt the delight of the Lamb'.
1146. Cf. Matt. 19:29, John 10:10.
1147ff. A saved child appears as one of the 144,000 virgins also in Chaucer's 'The Prioress's Tale' (*CT* VII.579–85). See Elizabeth Hart, **7a** 1927.
1149–52. 'Lord, how happily she behaved, she who was so white, among her companions! That sight caused me to resolve to wade (across) for love-longing in (my) great desire.' *Luf-longyng* (1152): though the primary sense of the word is secular, it is used elsewhere with a religious meaning, as in the Harley Lyric on the Five Joys of the Virgin (16) and Julian of Norwich, *Revelations of Divine Love* (chapter 71). Cf. 11n for the similar compound *luf-daungere.*

XX

Delyt me drof in yȝe and ere,   [f55ʳ]
My manez mynde to maddyng malte;
Quen I seȝ my frely, I wolde be þere,   1155
Byȝonde þe water þaȝ ho were walte.
I þoȝt þat noþyng myȝt me dere
To fech me bur and take me halte,
And to start in þe strem schulde non me stere,
To swymme þe remnaunt, þaȝ I þer swalte.   1160
Bot of þat munt I watz bitalt;
When I schulde start in þe strem astraye,
Out of þat caste I watz bycalt:
Hit watz not at my Pryncez paye.

Hit payed Hym not þat I so flonc   1165
Ouer meruelous merez, so mad arayd.
Of raas þaȝ I were rasch and ronk,
Ȝet rapely þerinne I watz restayed,
For ryȝt as I sparred vnto þe bonc,
Þat brathþe out of my drem me brayde.   1170
Þen wakned I in þat erber wlonk;

1170. brathþe] MS bratþe (þ *written over* h)

1153–1212. The concatenation word in the last section is *paye* 'pleasure', with the specific sense of the will of God (it is *Pryncez paye* in three of the five stanzas). Thus the concatenation emphasizes the Dreamer's progression from self-absorbed rebelliousness to obedience to God's will—a sense reinforced by the echoes of the beginning of the poem.

1153–60. 'Desire poured into me through eye and ear, dissolving my human mind to madness; when I saw my gracious one, I wanted to be there, though she was set beyond the water. I thought that nothing could harm me by dealing me a blow and offering obstruction to me, and no one would restrain me from plunging into the stream, and swimming the remainder, even if I died there.' *Malte* (1154): possibly intransitive (subj. *mynde*). *Walte* (1156): of two possible senses, 'set' (from OE *waldan*) is preferable to 'chosen, perceived' (cf. OIcel *velja*). *To fech me bur* (1158): Gollancz interprets this phrase as 'to take a preliminary spurt' and *take me halte* (1158) as 'in taking off'. (This would involve understanding *myȝt me dere* (1157) as 'would hinder me from'.) Implicit in this passage is the familiar metaphor drawn from secular love, of passion overcoming reason and the lover being smitten by beauty through the eyes. Cf. 1152n.

1165–8. 'It did not please Him that I rushed over the miraculous waters like that, in such a state of frenzy. Though I was rash and impetuous to rush headlong, I was quickly restrained in that course'.

1171ff. The physical setting is unaltered (cf. 9–60); the change which has taken place is in the Dreamer's spiritual state. His immediate response is again one of passionate

My hede vpon þat hylle watz layde
Þeras my perle to grounde strayd.
I raxled, and fel in gret affray,
And, sykyng, to myself I sayd: 1175
'Now al be to þat Pryncez paye.'

Me payed ful ille to be outfleme
So sodenly of þat fayre regioun,
Fro alle þo syȝtez so quyke and queme.
A longeyng heuy me strok in swone,   1180
And rewfully þenne I con to reme:
'O perle,' quoþ I, 'of rych renoun,
So watz hit me dere þat þou con deme
In þys veray avysyoun!
If hit be ueray and soth sermoun   1185
Þat þou so strykez in garlande gay,
So wel is me in þys doel-doungoun
Þat þou art to þat Prynsez paye.'

To þat Pryncez paye hade I ay bente,   [f55ᵛ]
And ȝerned no more þen watz me geuen,   1190
And halden me þer in trwe entent,

1179.   quyke (Gollancz)] MS quykez
1185.   If] MS inf (ĭf)
1186.   strykez (Gollancz)] MS stykez

---

sorrow, but this is now controlled by his recognition of the place of human loss in the new structure of values he has learned in the vision.

1177–9.   'It pleased me very ill to be driven so suddenly out of that lovely country, away from all those sights so vivid and pleasing.'

1185–7.   'If it is a true and real account that you go thus in your bright garland (i.e. crown), then it is well with me in this dungeon of sorrow'. Gordon and Hillmann retain MS *stykez*, taking it intransitively to mean '(you) are set'. They interpret the *garlande gay* (1186) metaphorically to signify the heavenly procession, and refer to the parallel usage of *ghirlanda* in *Paradiso* X.91–3 and XII.19–20. But, as Ian Bishop points out (*RES*, ns 8 [1957], 12–21), the parallel is not precise, for Dante refers not to a procession but to a circle of the blessed. In view of the fact that the *corona* ('crown') was commonly understood to stand for the circle of the blessed, it is more likely that the *garlande* here signifies the Maiden's crown (previously described in 205ff) which itself symbolizes her heavenly setting. In the context of this interpretation, Gollancz's emendation of MS *stykez* to *strykez* 'go' is adopted.

1189–94.   'If I had all the time submitted to that Prince's pleasure, and yearned for no more than was allowed me, and been content with that in true resolve, as the pearl that was so fair had begged me, quite probably, drawn into God's presence, I would have been brought to more of His mysteries.' The speech is an acknowledgement of the Dreamer's lack of restraint in trying to cross the stream: cf. 1153–60n.

As þe perle me prayed þat watz so þryuen,
As helde, drawen to Goddez present,
To mo of His mysterys I hade ben dryuen.
Bot ay wolde man of happe more hente   1195
Þen moȝte by ryȝt vpon hem clyuen;
Þerfore my joye watz sone toriuen,
And I kaste of kythez þat lastez aye.
Lorde, mad hit arn þat agayn Þe stryuen,
Oþer proferen Þe oȝt agayn Þy paye.   1200

To pay þe Prince oþer sete saȝte
Hit is ful eþe to þe god Krystyin;
For I haf founden Hym, boþe day and naȝte,
A God, a Lorde, a frende ful fyin.
Ouer þis hyul þis lote I laȝte,   1205
For pyty of my perle enclyin,
And syþen to God I hit bytaȝte,
In Krystez dere blessyng and myn,
Þat in þe forme of bred and wyn
Þe preste vus schewez vch a daye.   1210
He gef vus to be His homly hyne
Ande precious perlez vnto His pay.
                    Amen.   Amen.

1196. moȝte (Gollancz)] MS moȝten

1199f. This statement would also serve as a summary of the moral of *Pat*: see *Pat* 1–
60, 524–31.

1201f. 'To please the Prince or be reconciled (to Him) is very easy to the good
Christian'. The possibility of resolution derived from *resoun* is recognized in 52; in
665, *resoun* is transformed into a personification of God. Here, resolution is finally
achieved through acceptance of God's will.

1205–10. 'On this mound this happened to me (*lit.* I received this chance), lying
prostrate for sorrow for my pearl, which I afterwards committed to God, with my
own (blessing) and the precious blessing of Christ, whom the priest shows us every
day in the form of bread and wine.' *Lote* (1205): probably 'happening, chance', but
with the possibility of a pun on the alternative meaning 'speech, word'. Norman
Davis, *RES*, ns 17 (1966), 403–5, and 18 (1967), 294 (also in Conley, **7a** 1970)
demonstrates that 1208 conforms to an idiom of epistolary subscription used by
parent to child, which is familiar in OE and ME. The suggestion of Hamilton, **7a**
1955, adopted by Hillmann—that *myn* is a noun meaning 'memorial'—is inciden-
tally proved to be untenable.

1211f. 'He granted us all to be humble servants and precious pearls to His pleasure.'
Alternatively, *gef* may be understood as pres. subjunctive 'may He grant' (cf. *G*
2068). *Homly:* perhaps also 'of (God's) household'. The last line echoes the first, and
brings the poem full circle.

Cleanness

Clannesse whoso kyndly cowþe comende,   [f57ʳ]
And rekken vp alle þe resounz þat ho by riȝt askez,
Fayre formez myȝt he fynde in forþering his speche,
And in þe contraré kark and combraunce huge.
For wonder wroth is þe Wyȝ þat wroȝt alle þinges   5
Wyth þe freke þat in fylþe folȝes Hym after—
As renkez of relygioun þat reden and syngen,
And aprochen to Hys presens, and prestez arn called;
Thay teen vnto His temmple and temen to Hymseluen,
Reken with reuerence þay rychen His auter,   10
Þay hondel þer His aune body and vsen hit boþe.

3. forþering] MS forering
10. rychen] MS r chen (*second letter blurred*)

1–4. 'Whoever were to commend cleanness fittingly, and reckon up all the arguments that she demands by right, lovely examples would he be able to find in advancing his discourse, and in the reverse enormous trouble and difficulty.' *Cowþe* (1): the exact force of the auxiliary is elusive but perhaps it comes close to the use of *con* as a past auxiliary (cf. *G* 2273, *Pe* 77–80n). *Formez* (3): 'examples, patterns', in allusion to the more positive of the illustrations which follow. *In þe contraré* (4) evidently balances *forþering* and must mean 'in speaking *against* cleanness'. The poet can hardly mean that one would have difficulty in illustrating the commendability of purity from stories of impurity, for this is precisely what he does in the three major *exempla*. See note to 27f.

5. *þe Wyȝ þat wroȝt alle þinges:* i.e. God. The four poems contain many such periphrases for God: cf. (for example) *Cl* 552, 1528; *G* 256, 1292; *Pat* 111, 397f; and especially *Pat* 206, which is almost identical.

9. Cf. *Pat* 316.

10. *rychen:* Both Gollancz and Menner read *rechen*, glossing respectively 'approach' and 'touch'. The second letter is blurred in the MS, but it is possible to make out the tops of two downstrokes; whereas these could not have formed an *e*, they could well have formed a *y*. Thus *rychen* is a more likely reading. *OED rich*, v.², sense 5, gives 'arrange, prepare (a thing)', which is more satisfactory than either of the meanings suggested for *rechen*. (Note that the first recorded use of *rich* in this sense is in *G* 2206, and that five of the six senses recorded under *rich* v.² are illustrated with citations from *G*.)

11. 'there they handle His own body and use it as well.' The priests handle Christ's body and use it sacramentally in the celebration of the eucharist. The same idea occurs in *Everyman* 739.

If þay in clannes be clos þay cleche gret mede;
Bot if þay conterfete crafte and cortaysye wont,
As be honest vtwyth and inwith alle fylþez,
Þen ar þay synful hemself, and sulpen altogeder   15
Boþe God and His gere, and Hym to greme cachen.
He is so clene in His courte, þe Kyng þat al weldez,
And honeste in His housholde, and hagherlych serued
With angelez enourled in alle þat is clene,
Boþe withinne and withouten in wedez ful bryȝt;   20
Nif He nere scoymus and skyg, and non scaþe louied,
Hit were a meruayl to much, hit moȝt not falle.
Kryst kydde hit Hymself in a carp onez,
Þeras He heuened aȝt happez and hyȝt hem her medez.
Me mynez on one amonge oþer, as Maþew recordez,   25
Þat þus of clannesse vnclosez a ful cler speche:
'Þe haþel clene of his hert hapenez ful fayre,
For he schal loke on oure Lorde with a leue chere';
As so saytz, to þat syȝt seche schal he neuer

---

15. sulpen (Gollancz)] MS sulped
28. leue (Gollancz)] MS bone

---

12. Here begins an extended 'clothing' metaphor—continued in *vtwyth ... inwith* (14), *withinne and withouten* (20), *hatz on* (30), *etc.*—which prepares the ground for the explicit parable of the Wedding Feast. The contrast is partly between a literal outward seemliness and inner turpitude (13–16), and partly between clean and unclean spiritual 'clothing' (33–5). The reference to priests and their possible defilement of God's *gere* (16) also broaches the theme of defilement of sacred vessels, which is explored in the story of Belshazzar.

15f. 'they are sinful themselves and altogether defile both God and His utensils, and drive Him to wrath.' *Sulpen:* '(they) defile'; MS *sulped* illustrates a scribal tendency to complete the sense of a line. Gollancz's emendation is therefore adopted. Menner reads *Loþe* (v. 'hate') for *Boþe* in 16.

21. 'if He were not scrupulous and fastidious, and (were it not true that He) loved no evil'.

23–6. 'Christ Himself once made it known in a speech, in which He extolled eight beatitudes and promised to them (i.e. the blessed) their rewards. I am thinking of one among them, as Matthew records, which discloses a clear statement about cleanness thus'. Christ's *carp* (23) is the Sermon on the Mount, in which the eight Beatitudes are specified (Matt. 5:1–11). This text is alluded to in a similar, but fuller, way in *Pat* (9ff).

27f. These lines paraphrase the sixth Beatitude: *Beati mundo corde: quoniam ipsi Deum videbunt* 'Blessed are the clean of heart: for they shall see God' (Matt. 5:8). In the next two lines (29f) the poet turns this statement around, and points out that the unclean shall not see God. This inversion foreshadows the method of the poem as a whole, for in it cleanness is celebrated mainly by means of a series of negative *exempla*—stories which describe the activities and downfalls of the unclean.

29–32. 'which is to say that anyone who has any uncleanness on, anywhere about him, shall never come to that sight; for He who banishes all filth far from His heart

Þat any vnclannesse hatz on, auwhere abowte;   30
For He þat flemus vch fylþe fer fro His hert
May not byde þat burre þat hit His body neȝe.
Forþy hyȝ not to heuen in haterez totorne,
Ne in þe harlatez hod, and handez vnwaschen.
For what vrþly haþel þat hyȝ honour haldez   35
Wolde lyke if a ladde com lyþerly attyred,
When he were sette solempnely in a sete ryche,   [f57ᵛ]
Abof dukez on dece, with dayntys serued?
Þen þe harlot with haste helded to þe table,
With rent cokrez at þe kne and his clutte traschez,   40
And his tabarde totorne, and his totez oute,
Oþer ani on of alle þyse, he schulde be halden vtter,
With mony blame ful bygge, a boffet peraunter,
Hurled to þe halle dore and harde þeroute schowued,
And be forboden þat borȝe to bowe þider neuer,   45
On payne of enprysonment and puttyng in stokkez;
And þus schal he be schent for his schrowde feble,
Þaȝ neuer in talle ne in tuch he trespas more.
And if vnwelcum he were to a wordlych prynce,
Ȝet hym is þe hyȝe Kyng harder in heuen;   50

32. neȝe (Gollancz)] MS neȝen
49. wordlych] MS worþlych
50. heuen] MS her euen

cannot endure the shock of its approaching Him (*lit.* that it should approach His body).' Gollancz's emendation provides the subjunctive singular required by the sense. *Byde þat burre* (32): cf. *Pat* 7 and *G* 290, 374. *His body* (32): cf. *his corse* (683n).

33ff. This passage anticipates the theme of the parable of the Wedding Feast which follows; see note to 134.

35. *hyȝ honour haldez:* 'possesses high rank'.

39-42. 'Then (if) the villain came hastily to the table, with leggings torn at the knee and his patched rags, and his smock torn and his shoes out at the toes, or any one of these, he would be put outside'.

43. *a boffet peraunter:* 'perhaps a blow'. The same half line occurs in *G* 2343.

48. 'though he never transgress further in word or in deed.'

49. *wordlych:* 'earthly'. The emendation restores the contrast between the earthly ruler in this line and the king of heaven in the next. The same contrast occurs between the beginning and the end of *Pe*: see *Pe* 1-4n.

49-160. The poet's account of the parable of the Wedding Feast draws on the versions in both St Luke (14: 16-24) and St Matthew (22: 1-14); both are printed in the Appendix.

50. 'yet the high King in heaven is harder to him'. The emendation is clearly required by the sense; possibly the scribe mistook an incidental mark in his copytext for an *-er* contraction sign.

As Maþew melez in his masse of þat man ryche,
Þat made þe mukel mangerye to marie his here dere,
And sende his sonde þen to say þat þay samne schulde,
And in comly quoyntis to com to his feste:
'For my boles and my borez arn bayted and slayne,   55
And my fedde foulez fatted with sclaȝt,
My polyle þat is penne-fed and partrykez boþe,
Wyth scheldez of wylde swyn, swanez and cronez,
Al is roþeled and rosted ryȝt to þe sete;
Comez cof to my corte, er hit colde worþe.'   60
When þay knewen his cal þat þider com schulde,
Alle excused hem by þe skyly he scape by moȝt.
On hade boȝt hym a borȝ, he sayde, by hys trawþe:
'Now turne I þeder als tyd þe toun to byholde.'
Anoþer nayed also and nurned þis cawse: 65
'I haf ȝerned and ȝat ȝokkez of oxen,
And for my hyȝez hem boȝt; to bowe haf I mester,
To see hem pulle in þe plow aproche me byhouez.'
'And I haf wedded a wyf,' so wer hym þe þryd;
'Excuse me at þe court, I may not com þere.'   70
Þus þay droȝ hem adreȝ with daunger vchone,
Þat non passed to þe place þaȝ he prayed were.

64. turne (Morris)] MS tne
72. place (Morris)] MS plate

51. *As Maþew melez in his masse:* 'as Matthew tells in his gospel read at mass.' See note to 49–160, *Pat* 9f, and *Pe* 493–8.
52–4. 'who made the great banquet for the marriage of (*lit.* to give in marriage) his beloved heir, and then set his message to say that they should assemble, and come to his feast in comely fine dress'.
56. *with sclaȝt:* 'in readiness for slaughter'; an unusual use of *with*, but evidently an extension from the primitive sense 'against'.
59. *ryȝt to þe sete:* probably 'ready for the sitting' (cf. *to sete*, G 72, 493). Contrast Menner 'appetizingly', Gollancz 'right to the proper point'.
61–4. 'When those who should have come there heard his invitation, each excused himself with whatever excuse he could escape by. One had bought himself an estate, he said, by his troth: "Now I am going there as soon as possible to see the homestead."' *By hys trawþe* (63): an indirect-speech form of '*by my trawþe*' (cf. note to G 2072f).
69. *so wer hym þe þryd:* 'thus the third excused himself'.
71f. 'Thus they held back with insolence, each one, so that no one went to the house though he was invited.'

Thenne þe ludych lorde lyked ful ille,   [f58ʳ]
And hade dedayn of þat dede; ful dryȝly he carpez.
He saytz: 'Now for her owne sorȝe þay forsaken habbez;   75
More to wyte is her wrange þen any wylle gentyl.
Þenne gotz forth, my gomez, to þe grete streetez,
And forsettez on vche a syde þe ceté aboute;
Þe wayferande frekez, on fote and on hors,
Boþe burnez and burdez, þe better and þe wers,   80
Laþez hem alle luflyly to lenge at my fest,
And bryngez hem blyþly to borȝe as barounez þay were,
So þat my palays plat ful be pyȝt al aboute;
Þise oþer wrechez iwysse worþy noȝt wern.'
Þen þay cayred and com þat þe cost waked,   85
Broȝten bachlerez hem wyth þat þay by bonkez metten,
Swyerez þat swyftly swyed on blonkez,
And also fele vpon fote, of fre and of bonde.
When þay com to þe courte keppte wern þay fayre,
Styȝtled with þe stewarde, stad in þe halle,   90
Ful manerly with marchal mad for to sitte,
As he watz dere of degré dressed his seete.
Þenne seggez to þe souerayn sayden þerafter:
'Lo! lorde, with your leue, at your lege heste
And at þi banne we haf broȝt, as þou beden habbez,   95
Mony renischche renkez, and ȝet is roum more.'
Sayde þe lorde to þo ledez, 'Laytez ȝet ferre,

---

86. metten] MS mettez *corrected to* metten

73ff. The similarity of this description to a number of accounts of God's reaction to human misdeeds in both *Pat* and *Cl* (e.g. *Pat* 129–32, 429–32; *Cl* 249–92, 557–600) may serve to emphasize that the earthly lord here represents God allegorically.

76. 'their misdeed is more blameworthy (*lit.* 'more to blame') than any gentile (i.e. heathen) perversity.' The point operates at the allegorical level. The Gentiles, who do not know God, are less to blame than the Jews, who, given the opportunity to know God, reject it (literally, refuse the invitation to the feast). Cf. 139n.

80. *þe better and þe wers:* i.e. of all social classes.

81f. 'invite them all courteously to stay at my feast, and bring them gladly to town as though they were barons'.

85. 'Then those that guarded the region went out and came back'.

89–92. 'When they came to the court they were well looked after, given places by the steward, set in the hall, by the marshal very courteously made to sit, the seat of each assigned according to his rank (*lit.* as he was noble in rank his seat placed).'

96. *renischche renkez:* 'strange men' (i.e. strangers to the lord).

97–104. Compare the lord's instructions with Luke 14:23.

Ferkez out in þe felde, and fechez mo gestez;
Waytez gorstez and greuez, if ani gomez lyggez;
Whatkyn folk so þer fare, fechez hem hider;   100
Be þay fers, be þay feble, forlotez none,
Be þay hol, be þay halt, be þay onyȝed,
And þaȝ þay ben boþe blynde and balterande cruppelez,
Þat my hous may holly by halkez by fylled.
For, certez, þyse ilk renkez þat me renayed habbe,   105
And denounced me noȝt now at þis tyme,
Schul neuer sitte in my sale my soper to fele,
Ne suppe on sope of my seue, þaȝ þay swelt schulde.'
Thenne þe sergauntez, at þat sawe, swengen þeroute,   [f 58ᵛ]
And diden þe dede þat watz demed, as he deuised hade,   110
And with peple of alle plytez þe palays þay fyllen;
Hit weren not alle on wyuez sunez, wonen with on fader.
Wheþer þay wern worþy oþer wers, wel wern þay stowed,
Ay þe best byfore and bryȝtest atyred,
Þe derrest at þe hyȝe dese, þat dubbed wer fayrest,   115
And syþen on lenþe bilooghe ledez inogh.
And ay as segges serly semed by her wedez,

---

98. Ferkez (Gollancz)] MS ferre
108. þaȝ] MS þaȝ þaȝ
110. watz] MS *om.*
117. as segges serly (Emerson)] MS a segge soerly

98. *Ferkez:* The MS reading *ferre* is probably an erroneous repetition of *ferre* at the end of the previous line. Gollancz's emendation improves the sense and fits into the pattern of clauses introduced by imperative verbs (*fechez, waytez*). The word *ferk* appears with a similar sense elsewhere in the MS (e.g. *Cl* 897, *Pat* 187, *G* 173, 2013).

99f. 'search gorse-heaths and woods (to see) if any men lie there; whatever kind of people are travelling there, bring them here'.

104. *by halkez by fylled:* 'be filled right to the corners.'

105–8. 'For, indeed, these same men who have refused me and proclaimed me not at all at this time, shall never sit in my room to taste my supper, nor eat one mouthful from my stew, even though they should die.' The failure to proclaim the lord (106) is a refusal to recognize his importance. This use of *denounce* is imitated from L *denuntiare*.

112. 'they were not all the sons of one wife (who were) begotten by one father': i.e. those who were begotten by one father did not all have the same mother—they were not all legitimate.

114f. 'the highest in rank and most splendidly attired in the forefront, the noblest, who were dressed most brilliantly, at the high table'.

117. 'And always as befitted men severally according to their clothes'. Emerson's (**5b** 1919) emendation, adopted here, makes acceptable sense of an obscure line. For *serly*, cf. the use of *serelych* (adv.) in *Pat* 193. Menner retains MS *soerly*, which he relates to OIcel *saurligr* 'unclean', and also to *sorȝe* 'filth' (846, *Pat* 275) and *sauerly* (*Pe* 226), which he would gloss 'base, vile'.

So with marschal at her mete mensked þay were.
Clene men in compaynye forknowen wern lyte,
And ȝet þe symplest in þat sale watz serued to þe fulle,   120
Boþe with menske and with mete and mynstrasy noble,
And alle þe laykez þat a lorde aȝt in londe schewe.
And þay bigonne to be glad þat god drink haden,
And vch mon with his mach made hym at ese.
Now inmyddez þe mete þe mayster hym biþoȝt   125
Þat he wolde se þe semblé þat samned was þere,
And rehayte rekenly þe riche and þe poueren,
And cherisch hem alle with his cher, and chaufen her joye.
Þen he bowez fro his bour into þe brode halle
And to þe best on þe bench, and bede hym be myry,   130
Solased hem with semblaunt and syled fyrre,
Tron fro table to table and talkede ay myrþe.
Bot as he ferked ouer þe flor, he fande with his yȝe—
Hit watz not for a halyday honestly arayed—
A þral þryȝt in þe þrong vnþryuandely cloþed,   135
Ne no festiual frok, bot fyled with werkkez;
Þe gome watz vngarnyst with god men to dele.
And gremed þerwith þe grete lorde, and greue hym he þoȝt.
'Say me, frende,' quoþ þe freke with a felle chere,
'Hov wan þou into þis won in wedez so fowle?   140
Þe abyt þat þou hatz vpon, no halyday hit menskez:
Þou, burne, for no brydale art busked in wedez.
How watz þou hardy þis hous for þyn vnhap to neȝe

---

127. poueren] MS pouener
143. to (Morris)] MS *om.*

119. 'Fine men were little (i.e. not) neglected in (that) company'.
122. *in londe:* 'in the world'.
127. *poueren:* The MS reading was caused by a scribe's writing the *-er* contraction sign after instead of before the letters *en*; a similar error occurs at *G* 124.
134. 'he was not dressed fittingly for a festival'. In biblical, devotional, and homiletic literature, foul or ragged clothes are often used to symbolize the soul stained by sin or neglected. Cf. 169–76n, and *Pat* 341–2n.
138. 'And the great lord became angry about that, and decided to punish him.'
139ff. The lord has specifically requested that people should wear their best clothes to his feast (53f), and therefore considers that the ill-dressed man is treating him with disdain. Modern readers may find the lord's reaction extreme or not entirely just; but it does not appear to have caused anxiety to medieval commentators, perhaps because the wedding garment could so readily be allegorized as good works—as indeed it is in 169ff—the lack of which was self-evidently reprehensible. It is also possible that at the literal level there was the understanding that wedding garments were available to all who chose to ask for them (cf. 4 Kgs. [AV 2 Kgs.] 10 : 22).

In on so ratted a robe and rent at þe sydez?
Þow art a gome vngoderly in þat goun febele;   [f 59ʳ]   145
Þou praysed me and my place ful pouer and ful gnede,
Þat watz so prest to aproche my presens hereinne.
Hopez þou I be a harlot þi erigaut to prayse?'
Þat oþer burne watz abayst of his broþe wordez,
And hurkelez doun with his hede, þe vrþe he biholdez;   150
He watz so scoumfit of his scylle, lest he skaþe hent,
Þat he ne wyst on worde what he warp schulde.
Þen þe lorde wonder loude laled and cryed,
And talkez to his tormenttourez: 'Takez hym,' he biddez,
'Byndez byhynde, at his bak, boþe two his handez,   155
And felle fetterez to his fete festenez bylyue;
Stik hym stifly in stokez, and stekez hym þerafter
Depe in my doungoun þer doel euer dwellez,
Greuing and gretyng and gryspyng harde
Of teþe tenfully togeder, to teche hym be quoynt.'   160
Thus comparisunez Kryst þe kyndom of heuen
To þis frelych feste þat fele arn to called;
For alle arn laþed luflyly, þe luþer and þe better,
Þat euer wern fulȝed in font, þat fest to haue.
Bot war þe wel, if þou wylt, þy wedez ben clene   165
And honest for þe halyday, lest þou harme lache,
For aproch þou to þat Prynce of parage noble,
He hates helle no more þen hem þat ar sowlé.

146.   gnede (Morris)] MS nede

148.   'Do you think that I am a beggar who would approve of your cloak?'
151.   'he was so out of his mind with confusion (*lit.* so disconcerted out of his reason) lest he should suffer'.
157–60.   Cf. *Pat* 79. The terms in which this punishment is described emphasize that it is an allegorical representation of the pains of hell.
159.   *gryspyng:* Gollancz emends to *gryspytyng.* The MS reading is retained here on the assumption that *gryspyng* is a contracted form (as suggested by *OED* and *MED*).
161ff.   Here the poet makes clear in true homiletic fashion the *significacio* of the parable. St Matthew's account of the parable of the Wedding Feast ends with the words *Multi enim sunt vocati, pauci vero electi* 'For many are called, but few are chosen' (22 : 14), the first part of which statement is paraphrased in *fele arn to called* (162). The fact that the poet omits any mention of the second part of this statement, which is not strictly relevant to the moral he draws from the parable, illustrates his willingness to modify biblical texts to suit his purpose as precisely as possible.
163f.   'for all, the worse and the better, who were ever baptized in the font, are graciously invited to have that feast.' The poet emphasizes the importance of baptism, which is also a central theme in *Pe*. Once more the symbolic association of dirty clothes and sin is evident (see note to 134).
167.   *For aproch þou:* 'for if you approach'.

Wich arn þenne þy wedez þou wrappez þe inne,
Þat schal schewe hem so schene schrowde of þe best? 170
Hit arn þy werkez, wyterly, þat þou wroȝt hauez,
And lyued with þe lykyng þat lyȝe in þyn hert;
Þat þo be frely and fresch fonde in þy lyue,
And fetyse of a fayr forme to fote and to honde,
And syþen alle þyn oþer lymez lapped ful clene; 175
Þenne may þou se þy Sauior and His sete ryche.
For feler fautez may a freke forfete his blysse,
Þat he þe Souerayn ne se, þen for slauþe one;
As for bobaunce and bost and bolnande priyde
Þroly into þe deuelez þrote man þryngez bylyue. 180
For couetyse and colwarde and croked dedez, [f 59ᵛ]
For monsworne and mensclaȝt and to much drynk,
For þefte and for þrepyng, vnþonk may mon haue;
For roborrye and riboudrye and resounez vntrwe,
And dysheriete and depryue dowrie of wydoez, 185
For marryng of maryagez and mayntnaunce of schrewez,
For traysoun and trichcherye and tyrauntyré boþe,
And for fals famacions and fayned lawez;
Man may mysse þe myrþe þat much is to prayse
For such vnþewez as þise, and þole much payne, 190
And in þe Creatores cort com neuermore,
Ne neuer see Hym with syȝt for such sour tournez.
Bot I haue herkned and herde of mony hyȝe clerkez,
And als in resounez of ryȝt red hit myseluen,
Þat þat ilk proper Prynce þat paradys weldez 195

---

177. feler (Gollancz)] MS fele

169f. 'What, then, are your clothes in which you wrap yourself, which must appear like lovely garments of the best (quality)?'
169–76. As a complement to the preceding account of the allegorical significance of foul clothes, the poet now states plainly (in a manner similar to that adopted in contemporary homiletic and devotional writings) that clean clothes stand for good works and virtuous living.
172. *lyued:* 'given life to' (see *OED live* v.²).
173. 'endeavour that those be beautiful and fresh in your life'.
177. *feler:* MS *fele* probably results from a scribe's having read line 177 in isolation, and having failed to realize that a comparative is required—as 178f indicates.
180. *deuelez þrote:* Hell mouth was often represented by the mouth of a whale, dragon, or less specific monster. See the account of Jonah being swallowed by the whale in *Pat* (247ff, especially 258n).
185. *dysheriete and depryue:* infinitives used as verbal nouns: 'disinheriting and depriving'.
187. *boþe:* 'also'.
194. *resounez of ryȝt:* 'discourses about righteousness'—i.e. expositions of morality.
195. The periphrasis *Prynce þat paradys weldez* also appears in *St Erkenwald* 161 and *Death and Life* 13. Similar epithets for God appear in 17, 644, and 1664. See also 5n.

Is displesed at vch a poynt þat plyes to scaþe;
Bot neuer ȝet in no boke breued I herde
Þat euer He wrek so wyþerly on werk þat He made,
Ne venged for no vilté of vice ne synne,
Ne so hastyfly watz hot for hatel of His wylle,   200
Ne neuer so sodenly soȝt vnsoundely to weng,
As for fylþe of þe flesch þat foles han vsed;
For, as I fynde, þer He forȝet alle His fre þewez,
And wex wod to þe wrache for wrath at His hert.

For þe fyrste felonye þe falce fende wroȝt   205
Whyl he watz hyȝe in þe heuen houen vpon lofte,
Of alle þyse aþel aungelez attled þe fayrest:
And he vnkyndely, as a karle, kydde a reward.
He seȝ noȝt bot hymself how semly he were,
Bot his Souerayn he forsoke and sade þyse wordez: 210
'I schal telde vp my trone in þe tramountayne,
And by lyke to þat Lorde þat þe lyft made.'
With þis worde þat he warp, þe wrake on hym lyȝt:
Dryȝtyn with His dere dom hym drof to þe abyme,
In þe mesure of His mode, His metz neuer þe lasse.   215
Bot þer He tynt þe tyþe dool of His tour ryche:

197ff. The poet's habit of describing and explaining God's actions, motivation, and even feelings in human terms is well exemplified in this passage; cf. (for example) 281–92, 557–600, 1143–52, 1501–2, and *Pat* 65–72 and 495–523. His attitude is in striking contrast to that of most Christian commentators, who normally try to avoid any suggestion of God behaving like a man.

204–8. 'and grew furious for vengeance as a result of the anger in His heart. For the false fiend committed the first crime while he was raised aloft high in heaven, designed to be the fairest of all the noble angels: and he made a recompense unnaturally, like a churl.' The fiend repays God's infinite generosity with treachery (cf. the response of the ill-clad guest to the lord's invitation in the parable of the Wedding Feast: see note to 139ff).

205–34. Cf. Isa. 14:12–15.

211. *tramountayne: OED* glosses 'the north pole star', adding in explanation 'so called in Italy and Provence, because visible beyond the Alps.' The context suggests that the word may here simply mean 'north'. The devil is traditionally associated with the north, an idea probably based on Isa. 14:12–13, and reflected in such works as the OE *Genesis* 31–4, *Cursor Mundi* 459, Chaucer, 'The Friar's Tale' (*CT* III.1413–16), *PPl* C.I.112, and Milton, *Paradise Lost* V.754–60.

212. *by:* 'be'.

213–15. 'As he spoke these words, the vengeance descended on him: God drove him to the abyss with (His) severe judgement, in the moderation of His anger, His mildness undiminished.' The poet emphasizes (as again in 230 and 247) that for the sins of Lucifer and Adam, however heinous, God's just punishment is given without the wrath which was aroused in Him by carnal sin (250). An additional connecting theme is suggested in the note to 235–48.

216. 'Yet He lost the tenth part of His noble entourage there (on that occasion)'.

Þaȝ þe feloun were so fers for his fayre wedez [f60ʳ]
And his glorious glem þat glent so bryȝt,
As sone as Dryȝtynez dome drof to hymseluen,
Þikke þowsandez þro þrwen þeroute, 220
Fellen fro þe fyrmament fendez ful blake,
Sweued at þe fyrst swap as þe snaw þikke,
Hurled into helle-hole as þe hyue swarmez.
Fylter fenden folk forty dayez lencþe,
Er þat styngande storme stynt ne myȝt; 225
Bot as smylt mele vnder smal siue smokez forþikke,
So fro heuen to helle þat hatel schor laste,
On vche syde of þe worlde aywhere ilyche.
Ȝis, hit watz a brem brest and a byge wrache,
And ȝet wrathed not þe Wyȝ; ne þe wrech saȝtled, 230
Ne neuer wolde, for wylfulnes, his worþy God knawe,
Ne pray Hym for no pité, so proud watz his wylle.
Forþy þaȝ þe rape were rank, þe rawþe watz lyttel;
Þaȝ he be kest into kare, he kepes no better.
Bot þat oþer wrake þat wex, on wyȝez hit lyȝt 235

---

231. wylfulnes] MS wylnesful
233. lyttel] MS lyttlel

---

217. *for:* 'on account of'.
217–23. Despite the fiend's excessive pride in his bright beauty (217f), once he and the rebel angels fall, they become *black* fiends (221). Their disadvantaged and discredited position is given further emphasis by the poet's technique of comparing them in successive similes (222f) to small and insignificant objects (cf. 226, 965f, 1791f, and *Pat* 268).
217–52. The left-hand side of f 60ʳ is severely blurred. However, a shadowy imprint of the beginning of each line appears in the right-hand margin of f 59ᵛ, and examination of this helps in the process of deciphering some words.
222. 'whirled at the first blow as thick as snow'.
224. 'The fiendish folk clung together for the duration of forty days'.
226f. 'but as sieved meal smokes very thickly under a fine sieve, so that vile shower stretched from heaven to hell'.
229–34. 'Yes, indeed, it was a terrible outrage and a supreme vengeance, and yet God was not enraged; nor did the wretch make peace, nor ever would, for wilfulness, acknowledge his worthy God, nor pray Him for pity, so proud was his will. Therefore though the blow was severe, the remorse was slight; though he is cast into sorrow, he behaves no better.' *Ȝis* (229): this word is blurred in the MS, but seems to be *ȝis* or *þis*. The former reading has been adopted for its superior sense: cf. the similar usages in 1113, *Pat* 117, 347, and *Pe* 635.
235. *þat oþer:* 'the second'.
235–48. The poet moves from the fall of the angels to the fall of man. He sees both as events in which the protagonist fails in *trawþe*, and neglects to fulfil his obligations to God. The biblical account of the fall of man is in Gen. 2–3; a brief discussion of the fall and redemption is given in *Pe* 636–60.

Þur3 þe faut of a freke þat fayled in trawþe,
Adam inobedyent, ordaynt to blysse.
Þer pryuély in paradys his place watz devised,
To lyue þer in lykyng þe lenþe of a terme,
And þenne enherite þat home þat aungelez forgart;   240
Bot þur3 þe eggyng of Eue he ete of an apple
Þat enpoysened alle peplez þat parted fro hem boþe,
For a defence þat watz dy3t of Dry3tyn Seluen,
And a payne þeron put and pertly halden.
Þe defence watz þe fryt þat þe freke towched,   245
And þe dom is þe deþe þat drepez vus alle;
Al in mesure and meþe watz mad þe vengiaunce,
And efte amended with a mayden þat make had neuer.
Bot in þe þryd watz forþrast al þat þryue schuld:
Þer watz malys mercyles and mawgré much scheued,   250
Þat watz for fylþe vpon folde þat þe folk vsed,
Þat þen wonyed in þe worlde withouten any maysterz.
Hit wern þe fayrest of forme and of face als,   [f60ᵛ]
Þe most and þe myriest þat maked wern euer,
Þe styfest, þe stalworþest þat stod euer on fete,   255
And lengest lyf in hem lent of ledez alle oþer.
For hit was þe forme foster þat þe folde bred,
Þe aþel aunceterez sunez þat Adam watz called,
To wham God hade geuen alle þat gayn were,

240. The idea that man was to inherit the place of the fallen angels in heaven was a commonplace. In the OE *Genesis* (356–441) the poet uses this idea to motivate Satan's envy of Adam and Eve and his plan to corrupt them.

241f. Cf. *St Erkenwald* 295f, *Death and Life* 273.

243f. 'because of a prohibition which was decreed by the Lord Himself, and a punishment assigned to it and openly kept.'

248. 'and afterwards remedied by a virgin who never had an equal.' In this context, *make* may mean either 'equal' or 'mate', and it is possible that both meanings are intended. The Virgin is called *makelez* ('peerless, without equal') in *Pe* 435. At this point her relevance consists not only in her peerlessness (the fact that she is the virgin mother of Christ), but also in the quality of that motherhood—the unique cleanness of the conception of Jesus: cf. note to 1069–88.

249. *þe þryd:* The Flood is seen as the third vengeance, the first two being the fall of the angels (205–34) and the fall of man (235–48).

249–528. The account of the Flood is based on Gen. 6:1–9:1.

250–52. 'there merciless anger and great displeasure was shown, which was because of the uncleanness practised on earth by the people who then lived without any masters in the world.' The failure of people to live chaste lives was traditionally seen as the cause of the Flood (cf., for instance, Chaucer, 'The Parson's Tale', *CT* X.839). Thus it is particularly relevant to the poet's theme; but see also Introduction, p. 25.

254. *þe most and þe myriest:* 'the biggest and the most graceful'. Cf. *G* 141f.

257f. 'For they were the first offspring that the earth bred, the sons of the noble ancestor who was called Adam'.

Alle þe blysse boute blame þat bodi my3t haue;   260
And þose lykkest to þe lede, þat lyued next after;
Forþy so semly to see syþen wern none.
Þer watz no law to hem layd bot loke to kynde,
And kepe to hit, and alle hit cors clanly fulfylle.
And þenne founden þay fylþe in fleschlych dedez,   265
And controeued agayn kynde contraré werkez,
And vsed hem vnþryftyly vchon on oþer,
And als with oþer, wylsfully, upon a wrange wyse:
So ferly fowled her flesch þat þe fende loked
How þe de3ter of þe douþe wern derelych fayre,   270
And fallen in fela3schyp with hem on folken wyse,
And engendered on hem jeauntez with her japez ille.
Þose wern men meþelez and ma3ty on vrþe,
Þat for her lodlych laykez alosed þay were;
He watz famed for fre þat fe3t loued best,   275
And ay þe bigest in bale þe best watz halden.
And þenne euelez on erþe ernestly grewen
And multyplyed monyfolde inmongez mankynde,
For þat þe ma3ty on molde so marre þise oþer
Þat þe Wy3e þat al wro3t ful wroþly bygynnez.   280
When He knew vche contré coruppte in hitseluen,
And vch freke forloyned fro þe ry3t wayez,
Felle temptande tene towched His hert.
As wy3e wo hym withinne, werp to Hymseluen:
'Me forþynkez ful much þat euer I mon made,   285
Bot I schal delyuer and do away þat doten on þis molde,
And fleme out of þe folde al þat flesch werez,
Fro þe burne to þe best, fro bryddez to fyschez;
Al schal doun and be ded and dryuen out of erþe   [f61ʳ]
Þat euer I sette saule inne; and sore hit Me rwez   290
Þat euer I made hem Myself; bot if I may herafter,
I schal wayte to be war her wrenchez to kepe.'
Þenne in worlde watz a wy3e wonyande on lyue,

260. *boute:* 'without'.
261f. 'and those who lived immediately after were most like the man (Adam); and so since then none have been so beautiful to look at.'
266. *agayn kynde:* 'against nature', i.e. unnatural.
269–72. This account is based on Gen. 6:1–4. *þe fende* (269): the fallen angels.
275f. 'he who loved fighting best was famed for being honourable, and always the one who did the greatest harm was considered the best.'
279f. 'because the mighty on earth so corrupt the others that the Being who created everything begins (to act) very angrily.'
284. 'Like a man sorrowful within, He said to Himself'. See 197ff and note.
286. 'but I shall destroy and do away with those on this earth who behave foolishly'.
292. 'I shall make sure to be careful that I take note of their deceitful deeds.'

Ful redy and ful ryȝtwys, and rewled hym fayre,
In þe drede of Dryȝtyn his dayez he vsez,   295
And ay glydande wyth his God, his grace watz þe more.
Hym watz þe nome Noe, as is innoghe knawen.
He had þre þryuen sunez, and þay þre wyuez:
Sem soþly þat on, þat oþer hyȝt Cam,
And þe jolef Japheth watz gendered þe þryd.   300
Now God in nwy to Noe con speke
Wylde wrakful wordez, in His wylle greued:
'Þe ende of alle kynez flesch þat on vrþe meuez
Is fallen forþwyth My face, and forþer hit I þenk.
With her vnworþelych werk Me wlatez withinne;   305
Þe gore þerof Me hatz greued and þe glette nwyed.
I schal strenkle My distresse, and strye al togeder,
Boþe ledez and londe and alle þat lyf habbez.
Bot make to þe a mancioun, and þat is My wylle,
A cofer closed of tres, clanlych planed.   310
Wyrk wonez þerinne for wylde and for tame,
And þenne cleme hit with clay comly withinne,
And alle þe endentur dryuen daube withouten.
And þus of lenþe and of large þat lome þou make:
Þre hundred of cupydez þou holde to þe lenþe,   315
Of fyfty fayre ouerþwert forme þe brede;
And loke euen þat þyn ark haue of heȝþe þretté,
And a wyndow wyd vponande wroȝt vpon lofte,

312. withinne] MS withinme
318. vponande (Gollancz) | MS vpon
      lofte] MS loste

301–44. This passage is based on Gen. 6:13–22. Though the poet expands the bib-
lical narrative and adds some extra touches, which contribute to the liveliness of the
passage and help to define the feelings and motives of God and Noah, he does not
alter the essential facts.

303f. 'The end of all kinds of flesh that move on earth has presented itself to me, and
I intend to carry it out.' Cf. Gen. 6:13: *Finis universae carnis venit coram me* 'The end of
all flesh is come before me'.

305f. 'I am sickened inwardly by their shameful practice; the filth of it has grieved
Me and the slime troubled Me.' The people's impurity is symbolized by physical
filth and slime: cf. *Pat* 269–344, where the foulness of the whale's belly symbolizes
Jonah's sinful state (see *Pat* 342n).

309. *to þe:* 'for yourself'.

312f. 'and then plaster it with clay fittingly within, and outside daub all the ham-
mered jointing' (i.e. pieces of wood which have been hammered tightly into place).

315–20. 'keep to three hundred cubits (for) the length, and make the breadth
precisely fifty across, and see that your ark has exactly thirty (cubits) in height, and a
wide opening window constructed above, the measure of a cubit square exactly; a
well fitting door, made in the side'.

In þe compas of a cubit kyndely sware;
A wel dutande dor, don on þe syde; 320
Haf hallez þerinne and halkez ful mony,
Boþe boskenz and bourez and wel bounden penez.
For I schal waken vp a water to wasch alle þe worlde,
And quelle alle þat is quik with quauende flodez,
Alle þat glydez and gotz and gost of lyf habbez; [f61ᵛ] 325
I schal wast with My wrath þat wons vpon vrþe.
Bot My forwarde with þe I festen on þis wyse,
For þou in reysoun hatz rengned and ryȝtwys ben euer:
Þou schal enter þis ark with þyn aþel barnez
And þy wedded wyf; with þe þou take 330
Þe makez of þy myry sunez; þis meyny of aȝte
I schal saue of monnez saulez, and swelt þose oþer.
Of vche best þat berez lyf busk þe a cupple,
Of vche clene comly kynde enclose seuen makez,
Of vche horwed in ark halde bot a payre, 335
For to saue Me þe sede of alle ser kyndez.
And ay þou meng with þe malez þe mete ho-bestez,
Vche payre by payre to plese ayþer oþer;
With alle þe fode þat may be founde frette þy cofer,
For sustnaunce to yowself and also þose oþer.' 340
Ful grayþely gotz þis god man and dos Godez hestes,
In dryȝ dred and daunger þat durst do non oþer.
Wen hit watz fettled and forged and to þe fulle grayþed,
Þenn con Dryȝttyn hym dele dryȝly þyse wordez.
'Now Noe,' quoþ oure Lorde, 'art þou al redy? 345
Hatz þou closed þy kyst with clay alle aboute?'
'Ȝe, Lorde, with Þy leue,' sayde þe lede þenne,
'Al is wroȝt at Þi worde, as Þou me wyt lantez.'
'Enter in, þenn,' quoþ He, 'and haf þi wyf with þe,
Þy þre sunez, withouten þrep, and her þre wyuez; 350

---

322. boskenz (Gollancz)] MS boskez

322. *boskenz:* Gollancz glosses 'the divisions of a cow-house which separate the animals from each other' (referring to *EDD* under *boskin*), and thus provides a far more satisfactory sense than the MS *boskez* 'bushes'.

333ff. This is a conflation of the two accounts of God's injunction to Noah in Gen. 6:20 and 7:2.

343f. 'When it was prepared and constructed and fully made ready, then God solemnly uttered these words to him.'

348. 'all is done according to Your instructions, as You granted me wisdom.' Noah's point is that the plans devised by God's infinite wisdom have been carried out by a man whose intellectual capacity, though God-given, is comparatively limited.

Bestez, as I bedene haue, bosk þerinne als,
And when ȝe arn staued, styfly stekez yow þerinne.
Fro seuen dayez ben seyed I sende out bylyue
Such a rowtande ryge þat rayne schal swyþe
Þat schal wasch alle þe worlde of werkez of fylþe;   355
Schal no flesch vpon folde by fonden onlyue,
Outtaken yow aȝt in þis ark staued
And sed þat I wyl saue of þyse ser bestez.'
Now Noe neuer styntez—þat niyȝt he bygynnez—
Er al wer stawed and stoken as þe steuen wolde.   360
Thenne sone com þe seuenþe day, when samned wern alle,   [f62ʳ]
And alle woned in þe whichche, þe wylde and þe tame.
Þen bolned þe abyme, and bonkez con ryse,
Waltes out vch walle-heued in ful wode stremez;
Watz no brymme þat abod vnbrosten bylyue;   365
Þe mukel lauande loghe to þe lyfte rered.
Mony clustered clowde clef alle in clowtez;
Torent vch a rayn-ryfte and rusched to þe vrþe,
Fon neuer in forty dayez. And þen þe flod ryses,
Ouerwaltez vche a wod and þe wyde feldez.   370
For when þe water of þe welkyn with þe worlde mette,
Alle þat deth moȝt dryȝe drowned þerinne.
Þer watz moon for to make when meschef was cnowen,

---

359. styntez] MS stystez
niyȝt] MS niyȝ

351–5. 'also, as I have ordered, bring beasts in there, and when you are lodged, shut yourselves up in there securely. When seven days have passed I shall swiftly send forth such a rushing tempest which will rain so hard that it will wash all the world (clean) of deeds of filth'.

360. 'until all were lodged and enclosed in accordance with the command.'

363ff. This description of the storm which accompanies the Flood may be compared with the account of the storm in *Pat* (137ff). In both instances, the biblical narrative is greatly expanded. Descriptions of storms at sea are a favourite device in alliterative poetry: see Nicolas Jacobs, *Spec.*, 47 (1972), 695–719.

364. *wode stremez:* cf. *Pat* 162.

365–8. 'soon there was no bank that remained unburst; the great flowing flood rose up to the sky. Many a clustered cloud split all in shreds; each rain-rift tore open and (rain) rushed to the earth'. As the clouds break apart, a gap appears, through which the rain pours.

371ff. The poet evokes considerable sympathy for the victims of the Flood: see Introduction, p. 3of.

373–6. 'there was cause for lamentation when the calamity was known—that there was no help for it but to die in the deep streams; the water grew ever more powerful, destroying homes, rushed into each house, seized those who lived there.' The clause of 374 is in apposition to *meschef* (373).

Þat noȝt dowed bot þe deth in þe depe stremez;
Water wylger ay wax, wonez þat stryede, 375
Hurled into vch hous, hent þat þer dowelled.
Fyrst feng to þe flyȝt alle þat fle myȝt;
Vuche burde with her barne þe byggyng þay leuez
And bowed to þe hyȝ bonk þer brentest hit wern,
And heterly to þe hyȝe hyllez þay haled on faste. 380
Bot al watz nedlez her note, for neuer cowþe stynt
Þe roȝe raynande ryg, þe raykande wawez,
Er vch boþom watz brurdful to þe bonkez eggez,
And vche a dale so depe þat demmed at þe brynkez.
Þe moste mountaynez on mor þenne watz no more dryȝe, 385
And þeron flokked þe folke, for ferde of þe wrake.
Syþen þe wylde of þe wode on þe water flette;
Summe swymmed þeron þat saue hemself trawed,
Summe styȝe to a stud and stared to þe heuen,
Rwly wyth a loud rurd rored for drede. 390
Harez, herttez also, to þe hyȝe runnen;
Bukkez, bausenez, and bulez to þe bonkkez hyȝed;
And alle cryed for care to þe Kyng of heuen,
Recouerer of þe Creator þay cryed vchone,

380. haled] MS aled

379. *bonk:* This is taken as an alternative (uninflected) pl. form, in view of the fact that, both here and in *Pat* 343, it is used in concord with a pl. verb.

381–4. 'But their efforts were all in vain, for the wild raining tempest, the sweeping waves, never ceased until each valley was brimful to the edges of the hills, and each valley so deep (with water) that it was filled to the brink.' The poet visualizes the hills surrounding valleys transformed into the shores of huge lakes. *Bot al watz nedlez her note* (381): cf. *Pat* 220. *Ryg* (382), some editors have felt the need to insert a word after *ryg:* Gollancz supplying *ne* and Morris *and.* Of these, the poet is more likely to have written *ne,* but the emendation is not strictly necessary.

385. Suggesting that the sense of this line in the MS is suspect, Gollancz emends *watz no* to *on.* The MS reading is here retained. The line is taken to suggest that even the mountains were becoming wet, but that the people flocked there nevertheless because these were the highest places and would be the last to be flooded.

386. *for ferde:* ME had a number of *for* + adj. (or pp.) phrases in which *for* is a prep. 'because of' and the adj. equivalent to a noun—thus *for fetys* (1103) and here *for ferde* 'because of fear'. *For* could also be used as an intensive prefix to adjs. and pps., however: thus *fordolked* 'grievously wounded' (*Pe* 11). Therefore in some contexts (given the unsystematic nature of the word division in the MS) the construction is ambiguous and the modern editor must make an arbitrary choice. See also Robinson's note to 'The Knight's Tale', *CT* I.2143.

388. *þat saue hemself trawed:* 'hoping to save themselves'. Relative clauses sometimes have explanatory, rather than qualifying, force—cf. 375, *Pat* 155, *G* 331.

394f. 'each one of them cried for rescue from the Creator, so that the confusion signified that His mercy had passed'. The idea seems to be that their cries for mercy,

Þat amounted þe mase His mercy watz passed, 395
And alle His pyté departed fro peple þat He hated.
Bi þat þe flod to her fete floȝed and waxed, [f62ᵛ]
Þen vche a segge seȝ wel þat synk hym byhoued.
Frendez fellen in fere and faþmed togeder,
To dryȝ her delful destyné and dyȝen alle samen; 400
Luf lokez to luf and his leue takez,
For to ende alle at onez and for euer twynne.
By forty dayez wern faren, on folde no flesch styryed
Þat þe flod nade al freten with feȝtande waȝez;
For hit clam vche a clyffe, cubites fyftene 405
Ouer þe hyȝest hylle þat hurkled on erþe.
Þenne mourkne in þe mudde most ful nede
Alle þat spyrakle inspranc—no sprawlyng awayled—
Saue þe haþel vnder hach and his here straunge,
Noe þat ofte neuened þe name of oure Lorde, 410
Hym aȝtsum in þat ark, as aþel God lyked,
Þer alle ledez in lome lenged druye.
Þe arc houen watz on hyȝe with hurlande gotez,
Kest to kythez vncouþe þe clowdez ful nere.
Hit waltered on þe wylde flod, went as hit lyste, 415

395. þe mase] MS þe masse þe mase
400. destyné] MS deystyne

which are not answered, indicate that God is set on revenge. Alternatively, *þe mase* could be a euphemism for 'damnation' (a sense to which *PPl* B.Prol.196 and I.6 seem to point; cf. *PPl* B.Prol.196: *þe mase amonge vs alle*), in which case 395 would mean 'it came to damn-all: His mercy had passed.' The definite article also occurs in *PPl* B.I.5f: *sestow þis poeple, How bisi þei ben abouten þe mase?*, where 'damn-all' again makes good sense (cf. *OED* sense 1 [a], delirium, delusion, disappointment). The MS reading clearly involves erroneous repetition; perhaps the second word was intended as a correction, since *þe mase* makes better sense than *þe masse*.

397–404. 'By the time the flood had grown and flowed as high as their feet, then each man saw clearly that he must drown. Friends came together and embraced each other, to suffer their sorrowful fate and all die together; love looks at loved one and takes his leave, to end all at the same time and part for ever. By the time forty days were ended, no flesh stirred on earth which the flood had not entirely devoured with contending waves'. There is a slight logical inconsistency in this last statement: the poet means that the flood has killed all living creatures.

408. 'all that the breath (of life) sprang into—no struggling availed'. *Spyrakle:* cf. Vulgate *spiraculum* 'breath of life' (Gen. 7:22).

411f. 'he and seven others in the ark, where everyone stayed dry in the vessel, as it pleased glorious God.' *Aȝtsum* descends from OE idiom of the type *eahta* (gen. pl.) *sum* 'one of eight', i.e. 'with seven companions'.

415ff. The ark's lack of navigational gear, which is not mentioned in Genesis, is added by the poet to emphasize the total submission of Noah and his companions to

Drof vpon þe depe dam, in daunger hit semed,
Withouten mast, oþer myke, oþer myry bawelyne,
Kable, oþer capstan to clyppe to her ankrez,
Hurrok, oþer hande-helme hasped on roþer,
Oþer any sweande sayl to seche after hauen,   420
Bot flote forthe with þe flyt of þe felle wyndez.
Whederwarde so þe water wafte, hit rebounde;
Ofte hit roled on rounde and rered on ende;
Nyf oure Lorde hade ben her lodezmon hem had lumpen harde.
Of þe lenþe of Noe lyf to lay a lel date,   425
Þe sex hundreth of his age and none odde ȝerez,
Of secounde monyth þe seuentenþe day ryȝtez,
Towalten alle þyse welle-hedez and þe water flowed;
And þryez fyfty þe flod of folwande dayez;
Vche hille watz þer hidde with yþez ful graye.   430
Al watz wasted þat wonyed þe worlde withinne,
Þat euer flote, oþer flwe, oþer on fote ȝede,
That roȝly watz þe remnaunt þat þe rac dryuez   [f63ʳ]

427. seuentenþe] MS seuenþe
430. yþez (Morris)] MS yrez
431. þat (Gollancz)] MS þat þer
432. Þat (Gollancz)] MS þer

the will of God. There are records of holy men in the early Celtic church going to sea in boats without rudders and oars specifically to demonstrate their willingness to be sent wherever God might wish: see, for instance, the entry in the *Anglo-Saxon Chronicle* (Parker MS) for 891.

419. *Hurrok:* The precise meaning of this word is uncertain. *OED* and *MED* define it as a part of a boat between the sternmost seat and the stern. Neither here nor in *Pat* 185 is this definition convincing. Bertil Sandahl (*Middle English Sea Terms: 1. The Ship's Hull* [Uppsala, 1951], pp. 126f) offers the more satisfactory suggestion that the *hurrok* is a rudder-band encircling the rudder to keep it in position. This sense is adopted here, and, following Anderson, in *Pat* 185.

422. *hit:* i.e. the ark.

423. Cf. *Pat* 147.

424. Cf. *Pat* 257ff, where Jonah's survival inside the whale is attributed to the protection of God.

425. 'To specify an exact point in the length of Noah's life'—which is specified in the following lines.

427. *seuentenþe:* The emendation is supported by Genesis: *septimodecimo die* 'the seventeenth day' (7:11).

429. 'and the flood (lasted) thrice fifty days afterwards'.

433f. 'so that it was fortunate for the remnant that the storm drives, that all species, so lodged, were united within.' The identification of *roȝly* is uncertain. It usually means 'rough' (as in *Pat* 64), but this would be inappropriate here. The suggestion, first made by Skeat (R. Morris and W. W. Skeat, *Specimens of Early English*, Part II [Oxford, rev. edn. 1894] p. 324) and elaborated by Gollancz, that *roȝly* means

Þat alle gendrez so joyst wern joyned wythinne.
Bot quen þe Lorde of þe lyfte lyked Hymseluen   435
For to mynne on His mon His meth þat abydez,
Þen He wakened a wynde on watterez to blowe;
Þenne lasned þe llak þat large watz are.
Þen He stac vp þe stangez, stoped þe wellez,
Bed blynne of þe rayn: hit batede as fast;   440
Þenne lasned þe loȝ lowkande togeder.
After harde dayez wern out an hundreth and fyfté,
As þat lyftande lome luged aboute,
Where þe wynde and þe weder warpen hit wolde,
Hit saȝtled on a softe day, synkande to grounde;   445
On a rasse of a rok hit rest at þe laste,
On þe mounte of Ararach of Armene hilles,
Þat oþerwayez on Ebrv hit hat þe Thanes.
Bot þaȝ þe kyste in þe cragez were closed to byde,
Ȝet fyned not þe flod ne fel to þe boþemez,   450
Bot þe hyȝest of þe eggez vnhuled wern a lyttel,
Þat þe burne bynne borde byhelde þe bare erþe.
Þenne wafte he vpon his wyndowe, and wysed þeroute

---

447. Ararach (Gollancz)] MS mararach
449. were] MS wern

'fortunate'—cf. OE *row* 'mild', OIcel *rolligr*—is therefore tentatively adopted. Alternatively, this word could be identified with *rwly* 'pitiful' (cf. 390), in which case, after affirming the complete destruction of life outside the ark, the poet draws attention to its precarious survival within.

435f. 'But when it pleased the Lord of the sky to think of His man who waits for His mercy'.

438–41. 'then the flood, which had been great before, subsided. Then He closed up the pools, stopped the wells, commanded the rain to cease: it abated immediately; then the sea subsided, shrinking in on itself.'

445. 'it came to rest on a mild day, sinking to the ground'.

447. *Ararach:* It is likely that the MS *mararach* results from a scribal error. The poet would probably have known the name Ararach: though not in Genesis, it appears in encyclopedic sources such as Bartholomaeus (see Trevisa XIV.3), and (as Gollancz points out) occurs in the French Mandeville.

448. Gollancz suggests that this is derived from the French Mandeville: 'Mes ly Iuys lappellant Thanez' (*The Buke of John Maundeuill*, ed. G. F. Warner [Roxburgh Club, 1889], p. 195). He reports that, among the variant readings for *Thanez, Chano* is the closest to the word from which this name is derived, the Persian for *Ararat, Kuh-i-Noh* 'Noah's mountain'.

449–54. 'But though the ark remained enclosed by the crags, the flood did not yet end or sink to the floors of the valleys, but the highest of the ridges were uncovered a little, so that the man on board beheld the bare earth. Then he pushed open his window, and sent out a messenger from that company to seek lands for them'.

A message fro þat meyny hem moldez to seche:
Þat watz þe rauen so ronk, þat rebel watz euer;   455
He watz colored as þe cole, corbyal vntrwe.
And he fongez to þe flyȝt and fannez on þe wyndez,
Halez hyȝe vpon hyȝt to herken tyþyngez.
He croukez for comfort when carayne he fyndez
Kast vp on a clyffe þer costese lay drye;   460
He hade þe smelle of þe smach and smoltes þeder sone,
Fallez on þe foule flesch and fyllez his wombe,
And sone ȝederly forȝete ȝisterday steuen,
How þe cheuetayn hym charged þat þe chyst ȝemed.
Þe rauen raykez hym forth, þat reches ful lyttel   465
How alle fodez þer fare, ellez he fynde mete;
Bot þe burne bynne borde þat bod to hys come
Banned hym ful bytterly with bestes alle samen.
He sechez anoþer sondezmon, and settez on þe douue,   [f63ᵛ]
Bryngez þat bryȝt vpon borde, blessed, and sayde: 470
'Wende, worþelych wyȝt, vus wonez to seche;
Dryf ouer þis dymme water; if þou druye fyndez
Bryng bodworde to bot blysse to vus alle.
Þaȝ þat fowle be false, fre be þou euer.'

464. chyst (Fischer)] MS kyst
469. douue] MS doune

456. *vntrwe:* The raven proves *vntrwe* in that it fails to honour its obligation to Noah, and return to the ark with news: this is emphasized in 463f. *Vntrawþe* is a recurrent theme in the poem: see note to 235–48, and Introduction, pp. 24–9.

459–64. Though there is no scriptural authority for this account of the raven's being lured from its duty to Noah by the desire to gorge itself on carrion, it is a common-place in the works of commentators, encyclopedists, and homilists, and is also reflected in the mystery plays. The unworthiness of the raven's actions is given emphasis by the repulsive physical details of 461f.

460. 'cast up on a cliff where the shores lay dry'.

463f. 'and immediately entirely forgot the order of yesterday, how the captain who ruled the ark had instructed him.' *Chyst:* the alliteration shows that the poet's form must have been the more southerly *chyst.*

466–8. 'how all people there fare, provided that he finds food. But the man on board who awaited his return cursed him very bitterly together with all other animals.'

469. *douue:* The scribe appears to have had difficulty with this word, which he spells successively *doūe* [= *doune*), *doveue* (481), and *dowue* (485). It may be inferred that the spelling of the word in his exemplar was strange to him and that only at the third encounter did he recognize it and convert it to his usual spelling. If so, his exemplar possibly had a diphthongal spelling *doueue* (see further 1707n).

470. 'brings that beautiful creature on board, blessed her, and said'.

473. 'bring a message to proclaim joy to us all.'

474. *þat fowle:* i.e. the raven.

Ho wyrled out on þe weder on wyngez ful scharpe,   475
Dreȝly alle alonge day þat dorst neuer lyȝt;
And when ho fyndez no folde her fote on to pyche,
Ho vmbekestez þe coste and þe kyst sechez.
Ho hittez on þe euentyde and on þe ark sittez;
Noe nymmes hir anon and naytly hir stauez.   480
Noe on anoþer day nymmez efte þe dowue,
And byddez hir bowe ouer þe borne efte bonkez to seche;
And ho skyrmez vnder skwe and skowtez aboute,
Tyl hit watz nyȝe at þe naȝt, and Noe þen sechez.
On ark on an euentyde houez þe dowue;   485
On stamyn ho stod and stylle hym abydez.
What! ho broȝt in hir beke a bronch of olyue,
Gracyously vmbegrouen al with grene leuez;
Þat watz þe syngne of sauyté þat sende hem oure Lorde,
And þe saȝtlyng of Hymself with þo sely bestez.   490
Þen watz þer joy in þat gyn where jumpred er dryȝed,
And much comfort in þat cofer þat watz clay-daubed.
Myryly on a fayr morn, monyth þe fyrst,
Þat fallez formast in þe ȝer, and þe fyrst day,
Ledez loȝen in þat lome and loked þeroute,   495
How þat watterez wern woned and þe worlde dryed.
Vchon loued oure Lorde, bot lenged ay stylle
Tyl þay had typyng fro þe Tolke þat tyned hem þerinne.
Þen Godez glam to hem glod þat gladed hem alle,
Bede hem drawe to þe dor: delyuer hem He wolde.   500
Þen went þay to þe wykket, hit walt vpon sone;
Boþe þe burne and his barnez bowed þeroute,

---

475. wyrled (Gollancz)] MS wyrle
481. dowue] MS doveue

485f. 'One evening the dove rests on the ark; she stood on the prow and quietly
awaits him (Noah).'
487. *What!:* Cf. *G* 2201–4n.
489f. 'that was the sign of safety which our Lord sent them, and of the reconciliation
of Himself with those harmless beasts.'
491. 'Then there was joy in that craft where those jumbled together suffered before'.
Here *jumpred* is taken as pp. of the verb *jumpre* 'jumble' used as subject. It has also
been interpreted as a noun 'confusion, uncertainty, bewilderment, grief', as in *MED*
and Menner.
492. *þat watz clay-daubed:* This is emphasized in the account of the construction of the
ark: see 312f, 346.
497. *loued:* 'praised'.
499. Cf. *Pat* 63.
501. *hit walt vpon sone:* 'they threw it open at once'.

Her wyuez walkez hem wyth and þe wylde after,
Þroly þrublande in þronge, þrowen ful þykke.
Bot Noe of vche honest kynde nem out an odde, [f64ʳ] 505
And heuened vp an auter and halȝed hit fayre,
And sette a sakerfyse þeron of vch a ser kynde
Þat watz comly and clene: God kepez non oþer.
When bremly brened þose bestez, and þe breþe rysed,
Þe sauour of his sacrafyse soȝt to Hym euen 510
Þat al spedez and spyllez; He spekes with þat ilke
In comly comfort ful clos and cortays wordez:
'Now, Noe, no more nel I neuer wary
Alle þe mukel mayny on molde for no mannez synnez,
For I se wel þat hit is sothe þat alle seggez wyttez 515
To vnþryfte arn alle þrawen with þoȝt of her herttez,
And ay hatz ben, and wyl be ȝet; fro her barnage
Al is þe mynde of þe man to malyce enclyned.
Forþy schal I neuer schende so schortly at ones
As dysstrye al for manez dedez, dayez of þis erþe. 520
Bot waxez now and wendez forth and worþez to monye,
Multyplyez on þis molde, and menske yow bytyde.
Sesounez schal yow neuer sese of sede ne of heruest,
Ne hete, ne no harde forst, vmbre ne droȝþe,
Ne þe swetnesse of somer, ne þe sadde wynter, 525
Ne þe nyȝt, ne þe day, ne þe newe ȝerez,
Bot euer renne restlez: rengnez ȝe þerinne.'

---

514. on (Morris)] MS *om*.
515. seggez (Gollancz)] MS mannez
520. dedez (Menner)] MS synne

504–6. 'vigorously jostling in a throng, packed in a dense crowd (*lit.* very densely). But Noah took out an odd one of each clean species, and raised up an altar and consecrated it reverently'.

510–13. 'the smell of his sacrifice reached right to Him who quickens and destroys all things; He speaks in gracious solace very intimate and courteous words to him: "Now, Noah, I will never again curse" '. See note to 197ff.

514. *on:* Morris's emendation clarifies the meaning. The MS reading is retained by Emerson (**5b** 1919), who takes *mayny* as an adj. meaning 'great, powerful', and Gollancz, who hyphenates *mayny-molde* and glosses 'earth'.

515. *seggez:* Gollancz's emendation, which restores the alliteration, is adopted. As he points out, *mannez* was probably copied from the previous line.

520. *dedez:* The MS *synne* is added above the line in a later hand. It seems probable that a reader, noticing this line's lack of a noun, added *synne* (perhaps, as Menner suggests, on the analogy of 514). Here Menner's emendation, which restores both sense and alliteration, is adopted. *Dayez of þis erþe:* 'during the existence of this earth'.

521. *waxez, wendez, worþez:* imperatives; so also *multyplyez* (522) and *rengnez ȝe* (527).

Þerwyth He blessez vch a best, and bytaȝt hem þis erþe.
Þen watz a skylly skyualde, quen scaped alle þe wylde,
Vche fowle to þe flyȝt þat fyþerez myȝt serue,   530
Vche fysch to þe flod þat fynne couþe nayte,
Vche beste to þe bent þat bytes on erbez;
Wylde wormez to her won wryþez in þe erþe,
Þe fox and þe folmarde to þe fryth wyndez,
Herttes to hyȝe heþe, harez to gorstez,   535
And lyounez and lebardez to þe lake-ryftes;
Hernez and hauekez to þe hyȝe rochez,
Þe hole-foted fowle to þe flod hyȝez,
And vche best at a brayde þer hym best lykez;
Þe fowre frekez of þe folde fongez þe empyre.   540
Lo! suche a wrakful wo for wlatsum dedez   [f64ᵛ]
Parformed þe hyȝe Fader on folke þat He made;
Þat He chysly hade cherisched He chastysed ful hardee,
In devoydynge þe vylanye þat venkquyst His þewez.
Forþy war þe now, wyȝe þat worschyp desyres   545
In His comlych courte þat Kyng is of blysse,
In þe fylþe of þe flesch þat þou be founden neuer,
Tyl any water in þe worlde to wasche þe fayly.
For is no segge vnder sunne so seme of his craftez,
If he be sulped in synne, þat syttez vnclene;   550
On spec of a spote may spede to mysse

532. þat] MS þat þat

528. *and bytaȝt hem þis erþe:* 'and committed this earth to them.'
529. *skylly skyualde:* 'wise separation'. This would allude to the fact that, though God
gives all beasts the same freedom to inhabit the world, the various species live in
different ways, places, even elements: the rich variety in nature is the subject of 530ff.
Though it is a noun in 62, *skylly* here appears to be an adj. After Luttrell **6**, *skyualde*
would derive from ON **skifald*, a noun related to *skifa* 'to cut into slices'. Morris
and Menner, on the other hand, interpret *skylly* as a noun, and take *skyualde* as
pa.t. of a verb, glossing 'ordered (*or* manifested) design (*or* separation)'. Gollancz
emends MS *skyualde/skynalde* to *skylnade*, relating this to OIcel *skilnaðr* 'separation'.
540. 'the four men take control of the earth.'
543–50. 'that which He had dearly cherished He punished very severely in destroying
the evil that overcame His virtues (i.e. the virtues which He had established). There-
fore take care now, man who desires honour in the noble court of Him who is King
of bliss, that you are never discovered in the filth of the flesh, so that any water in the
world would fail to wash you. For there is no man under the sun, however seemly in
his deeds, who, if he is defiled in sin, will sit down unclean (i.e. in that unclean
state)'.
545–56. The story of the Flood concluded, the poet points out, in typical homiletic
fashion, the moral lessons it may provide for the edification of his audience.

Of þe syȝte of þe Souerayn þat syttez so hyȝe;
For þat schewe me schale in þo schyre howsez,
As þe beryl bornyst byhouez be clene,
Þat is sounde on vche a syde and no sem habes—   555
Withouten maskle oþer mote, as margerye-perle.
Syþen þe Souerayn in sete so sore forþoȝt
Þat euer He man vpon molde merked to lyuy,
For he in fylþe watz fallen, felly He uenged,
Quen fourferde alle þe flesch þat He formed hade.   560
Hym rwed þat He hem vprerde and raȝt hem lyflode;
And efte þat He hem vndyd, hard hit Hym þoȝt.
For quen þe swemande sorȝe soȝt to His hert,
He knyt a couenaunde cortaysly with monkynde þere,
In þe mesure of His mode and meþe of His wylle,   565
Þat He schulde neuer for no syt smyte al at onez,
As to quelle alle quykez for qued þat myȝt falle,
Whyl of þe lenþe of þe londe lastez þe terme.
Þat ilke skyl for no scaþe ascaped Hym neuer.
Wheder wonderly He wrak on wykked men after,   570
Ful felly for þat ilk faute forferde a kyth ryche,
In þe anger of His ire, þat arȝed mony;
And al watz for þis ilk euel, þat vnhappen glette,
Þe venym and þe vylanye and þe vycios fylþe
Þat bysulpez mannez saule in vnsounde hert,   575

553f. 'so that one shall appear in those bright dwellings, it is necessary to be pure like the shining beryl'.

554ff. Jewels are used to symbolize spiritual cleanness throughout *Pe*. The wording of 556 may be compared with *Pe* 721–80, where a similar phrase is used in the concatenation; the brightness and purity of the beryl is also observed in *Pe* 110 and 1011.

557–60. 'Because it very deeply grieved the Sovereign on (His) throne that He had ever placed mankind to live on earth, because he had fallen into filth, He fiercely took vengeance, when all the flesh that He had made perished.'

557–600. These lines provide moral generalization based on the preceding account of particular sin and retribution, and function as a transitional passage between the story of the Flood and that of Abraham. The attribution of human feelings to God is once more striking, particularly that of regret for the Flood, as this has no scriptural basis: see note to 197ff.

563. Cf. *Pat* 507.

564–8. Cf. Gen. 9:11.

567. 'so as to kill all living creatures for (any) evil that might befall'.

569. 'That particular judgement (i.e. total destruction) never passed His lips on account of any sin.'

571f. 'for that same sin very fiercely destroyed a rich region, in the anger of His wrath, so that many were afraid'.

574. Cf. *Pat* 71.

Þat he his Saueour ne see with syȝt of his yȝen.
Alle illez He hates as helle þat stynkkez;   [f65ʳ]
Bot non nuyez Hym on naȝt ne neuer vpon dayez
As harlottrye vnhonest, heþyng of seluen:
Þat schamez for no schrewedschyp, schent mot he worþe.   580
Bot sauyour, mon, in þyself, þaȝ þou a sotte lyuie,
Þaȝ þou bere þyself babel, byþenk þe sumtyme
Wheþer He þat stykked vche a stare in vche steppe yȝe—
Ȝif Hymself be bore blynde hit is a brod wonder;
And He þat fetly in face fettled alle eres,   585
If He hatz losed þe lysten hit lyftez meruayle:
Trave þou neuer þat tale—vntrwe þou hit fyndez.
Þer is no dede so derne þat dittez His yȝen;
Þer is no wyȝe in his werk so war ne so stylle
Þat hit ne þrawez to Hym þro er he hit þoȝt haue.   590
For He is þe gropande God, þe grounde of alle dedez,
Rypande of vche a ring þe reynyez and hert.
And þere He fyndez al fayre a freke wythinne,
With hert honest and hol, þat haþel He honourez,

577.   Alle (Gollancz)] MS þat alle
584.   Hymself] MS hymsele
586.   He] MS he he
590.   þro] MS þre
594.   With (Gollancz)] MS þat

576.   'so that he may not see his Saviour with the sight of his eyes.' Thus the poet
       argues that those of *vnsounde hert* will miss the reward promised in the sixth Beatitude:
       Beati mundo corde 'Blessed are the clean of heart' (Matt. 5:8).
577.   *Alle:* As Gollancz suggests, it is probable that MS *þat alle* results from a scribe's
       erroneously catching *þat* from the preceding line. *Helle þat stynkkez:* Cf. *Pat* 274n.
580.   'he who is not ashamed for any wickedness, he must be disgraced.'
581.   *sauyour:* a form of *sauour* 'know, apprehend'.
583f. 'whether He who set the power of sight in each bright eye—if He was born
       blind, it is a great wonder'. Cf. Ps. 93 (AV 94) : 9, and *Pat* 121–4n.
586.   'if He has lost the power of hearing, it is more than strange (*lit.* arouses wonder)'.
587.   *vntrwe þou hit fyndez:* 'you will find it untrue.'
589f. 'there is no man so cautious or so secretive in his conduct that it does not rush
       swiftly to Him before he has thought it.'
592.   Cf. Rev. 2:23. *Reynyez:* 'kidneys' or 'loins'; the kidneys were traditionally the
       seat of the affections. The poet is arguing that God has insight into man's most
       personal thoughts and wishes, including those concerning sexuality and emotions;
       one might translate: 'searching out the sexual and emotional longings of every man.'
593.   *þere:* 'where'.
594.   *With:* MS *þat* probably results from a scribe's having been influenced by the
       occurrence of *þat* at the beginning of the second half of the line.

Sendez hym a sad sy3t: to se His auen face, 595
And harde honysez þise oþer, and of His erde flemez.
Bot of þe dome of þe douþe for dedez of schame—
He is so skoymos of þat skaþe, He scarrez bylyue;
He may not dry3e to draw allyt, bot drepez in hast:
And þat watz schewed schortly by a schaþe onez. 600
Olde Abraham in erde onez he syttez
Euen byfore his hous-dore, vnder an oke grene;
Bry3t blykked þe bem of þe brode heuen;
In þe hy3e hete þerof Abraham bidez:
He watz schunt to þe schadow vnder schyre leuez. 605
Þenne watz he war on þe waye of wlonk Wy3ez þrynne;
If Þay wer farande and fre and fayre to beholde
Hit is eþe to leue by þe last ende.
For þe lede þat þer laye þe leuez anvnder,
When he hade of Hem sy3t he hy3ez bylyue, 610
And as to God þe goodmon gos Hem agaynez
And haylsed Hem in onhede, and sayde: 'Hende Lorde,
3if euer Þy mon vpon molde merit disserued, [f65ᵛ]
Lenge a lyttel with Þy lede, I lo3ly biseche;
Passe neuer fro Þi pouere, 3if I hit pray durst, 615

600. schaþe (Gollancz)] MS scaþe

595. 'sends him a solemn vision: to see His own face'. The poet is speaking of the revelation of divine truth achieved by the righteous, and alluding once more to the Beatitude 'Blessed are the clean of heart: for they shall see God' (AV 'pure in heart': Matt. 5:8; cf. 27f, 176, 576).

597–9. 'But as to the judgement of men for deeds of shame—He has such repugnance of that sin, He is provoked immediately; He cannot bear to hold back, but destroys (them) quickly'.

600. Thus the story of Abraham is introduced specifically as an *exemplum*: cf. *Pat* 57–60.

601–1012. This section of the poem is based on Gen. 18:1–19:28.

608. 'it is easy to believe from the final outcome.'

611–780. The poet alternates between singular and plural forms in referring to the divine presence. The point is that it is at once singular (God) and plural (three persons). A similar device occurs in the corresponding biblical narrative, Gen. 18—a text which was used by commentators to illustrate the nature of the Trinity.

612. *haysled Hem in onhede:* 'greeted Them in unity'. Abraham here addresses the divine persons in the singular: see note to 611–780.

612ff. Abraham's position as a servant of God is emphasized, specifically at 639. The relationship between an earthly lord and his servants is used as a metaphor for the relationship between God and man elsewhere in the poems, for instance in the parable of the Wedding Feast in *Cl*, and in *Pe* 1189–1212.

615–18. 'if I dare ask for it, never go from Your poor servant until You have stayed with Your man and rested under the bough (i.e. in the shade), and I shall quickly get You a little water, and swiftly set about having Your feet washed.'

Er Þou haf biden with Þi burne and vnder boȝe restted,
And I schal wynne Yow wyȝt of water a lyttel,
And fast aboute schal I fare Your fette wer waschene.
Resttez here on þis rote and I schal rachche after
And brynge a morsel of bred to baume Your hertte.'   620
'Fare forthe,' quoþ þe Frekez, 'and fech as þou seggez;
By bole of þis brode tre We byde þe here.'
Þenne orppedly into his hous he hyȝed to Saré,
Comaunded hir to be cof and quyk at þis onez:
'Þre mettez of mele menge and ma kakez;   625
Vnder askez ful hote happe hem byliue;
Quyl I fete sumquat fat, þou þe fyr bete,
Prestly at þis ilke poynte sum polment to make.'
He cached to his covhous and a calf bryngez,
Þat watz tender and not toȝe, bed tyrue of þe hyde,   630
And sayde to his seruaunt þat he hit seþe faste;
And he deruely at his dome dyȝt hit bylyue.
Þe burne to be bare-heued buskez hym þenne,
Clechez to a clene cloþe and kestez on þe grene,
Þrwe þryftyly þeron þo þre þerue kakez,   635
And bryngez butter wythal and by þe bred settez;
Mete messez of mylke he merkkez bytwene,
Syþen potage and polment in plater honest.
As sewer in a god assyse he serued Hem fayre,

---

620.   baume (Gollancz)] MS baune

620.   *baume:* This translates the Vulgate *confortate* (Gen. 18:5).
625f.   'Mix three measures of meal and make cakes; quickly cover them under very
hot ashes'.
627.   *Quyl I fete sumquat fat:* Probably 'while I fetch something fattened (i.e. ready to
kill)'—which is precisely what Abraham does in 629f, when he fetches the calf. This
interpretation takes *fat* as an adj. meaning 'fattened' (*MED* sense 1). Gollancz and
Menner both take *fat* as a n., respectively glossing *sumquat fat* as 'some kind of
vessel' (cf. 802) and 'a little fat'. Gollancz's interpretation is possible, though not
very likely—there is no further mention of any vessel. Menner's is not convincing, for
though the pron. followed by a partitive construction is common, it does not occur
without *of* or a genitive (e.g. 'somewhat of lust, somewhat of lore' [Gower, *Confessio
Amantis*, Prol. 19]; *what nwez, G* 1407).
632.   'and he (the servant) quickly at his (Abraham's) command prepared it im-
mediately.'
633.   Abraham removes his hat as a mark or respect: cf. *Pe* 237n.
639-42.   'Like a *sewer* (i.e. a chief servant in charge of seating, service, food, etc.) in a
worthy manner he humbly served whatever he had to Them, with a dignified and
courteous demeanour; and God, like a happy guest who was pleased to meet his
friend, made merry and praised his feast.' The demeanour of the Maiden in *Pe* is
similarly described as *sadde* (211).

Wyth sadde semblaunt and swete of such as he hade; 640
And God as a glad gest mad god chere
Þat watz fayn of his frende, and his fest praysed.
Abraham, al hodlez, with armez vp-folden,
Mynystred mete byfore þo Men þat myȝtes al weldez.
Þenne Þay sayden as Þay sete samen alle þrynne, 645
When þe mete watz remued and Þay of mensk speken,
'I schal efte hereaway, Abram,' Þay sayden,
'Ȝet er þy lyuez lyȝt leþe vpon erþe,
And þenne schal Saré consayue and a sun bere, [f66ʳ]
Þat schal be Abrahamez ayre and after hym wynne 650
With wele and wyth worschyp þe worþely peple
Þat schal halde in heritage þat I haf men ȝarked.'
Þenne þe burde byhynde þe dor for busmar laȝed;
And sayde sothly to hirself Saré þe madde:
'May þou traw for tykle þat þou teme moȝtez, 655
And I so hyȝe out of age, and also my lorde?'
For soþely, as says þe wryt, he wern of sadde elde,
Boþe þe wyȝe and his wyf, such werk watz hem fayled
Fro mony a brod day byfore; ho barayn ay bydene,
Þat selue Saré, withouten sede into þat same tyme. 660
Þenne sayde oure Syre þer He sete: 'Se! so Saré laȝes,

---

652. ȝarked (Fischer)] MS ȝark
655. teme (Emerson)] MS tonne
659. bydene (Gollancz)] MS byene

644. *þat myȝtes al weldez:* This is typical of the epithets the poet habitually applies to God (see 5n): its application to the three persons stresses their identification with God.

647f. '"I shall return here, Abraham," They said, "once more before your spark of life on earth ceases"'.

652. 'who will hold in heritage what I have granted to men.' Gollancz's emendation of *men* to *hem* is unnecessary.

654. *sothly:* 'softly, quietly' (cf. *G* 673n).

655. 'Can you believe that it is unlikely that you may conceive?' Sarah's words to herself are ironic, mocking the notion that she should be expected to believe that this could happen. Like the Dreamer in *Pe* and Jonah in *Pat*, she fails to distinguish between what is possible to God and what is possible to man. Cf. 581–90, *Pat* 121–4n.

657. *as says þe wryt:* The reference is to Gen. 18:11. *He wern:* the plural verb appears to be used in anticipation of the compound subject *Boþe þe wyȝe and his wyf* substituted in the next line (cf. *G* 2411f for a similar revision of the indirect object, not involving grammatical agreement). Gollancz suggests emending to *hit wern* (cf. 112); however, in view of the freedom of ME pronominal usage in regard to agreement of number (cf. T. F. Mustanoia, *A Middle English Syntax*, Part I, Parts of Speech [Helsinki, 1960], p. 141f), the MS reading may be genuine. Cf. 378, 889, *G* 1984–6.

Not trawande þe tale þat I þe to schewed.
Hopez ho oȝt may be harde My hondez to work?
And ȝet I avow verayly þe avaunt þat I made;
I schal ȝeply aȝayn and ȝelde þat I hyȝt,   665
And sothely sende to Saré a soun and an hayre.'
Þenne swenged forth Saré and swer by hir trawþe
Þat for lot þat Þay laused ho laȝed neuer.
'Now innoghe: hit is not so,' þenne nurned þe Dryȝtyn,
'For þou laȝed aloȝ, bot let we hit one.'   670
With þat Þay ros vp radly, as Þay rayke schulde,
And setten toward Sodamas Her syȝt alle at onez;
For þat cité þerbysyde watz sette in a vale,
No mylez fro Mambre mo þen tweyne,
Whereso wonyed þis ilke wyȝ, þat wendez with oure Lorde   675
For to tent Hym with tale and teche Hym þe gate.
Þen glydez forth God; þe godmon Hym folȝez;
Abraham heldez Hem wyth, Hem to conueye
Towarde þe cety of Sodamas þat synned had þenne
In þe faute of þis fylþe. Þe Fader hem þretes,   680
And sayde þus to þe segg þat sued Hym after:
'How myȝt I hyde Myn hert fro Habraham þe trwe,
Þat I ne dyscouered to his corse My counsayl so dere,
Syþen he is chosen to be chef chyldryn fader,
Þat so folk schal falle fro to flete alle þe worlde,   [f66ᵛ]   685
And vche blod in þat burne blessed schal worþe?
Me bos telle to þat tolk þe tene of My wylle,
And alle Myn atlyng to Abraham vnhaspe bilyue.
The grete soun of Sodamas synkkez in Myn erez,
And þe gult of Gomorre garez Me to wrath.   690

679.   Towarde] MS in towarde

663.   'does she think that anything can be difficult for My hands to accomplish?'
665.   'I shall soon come again and give what I promised'. Cf *G* 1981.
668.   'that she had not laughed at the speech They uttered.'
670.   'for you laughed softly, but let us leave that alone.'
674–6. 'no more than two miles from Mambre, where lived this same man (Abraham), who goes with our Lord in order to attend Him with conversation and show Him the way.'
679.   *Towarde:* MS *in* appears to have been caught up from the beginning of the following line.
682.   Once again, God's response and motivation are seen in human terms: see note to 197ff.
683.   *his corse:* 'him'. Cf. *my cors, G* 1237n.
684–6. 'since he is chosen to be the chief father of children, from whom people will spring so as to fill all the world, and each descendant shall be blessed because of that man?'

I schal lyȝt into þat led and loke Myseluen
If þay haf don as þe dyne dryuez on lofte.
Þay han lerned a lyst þat lykez me ille,
Þat þay han founden in her flesch of fautez þe werst:
Vch male matz his mach a man as hymseluen,   695
And fylter folyly in fere on femmalez wyse.
I compast hem a kynde crafte and kende hit hem derne,
And amed hit in Myn ordenaunce oddely dere,
And dyȝt drwry þerinne, doole alþer-swettest,
And þe play of paramorez I portrayed Myseluen,   700
And made þerto a maner myriest of oþer:
When two true togeder had tyȝed hemseluen,
Bytwene a male and his make such merþe schulde come,
Welnyȝe pure paradys moȝt preue no better;
Ellez þay moȝt honestly ayþer oþer welde,   705
At a stylle stollen steuen, vnstered wyth syȝt,
Luf-lowe hem bytwene lasched so hote
Þat alle þe meschefez on mold moȝt hit not sleke.
Now haf þay skyfted My skyl and scorned natwre,
And henttez hem in heþyng an vsage vnclene.   710
Hem to smyte for þat smod smartly I þenk,
Þat wyȝez schal be by hem war, worlde withouten ende.'
Þenne arȝed Abraham and alle his mod chaunged,
For hope of þe harde hate þat hyȝt hatz oure Lorde.

---

692. if] MS inf (īf)
703. come] MS conne
713. chaunged] MS chaunge

---

695. *as:* 'like'.
697–700. 'I devised a natural way for them and taught it to them secretly, and esteemed it in My ordinance singularly precious, and set love within it, intercourse sweetest of all, and I Myself devised the play of love'. *Doole:* though the primary sense is probably 'sharing, intercourse' (*OED dole* sb¹, sense 7), there may be also a punning allusion to *do(e)l* 'grief, lamentation' and to the commonplace of the sweet sorrow of love.
697–708. This emphatic statement of the value of sexual love is a startlingly unusual attitude to find in a medieval homiletic poem—particularly as the poet gives these words to God (see Introduction, p. 24f).
705–8. 'provided that they would possess each other in a proper manner, at a quiet secret meeting, undisturbed by sight, the flame of love would blaze so hot between them that all the evils on earth would not be able to quench it.'
711f. 'I intend to smite them severely for that filth, so that men will be warned by them, for ever and ever.' God states his intention to make examples of the inhabitants of Sodom and Gomorrah—an idea not derived from the account in Gen. (The poet himself is, of course, using their story in precisely this way.)
714. *For hope of:* 'in the expectation of'.

Al sykande he sayde: 'Sir, with Yor leue,   715
Schal synful and saklez suffer al on payne?
Weþer euer hit lyke my Lorde to lyfte such domez
Þat þe wykked and þe worþy schal on wrake suffer,
And weye vpon þe worre half þat wrathed Þe neuer?
Þat watz neuer Þy won þat wroȝtez vus alle.   720
Now fyfty fyn frendez wer founde in ȝonde toune,   [f67ʳ]
In þe cety of Sodamas and also Gomorre,
Þat neuer lakked Þy laue, bot loued ay trauþe,
And reȝtful wern and resounable and redy Þe to serue,
Schal þay falle in þe faute þat oþer frekez wroȝt,   725
And joyne to her juggement, her juise to haue?
Þat nas neuer Þyn note, vnneuened hit worþe,
Þat art so gaynly a God and of goste mylde.'
'Nay, for fyfty,' quoþ þe Fader, 'and þy fayre speche,
And þay be founden in þat folk of her fylþe clene,   730
I schal forgyue alle þe gylt þurȝ My grace one,
And let hem smolt al unsmyten smoþely at onez.'
'Aa! blessed be Þow,' quoþ þe burne, 'so boner and þewed,
And al haldez in Þy honde, þe heuen and þe erþe;
Bot, for I towched haf þis talke, tatz to non ille   735
Ȝif I mele a lyttel more þat mul am and askez.
What if fyue faylen of fyfty þe noumbre,
And þe remnaunt be reken, how restes Þy wylle?'
'And fyue wont of fyfty,' quoþ God, 'I schal forȝete alle
And wythhalde My honde for hortyng on lede.'   740
'And quat if faurty be fre and fauty þyse oþer:
Schalt Þow schortly al schende and schape non oþer?'

---

735.   towched] MS *om.*

717–19.   'Would it ever please my Lord to decree such judgements that the wicked
and the worthy must suffer the same punishment, and to weigh on the more wicked
side those who never angered You?'

721.   'Now if fifty good friends were found in yonder town'.

726.   'and share in their judgement, to have their doom?'

727.   *vnneuened hit worþe:* 'let it be unthought of (*lit.* unnamed).'

730.   *And:* 'if'.

735.   *towched:* A verb beginning with *t* is almost certainly missing from the line.
Though this emendation is conjectural, there are in fact relatively few words in the
vocabulary of the MS which would fit both the alliterative pattern and the sense. Cf.
1437 and *G* 1541, where *towche* alliterates with *tale*. *Tatz to non ille:* cf. *G* 1811.

736.   'if I who am dust and ashes speak a little more.' Cf. 747 and *Pe* 905.

737f.   'What if five be lacking from the total of fifty, and the rest are pure—how does
Your wish stand?'

740.   *for hortyng on lede:* 'from harming one man'.

'Nay, þaʒ faurty forfete, ʒet fryst I a whyle,
And voyde away My vengaunce, þaʒ Me vyl þynk.'
Þen Abraham obeched Hym and loʒly Him þonkkez: 745
'Now sayned be Þou, Sauiour, so symple in Þy wrath!
I am bot erþe ful euel and vsle so blake,
For to mele wyth such a Mayster as myʒtez hatz alle.
Bot I haue bygonnen wyth my God, and He hit gayn þynkez;
ʒif I forloyne as a fol Þy fraunchyse may serue. 750
What if þretty þryuande be þrad in ʒon tounez,
What schal I leue of my Lorde—if He hem leþe wolde?'
Þenne þe godlych God gef hym onsware:
'ʒet for þretty in þrong I schal My þro steke,
And spare spakly of spyt in space of My þewez, 755
And My rankor refrayne four þy reken wordez.'
'What for twenty,' quoþ þe tolke, 'vntwynez Þou hem þenne?' [f67ᵛ]
'Nay, ʒif þou ʒernez hit ʒet, ʒark I hem grace;
If þat twenty be trwe, I tene hem no more,
Bot relece alle þat regioun of her ronk werkkez.' 760
'Now, aþel Lorde,' quoþ Abraham, 'onez a speche,
And I schal schape no more þo schalkkez to helpe.
If ten trysty in toune be tan in Þi werkkez,
Wylt Þou mese Þy mode and menddyng abyde?'
'I graunt,' quoþ þe grete God, 'Graunt mercy,' þat oþer; 765
And þenne arest þe renk and raʒt no fyrre.
And Godde glydez His gate by þose grene wayez,

---

752. of] MS if

743. 'No, if forty were to lose their right, yet I would delay for a while'.
744. Cf. *Pat* 284.
745. This line is irregular in alliteration, and may therefore be faulty. Previous editors have suggested various emendations, but, as none of these is particularly convincing and the unemended line makes good sense, it has been allowed to stand.
749f. 'But I have begun (to speak) with my God, and it seems good to Him (i.e. God has approved so far); if I, as a fool, go astray, Your magnanimity will suffice.' Abraham realizes that God's wisdom and mercy is not subject to human limitations—a point which Sarah has earlier failed to understand (see 655n).
752. 'what shall I believe of my Lord—would He be merciful to them?'
754f. 'Even for thirty in the throng I shall restrain My anger, and immediately hold back from wrath in the delay afforded by My noble qualities'.
758. 'No, if you still desire it, I will grant them grace'.
761. *onez a speche:* 'one word more'.
763f. 'If ten citizens faithful in Your works are found, will You moderate Your anger and await amendment?' Presumably Abraham, asking God to pardon the sinful majority for the sake of the virtuous minority, is merely expressing the hope that God's patience would be rewarded by the sinners mending their ways.

And he conueyen Hym con with cast of his y3e;
And als he loked along þereas oure Lorde passed,
3et he cryed Hym after with careful steuen: 770
'Meke Mayster, on Þy mon to mynne if Þe lyked,
Loth lengez in 3on leede þat is my lef broþer;
He syttez þer in Sodomis, Þy seruaunt so pouere,
Among þo mansed men þat han Þe much greued.
3if Þou tynez þat toun, tempre Þyn yre,   775
As Þy mersy may malte, Þy meke to spare.'
Þen he wendez his way, wepande for care,
Towarde þe mere of Mambre, mornande for sorewe;
And þere in longyng al ny3t he lengez in wones,
Whyl þe Souerayn to Sodamas sende to spye.   780
His sonde into Sodamas watz sende in þat tyme,
In þat ilk euentyde, by aungels tweyne,
Meuand mekely togeder as myry men 3onge,
As Loot in a loge dor lened hym alone,
In a porche of þat place py3t to þe 3ates,   785
Þat watz ryal and ryche so watz þe renkes seluen.
As he stared into þe strete þer stout men played,

777. wendez] MS *repeats*
778. mornande (Menner)] MS wepande
781. sonde (Gollancz)] MS sondes
783. Meuand] MS *repeats*

768. 'and he followed Him with his eyes (*lit.* with the glance of his eye)'.
771–6. This special plea of Abraham for Lot is not in the biblical account.
771. 'Merciful Master, if it would please You to remember Your man'.
772. *broþer:* Abraham is in fact Lot's uncle: see 924n.
773. *pouere:* 'poor'. In terms of worldly possessions, Lot is rich (see 786n, 812, 878). The word *pouere* is probably here intended to suggest spiritual poverty, the quality celebrated in the first beatitude (Matt. 5:3), and consisting in humble obedience to the will of God.
775f. 'If You destroy that town, temper Your wrath, as Your mercy may soften (it), to spare Your meek (follower).'
778. *mornande for sorewe:* The MS reads *wepande for care*, as the result of a scribe's erroneously copying the last three words of the previous line. *Care* is altered to *sorewe* by a later (but still medieval) hand. *Wepande* is emended to *mornande* to avoid repetition and to fit the alliterative pattern. (There is considerable evidence of scribal inattention at this point in the MS—777, 778, and 783 all containing minor errors.)
780. 'while the Sovereign sent someone to Sodom to investigate.'
781. *sonde:* The sense is evidently 'message' and the singular form agrees with the following verb; the scribal *sondes* may have arisen from misinterpretation of the word as 'messenger'.
786. 'which was royal and rich as was the man himself.' Lot's wealth was traditional: see 773n, 812, 878.

He syȝe þer swey in asent swete men tweyne;
Bolde burnez wer þay boþe with berdles chynnez,
Ryol rollande fax to raw sylk lyke,   790
Of ble as þe brere-flour whereso þe bare scheweed.
Ful clene watz þe countenaunce of her cler yȝen;
Wlonk whit watz her wede and wel hit hem semed.   [f68ʳ]
Of alle feturez ful fyn and fautlez boþe;
Watz non aucly in ouþer, for aungels hit wern,   795
And þat þe ȝep vnderȝede þat in þe ȝate syttez;
He ros vp ful radly and ran hem to mete,
And loȝe he loutez hem to, Loth, to þe grounde,
And syþen soberly: 'Syrez, I yow byseche
Þat ȝe wolde lyȝt at my loge and lenge þerinne.   800
Comez to your knaues kote, I craue at þis onez;
I schal fette yow a fatte your fette for to wasche;
I norne yow bot for on nyȝt neȝe me to lenge,
And in þe myry mornyng ȝe may your waye take.'
And þay nay þat þay nolde neȝ no howsez,   805
Bot stylly þer in þe strete as þay stadde wern
Þay wolde lenge þe long naȝt and logge þeroute:
Hit watz hous innoȝe to hem þe heuen vpon lofte.
Loth laþed so longe wyth luflych wordez
Þat þay hym grauntet to go and gruȝt no lenger.   810
Þe bolde to his byggyng bryngez hem bylyue,
Þat watz ryally arayed, for he watz ryche euer.
Þe wyȝez wern welcom as þe wyf couþe;
His two dere doȝterez deuoutly hem haylsed,
Þat wer maydenez ful meke, maryed not ȝet,   815

790. Ryol] MS royl
795. aucly] MS autly
812. Þat watz (Morris)] MS þat

788. 'he saw two fair men walking there together'.

789ff. In medieval portraits, both verbal and pictorial, angels are normally characterized by fair boyish beauty: see J. Villette, *L'Ange dans L'Art Occident du XII–XVI*ᵉ *Siècle* (Paris, 1940).

790. *Ryol:* The reversal of *yo* is probably scribal; this word is consistently spelled *ry-* or *ri-*.

795f. 'none (i.e. no feature) was unbecoming in either, for they were angels, and the alert man who sits in the gate understood that'.

799ff. Lot immediately recognizes the angels for what they are, and adopts the role and manner of a servant before his lord: cf. note to 612ff.

802f. 'I shall fetch you a tub to wash your feet; I entreat you to stay with me for just one night'. Cf. 618.

805. 'And they said that they would not come near any house'. Cf. *G* 1836.

809f. 'Lot urged them so long with courteous words that they consented to come with him and no longer refused.'

813. *as:* 'as well as'.

And þay wer semly and swete, and swyþe wel arayed.
Loth þenne ful lyȝtly lokez hym aboute,
And his men amonestes mete for to dyȝt:
'Bot þenkkez on hit be þrefte what þynk so ȝe make,
For wyth no sour ne no salt seruez hym neuer.'   820
Bot ȝet I wene þat þe wyf hit wroth to dyspyt,
And sayde softely to hirself: 'Þis vnsaueré hyne
Louez no salt in her sauce; ȝet hit no skyl were
Þat oþer burne be boute, þaȝ boþe be nyse.'
Þenne ho sauerez with salt her seuez vchone,   825
Agayne þe bone of þe burne þat hit forboden hade,
And als ho scelt hem in scorne þat wel her skyl knewen.
Why watz ho, wrech, so wod? Ho wrathed oure Lorde.
Þenne seten þay at þe soper, wern serued bylyue,   [f68ᵛ]
Þe gestes gay and ful glad, of glam debonere,   830
Welawynnely wlonk, tyl þay waschen hade,
Þe trestes tylt to þe woȝe and þe table boþe.
Fro þe seggez haden souped and seten bot a whyle,
Er euer þay bosked to bedde, þe borȝ watz al vp,
Alle þat weppen myȝt welde, þe wakker and þe stronger,   835
To vmbelyȝe Lothez hous þe ledez to take.
In grete flokkez of folk þay fallen to his ȝatez;
As a scowte-wach scarred so þe asscry rysed;

---

822. vnsaueré (Morris)] MS vnfauere

817ff. The episode in which Lot's wife puts salt into the food does not occur in the Bible, but the story and its thematic link with her ultimate fate (see 996–1000) are well known in Hebraic tradition; see O. F. Emerson, *MLR*, 10 (1915), 373–5.

819–24. '"But remember that whatever you make must be unleavened, for you must never serve them with leaven nor with salt." But yet I think the woman turned it to defiance, and said quietly to herself: "These disagreeable fellows like no salt in their sauce; yet it would be unreasonable that anyone else should go without, even though both of them are fastidious."' The application by Lot's wife of the disrespectful term *vnsaueré hyne* to the angels emphasizes the contrast between her attitude to divine authority and Lot's. Gollancz (2nd edn., p. xxvi) explains that 'the angels must not be offered leaven, which sets up fermentation, a form of corruption'.

827. 'and also she reviled with scorn those who well perceived her attitude.'

828. Cf. the similar tone in *Pat* 113f.

831. *tyl þay waschen hade:* 'until they had washed': i.e. until the meal was finished.

832. 'both the trestles and the tables leant against the wall.' Cf. *G* 884, 1648.

833. *Fro:* 'after'.

836. *þe ledez:* i.e. the angels.

838f. 'the shout rose as though from a terrified watchman; with stout clubs they clatter on the walls of that house'. The word *clos* should perhaps be translated 'enclosure': the poet probably has in mind a house and land enclosed by a perimeter wall. *Clatrez* (839): a verb *clatz* is not elsewhere attested: a scribe appears to have omitted the 're' abbreviation.

With kene clobbez of þat clos þay clatrez on þe wowez,
And wyth a schrylle scharp schout þay schewe þyse wordez: 840
'If þou louyez þy lyf, Loth, in þyse wones,
Ӡete vus out þose ӡong men þat ӡore-whyle here entred,
Þat we may lere hym of lof, as oure lyst biddez,
As is þe asyse of Sodomas to seggez þat passen.'
Whatt! þay sputen and speken of so spitous fylþe,   845
What! þay ӡeӡed and ӡolped of ӡestande sorӡe,
Þat ӡet þe wynd and þe weder and þe worlde stynkes
Of þe brych þat vpbraydez þose broþelych wordez.
Þe godman glyfte with þat glam and gloped for noyse;
So scharpe schame to hym schot, he schrank at þe hert.   850
For he knew þe costoum þat kyþed þose wrechez,
He doted neuer for no doel so depe in his mynde.
'Allas!' sayd hym þenne Loth, and lyӡtly he rysez,
And bowez forth fro þe bench into þe brode ӡates.
What! he wonded no woþe of wekked knauez,   855
Þat he ne passed þe port þe peril to abide.
He went forthe at þe wyket and waft hit hym after,
Þat a clyket hit cleӡt clos hym byhynde.
Þenne he meled to þo men mesurable wordez,
For harlotez with his hendelayk he hoped to chast: 860
'Oo, my frendez so fre, your fare is to strange;
Dotz away your derf dyn and derez neuer my gestes.
Avoy! hit is your vylaynye, ӡe vylen yourseluen;

---

839. clatrez] MS clatz (Gollancz: claterz)
840. wordez] MS worde
856. peril] MS pil

841–4. 'If you love (i.e. value) your life, Lot, in these lands, send out to us those young men who entered here a little while ago, so we can teach them about love, as our desire prompts, as the custom of Sodom is to men who pass through.'
845f. *What(t)!:* Cf. *G* 2201–4n.
847f. 'so that the wind and the sky and the earth still stink from the vomit that those venomous words throw up.' Sin is often associated with foul smell: see the description of the belly of the whale in *Pat* (especially 274f).
855f. 'Lo! he feared no harm from wicked knaves, which would stop him from passing through the gate to face the danger.'
860. 'for he hoped to restrain evil men with his courtesy'.
861–72. Rabanus Maurus, in his *Commentary on Genesis* (*PL* 107: 555), suggests, as compensation for Lot's sin in offering to prostitute his daughters, his concern for his guests, his wish to avoid a greater wrong (the insult to the angels), and his perturbation of mind. Nevertheless, Rabanus gravely remarks that Lot's conduct *nullo modo imitanda est* ('is by no means to be imitated'). We need not suppose that, however sympathetically the poet presents Lot, he entirely endorses Lot's behaviour in this respect. (See Introduction, p. 24f.)

And 3e are jolyf gentylmen, your japez ar ille.
Bot I schal kenne yow by kynde a crafte þat is better: [f69ʳ]   865
I haf a tresor in my telde of tow my fayre de3ter,
Þat ar maydenez vnmard for alle men 3ette;
In Sodamas, þa3 I hit say, non semloker burdes;
Hit arn ronk, hit arn rype, and redy to manne;
To samen wyth þo semly þe solace is better.   870
I schal biteche yow þo two þat tayt arn and quoynt,
And laykez wyth hem as yow lyst, and letez my gestes one.'
Þenne þe rebaudez so ronk rerd such a noyse
Þat a3ly hurled in his erez her harlotez speche:
'Wost þou not wel þat þou wonez here a wy3e strange,   875
An outcomlyng, a carle? We kylle of þyn heued!
Who joyned þe be jostyse oure japez to blame,
Þat com a boy to þis bor3, þa3 þou be burne ryche?'
Þus þay þrobled and þrong and þrwe vmbe his erez,
And distresed hym wonder strayt with strenkþe in þe prece,   880
Bot þat þe 3onge men, so 3epe, 3ornen þeroute,
Wapped vpon þe wyket and wonnen hem tylle,
And by þe hondez hym hent and horyed hym withinne,
And steken þe 3ates ston-harde wyth stalworth barrez.
Þay blwe a boffet inblande þat banned peple,   885
Þat þay blustered, as blynde as Bayard watz euer;
Þay lest of Lotez logging any lysoun to fynde,
Bot nyteled þer alle þe ny3t for no3t at þe last.
Þenne vch tolke ty3t hem, þat hade of tayt fayled,
And vchon roþeled to þe rest þat he reche mo3t;   890
Bot þay wern wakned al wrank þat þer in won lenged,

875–8. According to Gen. 13:12, Lot went to live in the cities of the plain after his separation from Abraham.

877. *joyned:* 'appointed' (as in *Pat* 62).

880f. 'and would have harrassed him very hard, by force in the throng, but that the young men, so prompt, ran out'.

885f. 'They (the angels) struck a blow among that cursed people, so that they strayed about, as blind as Bayard ever was'. With *inblande,* cf. *inmyddes* (*G* 167, 1932); the word is probably identical with the prep. *ebland* (*Wars of Alexander* 4086, 4315, 5444). The blindness of Bayard, supposedly Charlemagne's horse, was proverbial (see Whiting, B.71).

889. *hem:* cf. 657n.

891f. 'but those who lived in the town there were woken quite awry by the very ugliest calamity ever suffered on earth.' *Wakned al wrank* appears to be grimly humorous understatement (cf. Towneley Plays, No. 13, 381). *On þe vglokest* (892): see *G* 137n. Gollancz's emendation clarifies both syntax and sense.

Of on þe vglokest vnhap euer on erd suffred.
Ruddon of þe day-rawe ros vpon vȝten,
When merk of þe mydnyȝt moȝt no more last.
Ful erly þose aungelez þis haþel þay ruþen,   895
And glopnedly on Godez halue gart hym vpryse;
Fast þe freke ferkez vp ful ferd at his hert;
Þay comaunded hym cof to cach þat he hade,
'Wyth þy wyf and þy wyȝez and þy wlonc deȝtters,
For we laþe þe, sir Loth, þat þou þy lyf haue.   900
Cayre tid of þis kythe er combred þou worþe,   [f69ᵛ]
With alle þi here vpon haste, tyl þou a hil fynde;
Foundez faste on your fete; bifore your face lokes,
Bot bes neuer so bolde to blusch yow bihynde,
And loke ȝe stemme no stepe, bot strechez on faste;   905
Til ȝe reche to a reset, rest ȝe neuer.
For we schal tyne þis toun and trayþely disstrye,
Wyth alle þise wyȝez so wykke wyȝtly devoyde,
And alle þe londe with þise ledez we losen at onez;
Sodomas schal ful sodenly synk into grounde,   910
And þe grounde of Gomorre gorde into helle,
And vche a koste of þis kythe clater vpon hepes.'
Þen laled Loth: 'Lorde, what is best?
If I me fele vpon fote þat I fle moȝt,
Hov schulde I huyde me fro Hym þat hatz His hate kynned   915
In þe brath of His breth þat brennez alle þinkez?
To crepe fro my Creatour I know not wheder,
Ne wheþer His fooschip me folȝez bifore oþer bihynde.'
Þe freke sayde: 'No foschip oure Fader hatz þe schewed,
Bot hiȝly heuened þi hele fro hem þat arn combred.   920

892. euer (Gollancz)] MS þat euer
915. Hym (Gollancz)] MS hem
917. I (Gollancz)] MS and (ꞇ)

896. 'and made him get up in alarm, in the name of God'.
901–6. 'Go quickly from this country before you are destroyed, in haste with all your household, till you find a hill; go quickly on your feet; look in front of your face, but never be so bold as to look behind you, and see that you do not delay a step, but press on fast; till you reach refuge, never rest.'
910–13. Compare Jonah's prophecy about Nineveh: *Pat* 361–4.
913–18. Unlike Jonah (*Pat* 83–8, 109–28), Lot realizes that it is impossible to hide from the wrath of God. It is a characteristic of the positive characters in the poem that they understand something of the nature of God, as does Abraham: see notes to 655 and 749f.
914–16. 'If I were to conceal myself as far as I could flee on foot (i.e. as far as my legs could carry me), how should I hide myself from Him who has aroused His hate in the ferocity of His breath, which burns all things?'

Nov wale þe a wonnyng þat þe warisch myȝt,
And He schal saue hit for þy sake þat hatz vus sende hider,
For þou art oddely þyn one out of þis fylþe,
And als Abraham þyn eme hit at Himself asked.'
'Lorde, loued He worþe,' quoþ Loth, 'vpon erþe!   925
Þer is a cité herbisyde þat Segor hit hatte—
Here vtter on a rounde hil hit houez hit one.
I wolde, if His wylle wore, to þat won scape.'
'Þenn fare forth,' quoþ þat fre, 'and fyne þou neuer,
With þose ilk þat þow wylt þat þrenge þe after,   930
And ay goande on your gate, wythouten agayn-tote,
For alle þis londe schal be lorne longe er þe sonne rise.'
Þe wyȝe wakened his wyf and his wlonk deȝteres,
And oþer two myri men þo maydenez schulde wedde;
And þay token hit as tayt and tented hit lyttel;   935
Þaȝ fast laþed hem Loth, þay leȝen ful stylle.
Þe aungelez hasted þise oþer and aȝly hem þratten,   [f 70ʳ]
And enforsed alle fawre forth at þe ȝatez:
Þo wern Loth and his lef, his luflyche deȝter;
Þer soȝt no mo to sauement of cities aþel fyue.   940
Þise aungelez hade hem by hande out at þe ȝatez,
Prechande hem þe perile, and beden hem passe fast:

926. þer] MS þen
935. tayt (Menner)] MS tyt

921–8. '"Now chose yourself a dwelling place which may protect you, and He who
has sent us here will preserve it for your sake, for you entirely alone are free from this
filth, and also Abraham your uncle asked (God) Himself for it." "Lord, may He be
praised on earth!" said Lot. There is a city near here that is called Zoar—outside
here it stands alone on a round hill. I would like, if it is His will, to escape to that
city." ' *þyn eme* (924): the letters *n eme* have been partially erased, and the word
broþer written over them in a later hand. This alteration may well have been inspired
by a literal interpretation of the statement in 772.

933–9. 'The man wakened his wife and his noble daughters, and two other excellent
men that those maidens were intended to marry; and they took it as sport and gave it
little attention; though Lot called them earnestly, they lay quite still. The angels
hastened the others and urged them on menacingly, and drove all four out of the
gates: these were Lot and his dear (wife) and his lovely daughters'. Though 933f is
about Lot's wife, daughters, and two prospective sons in law, *þay* in 935f denotes
only the two young men—who refuse to leave (cf. Gen. 19:14–16). Clearly, *þise oþer*
(937) refers to Lot's wife and daughters: 938f and Gen. 19:13–16 indicate that the
only survivors are these three and Lot. The subsequent well-known story about Lot's
incest with his daughters (Gen. 19:20–28) depends on their not having husbands.
Tayt (935): Menner's emendation is adopted. The MS reading probably resulted
from a scribe's mistaking *as tayt* for the common *as tyt* ('quickly').

940. *cities aþel fyue*: see 1015n.

'Lest ȝe be taken in þe teche of tyrauntez here,
Loke ȝe bowe now bi bot; bowez fast hence!'
And þay kayre ne con, and kenely flowen. 945
Erly, er any heuen-glem, þay to a hil comen.
Þe grete God in His greme bygynnez on lofte
To waken wederez so wylde; þe wyndez He callez,
And þay wroþely vpwafte and wrastled togeder,
Fro fawre half of þe folde flytande loude. 950
Clowdez clustered bytwene kesten vp torres,
Þat þe þik þunder-þrast þirled hem ofte.
Þe rayn rueled adoun, ridlande þikke
Of felle flaunkes of fyr and flakes of soufre,
Al in smolderande smoke smachande ful ille, 955
Swe aboute Sodamas and hit sydez alle,
Gorde to Gomorra, þat þe grounde laused,
Abdama and Syboym, þise ceteis alle faure
Al birolled wyth þe rayn, rostted and brenned,
And ferly flayed þat folk þat in þose fees lenged. 960
For when þat þe Helle herde þe houndez of heuen,
He watz ferlyly fayn, vnfolded bylyue;
Þe grete barrez of þe abyme he barst vp at onez,
Þat alle þe regioun torof in riftes ful grete,
And clouen alle in lyttel cloutes þe clyffez aywhere, 965
As lauce leuez of þe boke þat lepes in twynne.
Þe brethe of þe brynston bi þat hit blende were,

948. waken] MS wakan

943–5. '"Lest you are caught in the sin of evil men here, see that you obey the command now; go quickly from here!" And they did not lament, but quickly fled.' With 943 cf. *G* 2488. With the *traductio* (word-play) of 944 cf. *G* 2276.
947ff. Cf. the description of the winds in *Pat* 131ff, and *G* 525.
951. *torres*: 'towers'—i.e. towering clouds, perhaps specifically thunder clouds: see *Pe* 875n.
957. 'struck Gomorrah, so that the ground opened'.
960. 'and the people who dwelt in those cities greatly terrified.'
961f. 'For when Hell heard the hounds of heaven, he was wonderfully glad, and opened at once'. Hell is personified, as it is systematically in the Gospel of Nicodemus. Gollancz observes that the *houndez of heuen* may be related to the Northern tradition of the 'Gabriel hounds', a mysterious pack whose appearance in the sky presaged disaster. One might also compare the Greyhound in Dante's *Inferno* I.100–111.
966. 'as leaves split away from a book that bursts apart.' The startling perspective of the image emphasizes man's feebleness in relation to God's enormous power: cf. *Pat* 268, which has a similar effect.
967–9. 'By the time the smoke from the brimstone had ceased, all those cities and their surroundings sank into hell. Those great crowds of men within did not know what to do (*lit.* were without counsel)'.

Al þo citees and her sydes sunkken to helle.
Rydelles wern þo grete rowtes of renkkes withinne,
When þay wern war of þe wrake þat no wyȝe achaped;   970
Such a ȝomerly ȝarm of ȝeĺlyng þer rysed,
Þerof clatered þe cloudes, þat Kryst myȝt haf rawþe.
Þe segge herde þat soun to Segor þat ȝede,   [f 70ᵛ]
And þe wenches hym wyth þat by þe way folȝed;
Ferly ferde watz her flesch þat flowen ay ilyche,   975
Trynande ay a hyȝe trot, þat torne neuer dorsten.
Loth and þo luly-whit, his lefly two deȝter,
Ay folȝed here face, bifore her boþe yȝen;
Bot þe balleful burde, þat neuer bode keped,
Blusched byhynden her bak þat bale for to herkken.   980
Hit watz lusty Lothes wyf þat ouer her lyfte schulder
Ones ho bluschet to þe burȝe, bot bod ho no lenger
Þat ho nas stadde a stiffe ston, a stalworth image,
Al so salt as ani se—and so ho ȝet standez.
Þay slypped bi and syȝe hir not þat wern hir samen-feres,   985
Tyl þay in Segor wern sette, and sayned our Lorde;
Wyth lyȝt louez vplyfte þay loued Hym swyþe,
Þat so His seruauntes wolde see and saue of such woþe.
Al watz dampped and don and drowned by þenne;
Þe ledez of þat lyttel toun wern lopen out for drede   990
Into þat malscrande mere, marred bylyue,
Þat noȝt saued watz bot Segor, þat sat on a lawe.
Þe þre ledez þerin lent, Loth and his deȝter;
For his make watz myst, þat on þe mount lenged

---

981. her (Morris)] MS he
993. lent (Gollancz)] MS *om.*

973–6. 'The man who was going to Zoar heard that sound, and the girls with him
who accompanied him on the way; they were (*lit.* their flesh was) terribly frightened
as they continued to flee, going all the time at a quick run, and never daring to turn.'
979. 'but the wretched woman, who never obeyed a command'.
982–5. 'she looked at the city once, but she waited no longer before she was fixed a
rigid stone, a sturdy statue, as salt as any sea—and thus she still stands. Those who
were her companions slipped by and did not see her'.
986–8. Their response to survival is similar to that of Noah and his companions: cf.
497.
988. 'who was thus prepared to look after and save His servants from such harm.'
992. 'so that nothing was saved but Zoar, that was set on a hill.'
993. *lent:* 'dwelt, remained'. Gollancz's emendation makes good the lack of a verb
and of an alliterative stave. However, he reads *lent þerin:* here the word order *þerin
lent*, which provides better alliterative rhythm, is adopted.

In a stonen statue þat salt sauor habbes,⠀⠀⠀⠀⠀⠀⠀⠀⠀⠀⠀995
For two fautes þat þe fol watz founde in mistrauþe:
On, ho serued at þe soper salt bifore Dryȝtyn,
And syþen, ho blusched hir bihynde, þaȝ hir forboden were;
For on ho standes a ston, and salt for þat oþer,
And alle lyst on hir lik þat arn on launde bestes.⠀⠀⠀⠀⠀⠀1000
Abraham ful erly watz vp on þe morne,
Þat alle naȝt much niye hade nomen in his hert,
Al in longing for Loth leyen in a wache;
Þer he lafte hade oure Lorde he is on lofte wonnen;
He sende toward Sodomas þe syȝt of his yȝen,⠀⠀⠀⠀⠀⠀1005
Þat euer hade ben an erde of erþe þe swettest,
As aparaunt to paradis, þat plantted þe Dryȝtyn;
Nov is hit plunged in a pit like of pich fylled.
Suche a roþun of a reche ros fro þe blake,⠀⠀⠀⠀⠀⠀[f71ʳ]
Askez vpe in þe ayre and vsellez þer flowen,⠀⠀⠀⠀⠀1010
As a fornes ful of flot þat vpon fyr boyles
When bryȝt brennande brondez ar bet þeranvnder.
Þis watz a uengaunce violent þat voyded þise places,
Þat foundered hatz so fayr a folk and þe folde sonkken.
Þer þe fyue citées wern set nov is a see called,⠀⠀⠀⠀1015
Þat ay is drouy and dym, and ded in hit kynde,
Blo, blubrande, and blak, vnblyþe to neȝe;
As a stynkande stanc þat stryed synne,

1002. nomen (Menner)] MS no mon
1015. Þer þe fyue] MS þer faure (*see* note)

---

996. 'for two misdeeds in which the fool was found unfaithful'. Once more, human misconduct is seen in terms of a failure of *trawþe*: see note to 235–48 and Introduction, pp. 24–9.

1000. 'and all that are beasts in the field like to lick her.'

1004. 'he made his way up to (the place) where he had left our Lord'.

1006f. 'that had always been the sweetest region on earth, like a colony of paradise, which God established'. The comparison is from Gen. 13:10: *antequam subverteret Dominus Sodomam et Gomorrham, sicut paradisus Domini* 'before the Lord destroyed Sodom and Gomorrha, as the paradise of the Lord.'

1009. 'Such a red smoke (*lit*. redness of a smoke) arose from the black'.

1013. Cf. *Pat* 370: the destruction of the cities is of course very similar to the fate with which Jonah threatens the Ninevites.

1015. *Þer þe fyue:* The words of the original scribe have been erased and *þer faure* written over them in a later hand. However, traces of the original words remain; they probably read *þer þe fyue*. The later scribe probably made his emendation for the sake of consistency with 956ff, where the poet names four cities which are to be destroyed. In 926 God undertakes to spare Zoar (which would have been the fifth), and in 992 the poet confirms that it was spared. According to tradition it was destroyed many years later.

1018. 'that destroyed sin (is) like a stinking pool'.

Þat euer of smelle and of smach smart is to fele.
Forþy þe derk Dede See hit is demed euermore,   1020
For hit dedez of deþe duren þere ȝet;
For hit is brod and boþemlez, and bitter as þe galle,
And noȝt may lenge in þat lake þat any lyf berez,
And alle þe costez of kynde hit combrez vchone.
For lay þeron a lump of led, and hit on loft fletez,   1025
And folde þeron a lyȝt fyþer, and hit to founs synkkez;
And þer water may walter to wete any erþe
Schal neuer grene þeron growe, gresse ne wod nawþer.
If any schalke to be schent wer schowued þerinne,
Þaȝ he bode in þat boþem broþely a monyth,   1030
He most ay lyue in þat loȝe in losyng euermore,
And neuer dryȝe no dethe to dayes of ende.
And as hit is corsed of kynde and hit coostez als,
Þe clay þat clenges þerby arn corsyes strong,
As alum and alkaran, þat angré arn boþe,   1035
Soufre sour and saundyuer, and oþer such mony;
And þer waltez of þat water in waxlokes grete
Þe spumande aspaltoun þat spyserez sellen;
And suche is alle þe soyle by þat se halues,
Þat fel fretes þe flesch and festres bones.   1040
And þer ar tres by þat terne of traytoures,
And þay borgounez and beres blomez ful fayre,
And þe fayrest fryt þat may on folde growe,

1019.   smelle (Morris)] MS synne
1038.   spumande] MS spuniande
1040.   festres (Morris, Menner)] MS festred

1019.   *smelle:* It is probable that a scribe erroneously repeated *synne* from the previous
line. *Smelle* alliterates with *smach*, and they appear together in 461.
1021.   'for its deeds of death continue there yet'.
1025ff.   As the Dead Sea was brought about by sin—the perverse reversal of God's
natural order—so it is characterized by these reversals of natural properties and
functions. The poet's account draws details from *Mandeville's Travels (ed. cit. Cl* 448n,
50–51).
1029–32.   'If any man were pushed into it to be destroyed, though he might remain
wretchedly in that deep place for a month, he must always live in that lake in
perdition evermore, and never suffer death until the last days (i.e. the Last
Judgement).'
1037f.   'and there flows from that water in lumps of wax the foaming asphalt that
spicers sell'.
1043–8.   The ultimate source of this description of the bitter apples by the Dead Sea is
Josephus (*Wars* IV.viii.4), but the idea had become a commonplace in medieval
commentaries and encyclopedic writing. The poet emphasizes the contrast between
the apples' beautiful outer appearance and the bitterness of their inner substance:
thus they are made a telling symbol of the false seeming of sin. This sense is sup-

As orenge and oþer fryt and apple-garnade,
Also red and so ripe and rychely hwed   [f71ᵛ]   1045
As any dom myȝt deuice of dayntyez oute;
Bot quen hit is brused oþer broken, oþer byten in twynne,
No worldez goud hit wythinne, bot wyndowande askes.
Alle þyse ar teches and tokenes to trow vpon ȝet,
And wittnesse of þat wykked werk, and þe wrake after   1050
Þat oure Fader forþrede for fylþe of þose ledes.
Þenne vch wyȝe may wel wyt þat He þe wlonk louies;
And if He louyes clene layk þat is oure Lorde ryche,
And to be couþe in His courte þou coueytes þenne,
To se þat Semly in sete and His swete face,   1055
Clerrer counseyl con I non, bot þat þou clene worþe.
For Clopyngnel in þe compas of his clene *Rose*,
Þer he expounez a speche to hym þat spede wolde
Of a lady to be loued: 'Loke to hir sone
Of wich beryng þat ho be, and wych ho best louyes,   1060
And be ryȝt such in vch a borȝe of body and of dedes,
And folȝ þe fet of þat fere þat þou fre haldes;
And if þou wyrkkes on þis wyse, þaȝ ho wyk were,
Hir schal lyke þat layk þat lyknes hir tylle.'
If þou wyl dele drwrye wyth Dryȝtyn þenne,   1065

1051. forþrede] MS forferde (Gollancz forþerde)
1056. counseyl] MS repeats

---

ported by the way in which they bring to mind the apple in the Garden of Eden. (Cf. Milton, *Paradise Lost* X.556–72.) A similar example of perverted nature is found in Dante, *Inferno* XII.1–6, where the ugly, twisted trees of the forest in hell are described.

1053f. 'and if He who is our noble Lord loves behaviour that is pure, and you desire to be known in His court then'.

1057–9. 'For Clopignel, in the course of his pure *Romance of the Rose*, where he sets forth a discourse to him who wishes to succeed in being loved by a lady, (says): "Look at her without delay"'. *Clopyngnel* is Jean de Meun. This passage (1057–64) alludes to *Le Roman de la Rose* 7689–7764 (ed. F. Lecoy, Paris, 1970). Jean's account concerns romantic love; the poet deliberately transforms its significance to the plane of divine love. *To be loued* complements *spede wolde*.

1061. *in vch a borȝe:* i.e. everywhere.

1062–4. 'and follow the example (*lit.* the footprints) of that mistress you consider noble; and if you behave in this way, even if she were disagreeable, she will be pleased by that behaviour which is like her own.' *Wyk* (1063): possibly 'difficult', with connotations of Dangier of the *Roman*.

1065–8. 'If, then, you wish to exchange love with God, and loyally love your Lord and become His beloved, then make yourself clean, and model yourself upon Christ, who is always polished as smooth as the pearl itself.' A well-known tradition, going back ultimately to the parable of the Pearl of Price (Matt. 13:45–6) associates the pearl with heaven and salvation. This association is, of course, essential to *Pe*: see note to 1111–48.

And lelly louy þy Lorde and His leef worþe,
Þenne confourme þe to Kryst, and þe clene make,
Þat euer is polyced als playn as þe perle seluen.
For, loke, fro fyrst þat He lyȝt withinne þe lel mayden,
By how comly a kest He watz clos þere,   1070
When venkkyst watz no vergynyté, ne vyolence maked,
Bot much clener watz hir corse, God kynned þerinne.
And efte when He borne watz in Beþelen þe ryche,
In wych puryté þay departed; þaȝ þay pouer were,
Watz neuer so blysful a bour as watz a bos þenne,   1075
Ne no schroude hous so schene as a schepon þare,
Ne non so glad vnder God as ho þat grone schulde.
For þer watz seknesse al sounde þat sarrest is halden,
And þer watz rose reflayr where rote hatz ben euer,
And þer watz solace and songe wher sorȝ hatz ay cryed;   1080
For aungelles with instrumentes of organes and pypes,   [f 72ʳ]
And rial ryngande rotes and þe reken fyþel,
And alle hende þat honestly moȝt an hert glade,
Aboutte my lady watz lent quen ho delyuer were.
Þenne watz her blyþe Barne burnyst so clene   1085
Þat boþe þe ox and þe asse Hym hered at ones;
Þay knewe Hym by His clannes for Kyng of nature,
For non so clene of such a clos com neuer er þenne.
And ȝif clanly He þenne com, ful cortays þerafter,
Þat alle þat longed to luþer ful lodly He hated,   1090
By nobleye of His norture He nolde neuer towche
Oȝt þat watz vngoderly oþer ordure watz inne.

1069–88. Like the Dead Sea, the Virgin Birth is presented in terms of the breaking of the laws of nature—though in this case with a supernaturally creative instead of a supernaturally destructive effect. The uniqueness of the birth of Christ is given emphasis by the repeated assertions (1078ff) of its difference from the expected norms of childbirth. This was a familiar theme in medieval Christian literature. In the mystery plays, for instance, emphasis is given to the painlessness of the birth and Mary's cleanness afterwards (e.g. York No. 17, 293f, Ludus Coventriae No. 15, 203f, 229ff, 302ff). The freedom from pain produces a symbolic reversal, in that the pain of childbirth was a curse of the Fall (see, e.g., Chester No. 2, 313ff). The Virgin Birth was also seen as one of the Five Joys of Mary—itself one of the symbolic 'fives' well known in the Middle Ages (cf. *G* 631–65).

1074. *In wych puryté þay departed:* 'in what purity they separated'.

1081–8. The singing of the angels and the adoration of the ox and ass are traditional elements derived from apocryphal writings. Both are reflected, for instance, in the mystery plays and in contemporary religious art.

1083. 'and all gracious things that might properly gladden a heart'.

1089–93. 'And if He came cleanly thence, most courteous afterwards, He who hated with loathing everything that pertained to evil, by the nobility of His nurture He would never touch anything that was base or in which there was filth. Yet loathsome people came to that Prince, such as many leprous beggars'.

ʒet comen lodly to þat Lede, as lazares monye,
Summe lepre, summe lome, and lomerande blynde,
Poysened, and parlatyk, and pyned in fyres, 1095
Drye folk and ydropike, and dede at þe laste,
Alle called on þat Cortayse and claymed His grace.
He heled hem wyth hynde speche of þat þay ask after,
For whatso He towched also tyd tourned to hele,
Wel clanner þen any crafte cowþe devyse. 1100
So hende watz His hondelyng vche ordure hit schonied,
And þe gropyng so goud of God and Man boþe,
Þat for fetys of His fyngeres fonded He neuer
Nauþer to cout ne to kerue with knyf ne wyth egge;
Forþy brek He þe bred blades wythouten, 1105
For hit ferde freloker in fete in His fayre honde,
Displayed more pryuyly when He hit part schulde,
Þenne alle þe toles of Tolowse moʒt tyʒt hit to kerue.
Þus is He kyryous and clene þat þou His cort askes:
Hov schulde þou com to His kyth bot if þou clene were? 1110

1101. hende (Gollancz)] MS clene

1093–1108. Though Christ is characterized by a special, superhuman cleanness (1085–92), it is particularly fitting that the unclean should come to Him for help. The symbolic association of physical sickness and healing with spiritual sickness and healing is a strong and ancient tradition, in which the most significant influence is the NT portrayal of Christ as physical and spiritual healer. The diseases specified here include those normally regarded in the Middle Ages as resulting from unclean or incontinent living of one kind or another.

1095. *fyres:* Previous editors have incorrectly glossed 'fevers'. This word is in fact used to designate diseases involving inflammation of the skin and putrefaction of the flesh.

1096. *Drye:* with an excess of the dry humours—colera and melancholia.

1098. *of þat þay ask after:* 'from what they ask'—i.e. from the disease or disability in question.

1101. 'His touch was so gracious that all filth shunned it'. The alliterative pattern suggests that MS *clene* is erroneous; Gollancz's emendation restores the alliteration without damaging the sense. Both *hondelyng* and *gropyng* (1102) are words used in medical writings to designate the manipulation of diseased or incapacitated parts.

1105–8. 'therefore He broke bread without blades, for indeed it behaved more perfectly in His fair hands, and was exposed more mysteriously when He wished to part it, than all the knives of Toulouse might endeavour to cut it.' This idea developed around the account of the supper at Emmaus in Luke 24:35, where Christ is recognized by the disciples by means of the way in which he breaks bread. Toulouse was not normally associated with knives, and it is therefore probable (as Gollancz points out) that the poet intended Toledo, which was. A reference to the blades of Toledo is made in the *Chanson de Roland* 1611.

1109. 'To that extent is He whose court you seek fastidious and pure'.

Nov ar we sore and synful and sovly vchone;
How schulde we se, þen may we say, þat Syre vpon throne?
ʒis, þat Mayster is mercyable, þaʒ þou be man fenny,
And al tomarred in myre whyle þou on molde lyuyes;
Þou may schyne þurʒ schryfte, þaʒ þou haf schome serued,   1115
And pure þe with penaunce tyl þou a perle worþe.
Perle praysed is prys þer perré is schewed,   [f 72ᵛ]
Þaʒ hyt not derrest be demed to dele for penies.
Quat may þe cause be called bot for hir clene hwes,
Þat wynnes worschyp abof alle whyte stones?   1120
For ho schynes so schyr þat is of schap rounde,
Wythouten faut oþer fylþe ʒif ho fyn were,
And wax euer in þe worlde in weryng so olde,
ʒet þe perle payres not whyle ho in pryse lasttes;
And if hit cheue þe chaunce vncheryst ho worþe,   1125
Þat ho blyndes of ble in bour þer ho lygges,
Nobot wasch hir wyth wourchyp in wyn as ho askes,
Ho by kynde schal becom clerer þen are.
So if folk be defowled by vnfre chaunce,
Þat he be sulped in sawle, seche to schryfte,   1130

1118. hyt (Gollancz)] MS hym
1124. pryse] MS pyese

1111–48. This passage of moral commentary between narratives tackles the question
of how a man may apply the lessons illustrated in the stories to his own life: of how he
may find salvation. Thus the penitential nature of the poem is made clear (par-
ticularly in 1113–16 and 1129–32). The use of mire to symbolize sin recurs through-
out *Cl* (and is seen in the whale episode in *Pat*: cf. 342n). Here the poet also alludes
to the traditional idea of the pearl surviving untarnished its burial in mire, which
often represented allegorically the relationship between the soul and the body: see
Kean, **7a** 1967, 147ff and *Pe* 22f and n. The symbolic identification of the pearl with
the righteous soul and salvation is central to the symbolism, structure, and meaning
of *Pe*.
1116. *tyl þou a perle worþe:* 'until you become a pearl': i.e. until you achieve salvation.
1117f. 'Pearl is highly valued where jewelry is displayed, though it is not considered
the most valuable to exchange for money.' The idea that the pearl is undervalued by
the worldly, derived perhaps from commentary on the parable of not casting pearls
before swine (Matt. 7:6), is commonplace in medieval religious writings: see Kean,
7a 1967, 148ff. *Hyt:* the emendation supplies the necessary subject form. In *Pe* both
neuter and feminine pronouns are similarly applied to the pearl (see note to *Pe* 3f).
1121. Cf. 555f, *Pe* 737f.
1122. *ʒif ho fyn were:* 'if it was perfect (to begin with)'.
1124. *pryse:* The emendation was suggested but not adopted by Menner.
1125–8. 'and if it happens by chance that she is neglected, so that she becomes dim of
colour in the room where she lies, only wash her with reverence in wine as she
requires, and by nature she will become brighter than before.'
1129. *folk:* here 'a person', 'somebody'.

And he may polyce hym at þe prest, by penaunce taken,
Wel bryȝter þen þe beryl oþer browden perles.
Bot war þe wel, if þou be waschen wyth water of schryfte,
And polysed als playn as parchmen schauen,
Sulp no more þenne in synne þy saule þerafter,   1135
For þenne þou Dryȝtyn dyspleses with dedes ful sore,
And entyses Hym to tene more trayþly þen euer,
And wel hatter to hate þen hade þou not waschen.
For when a sawele is saȝtled and sakred to Dryȝtyn,
He holly haldes hit His and haue hit He wolde;   1140
Þenne efte lastes hit likkes, He loses hit ille,
As hit were rafte wyth vnryȝt and robbed wyth þewes.
War þe þenne for þe wrake: His wrath is achaufed
For þat þat ones watz His schulde efte be vnclene,
Þaȝ hit be bot a bassyn, a bolle oþer a scole,   1145
A dysche oþer a dobler, þat Dryȝtyn onez serued.
To defowle hit euer vpon folde fast He forbedes,
So is He scoymus of scaþe þat scylful is euer.
And þat watz bared in Babyloyn in Baltazar tyme,
Hov harde vnhap þer hym hent and hastyly sone,   1150
For he þe vesselles avyled þat vayled in þe temple
In seruyse of þe Souerayn sumtyme byfore.
Ȝif ȝe wolde tyȝt me a tom telle hit I wolde,   [f 73ʳ]
Hov charged more watz his chaunce þat hem cherych nolde
Þen his fader forloyne þat feched hem wyth strenþe,   1155

1131. The figure of 'polishing the soul' is a commonplace of religious instruction: see, for example, *Ancrene Wisse* (EETS OS 249) p. 196, 19–26.

1134. This comparison is also found (in more extended form) in a 12th c. sermon designed to appeal to illuminators of manuscripts: 'Let us consider how we may become scribes of the Lord. The parchment on which we write for him is a pure conscience, whereon all our good works are noted by the pen of memory, and make us acceptable to God. The knife wherewith it is scraped is the fear of God, which removes from our conscience by repentance all the roughness and unevenness of sin and vice. The pumice wherewith it is made smooth is the discipline of heavenly desires . . .' (see R. A. B. Mynors, *Durham Cathedral Manuscripts* [Oxford, 1939] 9).

1140–42. 'He considers it completely His and wishes to keep it; when it again tastes vices He loses it with ill will, as though it were seized wrongfully and stolen by thieves.'

1143–8. Here the poet makes the thematic transition from the subject of the uncleanness of men to the related subject of the desecration of holy vessels. This passage is necessary in order to demonstrate the thematic relevance of the final narrative. The unifying factor is the symbol of the vessel dedicated to God, which may be both a vessel literally and represent a man symbolically: see Charlotte C. Morse, **7b** 1970–71, and Introduction, p. 25f. Cf. 12–16 and note to 12.

1153. Cf. *Pat* 59f.

1154–6. 'how the fortune of him who would not take care of them was heavier than that of his erring father who seized them by force, and robbed the Church of all holy objects.'

And robbed þe relygioun of relykes alle.
Danyel in his dialokez devysed sumtyme,
As ȝet is proued expresse in his profecies,
Hov þe gentryse of Juise and Jherusalem þe ryche
Watz disstryed wyth distres, and drawen to þe erþe.   1160
For þat folke in her fayth watz founden vntrwe,
Þat haden hyȝt þe hyȝe God to halde of Hym euer;
And He hem halȝed for His and help at her nede
In mukel meschefes mony, þat meruayl is to here.
And þay forloyne her fayth and folȝed oþer goddes,   1165
And þat wakned His wrath and wrast hit so hyȝe
Þat He fylsened þe faythful in þe falce lawe
To forfare þe falce in þe faythe trwe.
Hit watz sen in þat syþe þat Zedechyas rengned
In Juda, þat justised þe Juyne kynges.   1170
He sete on Salamones solie on solemne wyse,
Bot of leauté he watz lat to his Lorde hende:
He vsed abominaciones of idolatrye,
And lette lyȝt bi þe lawe þat he watz lege tylle.
Forþi oure Fader vpon folde a foman hym wakned: 1175
Nabigodenozar nuyed hym swyþe.
He pursued into Palastyn with proude men mony,
And þer he wast wyth werre þe wones of þorpes;
He herȝed vp alle Israel and hent of þe beste,
And þe gentylest of Judée in Jerusalem biseged,   1180
Vmbewalt alle þe walles wyth wyȝes ful stronge,
At vche a dor a doȝty duk, and dutte hem wythinne;

1164.   is (Morris)] MS *om.*
1169.   Zedechyas] MS Zedethyas
1178.   wyth] MS wyth with

1157–74.   This account is based on 2 Chron. 36:11–14.
1161.   Thus the destruction of Jerusalem is related to the poem's secondary theme, *vntrawþe:* see Introduction, pp. 24–9.
1162–4.   'who had promised the supreme God to be faithful to Him ever; and He consecrated them as His and helped them in their need in many great misfortunes, as it is marvellous to hear.'
1167–70.   'that He aided those faithful to the false religion to destroy those false to the true faith. This was seen in the time when Zedechiah reigned in Judah, which the kings of the Jews ruled.' The rhetoric of 1167f may be compared to that of *G* 3f.
1172.   'but he was slow in loyalty to his gracious Lord'.
1174.   'and cared little for the religion to which he owed allegiance.'
1175.   *hym:* 'for him'.
1175–1292.   This narrative is based mainly on Jer. 52:4–19.
1179.   *hent of þe beste:* 'took the nobles prisoner'.
1182, 1184.   *hem wythinne, hem þeroute:* 'those inside', 'those outside'.

For þe borȝ watz so bygge batayled alofte,
And stoffed wythinne with stout men to stalle hem þeroute.
Þenne watz þe sege sette þe ceté aboute,   1185
Skete skarmoch skelt, much skaþe lached;
At vch brugge a berfray on basteles wyse
Þat seuen syþe vch a day asayled þe ȝates;   [f73ᵛ]
Trwe tulkkes in toures teueled wythinne,
In bigge brutage of borde bulde on þe walles;   1190
Þay feȝt and þay fende of, and fylter togeder
Til two ȝer ouertorned, ȝet tok þay hit neuer.
At þe laste, vpon longe, þo ledes wythinne,
Faste fayled hem þe fode, enfamined monie;
Þe hote hunger wythinne hert hem wel sarre   1195
Þen any dunt of þat douthe þat dowelled þeroute.
Þenne wern þo rowtes redles in þo ryche wones;
Fro þat mete watz myst, megre þay wexen,
And þay stoken so strayt þat þay ne stray myȝt
A fote fro þat forselet to forray no goudes.   1200
Þenne þe kyng of þe kyth a counsayl hym takes
Wyth þe best of his burnes, a blench for to make;
Þay stel out on a stylle nyȝt er any steuen rysed,
And harde hurles þurȝ þe oste er enmies hit wyste.
Bot er þay atwappe ne moȝt þe wach wythoute   1205
Hiȝe skelt watz þe askry þe skewes anvnder.
Loude alarom vpon launde lulted watz þenne;
Ryche, ruþed of her rest, ran to here wedes,

1183. batayled] MS baytayled
1194. enfamined] MS enfannined

1186f. 'skirmishes sharply launched, much injury received; at each drawbridge a movable tower of the kind mounted on wheels'. This translation and the definitions in the Glossary are based on the supposition that *bastel* is used to add a further qualification to *berfray*. Alternatively, it is possible that the poet did not intend to differentiate between their meanings, but is duplicating nouns for purposes of metre and effect.

1189f. 'faithful men fought from within towers, and on strong wooden platforms built on the walls'. Stone, 4 1971, 127, points out that during the Middle Ages temporary wooden platforms were sometimes built on to battlements; from these soldiers could foil the efforts of besiegers trying to scale the walls. Cf. 1384.

1199f. 'and they were enclosed so tightly that they could not stray a foot from that fortress to plunder any goods.'

1205f. 'But before they could escape the (notice of the) watch outside the alarm was launched high under the skies.'

1208. *Ryche:* 'noblemen'.

Hard hattes þay hent and on hors lepes;
Cler claryoun crak cryed on lofte.   1210
By þat watz alle on a hepe hurlande swyþee,
Folȝande þat oþer flote, and fonde hem bilyue,
Ouertok hem as tyd, tult hem of sadeles,
Tyl vche prynce hade his per put to þe grounde.
And þer watz þe kyng kaȝt wyth Caldé prynces,   1215
And alle hise gentyle forjusted on Jerico playnes,
And presented wern as presoneres to þe prynce rychest,
Nabigodenozar, noble in his chayer;
And he þe faynest freke þat he his fo hade,
And speke spitously hem to, and spylt þerafter.   1220
Þe kynges sunnes in his syȝt he slow euervch one,
And holkked out his auen yȝen heterly boþe,
And bede þe burne to be broȝt to Babyloyn þe ryche,
And þere in dongoun be don to dreȝe þer his wyrdes.   [f 74ʳ]
Now se, so þe Souerayn set hatz His wrake: 1225
Nas hit not for Nabugo ne his noblé nauþer
Þat oþer depryued watz of pryde with paynes stronge,
Bot for his beryng so badde agayn his blyþe Lorde;
For hade þe Fader ben his frende, þat hym bifore keped,
Ne neuer trespast to Him in teche of mysseleue,   1230
To colde wer alle Caldé and kythes of Ynde,
Ȝet take Torkye hem wyth—her tene hade ben little.
Ȝet nolde neuer Nabugo þis ilke note leue
Er he hade tyrued þis toun and torne hit to grounde.
He joyned vnto Jerusalem a gentyle duc þenne—   1235
His name watz Nabuzardan—to noye þe Jues;
He watz mayster of his men and myȝty himseluen,
Þe chef of his cheualrye his chekkes to make;
He brek þe bareres as bylyue, and þe burȝ after,

1225. Souerayn] MS soueray
1234. tyrued (Gollancz)] MS tuyred

1211f. 'By that time all were rushing fast in a crowd, following the other troop, and
soon found them'.
1215. *wyth:* 'by'.
1219. 'and he (was) the gladdest man because he had his enemy'.
1222. 'and cruelly dug out both his (the king's) eyes'.
1226. *Nabugo:* the first element of *Nabugodenozar*.
1229–32. 'for had the Father, who previously preserved him, been his friend, and had
he never trespassed against Him in the sin of misbelief, all Chaldea and the countries
of India—even include Turkey with them—would have been too lacking in zeal and
would have done little harm.'

And enteres in ful ernestly, in yre of his hert.   1240
What! þe maysterry watz mene: þe men wern away,
Þe best boȝed wyth þe burne þat þe borȝ ȝemed,
And þo þat byden wer so biten with þe bale hunger
Þat on wyf hade ben worþe þe welgest fourre.
Nabizardan noȝt forþy nolde not spare,   1245
Bot bede al to þe bronde vnder bare egge;
Þay slowen of swettest semlych burdes,
Baþed barnes in blod and her brayn spylled;
Prestes and prelates þay presed to deþe,
Wyues and wenches her wombes tocoruen,   1250
Þat her boweles outborst aboute þe diches,
And al watz carfully kylde þat þay cach myȝt.
And alle þat swypped, vnswolȝed of þe sworde kene,
Þay wer cagged and kaȝt on capeles al bare,
Festned fettres to her fete vnder fole wombes,   1255
And broþely broȝt to Babyloyn þer bale to suffer,
To sytte in seruage and syte, þat sumtyme wer gentyle.
Now ar chaunged to chorles and charged wyth werkkes,
Boþe to cayre at þe kart and þe kuy mylke,
Þat sumtyme sete in her sale syres and burdes. [f 74ᵛ] 1260
And ȝet Nabuzardan nyl neuer stynt
Er he to þe tempple tee wyth his tulkkes alle;
Betes on þe barers, brestes vp þe ȝates,
Slouen alle at a slyp þat serued þerinne,
Pulden prestes bi þe polle and plat of her hedes,   1265
Diȝten dekenes to deþe, dungen doun clerkkes,
And alle þe maydenes of þe munster maȝtyly hokyllen
Wyth þe swayf of þe sworde þat swolȝed hem alle.
Þenne ran þay to þe relykes as robbors wylde,

1243. so] MS fo
1253. þat (Morris)] MS *om.*

1241–4. 'Well! the victory was poor: the men were away, the nobles gone with the man who ruled the city, and those who remained were so tormented with dire hunger that one woman would have been worth the strongest four.'

1245–60. This passage is based on 2 Chron. 36:17–21, with characteristically vivid elaboration, especially of the violence and horror.

1245. *noȝt forþy:* 'however'.

1247. 'they killed lovely maidens of the fairest'.

1253–5. 'And all who escaped, unconsumed by the sharp sword, were bound and taken on horses quite naked, fetters fastened to their feet under the horses' bellies'.

1261–92. This passage is based on Jer. 52:13–19.

1267. *hokyllen:* Menner emends to *he kyllen,* which is grammatically unacceptable. Here, following Gollancz, *hokyllen* is retained, and taken as a form of *hockle* 'to cut up stubble', in this case 'to cut to pieces'.

And pyled alle þe apparement þat pented to þe kyrke—   1270
Þe pure pyleres of bras pourtrayd in golde,
And þe chef chaundeler charged with þe lyʒt,
Þat ber þe lamp vpon lofte þat lemed euermore
Bifore þe *sancta sanctorum* þer selcouth watz ofte.
Þay caʒt away þat condelstik, and þe crowne als   1275
Þat þe auter hade vpon, of aþel golde ryche,
Þe gredirne and þe goblotes garnyst of syluer,
Þe bases of þe bryʒt postes and bassynes so schyre,
Dere disches of golde and dubleres fayre,
Þe vyoles and þe vesselment of vertuous stones.   1280
Now hatz Nabuzardan nomen alle þyse noble þynges,
And pyled þat precious place and pakked þose godes;
Þe golde of þe gazafylace to swyþe gret noumbre,
Wyth alle þe vrnmentes of þat hous, he hamppred togeder;
Alle he spoyled spitously in a sped whyle   1285
Þat Salomon so mony a sadde ʒer soʒt to make.
Wyth alle þe coyntyse þat he cowþe clene to wyrke,
Deuised he þe vesselment, þe vestures clene;
Wyth slyʒt of his ciences, his Souerayn to loue,
Þe hous and þe anournementes he hyʒtled togedere.   1290
Now hatz Nabuzardan nummen hit al samen,
And syþen bet doun þe burʒ and brend hit in askes.
Þenne wyth legiounes of ledes ouer londes he rydes,
Herʒez of Israel þe hyrnez aboute;
Wyth charged chariotes þe cheftayn he fyndez,   1295
Bikennes þe catel to þe kyng, þat he caʒt hade;   [f75ʳ]

1274. þe] MS þ
1291. nummen] MS numnend
1294. hyrnez] MS hyrne
1295. fyndez] MS fynde

1271. *pourtrayd in:* 'adorned with'.
1274. *þer selcouth watz ofte:* 'where wonders often occurred.'
1275. *þe crowne:* see 1443–50n.
1286f. Solomon's temple project is described in 3 Kgs. (AV 1 Kgs.) 5–7 and 2 Chron. 2–5.
1287–92. 'With all the wisdom that he could (had), in order to work righteously, he devised the vessels and the pure vestments; with the skill of his knowledge, in order to praise his Lord, he decorated the church and the ornaments together. Now Nebuzaradan has seized it all together, and then beaten down the city and burnt it to ashes.' With 1292 cf. *G* 2.
1293–1419. This passage is not based on a biblical narrative.
1294. 'harries the corners of Israel about'.
1296–9. 'delivers to the king the property that he had seized; presented to him the prisoners that they had taken as booty—many men worthy while their worldly prosperity lasted, many sons of seemly lords, and very rich maidens'.

Presented him þe prisoneres in pray þat þay token—
Moni a worþly wyȝe whil her worlde laste,
Moni semly syre soun, and swyþe rych maydenes,
Þe pruddest of þe prouince, and prophetes childer,   1300
As Ananie, and Azarie, and als Mizael,
And dere Daniel also, þat watz deuine noble,
With moni a modey moder-chylde mo þen innoghe.
And Nabugodenozar makes much joye,
Nov he þe kyng hatz conquest and þe kyth wunnen,   1305
And dreped alle þe doȝtyest and derrest in armes,
And þe lederes of her lawe layd to þe grounde,
And þe pryce of þe profecie prisoners maked.
Bot þe joy of þe juelrye so gentyle and ryche,
When hit watz schewed hym so schene, scharp watz his wonder;   1310
Of such vessel auayed, þat vayled so huge,
Neuer ȝet nas Nabugodenozar er þenne.
He sesed hem with solemneté, þe Souerayn he praysed
Þat watz aþel ouer alle, Israel Dryȝtyn;
Such god, such gounes, such gay vesselles,   1315
Comen neuer out of kyth to Caldée reames.
He trussed hem in his tresorye in a tryed place,
Rekenly, wyth reuerens, as he ryȝt hade;
And þer he wroȝt as þe wyse, as ȝe may wyt hereafter,
For hade he let of hem lyȝt, hym moȝt haf lumpen worse.   1320
Þat ryche in gret rialté rengned his lyue,
As conquerour of vche a cost he cayser watz hatte,
Emperour of alle þe erþe and also þe saudan,
And als þe god of þe grounde watz grauen his name.
And al þurȝ dome of Daniel, fro he deuised hade   1325
Þat alle goudes com of God, and gef hit hym bi samples,
Þat he ful clanly bicnv his carp bi þe laste,

1308. profecie] MS profetie
1315. gounes (Gollancz)] MS gomes

1308. *pryce of þe profecie:* 'chief of the company of prophets'.
1311f. 'Nebuchadnezzar had never before then been informed of such vessels, which were worth so much.'
1317–20. Here the contrast between the way in which Nebuchadnezzar treats the holy vessels and the way in which Belshazzar will do so (the main subject of 1357–1804) is anticipated.
1320. 'for had he neglected them, something worse might have happened to him.'
1321. *Þat ryche:* 'that noble man'.
1325–8. 'And (it was) all through the judgement of Daniel, after he had explained that all good things come from God, and revealed it to him by examples, that he completely acknowledged his (Daniel's) discourse at last, and often it humbled his spirit, his arrogant deeds.'

And ofte hit mekned his mynde, his maysterful werkkes.
Bot al drawes to dyȝe with doel vpon ende:
Bi a haþel neuer so hyȝe, he heldes to grounde.   1330
And so Nabugodenozar, as he nedes moste,
For alle his empire so hiȝe in erþe is he grauen.   [f75ᵛ]
Bot þenn þe bolde Baltazar, þat watz his barn aldest,
He watz stalled in his stud, and stabled þe rengne
In þe burȝ of Babiloyne, þe biggest he trawed,   1335
Þat nauþer in heuen ne on erþe hade no pere;
For he bigan in alle þe glori þat hym þe gome lafte,
Nabugodenozar, þat watz his noble fader.
So kene a kyng in Caldée com neuer er þenne;
Bot honoured he not Hym þat in heuen wonies.   1340
Bot fals fantummes of fendes, formed with handes,
Wyth tool out of harde tre, and telded on lofte,
And of stokkes and stones, he stoute goddes callz,
When þay ar gilde al with golde and gered wyth syluer;
And þere he kneles and callez and clepes after help.   1345
And þay reden him ryȝt rewarde he hem hetes,
And if þay gruchen him his grace, to gremen his hert,
He cleches to a gret klubbe and knokkes hem to peces.
Þus in pryde and olipraunce his empyre he haldes,
In lust and in lecherye and loþelych werkkes,   1350
And hade a wyf for to welde, a worþelych quene,
And mony a lemman, neuer þe later, þat ladis wer called.
In þe clernes of his concubines and curious wedez,
In notyng of nwe metes and of nice gettes,
Al watz þe mynde of þat man on misschapen þinges,   1355
Til þe Lorde of þe lyfte liste hit abate.
Thenne þis bolde Baltazar biþenkkes hym ones
To vouche on avayment of his vayneglorie;

1329. vpon] MS vpn
1336. on] MS no
1339. neuer] MS neū
1358. vayneglorie] MS vayne gorie

1330. 'however great a man is, he falls to the ground.'
1334–6. 'he (Belshazzar) was installed in his (Nebuchadnezzar's) place, and established the reign in the city of Babylon (a reign) he believed the greatest, having no equal either in heaven or on earth'.
1346–8. 'If they advise him correctly he promises them reward, and if they refuse him his favour, angering his heart, he seizes a great club and knocks them to pieces.' The poet presents Belshazzar's conduct as not only sinful but also comic in its folly.
1353–6. 'The mind of that man was entirely (fixed) on wicked things, on the beauty of his concubines and exquisite clothes, on using new foods and foolish fashions, until it pleased the Lord of the heavens to end it.'

Hit is not innoghe to þe nice al noȝty þink vse
Bot if alle þe worlde wyt his wykked dedes.   1360
Baltazar þurȝ Babiloyn his banne gart crye,
And þurȝ þe cuntré of Caldée his callyng con spryng,
Þat alle þe grete vpon grounde schulde geder hem samen
And assemble at a set day at þe saudans fest.
Such a mangerie to make þe man watz auised,   1365
Þat vche a kythyn kyng schuld com þider,
Vche duk wyth his duthe, and oþer dere lordes,
Schulde com to his court to kyþe hym for lege,   [f 76ʳ]
And to reche hym reuerens, and his reuel herkken,
To loke on his lemanes and ladis hem calle.   1370
To rose hym in his rialty rych men soȝtten,
And mony a baroun ful bolde, to Babyloyn þe noble.
Þer bowed toward Babiloyn burnes so mony,
Kynges, cayseres ful kene, to þe court wonnen,
Mony ludisch lordes þat ladies broȝten,   1375
Þat to neuen þe noumbre to much nye were.
For þe bourȝ watz so brod and so bigge alce,
Stalled in þe fayrest stud þe sterrez anvnder,
Prudly on a plat playn, plek alþer-fayrest,
Vmbesweyed on vch a syde with seuen grete wateres,   1380
With a wonder wroȝt walle wruxeled ful hiȝe,
With koynt carneles aboue, coruen ful clene,
Troched toures bitwene, twenty spere lenþe,
And þiker þrowen vmbeþour with ouerþwert palle.
Þe place þat plyed þe pursaunt wythinne   1385
Watz longe and ful large and euer ilych sware,
And vch a syde vpon soyle helde seuen myle,
And þe saudans sete sette in þe myddes.

1359. 'it is not enough to the foolish person to practise every wicked thing'.

1365f. 'The man intended to make such a feast that the king of every land should come to it'. *Vche a kythyn kyng:* cf. *mony ludisch lordes* (1375).

1371f. 'To praise him in his royal state rich men and many a bold baron came to Babylon the noble.'

1377–1492. This description is partially based on Mandeville (*ed. cit. Cl* 448n, 105–7, 136).

1382–4. 'with elegant battlements above, carved very skilfully, crocketed towers at intervals of twenty spear lengths, and (others) more closely crowded around the outside, with wooden platforms placed at right angles.' See note to 1189f. *Troched* (1383): *OED* glosses *troche* as 'a cluster of three or more tines at the summit of a deer's horn' (as in *The Parlement of the Thre Ages* 67); thus *troched* as an architectural term embodies a simile comparing crocketed towers to branching antlers (as in *G* 795).

1385f. 'The palace which was contained within the precinct was long and very broad and square on all sides'. The poet turns from describing the outer wall of the *bourȝ* (Babylon conceived as a medieval castle or fortified town) to describing the palace (*place* in the sense of 'house, hall').

Þat watz a palayce of pryde passande alle oþer,
Boþe of werk and of wunder, and walled al aboute;   1390
Heȝe houses withinne, þe halle to hit med,
So brod bilde in a bay þat blonkkes myȝt renne.
When þe terme of þe tyde watz towched of þe feste,
Dere droȝen þerto and vpon des metten,
And Baltazar vpon bench was busked to sete,   1395
Stepe stayred stones of his stoute throne.
Þenne watz alle þe halle flor hiled with knyȝtes,
And barounes at þe sidebordes bounet aywhere,
For non watz dressed vpon dece bot þe dere seluen,
And his clere concubynes in cloþes ful bryȝt.   1400
When alle segges were þer set þen seruyse bygynnes,
Sturne trumpen strake steuen in halle,
Aywhere by þe wowes wrasten krakkes,
And brode baneres þerbi blusnande of gold,   [f 76ᵛ]
Burnes berande þe bredes vpon brode skeles   1405
Þat were of sylueren syȝt, and served þerwyth,
Lyfte logges þerouer and on lofte coruen,
Pared out of paper and poynted of golde,
Broþe baboynes abof, besttes anvnder,
Foles in foler flakerande bitwene,   1410

1390. walled (Gollancz)] MS walle
1402. Sturne] MS sturnen
1405. þe] MS þe þe
1406. served] MS severed
1408. golde] MS glolde

1391. *med:* This is probably a form of *mete* 'proportionate', with an inverted spelling, *d* for *t*, due to the characteristic West Midland unvoicing of final *d* (cf. *coumforde* 'comfort', *Pe* 369, *marked* 'market', *Pe* 513).
1392. 'built with so broad a space between the columns that horses might run there.'
1396. 'ascended the stone steps (*lit.* the stones arranged as steps) of his massive throne.'
1399. *þe dere:* 'the noble one'—i.e. Belshazzar. Cf. *G* 928.
1402f. 'harsh trumpets sound notes in the hall, everywhere their blasts resound by the walls'. The fanfare at Arthur's feast is similarly described in *G* 116–20.
1406. *of sylueren syȝt:* 'with the appearance of silver ones'. Perhaps the point is that the dishes were so large that one would not expect them to be real silver, but nevertheless they looked as if they were.
1407–12. 'raised canopies over them, carved on top, cut out of paper and tipped with gold, fierce baboons above, beasts underneath, birds in foliage fluttering between, and all enamelled richly in azure and indigo; and it was all carried in by men on horseback.' This describes a rather exotic version of the elaborate table decoration fashionable during the late Middle Ages. *Pared out of paper* (1408): cf. *G* 802, where the castle momentarily looks like one of these table decorations, and see note.

And al in asure and ynde enaumayld ryche;
And al on blonkken bak bere hit on honde.
And ay þe nakeryn noyse, notes of pipes,
Tymbres and tabornes, tulket among,
Symbales and sonetez sware þe noyse,   1415
And bougounz busch batered so þikke.
So watz serued fele syþe þe sale alle aboute,
With solace at þe sere course, bifore þe self lorde,
Þer þe lede and alle his loue lenged at þe table;
So faste þay weʒed to him wyne hit warmed his hert   1420
And breyþed vppe into his brayn and blemyst his mynde,
And al waykned his wyt, and welneʒe he foles;
For he waytez on wyde, his wenches he byholdes,
And his bolde baronage aboute bi þe woʒes.
Þenne a dotage ful depe drof to his hert,   1425
And a caytif counsayl he caʒt bi hymseluen;
Maynly his marschal þe mayster vpon calles,
And comaundes hym cofly coferes to lauce,
And fech forþ þe vessel þat his fader broʒt,
Nabugodenozar, noble in his strenþe,   1430
Conquerd with his knyʒtes and of kyrk rafte
In Judé, in Jerusalem, in gentyle wyse:
'Bryng hem now to my borde, of beuerage hem fylles,
Let þise ladyes of hem lape—I luf hem in hert;
Þat schal I cortaysly kyþe, and þay schin knawe sone,   1435

1429. forþ þe] MS forþe

1413. *nakeryn noyse:* 'the sound of kettle-drums'. Cf. *G* 118.
1417-1660. This passage is partly based on Dan. 5:1-20.
1421. 'and rose as a vapour into his brain and impaired his mind'. Gollancz and Menner both gloss *breyþed* 'rushed', deriving the word from ON (cf. OIcel *bregða*); this is the only occurrence listed in *MED*. Though the word may possibly be influenced in form by the ON word, it is much more likely that the meaning is to be related to ME *breþen* 'breathe', in this case 'rise as a vapour'—the well-attested *MED* sense 3(*a*). It was believed that the effect of wine on the mind was caused by vapours rising from the stomach into the brain (see Trevisa, VII.1)—clearly the process described here.
1431f. '(which he) conquered with his knights and seized from the church in Judea, in Jerusalem, in a noble manner'. The pillage of the temple is described in 1269-90, and Nebuchadnezzar's reverent attitude to the treasure in 1309-20.
1434. *þise ladyes:* the concubines—whom Belshazzar calls ladies (see 1352, 1370).
1435-7. '"I shall graciously show, and they will soon know, that there is no liberality in any man like the gracious deeds of Belshazzar." Then this order was immediately told to the treasurer.'

Þer is no bounté in burne lyk Baltazar þewes.'
Þenne towched to þe tresour þis tale watz sone,
And he with keyes vncloses kystes ful mony;
Mony burþen ful bryȝt watz broȝt into halle,
And couered mony a cupborde with cloþes ful quite.   [f 77ʳ]   1440
Þe jueles out of Jerusalem with gemmes ful bryȝt
Bi þe syde of þe sale were semely arayed;
Þe aþel auter of brasse watz hade into place,
Þe gay coroun of golde gered on lofte.
Þat hade ben blessed bifore wyth bischopes hondes   1445
And wyth besten blod busily anoynted,
In þe solempne sacrefyce þat goud sauor hade
Bifore þe Lorde of þe lyfte in louyng Hymseluen,
Now is sette, for to serue Satanas þe blake,
Bifore þe bolde Baltazar wyth bost and wyth pryde;   1450
Houen vpon þis auter watz aþel vessel
Þat wyth so curious a crafte coruen watz wyly.
Salamon sete him seuen ȝere and a syþe more,
With alle þe syence þat hym sende þe souerayn Lorde,
For to compas and kest to haf hem clene wroȝt.   1455
For þer wer bassynes ful bryȝt of brende golde clere,
Enaumaylde with azer, and eweres of sute,
Couered cowpes foul clene, as casteles arayed,

1452. so] MS fo
1453. seuen (Morris)] MS s . . . n (*letters blurred*)

1440. 'and many sideboards were covered with very white cloths.'
1443–50. 'the noble altar of brass was brought in (*or:* into hall), with the splendid cincture of gold arrayed upon it. That which had before been blessed by the hands of bishops and carefully anointed with the blood of beasts, in the solemn sacrifice which had good aroma before the Lord of the heaven in His praise, is now placed, to serve the black Satan, before the bold Belshazzar with boasting and pride'. Since no crown is mentioned among the vessels commissioned by Solomon for the Temple, the word *coroun* in 1444 (like *crowne*, 1275) appears to designate a gold cincture or moulding, such as surrounded the ark of the covenant and the incense-altar made by Bezalel for the Tabernacle of Moses (see Exod. 25:24–5, 37:1–3 and 25–7, where the Heb *zer* 'border, edge' is translated by *corona* 'crown' in the Vulgate). The link between Solomon's altar of brass and the altars of Bezalel may have been provided for the poet by 2 Chron. 1:5, where it is stated that before building the Temple, Solomon offered sacrifices on the brazen sacrificial altar made for Moses by Bezalel.
1451f. 'raised upon this altar were noble vessels that had been cleverly fashioned with such rare skill.'
1453–5. This is a point made earlier: 1285–90.
1458–64. 'very fair covered cups, adorned like castles, fortified under the battlement with skilfully made bantels (i.e. projecting horizontal coursings), and carved out in figures of wonderful shapes. The tops of the covers which rose up from the cups were elegantly formed into long turrets, pinnacles plainly set there jutted out at intervals,

Enbaned vnder batelment with bantelles quoynt,
And fyled out of fygures of ferlylé schappes.   1460
Þe coperounes of þe couacles þat on þe cuppe reres
Wer fetysely formed out in fylyoles longe;
Pinacles py3t þer apert þat profert bitwene,
And al bolled abof with braunches and leues,
Pyes and papejayes purtrayed withinne,   1465
As þay prudly hade piked of pomgarnades;
For alle þe blomes of þe bo3es wer blyknande perles,
And alle þe fruyt in þo formes of flaumbeande gemmes,
Ande safyres, and sardiners, and semely topace,
Alabaundarynes, and amaraunz, and amaffised stones,   1470
Casydoynes, and crysolytes, and clere rubies,
Penitotes, and pynkardines, ay perles bitwene;
So trayled and tryfled atrauerce wer alle,
Bi vche bekyr ande bolle, þe brurdes al vmbe;
Þe gobelotes of golde grauen aboute,   1475
And fyoles fretted with flores and fleez of golde;   [f 77ᵛ]
Vpon þat avter watz al aliche dresset.
Þe candelstik bi a cost watz cayred þider sone,
Vpon þe pyleres apyked, þat praysed hit mony,
Vpon hit basez of brasse þat ber vp þe werkes,   1480
Þe bo3es bry3t þerabof, brayden of golde,
Braunches bredande þeron, and bryddes þer seten

1461. couacles (Menner)] MS cauacles
1474. bolle (Bateson)] MS þe bolde

and all embossed above with branches and leaves'. *Enbaned* (1459): cf. *G* 790; *bantelles* (1459): cf. *Pe* 992n, 1017.

1466. *As:* 'as though'.

1472. *Penitotes:* The usual form of the word is *peritot*, from OF *peridot*. In arguing against emendation to *peritotes*, Gollancz points out that *penitotes* is not an unlikely form, given the English tendency to modify OF *r* to *n*.

1473f. 'all were thus ornamented from side to side with trailing patterns and trefoils, all around the rims of each beaker and bowl'.

1478–80. 'The candlestick was at once brought there by a device, so that many praised it, arrayed on the pillars, upon its bases of brass which supported the structure'. The poet follows Dan. 5:5 in alluding to only one candlestick (the accounts of the furnishing of the Temple of Solomon mention, in 2 Chron. 4:7 and 3 Kgs. [AV 1 Kgs] 7:49, ten candelabra). For the description of the candelabrum here, the poet turns again (cf. 1443–50n) to the description of the construction of Moses's tabernacle and the account of the single candelabrum there (Exod. 25:31ff and 37:17ff). The idea of the *cost* (evidently a kind of trolley) and the *basez of brasse*, however, appears to have been adopted by the poet from 3 Kgs. 7:27ff, where we are told that for Solomon's Temple Hiram made ten bases of brass on wheels, to support the ten lavers of brass.

Of mony koynt kyndes, of fele kyn hues,
As þay with wynge vpon wynde hade waged her fyþeres.
Inmong þe leues of þe lyndes lampes wer grayþed,   1485
And oþer louflych lyȝt þat lemed ful fayre,
As mony morteres of wax merkked withoute
With mony a borlych best al of brende golde.
Hit watz not wonte in þat wone to wast no serges,
Bot in temple of þe trauþe trwly to stonde   1490
Bifore þe *sancta sanctorum*, þer soþefast Dryȝtyn
Expouned His speche spiritually to special prophetes.
Leue þou wel þat þe Lorde þat þe lyfte ȝemes
Displesed much at þat play in þat plyt stronge,
Þat His jueles so gent wyth jaueles wer fouled,   1495
Þat presyous in His presens wer proued sumwhyle.
Soberly in His sacrafyce summe wer anoynted,
Þurȝ þe somones of Himselfe þat syttes so hyȝe;
Now a boster on benche bibbes þerof
Tyl he be dronkken as þe deuel, and dotes þer he syttes.   1500
So þe Worcher of þis worlde wlates þerwyth
Þat in þe poynt of her play He poruayes a mynde;
Bot er harme hem He wolde in haste of His yre,
He wayned hem a warnyng þat wonder hem þoȝt.
Nov is alle þis guere geten glotounes to serue,   1505
Stad in a ryche stal, and stared ful bryȝte;

1483.   koynt] MS *om.*
1485.   lyndes] MS *om.*
1491.   þer (Emerson)] MS *om.*
1506.   bryȝte] MS bryȝtz

1483.   *koynt:* It is likely that the line lacks an alliterating adj. at this point. Various
other editorial suggestions have been made, among them *curious* (Bülbring **5b**, fol-
lowed by Menner), *cler* (Gollancz), and *coloured* (Bateson **5b**: *mony kyndes
coloured*).

1485.   *lyndes:* The line clearly lacks an alliterating noun: cf. 1483n. With this conjec-
ture, *lyndes*, cf. the usage in *G* 526. There have been various other suggestions, among
them *launces* (Bülbring **5b**, followed by Menner), and *lefsel* (Gollancz).

1493–6.   'You may well believe that the Lord that rules the sky was greatly displeased
by that revelry in that strange situation, that His treasures so noble, which before
had proved precious in His presence, were defiled by louts.'

1501f.   'The Creator of this world is so disgusted at this that at the height of their sport
He settles on a purpose'.

1505–8.   'Now all these utensils have been fetched to serve gluttons, set in a rich place,
and shone very brightly. Belshazzar in a sudden impulse: "Serve us from them! Bring
wine in this house! Wassail!" he cries.' The difficulties of line 1507 are resolved by
starting Belshazzar's speech at *bede* (instead of at the beginning of 1508, as in other
editions): cf. 1622. Gollancz takes *vus* as the verb 'use', while Menner emends
to *bus* 'drink'. *Wassayl* (1508) is derived from OE *wes hal* 'may you have good health'.

Baltazar in a brayd: 'Bede vus þerof!
Weȝe wyn in þis won! Wassayl!' he cryes.
Swyfte swaynes ful swyþe swepen þertylle,
Kyppe kowpes in honde kyngez to serue;   1510
In bryȝt bollez ful bayn birlen þise oþer,
And vche mon for his mayster machches alone.   [f 78ʳ]
Þer watz rynging, on ryȝt, of ryche metalles,
Quen renkkes in þat ryche rok rennen hit to cache;
Clatering of couaclez þat kesten þo burdes   1515
As sonet out of sauteray songe als myry.
Þen þe dotel on dece drank þat he myȝt;
And þenne derfly arn dressed dukez and pryncez,
Concubines and knyȝtes, bi cause of þat merthe;
As vchon hade hym inhelde he haled of þe cuppe.   1520
So long likked þise lordes þise lykores swete,
And gloryed on her falce goddes, and her grace calles,
Þat were of stokkes and stones, stille euermore—
Neuer steuen hem astel, so stoken is hor tonge.
Alle þe goude golden goddes þe gaulez ȝet neuenen,   1525
Belfagor and Belyal, and Belssabub als,
Heyred hem as hyȝly as heuen wer þayres,
Bot Hym þat alle goudes giues, þat God þay forȝeten.

1516. sauteray (Morris)] MS saueray
1518. derfly] MS *om.*
1524. is] MS ins (īs)

1511–16. 'others very readily pour (wine) into bright bowls, and each man exerts himself on behalf of his master alone. Truly there was ringing of rich metals when men in that magnificent castle ran to take it (the wine); the clattering of lids which those ladies threw rang out as merrily as music from a psaltery.' *Rok* (1514) probably means 'castle' (OF *roque*), but note Gollancz's gloss 'crowd' (i.e. 'ruck').

1517. *þat he myȝt:* 'as hard as he could'.

1518. *derfly:* The line in the MS is short, and it is probable that an alliterating word is missing. Cf. Emerson's **5b** *derely*. Other emendations have been more elaborate: e.g. *þat derrest* (Gollancz); *drinkez arn dressed for* (Bülbring **5b**); and *drinkez arn dressed to* (Menner).

1520. 'as each one had (wine) poured for him he drained the cup.'

1522. *calles:* 'entreats'.

1523–5. 'who were (made) of wooden blocks and stones, dumb for ever; no sound ever stole forth from them, their tongues were so fastened. The wretches still call on all the good golden gods'. Cf. the earlier description of Nebuchadnezzar's false gods, 1341–8.

1526. *Belfagor* is a false god associated with pride (see Num. 25:3). *Belyal* means 'evil' in Heb., and becomes personified in biblical tradition (see 2 Cor. 6:15). *Belssabub* was traditionally chief of the false gods; his name means 'lord of the flies' in Heb. (see Matt. 12:24).

Forþy a ferly bifel þat fele folk seȝen;
Fyrst knew hit þe kyng and alle þe cort after: 1530
In þe palays pryncipale, vpon þe playn wowe,
In contrary of þe candelstik, þer clerest hit schyned,
Þer apered a paume, with poyntel in fyngres,
Þat watz grysly and gret, and grymly he wrytes;
Non oþer forme bot a fust faylande þe wryste   1535
Pared on þe parget, purtrayed lettres.
When þat bolde Baltazar blusched to þat neue,
Such a dasande drede dusched to his hert
Þat al falewed his face and fayled þe chere;
Þe stronge strok of þe stonde strayned his joyntes,   1540
His cnes cachches toclose, and cluchches his hommes,
And he with plattyng his paumes dispyses his leres,
And romyes as a rad ryth þat rorez for drede,
Ay biholdand þe honde til hit hade al grauen
And rasped on þe roȝ woȝe runisch sauez.   1545
When hit þe scrypture hade scraped wyth a scrof penne,
As a coltour in clay cerues þe forȝes,
Þenne hit vanist verayly and voyded of syȝt,   [f 78ᵛ]
Bot þe lettres bileued ful large vpon plaster.
Sone so þe kynge for his care carping myȝt wynne,   1550
He bede his burnes boȝ to þat were bok-lered,

1529. Forþy (Gollancz)] MS for þer
1532. þer (Gollancz)] MS þat
1542. dispyses] MS displayes
1546. scrof] MS strof
1547. þe] MS þo

1529. *Forþy:* The context supports the emendation to a conj. meaning 'therefore'.
1532. *In contrary of:* 'opposite': Vulgate *contra* 'over against' (Dan. 5:5).
1541f. 'his knees knock together and his thighs bend, and with the striking of his palms he treat his cheeks with scorn'. These difficult lines have been variously interpreted and emended. Only one emendation is made here: that of the difficult *displayes* to *dispyses* 'treats with scorn' (as in 1790). MS *leřs* is read *leres* and understood to mean 'cheeks' (cf. *G* 318, 943, 2228, and *Pe* 398). These lines may be regarded as a loose translation of the Vulgate *Tunc facies regis commutata est, et cogitationes ejus conturbabant eum: et compages renum ejus solvebantur, et genua ejus ad se invicem collidebantur* 'Then the king's countenance changed, and his thoughts troubled him: and the joints of his loins were loosed, and his knees struck one against the other' (Dan. 5:6).
1546. *scrypture:* 'inscription'.
1550–52. 'As soon as the king was able to speak again for his distress, he ordered his men who were book-learned to come, to examine the writing (to see) what it meant, and to tell him clearly'.

To wayte þe wryt þat hit wolde, and wyter hym to say—
'For al hit frayes my flesche, þe fyngres so grymme.'
Scoleres skelten þeratte þe skyl for to fynde,
Bot þer watz neuer on so wyse couþe on worde rede,   1555
Ne what ledisch lore ne langage nauþer,
What typyng ne tale tokened þo draȝtes.
Þenne þe bolde Baltazar bred ner wode,
And bede þe ceté to seche segges þurȝout
Þat wer wyse of wychecrafte, and warlaȝes oþer   1560
Þat con dele wyth demerlayk and deuine lettres.
'Calle hem alle to my cort, þo Caldé clerkkes,
Vnfolde hem alle þis ferly þat is bifallen here,
And calle wyth a hiȝe cry: "He þat þe kyng wysses,
In expounyng of speche þat spredes in þise lettres,   1565
And makes þe mater to malt my mynde wythinne,
Þat I may wyterly wyt what þat wryt menes,
He schal be gered ful gaye in gounes of porpre,
And a coler of cler golde clos vmbe his þrote;
He schal be prymate and prynce of pure clergye,   1570
And of my þreuenest lordez þe þrydde he schal,
And of my reme þe rychest to ryde wyth myseluen,
Outtaken bare two, and þenne he þe þrydde."'
Þis cry watz vpcaste, and þer comen mony
Clerkes out of Caldye þat kennest wer knauen,   1575
As þe sage sathrapas þat sorsory couþe,
Wychez and walkyries wonnen to þat sale,
Deuinores of demorlaykes þat dremes cowþe rede,
Sorsers of exorsismus and fele such clerkes;

1559. bede (Morris)] MS ede
1566. makes] MS make
1579. of (Gollancz)] MS̄ and (τ)

1554. 'Scholars hastened to it to discover the significance'.
1559. 'and ordered the city (i.e. the citizens) to seek men everywhere'.
1566f. 'and resolves the matter (*lit.* makes the matter be resolved) within my mind, so that I may clearly understand what the writing means'.
1570. *clergye:* 'learning'.
1575. *þat kennest wer knauen:* 'who were acknowledged to be the wisest'.
1576. *sathrapas:* 'wise men'. The precise biblical meaning of *satrap*—'provincial governor'—was not known in ME.
1577. *Wychez and walkyries:* Gollancz suggests that this may be an alliterative formula derived from OE *wiccean and wælcyrian*. Like *satrap*, *valkyrie* had lost its precise meaning, and is here used unspecifically to signify a wizard or sorcerer.
1579. *Sorsers of exorsismus:* 'sorcerers who called up spirits'.

And alle þat loked on þat letter as lewed þay were   1580
As þay had loked in þe leþer of my lyft bote.
Þenne cryes þe kyng and kerues his wedes.
What! he corsed his clerkes and calde hem chorles;
To henge þe harlotes he heȝed ful ofte: [f79ʳ]
So watz þe wyȝe wytles he wed wel ner.   1585
Ho herde hym chyde to þe chambre þat watz þe chef quene.
When ho watz wytered bi wyȝes what watz þe cause—
Suche a chaungande chaunce in þe chef halle—
Þe lady, to lauce þat los þat þe lorde hade,
Glydes doun by þe grece and gos to þe kyng.   1590
Ho kneles on þe colde erþe and carpes to hymseluen
Wordes of worchyp wyth a wys speche.
'Kene kyng,' quoþ þe quene, 'kayser of vrþe,
Euer laste þy lyf in lenþe of dayes!
Why hatz þou rended þy robe for redles hereinne,   1595
Þaȝ þose ledes ben lewed lettres to rede,
And hatz a haþel in þy holde, as I haf herde ofte,
Þat hatz þe gost of God þat gyes alle soþes?
His sawle is ful of syence, saȝes to schawe,
To open vch a hide þyng of aunteres vncowþe.   1600
Þat is he þat ful ofte hatz heuened þy fader
Of mony anger ful hote with his holy speche.
When Nabugodenozar watz nyed in stoundes,
He devysed his dremes to þe dere trawþe;
He keuered hym with his counsayl of caytyf wyrdes;   1605

1598.   gost (Gollancz)] MS gostes

1580f.   'and all who looked at that inscription were as ignorant as though they had looked at the leather of my left boot.' The poet's unexpected use of this piece of colloquial humour does not only serve to amuse: it also suggests the emptiness of the sorcerers' pretensions to knowledge.

1584.   *heȝed:* Gollancz glosses 'shouted', deriving this from the ME interjection *hei*; Menner takes it as pa.t. of *hyȝe* 'hasten'. Neither of these interpretations is really supported by the context. It is more likely that *heȝed* is a form of *hyȝt* 'vowed', pa.t. of *hete*; cf. the similar suggestion in Fowler, **5b** 1972–3, 334.

1585.   *he wed wel ner:* 'he very nearly went mad.'

1586–90.   'She who was the chief queen heard him scolding from her bedroom. When she was informed by servants what the cause was—such a change of fortune in the main hall—the lady, to relieve the harm that the lord had (suffered), moves down by the stairs and goes to the king.'

1591.   *hymseluen:* 'him'. Cf. *G* 113n.

1595–8.   'Why have you rent your robe for lack of advice in this matter, though those men are ignorant to read letters, when you have a man in your dominion, as I have often heard, who has the spirit of God who rules all truths?'

1605–8.   'with his advice he restored him (Nebuchadnezzar) from evil fortunes; everything that he (Nebuchadnezzar) asked him, in time he explained completely, through the aid of the spirit, which was present within him, of the most gracious gods which avail everywhere.'

Alle þat he spured hym, in space he expowned clene,
Þurȝ þe sped of þe spyryt, þat sprad hym withinne,
Of þe godeliest goddez þat gaynes aywhere.
For his depe diuinité and his dere sawes,
Þy bolde fader Baltazar bede by his name,   1610
Þat now is demed Danyel, of derne coninges,
Þat caȝt watz in þe captyuidé in cuntré of Jues;
Nabuzardan hym nome, and now is he here,
A prophete of þat prouince and pryce of þe worlde.
Sende into þe ceté to seche hym bylyue,   1615
And wynne hym with þe worchyp to wayne þe bote;
And þaȝ þe mater be merk þat merked is ȝender,
He schal declar hit also cler as hit on clay stande.'
Þat gode counseyl at þe quene watz cached as swyþe;
Þe burne byfore Baltazar watz broȝt in a whyle.   [f 79ᵛ]   1620
When he com bifore þe kyng and clanly had halsed,
Baltazar vmbebrayde hym, and 'Beue sir,' he sayde,
'Hit is tolde me bi tulkes þat þou trwe were
Profete of þat prouynce þat prayed my fader,
Ande þat þou hatz in þy hert holy connyng,   1625
Of sapyence þi sawle ful, soþes to schawe;
Goddes gost is þe geuen þat gyes alle þynges,

1608. godeliest] MS godelest
1618. cler (Gollancz)] MS *om.*
1619. as] MS as as
1622. Beue (Gollancz)] MS leue

1610. *Baltazar:* Vulgate *Baltassar* (Dan. 1:7). The poet follows the Vulgate in identifying the earlier name of Daniel with that of Belshazzar. The AV, in contrast, has *Belteshazzar. By:* 'to be'.
1612f. This event is described in 1293–1308.
1614. *pryce of þe worlde:* 'best in the world.'
1616–18. 'and persuade him by (promise of) honour to bring you help; and though the matter that is written over there is obscure, he will interpret it as clearly as it stands on the clay wall.' In 1632–40 Belshazzar carries out the advice given by his wife in 1616.
1619. *at:* 'from'.
1620. *þe burne:* i.e. Daniel.
1622. *Beue:* a form of *beau* 'fine, handsome': cf. *G* 1222. The emendation is supported by the alliterative pattern.
1623f. 'men tell me that you were a true prophet of that province that my father plundered'.
1627f. 'the spirit of God who rules all things is revealed to you, and you uncover every secret thing that the King of heaven purposes.'

And þou vnhyles vch hidde þat Heuen-Kyng myntes.
And here is a ferly byfallen, and I fayn wolde
Wyt þe wytte of þe wryt þat on þe wowe clyues,   1630
For alle Caldé clerkes han cowwardely fayled.
If þou with quayntyse con quere hit, I quyte þe þy mede:
For if þou redes hit by ry3t and hit to resoun brynges,
Fyrst telle me þe tyxte of þe tede lettres,
And syþen þe mater of þe mode mene me þerafter,   1635
And I schal halde þe þe hest þat I þe hy3t haue,
Apyke þe in porpre cloþe, palle alþer-fynest,
And þe by3e of bry3t golde abowte þyn nekke,
And þe þryd þryuenest þat þrynges me after,
Þou schal be baroun vpon benche, bede I þe no lasse.'   1640
Derfly þenne Danyel deles þyse wordes:
'Ryche kyng of þis rengne, rede þe oure Lorde!
Hit is surely soth þe Souerayn of heuen
Fylsened euer þy fader and vpon folde cheryched,
Gart hym grattest to be of gouernores alle,   1645
And alle þe worlde in his wylle welde as hym lyked.
Whoso wolde wel do, wel hym bityde,
And quos deth so he dezyre, he dreped als fast;
Whoso hym lyked to lyft, on lofte watz he sone,
And quoso hym lyked to lay watz lo3ed bylyue.   1650
So watz noted þe note of Nabugodenozar,
Styfly stabled þe rengne bi þe stronge Dry3tyn,
For of þe Hy3est he hade a hope in his hert,
Þat vche pouer past out of þat Prynce euen.
And whyle þat counsayl watz cle3t clos in his hert   1655
Þere watz no mon vpon molde of my3t as hymseluen;
Til hit bitide on a tyme towched hym pryde   [f80ʳ]
For his lordeschyp so large and his lyf ryche;

1646. lyked (Emerson)] MS lykes
1655. counsayl (Bülbring)] MS *om.*

1634. *tede:* 'joined together'. The poet may have been influenced by the Vulgate *ligata* 'difficult (*lit.* bound) things' (Dan. 5 : 16). Cf. *G* 35: *with lel letteres loken.*
1636. 'and I shall keep the promise that I have made to you'.
1642. 'Great king of this realm, may our Lord guide you!'
1647. 'Whoever he wished to do good to, good came to him'.
1651–4. 'Thus the renown of Nebuchadnezzar was made famous, his kingdom firmly established by the mighty Lord, because he had a belief in his heart concerning the Highest, that all power came directly from that Prince.'
1655. *counsayl:* An alliterating noun appears to have been lost. Bülbring's **5b** suggestion seems to fit the context better than Gollancz's *coyntise.*

He hade so huge an insy3t to his aune dedes
Þat þe power of þe hy3e Prynce he purely for3etes.　　　　1660
Þenne blynnes he not of blasfemy on to blame þe Dry3tyn;
His my3t mete to Goddes he made with his wordes:
"I am god of þe grounde, to gye as me lykes.
As He þat hy3e is in heuen, His aungeles þat weldes.
If He hatz formed þe folde and folk þervpone,　　　　1665
I haf bigged Babiloyne, bur3 alþer-rychest,
Stabled þerinne vche a ston in strenkþe of myn armes;
Mo3t neuer my3t bot myn make such anoþer."
Watz not þis ilke worde wonnen of his mowþe
Er þenne þe Souerayn sa3e souned in his eres:　　　　1670
"Now Nabugodenozar inno3e hatz spoken,
Now is alle þy pryncipalté past at ones,
And þou, remued fro monnes sunes, on mor most abide
And in wasturne walk and wyth þe wylde dowelle,
As best, byte on þe bent of braken and erbes,　　　　1675
With wroþe wolfes to won and wyth wylde asses."
Inmydde þe poynt of his pryde departed he þere
Fro þe soly of his solempneté; his solace he leues,
And carfully is outkast to contré vnknawen,
Fer into a fyr fryth þere frekes neuer comen.　　　　1680
His hert heldet vnhole; he hoped non oþer
Bot a best þat he be, a bol oþer an oxe.
He fares forth on alle faure, fogge watz his mete,
And ete ay as a horce when erbes were fallen;
Þus he countes hym a kow þat watz a kyng ryche,　　　　1685
Quyle seuen syþez were ouerseyed, someres I trawe.

1669. mowþe (Menner)] MS *adds* one (*in a later hand*)

1661f. 'Then he does not hold back from blasphemy so as to disparage the Lord; with his words he made his might equal to God's'.

1661-1798. The poet bases this part of the narrative on Dan. 4:27-33 and 5:21-31.

1666-8. 'I have built Babylon, richest city of all, established every stone there through the strength of my arms; no power but mine could ever make another such (city).'

1670. Cf. *Pat* 63f.

1675. 'like a beast, eat bracken and grass in the field'. Cf. *Pat* 392.

1681f. 'His mind became unsound; he thought no other than that he was a beast, a bull or an ox.'

1684. 'and ate hay like a horse when plants were dead': i.e. in the winter.

1686. 'until seven periods had passed, summers I believe.' *Someres I trawe* is an interpretative comment on the Vulgate's rather vague *tempora* (the line being adapted from *septem tempora mutabuntur super te* 'seven times shall pass over thee' [Dan. 4:29]).

By þat mony þik fytherez þry3t vmbe his lyre,
Þat alle watz dubbed and dy3t in þe dew of heuen;
Faxe, fyltered and felt, flo3ed hym vmbe,
Þat schad fro his schulderes to his schere-wykes,   1690
And twenty-folde twynande hit to his tos ra3t,
Þer mony clyuy as clyde hit cly3t togeder.
His berde ibrad alle his brest to þe bare vrþe,
His browes bresed as breres aboute his brode chekes;   [f80ᵛ]
Hol3e were his y3en and vnder campe hores,   1695
And al watz gray as þe glede, with ful grymme clawres
Þat were croked and kene as þe kyte paune;
Erne-hwed he watz and al ouerbrawden,
Til he wyst ful wel who wro3t alle my3tes,
And cowþe vche kyndam tokerue and keuer when Hym lyked.   1700
Þenne He wayned hym his wyt, þat hade wo soffered,
Þat he com to knawlach and kenned hymseluen;
Þenne he loued þat Lorde and leued in trawþe
Hit watz non oþer þen He þat hade al in honde.
Þenne sone watz he sende agayn, his sete restored;   1705
His barounes bo3ed hym to, blyþe of his come,

1687.   fytherez] MS thy3e
1689.   flo3ed (Fowler)] MS flosed
1690.   schere-wykes (Menner)] MS schyre wykes

1687.   This line has caused great difficulty. Gollancz's emendation to *the3e* 'sinews' is entirely unacceptable. Menner translates 'By that time many thick (tufts of hair) were growing about his flesh', taking *thy3e* as 'were growing' (from the verb *the*), *þry3t* as pp. of *þryche* 'to crowd' used as an adj., and *þik* as an adj. used substantively to mean 'thick (tufts of hair)'. However, the sense 'grow' for *the* is strained; and *mony þik* hardly follows the usual pattern for the substantive adj., in that it does not possess the essential quality of the object designated. Our emendation derives support from the Vulgate (Dan. 4:30) *donec capilli ejus in similitudinem aquilarum crescerent* 'till his hairs grew like the feathers of eagles'. Furthermore, there is a mark above the *y* of *thy3e* which looks like an abortive *-er* abbreviation sign. *þry3t* is taken as pa.t. rather than pp., and the line translated 'By that time many thick feathers crowded around his face.'

1689–98.   Compare the description of the giant in the alliterative *Morte Arthure* 1078–90.

1689.   'hair, tangled and matted, flowed all around him'. Fowler's **5b** emendation, assuming a simple scribal error, clarifies an otherwise obscure line.

1691f.   'and entwining twenty-fold it reached to his toes, where many (hairs) clung as though plaster stuck it together.'

1701f.   'Then He restored his reason to him who had suffered sorrow, so that he recovered his senses and knew himself'. Like Jonah, Nebuchadnezzar learns through suffering: cf. *Pat* 296.

1704.   *hade al in honde:* 'controlled everything'.

Haȝerly in his aune hwef his heued watz couered,
And so ȝeply watz ȝarked and ȝolden his state.
Bot þou, Baltazar, his barne and his bolde ayre,
Seȝ þese syngnes with syȝt and set hem at lyttel,   1710
Bot ay hatz hofen þy hert agaynes þe hyȝe Dryȝtyn,
With bobaunce and with blasfamye bost at Hym kest,
And now His vessayles avyled in vanyté vnclene,
Þat in His hows Hym to honour were heuened of fyrst;
Bifore þe barounz hatz hom broȝt, and byrled þerinne   1715
Wale wyne to þy wenches in waryed stoundes;
Bifore þy borde hatz þou broȝt beuerage in þ'edé,
Þat blyþely were fyrst blest with bischopes hondes,
Louande þeron lese goddez þat lyf haden neuer,
Made of stokkes and stonez þat neuer styry moȝt.   1720
And for þat froþande fylþe, þe Fader of heuen
Hatz sende into þis sale þise syȝtes vncowþe,
Þe fyste with þe fyngeres þat flayed þi hert,
Þat rasped renyschly þe woȝe with þe roȝ penne.
Þise ar þe wordes here wryten, withoute werk more,   1725

1707. hwef] MS hwe
1711. Dryȝtyn] MS dryȝtn
1722. Hatz sende] MS *repeats*

1707. 'his head was covered fittingly with his own headdress'. In the context of 1706–8 this is evidently a reference to the solemn reinstatement of Nebuchadnezzar (Vulgate *et in regno meo restitutus sum* 'and I was restored to my kingdom' [Dan. 4:33]), which is symbolized by a new coronation. Though Gollancz did not emend in this instance, he later recognized (see his note to *G* 1738) that MS *hwe* here represents OE *hūfe* 'head covering'. It seems possible that the form which lies behind MS *hwe(z)* here and at *G* 1738 is *hwef*, representing a diphthongized pronunciation. The scribe's treatment of the similar word *douue* (OE *dūfa*; see 469n) suggests that words of this structure could have had a diphthongized form in the exemplar.

1717. *þ'edé*: MS *þede* has caused much difficulty. Clearly the sense requires a word meaning 'vessels'. Menner retains *þede*, acknowledging the *OED* definition 'a brewer's strainer', but suggesting that it is here used to mean 'vessel'. Gollancz offers a bold emendation to *þ'ydres* 'the vessels', which he derives from Latin *hydria*. Here *þ'edé* is taken as a substantive use of the adj. *edé, edi*: 'the blessed vessels'. *MED*, *edi* sense 2(*a*) provides evidence that *the edi* is used in ME to mean 'the blessed one'. This interpretation has the advantage of maintaining the contrast between the sacredness of the vessels and the blasphemous use to which they are being put.

1719f. These false gods have been described twice previously, in 1341–8 and 1523–5.

1725f. 'Without more ado, these are the words here written, with each character, as I find (it), as it pleases our Father'.

By vch fygure, as I fynde, as oure Fader lykes:
Mane, Techal, Phares: merked in þrynne,
Þat þretes þe of þyn vnþryfte vpon þre wyse.
Now expowne þe þis speche spedly I þenk:
Mane menes als much as "Maynful Gode   [f81ʳ] 1730
Hatz counted þy kyndam bi a clene noumbre,
And fulfylled hit in fayth to þe fyrre ende".
To teche þe of *Techal,* þat terme þus menes:
"Þy wale rengne is walt in weȝtes to heng,
And is funde ful fewe of hit fayth-dedes."   1735
And *Phares* folȝes for þose fawtes, to frayst þe trawþe;
In *Phares* fynde I forsoþe þise felle saȝes:
"Departed is þy pryncipalté, depryued þou worþes,
Þy rengne rafte is þe fro, and raȝt is þe Perses;
Þe Medes schal be maysteres here, and þou of menske schowued."'   1740
Þe kyng comaunded anon to cleþe þat wyse
In frokkes of fyn cloþ, as forward hit asked;
Þenne sone watz Danyel dubbed in ful dere porpor,
And a coler of cler golde kest vmbe his swyre.
Þen watz demed a decre bi þe duk seluen: 1745
Bolde Baltazar bed þat hym bowe schulde
Þe comynes al of Caldé þat to þe kyng longed,
As to þe prynce pryuyest preued þe þrydde,
Heȝest of alle oþer saf onelych tweyne,
To boȝ after Baltazar in borȝe and in felde.   1750
Þys watz cryed and knawen in cort als fast,
And alle þe folk þerof fayn þat folȝed hym tylle.
Bot howso Danyel watz dyȝt, þat day ouerȝede;

1744. coler] MS cloler
1746. Baltazar] MS Baltaza

1728. *of:* 'for'.
1730–32. '*Mene* is as much as to say: "Mighty God has reckoned your kingdom by an exact number, and in faith has completed it to its latter end."' The poet is rendering the mysterious message of Dan. 5:26.
1734f. 'Your noble kingdom is chosen to hang in the scales, and has been found very lacking in deeds of faith.'
1742. *as forward hit asked:* 'as the agreement required'. Belshazzar gives Daniel the rewards promised in 1623–40.
1746–50. 'noble Belshazzar commanded that all the common people of Chaldea who belonged to the king should bow to him (Daniel), as (one) acknowledged as third nearest to the prince, highest of all save two, to follow Belshazzar in city and country.'
1753–6. 'But however Daniel was dressed (i.e. honoured), that day passed; night approached immediately with very many troubles, for another day never dawned, after that same darkness, before that very judgement that Daniel had expounded was executed.'

Ny3t ne3ed ry3t now with nyes fol mony,
For da3ed neuer anoþer day, þat ilk derk after, 1755
Er dalt were þat ilk dome þat Danyel deuysed.
Þe solace of þe solempneté in þat sale dured
Of þat farand fest, tyl fayled þe sunne;
Þenne blykned þe ble of þe bry3t skwes,
Mourkenes þe mery weder, and þe myst dryues 1760
Þor3 þe lyst of þe lyfte, bi þe lo3 medoes.
Vche haþel to his home hy3es ful fast,
Seten at her soper and songen þerafter;
Þen foundez vch a fela3schyp fyrre at forþ na3tes.
Baltazar to his bedd with blysse watz caryed; 1765
Reche þe rest as hym lyst: he ros neuer þerafter. [f81ᵛ]
For his foes in þe felde in flokkes ful grete,
Þat longe hade layted þat lede his londes to strye,
Now ar þay sodenly assembled at þe self tyme.
Of hem wyst no wy3e þat in þat won dowelled. 1770
Hit watz þe dere Daryus, þe duk of þise Medes,
Þe prowde prynce of Perce, and Porros of Ynde,
With mony a legioun ful large, with ledes of armes,
Þat now hatz spyed a space to spoyle Caldéez.
Þay þrongen þeder in þe þester on þrawen hepes, 1775
Asscaped ouer þe skyre watteres and scayled þe walles,
Lyfte laddres ful longe and vpon lofte wonen,
Stelen stylly þe toun er any steuen rysed.
Withinne an oure of þe niy3t an entré þay hade,
3et afrayed þay no freke. Fyrre þay passen, 1780
And to þe palays pryncipal þay aproched ful stylle,
Þenne ran þay in on a res on rowtes ful grete;
Blastes out of bry3t brasse brestes so hy3e,
Ascry scarred on þe scue, þat scomfyted mony.
Segges slepande were slayne er þay slyppe my3t; 1785
Vche hous heyred watz withinne a hondewhyle.
Baltazar in his bed watz beten to deþe,

1776. scayled (Gollancz)] MS scaþed

1761. *Þor3 þe lyst of þe lyfte:* 'through the edge of the sky': i.e. along the horizon.
1764. 'then each company goes on its way late at night.' The groups of feasters finally disperse to bed.
1766. 'let him obtain rest as it pleases him: he never rose again.'
1774. 'who has now spied an opportunity to plunder Chaldea (*lit.* Chaldeans).'
1783f. 'blasts from bright brass trumpets burst out so loud, an alarmed clamour in the sky, which daunted many.'

Þat boþe his blod and his brayn blende on þe cloþes;
The kyng in his cortyn watz kaȝt bi þe heles,
Feryed out bi þe fete and fowle dispysed. 1790
Þat watz so doȝty þat day and drank of þe vessayl
Now is a dogge also dere þat in a dych lygges.
For þe mayster of þyse Medes on þe morne ryses,
Dere Daryous þat day dyȝt vpon trone,
Þat ceté seses ful sounde, and saȝtlyng makes 1795
Wyth alle þe barounz þeraboute, þat bowed hym after.
And þus watz þat londe lost for þe lordes synne,
And þe fylþe of þe freke þat defowled hade
Þe ornementes of Goddez hous þat holy were maked.
He watz corsed for his vnclannes, and cached þerinne, 1800
Done doun of his dyngneté for dedez vnfayre,
And of þyse worldes worchyp wrast out for euer, [f82ʳ]
And ȝet of lykynges on lofte letted, I trowe:
To loke on oure lofly Lorde late bitydes.
Þus vpon þrynne wyses I haf yow þro schewed 1805
Þat vnclannes tocleues in corage dere
Of þat wynnelych Lorde þat wonyes in heuen,
Entyses Hym to be tene, teldes vp His wrake;
Ande clannes is His comfort, and coyntyse He louyes,
And þose þat seme arn and swete schyn se His face. 1810
Þat we gon gay in oure gere þat grace He vus sende,
Þat we may serue in His syȝt, þer solace neuer blynnez.
                                                Amen.

1808. teldes (Menner)] MS telled

1791–1800. This passage serves as a statement of the relationship between the story of
Belshazzar and the theme of cleanness.
1791f. 'He who was so bold that day and drank from the vessels is now as noble as
a dog that lies in a ditch.'
1795f. 'seizes the city entirely undamaged, and is reconciled with all the barons
thereabout, who followed after him.'
1803f. 'and also deprived of pleasures above, I believe: to look on our lovely Lord will
happen late (for him)': i.e. he will never do so.
1805. The three stories alluded to are those of the Flood, the Destruction of the Cities,
and Belshazzar's Feast: see Introduction, pp. 26–9.
1806f. 'that uncleanness cleaves asunder the noble heart of that gracious Lord who
dwells in heaven'.
1810. This line is reminiscent of the Beatitudes: see 23–8 and notes, and *Pat* 9–33.
1811f. 'May He send us that grace that we may go brightly in our apparel, so that we
may serve in His sight, where joy never ceases.' The bright clothes are again symbolic
of purity, and thus of salvation.

Patience

Pacience is a poynt, þaȝ hit displese ofte.   [f83ʳ]
When heuy herttes ben hurt wyth heþyng oþer elles,
Suffraunce may aswagen hem and þe swelme leþe,
For ho quelles vche a qued and quenches malyce;
For quoso suffer cowþe syt, sele wolde folȝe,   5
And quo for þro may noȝt þole, þe þikker he sufferes.
Þen is better to abyde þe bur vmbestoundes
Þen ay þrow forth my þro, þaȝ me þynk ylle.
I herde on a halyday, at a hyȝe masse,
How Mathew melede þat his Mayster His meyny con teche.   10
Aȝt happes He hem hyȝt and vcheon a mede,
Sunderlupes, for hit dissert, vpon a ser wyse:
Thay arn happen þat han in hert pouerté,
For hores is þe heuen-ryche to holde for euer;
Þay ar happen also þat haunte mekenesse,   15
For þay schal welde þis worlde and alle her wylle haue;
Thay ar happen also þat for her harme wepes,

---

3. aswagen] MS aswagend

1–8. 'Patience is a virtue, though it may often displease. When sorrowful hearts are
hurt by scorn or something else, long-suffering can ease them and assuage the heat,
for she (patience) kills everything bad and extinguishes malice. For if anyone could
endure sorrow, happiness would follow; and anyone who, through resentment, can-
not endure suffers the more intensely. So it is better (for me) to put up with the
onslaught from time to time, though this may be distasteful to me, than to give vent
continually to my resentment.' For *poynt* (1) 'virtue' cf. *G* 627n; Bateson gratuitously
supplies *noble* before *poynt* (to match 531). With 6 cf. *Pe* 344.

9f. Cf. *PPl* C.VI.272f. In the present Roman Missal the Beatitudes passage from St
Matthew is the Gospel for the Feast of All Saints (1 Nov.) and its Octave, that of St
Boniface (5 June) and of certain other martyrs. This association with the Feast of St
Boniface, the 8th c. English apostle to Saxony, may have been in the poet's mind in
prefacing it to the story of the unwilling prophet Jonah. For a briefer reference to St
Matthew and the Beatitudes, in somewhat similar wording, see *Cl* 23–8.

11f. 'He decreed them eight beatitudes, and for each one a reward, severally, accord-
ing to its merit, in a diverse manner'.

13–28. This passage is a fairly close rendering of Matt. 5:3–10.

17f. 'they are blessed also who weep for their wrong (sin), for they shall obtain
comfort in many countries'. *Harme* could mean either 'injury (done to them)' or 'sin'
(cf. *G* 2511)—the Vulgate has simply *Beati qui lugent* 'Blessed are they that mourn'—
but a common medieval gloss is *pro suis vel aliorum peccatis* ('for their own sins or those

For þay schal comfort encroche in kythes ful mony;
Þay ar happen also þat hungeres after ryȝt,
For þay schal frely be refete ful of alle gode;   20
Thay ar happen also þat han in hert rauþe,
For mercy in alle maneres her mede schal worþe;
Þay ar happen also þat arn of hert clene,
For þay her Sauyour in sete schal se with her yȝen;
Thay ar happen also þat halden her pese,   25
For þay þe gracious Godes sunes schal godly be called;
Þay ar happen also þat con her hert stere,
For hores is þe heuen-ryche, as I er sayde.
These arn þe happes alle aȝt þat vus bihyȝt weren,
If we þyse ladyes wolde lof in lyknyng of þewes: 30
Dame Pouert, Dame Pitée, Dame Penaunce þe þrydde,   [f83ᵛ]
Dame Mekenesse, Dame Mercy, and miry Clannesse,
And þenne Dame Pes, and Pacyence put in þerafter.
He were happen þat hade one; alle were þe better.
Bot syn I am put to a poynt þat pouerté hatte,   35

---

35. syn] MS fyn

---

of others'). It is probable that the poet has this interpretation in mind, for the
personification to which this Beatitude relates is called *Dame Penaunce* (31).

25. 'they are blessed also who remain quiet'. Cf. Vulgate *Beati pacifici* 'Blessed are the
peacemakers': as in 17, the English rendering is an interpretation rather than a
direct translation. It also reflects the influence of the commentaries: the *Glossa
Ordinaria* (*PL* 114 : 90) cites the following (Augustinian) definition: *Pacifici sunt qui
omnes motus animis componunt et rationi subjiciunt* ('The peaceful are those who quieten
all motions of the soul and subdue them to reason').

27. *þat con her hert stere:* 'who can control their hearts'. Cf. Vulgate *qui persecutionem
patiuntur propter justitiam* 'that suffer persecution for justice' sake'. This is the poet's
only radical departure from the Vulgate text of the Beatitudes in St Matthew. His
alteration places emphasis on self-control and moderation—a theme of major
relevance to the story of Jonah.

28. *as I er sayde* ('as I said before') draws attention to the similarity of the first and last
Beatitude (cf. 37–40).

30. *in lyknyng of þewes:* 'in imitation of (their) virtues'.

31–3. These figures personify the virtues celebrated in the Beatitudes. The phrasing of
31 and 32 shows the influence of tradition: in groups of three co-ordinate nouns,
particularly proper nouns, the last is often marked by an epithet: see *G* 553 and *Pe*
105 (and, for instance, *Beowulf* 61), and J. P. Oakden's observations in *RES*, 9
(1933), 50–53.

35f. The close connection between patience and poverty has biblical authority (see,
for example, Ps. 9 : 19), and is of major significance in *PPl* C.XIIf., XVI. *Play me*
(36) 'amuse myself' continues the figurative language of love begun in 30.

I schal me poruay pacence and play me with boþe,
For in þe tyxte þere þyse two arn in teme layde,
Hit arn fettled in on forme, þe forme and þe laste,
And by quest of her quoyntyse enquylen on mede.
And als, in myn vpynyoun, hit arn of on kynde: 40
For þeras pouert hir proferes ho nyl be put vtter,
Bot lenge wheresoeuer hir lyst, lyke oþer greme;
And þereas pouert enpresses, þaȝ mon pyne þynk,
Much, maugré his mun, he mot nede suffer;
Thus pouerté and pacence arn nedes playferes.   45
Syþen I am sette with hem samen, suffer me byhoues;
Þenne is me lyȝtloker hit lyke and her lotes prayse,
Þenne wyþer wyth and be wroth and þe wers haue.
Ȝif me be dyȝt a destyné due to haue,
What dowes me þe dedayn, oþer dispit make?   50
Oþer ȝif my lege lorde lyst on lyue me to bidde
Oþer to ryde oþer to renne to Rome in his ernde,

37–9. 'for in the passage (the Beatitudes) where these two are discussed, they are presented in one formula (as) the first and the last, and by pursuit of their wisdom (*or* beauty, courtliness) attain one (the same) reward.' *Quoyntyse* (39) suggests both the metaphorical beauty of the 'ladies' and the wisdom of the virtues they represent: cf. the metaphor of courtship in *Cl* 1057–64. This passage may also allude to the identification—often found in medieval commentaries, and made specifically in the morality play *Wisdom*—between Christ and wisdom (cf. 1 Cor. 1:24). Thus 39 could be interpreted as suggesting the pursuit of Christ: cf. *Pe* 689–94n.

40–45. The poet has already discussed the theoretical connection between poverty and patience; these lines now illustrate the reality of the connection in terms of human experience.

44. *maugré his mun:* 'in spite of anything he might say'. The original form of the phrase was *maugré his* 'in spite of him', but this is often extended for emphasis by the addition of a part of the body, as if *his* were possessive. Cf. 54, *G* 1565.

46. *sette with:* 'beset by'.

47. 'then it is easier for me to like it and praise their manners'.

49f. 'If it is ordained for me to receive an inevitable fate, what does indignation, or making resistance, avail me?' Man's reluctance to accept the destiny which God has determined for him is a central theme in both *Pat* and *Pe*.

52. *Rome:* This word has usually been interpreted as the verb *rome* 'roam'—which contributes little to the sense. Ekwall's **5c** suggestion that it means 'Rome' is preferable: thus the idea of going to Rome is used as a metaphor for any arduous journey (cf. the proverbial *from hence to Rome*, meaning 'a long way' [Whiting R.182]). Anderson points out similar usages in the Towneley play No. 30, 127f, and in *Ancrene Wisse* (EETS OS 249) 221. Possibly the preacher–narrator also implies the situation of a priest sent to Rome by his bishop (Chaucer's Pardoner refers to his bishop as *oure lige lorde* in 'The Pardoner's Prologue' [*CT* VI.337]). If so, this would serve to emphasize both the specific connection between Jonah and the narrator as men under an obligation to preach the Word of God, and (in more general terms) the universal relevance of the ensuing story of Jonah.

What grayþed me þe grychchyng bot grame more seche?
Much ȝif he me ne made, maugref my chekes,
And þenne þrat moste I þole and vnþonk to mede,   55
Þe had bowed to his bode bongré my hyure.
Did not Jonas in Judé suche jape sumwhyle?
To sette hym to sewrté, vnsounde he hym feches.
Wyl ȝe tary a lyttel tyne and tent me a whyle,
I schal wysse yow þerwyth as holy wryt telles.   60
Hit bitydde sumtyme in þe termes of Judé,
Jonas joyned watz þerinne Jentyle prophete;
Goddes glam to hym glod þat hym vnglad made,
With a roghlych rurd rowned in his ere:
'Rys radly,' He says, 'and rayke forth euen;   65
Nym þe way to Nynyue wythouten oþer speche,
And in þat ceté My saȝes soghe alle aboute,   [f84ʳ]
Þat in þat place, at þe poynt, I put in þi hert.
For iwysse hit arn so wykke þat in þat won dowellez
And her malys is so much, I may not abide,   70
Bot venge Me on her vilanye and venym bilyue;
Now sweȝe Me þider swyftly and say Me þis arende.'
When þat steuen watz stynt þat stowned his mynde,
Al he wrathed in his wyt, and wyþerly he þoȝt:
'If I bowe to His bode and bryng hem þis tale,   75

---

73.   stowned] MS støwnod

53–6.   'what good would complaining do me?—it would only invite more trouble. It would be a great thing (i.e. very fortunate) if he did not compel me, despite my objections, and then I would have to endure compulsion and vexation as my reward, who should have complied with his command in accordance with (the terms of) my hire.' *Much ȝif he me ne made* (54): see Grattan, **5c** 1914, 403, and cf. *Cl* 21f. *Hyure* (56) may remind us of the parable of the Vineyard, used in *Pe* to symbolize the relationship between God and man.

57.   *jape* anticipates the comic element in the poet's treatment of Jonah.

58.   'in his attempt to achieve security, he brings himself misfortune.'

59f.   Cf. *Cl* 1153, *G* 30f. Note the strong appeal to scriptural authority, and cf. 244. The story of Jonah is of course mainly based on the OT Book of Jonah. *Wysse yow þerwyth:* 'instruct you by means of it'.

62.   *Jentyle prophete:* 'prophet to the Gentiles'.

63.   Cf. *Cl* 499. The poet informs us immediately that God's message makes Jonah 'vnglad': thus anticipating his rebellious conduct.

64.   This line foreshadows the way in which God later works through the elements, in the storm and again in the episode of the woodbine: cf. 247n.

71.   'but will revenge Myself on their evil and malice immediately'. The future auxiliary is understood, perhaps from *may* in 70; *may* is sometimes a pure future auxiliary ('will') in ME.

72.   *Me:* 'for Me'.

And I be nummen in Nuniue, my nyes begynes:
He telles me þose traytoures arn typped schrewes;
I com wyth þose tyþynges, þay ta me bylyue,
Pynez me in a prysoun, put me in stokkes,
Wryþe me in a warlok, wrast out myn yȝen.   80
Þis is a meruayl message a man for to preche
Amonge enmyes so mony and mansed fendes,
Bot if my gaynlych God such gref to me wolde,
For desert of sum sake þat I slayn were.
At alle peryles,' quoþ þe prophete, 'I aproche hit no nerre.   85
I wyl me sum oþer waye þat He ne wayte after;
I schal tee into Tarce and tary þere a whyle,
And lyȝtly when I am lest He letes me alone.'
Þenne he ryses radly and raykes bilyue,
Jonas toward port Japh, ay janglande for tene   90
Þat he nolde þole for noþyng non of þose pynes,
Þaȝ þe Fader þat hym formed were fale of his hele.
'Oure Syre syttes,' he says, 'on sege so hyȝe
In His glowande glorye, and gloumbes ful lyttel
Þaȝ I be nummen in Nunniue and naked dispoyled,   95
On rode rwly torent with rybaudes mony.'
Þus he passes to þat port his passage to seche,
Fyndes he a fayr schyp to þe fare redy,
Maches hym with þe maryneres, makes her paye

84. For] MS fof
94. glowande] MS g wande (*nothing legible in space between* g *and* w)

77. *typped:* The exact sense is not certain, but there has been general agreement that it probably means 'consummate, extreme' (cf. ModE 'with knobs on').

79. *Pynez:* the spelling suggests 'torture', but 'pin, confine' is also possible and perhaps more appropriate in the context.

83f. 'unless my gracious God wishes such suffering to befall me, that I should be slain in recompense for some fault.'

83–8. Note the bitterness against God in Jonah's comments as he tries to justify his desire to shirk his duty. The futility of his plan to escape from God is demonstrated by the storm, and already suggested by 49ff.

86. The verb of motion is omitted after an auxiliary.

91. Cf. 6—which can provide a criticism of Jonah's attitude here.

92. *fale of:* 'indifferent about'.

95f. This description clearly suggests the Crucifixion (cf. *Pe* 806), encouraging the reader to see Jonah's conduct in comparison to Christ's. For a consideration of the implications of this connection, see Andrew, 7c 1972–3.

99–108. 'settles with the seamen, pays their fee to take him to Tarshish as soon as they could. Then he stepped on board that ship (*lit.* on those boards) and they prepare their tackle, hoist the mainsail, fasten ropes; quickly they weigh their anchors at the windlass, smartly fasten the spare bow-line to the bowsprit, haul at the guy-ropes,

For to towe hym into Tarce as tyd as þay myȝt.   100
Then he tron on þo tres, and þay her tramme ruchen,
Cachen vp þe crossayl, cables þay fasten,
Wiȝt at þe wyndas weȝen her ankres,   [f84ᵛ]
Spende spak to þe sprete þe spare bawelyne,
Gederen to þe gyde-ropes, þe grete cloþ falles,   105
Þay layden in on laddeborde, and þe lofe wynnes,
Þe blyþe breþe at her bak þe bosum he fyndes;
He swenges me þys swete schip swefte fro þe hauen.
Watz neuer so joyful a Jue as Jonas watz þenne,
Þat þe daunger of Dryȝtyn so derfly ascaped;   110
He wende wel þat þat Wyȝ þat al þe world planted
Hade no maȝt in þat mere no man for to greue.
Lo, þe wytles wrechche! For he wolde noȝt suffer,
Now hatz he put hym in plyt of peril wel more.
Hit watz a wenyng vnwar þat welt in his mynde,   115
Þaȝ he were soȝt fro Samarye, þat God seȝ no fyrre.
Ȝise, He blusched ful brode: þat burde hym by sure;
Þat ofte kyd hym þe carpe þat kyng sayde,
Dyngne Dauid on des þat demed þis speche
In a psalme þat he set þe sauter withinne: 120
'O folez in folk, felez oþerwhyle

---

the huge canvas falls; they put in (their oars) on the larboard side and gain the luff (i.e. the advantage of the wind). The happy (i.e. favourable) wind behind them finds the swelling sail; it swiftly swings this fine ship out of the harbour.' The abrupt half lines create a sense of the sailors' bustling activity and Jonah's anxiety to escape. *Spende* (104): it is not absolutely clear whether the scribe intended *spende*, *spynde*, or *sprude*. The word has usually been read as *sprude* 'spread', but the form is dubious and unrecorded, and the sense weak. Anderson suggests *spynde*, interpreting this as a form of the pa.t. of *spennan* 'fasten'. But the MS most probably reads *spende* ('fastened'): the angle of the hair-line is closer to that of the usual *e* than to that of the usual *y*. Cf. *spend* (pp.), *G* 587. *Me* (108): ethic dative (see *G* 1905n).

113. *For:* 'because'.

117f. 'Yes, He looked far and wide (*or* with eyes wide open: cf. *G* 446): of that he (Jonah) should have been sure; the speech which the king made often declared that to him'. Gollancz argues that *hym* (117) refers to God, translating the second half of the line: 'it beseemed Him, be sure!' It is more likely that *hym* refers to Jonah; as Anderson points out, *hym* in 118 unequivocally denotes Jonah, and the change in reference of the personal pronouns is less awkward in 117 than it would be in 118.

121-4. This is translated from Ps. 93 (AV 94) : 8–9; cf. the similar use of this text in *Cl* 581ff. *Stapen in folé* (122): the MS reading *stape fole* has caused some difficulty. Anderson suggests that *stape* is derived from OF *estapé* 'mad', and that *stape fole* means ' "quite mad", *lit.* "crazy-mad" '. Gollancz emends to *stape in folé*, which he glosses 'advanced in folly', with reference to OE *stæppan* 'step, advance'. Here Gollancz's suggestion is followed, except that the reading *stapen* is adopted, as a more likely pp. form. The emendation assumes omission of *in* at an earlier stage by homoeoteleuton.

And vnderstondes vmbestounde, þaȝ ȝe be stapen in folé:
Hope ȝe þat He heres not þat eres alle made?
Hit may not be þat He is blynde þat bigged vche yȝe.'
Bot he dredes no dynt þat dotes for elde.   125
For he watz fer in þe flod foundande to Tarce,
Bot I trow ful tyd ouertan þat he were,
So þat schomely to schort he schote of his ame.
For þe Welder of wyt þat wot alle þynges,
Þat ay wakes and waytes, at wylle hatz He slyȝtes.   130
He calde on þat ilk crafte He carf with His hondes;
Þay wakened wel þe wroþeloker for wroþely He cleped:
'Ewrus and Aquiloun þat on est sittes
Blowes boþe at My bode vpon blo watteres.'
Þenne watz no tom þer bytwene His tale and her dede,   135
So bayn wer þay boþe two His bone for to wyrk.
Anon out of þe norþ-est þe noys bigynes,
When boþe breþes con blowe vpon blo watteres.
Roȝ rakkes þer ros with rudnyng anvnder;   [f85ʳ]
Þe see souȝed ful sore, gret selly to here;   140
Þe wyndes on þe wonne water so wrastel togeder
Þat þe wawes ful wode waltered so hiȝe
And efte busched to þe abyme, þat breed fysches
Durst nowhere for roȝ arest at þe bothem.
When þe breth and þe brok and þe bote metten,   145
Hit watz a joyles gyn þat Jonas watz inne,
For hit reled on roun vpon þe roȝe yþes.
Þe bur ber to hit baft, þat braste alle her gere,
Þen hurled on a hepe þe helme and þe sterne;
Furst tomurte mony rop and þe mast after;   150

122.   ȝe (Zupitza)] MS he
      stapen] MS stape
      in (Gollancz)] MS *om.*

125. *elde:* There is no biblical support for this suggestion that Jonah's folly may result
from senility; neither has any source been found among the Christian commentators.
Stapen (122) may also have overtones of senility: cf. Chaucer, 'The Nun's Priest's
Tale', *CT* VII.2821.

131ff. These lines emphasize God's control over nature, which is a key factor in both
the storm and the woodbine episodes. In classical terminology, Eurus is a wind from
the east or south-east, and Aquilon from the north or north-north-east. Cf. Virgil,
Aeneid I.52ff.

132. 'they awakened so much the more angrily because He called angrily'.

137ff. The description of the storm may be compared to the account of the Flood in
Cl: see *Cl* 363ff and note.

147. Cf. *Cl* 423.

148. *þat braste alle her gere:* 'so that all their gear broke'.

Þe sayl sweyed on þe see, þenne suppe bihoued
Þe coge of þe colde water, and þenne þe cry ryses.
3et coruen þay þe cordes and kest al þeroute;
Mony ladde þer forth lep to laue and to kest—
Scopen out þe scaþel water þat fayn scape wolde—   155
For be monnes lode neuer so luþer, þe lyf is ay swete.
Þer watz busy ouer borde bale to kest,
Her bagges and her feþer-beddes and her bry3t wedes,
Her kysttes and her coferes, her caraldes alle,
And al to ly3ten þat lome, 3if leþe wolde schape.   160
Bot euer watz ilyche loud þe lot of þe wyndes,
And euer wroþer þe water and wodder þe stremes.
Þen þo wery forwro3t wyst no bote,
Bot vchon glewed on his god þat gayned hym beste:
Summe to Vernagu þer vouched avowes solemne,   165
Summe to Diana deuout and derf Neptune,
To Mahoun and to Mergot, þe mone and þe sunne,
And vche lede as he loued and layde had his hert.
Þenne bispeke þe spakest, dispayred wel nere:
'I leue here be sum losynger, sum lawles wrech,   170

---

152. colde] MS clolde
166. Neptune (Anderson)] MS Nepturne

154–6. 'many a fellow ran forward there to bale out and throw (overboard)—those who were anxious to escape scooped out the harmful water—for however wretched a man's way of life may be, life itself is still sweet.' Cf. the poet's similar comment in 280.

157ff. The implied contempt for the trappings of civilization gives a subdued moral tone to the narrative. As Wilson, **8** 1976, 61, points out, this passage echoes the conventional homiletic theme of the irrelevance of luxuries to the man facing imminent death.

160. *3if leþe wolde schape:* 'in case calm should fall.'

163. *þo wery forwro3t:* 'those (men) exhausted with toil'.

164–7. The names of these deities are not found in the Vulgate account, which says simply *clamaverunt viri ad deum suum* 'the men cried to their god' (1:5). *Vernagu* (165): a giant who appears in the Charlemagne romances. *Diana deuout* (166): Diana is 'devout' in the special sense of being devoted to chastity. *Neptune* (166): Gollancz suggests that MS *Nepturne* results from scribal confusion with the ending of *Saturne*, but does not emend. *Mahoun* (167): Mahomet, who was regarded as a false god by medieval Christians. In the mystery plays, evil characters (such as Herod) often swear by him and sometimes express allegiance to him. *Mergot* (167): Margot, a heathen god mentioned in the Charlemagne romances, and probably related to the biblical Magog (see Gen. 10:2, Ezek. 38:2).

168. *and layde had his hert:* 'and had committed his heart (i.e. his faith).'

170ff. The sailor's speech emphasizes the fact that Jonah, through his selfish desire to escape his duty, has endangered the lives of innocent people. Thus, once again, his conduct is in contrast to Christ's: see 95f and note.

Þat hatz greued his god and gotz here amonge vus.
Lo, al synkes in his synne and for his sake marres.
I lovue þat we lay lotes on ledes vchone,
And whoso lympes þe losse, lay hym þeroute;
And quen þe gulty is gon, what may gome trawe   [f85ᵛ] 175
Bot He þat rules þe rak may rwe on þose oþer?'
Þis watz sette in asent, and sembled þay were,
Herȝed out of vche hyrne to hent þat falles.
A lodesmon lyȝtly lep vnder hachches,
For to layte mo ledes and hem to lote bryng.   180
Bot hym fayled no freke þat he fynde myȝt,
Saf Jonas þe Jwe, þat jowked in derne.
He watz flowen for ferde of þe flode lotes
Into þe boþem of þe bot, and on a brede lyggede,
Onhelde by þe hurrok, for þe heuen wrache,   185
Slypped vpon a sloumbe-selepe, and sloberande he routes.
Þe freke hym frunt with his fot and bede hym ferk vp:
Þer Ragnel in his rakentes hym rere of his dremes!
Bi þe haspede hater he hentes hym þenne,
And broȝt hym vp by þe brest and vpon borde sette,   190
Arayned hym ful runyschly what raysoun he hade

189.   hater (Ekwall)] MS *om.*

173–6. 'I recommend (*lit.* praise) that we deal out lots to every man and whoever the
losing one falls to, put him overboard; and what can a man believe but that, when
the guilty one is gone, He who rules the storm-cloud will have pity on the others?'

181. 'But there was no man lacking to him (among those) that he could find'; i.e. 'but
there wasn't a man that he couldn't find'.

185. *Onhelde by þe hurrok:* 'huddled by the hurrock'. The precise sense of *hurrok* is not
certain, but it probably denotes a rudder-band encircling the rudder to keep it in
position: see *Cl* 419n.

186. 'slipped into a heavy sleep, and he slobbers and snores.' The description of Jonah
is most uncomplimentary, and his sleep is probably intended to symbolize moral
lassitude. Sleep is often used in medieval religious writings to signify lack of moral
awareness. Jonah's sleep at this point is specifically interpreted as the sleep of sin by
the 13th c. commentator Hugh of St Cher, in his *Postillae* (see R. H. Bowers, *The
Legend of Jonah* [The Hague, 1971], p. 58).

188. 'may Ragnel in his chains rouse him from his dreams!' For *þer* introducing a
blessing or curse, cf. *G* 839n. *Ragnel:* the name of a devil.

189. *haspede hater:* Anderson retains the MS reading, suggesting *haspede* = *hasp-hede*
'clasp-head'—but this compound is not elsewhere recorded. It is more likely that a
noun before or after *haspede* has been omitted through homoarchy. There have been
various emendations, including *here haspede* (Gollancz, 1st edn.), *hayre haspede*
(Gollancz, 2nd edn.), and *hater haspede* (Bateson, 2nd edn.). Ekwall's **5c** sugges-
tion *haspede hater* 'clasped garment' (i.e. garment fastened with a clasp) is adopted
here.

In such slaȝtes of sorȝe to slepe so faste.
Sone haf þay her sortes sette and serelych deled,
And ay þe lote vpon laste lymped on Jonas.
Þenne ascryed þay hym sckete and asked ful loude: 195
'What þe deuel hatz þou don, doted wrech?
What seches þou on see, synful schrewe,
With þy lastes so luþer to lose vus vchone?
Hatz þou, gome, no gouernour ne god on to calle,
Þat þou þus slydes on slepe when þou slayn worþes?   200
Of what londe art þou lent, what laytes þou here,
Whyder in worlde þat þou wylt, and what is þyn arnde?
Lo, þy dom is þe dyȝt, for þy dedes ille.
Do gyf glory to þy godde, er þou glyde hens.'
'I am an Ebru,' quoþ he, 'of Israyl borne;   205
Þat Wyȝe I worchyp, iwysse, þat wroȝt alle þynges, ·
Alle þe worlde with þe welkyn, þe wynde and þe sternes,
And alle þat wonez þer withinne, at a worde one.
Alle þis meschef for me is made at þys tyme,
For I haf greued my God and gulty am founden;   210
Forþy berez me to þe borde and baþes me þeroute,   [f86ʳ]
Er gete ȝe no happe, I hope forsoþe.'
He ossed hym by vnnynges þat þay vndernomen
Þat he watz flawen fro þe face of frelych Dryȝtyn;
Þenne such a ferde on hem fel and flayed hem withinne   215
Þat þay ruyt hym to rowwe, and letten þe rynk one.
Haþeles hyȝed in haste with ores ful longe,
Syn her sayl watz hem aslypped, on sydez to rowe,

194.   þe] MS þe þe
211.   baþes] MS baþeþes

194.   *ay:* 'always': presumably the poet imagines them casting lots several times; contrast the Vulgate account (1 : 7).
197.   *What seches þou:* 'Why are you trying?'
200.   *when þou slayn worþes:* 'when you are going to be killed.'
205–12.   It is significant that as soon as Jonah is challenged with his misdemeanours he accepts full responsibility for them and agrees that he should be thrown from the boat: the poet here introduces the positive side of Jonah's character.
206–8.   'I indeed worship that Person who created all things, all the world with the sky, the wind and the stars, and all that live in it, by a single word.'
212f.   '"until then you will get no good fortune, I truly believe." He showed them by signs that they understood'.
214.   *fro þe face of frelych Dryȝtyn:* cf. Vulgate *a facie Domini* 'from the face of the Lord' (1:3).
216.   'that they hasten to row, and let the man (Jonah) alone.'

Hef and hale vpon hyȝt to helpen hymseluen,
Bot al watz nedles note: þat nolde not bityde.   220
In bluber of þe blo flod bursten her ores.
Þenne hade þay noȝt in her honde þat hem help myȝt;
Þenne nas no coumfort to keuer, ne counsel non oþer,
Bot Jonas into his juis jugge bylyue.
Fyrst þay prayen to þe Prynce þat prophetes seruen   225
Þat He gef hem þe grace to greuen Hym neuer,
Þat þay in balelez blod þer blenden her handez,
Þaȝ þat haþel wer His þat þay here quelled.
Tyd by top and bi to þay token hym synne;
Into þat lodlych loȝe þay luche hym sone.   230
He watz no tytter outtulde þat tempest ne sessed:
Þe se saȝtled þerwith as sone as ho moȝt.
Þenne þaȝ her takel were torne þat totered on yþes,
Styffe stremes and streȝt hem strayned a whyle,
Þat drof hem dryȝlych adoun þe depe to serue,   235
Tyl a swetter ful swyþe hem sweȝed to bonk.
Þer watz louyng on lofte, when þay þe londe wonnen,
To oure mercyable God, on Moyses wyse,
With sacrafyse vpset, and solempne vowes,
And graunted Hym on to be God and graythly non oþer.   240
Þaȝ þay be jolef for joye, Jonas ȝet dredes;
Þaȝ he nolde suffer no sore, his seele is on anter;
For whatso worþed of þat wyȝe fro he in water dipped,
Hit were a wonder to wene, ȝif holy wryt nere.
Now is Jonas þe Jwe jugged to drowne;   245
Of þat schended schyp men schowued hym sone.

240. on] MS vn
245. to] MS to to

219f. 'heave and pull as strongly as possible to help themselves, but all this activity
was in vain: that (i.e. what they are trying to achieve) would not happen.' Cf. *Cl*
381.
225–8. The sailors, who have previously (164–8) addressed their supplications to a
variety of heathen gods, now address the true God, and do so again later in thanks
for their escape from the storm (237–40).
231. 'No sooner was he thrown out than the tempest ceased'.
233. 'Then though the tackle of those who tottered on the waves was torn'.
235. 'that drove them relentlessly down at the mercy of (*lit.* to serve) the deep'.
240. *on:* Most editors have adopted this emendation, without which the sense is
strained. The emended line means: 'and acknowledged Him alone to be God and
truly no other.'
242. The poet emphasizes that Jonah's fate results from his lack of patience: cf. 6.
244. Once again we are reminded of the story's scriptural authority: cf. 59f and note.

A wylde walterande whal, as Wyrde þen schaped,   [f86ᵛ]
Þat watz beten fro þe abyme, bi þat bot flotte,
And watz war of þat wyʒe þat þe water soʒte,
And swyftely swenged hym to swepe, and his swolʒ opened;   250
Þe folk ʒet haldande his fete, þe fysch hym tyd hentes;
Withouten towche of any tothe he tult in his þrote.
Thenne he swengez and swayues to þe se boþem,
Bi mony rokkez ful roʒe and rydelande strondes,
Wyth þe mon in his mawe malskred in drede,   255
As lyttel wonder hit watz, ʒif he wo dreʒed,
For nade þe hyʒe Heuen-Kyng, þurʒ His honde myʒt,
Warded þis wrech man in warlowes guttez,
What lede moʒt leue bi lawe of any kynde,
Þat any lyf myʒt be lent so longe hym withinne?   260
Bot he watz sokored by þat Syre þat syttes so hiʒe,

---

259.   leue (Gollancz)] MS lyue

247.   *Wyrde:* The OE word originally meant 'fate' but changed its meaning under the pressure of Christian philosophy (see B. J. Timmer, *Neophil.*, 26 (1940–41), 24–33 and 213–28). Here it clearly indicates providence controlled directly by God, rather than fate working in a random manner. The appearance of the whale at this juncture is an example of God's using, for a specific purpose, a component of divinely ordered nature—as similarly with the winds, the sun, the woodbine, and the worm (see 131–6, 443f, 467–72, and Introduction, p. 20).

248.   This is anticipated in 142–4, where the poet speaks of the fishes being unable to stay near the sea-bed because of the turbulence of the water.

253f.   'then he (the whale) swings and sweeps to the bottom of the sea, beside many very rough rocks and winnowing sands'. Anderson glosses *rydelande strondes* 'surging currents' (OF *rideler*, OE *strand*). However, the description at this point appears to be of the sea-bed, which the poet imagines as a submerged coastal landscape. If *strondes* has the sense 'beaches, sands' (cf. *Pe* 152), *rydelande* may mean 'sifting, winnowing' (OE *hriddel* 'sieve'); cf. *Cl* 953.

258.   *warlowes:* 'the devil's'. The symbolic connection between the whale and hell was a commonplace during the Middle Ages. Sea monster's jaws were used to represent hell mouth in performances of the mystery cycles, and appear with the same significance in 'doom' paintings on church walls. This tradition may rest upon Isaiah 5:14; its influence may be seen in, e.g., Isidore of Seville's *Etymologiae* (XII.6.8) and the ME *Bestiary*, where it is stated that the whale stands for the devil.

259.   *leue:* MS *lyue* is probably a scribal error caused through neglect of syntactical continuity with the following line. If it is retained it must be understood as a form of *leue* 'believe' (so Bateson and Anderson). There is only one other instance in the MS of the spelling *y* for OE *ē* (*Pat* 454 *wype*: OE *wēþe*); thus miscopying seems the more likely explanation of the form.

259ff.   Jonah's survival inside the whale, impossible according to the laws of nature, is brought about through the protection of God. Many commentators saw the fact that Jonah was not digested as miraculous.

Þaȝ were wanlez of wele in wombe of þat fissche,
And also dryuen þurȝ þe depe and in derk walterez.
Lorde, colde watz his cumfort, and his care huge,
For he knew vche a cace and kark þat hym lymped,   265
How fro þe bot into þe blober watz with a best lachched,
And þrwe in at hit þrote withouten þret more,
As mote in at a munster dor, so mukel wern his chawlez.
He glydes in by þe giles þurȝ glaym ande glette,
Relande in by a rop, a rode þat hym þoȝt,   270
Ay hele ouer hed hourlande aboute,
Til he blunt in a blok as brod as a halle;
And þer he festnes þe fete and fathmez aboute,
And stod vp in his stomak þat stank as þe deuel.
Þer in saym and in sorȝe þat sauoured as helle,   275
Þer watz bylded his bour þat wyl no bale suffer.
And þenne he lurkkes and laytes where watz le best,
In vche a nok of his nauel, bot nowhere he fyndez
No rest ne recouerer, bot ramel ande myre,
In wych gut so euer he gotz, bot euer is God swete;   280
And þer he lenged at þe last, and to þe Lede called:
'Now, Prynce, of Þy prophete pité Þou haue.
Þaȝ I be fol and fykel and falce of my hert,   [f87ʳ]
Dewoyde now Þy vengaunce, þurȝ vertu of rauthe;
Thaȝ I be gulty of gyle, as gaule of prophetes,   285
Þou art God, and alle gowdez ar grayþely Þyn owen.
Haf now mercy of Þy man and his mysdedes,
And preue Þe lyȝtly a Lorde in londe and in water.'

262.   'though he was without hope of well-being in the belly of that fish'.

266.   'how (in going) from the boat into the seething water (he) was seized by an animal'.

268.   This fine image, with its striking perspective, emphasizes Jonah's insignificance in relation to the vastness of the whale, and thus suggests the futility of his struggle against God. Though the belly is associated with the devil and hell (see 258n, 274f, 306), the entrance is compared to a *munster* ('cathedral') *dor*: see Andrew, **7c** 1976–7.

269.   *glaym ande glette:* 'slime and filth'. It is also possible to read *glaymande glette* ('slimy filth'). Cf. 279; G 46, 1426.

272.   'till he stopped in a compartment as broad as hall'.

274.   In medieval literature the devil and hell are often associated with foul smells: see, for instance, Towneley Play No. 2, 283, and Chaucer, 'An ABC' 56. Cf. also notes to 258 and 268.

276.   Thus the poet makes explicit the relevance of this event to the theme of patience.

277.   *le:* 'shelter'.

282–8.   Jonah has previously shown awareness of his misdeeds, when he accepts responsibility for them in the storm (205–12). Now we see that he is willing to ask God for forgiveness, and this brief speech is thus a prelude to his full confession in 305–36.

With þat he hitte to a hyrne and helde hym þerinne,
Þer no defoule of no fylþe watz fest hym abute;   290
Þer he sete also sounde, saf for merk one,
As in þe bulk of þe bote þer he byfore sleped.
So in a bouel of þat best he bidez on lyue,
Þre dayes and þre nyʒt, ay þenkande on Dryʒtyn,
His myʒt and His merci, His mesure þenne.   295
Now he knawez Hym in care þat couþe not in sele.
Ande euer walteres þis whal bi wyldren depe,
Þurʒ mony a regioun ful roʒe, þurʒ ronk of his wylle;
For þat mote in his mawe mad hym, I trowe,
Þaʒ hit lyttel were hym wyth, to wamel at his hert;   300
Ande as sayled þe segge, ay sykerly he herde
Þe bygge borne on his bak and bete on his sydes.
Þen a prayer ful prest þe prophete þer maked;
On þis wyse, as I wene, his wordez were mony:
'Lorde, to Þe haf I cleped in carez ful stronge;   305
Out of þe hole Þou me herde of hellen wombe;
I calde, and Þou knew myn vncler steuen.
Þou diptez me of þe depe se into þe dymme hert,
Þe grete flem of Þy flod folded me vmbe;
Alle þe gotez of Þy guferes and groundelez powlez,   310
And Þy stryuande stremez of stryndez so mony,
In on daschande dam dryuez me ouer.
And ʒet I sayde as I seet in þe se boþem:
"Careful am I, kest out fro Þy cler yʒen
And deseuered fro Þy syʒt; ʒet surely I hope   315
Efte to trede on Þy temple and teme to Þyseluen."'

294. þre nyʒt] MS þe nyʒt
313. sayde (Gollancz)] MS say

291. *merk one:* 'darkness alone'.
292ff. Jonah's spiritual state during his sleep in the boat, when he was ignoring his misdemeanours, is in sharp contrast to his state in this period inside the whale, during which he comes to a full awareness of his failings.
294. Commentators normally saw Jonah's three days in the belly as a type of Christ's three days in hell: see note to 95f.
296. This comment on Jonah would be equally true of the Dreamer in *Pe.*
300. *þaʒ hit lyttel were hym wyth:* 'though it was little in comparison with him'.
301f. 'and as the man floated along, assuredly he heard all the time the great flood on his (the whale's) back, beating on his sides.'
305–36. Cf. Ps. 68 (AV 69). In medieval psalters this psalm was often illustrated with a picture of Jonah, usually emerging from the whale.
308. 'You plunged me into the dim heart of the deep sea'.
310. Cf. *Pe* 608.
316. Cf. *Cl* 9.

I am wrapped in water to my wo stoundez;
Þe abyme byndes þe body þat I byde inne;
Þe pure poplande hourle playes on my heued; [f87ᵛ]
To laste mere of vche a mount, Man, am I fallen; 320
Þe barrez of vche a bonk ful bigly me haldes,
Þat I may lachche no lont, and Þou my lyf weldes.
Þou schal releue me, Renk, whil Þy ryʒt slepez,
Þurʒ myʒt of Þy mercy þat mukel is to tryste.
For when þ'acces of anguych watz hid in my sawle, 325
Þenne I remembred me ryʒt of my rych Lorde,
Prayande Him for peté His prophete to here,
Þat into His holy hous myn orisoun moʒt entre.
I haf meled with Þy maystres mony longe day,
Bot now I wot wyterly þat þose vnwyse ledes 330
Þat affyen hym in vanyté and in vayne þynges
For þink þat mountes to noʒt her mercy forsaken;
Bot I dewoutly awowe, þat verray betz halden,
Soberly to do Þe sacrafyse when I schal saue worþe,
And offer Þe for my hele a ful hol gyfte, 335
And halde goud þat Þou me hetes: haf here my trauthe.'
Thenne oure Fader to þe fysch ferslych biddez
Þat he hym sput spakly vpon spare drye.
Þe whal wendez at His wylle and a warþe fyndez,
And þer he brakez vp þe buyrne as bede hym oure Lorde. 340
Þenne he swepe to þe sonde in sluchched cloþes:
Hit may wel be þat mester were his mantyle to wasche.

---

317. *to my wo stoundez:* Gollancz's interpretation 'until my woe stupefies (me)' seems more idiomatic than Anderson's ' "(up) to my pangs of woe", i.e. "to my innermost anguish".' The Vulgate *usque ad animam* 'even to the soul' (2:6) is not particularly close to either.

319. *Þe pure poplande hourle:* 'the foaming sea itself'; *pure* is used as an intensive. A similar phrase occurs in *The Wars of Alexander* (Ashmole MS) 1154.

320f. In these lines the poet follows the Vulgate quite closely: cf. 2:7.

323f. The poet departs from the Vulgate text here. He may have in mind the Debate of the Four Daughters of God, a dramatization of Ps. 84 (AV 85): 10–11, in which the attributes of the godhead, Mercy, Truth, Peace, and Justice, are portrayed debating man's salvation.

329–32. 'I have spoken with Your learned men for many a long day, but now I know for sure that those foolish men who trust in vanity and empty things forsake the mercy which is (properly) theirs for something that is of no significance'. *Þose vnwyse ledes* (330) are probably not to be identified with *Þy maystres* (329).

333. *þat:* 'that which'.

338f. 'that he should spit him out quickly upon desert land. The whale goes, in accordance with His will, and finds a shore'.

342. One would expect Jonah's clothes to be dirty after he has spent three days and nights in the whale's belly, the foul and slimy nature of which the poet has emphasized; but it is clear that Jonah's soiled cloak also symbolizes the defilement of

Þe bonk þat he blosched to and bode hym bisyde
Wern of þe regiounes ryʒt þat he renayed hade.
Þenne a wynde of Goddez worde efte þe wyʒe bruxlez: 345
'Nylt þou neuer to Nuniue bi no kynnez wayez?'
'ʒisse, Lorde,' quoþ þe lede, 'lene me Þy grace
For to go at Þi gre: me gaynez non oþer.'
'Ris, aproche þen to prech, lo, þe place here.
Lo, My lore is in þe loke, lauce hit þerinne.'   350
Þenne þe renk radly ros as he myʒt,
And to Niniue þat naʒt he neʒed ful euen;
Hit watz a ceté ful syde and selly of brede;
On to þrenge þerþurʒe watz þre dayes dede.
Þat on journay ful joynt Jonas hym ʒede,   [f88ʳ] 355
Er euer he warpped any worde to wyʒe þat he mette,
And þenne he cryed so cler þat kenne myʒt alle
Þe trwe tenor of his teme; he tolde on þis wyse:
'ʒet schal forty dayez fully fare to an ende,
And þenne schal Niniue be nomen and to noʒt worþe;   360
Truly þis ilk toun schal tylte to grounde;
Vp-so-doun schal ʒe dumpe depe to þe abyme,
To be swolʒed swyftly wyth þe swart erþe,
And alle þat lyuyes hereinne lose þe swete.'
Þis speche sprang in þat space and spradde alle aboute,   365
To borges and to bacheleres þat in þat burʒ lenged;
Such a hidor hem hent and a hatel drede,
Þat al chaunged her chere and chylled at þe hert.
Þe segge sesed not ʒet, bot sayde euer ilyche:
'Þe verray vengaunce of God schal voyde þis place!'   370
Þenne þe peple pitosly pleyned ful stylle,
And for þe drede of Dryʒtyn doured in hert;

348. non] MS mon

sin. Cf. *PPl* B.XIII.272ff, where Haukyn is advised to wash his sin-stained coat;
interestingly, he is afterwards addressed by Patience on the subject of poverty. Cf.
also the symbolic use of dirty clothes in the parable of the Wedding Feast (*Cl* 51ff);
see notes to *Cl* 12, 134, and 169–76.
343f. These lines draw attention to the utter futility of Jonah's attempt to avoid
obeying God. *Bonk:* 'shores'; see *Cl* 379n.
346. 'Will you still not go to Nineveh on any account (*lit.* by any sort of way)?'
347. *ʒisse:* This is a strong affirmative ('yes, indeed'), often used (like ModFr *si*) in
contradicting a negative.
354f. 'merely to pass through it was three days' work. Jonah walked one day's jour-
ney continuously'. Cf. Jonah 3:3–4.
360–64. Jonah's prophecy may be compared with the description of the destruction of
Sodom and the other cities in *Cl* (947ff).
364. *lose þe swete:* 'lose the life-blood': thus 'die'.
365. *in þat space:* 'there and then'.

Heter hayrez þay hent þat asperly bited,
And þose þay bounden to her bak and to her bare sydez,
Dropped dust on her hede, and dymly bisoȝten   375
Þat þat penaunce plesed Him þat playnez on her wronge.
And ay he cryes in þat kyth tyl þe kyng herde,
And he radly vpros and ran fro his chayer,
His ryche robe he torof of his rigge naked,
And of a hep of askes he hitte in þe myddez.   380
He askez heterly a hayre and hasped hym vmbe,
Sewed a sekke þerabof, and syked ful colde;
Þer he dased in þat duste, with droppande teres,
Wepande ful wonderly alle his wrange dedes.
Þenne sayde he to his serjauntes: 'Samnes yow bilyue;   385
Do dryue out a decre, demed of myseluen,
Þat alle þe bodyes þat ben withinne þis borȝ quyk,
Boþe burnes and bestes, burdez and childer,
Vch prynce, vche prest, and prelates alle,
Alle faste frely for her falce werkes;   390
Sesez childer of her sok, soghe hem so neuer,   [f88ᵛ]
Ne best bite on no brom, ne no bent nauþer,
Passe to no pasture, ne pike non erbes,
Ne non oxe to no hay, ne no horse to water.
Al schal crye, forclemmed, with alle oure clere strenþe;   395
Þe rurd schal ryse to Hym þat rawþe schal haue;
What wote oþer wyte may ȝif þe Wyȝe lykes,
Þat is hende in þe hyȝt of His gentryse?
I wot His myȝt is so much, þaȝ He be myssepayed,
Þat in His mylde amesyng He mercy may fynde.   400
And if we leuen þe layk of oure layth synnes,
And stylle steppen in þe styȝe He styȝtlez Hymseluen,
He wyl wende of His wodschip and His wrath leue,
And forgif vus þis gult, ȝif we Hym God leuen.'
Þenne al leued on His lawe and laften her synnes,   405
Parformed alle þe penaunce þat þe prynce radde;
And God þurȝ His godnesse forgef as He sayde;
Þaȝ He oþer bihyȝt, withhelde His vengaunce.
Muche sorȝe þenne satteled vpon segge Jonas;
He wex as wroth as þe wynde towarde oure Lorde.   410

385-404. The King here orders that the Ninevites should admit their guilt and appeal to God for mercy: just as Jonah has done from the belly of the whale.

391. *soghe hem so neuer:* 'however much it may hurt them'.

392. Cf. *Cl* 1675.

397f. 'who knows or can know if it will please the Lord who is gracious in the excellence of His courtesy (to have pity)?'

407f. 'and God in His goodness forgave (them), as He said He would; though He had promised otherwise, He withheld His vengeance.'

410. *as wroth as þe wynde:* a formula of comparison often used in alliterative poetry: cf. *G* 319.

So hatz anger onhit his hert, he callez
A prayer to þe hyȝe Prynce, for pyne, on þys wyse:
'I biseche Þe, Syre, now Þou self jugge;
Watz not þis ilk my worde þat worþen is nouþe,
Þat I kest in my cuntré, when Þou Þy carp sendez   415
Þat I schulde tee to þys toun Þi talent to preche?
Wel knew I Þi cortaysye, Þy quoynt soffraunce,
Þy bounté of debonerté and Þy bene grace,
Þy longe abydyng wyth lur, Þy late vengaunce;
And ay Þy mercy is mete, be mysse neuer so huge.   420
I wyst wel, when I hade worded quatsoeuer I cowþe
To manace alle þise mody men þat in þis mote dowellez,
Wyth a prayer and a pyne þay myȝt her pese gete,
And þerfore I wolde haf flowen fer into Tarce.
Now, Lorde, lach out my lyf, hit lastes to longe.   425
Bed me bilyue my bale-stour and bryng me on ende,
For me were swetter to swelt as swyþe, as me þynk,   [f89ʳ]
Þen lede lenger Þi lore þat þus me les makez.'
Þe soun of oure Souerayn þen swey in his ere,
Þat vpbraydes þis burne vpon a breme wyse: 430
'Herk, renk, is þis ryȝt so ronkly to wrath
For any dede þat I haf don oþer demed þe ȝet?'
Jonas al joyles and janglande vpryses,
And haldez out on est half of þe hyȝe place,
And farandely on a felde he fettelez hym to bide,   435
For to wayte on þat won what schulde worþe after.
Þer he busked hym a bour, þe best þat he myȝt,
Of hay and of euer-ferne and erbez a fewe,

---

411. he] MS ye

413–16. 'I beseech You, Lord, now judge Yourself; was not this very thing that has come to pass what I said (*lit.* the speech which I uttered) in my country, when You sent Your word that I should go to this town to preach Your purpose?' *þat worþen is* qualifies *þis ilk*; *þat I kest* qualifies *my worde*. The answer to Jonah's question is, of course, 'no': he made no such prediction. Note the excessive concern with reputation throughout this speech, especially in 427f.

417–20. Jonah here criticizes God for possessing the very qualities to which he directed his prayer from the belly of the whale.

427. *me were swetter:* 'I should rather' (*lit.* 'it would be more pleasant to me').

428. This indicates that Jonah's grievance is that God considers it more important to save the Ninevites than to carry out his threat of destruction and thus show Jonah to be a true prophet.

433. *janglande:* This word is also used in 90 to describe Jonah's state of angry rebellion against God.

434. 'and goes out on the eastern side of the great city'.

436. 'to watch what would happen afterwards in that city.'

For hit watz playn in þat place for plyande greuez,
For to schylde fro þe schene oþer any schade keste. 440
He bowed vnder his lyttel boþe, his bak to þe sunne,
And þer he swowed and slept sadly al ny3t,
Þe whyle God of His grace ded growe of þat soyle
Þe fayrest bynde hym abof þat euer burne wyste.
When þe dawande day Dry3tyn con sende, 445
Þenne wakened þe wy3 vnder wodbynde,
Loked alofte on þe lef þat lylled grene;
Such a lefsel of lof neuer lede hade,
For hit watz brod at þe boþem, bo3ted on lofte,
Happed vpon ayþer half, a hous as hit were, 450
A nos on þe norþ syde and nowhere non ellez,
Bot al schet in a scha3e þat schaded ful cole.
Þe gome gly3t on þe grene graciouse leues,
Þat euer wayued a wynde so wyþe and so cole;
Þe schyre sunne hit vmbeschon, þa3 no schafte my3t 455
Þe mountaunce of a lyttel mote vpon þat man schyne.
Þenne watz þe gome so glad of his gay logge,
Lys loltrande þerinne lokande to toune;
So blyþe of his wodbynde he balteres þervnder,
Þat of no diete þat day þe deuel haf he ro3t. 460
And euer he la3ed as he loked þe loge alle aboute,
And wysched hit were in his kyth þer he wony schulde,
On he3e vpon Effraym oþer Ermonnes hillez: [f89ᵛ]
'Iwysse, a worþloker won to welde I neuer keped.'
And quen hit ne3ed to na3t nappe hym bihoued; 465
He slydez on a sloumbe-slep sloghe vnder leues,
Whil God wayned a worme þat wrot vpe þe rote,
And wyddered watz þe wodbynde bi þat þe wy3e wakned;
And syþen He warnez þe west to waken ful softe,
And sayez vnte Zeferus þat he syfle warme, 470
Þat þer quikken no cloude bifore þe cler sunne,
And ho schal busch vp ful brode and brenne as a candel.

---

459. þervnder] MS þervnde

439f. 'for it was bare in that place as regards waving groves, to shield from the sun (*lit.* bright one) or cast any shade.'
443. *ded growe of þat soyle:* 'caused to grow from that soil'.
450. *Happed vpon ayþer half:* 'enclosed upon each side'.
454. 'which a wind so light and so cool continually made to wave'. Alternatively: 'which continually wafted a wind so light and cool'.
460. The line is so idiomatic that it resists literal translation, but may be rendered: 'but he cared (*ro3t*) for no food that day—the devil take it.' *Þe deuel haf* apparently stands in place of an adverbial expression such as *no3t* '(not) at all'.
469. *þe west:* i.e. the west wind.

Þen wakened þe wyȝe of his wyl dremes,
And blusched to his wodbynde þat broþely watz marred,
Al welwed and wasted þo worþelych leues;　　　　　475
Þe schyre sunne hade hem schent er euer þe schalk wyst.
And þen hef vp þe hete and heterly brenned;
Þe warm wynde of þe weste, wertes he swyþez.
Þe man marred on þe molde þat moȝt hym not hyde;
His wodbynde watz away, he weped for sorȝe;　　　　480
With hatel anger and hot, heterly he callez:
'A, Þou Maker of man, what maystery Þe þynkez
Þus Þy freke to forfare forbi alle oþer?
With alle meschef þat Þou may, neuer Þou me sparez;
I keuered me a cumfort þat now is caȝt fro me,　　　485
My wodbynde so wlonk þat wered my heued.
Bot now I se Þou art sette my solace to reue;
Why ne dyȝttez Þou me to diȝe? I dure to longe.'
Ȝet oure Lorde to þe lede laused a speche:
'Is þis ryȝtwys, þou renk, alle þy ronk noyse,　　　490
So wroth for a wodbynde to wax so sone?
Why art þou so waymot, wyȝe, for so lyttel?'
'Hit is not lyttel,' quoþ þe lede, 'bot lykker to ryȝt;
I wolde I were of þis worlde wrapped in moldez.'
'Þenne byþenk þe, mon, if þe forþynk sore,　　　　495
If I wolde help My hondewerk, haf þou no wonder;
Þou art waxen so wroth for þy wodbynde,
And trauayledez neuer to tent hit þe tyme of an howre,
Bot at a wap hit here wax and away at anoþer,　　　[f90ʳ]
And ȝet lykez þe so luþer, þi lyf woldez þou tyne.　　500
Þenne wyte not Me for þe werk, þat I hit wolde help,
And rwe on þo redles þat remen for synne;

479. 'The man, who could not hide himself, suffered on the ground'. It is not uncommon for a relative clause to be separated from its antecedent (cf. *G* 145n). Jonah's suffering is also mentioned in the OT (4:8).

482. *what maystery þe þynkez:* 'what triumph does it seem to You?'

482–8. Jonah forgets that God has mercifully spared him in the belly of the whale, and appears even to claim credit for the provision of the woodbine (485). For the second time, he invites God to end his life (cf. 425–8).

493. *lykker to ryȝt:* 'more a matter of justice' (*lit.* 'more like justice'). Jonah is claiming that it is the principle of the matter that is important.

495ff. In this speech God explains his motives in terms identifiable with human emotional response. Thus it is a good instance of the poet's tendency to 'humanize' God: cf. 65–72, 345–50, 407f, and 429–32, and see Introduction, p. 20.

496. *My hondewerk:* God emphasizes his role as creator: cf. 131. In the OE poem *Genesis B* (455) Adam is referred to as *godes handgesceaft* 'God's handiwork'.

501. 'Then do not blame Me if I wish to help My creation'. The word *werk* denotes the Ninevites: cf. 496n.

Fyrst I made hem Myself of materes Myn one,
And syþen I loked hem ful longe and hem on lode hade.
And if I My trauayl schulde tyne of termes so longe,   505
And type doun ȝonder toun when hit turned were,
Þe sor of such a swete place burde synk to My hert,
So mony malicious mon as mournez þerinne.
And of þat soumme ȝet arn summe, such sottez formadde,
Bitwene þe stele and þe stayre disserne noȝt cunen,   510
What rule renes in roun bitwene þe ryȝt hande
And his lyfte, þaȝ his lyf schulde lost be þerfor;
As lyttel barnez on barme þat neuer bale wroȝt,
And wymmen vnwytté þat wale ne couþe
Þat on hande fro þat oþer, for alle þis hyȝe worlde.   515
And als þer ben doumbe bestez in þe burȝ mony,
Þat may not synne in no syt hemseluen to greue.
Why schulde I wrath wyth hem, syþen wyȝez wyl torne,
And cum and cnawe Me for Kyng and My carpe leue?
Wer I as hastif as þou heere, were harme lumpen;   520
Couþe I not þole bot as þou, þer þryued ful fewe.
I may not be so malicious and mylde be halden,
For malyse is noȝt to mayntyne boute mercy withinne.'

510–12. *follow* 513–15 *in* MS
515. for] MS fol
520. as þou] MS a þou
522. malicious] MS malcious
523. noȝt] MS noȝ

507f. The poet emphasizes that God's mercy is aroused by the repentance of the Ninevites, and we are reminded that he pardoned Jonah under similar circumstances. Cf. *Cl* 1699–1708.

509–15. In the MS 510–12 follow 513–15, producing a lack of continuity between 515 and 510 (numbering of this edition). The sequence adopted here was suggested by Gollancz but not implemented by him. He believed that 510–12 are displaced, and that they were cancelled by the poet and replaced by 513–15. In his text the lines are left as they stand in the MS, but 510–12 are enclosed in square brackets; in this he is followed by Anderson. But it is significant that both these editors were influenced by their desire to maintain the quatrain arrangement, which is disrupted by the retention of 510–12 (see *Note on Language and Metre*, p. 49). Whether the lines were cancelled by the poet remains hypothetical, but the above sequence does give a rationally ordered series of innocent groups—idiots, children, foolish women, and dumb beasts (516f).

510–12. 'they could not distinguish between the upright of a ladder and the rung, nor (could they see) what rule inscrutably applies to the right hand and what to the (*lit.* his) left, though they might lose their lives thereby'. Cf. Jonah 4:11, Matt. 6:3.

520. *heere:* 'in this instance': cf. *G* 2366n. (But note Anderson's suggestion that this is not an adv. but a noun meaning 'sir' [from OE *herra* 'lord'].)

523. 'for the power to do harm is not to be exercised without mercy within.'

Be noȝt so gryndel, godman, bot go forth þy wayes,
Be preue and be pacient in payne and in joye;　　　　　　　525
For he þat is to rakel to renden his cloþez
Mot efte sitte with more vnsounde to sewe hem togeder.
Forþy when pouerté me enprecez and paynez innoȝe
Ful softly with suffraunce saȝttel me bihouez;
Forþy penaunce and payne topreue hit in syȝt　　　　　　530
Þat pacience is a nobel poynt, þaȝ hit displese ofte.
　　　　　　　　　　　　　　　Amen.

524. Opinions have differed as to precisely where in this passage God's speech should end, and the voice of the narrator resume: editors have to decide where to place the final inverted comma. Gollancz puts it at the end of 527; we have chosen, with Bateson and Anderson, to put it at the end of 523. Both are legitimate interpretations. It can be argued on the one side that 524 sounds more like the tone of God speaking to Jonah than the narrator addressing his audience, and on the other side that the exhortation to patience in 525 picks up the concerns of the 'prologue', and is thus more appropriate to the narrator than to God. A definitive argument either way is difficult to envisage. This passage (524–7) functions as a bridge between the voice of God speaking to Jonah and the voice of the narrator in the *persona* of a preacher, God's representative on earth, addressing an audience on the principles of Christian conduct. Thus a certain similarity between the two voices is fitting, and the precise point at which the speaker changes remains elusive. *Gryndel* (524): 'fierce, angry' (possibly related to OE *Grendel* and OIcel *grindill* 'storm, wind'). The only other citation for this word in *MED* is *G* 2338, where it is used in the same phrase, in a passage of similar tone and significance.

526f. This metaphor may be compared with that at the centre of the parable of the Wedding Feast in *Cl* (51–192: see especially 144f).

Sir Gawain
and the Green Knight

I

Siþen þe sege and þe assaut watz sesed at Troye, [f91ʳ]
Þe borȝ brittened and brent to brondez and askez,
Þe tulk þat þe trammes of tresoun þer wroȝt
Watz tried for his tricherie, þe trewest on erthe.
Hit watz Ennias þe athel and his highe kynde, 5
Þat siþen depreced prouinces, and patrounes bicome
Welneȝe of al þe wele in þe west iles.
Fro riche Romulus to Rome ricchis hym swyþe,
With gret bobbaunce þat burȝe he biges vpon fyrst
And neuenes hit his aune nome, as hit now hat; 10
Ticius to Tuskan and teldes bigynnes,
Langaberde in Lumbardie lyftes vp homes,

3f. 'the man who framed the treasonable plots there was tried (and 'became famous', a pun) for his treachery, the most authentic example on earth.' Medieval legend associated Aeneas with the traitor Antenor in plotting with the Greeks (see, for instance, the ME alliterative *Destruction of Troy* [ed. D. Donaldson and G. A. Panton, EETS OS 39, 56], based on Guido del Colonna). It has been argued that Antenor is the traitor referred to here, but it seems likely that the poet is enunciating the motif of 'shame and success' (or *blysse and blunder*) which is dominant in the present adventure of Gawain, a descendant of Aeneas, and which can be discerned in the lives of other members of this *highe kynde*, Brutus and Arthur (see notes to 13, 2465f). The account in the *Laud Troy Book* (*c.* 1400), which does not attempt to exonerate Aeneas, relates the trial and exile of Aeneas and Antenor with their kin, after the departure of the Greeks; note especially

> And yit afftirward hit schop so
> That the traytoures bothe two
> For here ffalsnesse were afftir demed (*sentenced*)
> To be exiled & afftir flemed (*banished*)
> With al here kyn & here lynage.
> (Ed. J. E. Wülfing, EETS OS 121, 122, 18599–603)

J. D. Burnley (in *NQ*, 203 [1973], 83f) notes that the connection between *Hit watz* (5) and the *tulk* of 3 is confirmed by the similar syntax of *Cl* 979–81.
7. *þe west iles:* 'lands of the west'.
11. While Langaberde and Brutus are well known in medieval legend as eponymous founders of Lombardy and Britain respectively, the name Ticius is not recorded elsewhere. Recognized 'founders' of Tuscany include a Tuscus and a Tirius; the form Ticius may be either an adaption of, or a scribal error for, the latter. (See Silverstein, **7d** 1964–5.)

And fer ouer þe French flod, Felix Brutus
On mony bonkkes ful brode Bretayn he settez
    Wyth wynne,   15
    Where werre and wrake and wonder
    Bi syþez hatz wont þerinne
    And oft boþe blysse and blunder
    Ful skete hatz skyfted synne.

Ande quen þis Bretayn watz bigged bi þis burn rych   20
Bolde bredden þerinne, baret þat lofden,
In mony turned tyme tene þat wroʒten.
Mo ferlyes on þis folde han fallen here oft
Þen in any oþer þat I wot, syn þat ilk tyme.
Bot of alle þat here bult of Bretaygne kynges   25
Ay watz Arthur þe hendest, as I haf herde telle.
Forþi an aunter in erde I attle to schawe,   [f91ᵛ]
Þat a selly in siʒt summe men hit holden
And an outtrage awenture of Arthurez wonderez.
If ʒe wyl lysten þis laye bot on littel quile,   30
I schal telle hit astit, as I in toun herde,
    With tonge.
    As hit is stad and stoken
    In stori stif and stronge,
    With lel letteres loken,
    In londe so hatz ben longe.   35

13. *Felix:* this is unique as a praenomen of Brutus (great-grandson of Aeneas), though the epithet ('happy') is associated in Roman tradition with founders of cities, etc., and in the EME form *sæl*, it is applied to him by the poet Laʒamon in his chronicle-poem *Brut*. It is appropriately used of Brutus, who is said to have been fated to early misfortune (his mother died giving birth to him and he later killed his father by accident) but upon exile from Italy successfully founded Britain; the name is echoed by *Wyth wynne* 'with joy' 15.

25. *of Bretaygne kynges:* inverted construction: 'kings of Britain' (in apposition to *alle*).

27, 28. *in erde, in siʒt:* poetic tags, but see glossary.

28. *þat . . . hit:* relative construction (= 'which').

30. *laye:* an OF word used by Marie de France (12th c.) to designate the short Breton tales which she versified; originally 'a short narrative poem intended to be sung or recited', it had come to mean simply 'poem' or 'song' by the 14th c., though perhaps with some 'Celtic' associations of magic and love; the present context suggests that it was still associated with minstrelsy.

31–6. 'I shall tell it at once, aloud, as I have heard it in the court. The form in which it is (here) set down and fixed, in a brave and powerful story enshrined in true syllables, is that in which it has long existed.' For correlative *as . . . so*, cf. 244, *Cl* 226f. 33–5 are evidently a reference to the text of the present poem, which the reciter would have in front of him. Other interpretations of the passage are possible with different punctuation. 35 can also be read 'linked with true letters' and the ambiguity may be deliberate; while asserting the authenticity of his version, the poet may be making oblique reference to the accuracy of the metre in which it is embodied. 36 may also be an allusion to the antiquity of the alliterative style ('as has long been the custom in the land'). See also P. J. Frankis, *NQ*, 206 (1961), 329.

Þis kyng lay at Camylot vpon Krystmasse
With mony luflych lorde, ledez of þe best—
Rekenly of þe Rounde Table alle þo rich breþer—
With rych reuel oryȝt and rechles merþes.   40
Þer tournayed tulkes by tymez ful mony,
Justed ful jolilé þise gentyle kniȝtes,
Syþen kayred to þe court, caroles to make;
For þer þe fest watz ilyche ful fiften dayes,
With alle þe mete and þe mirþe þat men couþe avyse: 45
Such glaum ande gle glorious to here,
Dere dyn vpon day, daunsyng on nyȝtes—
Al watz hap vpon heȝe in hallez and chambrez
With lordez and ladies, as leuest him þoȝt.
With all þe wele of þe worlde þay woned þer samen,   50
Þe most kyd knyȝtez vnder Krystes Seluen
And þe louelokkest ladies þat euer lif haden,
And he þe comlokest kyng, þat þe court haldes;
For al watz þis fayre folk in her first age,
    On sille,   55
  Þe hapnest vnder heuen,
  Kyng hyȝest mon of wylle—
  Hit were now gret nye to neuen
  So hardy a here on hille.

Wyle Nw ȝer watz so ȝep þat hit watz nwe cummen,   60
Þat day doubble on þe dece watz þe douth serued.
Fro þe kyng watz cummen with knyȝtes into þe halle,
Þe chauntré of þe chapel cheued to an ende,
Loude crye watz þer kest of clerkez and oþer,

46. glaum ande] MS glaumande (*see Pat* 269n)
58. were] MS werere

37. According to French romance, Arthur held court five times a year on the great Christian festivals, Easter, Ascension, Whitsun, All Saints (cf. 536–7), and Christmas. In the *Livre de Carados*, possibly the poet's source for the story of the Beheading Game, the challenger enters Arthur's court at Carduel during the Whitsuntide feast.

43. *caroles:* courtly ring dances with singing; cf. the description in the Chaucerian translation of the *Roman de la Rose* 743ff.

51. *vnder Krystes Seluen:* 'except Christ Himself' or 'on earth'.

54. Arthur and his courtiers were all in their youth (*first age*); by implication this was also the golden age of Arthur's court and reign, before the appearance of the treachery which brought about the downfall of the Round Table. The theme of the first stanza (the rise and fall of kingdoms) is heard faintly in the background.

60. The whole line is a periphrasis for 'On New Year's Day'.

63. *cheued to an ende:* a participial phrase, 'having ended'.

64. *Loude crye:* the greeting *Nowel* ('Merry Christmas') of the next line (cf. *neuened ful ofte*).

Nowel nayted onewe, neuened ful ofte.   [f92ʳ] 65
And syþen riche forth runnen to reche hondeselle,
Ʒeʒed 'Ʒeres ʒiftes!' on hiʒ, ʒelde hem bi hond,
Debated busyly aboute þo giftes;
Ladies laʒed ful loude þoʒ þay lost haden
And he þat wan watz not wrothe—þat may ʒe wel trawe.   70
Alle þis mirþe þay maden to þe mete tyme.
When þay had waschen worþyly, þay wenten to sete,
Þe best burne ay abof, as hit best semed;
Whene Guenore ful gay grayþed in þe myddes,
Dressed on þe dere des, dubbed al aboute: 75
Smal sendal bisides, a selure hir ouer
Of tryed tolouse, of tars tapites innoghe
Þat were enbrawded and beten wyth þe best gemmes
Þat myʒt be preued of prys wyth penyes to bye
        In daye.   80
      Þe comlokest to discrye
      Þer glent with yʒen gray;
      A semloker þat euer he syʒe
      Soth moʒt no mon say.

Bot Arthure wolde not ete til al were serued;   85
He watz so joly of his joyfnes, and sumquat childgered.
His lif liked hym lyʒt; he louied þe lasse
Auþer to longe lye or to longe sitte,
So bisied him his ʒonge blod and his brayn wylde.
And also anoþer maner meued him eke,   90

88.   longe lye] MS lenge lye

65.   *onewe:* i.e. the festive spirit of Christmas Day was renewed on New Year's Day.
66ff.   *hondeselle* probably designates gifts to subordinates (Christmas boxes), *Ʒeres ʒiftes* those given to equals. The giving of the latter takes the form of a guessing game like Handy Dandy (cf. *bi hond* 67) with forfeits: if the lady fails to guess which hand the present is in, the knight wins a kiss (hence the somewhat arch comment of 69f).
73.   'the man of highest rank, in each case, in the higher position (i.e. in order of degree throughout), as was most fitting'.
79f.   'whose value could ever (*In daye*) be tested by buying them with money', i.e. 'that money could buy'.
81.   *comlokest: gemme* is understood, a metaphor which is picked up in *glent*: 'glanced' or 'sparkled'; Guenevere is meant, of course, a jewel beyond price in comparison with those of 78–80.
82.   *yʒen gray:* see *Pe* 254n.
86–9.   'he was so lively in his youthfulness, and somewhat boyish. He loved an active life; he didn't care much for lying in bed or sitting long, he was so agitated by his young blood and his restless mind.'

Þat he þurȝ nobelay had nomen: he wolde neuer ete
Vpon such a dere day, er hym deuised were
Of sum auenturus þyng, an vncouþe tale
Of sum mayn meruayle þat he myȝt trawe,
Of alderes, of armes, of oþer auenturus;   95
Oþer sum segg hym bisoȝt of sum siker knyȝt
To joyne wyth hym in justyng, in jopardé to lay,
Lede, lif for lyf, leue vchon oþer,
As fortune wolde fulsun hom, þe fayrer to haue.
Þis watz kynges countenaunce where he in court were,   100
At vch farand fest among his fre meny
      In halle.   [f92ᵛ]
    Þerfore of face so fere
    He stiȝtlez stif in stalle;
    Ful ȝep in þat Nw Ȝere,   105
    Much mirthe he mas with alle.

Thus þer stondes in stale þe stif kyng hisseluen,
Talkkande bifore þe hyȝe table of trifles ful hende.
There gode Gawan watz grayþed Gwenore bisyde,
And Agrauayn a la Dure Mayn on þat oþer syde sittes—   110
Boþe þe kynges sister-sunes and ful siker kniȝtes;
Bischop Bawdewyn abof biginez þe table,

95. Of] MS Of of

91. *Þat he . . . nomen:* probably a relative clause, 'which he had undertaken as a matter of honour'.

92–4. *er . . . meruayle:* 'until he had been told of some daring enterprise, a strange tale of some great wonder'.

95. *alderes:* either 'princes' (OE *aldor*) or 'ancestors' (OE *ældra*); the two are confused in ME in some contexts.

96–9. 'or else some man entreated him for a true knight to engage in jousting with him, for a man (*lede*) to lay life against life in jeopardy, either one to concede victory to the other, as fortune saw fit to help them.' 97–9 summarize the terms of honourable combat.

110. *a la Dure Mayn:* 'of the hard hand'. Agravain and Gawain were sons of Lot, King of Orkney; their mother was Arthur's half-sister, Anna (sometimes known as Belisent). Another half-sister of Arthur was Morgan, cf. 2463ff. *On þat oþer syde:* i.e. of Gawain. Guenevere sits on Arthur's left, at the centre of the table; Gawain and Agravain are to the left of her. On Arthur's right are Bishop Baldwin and Iwain.

112. *abof biginez þe table:* an idiomatic expression meaning 'sits in the place of honour' (at the right of the host, cf. 1001). When the host sat at the end of the table the guest of honour would occupy the first place on his right at the 'top' of the long side. The poet does not introduce the Round Table, though he uses the phrase for the abstract 'Arthur's court'; in general the background details of the romance are drawn from contemporary aristocratic life.

And Ywan, Vryn son, ette with hymseluen.
Þise were diȝt on þe des and derworþly serued,
And siþen mony siker segge at þe sidbordez.   115
Þen þe first cors come with crakkyng of trumpes
Wyth mony baner ful bryȝt, þat þerbi henged;
Nwe nakryn noyse with þe noble pipes,
Wylde werbles and wyȝt wakned lote,
Þat mony hert ful hiȝe hef at her towches.   120
Dayntés dryuen þerwyth of ful dere metes,
Foysoun of þe fresche, and on so fele disches
Þat pine to fynde þe place þe peple biforne
For to sette þe sylueren þat sere sewes halden
      On clothe.   125
      Iche lede as he loued hymselue
      Þer laght withouten loþe;
      Ay two had disches twelue,
      Good ber and bryȝt wyn boþe.

Now wyl I of hor seruise say yow no more,   130
For vch wyȝe may wel wit no wont þat þer were.
Anoþer noyse ful newe neȝed biliue,
Þat þe lude myȝt haf leue liflode to cach;
For vneþe watz þe noyce not a whyle sesed,
And þe fyrst cource in þe court kyndely serued,   135
Þer hales in at þe halle dor an aghlich mayster,
On þe most on þe molde on mesure hyghe;
Fro þe swyre to þe swange so sware and so þik,

113.   with] MS wit
124.   sylueren] MS syluener (cf. *Cl* 127n)

113.   *ette with hymseluen:* 'shared dishes with him' (i.e. with Baldwin), cf. 128. At the
       end of a line, *hymseluen* is frequently used for *him*, with no special emphasis.
116.   *cors:* A 'course' comprised a variety of dishes (enough to constitute a complete
       meal by any modern standard). A medieval banquet consisted of a number of these
       courses. Cf. 128.
117.   *Wyth . . . bryȝt:* 'resplendent with many a banner'.
119.   'spirited, piercing trills roused echoes'.
126.   *as . . . hymselue:* 'as he himself liked'.
132f. 'Another, quite new, noise drew near suddenly, so that the prince might have
       leave (i.e. which was to give the prince leave) to take food'; cf. 9off.
134.   'for scarcely a moment after the music had finished . . .' (cf. 116ff). The double
       negative is merely emphatic.
135.   *serued: watz* is understood from the previous line.
137.   'the very biggest man on earth in height'. *On þe most,* 'one the biggest' is an
       idiomatic superlative, not yet confused with the weaker 'one of the biggest'.

And his lyndes and his lymes so longe and so grete,
Half-etayn in erde I hope þat he were,   [f93ʳ]   140
Bot mon most I algate mynn hym to bene,
And þat þe myriest in his muckel þat myȝt ride;
For of bak and of brest al were his bodi sturne,
Both his wombe and his wast were worthily smale,
And alle his fetures folȝande in forme, þat he hade,   145
    Ful clene.
      For wonder of his hwe men hade,
      Set in his semblaunt sene;
      He ferde as freke were fade,
      And oueral enker grene.   150

Ande al grayþed in grene þis gome and his wedes:
A strayt cote ful streȝt þat stek on his sides,
A meré mantile abof, mensked withinne
With pelure pured apert, þe pane ful clene
With blyþe blaunner ful bryȝt, and his hod boþe,   155
Þat watz laȝt fro his lokkez and layde on his schulderes;
Heme wel-haled hose of þat same grene,
Þat spenet on his sparlyr, and clene spures vnder
Of bryȝt golde, vpon silk bordes barred ful ryche,
And scholes vnder schankes þere þe schalk rides.   160
And alle his vesture uerayly watz clene verdure,
Boþe þe barres of his belt and oþer blyþe stones
Þat were richely rayled in his aray clene
Aboutte hymself and his sadel, vpon silk werkez;

---

144. Both] MS bot

141f. '(that) I think he was half-giant on earth, but at any rate I suppose (declare?) him to be the biggest man (on earth), and moreover the most elegant for his size who could ride a horse'.

145f. 'and every part of him agreeing in proportion completely.' Possibly, however, *folȝande in forme* is an oblique reference to his colour (to be revealed in the following lines): 'matching in outward appearance (colour)'. This would enable us to understand *For* (147) in its usual sense. In either case, *þat he hade* qualifies *fetures*, repeating the force of *his* (cf. 327), rather than *forme* (note the absence of definite article). For other such separated relative clauses cf. 429, 785, 1456, 1914, etc.

154f. *þe pane . . . bryȝt:* 'the whole of the edging bright with lovely fur'. *Blaunner:* probably 'ermine' (OF *blanc* 'white' + *neir* 'black'); however, since the poet insists throughout the description on the greenness of the newcomer, it seems better to take the word in the more general sense of 'fur' here.

160. 'and the man rides there without any shoes on his feet (*lit.* under legs).' I.e. he wore only stockings or soft socks—considered appropriate wear for peaceful pursuits (e.g. hunting) in the 14th c. Knights in armour, on the other hand, wore steel shoes (*sabatounz*, cf. 574); the expression 'shoeless', therefore, accords with the assurance (203ff) that the Green Knight had no piece of armour about him.

Þat were to tor for to telle of tryfles þe halue 165
Þat were enbrauded abof, wyth bryddes and flyʒes,
With gay gaudi of grene, þe golde ay inmyddes.
Þe pendauntes of his payttrure, þe proude cropure,
His molaynes and alle þe metail anamayld was þenne,
Þe steropes þat he stod on stayned of þe same, 170
And his arsounz al after, and his aþel scurtes,
Þat euer glemered and glent al of grene stones.
Þe fole þat he ferkkes on fyn of þat ilke,
    Sertayn:
  A grene hors gret and þikke, 175
  A stede ful stif to strayne,
  In brawden brydel quik;
  To þe gome he watz ful gayn. [f93ᵛ]

Wel gay watz þis gome gered in grene
And þe here of his hed of his hors swete: 180
Fayre fannand fax vmbefoldes his schulderes.
A much berd as a busk ouer his brest henges,
Þat wyth his hiʒlich here þat of his hed reches
Watz euesed al vmbetorne abof his elbowes,
Þat half his armes þervnder were halched in þe wyse 185
Of a kyngez capados þat closes his swyre;
Þe mane of þat mayn hors much to hit lyke,
Wel cresped and cemmed, wyth knottes ful mony
Folden in wyth fildore aboute þe fayre grene,
Ay a herle of þe here, anoþer of golde; 190
Þe tayl and his toppyng twynnen of a sute
And bounden boþe wyth a bande of a bryʒt grene
Dubbed wyth ful dere stonez, as þe dok lasted,
Syþen þrawen wyth a þwong; a þwarle knot alofte,

---

168. þe] MS pe
171. scurtes] *so* MS. *Other edd. have read* sturtes, *and emended to* skyrtes
182. as] MS as as

165–7. The first *þat* is a demonstrative pronoun (cf. 719): 'It would be too difficult to relate half the details that were embroidered on it (i.e. *his aray clene*), including birds and butterflies, with lovely green beadwork everywhere amongst the gold.'
181. *fannand:* lit. 'fanning'; usually understood as 'waving, floating', but perhaps the sense is rather 'spreading out like a fan'. In 'The Miller's Tale', Absolon the fop (admittedly a different type of character) has curly, golden hair which *strouted* (spread out) *as a fanne large and brode* (*CT* I.3315). Cf. also *MED: fannen* 2(c).
185f. 'so that his upper arms were enclosed beneath it in the manner of a king's cape, which encircles (wraps round) his neck'. A *capados* was a short leather cape with a hood, cf. 572.
193. *as þe dok lasted:* 'to the end of the tuft'.
194f. 'then drawn up with a thong; (there was) an intricate knot at the top, on which many glittering bells of pure gold were ringing.'

Þer mony bellez ful bryʒt of brende golde rungen.   195
Such a fole vpon folde, ne freke þat hym rydes,
Watz neuer sene in þat sale wyth syʒt er þat tyme
    With yʒe.
    He loked as layt so lyʒt—
    So sayd al þat hym syʒe.   200
    Hit semed as no mon myʒt
    Vnder his dynttez dryʒe.

Wheþer, hade he no helme ne hawbergh nauþer
Ne no pysan ne no plate þat pented to armes
Ne no schafte ne no schelde to schwue ne to smyte;   205
Bot in his on honde he hade a holyn bobbe
(Þat is grattest in grene when greuez ar bare)
And an ax in his oþer, a hoge and vnmete,
A spetos sparþe to expoun in spelle quoso myʒt.
Þe hede of an elnʒerde þe large lenkþe hade,   210
Þe grayn al of grene stele and of golde hewen
Þe bit burnyst bryʒt, with a brod egge
As wel schapen to schere as scharp rasores.
Þe stele of a stif staf þe sturne hit bi grypte,
Þat watz wounden wyth yrn to þe wandez ende   [f94ʳ]   215
And al bigrauen with grene in gracios werkes;

---

203. hawbergh] MS hawbrgh

196ff. the redundancy of *vpon folde ... in þat sale ... er þat tyme*, and of *sene ... wyth syʒt ... With yʒe*, aptly conveys the stupefaction of the courtiers.

199. 'His glance was as swift as lightning (*layt*)'; *loked* means 'glanced a look' rather than 'appeared'.

203. Note the dramatic nature of the description; the speculation that 'it seemed as if no man might survive his blows' (201-2) leads the observer (as it were) to look more closely for armour and weapons.

206f. A branch carried in his hand was a sign of peace (cf. 265f and *Cl* 486-90). Messengers in the Middle Ages often carried an olive branch; it is entirely in keeping with the enigmatical humour of the Green Knight that he should carry a Christmas evergreen, like some wassailer wishing peace and joy to the house, while showing them an enormous weapon of war in the other hand.

209. 'a cruel battle-axe for anyone to describe in words.'

210. 'The axe-head was as long as an ell-rod' (i.e. 45 inches); cf. the second axe, 2225. Both axes evidently had half-moon shaped blades measuring about four feet from upper to lower extremity. In addition, the poet appears to describe this one, at least, as having a spike (*grayn*) sticking out at the back of the blade. D. Yerkes points out (in *NQ*, 220 [1975], 4) that the word *grayn* is used in the Percy Folio MS in the sense 'spike'.

213. *rasores:* 'razor's (edge)'.

214-16. 'The grim knight gripped it by the handle (*stele*), consisting of a strong staff which was bound with iron to the end of the shaft and carved all over with pleasing designs in green'.

A lace lapped aboute þat louked at þe hede
And so after þe halme halched ful ofte,
Wyth tryed tasselez þerto tacched innoghe
On botounz of þe bryƷt grene brayden ful ryche.   220
Þis haþel heldez hym in and þe halle entres,
Driuande to þe heƷe dece—dut he no woþe.
Haylsed he neuer one bot heƷe he ouerloked.
Þe fyrst word þat he warp, 'Wher is,' he sayd,
'Þe gouernour of þis gyng? Gladly I wolde   225
Se þat segg in syƷt and with hymself speke
    Raysoun.'
        To knyƷtez he kest his yƷe
        And reled hym vp and doun.
        He stemmed and con studie   230
        Quo walt þer most renoun.

Ther watz lokyng on lenþe þe lude to beholde,
For vch mon had meruayle quat hit mene myƷt
Þat a haþel and a horse myƷt such a hwe lach
As growe grene as þe gres and grener hit semed,   235
Þen grene aumayl on golde glowande bryƷter.
Al studied þat þer stod and stalked hym nerre
Wyth al þe wonder of þe worlde what he worch schulde.
For fele sellyez had þay sen bot such neuer are;
Forþi for fantoum and fayryƷe þe folk þere hit demed.   240
Þerfore to answare watz arƷe mony aþel freke
And al stouned at his steuen and ston-stil seten
In a swoghe sylence þurƷ þe sale riche.
As al were slypped vpon slepe so slaked hor lotez

---

236. glowande] MS lowande

224. *Þe fyrst word þat he warp:* a traditional formula for introducing a speech. Cf. also *Pat* 356, *Cl* 152, 213.

229. *reled hym:* possibly 'rolled them (his eyes)', cf. 304; but in view of *He stemmed* ('stopped') in the next line it is perhaps better to read 'swaggered up and down' or 'turned (rode) to and fro'.

236. Poetic inversion: 'shining brighter than green enamel on gold.'

237. 'All who were standing there stared and cautiously approached him'. These are presumably the servants, whose naïve curiosity is thus suitably differentiated from the stunned silence of the courtiers (241ff). The suggestion of M. Markus (*Neu.Mitt.*, 75 [1974], 625–9) that *þat þer stod* is an object phrase 'him who was standing there', while possible in itself, deprives *stalked* of its subject *al* (since 242 rules out the possibility that everybody in the hall approached him); Markus makes 'the Green Knight' the implied subject of *stalked hym* (taken as reflex.), but this, in turn, leaves 238 hanging.

244f. 'Their voices died away as suddenly as if they had all fallen asleep'.

In hy3e—   245
I deme hit not al for doute
Bot sum for cortaysye—
Bot let hym þat al schulde loute
Cast vnto þat wy3e.

Þenn Arþour, bifore þe hi3 dece, þat auenture byholdez   250
And rekenly hym reuerenced, for rad was he neuer,
And sayde, 'Wy3e, welcum iwys to þis place.
Þe hede of þis ostel, Arthour I hat.   [f94ᵛ]
Li3t luflych adoun and lenge, I þe praye,
And quatso þy wylle is we schal wyt after.'   255
'Nay, as help me,' quoþ þe haþel, 'He þat on hy3e syttes,
To wone any quyle in þis won hit watz not myn ernde;
Bot for þe los of þe, lede, is lyft vp so hy3e
And þy bur3 and þy burnes best ar holden,
Stifest vnder stel-gere on stedes to ryde,   260
Þe wy3test and þe worþyest of þe worldes kynde,
Preue for to play wyth in oþer pure laykez,
And here is kydde cortaysye, as I haf herd carp—
And þat hatz wayned me hider, iwyis, at þis tyme.
3e may be seker bi þis braunch þat I bere here   265
Þat I passe as in pes and no ply3t seche;
For had I founded in fere, in fe3tyng wyse,
I haue a hauberghe at home and a helme boþe,
A schelde and a scharp spere, schinande bry3t,
Ande oþer weppenes to welde, I wene wel, als;   270
Bot for I wolde no were, my wedez ar softer.
Bot if þou be so bold as alle burnez tellen,
Þou wyl grant me godly þe gomen þat I ask
        Bi ry3t.'

248f. 'but allowed him to whom all were duty bound to defer (i.e. Arthur) to address that man.' Possibly, however, *let* is to be read as imperative, addressed to the audience, as in 1994.

253. 'I, the head ot this house, am called Arthur.'

254. *I þe praye:* as king, Arthur properly uses the singular pronoun to everyone except Guenevere; his general manner towards the Green Knight is courteous and hospitable in the extreme. The latter's use of *thou* to Arthur, however, is a mark of disrespect (contrast Gawain's manner of addressing the king in 343ff).

256. *He þat on hy3e syttes:* a periphrasis for 'God'.

258. 'but because your renown, sir, is built up to such a height'.

262. *oþer pure laykez:* sc. 'than jousting'. He alludes to the beheading game.

267. *in fere:* either 'in company' or 'in martial fashion, array' from a phrase such as *in fere* (i.e. 'show, array') *of war*.

274. I.e. 'by prerogative of the Christmas season'.

> Arthour con onsware   275
> And sayd, 'Sir cortays kny3t,
> If þou craue batayl bare,
> Here faylez þou not to fy3t.'

'Nay, frayst I no fy3t, in fayth I þe telle;
Hit arn aboute on þis bench bot berdlez chylder.   280
If I were hasped in armes on a he3e stede,
Here is no mon me to mach, for my3tez so wayke.
Forþy I craue in þis court a Crystemas gomen,
For hit is 3ol and Nwe 3er, and here ar 3ep mony.
If any so hardy in þis hous holdez hymseluen,   285
Be so bolde in his blod, brayn in hys hede,
Þat dar stifly strike a strok for anoþer,
I schal gif hym of my gyft þys giserne ryche,
Þis ax, þat is heué innogh, to hondele as hym lykes,
And I schal bide þe fyrst bur as bare as I sitte.   [f95ʳ]   290
If any freke be so felle to fonde þat I telle,
Lepe ly3tly me to and lach þis weppen—
I quit-clayme hit for euer, kepe hit as his auen—
And I schal stonde hym a strok, stif on þis flet,
Ellez þou wyl di3t me þe dom to dele hym anoþer   295
> Barlay,

---

282. so] MS fo

277. *batayl bare:* 'battle without armour' (cf. 290). Barron, however, relates the phrase (which he takes in the sense 'single combat'—cf. *bare* 'single' 1141) to *in fere* (taken in the sense 'in company') 267.

278. 'you will not lack fighting here.'

280. *Hit arn . . . bot:* 'there are only .

285-7. 'If anyone in this house considers himself so brave, (to) be so bold-spirited, so reckless of mind, that (he) dares. . .'.

288. *giserne:* the term *gisarm* was usually applied to a battle-axe with a long blade in line with the shaft, sharpened on both sides and ending in a point, though the description in 209ff appears to distinguish the *grayn* (spike) from the blade. However, there is little doubt that the variations *ax*, *giserne*, *denez ax*, and *sparþe* are introduced mainly for the sake of alliteration and that they are all used as synonyms for 'battle-axe'.

291. 'If any warrior be so daring (as) to put to the test what I propose'.

292f. *Lepe . . . lach . . . kepe:* subjunctives, 'let him run, seize, keep'.

296. *Barlay:* usually identified with the dialect word *barley* used in children's games to call a truce or to lay first claim to something ('bags I'); perhaps 'I claim first blow'. A suggested etymology is OF *par loi*, *par lei* 'by law', which would agree with the regular stress pattern in the bob: x / (x). Another explanation is that the word is a noun meaning 'blow'. (See B. M. White, *Neophil.*, 37 [1953], 113-15.)

And ʒet gif hym respite
A twelmonyth and a day.
Now hyʒe, and let se tite
Dar any herinne oʒt say.'   300

If he hem stowned vpon fyrst, stiller were þanne
Alle þe heredmen in halle, þe hyʒ and þe loʒe.
Þe renk on his rouncé hym ruched in his sadel
And runischly his rede yʒen he reled aboute,
Bende his bresed broʒez, blycande grene,   305
Wayued his berde for to wayte quoso wolde ryse.
When non wolde kepe hym with carp he coʒed ful hyʒe
Ande rimed hym ful richly and ryʒt hym to speke.
'What, is þis Arþures hous,' quoþ þe haþel þenne,
'Þat al þe rous rennes of þurʒ ryalmes so mony?   310
Where is now your sourquydrye and your conquestes,
Your gryndellayk and your greme and your grete wordes?
Now is þe reuel and þe renoun of þe Rounde Table
Ouerwalt wyth a worde of on wyʒes speche,
For al dares for drede withoute dynt schewed!'   315
Wyth þis he laʒes so loude þat þe lorde greued;
Þe blod schot for scham into his schyre face
        And lere;
        He wex as wroth as wynde;

312. gryndellayk] n *illegible in* MS

298. A traditional expression meaning 'until the same day a year hence'. In the
present case, from 1 January 'a twelvemonth' would extend to 31 December, and the
extra day is mentioned to make it clear that the term expires on the following day, 1
January.

306. 'turned his head from side to side (*lit.* waved his beard) to see if anyone would
rise.'

307. *kepe hym with carp:* the preposition possibly governs *hym:* 'hold speech with him';
but in view of *Cl* 89 it seems equally possible to understand 'entertain him with
speech'. *Coʒed:* TG-Davis notes that this verb can be used of a wide range of vocal
sounds, and as a verb of saying (e.g. in *CT* I.3679f); here, however, it evidently
denotes a preparation for speech (cf. 308) and thus probably means 'coughed' or
'cleared his throat'.

309f. The scornful question, with its implication that they are failing to live up to their
reputation, is a technique also adopted later by the Lady of Hautdesert—see 1481ff
and cf. 1528.

310. *Þat . . . of:* 'of which'.

315. 'for everyone is cowering in fear without a blow being offered!' The ambiguity of
the last phrase (i.e. offered to them, or offered to him, in response to his request) is no
doubt deliberate.

316. *þe lorde greued:* 'the lord (Arthur) was offended'.

So did alle þat þer were.   320
Þe kyng, as kene bi kynde,
Þen stod þat stif mon nere,

Ande sayde, 'Haþel, by heuen þyn askyng is nys,
And as þou foly hatz frayst, fynde þe behoues.
I know no gome þat is gast of þy grete wordes.   325
Gif me now þy geserne, vpon Godez halue,
And I schal bayþen þy bone þat þou boden habbes.'
Lyȝtly lepez he hym to and laȝt hit at his honde.   [f95ᵛ]
Þen feersly þat oþer freke vpon fote lyȝtis.
Now hatz Arthure his axe and þe halme grypez   330
And sturnely sturez hit aboute, þat stryke wyth hit þoȝt.
Þe stif mon hym bifore stod vpon hyȝt,
Herre þen ani in þe hous by þe hede and more.
Wyth sturne schere þer he stod he stroked his berde
And wyth a countenaunce dryȝe he droȝ doun his cote,   335
No more mate ne dismayd for hys mayn dintez
Þen any burne vpon bench hade broȝt hym to drynk
      Of wyne.
   Gawan, þat sate bi þe quene,
   To þe kyng he can enclyne,   340
   'I beseche now with saȝez sene
   Þis melly mot be myne.'

'Wolde ȝe, worþilych lorde,' quoþ Wawan to þe kyng,

---

328. hit] MS *om.* (cf. 827)
336. hys] MS hyns (hȳs)
343. Wawan] MS Gawan

---

320. *þat þer were:* 'who were there'.
321. *as kene bi kynde:* 'like the brave man he was by nature', cf. 1104.
322. *nere:* strictly comparative of *neȝ*, i.e. 'nearer'.
324. 'and as you have asked for foolishness it behoves you to find it.'
328. 'Swiftly he springs towards him and received it from his hand.'
331. 'and fiercely brandishes it about, (like one) who intended to strike with it.'
335. *droȝ doun his cote:* i.e. from the back of his neck.
336. *for hys mayn dintez:* 'for his mighty blows'—i.e. either the ones he seemed prepared to deliver, or the blows he was practising at that moment; there is no implication (as has been supposed) that Arthur is actually attempting to behead the Green Knight at this point.
337f. *to drynk Of wyne:* 'some wine to drink'; this use of *of* is probably an imitation of Fr *de* (*du*, etc.), cf. 854.
340. *can enclyne:* 'bowed'.
341f. These two lines are probably to be understood as a brief summary of Gawain's speech to the king, which is given in its full elaboration in the next stanza; for the same device (*transitio*), cf. 387–9, 734–9, 2185–8, 2237f.
343. *Wolde ȝe:* 'If you would ... (bid me)'. *Wawan:* the poet several times uses the

'Bid me boȝe fro þis benche and stonde by yow þere,
Þat I wythoute vylanye myȝt voyde þis table,   345
And þat my legge lady lyked not ille,
I wolde com to your counseyl bifore your cort ryche.
For me þink hit not semly—as hit is soþ knawen—
Þer such an askyng is heuened so hyȝe in your sale,
Þaȝ ȝe ȝourself be talenttyf, to take hit to yourseluen,   350
Whil mony so bolde yow aboute vpon bench sytten
Þat vnder heuen I hope non haȝerer of wylle
Ne better bodyes on bent þer baret is rered.
I am þe wakkest, I wot, and of wyt feblest,
And lest lur of my lyf, quo laytes þe soþe.   355
Bot for as much as ȝe ar myn em I am only to prayse;
No bounté but your blod I in my bodé knowe.
And syþen þis note is so nys þat noȝt hit yow falles,
And I haue frayned hit at yow fyrst, foldez hit to me.
And if I carp not comlyly let alle þis cort rych   360
        Bout blame.'
        Ryche togeder con roun;
        And syþen þay redden alle same
        To ryd þe kyng wyth croun
        And gif Gawan þe game.   365

Þen comaunded þe kyng þe knyȝt for to ryse;   [f96ʳ]
And he ful radly vpros and ruchched hym fayre,
Kneled doun bifore þe kyng and cachez þat weppen.
And he luflyly hit hym laft and lyfte vp his honde
And gef hym Goddez blessyng, and gladly hym biddes   370
Þat his hert and his honde schulde hardi be boþe.
'Kepe þe, cosyn,' quoþ þe kyng, 'þat þou on kyrf sette,

alternative form with initial *W-* when he wishes to alliterate on *w* (as in 559, 906, etc.). The Celtic form of the name (like that of *Guenever*, which appears as *Wenore* in 945) began with *Gw-*, which alternated with *W-* in certain positions.

345. *wythoute vylanye:* 'without discourtesy'. Gawain's *cortaysye* shows in this stanza as an elaborate politeness of manner and speech.

346. 'and if that did not displease my sovereign lady (Guenevere)'; *þat* is subject.

347. *com to your counseyl:* 'give you advice'; cf. 'come to someone's help.'

348. *me þink:* a conflation of *I þink* and *me þinkeþ* ('it seems to me').

350. *to take hit:* sc. 'for you . . .'.

352. 'that I think none on earth (to be) more resourceful in courage'.

353. *on bent . . . rered:* 'on the field of battle'.

356. 'I am only praiseworthy in that you are my uncle'; (*only* repeats *Bot*).

358. *þis note is so nys:* 'this matter is so foolish'.

360f. 'and if I speak unfittingly let all this noble court (speak) without offence.' Other interpretations are possible, however: 'let all this noble court be free from blame' (see TG-Davis note), or (taking *rych* as a verb, meaning 'decide'): 'let all this court decide without reproach whether I speak fittingly or not.'

372. *Kepe þe:* 'Take care'. *Þat . . . sette:* 'that you strike one blow' (cf. 287, 294, and Gawain's words in 2252). For this use of *set*, see *OED set* v. III.20.

And if þou redez hym ryȝt, redly I trowe
Þat þou schal byden þe bur þat he schal bede after.'
Gawan gotz to þe gome with giserne in honde   375
And he baldly hym bydez—he bayst neuer þe helder.
Þen carppez to Sir Gawan þe knyȝt in þe grene,
'Refourme we oure forwardes, er we fyrre passe.
Fyrst I eþe þe, haþel, how þat þou hattes
Þat þou me telle truly, as I tryst may.'   380
'In god fayth,' quoþ þe goode knyȝt, 'Gawan I hatte
Þat bede þe þis buffet (quatso bifallez after)
And at þis tyme twelmonyth take at þe anoþer
Wyth what weppen so þou wylt—and wyth no wyȝ ellez
    On lyue.'   385
        Þat oþer onswarez agayn,
        'Sir Gawan, so mot I þryue
        As I am ferly fayn
        Þis dint þat þou schal dryue.'

'Bigog,' quoþ þe grene knyȝt, 'Sir Gawan, me lykes   390
Þat I schal fange at þy fust þat I haf frayst here.
And þou hatz redily rehersed, bi resoun ful trwe,
Clanly al þe couenaunt þat I þe kynge asked,
Saf þat þou schal siker me, segge, bi þi trawþe,
Þat þou schal seche me þiself, whereso þou hopes   395
I may be funde vpon folde, and foch þe such wages
As þou deles me today bifore þis douþe ryche.'
'Where schulde I wale þe?' quoþ Gauan. 'Where is þy place?
I wot neuer where þou wonyes, bi Hym þat me wroȝt,
Ne I know not þe, knyȝt, þy cort ne þi name.   400
Bot teche me truly þerto and telle me howe þou hattes,

384. so] MS fo
398. place] MS plate

373f. 'and if you deal with him properly, I fully believe that you will stand the blow
that he is to offer afterwards.' In addition to the humorous implication 'because he'll
be dead', there may well be a pun on *byden*, which can mean 'endure' or 'wait for'.
376. *he bayst neuer þe helder:* 'he was dismayed no more for that'.
379f. *how þat . . . truly:* 'that you tell me truly what you are called'.
384f. *and wyth . . . lyue:* If this means 'with no one else present' it was not included in
the challenge, unless in the obscure *barlay*, though Gawain does meet the Green
Knight alone (cf. especially 2149ff, 2242–6). However, the meaning is almost cer-
tainly 'at the hands of no other living person' (for *wyth:* 'at the hands of' cf. 681);
Gawain might be expected to insist on this point, which appears to give him a good
chance of escaping the return blow (cf. 373f, 410).
389. There is a suggestion of special stress on *þou*, which is echoed in the next stanza
and at 908ff and 2239ff.
391. *þat I haf frayst:* 'that which I have asked'.
401. 'But direct me faithfully to it and tell me what you are called'.

And I schal ware alle my wyt to wynne me þeder—
And þat I swere þe for soþe and by my seker traweþ.'
'Þat is innogh in Nwe Ʒer—hit nedes no more,'
Quoþ þe gome in þe grene to Gawan þe hende. 405
'Ʒif I þe telle trwly quen I þe tape haue
And þou me smoþely hatz smyten, smartly I þe teche
Of my hous and my home and myn owen nome,
Þen may þou frayst my fare and forwardez holde;
And if I spende no speche þenne spedez þou þe better, 410
For þou may leng in þy londe and layt no fyrre.
       Bot slokes!
    Ta now þy grymme tole to þe
    And let se how þou cnokez.'
       'Gladly, sir, forsoþe,' 415
    Quoþ Gawan; his ax he strokes.

The grene knyʒt vpon grounde grayþely hym dresses;
A littel lut with þe hede, þe lere he discouerez;
His longe louelych lokkez he layd ouer his croun,
Let þe naked nec to þe note schewe. 420
Gauan gripped to his ax and gederes hit on hyʒt;
Þe kay fot on þe folde he before sette,
Let hit doun lyʒtly lyʒt on þe naked,
Þat þe scharp of þe schalk schyndered þe bones
And schrank þurʒ þe schyire grece and schade hit in twynne, 425
Þat þe bit of þe broun stel bot on þe grounde.
Þe fayre hede fro þe halce hit to þe erþe,
Þat fele hit foyned wyth her fete þere hit forth roled;
Þe blod brayd fro þe body, þat blykked on þe grene.
And nawþer faltered ne fel þe freke neuer þe helder 430
Bot styþly he start forth vpon styf schonkes
And runyschly he raʒt out þereas renkkez stoden,
Laʒt to his lufly hed and lyft hit vp sone,

---

425. schade] MS scade
432. runyschly] MS ruyschly

---

404. The New Year is still a time for making solemn resolutions. The Green Knight discourages Gawain from taking a stronger oath.
409. *frayst my fare:* an idiom meaning 'call on me' (*lit.* 'ask how I am getting on'); cf. 2494.
410. *spedez þou þe better:* 'it will be all the better for you'.
412. *slokes:* several interpretations are possible; e.g. 'let us stop' (1 pl. imperat.), 'stop' (2 pl. imperat.), 'you are dawdling' (2 sing. indic.); the last is perhaps to be preferred.
416. *his ax he strokes:* i.e. to test its edge.
424. 'so that the man's sharp blade cut through the bones'.
429. *þat blykked:* qualifies *blod*.

And syþen boȝez to his blonk, þe brydel he cachchez,
Steppez into stel-bawe and strydez alofte,   435
And his hede by þe here in his honde haldez;
And as sadly þe segge hym in his sadel sette
As non vnhap had hym ayled, þaȝ hedlez nowe
    In stedde.
    He brayde his bluk aboute,   440
    Þat vgly bodi þat bledde.   [f97ʳ]
    Moni on of hym had doute,
    Bi þat his resounz were redde.

For þe hede in his honde he haldez vp euen,
Toward þe derrest on þe dece he dressez þe face   445
And hit lyfte vp þe yȝe-lyddez and loked ful brode
And meled þus much with his muthe as ȝe may now here:
'Loke, Gawan, þou be grayþe to go as þou hettez
And layte as lelly til þou me, lude, fynde
As þou hatz hette in þis halle, herande þise knyȝtes.   450
To þe Grene Chapel þou chose, I charge þe, to fotte
Such a dunt as þou hatz dalt—disserued þou habbez—
To be ȝederly ȝolden on Nw Ȝeres morn.
Þe Knyȝt of þe Grene Chapel men knowen me mony;
Forþi me for to fynde, if þou fraystez, faylez þou neuer.   455
Þerfore com, oþer recreaunt be calde þe behoues.'
With a runisch rout þe raynez he tornez,
Halled out at þe hal dor, his hed in his hande,
Þat þe fyr of þe flynt flaȝe fro fole houes.
To quat kyth he becom knwe non þere,   460
Neuer more þen þay wyste from queþen he watz wonnen.
    What þenne?
    Þe kyng and Gawen þare
    At þat grene þay laȝe and grenne,

---

438. nowe (Cawley)] MS howe
456. behoues] MS behoueus

442f. 'Many a one was frightened of him by the time he had finished speaking'—a good instance of the poet's use of the *wheel* for surprise and suspense.

445. *þe derrest:* probably 'the nobles', cf. *Cl* 115. It is suggested that Guenevere ('the noblest') is meant—Arthur is not yet seated—but, in spite of the motive revealed belatedly in 2460, this is not a very likely reading, since the words are addressed to Gawain.

447. *his* is neuter possessive at this time: 'with its mouth'.

450. *herande:* absolute use of the present participle: '(while) these knights (were) listening'.

454. *men knowen me mony:* 'I am widely known as'.

460f. A 'fairy' formula. Cf. *Sir Orfeo* (ed. A. J. Bliss, Oxford, 1954) 288: *No never he nist whider thai bicome* and 296: *Ac never he nist whider thai wold*; cf. also 2477f below.

Ʒet breued watz hit ful bare 465
A meruayl among þo menne.

Þaʒ Arþer þe hende kyng at hert hade wonder,
He let no semblaunt be sene bot sayde ful hyʒe
To þe comlych quene wyth cortays speche,
'Dere dame, today demay yow neuer. 470
Wel bycommes such craft vpon Cristmasse—
Laykyng of enterludez, to laʒe and to syng—
Among þise kynde caroles of knyʒtez and ladyez.
Neuerþelece to my mete I may me wel dres,
For I haf sen a selly I may not forsake.' 475
He glent vpon Sir Gawen and gaynly he sayde,
'Now sir, heng vp þyn ax, þat hatz innogh hewen.'
And hit watz don abof þe dece on doser to henge, [f97ᵛ]
Þer alle men for meruayl myʒt on hit loke
And bi trwe tytel þerof to telle þe wonder. 480
Þenne þay boʒed to a borde þise burnes togeder,
Þe kyng and þe gode knyʒt, and kene men hem serued
Of alle dayntyez double, as derrest myʒt falle,
Wyth alle maner of mete and mynstralcie boþe.
Wyth wele walt þay þat day, til worþed an ende 485
      In londe.
   Now þenk wel, Sir Gawan,
   For woþe þat þou ne wonde
   Þis auenture for to frayn
   Þat þou hatz tan on honde. 490

465f. Cf. 91-4, 474f.
470. 'Dear lady, do not be perturbed (*reflex.*) on a day like this.'
472f. 'playing of interludes, laughing and singing—among the courtly carols performed by knights and ladies.' The term *enterludez* (L *interludium*, *lit.* 'between play') was possibly first used of short dramatic or mimic entertainments between courses at a banquet. Though by the 14th c. it seems to have designated simply 'plays' (sometimes 'miracle plays'), the word may have retained a derogatory association with minstrelsy or mumming. In contrasting what they have just seen with the courtiers' own *caroles*, King Arthur conveys an aristocratic disdain for professional entertainment and at the same time contrives to suggest that the beheading may have been no more than an illusionist's trick (cf. *craft*).
477. Arthur aptly (*gaynly*) quotes a proverbial expression meaning 'cease from strife'.
479f. 'where everyone could look at it in amazement and relate the wonder of it by true right.' Possibly, however, *to telle* is grammatically parallel to *to henge:* the axe would tell its own wonderful story (cf. 626); in this case we should read *þerof* with *tytel* rather than with *wonder*.
483. *as derrest myʒt falle:* either 'in the noblest fashion possible' or 'as might be fitting to nobles'.
485f. 'They spent that day in enjoyment until it came to an end (*lit.* an end came).'
488-90. 'that you do not shrink because of the danger from making trial of this quest which you have undertaken.'

II

This hanselle hatz Arthur of auenturus on fyrst
In ʒonge ʒer for he ʒerned ʒelpyng to here.
Thaʒ hym wordez were wane when þay to sete wenten,
Now ar þay stoken of sturne werk, staf-ful her hond.
Gawan watz glad to begynne þose gomnez in halle 495
Bot þaʒ þe ende be heuy haf ʒe no wonder:
For þaʒ men ben mery in mynde quen þay han mayn drynk,
A ʒere ʒernes ful ʒerne and ʒeldez neuer lyke;
Þe forme to þe fynisment foldez ful selden.
Forþi þis ʒol ouerʒede, and þe ʒere after, 500
And vche sesoun serlepes sued after oþer:
After Crystenmasse com þe crabbed Lentoun,
Þat fraystez flesch wyth þe fysche and fode more symple,
Bot þenne þe weder of þe worlde wyth wynter hit þrepez,
Colde clengez adoun, cloudez vplyften, 505
Schyre schedez þe rayn in schowrez ful warme,
Fallez vpon fayre flat, flowrez þere schewen,
Boþe groundez and þe greuez grene ar her wedez,
Bryddez busken to bylde and bremlych syngen

491. *hatz:* 'has received'.

493. 'Though (such) speeches (i.e. the *ʒelpyng* of 492) were not forthcoming for him when they sat down' – an allusion to the beginning of the feast, 72–102. *Hym* may mean 'them' with little change of sense: 'Though they lacked such speeches'.

494. *staf-ful:* A word of obscure origin; if it is understood to mean 'as full as one's hand is when holding a staff' it contains an oblique ironical reference to the axe. Cf. also *OED staff-full.*

497. The similarity between this line and the beginning of Vernon Lyric 7 'Sometime Think on Yesterday' brings to the reader's notice the theme of mutability underlying this description of the passing of the seasons:

　Whon Men beoþ muriest at heor Mele,
　Wiþ mete & drink to maken hem glade,
　Wiþ worschip & wiþ worldlich wele
　Þei ben so set, þey conne not sade; . . .
　But in heor hertes I wolde þei hade,
　Whon þei gon ricchest men on array,
　Hou sone þat god hem may degrade,
　And sumtyme þenk on ʒusterday.

(*Minor Poems of the Vernon MS*, ed. C. Horstmann and F. J. Furnivall [EETS OS 98, 117], II, 675–80.) Cf. also the poet's use of *ʒisterdayez* in 529.

503. 'which tests the body with fish and plainer food'.

504. 'but then nature's weather (i.e. the coming of spring) contends (*þrepez*) with winter'. The changing of the seasons was traditionally imagined as a battle between Summer and Winter which manifested itself particularly in the equinoctial storms (cf. 523ff). In 2000, however, the phrase *wederez of þe worlde* refers to the storms of winter.

505. *Colde clengez adoun:* 'frost shrinks into the earth (dies)'.

For solace of þe softe somer þat sues þerafter   510
    Bi bonk,
And blossumez bolne to blowe
Bi rawez rych and ronk,
Þen notez noble innoȝe
Ar herde in wod so wlonk.   [f98ʳ] 515

After þe sesoun of somer wyth þe soft wyndez,
Quen Zeferus syflez hymself on sedez and erbez,
Wela wynne is þe wort þat waxes þeroute,
When þe donkande dewe dropez of þe leuez,
To bide a blysful blusch of þe bryȝt sunne.   520
Bot þen hyȝes Heruest and hardenes hym sone,
Warnez hym for þe wynter to wax ful rype;
He dryues wyth droȝt þe dust for to ryse,
Fro þe face of þe folde to flyȝe ful hyȝe;
Wroþe wynde of þe welkyn wrastelez with þe sunne,   525
Þe leuez laucen fro þe lynde and lyȝten on þe grounde,
And al grayes þe gres þat grene watz ere;
Þenne al rypez and rotez þat ros vpon fyrst,
And þus ȝirnez þe ȝere in ȝisterdayez mony
And wynter wyndez aȝayn, as þe worlde askez,   530
    No fage,
Til Meȝelmas mone
Watz cumen wyth wynter wage.
Þen þenkkez Gawan ful sone
Of his anious uyage.   535

Ȝet quyl Al Hal Day with Arþer he lenges;
And he made a fare on þat fest for þe frekez sake,
With much reuel and ryche of þe Rounde Table.

---

531. fage (Onions)] MS sage

518. *þeroute:* possibly 'outside, out of doors' (as in 2000) but better 'out of it (the seed)'.
520. *To bide:* 'to enjoy'; the subject is *wort* (518).
521. *hardenes hym:* as the next line makes clear, this is a play upon words: 'encourages him' (i.e. the *wort*) and 'makes him hard with fruit'; we might render 'puts heart into him'.
522. *for þe wynter:* 'against (the coming of) the winter'.
523. *He:* i.e. *Heruest:* 'with drought he (Autumn) makes the dust rise'.
525. The reference is to the equinoctial gales (cf. 504n).
528–31. 'then everything that grew in the beginning ripens and rots, and thus the year runs by in many yesterdays and winter comes back, as nature demands, in truth'. This use of 'yesterday' to suggest the mutability of earthly life (cf. Macbeth's 'And all our yesterdays have lighted fools The way to dusty death'), is no doubt reminiscent of texts such as Job 8 : 9 and Ps. 89 (AV 90) : 4, where early English versions invariably have 'yesterday' (*dæg gystran, yhistre-dai, etc.*) for *dies hesterna*.
533. *wyth wynter wage:* 'with pledge of winter'.
536. *Al Hal Day:* 'All Saints' Day', 1 November.

Kny3tez ful cortays and comlych ladies
Al for luf of þat lede in longynge þay were;   540
Bot neuer þe lece ne þe later þay neuened bot merþe.
Mony joylez for þat jentyle japez þer maden.
For aftter mete with mournyng he melez to his eme
And spekez of his passage, and pertly he sayde,
'Now, lege lorde of my lyf, leue I yow ask.   545
3e knowe þe cost of þis cace; kepe I no more
To telle yow tenez þerof – neuer bot trifel –
Bot I am boun to þe bur barely tomorne
To sech þe gome of þe grene, as God wyl me wysse.'
Þenne þe best of þe bur3 bo3ed togeder,   550
Aywan and Errik and oþer ful mony –
Sir Doddinaual de Sauage, þe Duk of Clarence,   [f98ᵛ]
Launcelot, and Lyonel, and Lucan þe gode,
Sir Boos and Sir Byduer, big men boþe,
And mony oþer menskful, with Mador de la Port.   555
Alle þis compayny of court com þe kyng nerre
For to counseyl þe kny3t, with care at her hert.
Þere watz much derue doel driuen in þe sale
Þat so worthé as Wawan schulde wende on þat ernde
To dry3e a delful dynt and dele no more   560
        Wyth bronde.
    Þe kny3t mad ay god chere
    And sayde, 'Quat schuld I wonde?
    Of Destinés derf and dere
    What may mon do bot fonde?'   565

He dowellez þer al þat day and dressez on þe morn,

---

541. *neuer . . . þe later:* a parallel expression to *neuer þe lece.*
542. 'Many who were joyless on account of that noble knight made jokes there.'
546f. 'You know the nature of this affair; I do not care to relate the troubles of it any
more to you – it would only be idle talk.'
549. *wyl me wysse:* 'sees fit to guide me.'
551ff. Some of the knights mentioned here (e.g. Eric, Lancelot, Bedevere) play an
important part in other Arthurian romances. Here their names are introduced (like
those of 110ff) in order to invest the story with authenticity for readers conversant
with the Arthurian background. *Aywan* is the Ywain of 113; *Sir Doddinaual de Sauage*
was so named for his love of hunting (OF *salvage*, L *silvaticus* 'of the woods'); *þe Duk
of Clarence* is a cousin (or brother) of Sir Dodinal. *Mador de la Port:* 'Mador the door-
keeper'.
558. *derue:* may be read as *derne* 'secret' (cf. 540–2).
559. *schulde wende:* 'should have to go'.
560f. *dele . . . bronde:* 'give none (i.e. blows) in return with his sword' – perhaps also
'never use his sword again'.
564f. 'What can one do but make trial of that which Destiny offers, whether painful or
pleasant?' (*Destinés* is possessive.)

Askez erly hys armez and alle were þay broȝt.
Fyrst a tulé tapit tyȝt ouer þe flet,
And miche watz þe gyld gere þat glent þeralofte.
Þe stif mon steppez þeron and þe stel hondelez,   570
Dubbed in a dublet of a dere tars,
And syþen a crafty capados, closed aloft,
Þat wyth a bryȝt blaunner was bounden withinne.
Þenne set þay þe sabatounz vpon þe segge fotez,
His legez lapped in stel with luflych greuez,   575
With polaynez piched þerto, policed ful clene,
Aboute his knez knaged wyth knotez of golde;
Queme quyssewes þen, þat coyntlych closed
His thik þrawen þyȝez, with þwonges to tachched;
And syþen þe brawden bryné of bryȝt stel ryngez   580
Vmbeweued þat wyȝ, vpon wlonk stuffe,
And wel bornyst brace vpon his boþe armes,
With gode cowters and gay and glouez of plate,
And alle þe godlych gere þat hym gayn schulde
        Þat tyde;   585
    Wyth ryche cote-armure,
    His gold sporez spend with pryde,
    Gurde wyth a bront ful sure
    With silk sayn vmbe his syde.

When he watz hasped in armes his harnays watz ryche: [f99ʳ] 590
Þe lest lachet oþer loupe lemed of golde.
So harnayst as he watz he herknez his masse
Offred and honoured at þe heȝe auter.
Syþen he comez to þe kyng and to his cort-ferez,
Lachez lufly his leue at lordez and ladyez,   595
And þay hym kyst and conueyed, bikende hym to Kryst.
Bi þat watz Gryngolet grayth and gurde with a sadel

591. oþer] MS ouer

571f. The armour was put on over the knight's clothes (the doublet and capados); cf. 2015.

574–7. 'Then they placed the steel shoes upon the man's feet; his legs (were) enclosed in steel by beautiful greaves to which were attached brightly polished knee pieces (*polaynez*), fastened about his knees with gold knots'.

579. *with . . . tachched:* 'tied on with laces'.

581. *vpon wlonk stuffe:* qualifies *ryngez*.

586. *cote-armure:* a knight's surcoat, or coat of arms, i.e. a cloth tunic worn over the armour and embroidered with his heraldic device (which hence itself receives the name 'coat-of-arms').

592f. *he herknez . . . honoured:* 'he hears his Mass offered and celebrated' (past participles).

Þat glemed ful gayly with mony golde frenges,
Ayquere naylet ful nwe, for þat note ryched,
Þe brydel barred aboute, with bryȝt golde bounden.   600
Þe apparayl of þe payttrure and of þe proude skyrtez,
Þe cropore, and þe couertor, acorded wyth þe arsounez.
And al watz, rayled on red, ryche golde naylez,
Þat al glytered and glent as glem of þe sunne.
Þenne hentes he þe helme and hastily hit kysses,   605
Þat watz stapled stifly and stoffed wythinne.
Hit watz hyȝe on his hede, hasped bihynde,
Wyth a lyȝtly vrysoun ouer þe auentayle,
Enbrawden and bounden wyth þe best gemmez
On brode sylkyn borde, and bryddez on semez,   610
As papjayez paynted peruyng bitwene,
Tortors and trulofez entayled so þyk
As mony burde þeraboute had ben seuen wynter
      In toune.
   Þe cercle watz more o prys   615
   Þat vmbeclypped hys croun,
   Of diamauntez a deuys
   Þat boþe were bryȝt and broun.

Then þay schewed hym þe schelde, þat was of schyr goulez
Wyth þe pentangel depaynt of pure golde hwez;   620
He braydez hit by þe bauderyk, aboute þe hals kestes.
Þat bisemed þe segge semlyly fayre
And quy þe pentangel apendez to þat prynce noble
I am in tent yow to telle, þof tary hyt me schulde.
Hit is a syngne þat Salamon set sumquyle   625

603. 'And it was all costly gold studs, set upon a red background'.
606. *stapled:* i.e. at the joints.
608. The *vrysoun* (OF *hourson*) was a band of embroidered silk which attached the *auentayle* (or *camail*), a piece of chain mail for the protection of the neck, to the bottom of the helmet.
611. 'such as parrots depicted between periwinkles (*peruyng*)'; the word may alternatively be read *pernyng* 'preening themselves', or perhaps 'flitting' (see B. James, *NQ*, 206 [1961], 9 and TG-Davis n); however, the present participle usually ends in *-ande* in this poem. As 'periwinkle' it must be understood collectively here, unless it is a corruption of *peruynkez.*
615–18. 'The circlet (band of gold) which ringed his head was (even) more valuable with perfect (*a deuys*) diamonds which were both clear and brown (i.e. of all tints).'
625. In the Middle Ages the idea developed that Solomon's magic seal bore a six-pointed star made of two interlaced triangles; in course of time this became identified with the five-pointed star (*pentangle, pentacle, pentalpha,* or *pentagramma*) which was used by the Pythagoreans and other sects as a symbol of health or perfection. In Christian eyes it was associated with black magic, but was sometimes made symbolic, instead, of the name Jesus or Maria (each of five letters), or of the five wounds of Christ. (See Green, **7d** 1962.)

In bytoknyng of trawþe, bi tytle þat hit habbez;
For hit is a figure þat haldez fyue poyntez [f99ᵛ]
And vche lyne vmbelappez and loukez in oþer
And ayquere hit is endelez (and Englych hit callen
Oueral, as I here, 'þe endeles knot'). 630
Forþy hit acordez to þis knyȝt and to his cler armez,
For ay faythful in fyue and sere fyue syþez,
Gawan watz for gode knawen and, as golde pured,
Voyded of vche vylany, wyth vertuez ennourned
    In mote. 635
    Forþy þe pentangel nwe
    He ber in schelde and cote,
    As tulk of tale most trwe
    And gentylest knyȝt of lote

Fyrst he watz funden fautlez in his fyue wyttez. 640
And efte fayled neuer þe freke in his fyue fyngres.

629. endelez] MS emdelez
634. vertuez] MS verertuez

626. *bi tytle þat hit habbez:* 'by its intrinsic right'. The complex unity of the figure makes it a 'natural' symbol of moral integrity, in the manner expounded in the lines which follow.

627. *poyntez:* a significant pun, in as much as the word can mean 'virtue, quality' in ME (cf. 654 and *Pat* 11). Perhaps it is also to be understood after *ay faythful in fyue* in 632.

628. 'and each line interlaces with and joins on to the others' (cf. 657). Each line of the pentangle passes over one, and under one, and joins the other two at its ends; see illustration:

630. *as I here:* to be read with *Oueral*: 'English people in all parts, I am told'. In fact, the phrase is not elsewhere recorded.

632f. 'for, always trustworthy in five ways, and five times in each way, Gawain was known as a virtuous knight'. The five pentads of virtue are detailed in the next stanza.

636. *nwe:* i.e. 'newly painted'; cf. 620. The adjective may also suggest the new significance given it in Christian use (see note to 625). Bennett argues (**5d** 1973, 7) that Gawain takes new arms for this enterprise.

641. *in his fyue fyngres:* i.e. 'in his deeds'(?) The symbolism is strained and uneven in parts.

And alle his afyaunce vpon folde watz in þe fyue woundez
Þat Cryst kaȝt on þe croys, as þe Crede tellez.
And queresoeuer þys mon in melly watz stad,
His þro þoȝt watz in þat, þurȝ alle oþer þyngez,   645
Þat alle his forsnes he fong at þe fyue joyez
Þat þe hende Heuen Quene had of hir Chylde.
(At þis cause þe knyȝt comlyche hade
In þe inore half of his schelde hir ymage depaynted,
Þat quen he blusched þerto his belde neuer payred.)   650
Þe fyft fyue þat I finde þat þe frek vsed
Watz fraunchyse and felaȝschyp forbe al þyng,
His clannes and his cortaysye croked were neuer,
And pité, þat passez alle poyntez – þyse pure fyue
Were harder happed on þat haþel þen on any oþer.   655
Now alle þese fyue syþez forsoþe were fetled on þis knyȝt
And vchone halched in oþer, þat non ende hade,
And fyched vpon fyue poyntez þat fayld neuer,
Ne samned neuer in no syde, ne sundred nouþer,
Withouten ende at any noke I oquere fynde,   660
Whereeuer þe gomen bygan or glod to an ende.
Þerfore on his schene schelde schapen watz þe knot,

---

659. nouþer] e *illegible*
660. oquere] MS quere (o *written above* u?); see TG-Davis n.

---

643. *Crede:* the Apostle's Creed (*crucifixus, mortuus, et sepultus*).
645f. 'his earnest intent was on this above all else: that he should get all his fortitude
from the five joys'. (*Fong* is pres. subj.; for similar examples of pres. subj. after pa.t.
see 738, 739.) The Five Joys of Mary were the Annunciation, Nativity, Resurrection,
Ascension, and Assumption; with the Five Wounds of Christ they form subjects of
popular devotions in the Middle Ages.
648f. In Geoffrey of Monmouth it is Arthur who has the image of the virgin painted
inside his shield.
651–5. The five virtues of chivalry are to be seen as forming a single group on a par
with the other pentads of 640, 641, 642, and 646. R. J. Spendal (*NQ,* 221 [1976],
147f) would identify the virtues of the fifth pentad (and perhaps of the whole pent-
angle) with Aquinas's Justice, which is sometimes called Truth (cf. *trawþe* 626), and
which includes the virtues of liberality (*liberalitas*), affability (*amicitia*), religion
(*religio*), observance (*observantia*), and piety (*pietas*).
653. *croked:* 'crooked, out of true' – an allusion to the symbolism of the lines of the
pentangle; cf. *poyntez* 654.
654. *Pity* and *piety* are not completely differentiated in meaning at this date (both
forms of the word go back, through OF, to L *pietas*). Here, among the virtues of
chivalry, the sense is primarily 'compassion' (cf. Chaucer's *For pitee renneth soone in
gentil herte*), but 'devotion to duty' is also of obvious importance in Gawain's story (as
in that of his ancestor Aeneas).
657. *þat . . . hade:* 'so that none (of them) came to an end'.
660. 'without end at any angle that I can find anywhere (*oquere*)'.

Ryally wyth red golde vpon rede gowlez,
Þat is þe pure 'pentaungel' wyth þe peple called   [f 100ʳ]
    With lore.   665
    Now grayþed is Gawan gay
    And laȝt his launce ryȝt þore
    And gef hem alle goud day –
    He wende for euermore.

He sperred þe sted with þe spurez and sprong on his way   670
So stif þat þe ston-fyr stroke out þerafter.
Al þat seȝ þat semly syked in hert
And sayde soþly al same segges til oþer,
Carande for þat comly, 'Bi Kryst, hit is scaþe
Þat þou, leude, schal be lost, þat art of lyf noble!   675
To fynde hys fere vpon folde, in fayth, is not eþe.
Warloker to haf wroȝt had more wyt bene
And haf dyȝt ȝonder dere a duk to haue worþed.
A lowande leder of ledez in londe hym wel semez,
And so had better haf ben þen britned to noȝt,   680
Hadet wyth an aluisch mon, for angardez pryde.
Who knew euer any kyng such counsel to take
As knyȝtez in cauelaciounz on Crystmasse gomnez?'
Wel much watz þe warme water þat waltered of yȝen
When þat semly syre soȝt fro þo wonez   685
    Þad daye.
    He made non abode
    Bot wyȝtly went hys way.
    Mony wylsum way he rode,
    Þe bok as I herde say.   690

Now ridez þis renk þurȝ þe ryalme of Logres,

683. cauelaciounz] MS cauelounz

664f. 'which is called the noble "pentangle" by learned people'; cf. 629f. This 'learned' name is an adaptation of the Fr *pentacle* (L *pentaculum*).
669. 'he thought (he was saying goodbye) for ever '
673. *soþly:* Gollancz notes that the context here requires the (now dialectal) word, meaning 'softly, quietly', and compares Keats's 'jellies soother than the creamy curd' (*Eve of St Agnes*) and the verb *to soothe*; the word occurs also in *Cl* 654.
675. *þat . . . noble:* '(you) who are (so) noble of life.'
677. *had more wyt bene:* 'would have made more sense'.
680. 'and it would have been better so than (for him to be) utterly destroyed'.
681. *for angardez pryde:* 'for arrogant pride'. The courtiers' underground criticism of Arthur, for his encouragement of the beheading bargain and for his acceptance of Gawain's obligation to keep his word, introduces into the poem a remarkably detached view of the ideals of chivalry. It also touches on the relation between games and morality, a theme which recurs throughout; cf. note to 1876–84.
683. 'as that of knights in trivial arguments about Christmas games?'
690. 'as I learned from the book': a conventional reference to the romance-writer's source, real or imaginary.
691. *Logres:* Geoffrey of Monmouth's name for Arthur's Britain (Welsh *Lloegyr*).

Sir Gauan, on Godez halue, þa3 hym no gomen þo3t –
Oft leudlez alone he lengez on ny3tez
Þer he fonde no3t hym byfore þe fare þat he lyked;
Hade he no fere bot his fole bi frythez and dounez,   695
Ne no gome bot God bi gate wyth to karp –
Til þat he ne3ed ful neghe into þe Norþe Walez.
Alle þe iles of Anglesay on lyft half he haldez
And farez ouer þe fordez by þe forlondez;
Ouer at þe Holy Hede, til he hade eft bonk   700
In þe wyldrenesse of Wyrale. Wonde þer bot lyte
Þat auþer God oþer gome wyth goud hert louied.   [f 100ᵛ]
And ay he frayned, as he ferde, at frekez þat he met
If þay hade herde any karp of a kny3t grene,
In any grounde þeraboute, of þe Grene Chapel.   705
And al nykked hym wyth 'Nay!'—þat neuer in her lyue
Þay se3e neuer no segge þat watz of suche hwez
            Of grene.

---

697. neghe] MS noghe
705. Chapel] MS clapel

692. *on Godez halue:* an exclamation, or perhaps lit. 'in the cause of God'.
698ff. *þe iles of Anglesay:* i.e. Anglesey itself and the neighbouring small islands (including Holy I. and Puffin I.). Gawain's journey takes him to Caernarvon and eastwards along the north coast of Wales. A 14th c. map in the Bodleian Library shows the usual route as passing through Bangor, Conway, Abergele, Rhuddlan, and Flint (see E. J. S. Parsons, *The Map of Great Britain Circa 1360, Known as The Gough Map: An Introduction to the Facsimile*, with 'The Roads of the Gough Map' by Sir Frank Stenton [Oxford, 1958]). With its geographical particularity, the description of this part of his journey contrasts with that of the beginning and end, which (appropriately enough) are clouded in a romantic vagueness. The poet, writing in the north-west midlands, probably knew, and expected his original audience to know, this part of the journey.
699. Apparently a reference to his crossing of the Conway and Clwyd. *Holy Hede* (700) may then be identifiable as Holywell, near Basingwerk Abbey, where the Roman road reaches the Dee. The lowest identifiable medieval fording place was at Shotwick, some eight miles up river, where the Dee is much narrower; the poet may have had a boat-crossing in mind here, however, as the phrase *hade eft bonk* perhaps suggests. The name has been much discussed; the only real certainty is that it does not refer to Holyhead in Anglesey (cf. 698). P. L. Heyworth (*MÆ*, 41 [1972], 124–7), leaving *Holy Hede* unexplained, would read 699 as a reference to the crossing of the Dee at Shotwick, between the headlands (*forlondez*) of Blacon Head and Burton Head; the plural *fordez* could be an allusion to the fact that the fording-places of the Dee changed frequently owing to the instability of its sands.
701f. 'in the wild country of Wirral. Very few lived there whom either God or a good-hearted man loved.' The forest of Wirral was a notorious refuge for outlaws in the 14th c.
706. Cf. 2471.

Þe knyȝt tok gates straunge
In mony a bonk vnbene.   710
His cher ful oft con chaunge,
Þat chapel er he myȝt sene.

Mony klyf he ouerclambe in contrayez straunge.
Fer floten fro his frendez, fremedly he rydez.
At vche warþe oþer water þer þe wyȝe passed   715
He fonde a foo hym byfore, bot ferly hit were,
And þat so foule and so felle þat feȝt hym byhode.
So mony meruayl bi mount þer þe mon fyndez
Hit were to tore for to telle of þe tenþe dole.
Sumwhyle wyth wormez he werrez and with wolues als,   720
Sumwhyle wyth wodwos þat woned in þe knarrez,
Boþe wyth bullez and berez, and borez oþerquyle,
And etaynez þat hym anelede of þe heȝe felle.
Nade he ben duȝty and dryȝe and Dryȝtyn had serued,
Douteles he hade ben ded and dreped ful ofte.   725
For werre wrathed hym not so much þat wynter nas wors,
When þe colde cler water fro þe cloudez schadde
And fres er hit falle myȝt to þe fale erþe.
Ner slayn wyth þe slete he sleped in his yrnes
Mo nyȝtez þen innoghe, in naked rokkez   730
Þeras claterande fro þe crest þe colde borne rennez
And henged heȝe ouer his hede in hard iisseikkles.
Þus in peryl and payne and plytes ful harde
Bi contray caryez þis knyȝt tyl Krystmasse Euen,
    Alone.   735
    Þe knyȝt wel þat tyde
    To Mary made his mone
    Þat ho hym red to ryde
    And wysse hym to sum wone.   [f101ʳ]

---

718. So] MS fo
726. nas (Davis)] MS was
727. schadde (Gollancz)] MS schadden

---

711. A play upon words (*significatio*): 'he looked this way and that' and 'his mood changed many times'; cf. 2169.
721. *wodwos*: pl. (OE *wudu wasa* 'wood man'); hairy woodland monsters of medieval imagination; they were often portrayed in medieval art and civic pageantry and seem to have appealed to alliterative writers particularly; see, e.g., *Wars of Alexander* (ed. W. W. Skeat, EETS ES 47) 1540, *Winner and Waster* (ed. Sir Israel Gollancz [London, 1931]) 70f.
725. 'there were many occasions when he would doubtless have been killed (*ded and dreped*).'
738. 'that she would direct his course'.

Bi a mounte on þe morne meryly he rydes   740
Into a forest ful dep, þat ferly watz wylde,
Hiȝe hillez on vche a halue and holtwodez vnder
Of hore okez ful hoge, a hundreth togeder.
Þe hasel and þe haȝþorne were harled al samen,
With roȝe raged mosse rayled aywhere,   745
With mony bryddez vnblyþe vpon bare twyges,
Þat pitosly þer piped for pyne of þe colde.
Þe gome vpon Gryngolet glydez hem vnder
Þurȝ mony misy and myre, mon al hym one,
Carande for his costes, lest he ne keuer schulde   750
To se þe seruyse of þat Syre þat on þat self nyȝt
Of a burde watz borne oure baret to quelle.
And þerfore sykyng he sayde, 'I beseche Þe, Lorde,
And Mary, þat is myldest moder so dere,
Of sum herber þer heȝly I myȝt here masse   755
Ande Þy matynez tomorne, mekely I ask,
And þerto prestly I pray my Pater and Aue
        And Crede.'
        He rode in his prayere
        And cryed for his mysdede.
        He sayned hym in syþes sere   760
        And sayde, 'Cros Kryst me spede.'

Nade he sayned hymself, segge, bot þrye
Er he watz war in þe wod of a won in a mote,
Abof a launde, on a lawe, loken vnder boȝez   765
Of mony borelych bole aboute bi þe diches,
A castel þe comlokest þat euer knyȝt aȝte,
Pyched on a prayere, a park al aboute,
With a pyked palays pyned ful þik,
Þat vmbeteȝe mony tre mo þen two myle.   770

---

751.   seruyse] MS seruy

---

740.   *on þe morne:* i.e. of Christmas Eve (cf. 755f). The stanza amplifies the preceding wheel. *Meryly:* at first sight a singularly inappropriate adv.; but *mery* (like *gay*) often has the sense 'elegant, splendid', cf. 142, 153.

756.   *Þy matynez:* i.e. Matins of Christmas Day.

761.   *in syþes sere:* each time he said one of the prayers, cf. 763.

762.   *Cros Kryst:* 'Christ's Cross'; the word order is French.

769.   'fenced in by a close palisade of spikes'. In the 13th c. French romance *La Mule Sans Frein,* in which a version of the Beheading Game occurs (as also in the German *Diu Krône,* apparently derived from it), Gawain arrives at a castle surrounded by a circle of stakes on each of which (with one exception!) is a human head. The *pyked palays* plays no such role in the English poem but its presence may be due to reminiscence of this version of the story.

770.   *mo þen two myle:* presumably in diameter.

Þat holde on þat on syde þe haþel auysed,
As hit schemered and schon þur3 þe schyre okez.
Þenne hatz he hendly of his helme and he3ly he þonkez
Jesus and Sayn Gilyan, þat gentyle ar boþe,
Þat cortaysly hade hym kydde and his cry herkened.   [f 101ᵛ] 775
'Now bone hostel,' coþe þe burne, 'I beseche yow 3ette!'
Þenne gederez he to Gryngolet with þe gilt helez
And he ful chauncely hatz chosen to þe chef gate,
Þat bro3t bremly þe burne to þe bryge ende
   In haste.   780
    Þe bryge watz breme vpbrayde,
    Þe 3atez wer stoken faste,
    Þe wallez were wel arayed –
    Hit dut no wyndez blaste.

Þe burne bode on bonk, þat on blonk houed,   785
Of þe depe double dich þat drof to þe place.
Þe walle wod in þe water wonderly depe
Ande eft a ful huge he3t hit haled vpon lofte,
Of harde hewen ston vp to þe tablez,
Enbaned vnder þe abataylment, in þe best lawe;   790
And syþen garytez ful gaye gered bitwene,
Wyth mony luflych loupe þat louked ful clene;
A better barbican þat burne blusched vpon neuer.
And innermore he behelde þat halle ful hy3e,
Towres telded bytwene, trochet ful þik,   795
Fayre fylyolez þat fy3ed, and ferlyly long,
With coruon coprounes, craftyly sle3e.
Chalk-whyt chymnées þer ches he inno3e,

774. Sayn] MS say
795. Towres] MS towre

773. 'Then he respectfully takes off his helmet and solemnly he thanks'.
774. *Sayn Gilyan:* St Julian, the patron saint of travellers.
776. *bone hostel:* a Fr phrase meaning 'good lodging', a standard invocation to St
Julian; cf. the Eagle in Chaucer's *House of Fame*, 1021–2:
   Now up the hed, for al ys wel;
   Seynt Julyan, loo, bon hostel!
781f. 'The drawbridge was firmly raised; the gates were securely shut'; (a description
of state, not action, of course).
785f. 'The horseman tarried, waiting on the bank of the deep double ditch which
surrounded the house.' (*Þat on blonk houed* qualifies *burne*.) The description in 787–93
is of the outer fortification (barbican).
790. 'fortified under the battlements in the best style'. (*Enbaned:* 'defended by horizon-
tal projecting courses'). Cf. *Pe* 992n, *Cl* 1458–64n.
796. *fylyolez:* 'pinnacles', apparently in quasi-apposition to *trochet.* Cf. *Cl* 1382–4n.

Vpon bastel rouez þat blenked ful quyte.
So mony pynakle payntet watz poudred ayquere   800
Among þe castel carnelez, clambred so þik,
Þat pared out of papure purely hit semed.
Þe fre freke on þe fole hit fayr innoghe þoȝt
If he myȝt keuer to com þe cloyster wythinne,
To herber in þat hostel whyl halyday lested,   805
    Auinant.
      He calde, and sone þer com
      A porter pure plesaunt;
      On þe wal his ernd he nome
      And haylsed þe knyȝt erraunt.   810

'Gode sir,' quoþ Gawan, 'woldez þou go myn ernde
To þe heȝ lorde of þis hous, herber to craue?'
'Ȝe, Peter!' quoþ þe porter, 'and purely I trowee   [f 102ʳ]
Þat ȝe be, wyȝe, welcum to won quyle yow lykez.'
Þen ȝede þe wyȝe ȝerne and com aȝayn swyþe   815
And folke frely hym wyth to fonge þe knyȝt.
Þay let doun þe grete draȝt and derely out ȝeden
And kneled doun on her knes vpon þe colde erþe
To welcum þis ilk wyȝ as worþy hom þoȝt.
Þay ȝolden hym þe brode ȝate, ȝarked vp wyde,   820
And he hem raysed rekenly and rod ouer þe brygge.
Sere seggez hym sesed by sadel quel he lyȝt
And syþen stabeled his stede stif men innoȝe.
Knyȝtez and swyerez comen doun þenne
For to bryng þis buurne wyth blys into halle.   825
Quen he hef vp his helme þer hiȝed innoghe

---

803. innoghe] MS innghe
813. trowee] MS trowoe
815. ȝerne and com (Davis)] MS *om.* (Gollancz: ȝare . . .)

---

799. 'which shone very white upon roofs of towers' (qualifying *chymnées*).
800. *pynacle payntet:* Fr word order.
802. 'that it looked as if it were all completely cut out of paper.' The castle is compared to the paper cut-outs which sometimes decorated food brought to table in 14th c. banquets. Chaucer's Parson speaks disapprovingly of *pride of the table . . . in . . . swich manere bake-metes and dissh-metes, brennynge of wilde fir and peynted and castelled with papir* (*CT* X.443f). Cf. also the description of Belshazzar's feast in *Cleanness* (especially 1408) and see Ackerman, *JEGP*, 56 (1957), 410–7.
804. 'if only he might manage to get inside the bailey'.
806. *Auinant:* 'pleasantly', or adj. 'pleasant' qualifying *hostel*.
813. *Peter:* 'by St Peter'—an appropriate oath for a porter (the half-line appears to be an adaptation of *(St) Peter the porter*—i.e. 'of heaven'—which occurs in *PPl* C.XVI.168.
819. *as . . . þoȝt:* 'in the way which seemed proper to them.'
821. *raysed:* i.e. he asked them to rise from their knees.

For to hent hit at his honde, þe hende to seruen;
His bronde and his blasoun boþe þay token.
Þen haylsed he ful hendly þo haþelez vchone
And mony proud mon þer presed þat prynce to honour.　　　　830
Alle hasped in his heȝ wede to halle þay hym wonnen,
Þer fayre fyre vpon flet fersly brenned.
Þenne þe lorde of þe lede loutez fro his chambre
For to mete wyth menske þe mon on þe flor.
He sayde, 'Ȝe ar welcum to welde, as yow lykez,　　　　835
Þat here is; al is yowre awen to haue at yowre wylle
　　　And welde.'
　'Graunt mercy,' quoþ Gawayn;
　'Þer Kryst hit yow forȝelde.'
As frekez þat semed fayn　　　　840
Ayþer oþer in armez con felde.

Gawayn glyȝt on þe gome þat godly hym gret,
And þuȝt hit a bolde burne þat þe burȝ aȝte,
A hoge haþel for þe nonez and of hyghe eldee.
Brode, bryȝt watz his berde and al beuer-hwed,　　　　845
Sturne, stif on þe stryþþe on stalworth schonkez,
Felle face as þe fyre, and fre of hys speche;
And wel hym semed forsoþe, as þe segge þuȝt,
To lede a lortschyp in lee of leudez ful gode.
Þe lorde hym charred to a chambre and chesly cumaundez　　　[f 102ᵛ]
To delyuer hym a leude hym loȝly to serue;　　　　851

850. chesly] MS clesly

833. The lord's chamber is to be imagined as a small room leading off a gallery, from which he comes down to greet Gawain in the hall. Later Gawain's bedroom is referred to as a *lofte* (1096, 1676).

835–7. 'You are welcome to enjoy whatever is here, as you please; it is all your own to have and use as you wish.' The repetition suggests that some dramatic irony is intended; cf. 1237f.

839. 'may Christ recompense you for it.' *þer(e)* is used idiomatically in ME to introduce blessings and curses.

840. 'In the manner of joyful men'.

844. *of hyghe eldee:* 'of mature age'. The portrait echoes, in muted tones, features of the description of the Green Knight (cf., e.g., 844 and 137ff, 845 and 182, 846 and 431).

847. *fre of hys speche:* 'courteous in speech', cf. 1031ff and contrast the arrogance of the Green Knight in Fitt I.

848f. 'and it appeared to Gawain that he was certainly a suitable person to exercise sovereignty in the castle over excellent knights.'

850. *chesly:* MS *clesly* is interpreted by edd. as an error for *chefly* (here perhaps 'quickly'). However, the MS form and the context point rather to *chesly* 'solicitously', a variant of *chysly*, *Cl* 543 (from OE *cīs* 'fastidious').

851. *To delyuer:* passive use of the infinitive: 'that a man should be assigned to him'.

And þere were boun at his bode burnez innoȝe
Þat broȝt hym to a bryȝt boure þer beddyng watz noble:
Of cortynes of clene sylk wyth cler golde hemmez
And couertorez ful curious with comlych panez   855
Of bryȝt blaunmer aboue, enbrawded bisydez,
Rudelez rennande on ropez, red golde ryngez,
Tapytez tyȝt to þe woȝe, of tuly and tars,
And vnder fete, on þe flet, of folȝande sute.
Þer he watz dispoyled, wyth spechez of myerþe,   860
Þe burn of his bruny and of his bryȝt wedez;
Ryche robes ful rad renkkez hem broȝten
For to charge and to chaunge and chose of þe best.
Sone as he on hent and happed þerinne,
Þat sete on hym semly, wyth saylande skyrtez,   865
Þe ver by his uisage verayly hit semed
Welneȝ to vche haþel, alle on hwes,
Lowande and lufly alle his lymmez vnder;
Þat a comloker knyȝt neuer Kryst made,
    Hem þoȝt.   870
      Wheþen in worlde he were,
      Hit semed as he moȝt
      Be prynce withouten pere
      In felde þer felle men foȝt.

A cheyer byfore þe chemné, þer charcole brenned,   875
Watz grayþed for Sir Gawan grayþely with cloþez:
Whyssynes vpon queldepoyntes, þat koynt wer boþe;
And þenne a meré mantyle watz on þat mon cast,
Of a broun bleeaunt, enbrauded ful ryche
And fayre furred wythinne with fellez of þe best,   880
Alle of ermyn in erde, his hode of þe same.
And he sete in þat settel semlych ryche

---

865. hym] MS hyn
872–4. moȝt . . . foȝt (Tolkien and Gordon)] MS myȝt . . . fyȝt
877. þat] MS þa

---

854. *Of cortynes:* cf. 337n.
864–8. 'As soon as he had taken one and had it on, one which looked well on him
with flowing skirts, truly it seemed to everyone from his appearance almost as if
spring (*ver*) had come in all its colours, all his limbs under the garment shining and
beautiful'. R. J. Menner's suggestion (*MLR*, 19 [1924], 205f), that *ver* (866) is a form
of OF *veir*, *vair* 'fur', should be noted. If this is adopted, the passage might be
rendered (with appropriate punctuation in the text): 'As soon as he had taken one
and had it on, one which looked well on him, with flowing skirts, the fur trimming
next to his face, it truly seemed resplendent to almost everyone, all his limbs under
the garment shining and beautiful'.

And achaufed hym chefly, and þenne his cher mended.
Sone watz telded vp a tabil on trestez ful fayre,
Clad wyth a clene cloþe þat cler quyt schewed,   885
Sanap and salure and syluerin sponez.
Þe wyȝe wesche at his wylle and went to his mete.   [f103ʳ]
Seggez hym serued semly innoȝe
Wyth sere sewes and sete, sesounde of þe best,
Doublefelde, as hit fallez, and fele kyn fischez—   890
Summe baken in bred, summe brad on þe gledez,
Summe soþen, summe in sewe sauered with spyces—
And ay sawses so sleȝe þat þe segge lyked.
Þe freke calde hit a fest ful frely and ofte
Ful hendely, quen alle þe haþeles rehayted hym at onez   895
    As hende,
    'Þis penaunce now ȝe take
    And eft hit schal amende.'
    Þat mon much merþe con make,
    For wyn in his hed þat wende.   900

Þenne watz spyed and spured vpon spare wyse,
Bi preué poyntez of þat prynce put to hymseluen,
Þat he beknew cortaysly of þe court þat he were
Þat aþel Arthure þe hende haldez hym one,
Þat is þe ryche ryal kyng of þe Rounde Table,   905
And hit watz Wawen hymself þat in þat won syttez,
Comen to þat Krystmasse, as case hym þen lymped.
When þe lorde hade lerned þat he þe leude hade,
Loude laȝed he þerat, so lef hit hym þoȝt,
And alle þe men in þat mote maden much joye   910
To apere in his presense prestly þat tyme
Þat alle prys and prowes and pured þewes
Apendes to hys persoun and praysed is euer,
Byfore alle men vpon molde his mensk is þe most.
Vch segge ful softly sayde to his fere,   915

883.   chefly] MS cefly
884.   tabil (Gollancz)] MS tapit
893.   sawses ... sleȝe (Napier)] MS sawes ... sleȝez

894–8.   'The knight very courteously and graciously called it a feast again and again
when all together the men, equally courteously (*As hende*), pressed him (with the
words)'. *As* may, however, introduce a polite imperative in ME: 'Do, gracious sir,
accept this penance for the time being'.
897f.   They modestly refer to the meal as a 'penance' (Christmas Eve being a day of
abstinence) and promise him better fare later (i.e. on Christmas Day).
900.   'because of the wine, which went to his head.'
912f.   *Þat ... to hys:* a form of the relative, 'to whose'.

'Now schal we semlych se sleʒtez of þewez
And þe teccheles termes of talkyng noble.
Wich spede is in speche vnspurd may we lerne,
Syn we haf fonged þat fyne fader of nurture.
God hatz geuen vus His grace godly forsoþe,   920
Þat such a gest as Gawan grauntez vus to haue
When burnez blyþe of His burþe schal sitte
    And synge.
    In menyng of manerez mere
    Þis burne now schal vus bryng.   [f103ᵛ] 925
    I hope þat may hym here
    Schal lerne of luf-talkyng.'

Bi þat þe diner watz done and þe dere vp
Hit watz neʒ at þe niyʒt neʒed þe tyme.
Chaplaynez to þe chapeles chosen þe gate,   930
Rungen ful rychely, ryʒt as þay schulden,
To þe hersum euensong of þe hyʒe tyde.
Þe lorde loutes þerto and þe lady als;
Into a cumly closet coyntly ho entrez.
Gawan glydez ful gay and gos þeder sone.   935
Þe lorde laches hym by þe lappe and ledez hym to sytte
And couþly hym knowez and callez hym his nome
And sayde he watz þe welcomest wyʒe of þe worlde.
And he hym þonkked þroly; and ayþer halched oþer
And seten soberly samen þe seruise quyle.   940
Þenne lyst þe lady to loke on þe knyʒt;
Þenne com ho of hir closet with mony cler burdez.

930. Chaplaynez] MS claplaynez

918. 'Now we can learn, without asking, what sort of thing success in conversation is'.

919. *þat fyne fader of nurture:* in many medieval romances Gawain is the *beau idéal* of courtesy, though not of chastity; from the 13th c. onwards, however, his character tends to be denigrated by writers whose chief aim is to idealize other knights (e.g. Lancelot or Tristan). This development accounts for the contradiction in Malory's treatment of Gawain and for Tennyson's unsympathetic attitude towards him. (See B. J. Whiting, *Mediaeval Studies*, 9 (1947), 189; excerpts in Fox, **7d** 1968; see also Owen, **7d** 1968.)

921. 'who allows us to receive such a guest as Gawain'.

926f. 'I believe anyone who has the opportunity of listening to him will learn something of the art of conversing about love.'

928. 'By the time dinner was over and the noble knight had risen'.

930. *þe chapeles:* the poet has in mind a large castle with several chapels, like Caernarvon.

934. Her closed pew is evidently in the chancel; cf. 942–6.

937. *hym knowez:* 'acknowledges him'.

Ho watz þe fayrest in felle, of flesche and of lyre
And of compas and colour and costes, of alle oþer,
And wener þen Wenore, as þe wyȝe þoȝt.   945
Ho ches þurȝ þe chaunsel to cheryche þat hende.
Anoþer lady hir lad bi þe lyft honde
Þat watz alder þen ho, an auncian hit semed,
And heȝly honowred with haþelez aboute.
Bot vnlyke on to loke þo ladyes were: 950
For if þe ȝonge watz ȝep, ȝolȝe watz þat oþer;
Riche red on þat on rayled ayquere,
Rugh ronkled chekez þat oþer on rolled;
Kerchofes of þat on wyth mony cler perlez;
Hir brest and hir bryȝt þrote, bare displayed,   955
Schon schyrer þen snawe þat schedes on hillez;
Þat oþer wyth a gorger watz gered ouer þe swyre,
Chymbled ouer hir blake chyn with chalk-quyte vayles,
Hir frount folden in sylk, enfoubled ayquere,
Toret and treleted with tryflez aboute,   960
Þat noȝt watz bare of þat burde bot þe blake broȝes,   [f 104ʳ]
Þe tweyne yȝen and þe nase, þe naked lyppez,
And þose were soure to se and sellyly blered,

946. Ho(Wright)] MS he; cf. 971
956. schedes] MS scheder
958. chalk-quyte (Onions)] MS mylk quyte

943f. 'She was the most beautiful creature alive (*fayrest in felle ... of alle oþer*) in respect of flesh, face, figure, complexion, and deportment'; *in felle* (lit. 'in skin') is best taken as a tag ('creature, person'); note the change of construction from *in* . . . to *of* . . . *of* . . . *of* . . .

943–69. The rhetoric of this double portrait of the ladies is examined in Pearsall, **7d** 1955. The contrast effectively sets off the lustrous beauty of the young lady against the wrinkled decrepitude of the old (identified in 2463 as Morgan le Faye), who is here described in terms reminiscent of religious lyrics of the 'Signs of Old Age' and 'Signs of Death' types. (Cf., for instance, *English Lyrics of the Thirteenth Century*, ed. Carleton Brown [Oxford, repr. 1950], 130, 220ff, and see, for a discussion of the tradition, Rosemary Woolf, *English Religious Lyric in the Middle Ages* [Oxford, 1968], 78ff, 102ff.) Obliquely, therefore, the portraits suggest the homiletic theme that old age is a mirror of the frailty of the flesh.

950. *vnlyke on to loke:* 'dissimilar in appearance (*lit.* to look upon)'.

952. 'a glowing pink everywhere adorned the first one'.

953. *þat oþer on rolled:* 'sagged on the other'.

954–6. 'the first lady's kerchiefs (were adorned) with many bright pearls; her breast and her bright throat, exposed bare, shone more brightly than snow which falls on hills'. This reading of the syntax of these lines is due to M. Markus, *Neu.Mitt.*, 75 (1974), 625–9.

960. '(her forehead) framed by embroidered hems (*Toret*) and veiled in lattice work (*treleted*), covered in fine stitching' (all in fuller description of the *sylk* of 959).

A mensk lady on molde mon may hir calle,
    For Gode!
    Hir body watz schort and þik,
    Hir buttokez balȝ and brode;
    More lykkerwys on to lyk
    Watz þat scho hade on lode.

965

When Gawayn glyȝt on þat gay þat graciously loked,
Wyth leue laȝt of þe lorde, he lent hem aȝaynes.
Þe alder he haylses, heldande ful lowe,
Þe loueloker he lappez a lyttel in armez.
He kysses hir comlyly and knyȝtly he melez.
Þay kallen hym of aquoyntaunce and he hit quyk askez
To be her seruaunt sothly, if hemself lyked.
Þay tan hym bytwene hem, wyth talkyng hym leden
To chambre, to chemné, and chefly þay asken
Spycez, þat vnsparely men speded hom to bryng,
And þe wynnelych wyne þerwith vche tyme.
Þe lorde luflych aloft lepez ful ofte,
Mynned merthe to be made vpon mony syþez,
Hent heȝly of his hode and on a spere henged
And wayned hom to wynne þe worchip þerof
Þat most myrþe myȝt meue þat Crystenmas whyle.
'And I schal fonde, bi my fayth, to fylter wyth þe best,
Er me wont þe wede, with help of my frendez.'
Þus wyth laȝande lotez þe lorde hit tayt makez
For to glade Sir Gawayn with gomnez in halle
    Þat nyȝt,
    Til þat hit watz tyme
    Þe lord comaundet lyȝt.
    Sir Gawen his leue con nyme
    And to his bed hym diȝt.

970

975

980

985

990

---

967. balȝ (Tolkien and Gordon)] MS baȝ
971. lent (S. O. Andrew)] MS went
987. wede] MS wedez
992. lord (Gollancz)] MS kyng

969. *þat:* 'that which' (i.e. the younger lady).
971. 'having excused himself from the lord, he went towards them.'
975f. 'They beg the favour of his company and he swiftly asks to be their servant truly, if it pleased them' (*hit* anticipates the next phrase; *seruaunt* has its courtly connotation, 'admirer').
979. *hom to bryng:* 'to bring to them'.
981–7. 'The lord often leaps to his feet in friendly manner, reminded them over and over again to make merry, ceremoniously took off his hood and hung it on a spear and directed that those who devised most amusement during Christmas were to win it as a trophy: "And, on my honour, I shall try with the help of my friends to contend with the best, before I lose the garment."'

On þe morne, as vch mon mynez þat tyme   995
Þat Dryȝtyn for oure destyné to deȝe watz borne,
Wele waxez in vche a won in worlde for His sake.
So did hit þere on þat day, þurȝ dayntés mony:
Boþe at mes and at mele messes ful quaynt   [f 104ᵛ]
Derf men vpon dece drest of þe best.   1000
Þe olde auncian wyf heȝest ho syttez;
Þe lorde lufly her by lent as I trowe.
Gawan and þe gay burde togeder þay seten
Euen inmyddez, as þe messe metely come,
And syþen þurȝ al þe sale, as hem best semed,   1005
Bi vche grome at his degré grayþely watz serued.
Þer watz mete, þer watz myrþe, þer watz much joye,
Þat for to telle þerof hit me tene were,
And to poynte hit ȝet I pyned me parauenture.
Bot ȝet I wot þat Wawen and þe wale burde   1010
Such comfort of her compaynye caȝten togeder
Þurȝ her dere dalyaunce of her derne wordez,
Wyth clene cortays carp closed fro fylþe,
Þat hor play watz passande vche prynce gomen,
          In vayres.   1015
    Trumpez and nakerys,
    Much pypyng þer repayres.
    Vche mon tented hys
    And þay two tented þayres.

Much dut watz þer dryuen þat day and þat oþer,   1020

---

996. Þat] þ *from offset*
1014. Þat] MS and (τ)

---

995. *On þe morne:* 'On the morrow'. The two lines are a periphrasis for 'On Christmas Day'; cf. 6on.

999. *messes ful quaynt:* direct object of (*Derf men*) *drest.*

1001. *heȝest:* 'in the place of honour'; cf. 112.

1002. *lufly her by lent:* 'courteously took his place beside her'.

1004–6. 'right in the centre, where the food properly came and afterwards (went) around the whole hall, as seemed most fitting to them, until each man in order of his degree was duly served.'

1009. 'even if, perchance, I were to take pains to describe it in detail.'

1011. 'found such pleasure in each other's company'.

1014f. 'that their pleasant occupation surpassed the pleasure of any nobleman (there), in truth.'

1016–19. 'There were trumpets, kettledrums and much piping present. Each man attended to his own pleasure (understood from *play*, 1014) and those two attended to theirs.'

And þe þryd as þro þronge in þerafter—
Þe joye of Sayn Jonez day watz gentyle to here
And watz þe last of þe layk leudez þer þoȝten.
Þer wer gestes to go vpon þe gray morne;
Forþy wonderly þay woke and þe wyn dronken,   1025
Daunsed ful dreȝly wyth dere carolez.
At þe last, when hit watz late, þay lachen her leue,
Vchon to wende on his way þat watz wyȝe stronge.
Gawan gef hym god day; þe godmon hym lachchez,
Ledes hym to his awen chambre, þe chymné bysyde,   1030
And þere he draȝez hym on dryȝe and derely hym þonkkez
Of þe wynne worschip þat he hym wayned hade
As to honour his hous on þat hyȝe tyde
And enbelyse his burȝ with his bele chere.
'Iwysse, sir, quyl I leue me worþez þe better   1035
Þat Gawayn hatz ben my gest at Goddez awen fest.'   [f 105ʳ]
'Grant merci, sir,' quoþ Gawayn, 'in god fayth hit is yowrez,
Al þe honour is your awen—þe heȝe Kyng yow ȝelde—
And I am, wyȝe, at your wylle to worch youre hest,
As I am halden þerto in hyȝe and in loȝe   1040
        Bi riȝt.'
    Þe lorde fast can hym payne
    To holde lenger þe knyȝt;
    To hym answrez Gawayn
    Bi non way þat he myȝt.   1045

Then frayned þe freke ful fayre at himseluen
Quat derue dede had hym dryuen at þat dere tyme

1030. chymné] MS hymne
1032. þat] MS and (τ)
1037. merci] MS nerci

1021ff. *þe þryd* (St John's Day) is 27 December; but the hunting (which begins on the morning when the guests leave) occupies the last three days of December. So 28 December—Holy Innocents' Day—is unaccounted for. Perhaps, as Gollancz suggested, it was referred to in a line between 1022 and 1023, now lost.

1027ff. The guests who are leaving early next morning take their leave before going to bed (cf. 1120, 1126f). The situation is repeated in 1960ff.

1029. 'Gawain said goodbye to him (but) the host seizes him'.

1033f. Though in indirect speech, the words are chosen to suggest the Host's *frenkysch fare* (1116), which is evident not only in his generous choice of the French terms *honour*, *enbelyse* and *bele chere* in reference to Gawain, but also in his modest use of the homely *hous* and *burȝ* of his own castle. Cf. *Cl* 785f and Lot's words in 799–801.

1035. 'Indeed, sir, it will be the better for me as long as I live'.

1042f. 'The lord earnestly endeavoured to keep the knight longer (i.e. in the castle)'.

1045. 'that he could by no means (stay longer).' Cf. 2471.

1047–9. 'what terrible deed had compelled him to ride away so eagerly from the king's court all by himself at the festal time, before the holidays were completely

So kenly fro þe kyngez kourt to kayre al his one,
Er þe halidayez holly were halet out of toun.
'Forsoþe, sir,' quoþ þe segge, 'ȝe sayn bot þe trawþe. 1050
A heȝe ernde and a hasty me hade fro þo wonez,
For I am sumned myselfe to sech to a place
I not in worlde whederwarde to wende hit to fynde.
I nolde bot if I hit negh myȝt on Nw Ȝeres morne
For alle þe londe inwyth Logres, so me oure Lorde help! 1055
Forþy, sir, þis enquest I require yow here:
Þat ȝe me telle with trawþe, if euer ȝe tale herde
Of þe Grene Chapel, quere hit on grounde stondez,
And of þe knyȝt þat hit kepes, of colour of grene.
Þer watz stabled bi statut a steuen vus bytwene 1060
To mete þat mon at þat mere, ȝif I myȝt last;
And of þat ilk Nw Ȝere bot neked now wontez,
And I wolde loke on þat lede, if God me let wolde,
Gladloker, bi Goddez Sun, þen any god welde!
Forþi, iwysse, bi ȝowre wylle, wende me bihoues; 1065
Naf I now to busy bot bare þre dayez,
And me als fayn to falle feye as fayly of myyn ernde.'
Þenne laȝande quoþ þe lorde, 'Now leng þe byhoues,
For I schal teche yow to þat terme bi þe tymez ende.
Þe Grene Chapayle vpon grounde greue yow no more 1070
Bot ȝe schal be in yowre bed, burne, at þyn ese
Quyle forth dayez and ferk on þe fyrst of þe ȝere
And cum to þat merk at mydmorn, to make quat yow likez [f 105ᵛ]
    In spenne.
        Dowellez whyle New Ȝeres daye 1075
        And rys and raykez þenne.
        Mon schal yow sette in waye;
        Hit is not two myle henne.'

1053. not] MS wot (cf. 726)
1069. þat] MS þa

over.' *Out of toun* (*lit*. 'from the homestead') is a conventional tag here, 'away'. The Host's apparently innocent inquiry may contain a humorous covert allusion to the beheading (see R. A. Waldron, *NQ*, 207 [1962], 366).
1054. 'I would not fail to reach it on New Year's morning' (*lit*. 'I would not wish otherwise than that I might').
1061. *ȝif I myȝt last:* 'if I happened to live so long'.
1064. *bi Goddez Sun:* i.e. 'by Christ'.
1070. 'Let the whereabouts of the Green Chapel bother you no more'.
1072. *Quyle forth dayez:* 'until late in the day'; presumably the Host here means 'on the day you leave', emphasizing the nearness of the Green Chapel. He later suggests a lie-in for Gawain on the next day (1093ff).
1074. A tag of obscure origin, meaning 'there'.
1077. 'You shall be put on the right road'.

Þenne watz Gawan ful glad and gomenly he laȝed:
'Now I þonk yow þryuandely þurȝ alle oþer þynge.   1080
Now acheued is my chaunce, I schal at your wylle
Dowelle and ellez do quat ȝe demen.'
Þenne sesed hym þe syre and set hym bysyde,
Let þe ladiez be fette to lyke hem þe better.
Þer watz seme solace by hemself stille;   1085
Þe lorde let for luf lotez so myry
As wyȝ þat wolde of his wyte, ne wyst quat he myȝt.
Þenne he carped to þe knyȝt, criande loude,
"Ȝe han demed to do þe dede þat I bidde—
Wyl ȝe halde þis hes here at þys onez?'   1090
'Ȝe, sir, forsoþe,' sayd þe segge trwe,
'Whyl I byde in yowre borȝe be bayn to ȝowre hest.'
'For ȝe haf trauayled,' quoþ þe tulk, 'towen fro ferre,
And syþen waked me wyth, ȝe arn not wel waryst
Nauþer of sostnaunce ne of slepe, soþly I knowe.   1095
Ȝe schal lenge in your lofte and lyȝe in your ese
Tomorn quyle þe messequyle and to mete wende
When ȝe wyl wyth my wyf, þat wyth yow schal sitte
And comfort yow with compayny til I to cort torne.
    Ȝe lende   1100
    And I schal erly ryse;
    On huntyng wyl I wende.'
    Gauayn grantez alle þyse,
    Hym heldande, as þe hende.

'Ȝet firre,' quoþ þe freke, 'a forwarde we make: 1105
Quatsoeuer I wynne in þe wod hit worþez to yourez
And quat chek so ȝe acheue chaunge me þerforne.

1092. ȝowre] MS ȝowe

1080. *þurȝ . . . þynge:* i.e. 'beyond all your other kindnesses.'
1083. *set hym bysyde:* 'seated Gawain beside himself'.
1087. '(he seemed) like a man who was about to go off his head, who didn't know what he might (do).' The last expression has an idiomatic appearance: cf. the OE poem *Judith* 68–9, *swa he nyste ræda nanne/on gewitlocan,* of the drunken Holofernes (who appears to have been actually unconscious, however).
1104. 'bowing (*Hym heldande* reflex.), like the courteous man he was.'
1105. *we make:* 'let us make'.
1106f. 'whatever I win in the forest becomes yours and you give me in exchange for it whatever bad luck you have.' The antithetical *chek* is outwardly expressive of the host's courtly generosity (cf. *lere* 1109) but has sinister overtones: in chess, it is 'check(mate)' (suggestive of the battle of wits in the bedroom episodes), and in hawking 'A false stoop, when a hawk forsakes her quarry for baser game' (*OED*), (suggesting Gawain's lapse from the pursuit of the highest ideals). The word has an unequivocally negative sense at 1857 and 2195.

Swete, swap we so: sware with trawþe,
Queþer leude so lymp lere oþer better.'
'Bi God,' quoþ Gawayn þe gode, 'I grant þertylle;   1110
And þat yow lyst for to layke lef hit me þynkes.'   [f 106ʳ]
'Who bryngez vus þis beuerage, þis bargayn is maked,'
So sayde þe lorde of þat lede; þay laȝed vchone.
Þay dronken and daylyeden and dalten vntyȝtel,
Þise lordez and ladyez, quyle þat hem lyked,   1115
And syþen with frenkysch fare and fele fayre lotez
Þay stoden and stemed and stylly speken,
Kysten ful comlyly and kaȝten her leue.
With mony leude ful lyȝt and lemande torches
Vche burne to his bed watz broȝt at þe laste   1120
    Ful softe.
    To bed ȝet er þay ȝede,
    Recorded couenauntez ofte;
    Þe olde lorde of þat leude
    Cowþe wel halde layk alofte.   1125

III

Ful erly bifore þe day þe folk vprysen.
Gestes þat go wolde hor gromez þay calden
And þay busken vp bilyue blonkkez to sadel,
Tyffen her takles, trussen her males;
Richen hem þe rychest, to ryde alle arayde,   1130
Lepen vp lyȝtly, lachen her brydeles,
Vche wyȝe on his way þer hym wel lyked.
Þe leue lorde of þe londe watz not þe last
Arayed for þe rydyng with renkkez ful mony;
Ete a sop hastyly, when he hade herde masse,   1135
With bugle to bent-felde he buskez bylyue.

1129.   her takles] MS he takles

1108f. 'My dear man, let us strike a bargain (*swap*) on these terms: to answer honourably, to whichever man may fall the worse lot or the better.' *Queþer ... so:* 'whichever (of two)' (cf. *quat ... so*); *lere:* quasi-compar. adj. 'worse' (?) (cf. *lur* 'loss').

1112. 'If someone will bring us the drink (to pledge our word), this bargain is made'; *beuerage* became a technical term in this sense in ME and was also used for 'bargain' itself (cf. also 1409, 1684).

1124f. 'he who had long been lord of that people certainly knew how to keep up the fun.'

1128. *And þay:* i.e. 'the servants'. In 1130 the subject changes back to 'the nobles' (*þe rychest*).

By þat any dayly3t lemed vpon erþe,
He with his haþeles on hy3e horsses weren.
Þenne þise cacheres þat couþe cowpled hor houndez,
Vnclosed þe kenel dore and calde hem þeroute,   1140
Blwe bygly in buglez þre bare mote.
Braches bayed þerfore and breme noyse maked;
And þay chastysed and charred on chasyng þat went,
A hundreth of hunteres, as I haf herde telle,
    Of þe best.   1145
      To trystors vewters 3od,
      Couples huntes of kest;
    Þer ros for blastez gode   [f 106ᵛ]
    Gret rurd in þat forest.

At þe fyrst quethe of þe quest quaked þe wylde.   1150
Der drof in þe dale, doted for drede,
Hi3ed to þe hy3e, bot heterly þay were
Restayed with þe stablye, þat stoutly ascryed.
Þay let þe herttez haf þe gate, with þe hy3e hedes,
Þe breme bukkez also, with hor brode paumez;   1155
For þe fre lorde hade defende in fermysoun tyme
Þat þer schulde no mon meue to þe male dere.
Þe hindez were halden in with 'Hay!' and 'War!'
Þe does dryuen with gret dyn to þe depe sladez.

1137. þat] MS þat þat

1139. 'Then hunters who were expert leashed their hounds in pairs'; *þis* and *þise* are used idiomatically to refer to something familiar to the listener though not necessarily present, cf. 473, 1112, 1514, 1914, 2423, *Cl* 428, etc.

1141. *þre bare mote:* 'three single notes of the horn' (the signal for unleashing the hounds).

1143. 'and they scolded and turned back (the hounds) that chased false scents'.

1146f. 'Keepers of hounds (*vewters*) went to their hunting-stations (*trystors*), huntsmen took off the leashes (*couples*)'.

1150. 'At the first sound of the baying of hounds on the scent the wild animals trembled.'

1153. 'turned back by the ring of beaters, who shouted loudly.' The purpose of the ring of beaters (*stablye*) which encircled the hunting area was to drive the quarry towards the arrows of the huntsmen (1160). Those which were not killed outright were pulled down by hounds at the receiving stations (1168).

1154–9. The close-season (*fermysoun*) for the male deer, harts (*herttez*) and bucks (*bukkez*), was 14 September–24 June; these the beaters allow to pass. The females, hinds and does, could be hunted during the winter, however, and were therefore prevented from escaping and driven back (1158–9).

1159. *dryuen* could be pa.t.pl. (as in 121; cf. 1151), 'ran (poured) with great clamour'; but if 1158 is a parallel, it seems better to take it as pp., '(were) driven by loud shouting'.

Þer myȝt mon se, as þay slypte, slentyng of arwes; 1160
At vche wende vnder wande wapped a flone,
Þat bigly bote on þe broun with ful brode hedez.
What! þay brayen and bleden, bi bonkkez þay deȝen,
And ay rachches in a res radly hem folȝes,
Hunterez wyth hyȝe horne hasted hem after 1165
Wyth such a crakkande kry as klyffes haden brusten.
What wylde so atwaped wyȝes þat schotten
Watz al toraced and rent at þe resayt,
Bi þay were tened at þe hyȝe and taysed to þe wattrez,
Þe ledez were so lerned at þe loȝe trysteres; 1170
And þe grehoundez so grete þat geten hem bylyue
And hem tofylched as fast as frekez myȝt loke
    Þer ryȝt.
    Þe lorde, for blys abloy,
    Ful oft con launce and lyȝt, 1175
    And drof þat day wyth joy
    Thus to þe derk nyȝt.

Þus laykez þis lorde by lynde-wodez euez
And Gawayn þe god mon in gay bed lygez,
Lurkkez quyl þe daylyȝt lemed on þe wowes, 1180
Vnder couertour ful clere, cortyned aboute.
And as in slomeryng he slode, sleȝly he herde
A littel dyn at his dor and derfly vpon;
And he heuez vp his hed out of þe cloþes,
A corner of þe cortyn he caȝt vp a lyttel,   [f107ʳ] 1185
And waytez warly þiderwarde quat hit be myȝt.
Hit watz þe ladi, loflyest to beholde,
Þat droȝ þe dor after hir ful dernly and stylle
And boȝed towarde þe bed; and þe burne schamed
And layde hym doun lystyly and let as he slepte. 1190

1160–62. 'There could be seen the slanting flight of arrows as they slipped (from the bow); at every turning in the wood an arrow swished (*wapped*), burying their broad heads deep in the brown flesh.'

1166. *as . . . brusten:* 'as if rocks were splitting.'

1167–73. 'Any animal that escaped the archers was pulled down and slaughtered (with the knife) at the receiving line, when they had been harassed on the heights and driven (*taysed*) down to the streams, so skilful were the men at the low stations; and so huge were the greyhounds that (they) quickly seized them and pulled them down as fast as men could turn and look (*lit.* look right there).'

1174f. 'The lord, transported with delight, galloped forward and dismounted again and again'.

1182f. 'And as he drifted in sleep (dozed) he heard a little stealthy sound at his door and (heard it) quickly open (*vpon* v.)'; *sleȝly* is to be loosely construed with the next line, rather than with *herde*. It has been plausibly suggested that *derfly* (here translated 'quickly') is a scribal error for *dernly* 'secretly' (*n* misread as *u*, and written *f*); cf. 1188.

And ho stepped stilly and stel to his bedde,
Kest vp þe cortyn and creped withinne
And set hir ful softly on þe bed-syde
And lenged þere selly longe to loke quen he wakened.
Þe lede lay lurked a ful longe quyle,   1195
Compast in his concience to quat þat cace myȝt
Meue oþer amount. To meruayle hym þoȝt;
Bot ȝet he sayde in hymself, 'More semly hit were
To aspye wyth my spelle in space quat ho wolde.'
Þen he wakenede and wroth and to hir warde torned   1200
And vnlouked his yȝe-lyddez and let as hym wondered
And sayned hym, as bi his saȝe þe sauer to worthe,
        With hande.
    Wyth chynne and cheke ful swete,
    Boþe quit and red in blande,   1205
    Ful lufly con ho lete
    Wyth lyppez smal laȝande:

'God moroun, Sir Gawayn,' sayde þat gay lady,
'Ȝe ar a sleper vnslyȝe, þat mon may slyde hider.
Now ar ȝe tan astyt! Bot true vus may schape,   1210
I schal bynde yow in your bedde—þat be ȝe trayst.'
Al laȝande þe lady lauced þo bourdez.
'Goud moroun, gay,' quoþ Gawayn þe blyþe,
'Me schal worþe at your wille and þat me wel lykez,
For I ȝelde me ȝederly and ȝeȝe after grace;   1215
And þat is þe best, be my dome, for me byhouez nede!'
(And þus he bourded aȝayn with mony a blyþe laȝter.)
'Bot wolde ȝe, lady louely, þen, leue me grante
And deprece your prysoun and pray hym to ryse,
I wolde boȝe of þis bed and busk me better;   1220
I schulde keuer þe more comfort to karp yow wyth.'

1199. in] n *illegible*
1208. gay (Tolkien and Gordon)] MS fayr
1214. your] MS þourr
        wel] *above line, another hand*
1216. be] MS he

1196f. 'pondered in his mind what the circumstance could portend or signify. It seemed amazing to him'.
1199. 'by talking to her, to discover in due course what she wants.'
1202. *as . . . worthe:* 'as if to become the safer by his prayer'.
1206f. 'she spoke very amiably with slender laughing lips' (for *lete* 'speak', cf. 1086).
1210. *Bot . . . schape:* 'Unless we can arrange a truce between ourselves'. The subject *we* is omitted.
1214. *Me . . . wille:* 'My fate shall be as you determine'.

'Nay forsoþe, beau sir,' sayd þat swete, [f 107ᵛ]
'Ʒe schal not rise of your bedde. I rych yow better:
I schal happe yow here þat oþer half als
And syþen karp wyth my knyʒt þat I kaʒt haue.   1225
For I wene wel, iwysse, Sir Wowen ʒe are,
Þat alle þe worlde worchipez; querso ʒe ride,
Your honour, your hendelayk is hendely praysed
With lordez, wyth ladyes, with alle þat lyf bere.
And now ʒe ar here, iwysse, and we bot oure one;   1230
My lorde and his ledez ar on lenþe faren,
Oþer burnez in her bedde, and my burdez als,
Þe dor drawen and dit with a derf haspe;
And syþen I haue in þis hous hym þat al lykez,
I schal ware my whyle wel, quyl hit lastez,   1235
     With tale.
        Ʒe ar welcum to my cors,
        Yowre awen won to wale,
        Me behouez of fyne force
        Your seruaunt be, and schale.'   1240

'In god fayth,' quoþ Gawayn, 'gayn hit me þynkkez.
Þaʒ I be not now he þat ʒe of speken—
To reche to such reuerence as ʒe reherce here
I am wyʒe vnworþy, I wot wel myseluen—
Bi God, I were glad and yow god þoʒt   1245
At saʒe oþer at seruyce þat I sette myʒt
To þe plesaunce of your prys; hit were a pure joye.'
'In god fayth, Sir Gawayn,' quoþ þe gay lady,
'Þe prys and þe prowes þat plesez al oþer,
If I hit lakked oþer set at lyʒt, hit were littel daynté.   1250
Bot hit ar ladyes innoʒe þat leuer wer nowþe
Haf þe, hende, in hor holde, as I þe habbe here,

1230. *bot oure one:* 'quite by ourselves'.

1237f. The lady's declaration is not as unequivocal as it appears to the modern reader: *my cors* is used in ME as a periphrasis for 'me' (cf. *His body, Cl* 32, *his corse, Cl* 683, 'him'); the line can therefore be understood as 'I am pleased to have you here', and this is how Gawain chooses to take it (cf. 1241). The bolder suggestion is, however, apparent in the next line: 'to take your own pleasure'. (See TG-Davis n).

1239f. 'I must of necessity be your servant, and shall be.' Basing her argument on Gawain's illustrious reputation as a courtier (borne out, she says, by his behaviour in her house) the lady attempts to reverse the usual roles and become *his* 'servant' (cf. 1214–16); *of fyne force* implies 'by the logic of the situation'.

1243. 'to attain to such an honour as you have just mentioned'—i.e. at 1240.

1245–7. 'by God, I should be glad if you saw fit that I should devote myself, by word or deed, to obliging your worthy self; it would be a sheer joy.'

To daly with derely your daynté wordez
Keuer hem comfort and colen her carez,
Þen much of þe garysoun oþer golde þat þay hauen.   1255
Bot I louue þat ilk Lorde þat þe lyfte haldez
I haf hit holly in my honde þat al desyres,
    Þurȝe grace.'
      Scho made hym so gret chere,
    Þat watz so fayr of face.   [f 108ʳ]   1260
      Þe knyȝt with speches skere
    Answared to vche a cace.

'Madame,' quoþ þe myry mon, 'Mary yow ȝelde,
For I haf founden, in god fayth, yowre fraunchis nobele;
And oþer ful much of oþer folk fongen hor dedez;   1265
Bot þe daynté þat þay delen for my disert nys euer—
Hit is þe worchyp of yourself, þat noȝt bot wel connez.'
'Bi Mary,' quoþ þe menskful, 'me þynk hit an oþer;
For were I worth al þe wone of wymmen alyue,
And al þe wele of þe worlde were in my honde,   1270
And I schulde chepen and chose to cheue me a lorde,
For þe costes þat I haf knowen vpon þe, knyȝt, here
Of bewté and debonerté and blyþe semblaunt—
And þat I haf er herkkened and halde hit here trwee—
Þer schulde no freke vpon folde bifore yow be chosen.'   1275
'Iwysse, worþy,' quoþ þe wyȝe, 'ȝe haf waled wel better;
Bot I am proude of þe prys þat ȝe put on me
And, soberly your seruaunt, my souerayn I holde yow
And yowre knyȝt I becom, and Kryst yow forȝelde.'
Þus þay meled of muchquat til mydmorn paste   1280
And ay þe lady let lyk a hym loued mych.

1255. þat] MS þat þat
1262. Answared] MS aswared
1266. nys euer] MS nyseu (er *abbr. om.*)

1253f. 'to make courtly play with your charming words, to find solace for themselves and assuage their longings'.
1257. *þat al desyres:* 'that which (i.e. him whom) everyone wants'.
1265–7. 'and some people take their line of conduct a good deal from others; but the honour which they bestow is not at all my deserving—it does credit to yourself, revealing the goodness of your own heart (*lit.* who can only behave generously).'
The passage is somewhat elliptical, perhaps reflecting Gawain's tact; he wants to dismiss his reputation (especially among women—cf. 1249ff) as mere tittle-tattle, without implying too strongly that *she* is over-credulous.
1268. *me þynk:* cf. 348n.
1274. 'for this is what I have heard before and now believe it to be true'. The lady is rebutting Gawain's modest denial at 1266.
1281f. 'And all the time the lady behaved as if (*lyk*) she loved him a great deal. The man acted guardedly and behaved most politely'.

Þe freke ferde with defence and feted ful fayre;
Þaȝ ho were burde bryȝtest þe burne in mynde hade,
Þe lasse luf in his lode for lur þat he soȝt
    Boute hone—   1285
    Þe dunte þat schulde hym deue,
    And nedez hit most be done.
    Þe lady þenn spek of leue;
    He granted hir ful sone.

Þenne ho gef hym god day and wyth a glent laȝed;   1290
And as ho stod ho stonyed hym wyth ful stor wordez:
'Now He þat spedez vche spech þis disport ȝelde yow,
Bot þat ȝe be Gawan hit gotz in mynde!'
'Querfore?' quoþ þe freke, and freschly he askez,
Ferde lest he hade fayled in fourme of his castes.   1295
Bot þe burde hym blessed and 'Bi þis skyl' sayde:
'So god as Gawayn gaynly is halden,   [f108ᵛ]
And cortaysye is closed so clene in hymseluen,
Couth not lyȝtly haf lenged so long wyth a lady
Bot he had craued a cosse bi his courtaysye,   1300
Bi sum towch of summe tryfle at sum talez ende.'
Þen quoþ Wowen: 'Iwysse, worþe as yow lykez;
I schal kysse at your comaundement, as a knyȝt fallez,
And fire lest he displese yow; so plede hit no more.'
Ho comes nerre with þat and cachez hym in armez,   1305
Loutez luflych adoun and þe leude kyssez.
Þay comly bykennen to Kryst ayþer oþer;

1283. ho ... burne (Morris)] MS I ... burde
1286. schulde] MS sculde
1304. so] MS fo

1283–6. 'though she may have been the loveliest lady the warrior had ever known (*lit.* remembered—cf. 943ff), he had brought with him so much the less love because of the penalty he was going to meet forthwith'. Morris's emendations to 1283, which are adopted here (though with different punctuation), avoid the difficulty of the repeated *burde* as well as the momentary inconsistency of narrative point of view. The error could have arisen through misunderstanding of *in mynde hade*. G. Sanderlin (*ChR*, 8 [1973], 60–4) argues for retention of the MS reading despite the change of point of view.

1296. *hym blessed* here seems to mean 'exclaimed "God bless you"' (see *OED bless*); *Bi þis skyl:* 'For this reason'. Cf. *Pe* 673f and note.

1297f. 'Anyone as good as Gawain is rightly (*gaynly*) considered to be and in whom courtesy is so completely embodied'.

1301. 'by some trifling hint at the end of a speech.'

1304. *And fire:* perhaps 'and in addition' (as in 2121), introducing Gawain's second reason for agreeing to kiss her. Burrow (*NQ* 217 [1972], 43–5), on the other hand, takes *fire* with *plede:* 'And do not continue to press your claims in this way (*so*) any further, lest he (i.e. I) incur your displeasure (by having to refuse).'

Ho dos hir forth at þe dore withouten dyn more,
And he ryches hym to ryse and rapes hym sone,
Clepes to his chamberlayn, choses his wede,   1310
Boȝez forth, quen he watz boun, blyþely to masse;
And þenne he meued to his mete, þat menskly hym keped,
And made myry al day til þe mone rysed,
  With game.
   Watz neuer freke fayrer fonge   1315
   Bitwene two so dyngne dame,
   Þe alder and þe ȝonge;
   Much solace set þay same.

And ay þe lorde of þe londe is lent on his gamnez,
To hunt in holtez and heþe at hyndez barayne;   1320
Such a sowme he þer slowe bi þat þe sunne heldet,
Of dos and of oþer dere, to deme were wonder.
Þenne fersly þay flokked in, folk, at þe laste,
And quykly of þe quelled dere a querré þay maked.
Þe best boȝed þerto with burnez innoghe,   1325
Gedered þe grattest of gres þat þer were
And didden hem derely vndo as þe dede askez.
Serched hem at þe asay summe þat þer were;
Two fyngeres þay fonde of þe fowlest of alle.
Syþen þay slyt þe slot, sesed þe erber,   1330
Schaued wyth a scharp knyf, and þe schyre knitten.
Syþen rytte þay þe foure lymmes and rent of þe hyde;

1315. Watz] MS with

1327. 'and had them gracefully cut open, in the prescribed manner.' The breaking of only one deer is described but the description is evidently meant to be representative. The breaking (or brittling) of the deer is a romance convention which reflects the importance attached to hunting skills as aristocratic accomplishments; cf., e.g., *The Parlement of the Thre Ages* (ed. M. Y. Offord, EETS OS 246), 66ff, for a similar alliterative description, and the *Tristan* of Gottfried von Strassburg (*fl.* 1210), English translation by A. T. Hatto (Penguin Books, 1960), chapter 4.
1328f. 'Some who were there examined them at the "assay"; they found two fingers' breadth of flesh on the poorest of them all.' The 'assay' was a ceremonious testing of the quality of the game; the word was also used of the part of the breast where the cut was made (cf. *The Parlement of the Thre Ages*, 70).
1330–52. 'Then they slit the hollow at the base of the throat (*slot*), took hold of the gullet, scraped it with a sharp knife and tied up the flesh. Then they cut off the four legs, and stripped off the skin; then they opened the belly, drew the bowels carefully to avoid undoing (*for laucyng*) the ligature (*lere*) of the knot (cf. 1331). (1335:) They seized the throat (*gargulun*) and properly separated the gullet (*wesaunt*) from the wind-pipe and tossed (*walt*) out the guts. Then they cut out the shoulder-joints with their sharp knives, drawing them through a small hole so as to keep the sides intact; then they cut open the breast and divided it in two. (1340:) And then one of them (*on*) begins once again (*eft*) at the neck, quickly cuts the carcase open right to the fork (*byȝt*), removes the neck offal (*avanters*) and truly after that they promptly loosen

Þen brek þay þe balé, þe bowelez out token,
Lystily for laucyng þe lere of þe knot.
Þay gryped to þe gargulun and grayþely departed　　　　　1335
Þe wesaunt fro þe wynt-hole and walt out þe guttez.
Þen scher þay out þe schulderez with her scharp knyuez,
Haled hem by a lyttel hole to haue hole sydes;
Siþen britned þay þe brest and brayden hit in twynne.
And eft at þe gargulun bigynez on þenne,　　　　　　　1340
Ryuez hit vp radly ry3t to þe by3t,
Voydez out þe avanters and verayly þerafter
Alle þe rymez by þe rybbez radly þay lauce;
So ryde þay of by resoun bi þe rygge bonez
Euenden to þe haunche, þat henged alle samen,　　　　　1345
And heuen hit vp al hole and hwen hit of þere—
And þat þay neme for þe 'noumbles' bi nome, as I trowe,
　　　Bi kynde.
　　Bi þe by3t al of þe þy3es
　　Þe lappez þay lauce bihynde;　　　　　　　　　　　1350
　　To hewe hit in two þay hy3es,
　　Bi þe bakbon to vnbynde.

Boþe þe hede and þe hals þay hwen of þenne
And syþen sunder þay þe sydez swyft fro þe chyne
And þe corbeles fee þay kest in a greue.　　　　　　　1355
Þenn þurled þay ayþer þik side þur3 bi þe rybbe
And henged þenne ayþer bi ho3ez of þe fourchez,
Vche freke for his fee as fallez for to haue.
Vpon a felle of þe fayre best fede þay þayr houndes
Wyth þe lyuer and þe ly3tez, þe leþer of þe paunchez,　　1360
And bred baþed in blod blende þeramongez.

1333.　bowelez] MS balez
1334.　þe lere (Gollancz)] MS and (τ) lere
1344.　So] MS fo
1357.　ayþer] MS aþer

all the membranes (*rymez*) on the ribs; (1344:) thus they correctly clear out the offal along the bones of the back right down (*Euenden*) to the haunch, so that it all hung together, and they lift it up quite intact and cut it off there—and that, I believe, they properly (*Bi kynde*) designate the "numbles". Then they loosen the folds of skin (*lappez*) behind the fork of the thighs; they make haste to cut the carcase in two, dividing it along the backbone.'

1355.　*corbeles fee:* 'raven's fee'; a piece of gristle from the end of the breast-bone, traditionally thrown to the crows or ravens.
1358.　'each man receiving what befits him for his fee (prize).'
1360.　*leþer of þe paunchez:* 'lining of the stomachs'.

Baldely þay blw prys, bayed þayr rachchez,
Syþen fonge þay her flesche, folden to home,
Strakande ful stoutly mony stif motez.
Bi þat þe dayly3t watz done þe douthe watz al wonen   1365
Into þe comly castel, þer þe kny3t bidez
     Ful stille,
       Wyth blys and bry3t fyr bette.
     Þe lorde is comen þertylle:
       When Gawayn wyth hym mette   1370
     Þer watz bot wele at wylle.

Thenne comaunded þe lorde in þat sale to samen alle þe meny,   [f 109ᵛ]
Boþe þe ladyes on loghe to ly3t with her burdes.
Bifore alle þe folk on þe flette frekez he beddez
Verayly his venysoun to fech hym byforne;   1375
And al godly in gomen Gawayn he called,
Techez hym to þe tayles of ful tayt bestes,
Schewez hym þe schyree grece schorne vpon rybbes:
'How payez yow þis play? Haf I prys wonnen?
Haue I þryuandely þonk þur3 my craft serued?'   1380
'3e iwysse,' quoþ þat oþer wy3e, 'here is wayth fayrest
Þat I se3 þis seuen 3ere in sesoun of wynter.'
'And al I gif yow, Gawayn,' quoþ þe gome þenne,
'For by acorde of couenaunt 3e craue hit as your awen.'
'Þis is soth,' quoþ þe segge, 'I say yow þat ilke: 1385
Þat I haf worthyly wonnen þis wonez wythinne
Iwysse with as god wylle hit worþez to 3ourez.'
He hasppez his fayre hals his armez wythinne
And kysses hym as comlyly as he couþe awyse:
'Tas yow þere my cheuicaunce; I cheued no more.   1390

1376. Gawayn] MS gaway
1386. Þat (Gollancz)] MS and (ᴄ)
      wonnen] MS *om.*
1389. he (Madden)] MS ho

1362. *bayed þayr rachchez:* 'their hounds barked (bayed)'.
1371. 'there was all the happiness that could be desired.'
1377. 'directs his attention to the number (tails) of extremely well-grown beasts'. The parallel structure of 401 and 1069 suggests that *to* governs *þe tayles* rather than *hym*. *Tayles* appears to contain a deliberate pun ('tails' and 'tallies'); the tails were left on the carcases and would serve as tallies.
1379. *play:* 'sport'; but implying the product rather than the activity (cf. *gomen* 1635, and the modern *game*).
1382. *þis seuen 3ere:* i.e. 'for many a year'. For a parallel use of the figure five as a round number, cf. *Pe* 449–52n.

I wowche hit saf fynly, þaȝ feler hit were.'
'Hit is god,' quoþ þe godmon, 'grant mercy þerfore.
Hit may be such hit is þe better, and ȝe me breue wolde
Where ȝe wan þis ilk wele bi wytte of yorseluen.'
'Þat watz not forward,' quoþ he; 'frayst me no more,   1395
For ȝe haf tan þat yow tydez; trawe ȝe non oþer
      Ȝe mowe.'
    Þay laȝed and made hem blyþe
    Wyth lotez þat were to lowe.
    To soper þay ȝede asswyþe,   1400
    Wyth dayntés nwe innowe.

And syþen by þe chymné in chamber þay seten,
Wyȝez þe walle wyn weȝed to hem oft,
And efte in her bourdyng þay bayþen in þe morn
To fylle þe same forwardez þat þay byfore maden: 1405
Wat chaunce so bytydez hor cheuysaunce to chaunge,
What nwez so þay nome, at naȝt quen þay metten.
Þay acorded of þe couenauntez byfore þe court alle —
Þe beuerage watz broȝt forth in bourde at þat tyme —   [f110ʳ]
Þenne þay louelych leȝten leue at þe last;   1410
Vche burne to his bedde busked bylyue.
Bi þat þe coke hade crowen and cakled bot þryse,
Þe lorde watz lopen of his bedde, þe leudez vchone,
So þat þe mete and þe masse watz metely delyuered,
Þe douthe dressed to þe wod, er any day sprenged,   1415
      To chace.
    Heȝ with hunte and hornez,
    Þurȝ playnez þay passe in space,
    Vncoupled among þo þornez
    Rachez þat ran on race.   1420

1394. yorseluen] MS horseluen
1406. Wat (Tolkien and Gordon)] MS þat
1412. crowen] MS crowez

1391. 'I bestow (vouchsafe) it completely (and would do so) even if there were more.'
1393f. 'It may be of such a nature that it would turn out to be the better prize, if only
you would tell me from whom'.
1396f. 'for you have received what is due to you; rest assured you cannot (have)
anything else.' Gawain may be conscious that the kisses were Bertilak's by right of a
husband as well as of the game.
1401. 'with many (*innowe*) new delicacies.'
1407. *What nwez so:* partitive genitive, *lit.* 'whatever of new'—i.e. 'whatever new
thing'.
1409. *beuerage:* see 1112n, 1684.
1412-15. See 2008n.
1419. *Vncoupled:* cf. 1139n; *among þo þornez:* an indication that they are to hunt the
boar, which lived among thorns and thick bushes.

Sone þay calle of a quest in a ker syde;
Þe hunt rehayted þe houndez þat hit fyrst mynged,
Wylde wordez hym warp wyth a wrast noyce.
Þe howndez þat hit herde hastid þider swyþe
And fellen as fast to þe fuyt, fourty at ones.   1425
Þenne such a glauer ande glam of gedered rachchez
Ros þat þe rocherez rungen aboute.
Hunterez hem hardened with horne and wyth muthe;
Þen al in a semblé sweyed togeder
Bitwene a flosche in þat fryth and a foo cragge.   1430
In a knot bi a clyffe at þe kerre syde,
Þeras þe rogh rocher vnrydely watz fallen,
Þay ferden to þe fyndyng, and frekez hem after.
Þay vmbekesten þe knarre and þe knot boþe,
Wyȝez, whyl þay wysten wel wythinne hem hit were   1435
Þe best þat þer breued watz wyth þe blodhoundez.
Þenne þay beten on þe buskez and bede hym vpryse;
And he vnsoundyly out soȝt, seggez ouerþwert.
On þe sellokest swyn swenged out þere,
Long sythen fro þe sounder þat soȝt for olde,   1440
For he watz borelych and brode, bor alþer-grattest,
Ful grymme quen he gronyed; þenne greued mony,
For þre at þe fyrst þrast he þryȝt to þe erþe

1426. glauer ande] MS glauerande; *see Pat* 269n
1435. wythinne] MS wyt inne
1440. fro] MS for
   soȝt] MS wiȝt
1441. borelych and] MS *om.*
   brode] *illegible*
1442–5. MS *blurred at left; some readings from offset on* 109ᵛ

1421–3. 'Soon the hounds signal (by baying) that they have a scent at the edge of a wooded marsh (cf. 1150); the huntsman urged on the hounds who had first drawn attention to the scent, uttered excited words to them with a loud noise.'

1431–6. 'In the middle of a wooded mound beside a high rock at the edge of the marsh, where the rough hillside had fallen in confusion, the hounds went to the dislodgement, with the men after them. The men cast about both the crag and the wooded knoll until they were sure they had contained the beast whose presence had been revealed by the voices of the bloodhounds.' *Hit* (1435): anticipatory subject, *lit.* 'there was (within their ring)'. *Blodhoundez* (1436): larger hounds (resembling the modern bloodhound), which were used, especially in boar-hunting, to attack the game at close quarters.

1438. 'and he came out menacingly straight across the line of men.'

1440. 'which had long since left (*soȝt fro*) the herd on account of age'. *Sounder* is the technical term for a herd of wild pig; *for olde:* 'on account of age' (see *Cl* 386n).

1441. *brode:* the word is illegible: also, the half-line appears to lack a stress (unless the first falls on *he*). For the emendation adopted above, cf. *The Parlement of the Thre Ages* 32: *And þer-to borely and brode and of body grete* (of a hart).

1443. *þre:* it is clear from 1438 and 1445 that this means 'three men'.

And sparred forth good sped boute spyt more.
Þise oþer halowed 'Hyghe!' ful hyȝe, and 'Hay! Hay!' cryed,   1445
Haden hornez to mouþe, heterly rechated.   [f110ᵛ]
Mony watz þe miyry mouthe of men and of houndez
Þat buskkez after þis bor with bost and wyth noyse,
    To quelle.
        Ful oft he bydez þe baye   1450
        And maymez þe mute innmelle.
        He hurtez of þe houndez, and þay
        Ful ȝomerly ȝaule and ȝelle.

Schalkez to schote at hym schowen to þenne,
Haled to hym of her arewez, hitten hym oft;   1455
Bot þe poyntez payred at þe pyth, þat pyȝt in his scheldez,
And þe barbez of his browe bite non wolde;
Þaȝ þe schauen schaft schyndered in pecez,
Þe hede hypped aȝayn weresoeuer hit hitte.
Bot quen þe dyntez hym dered of her dryȝe strokez,   1460
Þen, braynwod for bate, on burnez he rasez,
Hurtez hem ful heterly þer he forth hyȝez;
And mony arȝed þerat and on lyte droȝen.
Bot þe lorde on a lyȝt horce launces hym after,
As burne bolde vpon bent his bugle he blowez,   1465
He rechated, and rode þurȝ ronez ful þyk,
Suande þis wylde swyn til þe sunne schafted.
Þis day wyth þis ilk dede þay dryuen on þis wyse,
Whyle oure luflych lede lys in his bedde,
Gawayn, grayþely at home in gerez ful ryche   1470
        Of hewe.
        Þe lady noȝt forȝate
        To com hym to salue;

1466.   rode] MS *blurred*
1473.   To com] MS com to

1452. *of þe houndez:* 'some of the hounds'.
1456f. 'but the points which struck his shoulders were blunted (*payred*) by the
toughness (*pyth*) (of them) and none would penetrate the bristles (*barbez*) of his
brow'. Standing at bay, the boar presents to the archers the toughened skin of his
shoulders and the coarse hair of his brow; either is capable of deflecting an arrow,
however hard it may strike (1458f). See Savage, *MLN*, 52 (1937), 36–8. *Barbez* has
usually been understood as 'arrow-heads' (*MED* 3(a)) but the pronoun *non*
(antecedent *poyntez*) is an adequate subject for *wolde bite*, and *of his browe* is more
naturally construed with *barbez* than with *bite*, which is usually followed by *in* or *on*
(cf. 426, 1162).
1473. Given the similarity of *c* and *t* in the handwriting of the time, the MS reading
com to is a fairly easy scribal error for *to com*; the emendation is not strictly necessary,
but greatly improves both syntax and metre.

Ful erly ho watz hym ate,
His mode for to remwe.   1475

Ho commes to þe cortyn and at þe kny3t totes.
Sir Wawen her welcumed worþy on fyrst,
And ho hym 3eldez a3ayn ful 3erne of hir wordez,
Settez hir sofly by his syde and swyþely ho la3ez
And wyth a luflych loke ho layde hym þyse wordez: 1480
'Sir, 3if 3e be Wawen, wonder me þynkkez,
Wy3e þat is so wel wrast alway to god
And connez not of compaynye þe costez vndertake,
And if mon kennes yow hom to knowe, 3e kest hom of your mynde: [f111ʳ]
Þou hatz for3eten 3ederly þat 3isterday I ta3t te   1485
Bi alder-truest token of talk þat I cowþe.'
'What is þat?' quoþ þe wyghe. 'Iwysse I wot neuer.
If hit be sothe þat 3e breue, þe blame is myn awen.'
'3et I kende yow of kyssyng,' quoþ þe clere þenne,
'Quereso countenaunce is couþe, quikly to clayme;   1490
Þat bicumes vche a kny3t þat cortaysy vses.'
'Do way,' quoþ þat derf mon, 'my dere, þat speche,
For þat durst I not do, lest I deuayed were.
If I were werned, I were wrang, iwysse, 3if I profered.'
'Ma fay,' quoþ þe meré wyf, '3e may not be werned;   1495
3e ar stif innoghe to constrayne wyth strenkþe, 3if yow lykez,
3if any were so vilanous þat yow devaye wolde.'
'3e, be God,' quoþ Gawayn, 'good is your speche;
Bot þrete is vnþryuande in þede þer I lende,
And vche gift þat is geuen not with goud wylle.'   1500

1474f. *watz hym ate:* no doubt deliberately ambiguous: 'Very early she visited him (or 'was pestering him') in order to bring about a change in his attitude.'

1478. *ful 3erne of hir wordez:* possibly 'using very eager language'; *3erne*, however, may be adverbial and *of hir wordez* dependent on *3eldez a3ayn:* 'she quickly replied to him'.

1483. *compaynye* already has some of the amorous connotation of the modern 'keep company', as it has also in Chaucer's lines on the Wife of Bath:
Housbondes at chirche dore she hadde fyve,
Withouten oother compaignye in youthe (*CT* I.46of)

1485f. 'you have quickly forgotten what I taught you (*te:* thee) yesterday in the very truest teaching I could put into words.'

1490. 'to claim it immediately wherever favour is clearly shown'.

1493. Gawain is not, as at first appears, reproving her for freedom of conduct.

1494. 'If I proffered (a kiss) and were refused, I would indeed be (put in the) wrong.'

1495. *Ma fay:* 'By my faith'.

1499. 'but force is (considered) ignoble in the land where I live'. Gawain skilfully counters her argument on her own terms and once more politely declares his un-willingness to take the initiative.

I am at your comaundement, to kysse quen yow lykez;
Ʒe may lach quen yow lyst and leue quen yow þynkkez,
    In space.'
    Þe lady loutez adoun
    And comlyly kysses his face.   1505
    Much speche þay þer expoun
    Of druryes greme and grace.

'I woled wyt at yow, wyʒe,' þat worþy þer sayde,
'And yow wrathed not þerwyth, what were þe skylle
Þat so ʒong and so ʒepe as ʒe at þis tyme,   1510
So cortayse, so knyʒtyly, as ʒe ar knowen oute—
And of alle cheualry to chose, þe chef þyng alosed
Is þe lel layk of luf, þe lettrure of armes;
For to telle of þis teuelyng of þis trwe knyʒtez,
Hit is þe tytelet token and tyxt of her werkkez   1515
How ledez for her lele luf hor lyuez han auntered,
Endured for her drury dulful stoundez,
And after wenged with her walour and voyded her care
And broʒt blysse into boure with bountées hor awen—
And ʒe ar knyʒt comlokest kyd of your elde,   1520
Your worde and your worchip walkez ayquere,   [fiii^v]
And I haf seten by yourself here sere twyes,
Ʒet herde I neuer of your hed helde no wordez
Þat euer longed to luf, lasse ne more.

    1514.   For] r *illegible*
    1516.   ledez] dez *illegible*
              for] r *illegible*

1507. 'about the punishments and favours of love.' The phrase is reminiscent of Chaucer's: *his* (the God of Love's) *myrakles and his crewel yre* (*The Parlement of Foules* 11).

1512f. 'and from among the whole (code) of chivalry, the thing principally praised is the faithful practice of love'. The syntax of the speech effectively suggests the informality of conversation (cf. 2446–58); after this long parenthesis (1512–19) giving the lady's views on the importance of love in the code of chivalry, the construction begun at 1509 is loosely resumed. *Þe lettrure of armes:* 'the (very) doctrine of knighthood'; as 1515–19 show, the rules of love are conceived as a set of guiding principles for active knighthood.

1514–16. 'for to speak of the striving (*teuelyng*) of true knights, (for *þis*, 'these', see 1139n) it is the rubric written at the head of their works, and the very words themselves, how men . . .'; *werkkez* contains a pun on 'deeds' and '(literary) works'— i.e. romances of chivalry.

1518. 'and later avenged and dispelled their sorrow through their valour'.

1519. I.e. they made their ladies happy by their achievements.

1524. *lasse ne more:* 'smaller or larger', i.e. 'at all'.

And ȝe, þat ar so cortays and coynt of your hetes,   1525
Oghe to a ȝonke þynk ȝern to schewe
And teche sum tokenez of trweluf craftes.
Why! ar ȝe lewed, þat alle þe los weldez,
Oþer elles ȝe demen me to dille your dalyaunce to herken?
    For schame!   1530
      I com hider sengel and sitte
      To lerne at yow sum game;
      Dos techez me of your wytte,
      Whil my lorde is fro hame.'

'In goud fayþe,' quoþ Gawayn, 'God yow forȝelde!   1535
Gret is þe gode gle, and gomen to me huge,
Þat so worþy as ȝe wolde wynne hidere
And pyne yow with so pouer a mon, as play wyth your knyȝt
With anyskynnez countenaunce; hit keuerez me ese.
Bot to take þe toruayle to myself to trwluf expoun   1540
And towche þe temez of tyxt and talez of armez
To yow, þat (I wot wel) weldez more slyȝt
Of þat art, bi þe half, or a hundreth of seche
As I am, oþer euer schal in erde þer I leue,
Hit were a folé felefolde, my fre, by my trawþe.   1545
I wolde yowre wylnyng worche at my myȝt,
As I am hyȝly bihalden, and euermore wylle
Be seruaunt to yourseluen, so saue me Dryȝtyn!'
Þus hym frayned þat fre and fondet hym ofte,
For to haf wonnen hym to woȝe, whatso scho þoȝt ellez;   1550
Bot he defended hym so fayr þat no faut semed,
Ne non euel on nawþer halue, nawþer þay wysten
    Bot blysse.

1526. *a ȝonke þynk:* 'a young thing' (herself); *ȝern* is adverbial: 'eagerly'.
1534. *fro hame:* 'away from home'.
1540f. 'But to take upon myself the task (*toruayle*) of expounding true love (*to . . .
expoun*, split infin.) and of treating of the subject-matter (*temez of tyxt*) and stories of
knighthood'.
1544. *oþer . . . leue:* 'or ever shall (be) in the country where I live (come from)'.
1550. 'in order to bring him to grief (wrong), whatever else she intended'. The poet
appears to wish to exonerate the lady. Alternatively *woȝe* can be interpreted as a verb
'woo' (so TG-Davis n) and the second half-line would then imply 'though she had no
genuine desire for his advances'. However, the closest syntactic parallel (831) leads
one to expect a noun rather than a verb here; also the whole tone of the comment
(cf. *fondet* 'tempted' 1549) favours the sense 'wrong, sin' (or perhaps 'harm', in view
of the possible consequences).
1552f. *nawþer . . . blysse:* 'nor were they aware of anything but pleasure.'

Þay laȝed and layked longe;
At þe last scho con hym kysse,   1555
Hir leue fayre con scho fonge,
And went hir waye, iwysse.

Then ruþes hym þe renk and ryses to þe masse,
And siþen hor diner watz dyȝt and derely serued.   [f112ʳ]
Þe lede with þe ladyez layked alle day   1560
Bot þe lorde ouer þe londez launced ful ofte,
Swez his vncely swyn, þat swyngez bi þe bonkkez
And bote þe best of his brachez þe bakkez in sunder
Þer he bode in his bay, tel bawemen hit breken
And madee hym mawgref his hed for to mwe vtter,   1565
So felle flonez þer flete when þe folk gedered.
Bot ȝet þe styffest to start bi stoundez he made,
Til at þe last he watz so mat he myȝt no more renne
Bot in þe hast þat he myȝt he to a hole wynnez
Of a rasse, bi a rokk þer rennez þe boerne.   1570
He gete þe bonk at his bak, bigynez to scrape—
Þe froþe femed at his mouth vnfayre bi þe wykez—
Whettez his whyte tuschez. With hym þen irked
Alle þe burnez so bolde þat hym by stoden
To nye hym onferum, bot neȝe hym non durst   1575
    For woþe;
  He hade hurt so mony byforne
  Þat al þuȝt þenne ful loþe
  Be more wyth his tusches torne,
  Þat breme watz and braynwod bothe.   1580

Til þe knyȝt com hymself, kachande his blonk,
Syȝ hym byde at þe bay, his burnez bysyde.

1580. and] MS *om.*

1564. *hit breken:* 'broke it (his stand)'.
1565. 'and made him move out into the open despite all he could do (*mawgref his hed*)'. Cf. *Pat* 44n.
1571ff. When at bay, the boar sharpens his lower tusks against his upper ones and scrapes the ground with his feet. The description of an angry boar in *The Seven Sages* (ed. Karl Brunner, EETS OS 191, 897–9) is very similar.
1572. 'the froth foamed hideously at the corners of his mouth'.
1573–6. *With hym . . . :* 'Then all the very brave men who stood round him became weary of trying to hurt (*nye*) him from a distance (*onferum*), but none of them dared to go near him because of the danger'.
1578. 'that it then seemed very hateful to everyone'.

He lyȝtes luflych adoun, leuez his corsour,
Braydez out a bryȝt bront and bigly forth strydez,
Foundez fast þurȝ þe forth þer þe felle bydez.   1585
Þe wylde watz war of þe wyȝe with weppen in honde,
Hef hyȝly þe here; so hetterly he fnast
Þat fele ferde for þe freke, lest felle hym þe worre.
Þe swyn settez hym out on þe segge euen,
Þat þe burne and þe bor were boþe vpon hepez   1590
In þe wyȝtest of þe water. Þe worre hade þat oþer,
For þe mon merkkez hym wel, as þay mette fyrst,
Set sadly þe scharp in þe slot euen,
Hit hym vp to þe hult, þat þe hert schyndered
And he ȝarrande hym ȝelde and ȝedoun þe water   1595
    Ful tyt.   [f112ᵛ]
    A hundreth houndez hym hent,
    Þat bremely con hym bite;
    Burnez him broȝt to bent
    And doggez to dethe endite.   1600

There watz blawyng of prys in mony breme horne,
Heȝe halowing on hiȝe with haþelez þat myȝt;
Brachetes bayed þat best, as bidden þe maysterez,
Of þat chargeaunt chace þat were chef huntes.
Þenne a wyȝe þat watz wys vpon wodcraftez   1605
To vnlace þis bor lufly bigynnez.
Fyrst he hewes of his hed and on hiȝe settez,
And syþen rendez him al roghe bi þe rygge after,
Braydez out þe boweles, brennez hom on glede,
With bred blent þerwith his braches rewardez.   1610
Syþen he britnez out þe brawen in bryȝt brode cheldez,
And hatz out þe hastlettez, as hiȝtly bisemez,
And ȝet hem halchez al hole þe haluez togeder
And syþen on a stif stange stoutly hem henges.
Now with þis ilk swyn þay swengen to home.   1615

1583. luflych] MS luslych
1588. freke] MS frekez

1595. *ȝedoun:* for *ȝed doun* 'went down'—'was carried downstream'.
1600. *to dethe endite:* 'do him to death.'
1602. *Heȝe:* though the same word as *hiȝe* in *on hiȝe* ('loudly'), is probably to be
distinguished in sense here ('proud'). Such repetition with change of meaning
(*traductio*) was regarded as a stylistic embellishment in the Middle Ages; cf. 2276n.
1603f. 'hounds bayed at that beast, as the masters-of-game, who were the chief
huntsmen of that difficult chase, commanded.'
1608. *bi þe rygge after:* 'along the backbone'.
1613. 'moreover. he fastens the two complete sides together'.

Þe bores hed watz borne bifore þe burnes seluen
Þat him forferde in þe forþe þurӡ forse of his honde
    So stronge.
    Til he seӡ Sir Gawayne
    In halle, hym þoӡt ful longe;   1620
    He calde, and he com gayn,
    His feez þer for to fonge.

Þe lorde ful lowde with lote and laӡter myry,
When he seӡe Sir Gawayn, with solace he spekez.
Þe goude ladyez were geten, and gedered þe meyny;   1625
He schewez hem þe scheldez and schapes hem þe tale
Of þe largesse and þe lenþe, þe liþernez alse
Of þe were, of þe wylde swyn in wod þer he fled.
Þat oþer knyӡt ful comly comended his dedez
And praysed hit as gret prys þat he proued hade,   1630
For suche a brawne of a best, þe bolde burne sayde,
Ne such sydes of a swyn segh he neuer are.
Þenne hondeled þay þe hoge hed; þe hende mon hit praysed
And let lodly þerat, þe lorde for to here.   [f113ᵛ]
'Now, Gawayn,' quoþ þe godmon, 'þis gomen is your awen   1635
Bi fyn forwarde and faste, faythely ӡe knowe.'
'Hit is sothe,' quoþ þe segge, 'and as siker trwe,
Alle my get I schal yow gif agayn, bi my trawþe.'
He hent þe haþel aboute þe halse and hendely hym kysses
And eftersones of þe same he serued hym þere.   1640
'Now ar we euen,' quoþ þe haþel, 'in þis euentide,
Of alle þe couenauntes þat we knyt syþen I com hider,
    Bi lawe.'
    Þe lorde sayde, 'Bi Saynt Gile,
    Ӡe ar þe best þat I knowe!   1645
    Ӡe ben ryche in a whyle,
    Such chaffer and ӡe drowe.'

1623. laӡter (Davis)] MS laӡed
1639. hent] MS *om.*

1616f. *bifore ... forferde:* 'in front of the very knight who had killed it'.
1620. *hym þoӡt ful longe:* 'it seemed a long time to him'—i.e. 'he was impatient'.
1630. 'and praised his action as giving proof of great accomplishment'.
1634. 'and made a show of abhorrence at it, in order to praise the lord.'
1637. *siker trwe:* qualifies *I* in 1638: 'and as surely true (as you are)'.
1644. *Saynt Gile:* St Giles was a saint of the 7th c. who lived as a hermit in a forest near Nîmes with a hind for companion. This association makes him perhaps an appropriate saint for the hunting knight.
1647. 'if you carry on (*drowe*) such trade.' The knight means that Gawain has doubled his takings in one day.

Þenne þay teldet tablez trestes alofte,
Kesten cloþez vpon; clere lyȝt þenne
Wakned bi woȝez, waxen torches   1650
Seggez sette, and serued in sale al aboute.
Much glam and gle glent vp þerinne
Aboute þe fyre vpon flet; and on fele wyse
At þe soper and after, mony aþel songez,
As coundutes of Krystmasse and carolez newe,   1655
With alle þe manerly merþe þat mon may of telle.
And euer oure luflych knyȝt þe lady bisyde;
Such semblaunt to þat segge semly ho made,
Wyth stille stollen countenaunce, þat stalworth to plese,
Þat al forwondered watz þe wyȝe and wroth with hymseluen,   1660
Bot he nolde not for his nurture nurne hir aȝaynez
Bot dalt with hir al in daynté, how-se-euer þe dede turned
          Towrast.
     Quen þay hade played in halle
     As longe as hor wylle hom last,   1665
     To chambre he con hym calle
     And to þe chemné þay past.

Ande þer þay dronken and dalten and demed eft nwe
To norne on þe same note on Nwe Ȝerez Euen;
Bot þe knyȝt craued leue to kayre on þe morn,   1670
For hit watz neȝ at þe terme þat he to schulde.
Þe lorde hym letted of þat, to lenge hym resteyed,   [f 113ᵛ]
And sayde, 'As I am trwe segge, I siker my trawþe
Þou schal cheue to þe Grene Chapel þy charres to make,
Leude, on Nw Ȝerez lyȝt, longe bifore pryme.   1675
Forþy þow lye in þy loft and lach þyn ese
And I schal hunt in þis holt and halde þe towchez,
Chaunge wyth þe cheuisaunce bi þat I charre hider.
For I haf fraysted þe twys and faythful I fynde þe.
Now "Þrid tyme, þrowe best" þenk on þe morne;   1680

1648. *trestes alofte:* 'upon trestles'.
1655. *coundutes:* 'Christmas part-songs' (a *coundute*, L *conductus*, was originally a passage
sung while the priest was proceeding to the altar).
1661. *nurne hir aȝaynez:* an idiom of uncertain meaning; the context appears to
demand the sense 'repulse her (openly)' rather than 'return her advances'.
1662f. 'but behaved with complete courtesy towards her even though this might be
misconstrued.'
1666. *he:* the host; *hym:* Gawain.
1669. 'to do the same (*lit.* sing the same tune? propose the same business?) on New
Year's Eve'.
1671. *þat he to schulde:* 'to which he had to go'; the verb of motion is omitted and *to*
accordingly bears the stress and alliteration.
1678. 'exchange winnings with you (*wyth þe*) when I return hither.'
1680. 'Now remember tomorrow (the saying) "Third time, throw best"'. From the
game of dice: 'Third time lucky'.

Make we mery quyl we may and mynne vpon joye,
For þe lur may mon lach whenso mon lykez.'
Þis watz grayþely graunted and Gawayn is lenged;
Bliþe broȝt watz hym drynk and þay to bedde ȝeden
      With liȝt.   1685
      Sir Gawayn lis and slepes
      Ful stille and softe al niȝt;
      Þe lorde, þat his craftez kepes,
      Ful erly he watz diȝt.

After messe, a morsel he and his men token.   1690
Miry watz þe mornyng; his mounture he askes.
Alle þe haþeles þat on horse schulde helden hym after
Were boun busked on hor blonkkez bifore þe halle ȝatez.
Ferly fayre watz þe folde, for þe forst clenged;
In rede rudede vpon rak rises þe sunne   1695
And ful clere castez þe clowdes of þe welkyn.
Hunteres vnhardeled bi a holt syde;
Rocheres roungen bi rys for rurde of her hornes.
Summe fel in þe fute þer þe fox bade,
Traylez ofte atraueres bi traunt of her wyles.   1700
A kenet kryes þerof; þe hunt on hym calles;
His felaȝes fallen hym to, þat fnasted ful þike,
Runnen forth in a rabel in his ryȝt fare,
And he fyskez hem byfore; þay founden hym sone.
And quen þay seghe hym with syȝt þay sued hym fast,   1705
Wreȝande hym ful weterly with a wroth noyse,
And he trantes and tornayeez þurȝ mony tene greue,
Hauilounez and herkenez bi heggez ful ofte.
At þe last bi a littel dich he lepez ouer a spenné,   [f114ʳ]
Stelez out ful stilly bi a strothe rande,   1710
Went haf wylt of þe wode, with wylez, fro þe houndes.

1690. morsel] m *with extra minim*
1693. bifore] MS biforere
1696. castez] MS costez
1700. atraueres (Gollancz)] MS atrayteres
1706. hym] ym *illegible*
          weterly] *blurred* (w *from offset on* f114ʳ)

1695f. 'the sun rises red, its redness reflected upon a bank of cloud, and in its full brightness drives the clouds from the sky (or MS *costez* 'coasts', 'skirts'?)'.
1699–1701. 'Some (of the hounds) hit upon the scent where the fox was lurking, (and) trail again and again across it (*atraueres*) in their wily ingenuity. A small hound gives tongue at it (the scent); the huntsman calls him on'.
1706. 'vilifying him in no uncertain terms with a furious noise'.
1710. *bi a strothe rande:* 'at the edge (*rande*) of a wooded marsh'. *Strothe:* cf. *Pe* 113–16n.
1711. 'thought (*went*) to have escaped (*wylt*) out of the wood by tricks, away from the hounds.'

Þenne watz he went, er he wyst, to a wale tryster,
Þer þre þro at a þrich þrat hym at ones,
    Al graye.
    He blenched aȝayn bilyue   1715
    And stifly start onstray.
    With alle þe wo on lyue
    To þe wod he went away.

Thenne watz hit list vpon lif to lyþen þe houndez,
When alle þe mute hade hym met, menged togeder: 1720
Suche a sorȝe at þat syȝt þay sette on his hede
As alle þe clamberande clyffes hade clatered on hepes.
Here he watz halawed when haþelez hym metten,
Loude he watz ȝayned with ȝarande speche;
Þer he watz þreted and ofte 'þef' called,   1725
And ay þe titleres at his tayl, þat tary he ne myȝt.
Ofte he watz runnen at when he out rayked,
And ofte reled in aȝayn, so Reniarde watz wylé.
And ȝe! he lad hem bi lagmon, þe lorde and his meyny,
On þis maner bi þe mountes quyle myd ouer vnder,   1730
Whyle þe hende knyȝt at home holsumly slepes
Withinne þe comly cortynes, on þe colde morne.
Bot þe lady, for luf, let not to slepe,
Ne þe purpose to payre þat pyȝt in hir hert,
But ros hir vp radly, rayked hir þeder   1735
In a mery mantyle, mete to þe erþe,
Þat watz furred ful fyne with fellez wel pured;

    1712. to] MS to to
    1719. list vpon lif (Morris)] MS lif vpon list

1713f. 'where three fierce (hounds)—all greyhounds—came at him in a rush.'
1716. 'and leaped off violently in a changed direction (*onstray*).'
1719f. 'Then it was pleasure indeed to hear (*lyþen*) the hounds, (their voices) mingled (*menged*) together, when all the pack had met up with him'.
1728. *Reniarde* (also *Renaude*): 'Reynard'—popular medieval name for the fox.
1729. *lad hem bi lagmon:* 'led them in a string'; *lagmon* is a rare word, perhaps related to *lag* n. 'last person in a race, etc.'. See Menner, *PQ*, 10 (1931), 163–8, and *EDD*.
1730. *quyle myd ouer vnder:* an extremely vague indication of time, *lit.* 'until half-way past (through?) *vnder*'; but *vnder* may be used precisely for 'the third hour' (9 a.m.), as in *Pe* 513, or loosely for 'mid-morning', 'midday', or even 'afternoon'. Perhaps best translated 'until well on in the afternoon'.
1731. *holsumly:* 'for the good of his health'—with delicate ironic contrast.
1733f. 'But the lady, on account of her wooing, did not allow herself to sleep nor did she allow the purpose which stuck in her heart to become blunted'; *for luf* (as appears later) is to be taken as 'for wooing', though it obviously suits the poet's purpose for the time being to allow the reader to assume inclination on the lady's part. Cf. 1927n.

No hwef goud on hir hede, bot þe haȝer stones
Trased aboute hir tressour be twenty in clusteres;
Hir þryuen face and hir þrote þrowen al naked,   1740
Hir brest bare bifore, and bihinde eke.
Ho comez withinne þe chambre dore and closes hit hir after,
Wayuez vp a wyndow and on þe wyȝe callez
And radly þus rehayted hym with hir riche wordes,
  With chere: 1745
   'A! mon, how may þou slepe?
   Þis morning is so clere.'   [f114ᵛ]
  He watz in drowping depe,
  Bot þenne he con hir here.

In dreȝ droupyng of dreme draueled þat noble,   1750
As mon þat watz in mornyng of mony þro þoȝtes,
How þat Destiné schulde þat day dele hym his wyrde
At þe Grene Chapel when he þe gome metes
And bihoues his buffet abide withoute debate more.
Bot quen þat comly com he keuered his wyttes,   1755
Swenges out of þe sweuenes and swarez with hast.
Þe lady luflych com, laȝande swete,
Felle ouer his fayre face and fetly hym kyssed.
He welcumez hir worþily with a wale chere;
He seȝ hir so glorious and gayly atyred,   1760
So fautles of hir fetures and of so fyne hewes,
Wiȝt wallande joye warmed his hert.
With smoþe smylyng and smolt þay smeten into merþe,
Þat al watz blis and bonchef þat breke hem bitwene,
  And wynne.   1765

1738. hwef] MS hwez
1752. dele hym (Tolkien and Gordon)] MS *om.*
1755. com (Emerson)] MS *om.*

1738f. 'No seemly coif on her head, but the noble stones (i.e. pearls?) set about her hair-fret in clusters of twenty'. If Gollancz's suggestion is correct, that the MS *hwez* is a form of OE *hūfe* (ME *howve*) 'head-covering, coif', the implication here is that it would have been a more seemly head-dress for a married woman. Cf. the Wife of Bath's paraphrase of 1 Tim. 2:9:
 'In habit maad with chastitee and shame
 Ye wommen shul apparaille yow,' quod he,
 'And noght in tressed heer and gay peree (*precious stones*)
 As perles, ne with gold, ne clothes riche.' (*CT* III.342ff)
See also *Cl* 1707n, *Pe* 197–228n.
1752f. Since he is not to meet the Green Knight until the next day, we must construe: 'on that day when he meets the man at the Green Chapel'.

Þay lauced wordes gode,
Much wele þen watz þerinne.
Gret perile bitwene hem stod,
Nif Maré of hir knyȝt mynne.

For þat prynces of pris depresed hym so þikke,   1770
Nurned hym so neȝe þe þred, þat nede hym bihoued
Oþer lach þer hir luf oþer lodly refuse.
He cared for his cortaysye, lest craþayn he were,
And more for his meschef ȝif he schulde make synne
And be traytor to þat tolke þat þat telde aȝt.   1775
'God schylde!' quoþ þe schalk. 'Þat schal not befalle!'
With luf-laȝyng a lyt he layd hym bysyde
Alle þe spechez of specialté þat sprange of her mouthe.
Quoþ þat burde to þe burne, 'Blame ȝe disserue
Ȝif ȝe luf not þat lyf þat ȝe lye nexte,   1780
Bifore alle þe wyȝez in þe worlde wounded in hert,
Bot if ȝe haf a lemman, a leuer, þat yow lykez better,
And folden fayth to þat fre, festned so harde
Þat yow lausen ne lyst—and þat I leue nouþe!   [f115ʳ]
And þat ȝe telle me þat now trwly I pray yow;   1785
For alle þe lufez vpon lyue, layne not þe soþe
      For gile.'
      Þe knyȝt sayde, 'Be Sayn Jon'
      (And smeþely con he smyle)
      'In fayth I welde riȝt non,   1790
      Ne non wil welde þe quile.'

'Þat is a worde,' quoþ þat wyȝt, 'þat worst is of alle;
Bot I am swared forsoþe—þat sore me þinkkez.

1770.   prynces (Emerson)] MS prynce

1768f.   'There was great peril between them—unless Mary be mindful of her knight.'
The tenses of *stod* and *mynne* are partly governed by the rhymes; but sudden transitions between past tense and present tense are common (e.g. at 2307f).
1776.   In ME the negative connotation of a prohibition is regularly repeated in the noun clause and (but for the indicative *schal*) Gawain's thought might be interpreted 'God forbid that that should happen', and is usually so punctuated. The present punctuation (which is justified by *schal*, instead of *schulde*) makes the expression of his determination stronger.
1778.   *spechez of specialté:* 'expressions of affection'.
1779–84.   'Said that lady to the man, "You deserve blame if you do not love that person you are lying beside, (who is) wounded in heart more than everybody in the world, unless you have a sweetheart, someone dearer to you, who pleases you better, and (have) pledged your word to that noble one, confirmed so definitely that you do not care to break it (*lausen*)—and that I do believe now!'
1786.   *For alle þe lufez vpon lyue:* equivalent to 'For the love of God and all the saints'.
1788.   *Sayn Jon:* St John the Apostle, by tradition supremely dedicated to celibacy.

Kysse me now, comly, and I schal cach heþen;
I may bot mourne vpon molde, as may þat much louyes.'   1795
Sykande ho sweȝe doun and semly hym kyssed,
And siþen ho seueres hym fro and says as ho stondes,
'Now, dere, at þis departyng do me þis ese:
Gif me sumquat of þy gifte, þi gloue if hit were,
Þat I may mynne on þe, mon, my mournyng to lassen.'   1800
'Now iwysse,' quoþ þat wyȝe, 'I wolde I hade here
Þe leuest þing, for þy luf, þat I in londe welde,
For ȝe haf deserued, forsoþe, sellyly ofte
More rewarde bi resoun þen I reche myȝt.
Bot to dele yow, for drurye, þat dawed bot neked!—   1805
Hit is not your honour to haf at þis tyme
A gloue for a garysoun of Gawaynez giftez.
And I am here an erande in erdez vncouþe
And haue no men wyth no malez with menskful þingez
(Þat mislykez me, ladé) for luf, at þis tyme;   1810
Iche tolke mon do as he is tan—tas to non ille
     Ne pine.'
        'Nay, hende of hyȝe honours,'
     Quoþ þat lufsum vnder lyne,
        'Þaȝ I nade oȝt of yourez,   1815
        Ȝet schulde ȝe haue of myne.'

Ho raȝt hym a riche rynk of red golde werkez,
Wyth a starande ston stondande alofte,
Þat bere blusschande bemez as þe bryȝt sunne;
Wyt ȝe wel, hit watz worth wele ful hoge.   1820
Bot þe renk hit renayed and redyly he sayde,

1799. if] MS of
1810. tyme] MS tyne
1815. nade (Gollancz)] MS hade

1799. *if it were:* 'if only'.
1805–7. 'But to give you, as a love-token (*drurye*), something of little worth (*lit.* that which profited little)!—it is not equal to your dignity for you to have at this time a glove as a trophy given by Gawain.' 1805 can be interpreted 'But to make you a present for the sake of love—that would not be very fitting'; the punctuation and the translation adopted above are, however, better syntactically (the use of *dele* without direct object would be awkward) and also more in keeping with Gawain's intention not to *lodly refuse* (1772).
1808. *an* is the preposition: 'on a mission'.
1811f. *tas . . . pine:* 'do not take it amiss or be distressed.'
1814. *vnder lyne:* '(one) dressed in linen', i.e. 'lady'. Cf. *Pe* 775–80n.
1815. May be emended to *hade noȝt*, with same sense, but the emendation of Gollancz (above) keeps the vocalic alliteration and also assumes a somewhat more probable miscopying.

'I wil no giftez, for Gode, my gay, at þis tyme;   [f115ᵛ]
I haf none yow to norne ne noȝt wyl I take.'
Ho bede hit hym ful bysily and he hir bode wernes
And swere swyfte by his sothe þat he hit sese nolde;   1825
And ho soré þat he forsoke and sayde þerafter,
'If ȝe renay my rynk, to ryche for hit semez,
Ȝe wolde not so hyȝly halden be to me,
I schal gif yow my girdel, þat gaynes yow lasse.'
Ho laȝt a lace lyȝtly þat leke vmbe hir sydez,   1830
Knit vpon hir kyrtel, vnder þe clere mantyle;
Gered hit watz with grene sylke and with golde schaped,
Noȝt bot arounde brayden, beten with fyngrez.
And þat ho bede to þe burne and blyþely bisoȝt,
Þaȝ hit vnworþi were, þat he hit take wolde;   1835
And he nay þat he nolde neghe in no wyse
Nauþer golde ne garysoun, er God hym grace sende
To acheue to þe chaunce þat he hade chosen þere.
'And þerfore I pray yow displese yow noȝt
And lettez be your bisinesse, for I bayþe hit yow neuer   1840
     To graunte.
  I am derely to yow biholde
  Bicause of your sembelaunt,
  And euer in hot and colde
  To be your trwe seruaunt.'   1845

'Now forsake ȝe þis silke,' sayde þe burde þenne,
For hit is symple in hitself? And so hit wel semez:
Lo! so hit is littel and lasse hit is worþy.
Bot whoso knew þe costes þat knit ar þerinne,
He wolde hit prayse at more prys, parauenture;   1850
For quat gome so is gorde with þis grene lace,
While he hit hade hemely halched aboute
Þer is no haþel vnder heuen tohewe hym þat myȝt,

1825. swyfte by (Emerson)] MS swyftel (Madden: swyftely)
1830. þat] MS þat þat

1827. *to ryche for hit semez:* 'because it seems too costly'.
1833. *brayden, beten:* 'embroidered (and) inlaid', corresponding respectively to *grene sylke* and *golde*, 1832.
1835. *vnworþi:* 'of little value'. As in 1847f, the lady is being modest—or pretending to be: cf. 1832f, 2038f, 2430–2.
1836. *nay:* (pa.t. of *nie* 'say no'): 'he said he would not by any means touch (*neghe*)'.
1844. 'and ever (will be) in all circumstances (or 'through thick and thin')'; cf. 1547f.
1847f. *And so . . . .:* 'And so it seems, perhaps: look! it is no bigger than this and its value is even less (than it seems).'
1853. *tohewe:* 'cut down, cut to pieces'; the word is calculated to make Gawain think of his own plight, just as *slyȝt* 'skill, stratagem' (1854) seems designed to suggest that the girdle may be a match for the Green Knight's magical powers (cf. 1858).

For he my3t not be slayn for sly3t vpon erþe.'
Þen kest þe kny3t, and hit come to his hert   1855
Hit were a juel for þe jopardé þat hym jugged were:
When he acheued to þe chapel his chek for to fech,
My3t he haf slypped to be vnslayn þe sle3t were noble.
Þenne he þulged with hir þrepe and þoled hir to speke.   [f116ʳ]
And ho bere on hym þe belt and bede hit hym swyþe   1860
(And he granted and hym gafe with a goud wylle)
And biso3t hym for hir sake disceuer hit neuer
Bot to lelly layne fro hir lorde; þe leude hym acordez
Þat neuer wy3e schulde hit wyt, iwysse, bot þay twayne,
　　For no3te.   1865
　　He þonkked hir oft ful swyþe,
　　Ful þro with hert and þo3t;
　　Bi þat on þrynne syþe
　　Ho hatz kyst þe kny3t so to3t.

Thenne lachchez ho hir leue and leuez hym þere,   1870
For more myrþe of þat mon mo3t ho not gete.
When ho watz gon, Sir Gawayn gerez hym sone,
Rises and riches hym in araye noble,
Lays vp þe luf-lace þe lady hym ra3t,
Hid hit ful holdely þer he hit eft fonde.   1875
Syþen cheuely to þe chapel choses he þe waye,
Preuély aproched to a prest and prayed hym þere
Þat he wolde lyste his lyf and lern hym better
How his sawle schulde be saued when he schuld seye heþen.
Þere he schrof hym schyrly and schewed his mysdedez,   1880

1858. My3t he] MS my3 ho
1863. fro (Morris)] MS for
1872. ho (Madden)] MS he
1878. lyste (Burrow)] MS lyfte

1856. 'it would be a godsend (*lit.* jewel) for the hazard assigned to him'.
1858. 'if he could only escape without getting killed it would be a fine stratagem.'
1859. 'Then he gave in to her insistence and allowed her to speak.'
1868f. 'by that time she had kissed the hardy (*to3t*) knight three times'—i.e. she then gave him a third kiss (cf. 1758, 1796). The apparently singular form *on þrynne sype* is explained as the relic of an old dative pl. in *-um*; cf. *on his fote* 2229.
1876–84. Gawain's confession has been much discussed by critics in the light of the fact that he evidently does not confess his concealment of the *luf-lace* and his incipient violation of the exchange agreement with the Host. See especially **7d** Burrow, 1959–60, 1964; Hills, 1963; Field, 1971; Evans, 1973; Foley, 1974. Probably the most satisfactory solution is that it is only in retrospect, when he sees its full significance, that the concealment becomes a grave moral fault for him. At the time, to violate the rules of a parlour game (note the element of jest in the descriptions in 1112f, 1392–9, 1404, 1409, 1623, 1644–7, 1681–5 and 1932ff) would hardly have seemed a sin at all.
1878. *lyste his lyf:* 'hear his confession'; see Burrow, **7d** 1965, 105, and TG-Davis n.

Of þe more and þe mynne, and merci besechez,
And of absolucioun he on þe segge calles;
And he asoyled hym surely and sette hym so clene
As domezday schulde haf ben diȝt on þe morn.
And syþen he mace hym as mery among þe fre ladyes,   1885
With comlych caroles and alle kynnes joye,
As neuer he did bot þat daye, to þe derk nyȝt,
    With blys.
      Vche mon hade daynté þare
      Of hym, and sayde, 'Iwysse,   1890
      Þus myry he watz neuer are,
      Syn he com hider, er þis.'

Now hym lenge in þat lee, þer luf hym bityde!
Ȝet is þe lorde on þe launde ledande his gomnes.
He hatz forfaren þis fox þat he folȝed longe;   1895
As he sprent ouer a spenné to spye þe schrewe,
Þeras he herd þe howndes þat hasted hym swyþe,   [f116ᵛ]
Renaud com richchande þurȝ a roȝe greue,
And alle þe rabel in a res ryȝt at his helez.
Þe wyȝe watz war of þe wylde and warly abides,   1900
And braydez out þe bryȝt bronde and at þe best castez.
And he schunt for þe scharp and schulde haf arered;
A rach rapes hym to, ryȝt er he myȝt,
And ryȝt bifore þe hors fete þay fel on hym alle
And woried me þis wyly wyth a wroth noyse.   1905
Þe lorde lyȝtez bilyue and lachez hym sone,
Rased hym ful radly out of þe rach mouþes,
Haldez heȝe ouer his hede, halowez faste,
And þer bayen hym mony braþ houndez.
Huntes hyȝed hem þeder with hornez ful mony,   1910
Ay rechatande aryȝt til þay þe renk seȝen.

1906. lachez (Tolkien and Gordon)] MS cachez
      hym (Madden)] MS by
1909. braþ (Morris)] MS bray

1881. 'belonging to (*Of*) the greater and lesser (sins), and begs for forgiveness'; contemporary penitential manuals classify the branches of sin minutely.
1883. *he:* the priest.
1884. *As:* 'as if'.
1897. 'at a place where he (the knight) heard the hounds in full chase'; *hasted hym:* 'pressed hard upon him', or possibly reflexive.
1902. *schulde haf arered:* 'was about to retreat'.
1905. *me:* untranslatable in this context ('ethic dative'); it conveys a colloquial or ironic tone, suggesting the involvement of the narrator; cf. 1932, 2014, 2144, 2459, *Pat* 72, 108.
1907. *rach mouþes:* 'mouths of the dogs'.

Bi þat watz comen his compeyny noble,
Alle þat euer ber bugle blowed at ones
And alle þise oþer halowed, þat hade no hornes;
Hit watz þe myriest mute þat euer mon herde,　　　　　　　1915
Þe rich rurd þat þer watz raysed for Renaude saule
　　With lote.
　　Hor houndez þay þer rewarde,
　　Her hedez þay fawne and frote,
　　And syþen þay tan Reynarde　　　　　　　　　　　　1920
　　And tyruen of his cote.

And þenne þay helden to home, for hit watz nieȝ nyȝt,
Strakande ful stoutly in hor store hornez.
Þe lorde is lyȝt at þe laste at hys lef home,
Fyndez fire vpon flet, þe freke þerbyside,　　　　　　　1925
Sir Gawayn þe gode, þat glad watz with alle—
Among þe ladies for luf he ladde much joye.
He were a bleaunt of blwe, þat bradde to þe erþe,
His surkot semed hym wel, þat softe watz forred,
And his hode of þat ilke henged on his schulder;　　　　1930
Blande al of blaunner were boþe al aboute.
He metez me þis godmon inmyddez þe flore
And al with gomen he hym gret and goudly he sayde,
'I schal fylle vpon fyrst oure forwardez nouþe,
Þat we spedly han spoken, þer spared watz no drynk.'　　[f117ʳ]　1935
Þen acoles he þe knyȝt and kysses hym þryes
As sauerly and sadly as he hem sette coupe.
'Bi Kryst,' quoþ þat oþer knyȝt, 'ȝe cach much sele
In cheuisaunce of þis chaffer, ȝif ȝe hade goud chepez.'
'Ȝe, of þe chepe no charg,' quoþ chefly þat oþer,　　　1940
'As is pertly payed þe porchas þat I aȝte.'

1919. Her] MS her her
1936. þe] MS *om.*
1941. porchas] MS chepez, *perhaps miscopied from* 1939 (Gollancz: pray)

1927. *for luf:* 'on account of friendship'; the phrase is little more than a tag, however, a conventional accompaniment of *lady* (as perhaps in 1733).
1928. 'He wore a silk garment of blue, which reached to the ground'. Burrow, **7d** 1965, 111f, notes that blue is traditionally the colour of faithfulness; it is ironical that Gawain should wear it for his one act of duplicity.
1932. *me:* see 1905n.
1934. On the previous two evenings the host has been first.
1935. 'which we readily (happily?) affirmed when the drink flowed freely.'
1938–41. '"By Christ," said the other knight, "you have had a lot of good luck in obtaining this merchandise, if you found the market (or 'prices') good." "Oh never mind the market," said the other knight quickly, "since the gain which I obtained is publicly paid."' Some of the wit of these lines stems from the ambiguity of *chepe* 'trade, bargain, market, price'.

'Mary,' quoþ þat oþer mon, 'myn is bihynde,
For I haf hunted al þis day and noȝt haf I geten
Bot þis foule fox felle—þe Fende haf þe godez!—
And þat is ful pore for to pay for suche prys þinges   1945
As ȝe haf þryȝt me here þro, suche þre cosses
          So gode.'
          'Inoȝ,' quoþ Sir Gawayn,
          I þonk yow, bi þe Rode,'
          And how þe fox watz slayn   1950
          He tolde hym as þay stode.

With merþe and mynstralsye, wyth metez at hor wylle,
Þay maden as mery as any men moȝten,
With laȝyng of ladies, with lotez of bordes,
(Gawayn and þe godemon so glad were þay boþe),   1955
Bot if þe douthe had doted oþer dronken ben oþer.
Boþe þe mon and þe meyny maden mony japez,
Til þe sesoun watz seȝen þat þay seuer moste;
Burnez to hor bedde behoued at þe laste.
Þenne loȝly his leue at þe lorde fyrst   1960
Fochchez þis fre mon and fayre he hym þonkkez
'Of such a selly sojorne as I haf hade here.
Your honour at þis hyȝe fest þe Hyȝe Kyng yow ȝelde!
I ȝef yow me for on of yourez, if yowreself lykez,
For I mot nedes, as ȝe wot, meue tomorne,   1965
And ȝe me take sum tolke to teche, as ȝe hyȝt,
Þe gate to þe Grene Chapel, as God wyl me suffer
To dele on Nw Ȝerez Day þe dome of my wyrdes.'
'In god fayþe,' quoþ þe godmon, 'wyth a goud wylle
Al þat euer I yow hyȝt halde schal I redé.'   1970
Þer asyngnes he a seruaunt to sett hym in þe waye
And coundue hym by þe downez, þat he no drechch had,   [f117ᵛ]

1962. selly] MS sellyly

1954. *lotez of bordes:* 'jesting speeches'.
1956. The clause is dependent on *moȝten* (1953): 'as merry as any men could . . . unless the company had been demented, or else drunk'—i.e. without overstepping the bounds of propriety.
1962f. Usually punctuated as one sentence, on the assumption that *yow ȝelde* governs *Of* ('repay you for') and that *Your honour . . . fest* is in loose apposition to *sojorne.* However, in similar constructions *ȝelde* takes direct object (cf. 1292, 2410, 2441—all in the speech of Gawain). The punctuation adopted here makes *Of* dependent on *þonkkez* (cf. 1031ff); transition in mid-sentence from indirect to direct speech is quite common in ME and is also found in OE.
1964. 'I pledge (*lit.* give) myself to you (as your servant) in return for one of your men, if it pleases you' (cf. 1666f).
1966. *And:* 'if'.

For to ferk þurȝ þe fryth and fare at þe gaynest
   Bi greue.
  Þe lorde Gawayn con þonk   1975
  Such worchip he wolde hym weue.
  Þen at þo ladyez wlonk
  Þe knyȝt hatz tan his leue.

With care and wyth kyssyng he carppez hem tille
And fele þryuande þonkkez he þrat hom to haue;   1980
And þay ȝelden hym aȝayn ȝeply þat ilk.
Þay bikende hym to Kryst with ful colde sykyngez;
Syþen fro þe meyny he menskly departes.
Vche mon þat he mette he made hem a þonke
For his seruyse and his solace and his sere pyne   1985
Þat þay wyth busynes had ben aboute hym to serue;
And vche segge as soré to seuer with hym þere
As þay hade wonde worþyly with þat wlonk euer.
Þen with ledes and lyȝt he watz ladde to his chambre
And blyþely broȝt to his bedde to be at his rest.   1990
Ȝif he ne slepe soundyly say ne dar I,
For he hade much on þe morn to mynne, ȝif he wolde,
   In þoȝt.
  Let hym lyȝe þere stille;
  He hatz nere þat he soȝt.   1995
  And ȝe wyl a whyle be stylle,
  I schal telle yow how þay wroȝt.

IV

Now neȝez þe Nw Ȝere and þe nyȝt passez,
Þe day dryuez to þe derk, as Dryȝtyn biddez.
Bot wylde wederez of þe worlde wakned þeroute;   2000
Clowdes kesten kenly þe colde to þe erþe,
Wyth nyȝe innoghe of þe norþe þe naked to tene.

1973. ferk] MS frk
1981. aȝayn] MS aȝay

1975. The subject is *þe lorde*.
1985f. *and his sere . . . serue:* 'and for the special trouble they had each taken to serve
  him with solicitude' (*þat* stands for 'with which'; *aboute* 'engaged in').
1988. *As:* 'as if'.
1991. 'Whether or not he slept soundly I dare not say'. The next line implies that he
  probably did not; cf. also 2006ff.
2000. *wederez of þe worlde:* see 504n, and cf. *Cl* 948.
2001–4. 'clouds drove the cold keenly down to the earth and there was bitter wind
  enough from the north to torment the unprotected flesh. The snow showered down
  sharply, stinging (*þat snayped*) the wild animals; the whistling wind struck down from
  the high ground'. With 2001 cf. *Cl* 951.

Þe snawe snitered ful snart, þat snayped þe wylde;
Þe werbelande wynde wapped fro þe hyȝe
And drof vche dale ful of dryftes ful grete.   2005
Þe leude lystened ful wel, þat leȝ in his bedde—
Þaȝ he lowkez his liddez ful lyttel he slepes;
Bi vch kok þat crue he knwe wel þe steuen.
Deliuerly he dressed vp er þe day sprenged,   [f118ʳ]
For þere watz lyȝt of a laumpe þat lemed in his chambre.   2010
He called to his chamberlayn, þat cofly hym swared,
And bede hym bryng hym his bruny and his blonk sadel.
Þat oþer ferkez hym vp and fechez hym his wedez
And grayþez me Sir Gawayn vpon a grett wyse.
Fyrst he clad hym in his cloþez, þe colde for to were,   2015
And syþen his oþer harnays, þat holdely watz keped:
Boþe his paunce and his platez piked ful clene,
Þe ryngez rokked of þe roust of his riche bruny,
And al watz fresch as vpon fyrst, and he watz fayn þenne
        To þonk.   2020
    He hade vpon vche pece,
    Wypped ful wel and wlonk;
    Þe gayest into Grece
    Þe burne bede bryng his blonk.

Whyle þe wlonkest wedes he warp on hymseluen—   2025
His cote wyth þe conysaunce of þe clere werkez
Ennurned vpon veluet, vertuus stonez

2010.   laumpe] MS laupe
2027.   vertuus] MS vertuuus

2008. 'every time a cock crowed he was aware of the hour.' It was believed in the Middle Ages that cocks could tell the time by the sun and would crow exactly on the hour (as Chauntecleer does in Chaucer's 'The Nun's Priest's Tale'). In view of 2009, however, Cawley is probably right in seeing this as a reference to the belief that they crow 'three times during the night—at midnight, 3 a.m., and an hour before dawn'. Cf. 1412–15.

2010. *of:* 'from'.

2012. *and his blonk sadel:* 'and saddle his horse'.

2014. *me:* see 1905n.

2018. 'the rings of his splendid mail-coat rocked free of rust'; armour was rocked in a barrel of sand to remove rust.

2019–24. 'and he gave hearty thanks (for that). He had on him (now) every piece, polished (*Wypped*) most splendidly; the most elegant (knight) from here to Greece ordered the man (*þe burne*) to bring his horse.' With 2023 cf. *Pe* 231.

2026–9. his surcoat with the badge of bright workmanship (or 'pure deeds'—cf. 631) set upon velvet, with potent gems inlaid and clasped everywhere (*aboute*), the seams embroidered, and beautifully lined within with fine furs'; *vertuus:* jewels were thought to have power against various evils and diseases. Cf. *Pe* 1015n.

Aboute beten and bounden, enbrauded semez,
And fayre furred withinne wyth fayre pelures—
Ʒet laft he not þe lace, þe ladiez gifte;   2030
Þat forgat not Gawayn, for gode of hymseluen.
Bi he hade belted þe bronde vpon his balʒe haunchez,
Þenn dressed he his drurye double hym aboute,
Swyþe sweþled vmbe his swange, swetely, þat knyʒt;
Þe gordel of þe grene silke þat gay wel bisemed,   2035
Vpon þat ryol red cloþe, þat ryche watz to schewe.
Bot wered not þis ilk wyʒe for wele þis gordel,
For pryde of þe pendauntez, þaʒ polyst þay were,
And þaʒ þe glyterande golde glent vpon endez,
Bot for to sauen hymself when suffer hym byhoued,   2040
To byde bale withoute dabate, of bronde hym to were
        Oþer knyffe.
    Bi þat þe bolde mon boun
    Wynnez þeroute bilyue,
    Alle þe meyny of renoun   2045
    He þonkkez ofte ful ryue.

Thenne watz Gryngolet grayþe, þat gret watz and huge,   [f 118ᵛ]
And hade ben sojourned sauerly and in a siker wyse:
Hym lyst prik for poynt, þat proude hors þenne.
Þe wyʒe wynnez hym to and wytez on his lyre   2050
And sayde soberly hymself and by his soth swerez,
'Here is a meyny in þis mote þat on menske þenkkez.

2033–5. 'then he—happily (*swetely*), that knight—arranged his love-token twice about himself, wrapped it (*swepled*; or pp.) every inch (*Swype:* lit. much) about his waist; the girdle of green silk well suited the magnificent knight (*þat gay*)'. It is also possible to read *þe gordel of þe grene silke* as direct object of *swepled* and the rest of 2035 as a relative clause with relative pronoun omitted. The word-order of 2034 may be intended to convey an ironical tone (as at 2031).

2036. *ryol red cloþe:* i.e. his surcoat, which forms a red background to the gold pentangle; on his shield the pentangle is painted *Ryally wyth red golde vpon rede gowlez* (663). The poet's emphatic (and ironic) reference to the juxtaposition of pentangle and girdle is suggestive, for in failing to hand over the latter to the host he has fallen short of the high virtues symbolized by the former.

2041f. *of bronde . . . knyffe:* 'to defend him from sword or knife': parallel to *for to sauen hymself* 2040 (cf. 384: *Wyth what weppen so þou wylt* and 1853: *tohewe*).

2043–6. 'When the brave man accoutred (*boun:* ready) comes outside soon, he thanks all the noble household often and abundantly (*ful ryue*).' None of the household, except his servant, are present on this occasion, of course; he has, in fact, already said goodbye and thanked them individually the night before (1979–90). The quatrain is again an anticipatory summary of the following stanza (cf. 341f).

2049. 'that high mettled horse was in the mood to gallop then, because of his (fine) condition (*for poynt*).'

Þe mon hem maynteines, joy mot he haue;
Þe leue lady, on lyue luf hir bityde!
ʒif þay for charyté cherysen a gest   2055
And halden honour in her honde, þe Haþel hem ʒelde
Þat haldez þe heuen vpon hyʒe, and also yow alle!
And ʒif I myʒt lyf vpon londe lede any quyle,
I schuld rech yow sum rewarde redyly, if I myʒt.'
Þenn steppez he into stirop and strydez alofte;   2060
His schalk schewed hym his schelde, on schulder he hit laʒt,
Gordez to Gryngolet with his gilt helez,
And he startez on þe ston, stod he no lenger
        To praunce.
    His haþel on hors watz þenne,   2065
    Þat bere his spere and launce.
    'Þis kastel to Kryst I kenne,'
    He gef hit ay god chaunce.

The brygge watz brayde doun, and þe brode ʒatez
Vnbarred and born open vpon boþe halue.   2070
Þe burne blessed hym bilyue and þe bredez passed,
Prayses þe porter bifore þe prynce kneled—
Gef hym God and goud day, þat Gawayn He saue—
And went on his way with his wyʒe one,
Þat schulde teche hym to tourne to þat tene place   2075
Þer þe ruful race he schulde resayue.
Þay boʒen bi bonkkez þer boʒez ar bare;
Þay clomben bi clyffez þer clengez þe colde.

2053. he (Gollancz)] MS þay

2053f. 'The man (who) supports them, may he have joy; the dear lady—may she be
loved while she lives!' Gollancz's emendation of 2053 is justified by the parallel
structure of 2054.
2056. *And ... honde:* 'and dispense favour (hospitality)'.
2057. *and ... alle!:* addressed (*in petto*) to the whole household (cf. 2043-6n).
2061. *His schalk* (also *His haþel* 2065): the guide allotted to him, who acted as his
squire. He hands over Gawain's helmet and lance at 2143.
2068. 'He wished it good fortune for ever.' Alternatively, the line can be read as part
of Gawain's wish: 'may He give it good fortune for ever.'
2072f. '(he) compliments the porter (who) knelt before the prince (cf. 818)—(and the
porter) wished him good day and commended him to God, (praying) that He would
save Gawain'. 2073 is a compressed, indirect-speech rendering of three greetings: (*I*)
gif yow Gode 'I commend you to God', (*God*) *gif yow goud day* (see *OED good day*), and
God saue yow. The syllepsis *gif yow God and goud day* may have been used in direct
speech too. A close parallel to 2073f is found in *Le Bone Florence*:
    And betaght hur god and gode day
    And bad hur wende on hur way
Cf. also 1029, 2068, and—for an indirect rendering of *God blesse yow*—1296n.

Þe heuen watz vphalt, bot vgly þervnder.
Mist muged on þe mor, malt on þe mountez;   2080
Vch hille hade a hatte, a myst-hakel huge.
Brokez byled and breke bi bonkkez aboute,
Schyre schaterande on schorez, þer þay doun schowued.
Wela wylle watz þe way þer þay bi wod schulden,   [f119ʳ]
Til hit watz sone sesoun þat þe sunne ryses   2085
    Þat tyde.
      Þay were on a hille ful hyȝe;
      Þe quyte snaw lay bisyde.
      Þe burne þat rod hym by
      Bede his mayster abide.   2090

For I haf wonnen yow hider, wyȝe, at þis tyme,
And now nar ȝe not fer fro þat note place
Þat ȝe han spied and spuryed so specially after.
Bot I schal say yow for soþe, syþen I yow knowe
And ȝe ar a lede vpon lyue þat I wel louy: 2095
Wolde ȝe worch bi my wytte, ȝe worþed þe better.
Þe place þat ȝe prece to ful perelous is halden:
Þer wonez a wyȝe in þat waste, þe worst vpon erþe,
For he is stiffe and sturne and to strike louies,
And more he is þen any mon vpon myddelerde,   2100
And his body bigger þen þe best fowre
Þat ar in Arþurez hous, Hestor, oþer oþer.
He cheuez þat chaunce at þe Chapel Grene,
Þer passes non bi þat place so proude in his armes
Þat he ne dyngez hym to deþe with dynt of his honde;   2105
For he is a mon methles and mercy non vses.
For be hit chorle oþer chaplayn þat bi þe chapel rydes,
Monk oþer masseprest, oþer any mon elles,
Hym þynk as queme hym to quelle as quyk go hymseluen.
Forþy I say þe: as soþe as ȝe in sadel sitte,   2110

2105. dyngez (Napier)] MS dynnez

2079. 'The clouds were high (*vphalt:* drawn up) but threatening beneath.'
2081. *myst-hakel:* 'cap-cloud' (*lit.* 'cape of mist'—a poetic compound of a type very common in OE but less so in ME alliterative poetry).
2082–4. 'Brooks bubbled and splashed on the hillsides round about, dashing white on the banks, where they (the riders) made their way down. The path which they had to take through the wood was very devious (*wylle*)'.
2086. 'at that time of year.'
2096. 'if you would act according to my judgement it would be the better for you.'
2102. *Hestor:* either a variant of *Hector* (of Troy) or less probably a reference to the Arthurian knight Hector de la Mare.
2109. 'it seems to him as pleasant a thing to kill him as to remain alive himself.' Perhaps: 'killing is second nature to him.'

Com ӡe þere, ӡe be kylled, may þe knyӡt rede,—
Trawe ӡe me þat trwely—þaӡ ӡe had twenty lyues
   To spende.
He hatz wonyd here ful ӡore,
On bent much baret bende;   2115
Aӡayn his dyntez sore
Ӡe may not yow defende.

'Forþy, goude Sir Gawayn, let þe gome one
And gotz away sum oþer gate, vpon Goddez halue!
Cayrez bi sum oþer kyth, þer Kryst mot yow spede!   2120
And I schal hyӡ me hom aӡayn; and hete yow fyrre
Þat I schal swere "Bi God and alle His gode halӡez",   [f 119ᵛ]
"As help me God and þe halydam", and oþez innoghe,
Þat I schal lelly yow layne and lauce neuer tale
Þat euer ӡe fondet to fle for freke þat I wyst.'   2125
'Grant merci,' quoþ Gawayn, and gruchyng he sayde,
'Wel worth þe, wyӡe, þat woldez my gode,
And þat lelly me layne I leue wel þou woldez;
Bot helde þou hit neuer so holde, and I here passed,
Founded for ferde for to fle, in fourme þat þou tellez,   2130
I were a knyӡt kowarde, I myӡt not be excused.
Bot I wyl to þe chapel, for chaunce þat may falle,
And talk wyth þat ilk tulk þe tale þat me lyste,
Worþe hit wele oþer wo, as þe Wyrde lykez
   Hit hafe.   2135

2131. not] MS mot

2111. 'if you go there you will be killed, if the knight has his way' (for *rede* 'manage', cf. 373). Sisam, however (*Fourteenth Century Verse and Prose*, 219f), suggests the emendation: *may* [*y*] *þe, knyӡt, rede* 'I may warn you (*þe*), knight'; *þe/ӡe* variation is exemplified also in 2110. In some ways this is to be preferred, for the guide does not otherwise refer to the guardian of the chapel as a knight and, indeed, his notion of him would make that title seem inappropriate (cf. 2137n). It would be pressing inference too far to suppose that the word *knyӡt* here is a slip of the tongue occasioned by his knowledge that the Green Knight is really Sir Bertilak, but cf. E. M. Wright, *JEGP*, 34 (1935), 157–79.
2114. *ful ӡore:* 'for a long time'; Burrow notes that this conflicts with Sir Bertilak's own statement at 2459ff.
2123. *As . . . halydam:* 'As may God and the holy object help me'—a form of oath which originated in the practice of swearing on a sacred relic.
2125. 'that you ever attempted to flee because of any man I (ever) knew.'
2127. 'Good luck befall you, man, who intended to benefit me'.
2129. 'but no matter how faithfully you kept it, if I passed this place'.
2131. *I myӡt not:* 'I could not'.
2132. 'But I am determined to go to the chapel whatever happens'.
2134f. 'whether good or ill come of it, as Providence sees fit to dispose.' *Wyrde:* cf. 2138 and *Pat* 247n.

Þaȝe he be a sturn knape
To stiȝtel, and stad with staue,
Ful wel con Dryȝtyn schape
His seruauntez for to saue.'

'Mary!' quoþ þat oþer mon, 'now þou so much spellez   2140
Þat þou wylt þyn awen nye nyme to þyseluen
And þe lyst lese þy lyf, þe lette I ne kepe.
Haf here þi helme on þy hede, þi spere in þi honde,
And ryde me doun þis ilk rake, bi ȝon rokke syde,
Til þou be broȝt to þe boþem of þe brem valay.   2145
Þenne loke a littel on þe launde, on þi lyfte honde,
And þou schal se in þat slade þe self chapel
And þe borelych burne on bent þat hit kepez.
Now farez wel, on Godez half, Gawayn þe noble!
For alle þe golde vpon grounde I nolde go wyth þe,   2150
Ne bere þe felaȝschip þurȝ þis fryth on fote fyrre.'
Bi þat þe wyȝe in þe wod wendez his brydel,
Hit þe hors with þe helez as harde as he myȝt,
Lepez hym ouer þe launde, and leuez þe knyȝt þere
     Alone.   2155
     'Bi Goddez Self,' quoþ Gawayn,
     'I wyl nauþer grete ne grone;
     To Goddez wylle I am ful bayn
     And to Hym I haf me tone.'

Thenne gyrdez he to Gryngolet and gederez þe rake,   [f 120ʳ]   2160
Schowuez in bi a schore at a schaȝe syde,
Ridez þurȝ þe roȝe bonk ryȝt to þe dale.
And þenne he wayted hym aboute, and wylde hit hym þoȝt,
And seȝe no syngne of resette bisydez nowhere,
Bot hyȝe bonkkez and brent vpon boþe halue   2165

2137. and] MS and and
2150. go] MS ge

2137. *and stad with staue:* 'and armed with a club'. Gawain echoes the guide's description of the guardian of the chapel as a wild man of the woods, though there is no apparent reason for him to conceal the fact that he knows the Green Knight; if it is not a slip on the poet's part, we may perhaps interpret it as wishful thinking: Gawain would no doubt prefer an encounter with an ordinary *wodwos* (cf. 721) to another meeting with the Green Knight.
2142. and it pleases you to lose your life, I do not care to dissuade you.'
2144. *me:* see 1905n.
2151. *on fote fyrre:* 'one foot further'.
2161f. 'pushes in, past a rock (*schore*—the *rokke* of 2144), at the edge of a thicket, rides down through the wooded slope right to the bottom.'

And ruȝe knokled knarrez with knorned stonez;
Þe skwez of þe scowtes skayned hym þoȝt.
Þenne he houed and wythhylde his hors at þat tyde
And ofte chaunged his cher þe chapel to seche.
He seȝ non suche in no syde—and selly hym þoȝt— 2170
Saue, a lyttel on a launde, a lawe as hit were,
A balȝ berȝ bi a bonke þe brymme bysyde,
Bi a forȝ of a flode þat ferked þare;
Þe borne blubred þerinne as hit boyled hade.
Þe knyȝt kachez his caple and com to þe lawe, 2175
Liȝtez doun luflyly and at a lynde tachez
Þe rayne of his riche, with a roȝe braunche.
Þenne he boȝez to þe berȝe, aboute hit he walkez,
Debatande with hymself quat hit be myȝt.
Hit hade a hole on þe ende and on ayþer syde, 2180
And ouergrowen with gresse in glodes aywhere,
And al watz holȝ inwith, nobot an olde caue
Or a creuisse of an olde cragge—he couþe hit noȝt deme
　　With spelle.
　'We! Lorde,' quoþ þe gentyle knyȝt, 2185
　'Wheþer þis be þe Grene Chapelle?
　Here myȝt aboute mydnyȝt
　Þe Dele his matynnes telle!'

'Now iwysse,' quoþ Wowayn, 'wysty is here;
Þis oritore is vgly, with erbez ouergrowen. 2190
Wel bisemez þe wyȝe wruxled in grene
Dele here his deuocioun on þe Deuelez wyse;
Now I fele hit is þe Fende, in my fyue wyttez,
Þat hatz stoken me þis steuen to strye me here.

　　2171. were] MS we
　　2177. of] MS and (τ)
　　2178–82. MS *blurred at left; some readings from offset on f119ᵛ*
　　2187. Here] MS he

2166f. 'and rough, lumpy crags with rugged outcrops; the clouds seemed to him to be grazed (*skayned*) by (*of*) the jutting rocks (*scowtes*).'
2171–4. 'except, at a short distance across a glade, a sort of knoll, a smooth-surfaced barrow (*berȝ*) on the side of (*bi*) a slope beside the water's edge, by the channel (*forȝ*) of a stream which passed there; the burn surged in it (i.e. the channel) as if it were boiling.' For the construction of the last clause, cf. 2202, *Cl* 1466, 1484.
2183f. *he . . . spelle:* 'he could not say which it was.'
2186–8. 'is this the green chapel? The Devil might well recite his matins here about midnight!' In monastic houses, matins, the first of the canonical hours, were sung before daybreak; however, midnight is probably mentioned here as an appropriate hour for the Devil's.
2193. 'now I feel, in my five senses, that it is the Devil'.

Þis is a chapel of meschaunce, þat chekke hit bytyde!   2195
Hit is þe corsedest kyrk þat euer I com inne!'
With heȝe helme on his hede, his launce in his honde,   [f120ᵛ]
He romez vp to þe roffe of þo roȝ wonez.
Þene herde he of þat hyȝe hil, in a harde roche
Biȝonde þe broke, in a bonk, a wonder breme noyse.   2200
Quat! hit clatered in þe clyff as hit cleue schulde,
As one vpon a gryndelston hade grounden a syþe.
What! hit wharred and whette as water at a mulne;
What! hit rusched and ronge, rawþe to here.
Þenne 'Bi Godde,' quoþ Gawayn, 'þat gere, as I trowe,   2205
Is ryched at þe reuerence me renk to mete
      Bi rote.
   Let God worche! "We loo!"
   Hit helppez me not a mote.
   My lif þaȝ I forgoo,   2210
   Drede dotz me no lote.'

Thenne þe knyȝt con calle ful hyȝe,

2205. as (Madden)] MS at

2195. 'This is a chapel of doom, ill fortune befall it!' *þat . . . hit:* 'which'.

2199f. Presumably *þat hyȝe hil* refers to the hill he is standing on (or the 'chapel' itself) and in *a harde roche Biȝonde þe broke, in a bonk* to the source of the noise. See 2221n.

2201-4. *as hit . . .:* 'as if it (the cliff) would split, as if someone were grinding a scythe upon a grindstone (for syntax cf. 2174). What! it whirred and ground like water at a mill; what! it swished and rang, ghastly to hear.' *Quat!:* as also in OE (*Hwæt!*), the word is an exclamation of surprise or a call for attention; here it may also be intended to echo the sound itself (cf. 1163—the sound of the arrow?).

2206f. These lines have not been satisfactorily explained. The following interpretation (cf. TG, p. 117) suits the stress-pattern best, for it elevates *renk*, as the alliteration seems to demand: '(that contrivance, as I believe) is being prepared (*ryched*) in honour of (*at þe reuerence*) marking out (*to mete*, lit. measure) the field of combat (*renk*) for me, with due ceremony (*Bi rote*).' Though there is no direct evidence, *me renk to mete* is presumed to have a metaphorical sense 'to challenge me to a duel'; the syntactical pattern would be that of *me steuen to holde* 2213. Other interpretations are possible if we allow an extra stress on *me* and put it before the caesura (perhaps cross-alliterating with *mete*): e.g. 'in honour of me, in order to meet a knight (*renk*) with due ceremony.'

2208-11. 'Let God's will be done! (To cry) "Alas!" will not help me a bit. Even though I lose my life, no noise (*lote*) shall make me fear (*Drede* v.)'. Cf. the Vernon poem *Deo Gracias* I, 45-8:

   Though I weore out of bonchef brought,
      What help weore to me to seye 'Allas!'
   In the nome of God, whatever be wrought,
      I schal seie, '*Deo gracias.*'

(*Minor Poems of the Vernon MS*, ed. by C. Horstmann and F. J. Furnivall [EETS OS 98, 117], II, 665).

'Who stiȝtlez in þis sted, me steuen to holde?
For now is gode Gawayn goande ryȝt here.
If any wyȝe oȝt wyl, wynne hider fast,   2215
Oþer now oþer neuer, his nedez to spede.'
'Abyde!' quoþ on on þe bonke abouen ouer his hede,
'And þou schal haf al in hast þat I þe hyȝt ones.'
Ȝet he rusched on þat rurde rapely a þrowe
And wyth quettyng awharf, er he wolde lyȝt;   2220
And syþen he keuerez bi a cragge and comez of a hole,
Whyrlande out of a wro wyth a felle weppen:
A denez ax, nwe dyȝt, þe dynt with to ȝelde,
With a borelych bytte bende by þe halme,
Fyled in a fylor, fowre fote large—   2225
Hit watz no lasse, bi þat lace þat lemed ful bryȝt!—
And þe gome in þe grene gered as fyrst,
Boþe þe lyre and þe leggez, lokkez and berde,
Saue þat fayre on his fote he foundez on þe erþe,
Sette þe stele to þe stone and stalked bysyde.   2230
When he wan to þe watter, þer he wade nolde,
He hypped ouer on hys ax and orpedly strydez,
Bremly broþe on a bent þat brode watz aboute,
      On snawe.

2223. with to (Madden)] MS witho

2215. *oȝt wyl:* 'wants anything'; *wynne:* (subjunc.) 'let him come'.
2219f. 'Still he swished on hastily with that noise for a while (*þrowe*) and turned back (*awharf*) to his sharpening before he would come down'.
2221. The Green Knight (who is standing on the hill at the opposite side of the stream from Gawain) appears to descend by some sort of hidden passage. From the allusive nature of the description it would appear that the poet had an actual site in mind. This has been variously identified, but most convincingly by M. Day (in the introduction to the Gollancz edn., p. xx) as Wetton Mill, Staffs. Further discussion of implications for the text is provided by R. E. Kaske in *Medieval Literature and Folklore Studies: Essays in Honor of Francis Lee Utley*, ed. Jerome Mandel and B. A. Rosenberg (New Brunswick, N.J., 1970), pp. 111–21.
2225f. 'sharpened on a grindstone, four feet wide (i.e. from point to point)—it was no less, by that belt which shone very brightly!' In describing the earlier axe, the poet mentions a *lace* ('cord') which is wrapped about its handle (217–20); if a similar cord is alluded to here, however, it is difficult to see how it could play any part in an observer's assessment of the size of the blade. The best solution is that *bi . . . bryȝt* is an oath on the green girdle (cf. the description at 2038f), spoken *in petto* by Gawain; at the moment when he sees the axe, with its huge blade, it is understandable that his thoughts should fly to his magic charm. See S. Malarky and J. B. Toelken, *JEGP*, 63 (1964), 14–20, (repr. in Howard and Zacher, **7d** 1968).
2233. 'a fiercely violent creature against a broad field'; the point of view is Gawain's.
2234. *On snawe:* complements *strydez*.

Sir Gawayn þe knyȝt con mete; [f121ʳ] 2235
He ne lutte hym noþyng lowe.
Þat oþer sayde, 'Now, sir swete,
Of steuen mon may þe trowe.'

'Gawayn,' quoþ þat grene gome, 'God þe mot loke!
Iwysse þou art welcom, wyȝe, to my place, 2240
And þou hatz tymed þi trauayl as truee mon schulde;
And þou knowez þe couenauntez kest vus bytwene:
At þis tyme twelmonyth þou toke þat þe falled
And I schulde at þis Nwe Ȝere ȝeply þe quyte.
And we ar in þis valay verayly oure one; 2245
Here ar no renkes vs to rydde, rele as vus likez.
Haf þy helme of þy hede and haf here þy pay.
Busk no more debate þen I þe bede þenne
When þou wypped of my hede at a wap one.'
'Nay, bi God,' quoþ Gawayn, 'þat me gost lante, 2250
I schal gruch þe no grwe, for grem þat fallez;
Bot styȝtel þe vpon on strok and I schal stonde stylle
And warp þe no wernyng to worch as þe lykez
      Nowhare.'
      He lened with þe nek and lutte 2255
      And schewed þat schyre al bare,
      And lette as he noȝt dutte;
      For drede he wolde not dare.

Then þe gome in þe grene grayþed hym swyþe,
Gederez vp hys grymme tole, Gawayn to smyte; 2260
With alle þe bur in his body he ber hit on lofte,

2240. welcom] MS welcon
2247. þy helme] MS þy þy helme

2235–8. 'Sir Gawain greeted the knight, (but) hardly bowed to him at all. The latter said, "So, my dear sir, you can be trusted to keep an appointment."'
2239. *God þe mot loke!*: 'God guard you!' Cf. the greeting of the old man in Chaucer's 'Pardoner's Tale' (*CT* VI.715): 'Now, lordes, God yow see!'
2243. 'Twelve months ago at this time of year you were to take what fell to your lot' (i.e. the right to deliver the first blow); *þou toke* could be pa.t. subjunc. or pa.t. indic. but since the Green Knight is summarizing the terms of the agreement rather than what happened we should interpret it as subjunc.
2250. *þat me gost lante:* 'who gave me a soul'.
2251. 'I shall not bear you the slightest ill-will (*no grwe:* not a bit) whatever injury befalls me'.
2254. Can be understood literally: 'anywhere', 'here or anywhere else'. Gawain implies that the remoteness of the valley is immaterial, provided that the Green Knight intends to stick to the single blow of the agreement. *Bot* (2252): 'only'.
2257f. 'and acted as if he feared nothing; he did not intend to flinch for fear.'

Munt as maȝtyly as marre hym he wolde.
Hade hit dryuen adoun as dreȝ as he atled,
Þer hade ben ded of his dynt þat doȝty watz euer.
Bot Gawayn on þat giserne glyfte hym bysyde,   2265
As hit com glydande adoun on glode hym to schende,
And schranke a lytel with þe schulderes for þe scharp yrne.
Þat oþer schalk wyth a schunt þe schene wythhaldez
And þenne repreued he þe prynce with mony prowde wordez:
'Þou art not Gawayn,' quoþ þe gome, 'þat is so goud halden,   2270
Þat neuer arȝed for no here by hylle ne be vale,
And now þou fles for ferde er þou fele harmez!   [f 121ᵛ]
Such cowardise of þat knyȝt cowþe I neuer here.
Nawþer fyked I ne flaȝe, freke, quen þou myntest,
Ne kest no kauelacion in kyngez hous Arthor.   2275
My hede flaȝ to my fote and ȝet flaȝ I neuer;
And þou, er any harme hent, arȝez in hert.
Wherfore þe better burne me burde be called
      Þerfore.'
          Quoþ Gawayn, 'I schunt onez   2280
          And so wyl I no more;
          Bot þaȝ my hede falle on þe stonez
          I con not hit restore.

'Bot busk, burne, bi þi fayth, and bryng me to þe poynt—
Dele to me my destiné and do hit out of honde.   2285
For I schal stonde þe a strok and start no more
Til þyn ax haue me hitte—haf here my trawþe.'
'Haf at þe þenne!' quoþ þat oþer, and heuez hit alofte
And waytez as wroþely as he wode were.
He myntez at hym maȝtyly bot not þe mon rynez,   2290
Withhelde heterly his honde er hit hurt myȝt.
Gawayn grayþely hit bydez and glent with no membre
Bot stode stylle as þe ston oþer a stubbe auþer

2291. his] MS hs

2262. 'aimed (a blow) at him as forcibly as if he intended to destroy him.'
2264. 'he who was ever brave (i.e. Gawain) would have died there from his blow.'
2265. *glyfte hym bysyde:* 'glanced sideways'.
2273. *cowþe I neuer here:* 'I never did hear'; cf. *Cl* 1–4n.
2276. A play on words: *flaȝ* (1) 'flew', *flaȝ* (2) 'fled'.
2277. *er any harme hent:* absolute use of the past participle; cf. the modern 'no offence taken'.
2284f. *out of honde:* The fact that this is the earliest recorded instance of this phrase (*OED* and *MED*), as of *Haf at þe* (2288), reinforces the impression that the language of the speeches is often extremely up to date and colloquial; *bryng me to þe poynt:* 'come to the point with me'—but also a play on words (cf. 2392).
2293f. 'but stood as steady as the rock, or else a stump that is anchored in rocky soil with a hundred roots.'

Þat raþeled is in roché grounde with rotez a hundreth.
Þen muryly efte con he mele, þe mon in þe grene: 2295
'So, now þou hatz þi hert holle hitte me bihous.
Halde þe now þe hy3e hode þat Arþur þe ra3t
And kepe þy kanel at þis kest, 3if hit keuer may!'
Gawayn ful gryndelly with greme þenne sayde:
'Wy, þresch on, þou þro mon! Þou þretez to longe.   2300
I hope þat þi hert ar3e wyth þyn awen seluen.'
'Forsoþe,' quoþ þat oþer freke, 'so felly þou spekez,
I wyl no lenger on lyte lette þin ernde
    Ri3t nowe.'
    Þenne tas he hym stryþe to stryke   2305
    And frounsez boþe lyppe and browe.
    No meruayle þa3 hym myslyke
    Þat hoped of no rescowe.

He lyftes ly3tly his lome and let hit doun fayre
With þe barbe of þe bitte bi þe bare nek.   [f 122ʳ]   2310
Þa3 he homered heterly, hurt hym no more
Bot snyrt hym on þat on syde, þat seuered þe hyde.
Þe scharp schrank to þe flesche þur3 þe schyre grece,
Þat þe schene blod ouer his schulderes schot to þe erþe.
And quen þe burne se3 þe blode blenk on þe snawe,   2315
He sprit forth spenne-fote more þen a spere lenþe,
Hent heterly his helme and on his hed cast,
Schot with his schulderez his fayre schelde vnder,

2305. he] MS he he

2297f. 'May the noble order (*hy3e hode*—i.e. the order of knighthood) which Arthur bestowed upon you keep you now and (may it) preserve your neck at this stroke, if it is able to accomplish it!' Although Gawain does not realize it at this point, the outcome of the beheading game is made dependent on his conduct during his last three days in the castle. The Green Knight is implying, 'Let us see if your knighthood enabled you to resist the temptations of the third day.'

2301. 'I believe that you have struck fear into your own heart (*lit.* 'that your heart is afraid of yourself', or possibly 'within yourself'—cf. 1660).'

2307f. 'No wonder if it displease him who expected no rescue.' Cf. note to 1768f.

2311f. *no more Bot:* 'no more than (to)'.

2316. *spenne-fote:* 'with feet together'; Gawain's instinctive reaction is an unprepared standing-jump.

2318. *vnder* is an adv. 'down': 'with his shoulders he jerked down his fair shield'. Gawain is carrying his shield slung on his shoulder in readiness (cf. 2061, and contrast 621); the jerk is evidently a practised movement to make it slide down the left arm while he draws his sword with the other hand. The word can hardly imply that Gawain 'swung it under his arm' (TG-Davis n): such a movement could not have been performed easily and quickly enough, even with the relatively small 14th c. shield, and would, in any case, have brought the shield to the front upside-down.

Braydez out a bryȝt sworde and bremely he spekez—
Neuer syn þat he watz barne borne of his moder   2320
Watz he neuer in þis worlde wyȝe half so blyþe—
'Blynne, burne, of þy bur! Bede me no mo!
I haf a stroke in þis sted withoute stryf hent
And if þow rechez me any mo I redyly schal quyte
And ȝelde ȝederly aȝayn—and þerto ȝe tryst—   2325
          And foo.
     Bot on stroke here me fallez—
     Þe couenaunt schop ryȝt so,
     Festned in Arþurez hallez—
     And þerfore, hende, now hoo!'   2330

The haþel heldet hym fro and on his ax rested,
Sette þe schaft vpon schore and to þe scharp lened
And loked to þe leude þat on þe launde ȝede,
How þat doȝty, dredles, deruely þer stondez,
Armed ful aȝlez; in hert hit hym lykez.   2335
Þenn he melez muryly wyth a much steuen
And, wyth a rynkande rurde, he to þe renk sayde,
'Bolde burne, on þis bent be not so gryndel.
No mon here vnmanerly þe mysboden habbez,
Ne kyd bot as couenaunde at kyngez kort schaped.   2340
I hyȝt þe a strok and þou hit hatz—halde þe wel payed.
I relece þe of þe remnaunt of ryȝtes alle oþer.

2320. barne (S. O. Andrew)]: MS burne
2329. Festned (Cawley)] MS *nearly illegible* (Menner: fermed; Gollancz: fettled)
2337. rynkande (Napier)] MS rykande
2339. habbez (Napier)] MS habbe

2320f. The redundancy and slight incoherence of the poet's description suggest a jumble of feelings (cf. 2334f).
2326. 'and in hostility': i.e. 'in earnest'. Gawain is saying that he will no longer consider himself bound by the rules of the game, but will fight.
2327. 'Only one stroke falls to my lot here'.
2330. W. A. Davenport (*ELN*, 11 [1973], 88f) points out that *hoo* 'stop' occurs elsewhere in the context of chivalrous encounters; he suggests that, with *hende*, its overtones would remind the Green Knight of gentlemanly codes of conduct.
2331. *heldet hym fro:* 'moved away from him (i.e. Gawain)'.
2338. *be not so gryndel:* cf. *Pat* 524n.
2339f. 'No one has treated you discourteously here, nor acted otherwise than as the covenant at the king's court laid down.'
2342–4. 'I release you from all remaining obligations whatever. If I had been quick, I could perhaps have repaid a blow more harshly (and) have done you harm.' Bennett, **5d** 1976, suggests that *Iif* (MS *iif*) is an error for *nif*, which yields the more logical sense 'If I had *not* been dexterous I could perhaps have dealt you a blow to your harm.'

Iif I deliuer had bene, a boffet paraunter
I couþe wroþeloker haf waret, to þe haf wroȝt anger.
Fyrst I mansed þe muryly with a mynt one   2345
And roue þe wyth no rof-sore. With ryȝt I þe profered
For þe forwarde þat we fest in þe fyrst nyȝt;   [f 122ᵛ]
And þou trystyly þe trawþe and trwly me haldez:
Al þe gayne þow me gef, as god mon schulde.
Þat oþer munt for þe morne, mon, I þe profered: 2350
Þou kyssedes my clere wyf, þe cossez me raȝtez.
For boþe two here I þe bede bot two bare myntes
    Boute scaþe.
   Trwe mon trwe restore;
   Þenne þar mon drede no waþe.   2355
   At þe þrid þou fayled þore,
   And þerfor þat tappe ta þe.

For hit is my wede þat þou werez, þat ilke wouen girdel.
Myn owen wyf hit þe weued, I wot wel forsoþe.
Now know I wel þy cosses and þy costes als,   2360
And þe wowyng of my wyf. I wroȝt hit myseluen;
I sende hir to asay þe, and sothly me þynkkez
On þe fautlest freke þat euer on fote ȝede.
As perle bi þe quite pese is of prys more,
So is Gawayn, in god fayth, bi oþer gay knyȝtez.   2365
Bot here yow lakked a lyttel, sir, and lewté yow wonted;

2347. In the phrase *þe fyrst nyȝt* the host appears to conflate the evening *before* the first hunt, when the agreement was first made (*fest*), with the evening *of* the hunt, when it was carried out; the *morne* of 2350 is evidently the day of the second hunt.

2348. 'and you faithfully and honestly kept (*lit.* keep) your pledge to me'.

2354f. 'A true person must (*mon*) restore truly; then one (*mon*) need (*þar*) fear no danger.'

2356. *þore:* 'there', 'in that respect'—i.e. in honesty.

2357. *ta þe:* imperative sing. (reflex.), '(you must) take'.

2359. *Myn . . . weued:* 'My own wife gave it to you'.

2361. *þe wowyng of my wife:* 'my wife's wooing (of you)'.

2361f. While the shape-shifting and the beheading game are later attributed to the agency of Morgan (2446ff), the Green Knight himself here emphatically assumes responsibility for the testing of Gawain in his castle.

2362. *me þynkkez:* either 'you seem to me' or 'it seems to me (that you are)'.

2363. 'the most (cf. 137n) faultless knight who ever lived (*lit.* walked).'

2364. 'As the pearl in comparison with (*bi*) the white (i.e. dried) pea is of greater value'; *pese* is the old singular form.

2365. *in god fayth:* perhaps more than an exclamation—'in respect of good faith'.

2366. *here:* 'in this respect' (cf. *Pat* 520n); *yow lakked a lyttel* is impersonal: 'a little was lacking to you', i.e. 'you fell short a little'. The construction of *lewté yow wonted* is similar.

Bot þat watz for no wylyde werke, ne wowyng nauþer,
Bot for ȝe lufed your lyf—þe lasse I yow blame.'
Þat oþer stif mon in study stod a gret whyle,
So agreued for greme he gryed withinne;   2370
Alle þe blode of his brest blende in his face,
Þat al he schrank for schome þat þe schalk talked.
Þe forme worde vpon folde þat þe freke meled:
'Corsed worth cowarddyse and couetyse boþe!
In yow is vylany and vyse, þat vertue disstryez.'   2375
Þenne he kaȝt to þe knot and þe kest lawsez,
Brayde broþely þe belt to þe burne seluen:
'Lo! þer þe falssyng—foule mot hit falle!
For care of þy knokke, cowardyse me taȝt
To acorde me with couetyse, my kynde to forsake: 2380
Þat is larges and lewté, þat longez to knyȝtez.
Now am I fawty and falce, and ferde haf ben euer
Of trecherye and vntrawþe—boþe bityde sorȝe
        And care!
    I biknowe yow, knyȝt, here stylle,   [f123ʳ] 2385
    Al fawty is my fare.
    Letez me ouertake your wylle
    And efte I schal be ware.'

Thenn loȝe þat oþer leude and luflyly sayde,
'I halde hit hardily hole, þe harme þat I hade.   2390
Þou art confessed so clene, beknowen of þy mysses,
And hatz þe penaunce apert of þe poynt of myn egge,
I halde þe polysed of þat plyȝt and pured as clene
As þou hadez neuer forfeted syþen þou watz fyrst borne.
And I gif þe, sir, þe gurdel þat is golde-hemmed;   2395
For hit is grene as my goune, Sir Gawayn, ȝe maye
Þenk vpon þis ilke þrepe þer þou forth þryngez

2390. hardily] MS hardilyly

2367. *wylyde werke:* probably 'intricate (skilled) workmanship' (i.e. of the girdle); cf.
2430–2 and (for the author's statement of Gawain's motives) 2037–40.
2372. *þat . . . talked:* '(at) what the man said.'
2382–4. 'Now I am sinful and dishonourable, I who have always been afraid of
treachery and dishonesty—may sorrow and care betide both of them!'
2387. 'Let me understand your wish' (i.e. in respect of 'penance'). For both men the
scene takes on the character of a chivalric 'confession'; cf. 2390ff, and notes to
1876–84 and 2445.
2396–9. 'because it is green like my gown (tunic), Sir Gawain, you may think about
this bout of ours where you go back (*lit.* mingle forth) among noble princes, and
this will be (*þis:* an ellipsis for 'this is') a perfect (or noble) token of the exploit of
the Green Chapel in the dwellings of (*at*) chivalrous knights.' Note that it is Gawain
(2433ff) who stresses the humbling effect of the girdle; the Green Knight evidently
has in mind a social scene, like that of 2513–21.

Among prynces of prys, and þis a pure token
Of þe chaunce of þe Grene Chapel at cheualrous knyȝtez.
And ȝe schal in þis Nwe ȝer aȝayn to my wonez   2400
And we schyn reuel þe remnaunt of þis ryche fest
    Ful bene.'
    Þer laþed hym fast þe lorde
    And sayde, 'With my wyf, I wene,
    We schal yow wel acorde,   2405
    Þat watz your enmy kene.'

'Nay forsoþe,' quoþ þe segge, and sesed hys helme
And hatz hit of hendely and þe haþel þonkkez,
'I haf sojorned sadly—sele yow bytyde,
And He ȝelde hit yow ȝare þat ȝarkkez al menskes! ·   2410
And comaundez me to þat cortays, your comlych fere,
Boþe þat on and þat oþer, myn honoured ladyez,
Þat þus hor knyȝt wyth hor kest han koyntly bigyled.
Bot hit is no ferly þaȝ a fole madde
And þurȝ wyles of wymmen be wonen to sorȝe;   2415
For so watz Adam in erde with one bygyled,
And Salamon with fele sere, and Samson, eftsonez—
Dalyda dalt hym hys wyrde—and Dauyth, þerafter,
Watz blended with Barsabe, þat much bale þoled.
Now þese were wrathed wyth her wyles, hit were a wynne huge   2420
To luf hom wel and leue hem not, a leude þat couþe.
For þes wer forne þe freest, þat folȝed alle þe sele   [f 123ᵛ]
Exellently, of alle þyse oþer vnder heuen-ryche
    Þat mused;

2400. The infinitive 'come' is understood after *schal* 'must'; *aȝayn:* 'back'.
2401. *þe remnaunt:* probably adverbial, '(for) the remainder'.
2408. *hatz hit of:* 'takes it off'.
2417f. *eftsonez, þerafter:* 'next' or 'again' (in the succession of items in the list).
2419. *þat much bale þoled:* 'who suffered much grief'; qualifies *Dauyth* (cf. 145–6n). See
  2 Kgs. (AV 2 Sam.) 12 : 7–20.
2420–4. 'Since these were troubled by their wiles, it would be a great advantage
  (*wynne:* 'gain', or possibly 'joy') to love them well and not trust them (*leue:* believe),
  if a man could (*lit.* for a man who could). For these were of old the noblest, those
  who were pre-eminently (*Exellently*) favoured by fortune (*lit.* those whom all pro-
  sperity followed pre-eminently), of all those (*lit.* those others) upon earth (*vnder
  heuen-ryche*) who have wandered in mind'. The sense is: 'I have mentioned only the
  most noteworthy examples of the stupefying influence of women on men.' For the
  force of *þyse oþer*, cf. 1139n, 1914. For the sense of *mused* 'wandered in mind, doted',
  cf. Gavin Douglas *Aeneid* IV (*Poetical Works*, ed. J. Small [Edinburgh, 1874], II,
  164), Prologue 16: *Your curious thochtis quhat bot musardry* (in a list of love's contrar-
  ieties), and the OF, ME *musard* 'dreamer'. Some editors construe *Exellently* with *of*
  ('pre-eminently above') and take *mused* as 'thought' (= 'lived'); so 'whom all pro-
  sperity followed pre-eminently above all who lived on earth'.

And alle þay were biwyled   2425
With wymmen þat þay vsed.
Þaȝ I be now bigyled,
Me þink me burde be excused.

'Bot your gordel,' quoþ Gawayn, '—God yow forȝelde!—
Þat wyl I welde wyth guod wylle, not for þe wynne golde,   2430
Ne þe saynt, ne þe sylk, ne þe syde pendaundes,
For wele ne for worchyp, ne for þe wlonk werkkez;
Bot in syngne of my surfet I schal se hit ofte,
When I ride in renoun remorde to myseluen
Þe faut and þe fayntyse of þe flesche crabbed,   2435
How tender hit is to entyse teches of fylþe.
And þus, quen pryde schal me pryk for prowes of armes,
Þe loke to þis luf-lace schal leþe my hert.
Bot on I wolde yow pray, displeses yow neuer:
Syn ȝe be lorde of þe ȝonder londe þat I haf lent inne   2440
Wyth yow wyth worschyp—þe Wyȝe hit yow ȝelde
Þat vphaldez þe heuen and on hyȝ sittez—
How norne ȝe yowre ryȝt nome, and þenne no more?'
'Þat schal I telle þe trwly,' quoþ þat oþer þenne:
'Bertilak de Hautdesert I hat in þis londe.   2445

2426. With] MS with wyth

2425–8. 'And all these were deceived (*biwyled*) by women with whom they had rela-
tions. If I am now taken in, it seems to me that I ought to be excused.' Gawain's
'anti-feminism' has puzzled editors and commentators, since it seems 'scarcely in
keeping with the knight of courtesy' (Gollancz, p. 129). However, the tone of the
present stanza is very different from that of Gawain's speech at 2374–88, where he
bitterly condemns himself. The last line in particular (*Me þink me burde be excused*), if
taken quite seriously, would contradict everything else he says about his own culpab-
ility. Taken as a rueful witticism it echoes the tone of 2414 and 2420f and the speech
can be read as a tactful, half-jocular, use of the ecclesiastical commonplace of the
'eternal Eve' as a transition to the less impassioned, more urbane, conclusion of the
conversation. See also Brewer, **8** 1966, and D. Mills, *Neu.Mitt.*, 71 (1970), 635–40.
2431. 'nor for the girdle (itself) nor for the long (*syde* adj.) pendants'. Note the
chiasmus, 2430–1: *golde* . . . *saynt* . . . *sylk* . . . *pendaundes*. The speech from 2429 to
2438 is rhetorical in tone; perhaps Gawain is a little inclined to dramatize his
predicament.
2436. 'how liable it is to catch (*entyse*) blemishes (*teches*) of sin.' The analogy between
sin and disease is a medieval commonplace; cf. J. Huizinga, *The Waning of the Middle
Ages* (Harmondsworth, 1955), 221, and *Pe* 725n.
2438. 'the act of looking at this love-girdle shall humble (*leþe*) my heart.'
2439. *on:* 'one thing'.
2445. *de Hautdesert:* Since the Green Knight is here revealing his everyday name,
Hautdesert must be the name of his castle rather than another designation of the
Green Chapel. Nevertheless, the introduction of the title (? 'of the high hermitage')
at this point may remind us that the Green Knight performs some of the confessional
functions of the hermits of the spiritualized French Arthurian *Quest del saint Graal*; see

Þurȝ myȝt of Morgne la Faye, þat in my hous lenges,
And koyntyse of clergye, bi craftes wel lerned—
Þe maystrés of Merlyn mony ho hatz taken,
For ho hatz dalt drwry ful dere sumtyme
With þat conable klerk; þat knowes alle your knyȝtez   2450
    At hame.
    Morgne þe goddes
    Þerfore hit is hir name;
    Weldez non so hyȝe hawtesse
    Þat ho ne con make ful tame—   2455

'Ho wayned me vpon þis wyse to your wynne halle
For to assay þe surquidré, ȝif hit soth were
Þat rennes of þe grete renoun of þe Rounde Table;
Ho wayned me þis wonder your wyttez to reue,
For to haf greued Gaynour and gart hir to dyȝe   [f124ʳ]   2460
With glopnyng of þat ilke gome þat gostlych speked
With his hede in his honde bifore þe hyȝe table.
Þat is ho þat is at home, þe auncian lady;
Ho is euen þyn aunt, Arþurez half-suster,
Þe duches doȝter of Tyntagelle, þat dere Vter after   2465

2448. hatz (Madden)] MS *om.*
2461. glopnyng] MS gopnyng
     gome] MS gomen

Smithers, **7d** 1963. Henry, **7d** 1976, suggests, on the other hand, that the name may contain a pun on OF *haut desert* in the sense of 'great merit, high reward'.

2446ff. The loose conversational structure of this speech is comparable to that of 1508ff. Sir Bertilak picks up the thread in 2456, after the digression on the fame and history of Morgan.

2447–51. 'and (her) skill in learning, (she who is) well-instructed in magic arts—she has acquired many of the miraculous powers of Merlin, for she has formerly had very intimate love-dealings with that excellent scholar, as all your knights at home know.' For an alternative construction of 2447f, see Barron, note.

2454f. 'there is no one so exalted in pride (*hawtesse*) whom she cannot humble completely—'.

2456. *vpon þis wyse:* i.e. in his green guise.

2457–61. 'to make trial of your pride, (to see) if (the report) which is current, of the great renown of the Round Table, is true. She sent this marvel to deprive you of your senses, in order to distress Guenevere and cause her to die from terror at that man who spoke in supernatural manner (*gostlych*)'; *me* (2459) has possibly been miscopied from 2456, but can be taken as ethic dative, especially in this position in the line (see 1905n and cf. other examples given there).

2464. See 110n.

2465f. 'the daughter of the duchess of Tintagel (Igerne), upon whom the noble Uther later begot Arthur, who is now glorious.' The pointed contrast between Arthur's shameful origins (he was conceived out of wedlock) and present renown recalls one of the themes of the opening stanza of the poem (there in connection with Aeneas and Felix Brutus).

Hade Arþur vpon, þat aþel is nowþe.
Þerfore I eþe þe, haþel, to com to þyn aunt.
Make myry in my hous: my meny þe louies
And I wol þe as wel, wyȝe, bi my faythe,
As any gome vnder God, for þy grete trauþe.'   2470
And he nikked hym 'Naye!'—he nolde bi no wayes.
Þay acolen and kyssen and kennen ayþer oþer
To þe Prynce of paradise, and parten ryȝt þere
    On coolde.
      Gawayn on blonk ful bene   2475
      To þe kynges burȝ buskez bolde,
      And þe knyȝt in þe enker grene
      Whiderwarde-soeuer he wolde.

Wylde wayez in þe worlde Wowen now rydez
On Gryngolet, þat þe grace hade geten of his lyue;   2480
Ofte he herbered in house and ofte al þeroute,
And mony a venture in vale he venquyst ofte
Þat I ne tyȝt at þis tyme in tale to remene.
Þe hurt watz hole þat he hade hent in his nek
And þe blykkande belt he bere þeraboute,   2485
Abelef, as a bauderyk, bounden bi his syde,
Loken vnder his lyfte arme, þe lace, with a knot,
In tokenyng he watz tane in tech of a faute.
And þus he commes to þe court, knyȝt al in sounde.
Þer wakned wele in þat wone when wyst þe grete   2490

2472. and kennen (Tolkien and Gordon)] MS *om.* (Madden: bikennen)
2482. he (Gollancz)]: MS and (ꝥ)

2469f. 'and I bear you as much good will, sir, on my honour, as (I do) any man on earth, because of your great integrity.'
2471. See 706, 1045n.
2477f. See 460n.
2479f. 'Gawain, whose life had been reprieved, now rides wild pathways in the world on Gringolet'.
2481. *in house:* i.e. 'where he had a roof over his head'.
2482f. 'and many times overcame hazards in valleys, which I do not intend at this time to relate (*remene:* recall).' *In vale* is little more than a tag: cf. *in erde,* etc. The emendation normalizes the structure in respect of the relative clause (antecedent: *venture*), and resolves the ambiguity of *venquyst ofte* which (as it stands in the MS) could mean 'was often vanquished'. The scribe probably copied the ampersand from the line above, instead of *he*.
2488. 'in order to signify that he had been found guilty of a fault.'
2489. *al in sounde:* 'safe and sound' (perhaps with some reference to his wound; cf. 2484).
2490. *þe grete:* either 'the prince' (i.e. King Arthur) or 'the nobles'. The latter reading is to be preferred (2491 *hym* 'to them') in view of the references to individuals in 2492f.

Þat gode Gawayn watz commen; gayn hit hym þoȝt.
Þe kyng kyssez þe knyȝt and þe whene alce,
And syþen mony syker knyȝt þat soȝt hym to haylce,
Of his fare þat hym frayned; and ferlyly he telles,
Biknowez alle þe costes of care þat he hade,   2495
Þe chaunce of þe chapel, þe chere of þe knyȝt,
Þe luf of þe ladi, þe lace at þe last.   [f124ᵛ]
Þe nirt in þe nek he naked hem schewed
Þat he laȝt for his vnleuté at þe leudes hondes
    For blame.   2500
    He tened quen he schulde telle;
    He groned for gref and grame.
    Þe blod in his face con melle,
    When he hit schulde schewe, for schame.

'Lo! lorde,' quoþ þe leude, and þe lace hondeled,   2505
'Þis is þe bende of þis blame I bere in my nek.
Þis is þe laþe and þe losse þat I laȝt haue
Of couardise and couetyse, þat I haf caȝt þare;
Þis is þe token of vntrawþe þat I am tan inne.
And I mot nedez hit were wyle I may last;   2510
For mon may hyden his harme bot vnhap ne may hit,
For þer hit onez is tachched twynne wil hit neuer.'
Þe kyng comfortez þe knyȝt, and alle þe court als
Laȝen loude þerat and luflyly acorden
Þat lordes and ledes þat longed to þe Table,   2515
Vche burne of þe broþerhede, a bauderyk schulde haue,

2506. in (Madden)] MS *om.* (Gollancz: on)
2511. mon (S. O. Andrew)] MS. non
2515. ledes (Burrow)] MS ladis

2494. *and ferlyly he telles:* 'and he tells his amazing story'.
2499f. 'which he received at the knight's hands as a reproof (*blame*) for his faithlessness.'
2506–9. 'this (the belt) is the ribbon of this reproof (the scar) which I carry in my neck. This is the injury and the damage which I have obtained because of cowardice and covetousness, which infected me there. This is the token of infidelity in which I have been detected.' Gawain adopts the girdle as the ribbon of an 'order' of shame (contrast 2519f). The very fact that he identifies the belt and the scar as twin tokens of his fault makes the passage difficult to construe: *laȝt* means 'took' in relation to the belt, 'received' in relation to the punishment; the identification becomes complete in *hit* 2510. With *caȝt*, cf. *entyse* 2436n.
2510. *wyle I may last:* 'as long as I may live'.
2511. 'for one may conceal one's offence but one cannot remove it'.
2515. *ledes:* Burrow (*NQ* 217 [1972], 43–5) defends the emendation on the grounds that the context is entirely masculine (*burne, broþerhede, hym*) and that ladies would not belong to such a military brotherhood.

A bende abelef hym aboute, of a bryȝt grene,
And þat, for sake of þat segge, in swete to were.
For þat watz acorded þe renoun of þe Rounde Table
And he honoured þat hit hade, euermore after,   2520
As hit is breued in þe best boke of romaunce.
Þus in Arthurus day þis aunter bitidde—
Þe Brutus bokez þerof beres wyttenesse.
Syþen Brutus, þe bolde burne, boȝed hider fyrst,
After þe segge and þe asaute watz sesed at Troye,   2525
     Iwysse,
     Mony aunterez herebiforne
     Haf fallen suche er þis.
     Now þat bere þe croun of þorne,
     He bryng vus to His blysse!   2530
               Amen

HONY SOYT QUI MAL PENCE.

2519. 'For that was agreed (to be) the glory of the Round Table'.
2521. Cf. 690n.
2523. *Brutus bokez:* 'chronicles of Britain', Brutus being the legendary founder; cf. 13, 2524.
2527f. 'many exploits of this kind have happened in times past (*herebiforne* = *er þis*).'

HONY SOYT . . . : the Garter motto appears to have been added to the poem in order to associate it with that order (instituted by Edward III about 1348). Its colour, however, is blue and (despite some similarity of theme in Polydore Vergil's well-known account of its founding) it is doubtful whether the poet intended any such direct connection.

Glossary

The Glossary is intended as a practical aid to the reader in the interpretation of the text and should be used in conjunction with the notes. The aim has been to include all word-forms which may give difficulty to the modern reader; a word is omitted only if it has the same (or nearly the same) spelling in modern English and is used in the text in a sense which is still current.* Notes on regular inflexions are given on p. 45f above; irregular and less obvious inflected forms are recorded in the Glossary. When looking up a word, the reader should first look for the line-reference in question; if this is not separately recorded, one of the common meanings (which are entered without line-references, or with a few references followed by '*etc.*') may be assumed to apply. Normal alphabetical order is observed (ʒ follows *g*, þ follows *t*) and variations in spelling are fully cross-referenced.

a, aa! *interj.* ah!
a *see also* **ho**
abate *v.* end
abate *see also* **abyde**
abayst *pp.* abashed, confounded
Abdama *n.* Admah
abelef *adv.* diagonally
abide(n) *see* **abyde**
able *adj.* entitled, *Pe* 599
abloy *adj.* transported, carried away
abod *see* **abyde**
abode *n.* stay, delay, *G* 687
abof, aboue(n) *adv. & prep.* above; on top; in a higher place, *G* 73; in the place of honour, *G* 112
abominacion *n.* abominable practice
aboue(n) *see* **abof**
ab(o)ut(t)e, abowte *adv. & prep.* about, around, round about; on account of, *Pe* 268; engaged in, *G* 1986
Abraham, Habraham *n.* Abraham
abroched *pp.* given utterance, expressed
abyde, -i- *v.* (**abate, abod** *pa.t.,* **abiden** *pp.*) wait, stop, remain; await; endure, *Pe* 348, 1090, *Cl* 856, *Pat* 7, *G* 1754; delay, *Pat* 70
abydyng *n.* enduring, tolerance
abyme *n.* abyss
abyt *n.* clothing
acces *n.* accession, attack
achaped *pa.t.* escaped
achaufed *pa.t. & pp.* kindled, aroused, *Cl* 1143; warmed, *G* 883
acheue *v.* achieve, obtain, accomplish; **a. to** reach (*cf.* **cheue**)

acole *v.* embrace
acorde *n.* agreement; **of care and me made a.** made sorrow familiar to me, *Pe* 371
acorde *v.* agree; correspond, *Pe* 819; match, *G* 602, 631; reconcile, *G* 2380, 2405
acroche *v.* acquire
adaunt *v.* daunt
adoun *adv.* down
adreʒ *adv.* back. *See also* **dryʒ(e)**
(a)dubbement(e) adornment, splendour
adyte *v.* accuse, arraign
affray *n.* dismay
affyen *v.* trust
afrayed *pa.t.* frightened, disturbed
after *prep., adv. & conj.* after, afterwards, for; along, *Pe* 125, *G* 218, 1608; by, from, *Pe* 998; to match, *G* 171; over, *Pat* 86
afyaunce *n.* trust
agayn, aʒayn *adv.* in reply, in return, back (again); again, *Pe* 326
agayn(e), agaynes, agayn(e)z, aʒayn(ez) *prep.* against; contrary to; towards; **nurne a.** refuse, *G* 1661
agayntote *n.* looking back
aghlich *adj.* fearsome
aglyʒte *pa.t.* slipped away
Agrauayn *n.* Agravain
agrete *adv.* generally, without distinction, *Pe* 560
agreued *pp.* overcome (with), *G* 2370
aʒayn(ez) *see* **agayn(e)**
aʒlez *adj.* fearless
aʒly *adv.* terribly, menacingly
aʒt(e) *adj.* eight

*For a complete *index verborum* the reader is referred to Kottler and Markman, **8** 1966, to which the editors have been greatly indebted in the compilation of the present Glossary.

aȝt(e) *see also* **oghe**
aȝtsum *adj.* one of eight
aȝtþe *adj.* eighth
al *see* **al(le)**
alabaundarynes *n.* alamandines (precious stones), *Cl* 1470
alarom *n.* alarm, alarum
alce *see* **als(e)**
alder *compar. adj.* older, elder
alderes *n.* princes, *G* 95
aldermen *n.* elders, senators, *Pe* 887, 1119
alder-truest *adj.* truest of all
aldest *superl. adj.* oldest, eldest
alegge *v.* plead
algate *adv.* anyway, at any rate
aliche *adv.* alike, in similar manner
alkaran *n.* mineral pitch
al(le) *adj., adv., pron. & conj.* all, everything, everybody; *adv.* everywhere, completely, quite; *conj.* even though, *G* 143; **of a. and sum** in full, *Pe* 584; **a. kynez** of all kinds; **Al Hal Day,** All Saints' Day
allyt *see* **lyte**
almyȝt(y) *adj.* almighty
aloft(e) *prep. & adv.* upon, up, at the top, above
aloȝ *adv.* softly
alone *adv.* alone; only, *Pe* 933
along(e) *prep. & adv.* along; throughout
alosed *pp.* famed, *Cl* 274; praised, *G* 1512
alow *v.* recognize, *Pe* 634
aloynte *pp.* far removed
als(e), **also, alce** *adv.* also, as well. *See also* **as** *adv.*
altogeder *adv.* entirely, wholly
alþaȝ *conj.* although
alþer-fayrest *adj.* fairest of all
alþer-fynest *adj.* finest of all
alþer-grattest *adj.* greatest of all
alþer-rychest *adj.* richest of all
alþer-swettest *adj.* sweetest of all
aluisch *adj.* other-worldly
alway *adv.* always
alyue *adj.* alive; living, *Pe* 445
amaffised *n.* amethyst
amarauntz *n.* emeralds; *cf.* **emerad(e)**
amatyst *n.* amethyst
ame *n.* aim, mark
amed *pa.t.* considered, esteemed
amende *v.* improve, *G* 898; *pp.* remedied, *Cl* 248
amesyng *n.* gentleness
amonestes *v.* admonishes, warns
among *prep.* among; *adv.* mingled together, *Pe* 905; at intervals, *Cl* 1414
amount *v.* amount (to), signify, *Cl* 395n, *G* 1197
anamayld *pp.* enamelled
Ananie *n.* Hananiah
and(e) *conj.* and; and yet, but, *Pe* 273, 931, *etc.* *Pat* 322; if, *Pe* 598, *Cl* 730, 739, *G* 1009, 1245, *etc.*
anelede *pa.t.* pursued
anende, onende *prep.* concerning, about, of, *Pe* 186, 697; against, near, *Pe* 1136; **-z** *prep.* opposite, *Pe* 975

angardez *n.* of arrogance (arrogant), *G* 681
angelez *see* **a(u)ngelez**
angel-hauyng *n.* angelic bearing
anger *n.* anger, resentment; harm, *G* 2344
angré *adj.* sharp, bitter
anguych *n.* anguish
anious *adj.* arduous
anjoynt *adj.* united
ankres, -z *n.* anchors
anon *adv.* at once, immediately after
anoþer *adj. & pron.* another, a second
anournementes *n.* ornaments, decoration
answ(a)r(e) *see* **onsware**
anvnder, onvunder *prep. & adv.* under; below, at the foot of, *Pe* 166; *adv.* underneath, *Pe* 991
anyskynnez *adj.* of any kind (at all)
aparaunt *n.* dependency
apassed *pp.* passed
apende *v.* appertain
apere *v.* appear
apert *adj. & adv.* open(ly); plain(ly); exposed, *G* 154
Apocalyp(p)ez, -(e)ce, Apokalypez, -ce *n.* Apocalypse, Revelation
apparayl(mente) *n.* adornment, ornamentation
apparement *n.* equipment, ornaments
apple-garnade *n.* pomegranate
appose *v.* interrogate
apyke *v.* adorn, array
aqoyntaunce *n.* acquaintance, company
aquyle *v.* lead, *Pe* 691; obtain permission, *Pe* 967
Ararach *n.* Ararat
aray(e) *n.* dress, array; setting, *Pe* 5; position, rank, *Pe* 491
aray(e)**d, -de** *pp.* dressed, prepared, adorned; constructed, *G* 783; **mad a.** in a state of frenzy, *Pe* 1166
arayned *pa.t.* questioned
arc *see* **ark**
are *adv.* before, *Cl* 438, 1128, *G* 239, 1632, 1891
ar(e)nde *see* **er(a)nd(e)**
arered *pp.* retreated, *G* 1902n.
arest *v.* stop; remain, *Pat* 144
areþede *n.* (people of old); old times, *Pe* 711
arewez, arwes *n.* arrows
arȝe *adj.* afraid, *G* 241
arȝe *v.* be afraid
ark, arc *n.* ark
Armene *adj.* Armenian
armes, -ez *n.* feats of arms, chivalry, *G* 95, 1513, *etc.*; armour (and weapons), *Cl* 1306, 1773, *G* 204, 281, *etc.*; coat-of-arms, *G* 631(?)
ar(n)(e), **arnde** *see* **be, er(a)nd(e)**
aros *pa.t.* arose
Arraby *n.* Arabia
arsoun(e)**z** *n.* saddle-bows
arwes *see* **arewez**
aryȝt, o- *adv.* in proper fashion; straight on, *Pe* 112
aryue *v.* arrive
as *conj.* as, while; according as, *Cl* 92; where, *G* 1004; as if, as though, *Cl* 82, *etc.*; **also . . . a.** just as . . . as, *Cl* 1618

as, als(o) *adv.* like, as, such as; according to, *Pe* 595; (intensive) **a. bare** as plainly as possible, *Pe* 836; **a. helde** quite probably, *Pe* 1193; **a. tyd, a. bylyue, a. fast** very quickly, *Cl* 64, 1239, *etc.*
asaute *see* **as(s)aut(e)**
asay *see* **as(s)ay**
asayled *pa. t.* assailed
ascaped, asscaped *pa.t.* escaped, *Cl* 569, *Pat* 110; crossed safely, *Cl* 1776
ascry, asscry, askry *n.* outcry, clamour, alarm
ascrye *v.* shout; cry to, *Pat* 195
asent(e) *n.* accord, harmony; **in a.** together, *Cl* 788; **sette in a.** agreed, *Pat* 177
aske *v.* ask (for); demand, require, *Cl* 1127, 1742, *G* 530, 1327; seek, *Cl* 1109
askes, -z *n.* ashes
askry *see* **ascry**
askyng *n.* request
aslypped *pp.* slipped away
asoyled *pa.t.* absolved
aspaltoun *n.* asphalt
asperly *adv.* sharply
as(s)aut(e) *n.* assault, attack
as(s)ay *n. & v.* test
asscaped, asscry *see* **ascaped, ascry**
assemblé *n.* union, *Pe* 760
as(s)pye *v.* see, catch sight of; discover, *Pe* 704, *G* 1199
as(s)tate *n.* condition, *Pe* 393; rank, *Pe* 490
asswyþe *adv.* immediately
as(s)yse *n.* manner, fashion, custom
astate *see* **as(s)tate**
astel *pa.t.* stole forth
astit, -y- *adv.* at once, in a moment, quickly, soon
astount *pp.adj.* amazed, stupified, *Pe* 179n
astraye *adv.* wildly, off course, *Pe* 1162
astyt *see* **astit**
asure, azer *n.* lapis lazuli
aswagen *v.* assuage
asyngne *v.* assign
asyse *see* **as(s)yse**
at *pron.* which; **þat a.** what, *Pe* 536
at(e) *prep. & adv.* at; in; to, *G* 929, 1671; of, *Cl* 1619, *G* 359, *etc.*; from, *G* 328, 391, *etc.*; for, *G* 648, 1320; with, *Pe* 287, *G* 1474, 2399; according to, *Pe* 199, 1164, *Cl* 348, *Pat* 134, 339, *etc.*, *G* 1006, 1546
athel, atle *see* **aþel, at(t)le**
atlyng *n.* purpose, intention
atrauerce, -res *adv.* from side to side
atslyke *v.* be spent
atteny *v.* reach
at(t)le *v.* intend, *G* 27; pretend, *G* 2263; *pp.* designed (to be), *Cl* 207
at(t)yred *pp.* attired
atwap(p)e *v.* escape
aþel, athel *adj.* noble, glorious
auayed *pp.* informed
aucly *adj.* untoward, perverse
Aue *n.* Ave Maria
auen *see* **aune**
auentayle *n.* neck-guard, *G* 608n
auenture, av-, aw-, a(u)nter *n.* strange hap-

pening, marvel, exploit; quest, *Pe* 64, *G* 489; **on a.** in peril, *Pat* 242
auenturus *adj.* daring
auinant *adj. or adv.* pleasant(ly), *G* 806
auise, auyse, avyse, awyse *v.* devise, *G* 45, 1389; contemplate, *G* 771; **watz auised** intended, *Cl* 1365
aumayl *n.* enamel
aunceterez *n.* ancestor's, *Cl* 258
auncian *adj.* aged, venerable; *as n. G* 948
aune, auen, awen, owen, owne *adj. & pron.* own
a(u)ngelez, aungel(l)(e)s *n.* angels
aunter *see* **auenture**
auntered *pa.t.* ventured, risked, *G* 1516
auter *n.* altar
auþer *see* **oþer**
auwhere *adv.* anywhere
auyse *see* **auise**
avanters *n.* offal near the neck, *G* 1342
avaunt *n.* promise, boast
avayment *n.* display
aventure *see* **auenture**
avow, avowe *v.* promise, affirm
avoy *interj.* shame on you!, *Cl* 863
avyled *pa.t. & pp.* defiled, profaned
avysyoun *n.* vision
away(e) *adv.* away; gone, absent, *Pe* 258, *Cl* 1241, *Pat* 480, 499; **here a.** hither, (to) here, *Cl* 647
awayed *pp.* taught, instructed, *Pe* 710
awayled *pa.t.* availed
awen, awenture *see* **aune, auenture**
awharf *pa.t.* turned aside
awhyle *adv.* for a time
awowe, awyse *see* **avow, auyse**
ay *adv.* always, ever; all the time, *Pe* 56, 132, *etc.*, *Cl* 132, *etc.*, *G* 562, *etc.*; in each case, *Cl* 114, *G* 128, 190; everywhere, *Pe* 44, *G* 167, *etc.*
ay *n.* hay, *Cl* 1684
ayled *pp.* troubled
ayquere *adv.* everywhere
ayre *n.*[1] air
ayre, hayre, here *n.*[2] heir
ayþer *adj. & pron.* each, both; **a. oþer, a. ....oþer** each other
Aywan *n.* Iwain
aywhere *adv.* everywhere
Azarie *n.* Azariah
azer *see* **asure**

babel *adj. or adv.* foolish(ly), *Cl* 582
Babiloyn(e), Babyloyn *n.* Babylon
baboynes *n.* baboons
babtem *see* **baptem**
bachlerez, bacheleres *n.* young men
badde *adj.* bad, wicked
bade *see* **byde**
baft *adv.* abaft, astern
bagges *n.* bags
bak(bon) *n.* back(bone)
baken *pp.* baked
bald(e)ly *adv.* boldly, vigorously
bale *adj.* dire

bale *n.*[1] harm, pain, *Pe* 478, 651, *Cl* 276, *Pat* 276, 513; calamity, *Cl* 980, *G* 2041; sorrow, grief, *Pe* 18, 123, *etc.*, *Cl* 1256, *G* 2419
bale *n.*[2] cargo, *Pat* 157
balé *n.* belly, *G* 1333
balelez *adj.* innocent
bale-stour *n.* death agony, *Pat* 426
balȝ(e) *adj.* smooth and rounded
balleful *adj.* wretched
balke *n.* (grave) mound, *Pe* 62
Baltazar *n.* Belshazzar; Belteshazzar, *Cl* 1610n
balterande *adj.* stumbling
balteres *v.* rolls around
baly *n.* stronghold, *Pe* 1083
bande *see* **bende**
baner *n.* banner
banne *n.* proclamation, order
banned *pp.* cursed
bantelez, bantel(le)s *n.* bantels; tiers, coursings (of a building), *Pe* 992, 1017, *Cl* 1459n
baptem, babtem *n.* baptism, *Pe* 627, 653
barayne *adj.* barren, *Cl* 659; not breeding, *G* 1320
barbe *n.* point, *G* 2310; *pl.* bristles, *G* 1457
barbican *n.* fortified gateway
bare *adj.* bare, naked; single, *G* 1141; clear, *Pe* 1025; without armour, *G* 277, 290; mere, *G* 2352; *adv.* plainly, *Pe* 836; openly, *G* 465; only, *Cl* 1573, *G* 1066; *as n.* bare skin, *Cl* 791; **-ly** positively, *G* 548
bared *pp.* disclosed, made apparent, *Cl* 1149
bare-heued *adj.* bare-headed
barer(e)s *n.* barriers, defences
baret *n.* battle, strife; enmity (with God), *G* 752
barlay *see* *G* 296n
barme *n.* breast
barnage *n.* childhood
barne *n.* child; a child, *G* 2320 (MS: **burne**)
baronage *n.* company of barons
baroun *n.* baron; **b. vpon benche** lord of the king's council, *Cl* 1640
barred *pp.* decorated with bars, *G* 159, 600
barrez, -s *n.* bars; barriers, *Cl* 963; decorative bars, *G* 162
Barsabe *n.* Bathsheba
barst *see* **breste**
bases, basez *n.* bases
basse *n.* (lowest) course, *Pe* 1000
bassyn *n.* basin, vessel
bastel *n.* tower; assault tower mounted on wheels, *Cl* 1187n; **b. roues** roofs of towers, *G* 799
basyng *n.* foundation, *Pe* 992
batayl *n.* (a) duel, *G* 277
batayled *adj.* fortified with battlements
bate *n.* baiting, persistent attacks, *G* 1461
batede *pa.t.* abated, ceased
batelment *n.* battlement
batered *pa.t.* clattered
baþe *v.* bathe; *imperat.* plunge, *Pat* 211
bauderyk *n.* baldric, belt, strap
baume *v.* comfort
bausenez *n.* badgers
Bawdewyn *n.* Baldwin
bawelyne *n.* bowline (a rope fastening the sail to the bow), *Pat* 104, *Cl* 417

bawemen *n.* archers
bay *n.*[1] a space between columns, *Cl* 1392
bay, baye *n.*[2] baying of hounds; defensive stance; **byde (at) þe b.** *or* **in his b.** stand at bay
Bayard *n.* a bay horse, *Cl* 886n
baye *v.* bay (at)
bayly *n.* dominion, *Pe* 442; realm, *Pe* 315
bayn *adj.* obedient; willing, *Pe* 807, *Pat* 136; *adv.* readily, *Cl* 1511
baysment *n.* confusion, *Pe* 174
bayst *pa.t.* was dismayed, *G* 376
bayted *pp.* fattened
bayþe(n) *v.* agree (to), grant
be *see* **be(ne), bi**
beau, beue *adj.* beautiful, *Pe* 197; **b. sir** good sir, (*lit.* (my) handsome lord), *Cl* 1622, *G* 1222
beauté, bewté *n.* beauty
becom(e) *see* **bicum**
bed, bedd(e) *n.* bed
bed(de), bede(n)(e) *see* **bid(de)**
befalle, begyn(n)e *see* **bifalle, bygyn(n)e**
beholde, by- *v.* (**behelde** *pa.t.*, **bihaldèn, biholde** *pp.*) behold, look (at); *pp.* obliged
behoue *see* **bihoue**
beke *n.* beak
beknew, beknowe(n) *see* **biknowe**
bekyr *n.* beaker, goblet
belde *n.* courage, *G* 650
bele *adj.* gracious, pleasant, *G* 1034
bele *v.* burn, *Pe* 18
Belfagor *n.* Baalpeor
Belssabub *n.* Beelzebub
Belyal *n.* Belial
bem(e) *n.* beam, ray; (wooden) beam, *Pe* 814
ben *see* **be(ne)**
bench(e) *n.* bench; *see also* **baroun**
bende, bande *n.* band; ribbon, *G* 2506, 2517
bende *pa.t.* (**bende, bent(e)** *pp.*) (bent); arched, *G* 305; fastened (**bi:** to), *G* 2224; fixed, set, *Pe* 1017; attached, *Pe* 664; submitted, *Pe* 1189; caused, *G* 2115
bene *adj.* & *adv.* pleasant(ly), beautiful(ly); gentle, *Pat* 418; happily, *G* 2475
be(ne), by *v.* (**was(se), watz, wace, wore, ware, wer(e)(n)** *pa.t.*, **ben(e)** *pp.*) be
bent *n.* field, battlefield; grass, *Pat* 392; bank (of stream), *G* 1599; **burne on b.** warrior, *G* 1465, 2148; **bentfelde** hunting field, *G* 1136
ber *n.* beer, *G* 129
berde *n.* beard
berdles, -z *adj.* beardless
bere *v.* (**ber(e)** *pa.t.*, **born(e), bore** *pp.*) bear, lift, wear; swing, *G* 2070; keep, *G* 2151; press, *G* 1860; have, possess, *Pe* 100, 756, *Cl* 333, 1023; **b. lyf** live; **b. þe face** make for, *Pe* 67; **b. to** strike, *Pat* 148
b(e)rest(e) *see* **breste**
berez *n.* bears, *G* 722
berfray *n.* a movable tower used in sieges
berȝ(e) *n.* barrow, mound
beryng *n.* bearing, behaviour
bes *see* **be(ne)**
best *superl. adj.* & *adv.* best (in various contex-

tual senses) *G* 78, 1216, *etc.*; perfect, *Pe* 863; noblest, *Pe* 1131; noble one, *Pe* 279; of highest rank, *Cl* 1202, *G* 73; nobles, *Cl* 1179, *G* 550, 1325; **of þe b.** from among the best, *G* 38, *etc.*; in the best manner, *G* 889, 1000

best(t)(e) *n.* beast, animal (**besten** *gen. pl.*, or *adj. Cl* 1446)

bete *v.*[1] (**bet(e)(n)** *pa.t.*, **beten** *pp.*) beat; *pp.* driven, *Pat* 248; inlaid, embroidered, *G* 78, 1833, 2028

bete *v.*[2] (**bet(te)** *pp.*) kindle, mend, make up (a fire), *Cl* 627, 1012, *G* 1368; amend, *Pe* 757

better *compar. adj. & adv.* better; rather, *Pe* 341

betydes *see* **bityde**

betz *see* **be(ne)**

Beþelen *n.* Bethlehem

beue *see* **beau**

beuerage *n.* drink

beuer-hwed *adj.* the colour of beaver

bewté *see* **beauté**

beyng *n.* nature, *Pe* 446

bi, be, by *prep.* by, beside, along, according to, from; through, *Pe* 684, 751; beside, *Pe* 140; against, *G* 2310; *for phrases see also the nouns* **contray, skyl, sype(s)**, *etc.*; *conj.* until, *G* 1006; by the time that, *Cl* 403, *G* 1169; when, *G* 2032; **b. þat** *adv.* by that time, *G* 597, 1868; then, *G* 2152; *conj.* by the time that, *Pat* 468, *G* 443, *etc.*; when, *G* 1678, 1912, 2043

bibbes *v.* drinks

bicnv *see* **biknowe**

bicum, bicome, be- by- *v.* (**becom, bicome, bycom** *pa.t.*) become; arrive (at), *G* 460

bid(de), bydde, bedde, bede *v.* (**bed(e)(n)** *pa.t.*, **bedene, boden** *pp.*) bid, command, ask; offer, *Cl* 1640, *G* 374, 382, 1824, *etc.*

bide(n) *see* **byde**

bifalle, be-, by- *v.* (**bifel** *pa.t.*, **bifallen** *pp.*) happen

bifore, byfore *adv. & prep.* before (*of time or place*); formerly; in front (of)

bigan *see* **bygyn(n)e**

big(ge), byg(g)(e) *adj. & adv.* (**bygger** *compar.*, **big(g)est** *superl.*) big, great; strong, *Cl* 1190, 1377, *G* 554, 2101; *adv.* strongly, *Cl* 1183

big(g)e *v.* build, make

bigyled, by- *pp.* beguiled

bigly, bygly *adv.* strongly, powerfully

bigog! *interj.* by God! *G* 390

bigonne(n) *see* **bygyn(n)e**

bigrauen *pp.* carved, *G* 216

biȝonde *see* **byȝonde**

bihalde(n), biholde *see* **beholde**

bihoue, be-, by- *v.impers.* (**bihous, bos, boz** *pres3s.*, **bihoued, byhod(e)** *pa.t.*) behove, be obliged, must

bihyȝt *pa.t. & pp.* promised

bihynde, byhynde(n) *prep. & adv.* behind; inferior, *G* 1942

bikenne, by- *v.* (**bikende** *pa.t.*) commend; deliver, *Cl* 1296

biknowe, be- *v.* (**beknew, bicnv** *pa.t.*, **benowen** *pp.*) confess, acknowledge

bilde *see* **bylde**

bileued *pa.t.* remained, *C* 1549

biliue *see* **bylyue**

bilooghe *adv.* below, *Cl* 116

bilyue *see* **bylyue**

birlen *v.* (**byrled** *pp.*) pour (out)

birolled *pp.* drenched, covered

bischop, bisshop *n.* bishop; *gen.pl.* bishops' *Cl* 1445

biseche, bysech(e) *v.* (**bisoȝt(en)** *pa.t.*) beseech, implore

biseged *pa.t.* besieged

biseme, by- *v.impers.* suit, become, befit

bisides, bisied *see* **bisyde, busy**

bisinesse, busynes *n.* importunity, *G* 1840; solicitude, *G* 1986

bisoȝt(en) *see* **biseche**

bispeke *pa.t.* spoke

bisshop *see* **bischop**

bisyde, by-, be- *prep. & adv.* beside, near; at his side, *G* 1083; alongside, *G* 1582(?), 2230; round about, *G* 2088; **þer (her) b.** nearby; *see also* **lay**; **bisides, bisydez,** *adv.* round about, *G* 76, 856, 2164

bitalt *pp.* shaken, *Pe* 1161

bite, byte *v.* (**bot(e), bited** *pa.t.*, **biten, byten** *pp.*) bite; torment, *Cl* 1243, *Pat* 373; penetrate, *Pe* 355, *G* 1457; **b. (on)** eat, *Pe* 640, *Cl* 1675, *Pat* 392

biteche *v.* (**bytaȝt(e)** *pa.t.*) commit, deliver

bitid(d)e *see* **bityde**

bit(te), bytte *n.* blade

bitwene *see* **bytwene**

bityde, bitide, be-, by- *v.* (**bitid(d)e, bityde** *pa.t.*) happen, befall

biþenkke *v.* (**biþoȝt** *pa.t.*) resolve, consider, reflect

biwyled *pp.* deceived, *G* 2425

biys *n.* fine linen (garment), *Pe* 197

blades *n.* knives, *Cl* 1105

blaȝt *adj.* pure white, *Pe* 212

blak(e) *adj.* black; *as n. Cl* 1009

blame *n.* blame, reproach, guilt; reproof, rebuke, *Pe* 715, *Cl* 43, *G* 2500, 2506

blame *v.* blame; disparage, *Cl* 1661

blande *n.* **in b.** together, *G* 1205. *See also* **inblande**

blande *pp.* trimmed, *G* 1931

blasfemy(e) *n.* blasphemy

blasoun *n.* shield, *G* 828

blastes, -z *n.* blasts

blaunmer, blaunner *n.* ermine, fur

blayke *adj.* white, pale, *Pe* 27

ble *n.* colour, complexion; **b. of Ynde** indigo, *Pe* 76

ble(e)aunt *n.* silk (garment), mantle

blemyst *pa.t.* impaired

blench *n.* trick, stratagem

blenched *pa.t.* dodged

blende *see* **blende(n), blynne**

blended *pp.* deluded (**with:** by), *G* 2419

blende(n), blent(e) *pa.t. & pp.* blended, mingled; *pa.subjunc.* (should) steep, *Pat* 227; *pp.* situated, *Pe* 385

blenk(e) *v.* shine

blent(e) *see* **blende(n)**

blesse *v.* bless; cross (oneself), *Pe* 341(?), *G*

2071; say 'God bless you (me)', *Pe* 341(?), *G* 1296*n*
bliþe *see* **blyþe**
blo *adj.* livid, dark
blober *see* **bluber**
blod(e) *n.* blood; descendant, *Cl* 686; **blody** *adj. Pe* 705
blok *n.* compartment
blom *n.* bloom, flower; *fig.* perfection, *Pe* 578
blonk *n.* (**blonkken** *gen.pl.*) horse
blosched *see* **blusche**
blot *n.* stain
blowe *v.*[1] blow, bloom, *G* 512
blowe *v.*[2] (**blw(e), blowed** *pa.t.*) blow
bluber, blober *n.* seething water
blubrande *presp.adj.* bubbling, surging
blubred *pa.t.* surged
bluk *n.* trunk, torso, *G* 440
blunder *n.* turmoil, strife
blunt *adj.* stunned, dazed, *Pe* 176
blunt *pa.t.* stopped
blusch *n.* gleam, *G* 520
blusche, -o- *v.* look, gaze, glance; **-ande** *presp. adj.* flashing, *G* 1819
blusnande *see* **blysned**
blustered *pa.t.* blundered about, strayed about, *Cl* 886
blwe *adj. & n.* blue
blw(e) *see* **blowe** *v.*[2]
blycande, blykkande *presp.* shining
blykke *v.* shine
blykned *pa.t.* grew pale; **blyknande** shining, *Cl* 1467 (*cf.* **blycande, blykke**)
blynde *adj.* blind; dim, *Pe* 83; *as n. Cl* 1094
blynde *v.* become dim
blynne *v.* (**blende** *pp.*, *Cl* 967) cease (**of**: from)
blysful *adj.* blissful, full of bliss *or* blessing; joyful, happy; delightful; *as n. Pe* 421
blysned *pa.t.* shone, *Pe* 1048; **blysnande, blusn-** *presp.adj.* gleaming, shining
blysse *n.* bliss, joy
blyþe, -i- *adj. & adv.* glad, happy, joyful; gentle, kind, *Pe* 1131, *Cl* 1085, 1228; bright, lovely, *G* 155, 162; *adv.* happily, *G* 1684
blyþe *n.* mercy, *Pe* 354
blyþ(e)ly *adv.* gladly, happily, joyously
bob(b)aunce *n.* arrogance, pomp, pride
bobbe *n.* bunch, clump
bode, bot *n.* bidding, command; offer, *G* 1824; **bi b.** according to command, *Cl* 944*n*
bod(e) *see also* **byde**
bodé, bodi *see* **body**
boden *see* **bid(de)**
bodworde *n.* message
body, bodi, bodé *n.* body; person
bodyly *adj.* bodily, physical, of (in) the body
bo(e)rne *n.* sea, flood, *Cl* 482, *Pat* 302; burn, stream, *G* 731, 1570, 2174
boffet *see* **buffet**
boȝe *n.* bough
boȝ(e)(d), boȝt *see* **bowe, by(y)e**
boȝted *pp.adj.* vaulted
bok(e) *n.* book
bok-lered *adj.* book-learned
bol, bul(l) *n.* bull
bold(e) *adj. & adv.* bold, valiant, daring;

noble, fine, *Cl* 789, 1333 *etc.*; *as n. Cl* 811, *G* 21; *adv.* valiantly, *G* 2476
bolle *n.*[1] bowl, *Cl* 1511
bol(l)e *n.*[2] trunk (of tree), *Pe* 76, *Cl* 622, *G* 766
bolled *pp.* embossed
bolne *v.* swell
bonchef *n.* happiness
bonde *adj. or n.* in a state of serfdom, serfs
bone *adj.* good; *see also* **(h)ostel**
bon(e) *n.*[1] bone
bone *n.*[2] request, prayer, *Pe* 912, 916, *G* 327; command, commandment, *Cl* 826, *Pat* 136; boon, favour, *Pe* 1090
boner *adj.* kind, compassionate
bonerté *n.* beatitude, *Pe* 762
bongré *prep.* in accordance with
bonk(k)(e) *n.* hill, hillside, ridge; bank (of stream), *Pe* 106, 1169, *G* 785; shore, *Pat* 236, *G* 700 *etc.*; bank of water, *Cl* 363
Boos *n.* Bors
bor *n.*[1] boar, *Cl* 55, *G* 722, *etc.*
bor *n.*[2] *see also* **bo(u)r(e)**
borde *n.*[1] board; table; wood, *Cl* 1190; side (of ship), *Pat* 211; **vpon b.** on deck, *Cl* 470, *Pat* 190; **bynne b.** on board (ship)
borde *n.*[2] band (of material), *G* 159, 610
borde *see also* **bo(u)rde**
bore *see* **bere**
bor(e)lych *adj.* massive, huge; noble, *Cl* 1488
borges *n.* citizens
borgoune *v.* bud
borȝ(e), borlych *see* **burȝ(e), bor(e)lych**
born(e) *see* **bere, bo(e)rne**
bornyst(e), burnyst, -ist *pp.* burnished, shining
boroȝt *see* **bryng**
bos *n.* cow-stall, *Cl* 1075
bos *see also* **bihoue**
bose *n.* coarse, awkward person, *Pe* 911
bosk(ed) *see* **busk(ke)**
boskenz *n.* divisions between stalls, *Cl* 322*n*
bost *n.* boasting; clamour, *G* 1448
boster *n.* boaster
bostwys, bu- *adj.* rough, crude
bosum *n.* swelling (of sail), *Pat* 107
bot *adv., conj. & prep.* but, except, only; quite, *G* 1230; but that, *Pat* 176; **b. (if)** unless, *Pe* 308, 428 *etc.*, *Cl* 1110, 1360, *Pat* 83, *G* 716, 1782 *etc.*; **b. þat** were it not that, *Cl* 881; **no more b.** only to the extent of, *G* 2312; **neuer b.** only, *G* 547; **noȝt b.** nothing but, *Cl* 209 *etc.*, only, *G* 1267, completely, *G* 1833
bot *v.* announce, proclaim, *Cl* 473
bot(e) *n.*[1] help, remedy
bote *n.*[2] boot, shoe
bot(e) *n.*[3] boat
bot(e) *see also* **bite, bode**
both(e), boþe *adj., pron. & adv.* both; each, *G* 2070, 2165; also, as well, *Cl* 11, 57, *G* 129, *etc.*
botounz *n.* buttons
boþe *n.* booth, arbour
boþe *see also* **both(e)**
boþem, bothem, boþom *n.* bottom; valley; deep place, *Cl* 1030
boþemlez *adj.* bottomless

bouel *n.* (**boweles, -z** *pl.*) bowel
bougounz *n. gen.pl.* of drumsticks, *Cl* 1416
boun *adj.* ready; setting off, *G* 548; arranged, *Pe* 534; fixed, fastened, *Pe* 992, 1103
bounden *see* **bynde**
bounet *pp.* ready, prepared, *Cl* 1398
bounté *n.* virtue, merit; liberality, *Cl* 1436
bo(u)rde *n. & v.* joke, jest; **bourdyng** *n.* jesting, *G* 1404
bo(u)r(e) *n.* bower, bedroom, private room; house, home, *Pe* 964; stall, *Cl* 322
bourȝ, bourne *see* **burȝ(e), bu(u)rne**
bout(e) *prep.* without
bowe, boȝ(e) *v.* go, come; bow, submit, *Cl* 1746; stoop, *Pat* 441; **b. after** follow, *Cl* 1750; **b. to, bi** obey, comply with, *Cl* 944(1), *Pat* 56, 75
boweles, -ez *see* **bouel**
boy *n.* lout, ruffian
boyle *v.* boil
boz *see* **bihoue**
brace *n.* arm-pieces
brach(et)es, -ez *n.* hounds
brad *pp.* grilled, *G* 891
bradde *pa.t.* reached, *G* 1928
brade *see* **brod(e)**
brake *v.* spew, vomit, *Pat* 340
braken *n.* bracken
bras(se) *n.* brass; brass trumpets, *Cl* 1783
braste *see* **breste**
brath(þe) *n.* (**braþez** *pl.*) ferocity, *Cl* 916; impetuosity, *Pe* 1170; *pl.* agonies, *Pe* 346
braþ *see also* **broþe**
braunch(e), bronch *n.* branch
braundysch *v.* struggle
brawden *see* **brayde**
brawen, brawne *n.* boar's flesh, meat; **b. of a best** well-fleshed boar, *G* 1631
brayd(e) *n.* **at a b.** quickly, *Cl* 539; **in a b.** in a sudden impulse, suddenly, *Cl* 1507
brayde *v.* (**brayd(e)(n)** *pa.t.*, **brayden, brawden, browden** *pp.*) draw, pull; take, *G* 621; bring, *Pe* 712; jerk, *Pe* 1170; fling, *G* 2377; gush, *G* 429; *pp.* embroidered, woven, intertwined, linked, *Cl* 1132, 1481, *G* 177, 220, 580, 1833; **b. doun** let down, *G* 2069
brayn *adj.* mad, reckless, *G* 286
brayn *n.* brain, brains
braynwod *adj.* maddened
bred *n.* bread
brede *n.¹* breadth, *Pe* 1031, *Cl* 316
brede *n.²* board, *Pat* 184, *G* 2071
brede *n.³* *pl.* roast meats, *Cl* 1405
brede *v.¹* (**bred(den)** *pa.t.*) breed, *Cl* 257; grow, flourish, *Pe* 415, *Cl* 1482, *G* 21; become, *Cl* 1558
brede *v.²* stretch, *Pe* 814
bredful *adj.* brimful, *Pe* 126. (*Cf.* **brurdful**)
breed *adj.* terrified, *Pat* 143
bref *adj.* transitory, *Pe* 268
brek(e)(n) *pa.t.* (**broken** *pp.*) broke; opened, *G* 1333; burst forth, *G* 1764
brem(e) *adj. & adv.* fierce, wild, stern, loud; terrible, *Cl* 229; intense, *Pe* 863; firmly, *G* 781; **-ly(ch)** *adv.* loudly, fiercely; quickly, *G* 779

brenne *v.* (**bren(n)(e)d** *pa.t.*, **brent, brende,** *pp.*) burn; broil, *G* 1609; *pp.adj.* refined (by fire) *or* burnished, *Pe* 989, *Cl* 1456, 1488, *G* 195
brent *adj.* steep, *Pe* 106, *G* 2165; *superl. Cl* 379
brere-flour *n.* briar-rose
breres *n.* briars
bresed *pp.adj.* bristly
brest *n.* trespass, outrage, *Cl* 229
breste, bereste *n.* breast
breste *v.* (**barst, braste, bursten** *pa.t.*, **brusten** *pp.*) burst (out), break
Bretaygne, Bretayn *n.* Britain
breth(e), breþe *n.* breath, *Cl* 916; wind, *Pat* 107, 145; smoke, smell, *Cl* 509, 967
breþer *n.* brothers(-in-arms)
breue *v.* declare, tell; reveal, *G* 1436
breyþed *pa.t.* 'breathed', rose as a vapour, *Cl* 1421n
brit(t)en *v.* destroy, *G* 2, 680; cut open, *G* 1339; **b. out** cut up, *G* 1611
brod(e) *adj.* broad, wide, great; *of time* long; *adv.* broadly, widely; **ful b.** far and wide, *Pat* 117, with eyes wide open, *G* 446
broȝes, -z, broȝt(e)(n) *see* **browes, bryng(e)**
brok(e) *n.* brook; sea, *Pat* 145
brom *n.* broom
bronch *see* **braunch(e)**
bronde, bront *n.* sword; firebrand, *Cl* 1012; charred stick, *G* 2
broþe, braþ *adj.* angry, fierce
broþely *adv.* wretchedly, *Cl* 1030, 1256, *Pat* 474; violently, *G* 2377
broþelych *adj.* venomous, vile, *Cl* 848
broþer *n.* brother; kinsman, *Cl* 772
broun *adj.* brown; dark, *Pe* 537; burnished, bright, *Pe* 990, *G* 426
browden *see* **brayde**
browes, broȝes, -z *n.* eyebrows
brugge *see* **bryg(g)e**
brunt *n.* blow, shock
bruny, bryné *n.* coat of mail
brurdes *n.* rims, edges
brurdful *adj.* brimful, *Cl* 383. (*Cf.* **bredful**)
brused *pp.* bruised
brusten *see* **breste**
brutage *n.* wooden platforms, *Cl* 1190n
bruxle *v.* upbraid
brych *n.* sin, *fig.* vomit, *Cl* 848
bryd *n.* bride, *Pe* 769
brydale *n.* wedding-feast, *Cl* 142
bryddes, -z *n.* birds
brydel *n.* bridle
bryg(g)e, -u- *n.* drawbridge
bryȝt *adj. & adv.* bright(ly); shining; beautiful; *as n. Pe* 755, *Cl* 470; *superl.* the most beautiful, *G* 1283
brym(me) *n.* bank, (water's) edge, *Cl* 365, *Pe* 232, *G* 2172; surface, *Pe* 1074
bryné *see* **bruny**
bryng(e) *v.* (**broȝt(e)(n)** *pa.t.*, **b(o)roȝt** *pp.*) bring; **b. to resoun** explain, *Cl* 1633
brynkez *n.* brinks, edges
brynston *n.* brimstone
buffet, bo- *n.* blow
bukkez *n.* bucks

bulde, bult *see* **bylde**
bulk *n.* hold, *Pat* 292
bul(l)ez, bur *see* **bol, bur(re)**
burde *n.* maiden, lady, woman
burde *v.impers.* **me** (þe, *etc.*) **b.** I (you, *etc.*) ought (to)
burʒ(e), bo(u)rʒ(e), burghe *n.* city, castle; estate, *Cl* 63; **in vch a b.** everywhere, *Cl* 1061
burne, burnyst *see* **bu(u)rn(e), bornyst(e)**
bur(re) *n.* onslaught, blow; force, *G* 2261; shock, *Cl* 32; strong wind, *Pat* 148
bursten *see* **breste**
burþen *n.* load, *Cl* 1439
busch *n.* noise, beating, *Cl* 1416
busch *v.* dash, plunge, *Pat* 143; rise, shoot up, *Pat* 472
busily *see* **busyly**
busk *n.* bush, *G* 182, 1437
busk(ke), bosk *v.* prepare; go, hasten; dress, *Cl* 142, *G* 1220; bring, *Cl* 351, 1395
busmar *n.* scorn
bustwys *see* **bostwys**
busy *adj. as n.* hurry, *Pat* 157
busy *v.* (**bisied** *pa.t.*) stir, *G* 89; bestir oneself, *G* 1066; *reflex.* concern oneself, *Pe* 268
busyly, busily, bysily *adv.* earnestly; carefully, *Cl* 1446
busynes *see* **bisinesse**
bu(u)rn(e), bourne, buyrne *n.* man, warrior, knight; sir, *Pe* 397, *G* 1071, *etc.*
by *see* **bi, be(ne)**
bycalle *v.* (**bycalt** *pp.*) call upon, *Pe* 913; *pp.* summoned, *Pe* 1163
bycom, bydde *see* **bicum, bid(de)**
byde, bide *v.* (**bod(e), bade, byden** *pa.t.*, **biden** *pp.*) remain, wait (for); stay, *Cl* 616; live, *Pat* 318; lie, *Pe* 75; endure, *Pe* 664, *Cl* 32, *G* 290 *etc.*; enjoy, *G* 520; **b. to** await, *Cl* 467
bydene *adv.* directly, *Pe* 196; continuously, *Cl* 659
Byduer *n.* Bedivere
bye, byfallen, byfore, byg(g)(e) *see* **by(y)e, bifalle, bifore, big(ge)**
byg(g)yng *n.* building, house, home
bygly *adj.* (habitable); pleasant, *Pe* 963. *See also* **bigly**
bygyled *see* **bigyled**
bygyn(n)e, be-, bi- *v.* (**bygan, bygonne** *pa.t.*, **bygonne(n)** *pp.*) begin; found, *G* 11; **b. þe table** sit in the place of honour, *G* 112; **is bygonne** has its origin (in), *Pe* 33
bygynner *n.* originator, *Pe* 436
byʒe *n.* ring, bracelet, necklace
byʒonde, bi- *prep.* beyond, across
byʒt *n.* fork (of animal's legs), *G* 1341, 1349
byhod(e), byholde, byhoue, byhynde(n), bykenne *see* **bihoue, beholde, bihoue, bihynde, bikenne**
bylde *n.* dwelling, *Pe* 727, 963
bylde *v.* (**bylde, bult** *pa.t.*, **bilde, bulde, bylded** *pp.*) build; live, dwell, *G* 25; build up, *Pe* 123
byled *pa.t.* boiled, bubbled, *G* 2082; **boyled** *pp.*, *G* 2174

bylyue, bilyue, biliue, byliue *adv.* quickly, swiftly, immediately, soon; **as b.** as soon as possible, *Cl* 1239
bynde *n.* woodbine (climbing plant), *Pat* 444. *See also* **wodbynde**
bynde *v.* bind, tie; **bounden** *pp.* tied, fastened; lined, *G* 573; trimmed, adorned, *Pe* 198, *G* 600, 609, 2028
bynne *prep.* **b. borde** within board, on board ship
byrled *see* **birlen**
byrþ-whatez *n.* dates of birth
bysech(e), byseme, bysily *see* **biseche, biseme, busyly**
bysulpe *v.* defile
bysyde *see* **bisyde**
byswyke *v.* cheat, *Pe* 568
bytaʒt(e), byte(n) *see* **biteche, bite**
bytoknyng *n.* sign
bytte *see* **bitte**
bytterly *adv.* bitterly
bytwene, bi- *prep. & adv.* between; in between, here and there, at intervals; **b. hem** aside, by themselves, *G* 977
bytwyste *prep.* between
bytyde, byþenk *see* **bityde, biþenkke**
by(y)e *v.* (**boʒt** *pa.t. & pp.*) buy; redeem, *Pe* 651, 893

cable, k- *n.* cable
cace, cas(e) *n.* matter, affair, *Pe* 673, *G* 546, 1196; chance, *G* 907; **vche a c.** everything that turned up, *G* 1262, every misfortune, *Pat* 265
cach(ch)(e), kach *v.* (**cached, caʒt(e)(n), kaʒt(en)** *pa.t. & pp.*) catch, seize, take, snatch; knock, *Cl* 1541; **c. to** *Pe* 50, *G* 2376; receive, obtain, accept, *Cl* 1619, *G* 643, 1011, 1938; conceive, *Cl* 1426; become infected with, *G* 2508; urge on, spur, drive, *Cl* 16, *G* 1581, 2175; hasten, start, go, *Cl* 629, *G* 1794; **c. of** take off, *Pe* 237; **c. vp** lift, hoist, *Pat* 102, *G* 1185
cacheres *n.* hunters
cagge *v.* bind, tie up
caʒt(e)(n) *see* **cach(ch)(e)**
cal *n.* invitation
Caldé(e), Caldye *n.* Chaldea, Chaldean
Caldéez *n.* the Chaldeans
calder *see* **co(o)lde**
calle, k- *v.* call, call out, summon; entreat, *Cl* 1522; **c. of** beg for, ask for, *G* 975, 1882, signal, *G* 1421
callyng *n.* proclamation, summons
calsydoyne *n.* chalcedony
Cam *n.* Ham
cambe *n.* comb; **comly onvunder c.** (beautiful) lady, *Pe* 775
campe *adj.* shaggy
can *see* **con**
candel *n.* candle
candelstik, con- *n.* candlestick
capados *n.* hood, cape
cap(e)le *n.* horse
captyuidé *n.* captivity
caraldes *n.* casks

carayne *n.* carrion

care, kare *n.* sorrow, distress, trouble; **c. of** concern for, *G* 2379

care *v.* be concerned

careful *adj.* sorrowful, anxious

carf *see* **kerue**

carfully *adv.* wretchedly, in suffering

carle, karle *n.* churl

carneles, -z *n.* battlements

carole *n.* courtly ring-dance with singing

carp(e) *n.* speech, discourse, conversation

carping *n.* speech, power of speech

carp(p)(e), karp *v.* speak, say, talk; **here c.** hear tell, *G* 263

carye *v.* carry, *Cl* 1765

carye *see also* **cayre**

case(e) *see* **cace**

cast, kest(e) *v.* (**cast, kest(en)** *pa.t.*, **cast(e), kast(e), kest(e)** *pp.*) cast (out), throw (out); convey, *Pe* 66; direct, aim, *G* 228, 1901; speak, utter, *Pat* 415, *G* 64, 249, 2275; arrange, *G* 2242; consider, *G* 1855; devise, *Cl* 1455

cast(e), kest *n.* intention, *Pe* 1163; speech, *G* 1295; stroke, *G* 2298; glance, *Cl* 768; fastening, *G* 2376; device, trick, *G* 2413; contrivance, *Cl* 1070

castel, k- *n.* castle; **castel-walle** *n.* castle wall, *Pe* 917*n*

casydoynes *n.* chalcedonies

catel *n.* property

caue *n.* cave

cauelaciounz *see* **kauelacion**

cause, cawse *n.* cause, reason; case, *Pe* 702

cayre, kayre, carye (*G* 734) *v.* go, ride; traverse, *Pe* 1031; pull, *Cl* 1259; bring, *Cl* 1478 (*cf.* **carye**)

cayser, kayser *n.* emperor

caytif, caytyf *adj.* evil, base, wretched

cemmed *pp.* combed

cercle *n.* circlet

certez *adv.* certainly

cerues *see* **kerue**

ceté, -y, cité, cyté, -y *n.* city

ceuer *see* **keuer**

chace *n.* the chase, *G* 1416; hunt, *G* 1604

chace *v.* drive, oust, *Pe* 443

chaffer *n.* trade, merchandise

chalk-whyt, -quyte *adj.* chalk-white

chambre *n.* room, private room, bedroom; bridal chamber, *Pe* 904

chapayle, chapel(le) *n.* chapel

charde *see* **charre**

charg *n.* importance; **no c.** no matter

charge *v.* charge, instruct, *Cl* 464, *G* 451; put on, *G* 863; load, burden, *Cl* 1258; *pp.* heavy, *Cl* 1154; laden, *Cl* 1295; **c. with** carrying, *Cl* 1272

chargeaunt *adj.* onerous, demanding

chariotes *n.* waggons, carts

charre *v.* (**charred, charde** *pa.t.*) turn aside (*reflex.*), *G* 850; turn back, *G* 1143; return, *G* 1678; fail, *Pe* 608

charres *n.* business affairs, *G* 1674

chast *v.* correct, restrain

chastyse *v.* chastise, punish; scold, *G* 1143

chaufen *v.* warm, excite

chaunce *n.* chance, fortune; **for c. þat** whatever, *G* 2132; adventure, exploit, *G* 1081 *etc.*; deed, *Cl* 1129

chauncely *adv.* fortuitously

chaundeler *n.* candlestick stand

chaunge *v.* change, exchange. *See also* **cher(e)**

chaunsel *n.* chancel

chauntré *n.* singing of mass, *G* 63

chawlez *n.* jaws

chayer(e), cheyer *n.* throne; chair, *G* 875

chef *adj.* chief, main; first, *Cl* 684

chef *n.* head, commander

chefly, cheuely *adv.* quickly, especially, first of all

cheftayn, cheue(n)tayn *n.* chieftain, ruler; captain, *Cl* 464

cheke *n.* cheek; **maugref my chekes** despite my objections, *Pat* 54

chek(ke) *n.* bad luck; doom, *G* 1857; onslaught, attack, *Cl* 1238

chelde, chemné *see* **(s)chelde, chymné**

chepe *n.* trade, bargain, market, price, *G* 1939, 1940*n*

chepen *v.* haggle

cher(e), schere *n.* face, expression; demeanour, manner, mood; cheerfulness, friendliness, welcome, *Cl* 641, *G* 562, 1259, *etc.*; **make god c.** make merry, *Cl* 641, behave cheerfully, *G* 562; **chaunge c.** look about, *G* 711*n*, 2169

cherych(e), -yse, -isch *v.* welcome, entertain; cherish, take care of, *Cl* 543, 1154, 1644

ches(e), chesly *see* **chose, chysly**

cheualrye *n.* body of knights; knighthood

cheue *v.* get, *G* 1271, 1390; come, *G* 63; **c. to** reach, *G* 1674; **c. þat (þe) chaunce** bring it about, *G* 2103, happen, *Cl* 1125

cheuely, cheue(n)tayn *see* **chefly, cheftayn**

cheuisaunce (-y-c-) *n.* winnings; acquisition, *G* 1939

childer, childgered *see* **chylde**

chorle *n.* serf; villain, *Cl* 1583

chose *v.* (**ches(e), chos(en)** *pa.t.*, **ichose, chosen** *pp.*) choose; perceive, *Pe* 187, *G* 798; make one's way, go, *G* 451, *etc.* (also **c. þe gate, waye**); devote oneself to, *G* 1838

chyche *n.* niggard, skinflint

chyde *v.* chide, scold; **for to c.** complaining, *Pe* 403

chylde *n.* (**chylder, childer** *pl.*, **chyldryn** *gen. pl.*) child; **childgered** *adj.* boyish, highspirited, *G* 86

chylled *pa.t.* grew cold

chymbled *pp.* muffled up

chymné, chemné *n.* fireplace; chimney, *G* 798

chyne *n.* chine, backbone, *G* 1354

chyn(ne) *n.* chin

chysly, chesly *adv.* dearly, solicitously, *Cl* 543, *G* 850*n*

chyst, ciences, cité *see* **kyst(e), syence, ceté**

clad *pa.t. & pp.* dressed, covered

clam(be) *see* **clym**

clamberande *presp.*, **clambred** *pp.* clustering, crowding

clanly(ch) *adv.* purely, chastely, *Cl* 264, 1089; neatly, *Cl* 310; completely, wholly, *Cl* 1327, *G* 393; courteously. *Cl* 1621; radiantly *or* chastely, *Pe* 2

clanner *see* **clene**

clannes(se), Clannesse *n.* cleanness, purity; Purity (*personified*), *Pat* 32

claryoun *n.* clarion

clater *v.* clatter, rattle, crash; splash, echo, *G* 731

clawres *n.* claws

clay *n.* clay; clay wall, *Cl* 1618

clay-daubed *adj.* plastered with clay

clayme, clem *v.* claim

cleche *v.* (**cleʒt** *pa.t.*) obtain, *Cl* 12; hold, fasten, *Cl* 858; hold fast, *Cl* 1655; **c. to** seize. *See also* **clyʒt**

clef, cleʒt, clem *see* **cleue, cleche, clayme**

cleme *v.* plaster, daub, *Cl* 312

clene *adj. & adv.* (**clener, clanner** *compar.*) clean, pure, chaste; bright, fair, (*sometimes blended with* pure), *Pe* 227, 289, 737, *etc.*, *Cl* 792, *etc.*, *G* 158, 576, *etc.*; fine, *Cl* 119; exact, *Cl* 1731; *adv.* cleanly; neatly, skilfully, perfectly, *Cl* 1382, *G* 792; completely, *Pe* 754(?), *Cl* 1606, *G* 146, 161, 1298, *etc.*; righteously, *Cl* 1287; plainly, *Pe* 949; *compar. adv.* more perfectly, *Cl* 1100

clenge *v.* cling; shrink, *G* 505 (*cf.* **clynge**)

clente *pp.* (riveted); enclosed, *Pe* 259

clepe *v.* call

cler(e) *adj. & adv.* (**cler(r)er** *compar.*, **clerest** *superl.*) clear, bright; fair, lovely (*& as n.*); pure; plain, easily understood, *Cl* 26, 1056; *adv.* clearly

clergye *n.* learning

clerk(k), k- *n.* priest, scholar; physician, *Pe* 1091; choirman, *G* 64

clernes *n.* beauty, splendour

clerrer *see* **cler(e)**

cleþe *v.* clothe, dress

cleue *v.* (**clef, cleuen** *pa.t.*, **clouen** *pp.*) split (asunder); rise sheer, *Pe* 66

clobbez, clomben *see* **klubbe, clym**

Clopyngnel *n.* Clopinel, i.e. Jean de Meun, *Cl* 1057n

clos(e) *adj. & adv.* close, fast; enclosed, *Cl* 12, 1070; closed, *Pe* 183; secret, *Cl* 512; tight, secure, *Pe* 512

clos *n.* enclosure, house

close *v.* enclose; contain, *Pe* 271, *G* 1298; encircle, *G* 186; close, fasten, *Pe* 803, *Cl* 1569, *G* 572, 1742; set, *Pe* 2; **closed fro** free from, *G* 1013

closet *n.* closed pew

clot *n.* clod, earth; mound, hill, *Pe* 789

cloþ(e) *n.* cloth; tablecloth; canvas, sail, *Pat* 105; *pl.* (table-)cloths, coverings; clothes, garments; bed-clothes, *Cl* 1788, *G* 1184

cloþed *pp.* dressed, clothed

cloude, clouen *see* **clowde, cleue**

cloutes, clowtez *n.* pieces, shreds

clowde, cloude *n.* cloud

cloyster, -or *n.* castle bailey, *G* 804; city, city wall, *Pe* 969

cluchche *v.* bend, *Cl* 1541n

clutte *adj.* patched

clyde *n.* plaster

clyff(e), klyf(f)e *n.* cliff, crag, hillside

clyʒt *pa.t.* held, *Cl* 1692. *See also* **cleche**

clyket *n.* latch

clym, klymbe *v.* (**clam(be), clomben** *pa.t.*) climb

clynge *v.* waste away, *Pe* 857

clyppe *v.* fasten

clypper *n.* shearer, *Pe* 802

clyue(n), clyuy *v.* stick, cling (together); pertain, belong, *Pe* 1196

cnawe *see* **knaw(e)**

cnawyng *n.* understanding

cnes *see* **kne**

cnoke, knokke *v.* knock, *Pe* 727; strike, *G* 414

cnowen *see* **knaw(e)**

cof *adj. & adv.* quick; quickly

cofer *n.* coffer, chest, jewel-box; ship, ark

cofly *adv.* quickly, promptly

coge *n.* boat

coʒed *pa.t.* coughed, cleared his throat, *G* 307n

coke, kok *n.* cock(erel)

cokrez *n.* leggings

colde *see* **co(o)lde**

cole *adj. & adv.* cool(ly)

cole *n.* coal, *Cl* 456

colen *v.* cool, assuage

coler *n.* collar

colored *pp.* coloured

colo(u)r *n.* colour; hue (whiteness), *Pe* 215; (white) complexion, *Pe* 22, 753, *G* 944

coltour *n.* coulter

colwarde *n.* malice

com *see* **com(me)**

comaund, cu- *v.* command; commend, *G* 2411

comaundement *n.* command

combraunce *n.* difficulty

combre *v.* destroy

come *n.* coming, *Pe* 1117; return, *Cl* 467, 1706

come(n) *see also* **com(me)**

comende *v.* commend

comfort(e), coum-, cum-, coumforde *n.* comfort, relief, consolation; pleasure, *Cl* 459, 512, *Pat* 264, 485, *G* 1011, 1221, 1254

comfort *v.* amuse, *G* 1099; console, *G* 2513

comly(ch), cumly *adj. & adv.* (**comloker, -est** *compar. & superl.*) comely, fair, fine; proper, *Cl* 512; *as n.* noble (fair) one, *Pe* 775, *G* 674, 1755, 1794; *adv.* beautifully, fairly; **comlyly, comly(che)** *adv.* fittingly, *G* 360, 648, *etc.*; courteously, *G* 1307, *etc.*

com(me), cum *v.* (**com(e)(n)** *pa.t.*, **com(m)-en, cum(m)en** *pp.*) come, arrive, go

commune *adj.* belonging in common

comparisunez *v.* compares

compas *n.* circuit, path, *Pe* 1072; shape, figure, *G* 944; compass, limits, *Cl* 1057; measure, *Cl* 319

compas *v.* (**compast** *pa.t.*) devise, plan; ponder, *G* 1196

compayny(e), compeyny *n.* company

comynes *n.* common people

con, cunen *v.* (**cowþe, couth, couþe** *pa.t. & pp.*) be able, can, know how (to). *See also* next con, can *auxil. v.* (*orig. fr.* [be-]gan, *confused w. prec.*) did, *Pe* 78n, 81, 88, *etc.*, *Cl* 301, 344, 363, *etc.*, *Pat* 10, 138, *etc.*, *G* 230, 275, 340, *etc.*; cowþe *pa.t. of* con *v. used in same way G* 2273; con + *inf.* = *pres. tense Pe* 271, 495, 509, *etc.*; conez *pres2s. Pe* 482, 909, 925

conable *adj.* excellent

conciens, -ce *n.* mind, *G* 1196; conviction, *Pe* 1089

condelstik *see* candelstik

conez *see* con *auxil. v.*

confourme *v.* conform; c. þe to model yourself upon, *Cl* 1067

connyng, coning *n.* learning; *pl.* branches of learning, *Cl* 1611

conquerd *pa.t.* won

conquest *pp.* conquered, *Cl* 1305

consayue *v.* conceive

constrayne *v.* force

conterfete *see* co(u)nterfete

contraré, -y *adj.* contrary; unnatural, *Cl* 266; *as n. Cl* 4; in c. of opposite, *Cl* 1532

contray, co(u)ntré, cuntré *n.* country, region; bi c. across country, *G* 734

controeued *pa.t.* contrived

contryssyon *n.* contrition

conueye(n) *v.* accompany, conduct; follow, *Cl* 768; escort to gate, *G* 596

conysaunce *n.* cognisance, badge

co(o)lde *adj.* (calder *compar.*, *Pe* 320) cold; lacking in zeal, *Cl* 1231; melancholy, *Pat* 264, *G* 1982; chilling, grievous, *Pe* 50, 808; *as n.* cold, *G* 505, *etc.*, (wintry) ground, *G* 2474; in hot and c. through thick and thin, *G* 1844; *adv.* sadly, *Pat* 382

coostez *see* cost(e)

cop(e)rounes *n.* tops, finials

corage *n.* heart

corbel, corbyal *n.* raven

cordes *n.* ropes

coro(u)nde *pa.t. & pp.* crowned

c(o)roun(e), crowne *n.* crown, diadem; top of head, *G* 419, 616; cincture, *Cl* 1275, 1444n

cors, cource, course *n.*[1] course, *Cl* 264; course (of a meal) *Cl* 1418 (*pl.*), *G* 116, 135

cors(e) *n.*[2] body; mi c., his c. me, him, *Cl* 683n, *G* 1237n

corsed *pa.t. & pp.* cursed

corsour *n.* horse, charger

corsyes *n.* corrosives

cort, court(e), kort *n.* court

cort(a)yn *n.* bed-curtain; cortyned *pp.* curtained, *G* 1181

cortays(e), cortez *adj.* courteous, gracious, fair; *as n.* gracious one, *Pe* 481, *Cl* 1097, *G* 2411; -ly *adv.* courteously, graciously

cortaysy(e), -sé *see* co(u)rtaysy(e)

cortel, kyrtel *n.* kirtle, gown

cortez *see* cortays(e)

cort-ferez *n.* fellow courtiers

cortyn *see* cort(a)yn

coruen, coruon *see* kerue

coruppte *adj.* corrupt

cosse *n.* kiss

cost *n.*[1] nature, *G* 546; contrivance, *Cl* 1478; *pl.*

qualities, *Cl* 1024, *G* 1272, 1849; manners, *G* 944, 1483; actions, *G* 2360; observances, *G* 750; c. of care hardships, *G* 2495

cost(e), koste *n.*[2] (costese, coostez *pl.*, *Cl* 460, 1033) coast; region; shore

costoum *n.* custom

cosyn *n.* cousin (nephew), *G* 372

cote *n.* coat, tunic; surcoat, *G* 637, 2026 (= cote-armure, *G* 586n)

coþe *pa.t.* quoth, said

couacles, couaclez *n.* covers (of cups)

couardise, cowardise, coward(d)yse *n.* cowardice

couenaunt, -aunde *n.* covenant, agreement, contract; *pl.* conditions

couered *pa.t. & pp.* covered

couerto(u)r *n.* caparison (ornamental cloth covering for horse's trappings) *G* 602; counterpane, *G* 855, 1181

couetyse *n.* avarice

coueyte *v.* covet, desire

coumforde, -fort *see* comfort(e)

coundue *v.* conduct

coundutes *n.* part-songs, *G* 1655n

counsayl, counse(y)l *n.* counsel, advice; plan, purpose

counte *v.* count; reckon, consider

countenance *n.* expression, *Cl* 792, *G* 335; custom, *G* 100; favour, approval, *G* 1490, 1539 *pl.* looks, *G* 1659

co(u)nterfete *v.* feign; imitate; dotz hem vus to c. liken them to us, *Pe* 556

countes *n.* countess, *Pe* 489

co(u)ntré *see* contray

couple, cupple *n.* couple, pair, *Cl* 333; leash, *G* 1147

course, cource *see* cors *n.*[1]

court(e) *see* cort

co(u)rtaysy(e), -sé *n.* courtesy, chivalry; *fig.* goodness, moral virtue, generosity, (divine) grace, *Pe* 432, 444, *etc.*, *Cl* 13, *Pat* 417

cout *v.* cut

couth *see* con

couþe *pp.adj.* known; manifest, *G* 1490

couþ(e) *see also* con

couþly *adv.* familiarly

covhous *n.* cow-shed

cowpes *see* cuppe

cowpled *pa.t.* leashed in pairs, *G* 1139

cowters *n.* elbow-pieces

cowþe(z) *see* con

cowwardely *adv.* basely, disgracefully

coynt, k-, qu-, quaynt *adj.* skilfully made; beautiful, *Cl* 871; skilful, *Pe* 889; wise, *Pat* 417; wise, fastidious, *Cl* 160, *G* 1525; -ly(ch) *adv.* gracefully, daintily; cleverly, *G* 2413

coyntyse, koynt-, quaynt-, quoynt-, -is(e) *n.* wisdom, skill; fine dress, *Cl* 54; Koyntyse (person.) Wisdom; *Pe* 690n

crabbed *adj.* harsh, *G* 502; perverse, *G* 2435

craft(e) *n.* artistry, (display of) skill; power, *Pat* 131; wisdom, *Cl* 13; practice, way, method, *Cl* 697, 865; *pl.* arts, powers; deeds, *Cl* 549; sports, *G* 1688

crafty *adj.* skilfully made

craftyly *adv.* skilfully
crag(g)e *n.* crag
crak, krak *n.* blast, blare
crakkande *presp.* ringing
crakkyng *n.* blaring
craþayn *n.* churl, boor
craue *v.* ask (for), beg (for); claim, *G* 1384
Creato(u)r *n.* Creator
Crede *n.* Apostle's Creed
crepe *v.* creep
cresped *pp.* curled
cresse *n.* cress; **not a c.** not a jot
creste *n.* mountain-top, *G* 731; crest, (heraldic) device, *Pe* 856
creuisse *n.* fissure
criande *see* **crye**
croked *adj.* hooked, curve, *Cl* 1697; crooked, out of true, *G* 653; dishonest, *Cl* 181
crokez *n.* sickles
cronez *n.* cranes
cropure, cropore *n.* crupper
Cros Kryst Christ's Cross
crossayl *n.* cross-sail, square-sail (a mainsail placed square across the ship)
croukez *v.* croaks
croun, crowne *see* **c(o)roun(e)**
croys *n.* cross
crue *pa.t.*, **crowen** *pp.* crowed
cruppelez *n.* cripples
cry(e), kry *n.* cry; proclamation, *Cl* 1574; blast, *G* 1166
crye, k- *v.* (**criande** *presp.*) cry (out), call; give tongue, *G* 1701; proclaim, *Cl* 1361, 1751; plead for, *Cl* 394; weep, *Cl* 1080, *G* 760; resound, *Cl* 1210
crysolyt *n.* chrysolite
crysopase *n.* chrysoprase
Cryst(es), Cryst(en)masse *see* **Kryst(e)**
cubit, cupyd *n.* cubit
cum, cum(m)en *see* **com(me)**
cumaundez, cumfort, cumly, cunen, cuntré *see* **comaund, comfort(e), comly(ch), con, contray**
cupborde *n.* sideboard
cuppe, cowpe, k- *n.* cup
cupple, cupydez *see* **couple, cubit**
cure *n.* care
curious, kyryous *adj.* rare, exquisite; skilful, *Cl* 1452; fastidious, *Cl* 1109
cyté, cyty *see* **ceté**

dabate *see* **debate**
daȝed *pa.t.* dawned
dale *n.* dale, valley (bottom)
dalt(en), daly *see* **dele, daylye**
dalyaunce *n.* courtly conversation
Dalyda *n.* Delilah
dam *n.* (pool); stream, water, *Pe* 324; water, flood, *Cl* 416, *Pat* 312
dame, Dame *n.* lady, Lady; ladies, *G* 1316
dampned *pp.* condemned, *Pe* 641
dampped *pp.* **stifled**, *Cl* 989 (*cf. also* **dampned**)
damvsel(le) *n.* damsel, young lady
Danyel, Daniel *n.* Daniel
dar(e) *v.*[1] (**durst, dorst(e)(n)** *pa.t.*) dare

dare *v.*[2] shrink, cower, *G* 315, 2258; bow down, submit, *Pe* 609, 839
Dary(o)us *n.* Darius
dasande *presp.adj.* dazing, stupefying
daschande *adj.* dashing, rushing
dased *pa.t. & pp.* lay dazed, *Pat* 383; *pp.adj.* dazed, *Pe* 1085
date *n.* limit, *Pe* 493; (point of) time, *Pe* 504, 529, *Cl* 425; beginning, *Pe* 516, 517; end, *Pe* 528, 540, 541; date, *Pe* 1040; season, *Pe* 505; rank, *Pe* 492
daube *v.* daub, plaster
Dauid, -yth *n.* David
daunce, -se *v.* dance; leap, writhe, *Pe* 345
daunger *n.* danger; fear, *Cl* 342; power, *Pat* 110; coldness, insolence, *Cl* 71; (state of) deprivation, *Pe* 250
daunsyng *n.* dancing
dawande *adj.* dawning
dawed, dawez *see* **dowe, day**
day(e) *n.* (**dayez, dawez** *pl.*) day, daylight; **in d.** ever, *G* 80; (**vpon**) **dayez** (*gen.*) in the day, *G* 1072, by day, *Cl* 578; **out of dawez** out of existence, *Pe* 282 (*see* **do**); **dayez of ende** last days, days of Judgement, *Cl* 1032; **dayez** for the duration, *Cl* 520
day-glem *n.* light of day (i.e. sun), *Pe* 1094
daylye, daly *v.* converse, flirt; speak, *Pe* 313
daylyȝt *n.* daylight
daynté, daynty(e) *n.* honour, courtesy; delight (in), *G* 1889; *pl.* luxuries, delicacies; *adj.* charming, *G* 1253
day-rawe *n.* dawn, first light of day
debate, da- *n.* resistance; contention, *Pe* 390
debonere *adj.* gracious in manner
debonerté *n.* courtesy, graciousness; meekness, *Pe* 798
dece, des(e) *n.* dais; throne, *Pat* 119
declar *v.* interpret
declyne *v.* fall (from prosperity), *Pe* 333; **d. into acorde** come to an agreement, *Pe* 509
decre *n.* decree
ded *see* **do, ded(e)**
dedayn *n.* indignation
ded(e) *adj.* dead; *as n. Cl* 1096; **D. See** Dead Sea
dede *n.* deed, act, activity, work; action, *Pe* 481
defence *n.* prohibition, *Cl* 243, 245; circumspection, *G* 1282
defende *v.* defend; forbid, *G* 1156
defoule *n.* defilement, *Pat* 290
defowle *v.* defile, pollute
degré *n.* rank; *pl.* steps, *Pe* 1022
deȝe, diȝe, dyȝe(n) *v.* die
deȝt(t)er(e)(s) *see* **doȝter**
dekenes *n.* deacons
dele *v.* (**dalt(en)** *pa.t.*, **dalt, deled** *pp.*) deal (out), mete out; bestow (on), *G* 1266, 1805; utter, deliver, *Cl* 344, 1641; perform, execute, *Cl* 1756, *G* 2192; associate, *Cl* 137; behave (towards), *G* 1662; converse, *G* 1668; partake of, *Cl* 1968; exchange, buy, *Cl* 1118; **d. drury wyth** exchange love with, have the love of; **d. vntyȝtel** behave freely, let oneself go
del(e) *see also* **doel, deuel**

delful, dulful *adj.* sorrowful, grievous; **-ly** *adv.* *Pe* 706
delit, delyt *n.* delight, joy, pleasure; desire; **laȝt d.** conceived a wish, *Pe* 1128
deliuer, delyuer *adj.* quick, nimble, *G* 2243; delivered, *Cl* 1084; **-ly** *adv.* quickly, nimbly, *G* 2009
delyuer *v.* release, save; despatch, *G* 1414; destroy, *Cl* 286; assign, *G* 851
demay *reflex.v.* be perturbed, *G* 470
deme *v.* judge, consider, assess, think fit; expect, *Pe* 336; ordain, *Pe* 348; condemn, *Pe* 325; censure, *Pe* 349; agree, *G* 1089, 1668; allow, *Pe* 324; decree, declare, *Cl* 110, 1745, *Pat* 386, 432; utter, *Pat* 119; speak (of), say, *Pe* 337, 361, 1183, *G* 2183
demerlayk *n.* magic; **demorlaykes** *pl.* phantoms
demme *v.* be baffled, *Pe* 223; fill (with water), *Cl* 384
dene *n.* valley
denez ax *n.* Danish axe, battle-axe, *G* 2223 (*see G* 288*n*)
denned *pa.t.* lurked, lay deep, *Pe* 51
denounced *pp.* proclaimed, *Cl* 106*n*
departe *v.* depart, *Cl* 396, 1677; part, *G* 1983; separate, part, divide, *Pe* 378, *Cl* 1074, 1738, *G* 1335; **departyng** *n.* parting, *G* 1798
depaynt(ed) *pp.* painted, portrayed; adorned, *Pe* 1102
depe *adj. & adv.* deep(ly); great, profound, *Cl* 1425, 1609; intense (whiteness of complexion), *Pe* 215; *as n.* depths, *Pe* 109; sea, *Pat* 235, 263, *etc.*
deprece *v.*[1] release, *G* 1219
deprece, depres(e) *v.*[2] subjugate, *G* 6; press, *G* 1770; drive away, *Pe* 778
depryue *v.* take away, dispossess
dere *adj.*[1] (**derrest** *superl.*) dear, beloved, *Pe* 368, 758, 795, *Cl* 52, 814, *G* 470, 754; precious, *Pe* 1183, 1208, *Cl* 698, *etc.*, *G* 121, 193, *etc.*; private, privy, *Cl* 683; essential, *Cl* 1604; noble, worthy, splendid, *Pe* 72, 85, 97, 121, *etc.*; exalted, *Pe* 492; festal, *G* 92, 1047; pleasant, pleasing, *Pe* 400, 880, *G* 47, 564, *etc.*; intimate, *G* 2449; good, right, *Pe* 504; dear(ly), *Pe* 733; *as n.* noble one(s), *Pe* 777, *Cl* 1394, 1399, *G* 678, 928; *superl.* most precious, *Cl* 1118; noblest, *Cl* 115, 1306, *G* 445; **derrest** *adv.* most nobly, *G* 483
dere *adj.*[2] severe, harsh, *Cl* 214
der(e) *n.* deer
dere *v.* harm, hurt, *Pe* 1157, *Cl* 862, *G* 1460
derely *adv.* courteously, in courtly style; deeply, *G* 1842; splendidly, *Pe* 995; extremely, gloriously, *Cl* 270
derez *n.* injuries, hindrances; **did me d.** put obstacles in my way, *Pe* 102
derf, derue *adj.* bold. strong; loud, fierce, *Cl* 862; painful, *G* 558, 564; dreadful, *G* 1047; **-ly** *adv.* boldly, quickly; ?wickedly, *Cl* 1518
derk *adj.* dark; *as n.* darkness, *Pe* 629, *Cl* 1755, *Pat* 263
derne *adj.* secret, hidden; confidential, *G* 1012; profound; *Cl* 1611; *as n.* secret, *Pat* 182; *adv.* secretly, *Cl* 697; **-ly** *adv.* secretly

derrest *see* **dere** *adj.*[1]
derþe *n.* glory, splendour, *Pe* 99
derue(ly) *see* **derf**
derworth *adj.* splendid, *Pe* 109; **derworþly** *adv.* sumptuously, *G* 114
des(e) *see* **dece**
deseuered *pp.* separated, *Pat* 315
des(s)ert(e) *see* **dis(s)ert**
dessypelez *n.* disciples, *Pe* 715
destyné, destiné *n.* destiny, fate
desyre, dezyre *v.* desire
determynable *adj.* incontrovertible, *Pe* 594
deþe, deth(e) *n.* death
deuaye, -v- *v.* refuse
deue *v.* strike down
deuel, dele *n.* devil
deuely *adj.* desolating, *Pe* 51
deuice *see* **deuise**
deuine *n.* prophet, diviner
deuine *v.* interpret
deuinores *n.* diviners
deuise, -ce, deuyse, -v- *v.* contemplate, *Pe* 1129; conceive, *Cl* 1046; devise, *Cl* 1100, 1288; explain, expound, *Cl* 1157, 1325, *etc.*; describe, *Pe* 99, 984, 995, 1021; relate, *G* 92; order, *Cl* 110; appoint, *Cl* 238
deuocioun *n.* devotion
deuote, deuout *adj.* devoted, devout
deuoutly, dewoutly *adv.* devoutly, reverently
deuoyde, -v-, -w- *v.* dispel, *Pe* 15; destroy, annihilate, *Cl* 908; withdraw, forgo, *Pat* 284
deuys(e), *n.* division, *Pe* 139; **a d.** as fine as one could think, perfect, *G* 617; **at my d.** in my opinion, to my wish, *Pe* 199
deuyse *see* **deuise**
deuysement *n.* description
devaye *see* **deuaye**
devised, devyse(d) *see* **deuise**
devoyde *see* **deuoyde**
devoydynge *n.* destroying
dew(e) *n.* dew
dewoutly, dewoyde *see* **deuoutly, deuoyde**
dewyne, do- *v.* languish, pine away, *Pe* 11, 326
dezyre *see* **desyre**
dialokez *n.* discourses
diamauntez *n.* diamonds
dich(es) *see* **dych(e)**
did(en) *see* **do**
diete *n.* food
diȝe *see* **deȝe**
diȝt, dyȝt(t) *v.* (**diȝt, dyȝt** *pa.t.*, **dyȝt(e)** *pp.*) ordain, appoint; dispose, *Pe* 360; dress, adorn, *Pe* 202, 987, *Cl* 1688, 1753; prepare, *Cl* 632, *G* 1559, 1689, 2223; serve, *Cl* 818; set, place, *Pe* 920, *Cl* 699, 1794, *G* 114; *reflex.* direct oneself, *G* 994; **d. to deþe** put to death, *Cl* 1266
dille, dylle *adj.* stupid, *G* 1529; slow, *Pe* 680
dint *see* **dynt**
diptez, dipped *pa.t.* dipped, plunged
disceuer, discouer, dys- *v.* reveal, disclose
discrye *v.* discern
dishes *see* **dysche**
dispayred *adj.* in despair
dispit, dyspyt *n.* resistance, defiance

displayed *pa.t. intrans.* separated, was exposed; *pp.* displayed, revealed
displese, dys- *v.* displease; be displeased, *Cl* 1494; *reflex.* be offended, *Pe* 422, *G* 1839, 2439
disport *n.* pleasure
dispoyled *pp.* stripped, *Pat* 95; divested, *G* 860
dispyse *v.* treat with scorn, abuse
disserne *v.* distinguish
dis(s)ert, des(s)ert(e) *n.* desert, merit; **for d. of** in recompense for, *Pat* 84
disserue *v.* deserve, *Cl* 613, *G* 452, 1779, 1803
distresed *pa.t.subjunc.* would have harassed, *Cl* 880
distres(se), disstrye *see* **dys(s)tresse, dys(s)trye**
ditte *v.* (**dutte** *pa.t.*, **dit** *pp.*) close, shut, fasten; **dutande** *presp.adj.* fitting
diuinité *n.* learning in divinity, *Cl* 1609
do *n.* doe, *Pe* 345
do *v.* (**dos, dotz** *pres.*, **ded, did(en), dyd, dyt** (*Pe* 681) *pa.t.*, **don(e)** *pp.*) do, make, cause; put, *Pe* 250, 282, 366, 1042, *Cl* 1224, 1801, *G* 478; give, pay, *Pe* 424; have, cause to (be), *Pat* 443, *G* 1327; *reflex.* go, *G* 1308; *pp.* finished, *G* 928, 1365; ruined, *Cl* 989; **d. (a)way** stop, put an end to, *Pe* 718, 823, *Cl* 286, 862, *G* 1492; **d. down of** put down from, *Cl* 1801; **d. out of dawez** annihilate, *Pe* 282; **d. pyne** take trouble, *Pe* 511
dobler *n.* large plate; **dubleres** *pl.*
doc *see* **duk**
do(e)l, del(e) *n.* sorrow, grief, lamentation
doel-doungoun *n.* dungeon of sorrow, *Pe* 1187
doel-dystresse sorrow of grief, grief-and-sorrow, *Pe* 337
dogge *n.* dog
doȝter *n.* (**deȝt(t)er(e)s, doȝterez** *pl.*) daughter
doȝty *see* **duȝty**
dok *n.* tuft (of tail and forelock), *G* 193
dol *see* **do(e)l**
dole *see* **dool(e)**
dom(e) *n.* judgement, decre; trial; doom, *Pat* 203; command, *Cl* 632; award, *Pe* 580; right, *G* 295; mind, *Pe* 157, *Cl* 1046; **domezday** *n.* doomsday
don(e) *see* **do** *v.*
donkande *presp.adj.* moistening
dool(e), dole *n.* part, *Pe* 136, *Cl* 216, *G* 719; intercourse, *Cl* 699
dor(e) *n.* door
dorst(e)(n) *see* **dar(e)** *v.*¹
dos *see* **do** *v.*
doser *n.* tapestry, backcloth
dotage *n.* folly, madness
dote *v.* be demented, behave foolishly; be astonished, *Cl* 852; **doted** *pp.adj.* foolish, demented, *Pat* 196, *G* 1956; frenzied, *G* 1151
dotel *n.* fool
dotz *see* **do** *v.*
doublefelde *adv.* in double helpings, *G* 890
doumbe *adj.* dumb
doun *adv. & prep.* down
doun, down *n.* hill
doungoun *n.* dungeon

doured *pa.t.* grieved
dousour *n.* sweetness, *Pe* 429
doute *n.* fear, *G* 246, 442; doubt, *Pe* 928; **douteles** *adj.* doubtless
d(o)uth(e), -þe *n.* company of men; host, *Pe* 839; **þe d.** men, mankind, *Cl* 270, 597
douue *see* **dowue**
dowe *v.* (**dawed, dowed** *pa.t.*) avail, *Pat* 50, *Cl* 374; *pa.t.subjunc.* would be worth, *G* 1805
d(o)welle *v.* dwell, remain
down *see* **doun**
dowrie *n.* dowry
dowue, douue *n.* dove
dowyne *see* **dewyne**
draȝe, draw(e), drowe *v.* (**droȝ(en)** *pa.t.* **drawen** *pp.*) draw, pull; bring, *Pe* 699, 1116, *Cl* 1160; shut, *G* 1188, 1233; carry on, bring home, *G* 1647; move, go, *Cl* 500, 1329, 1394; **d. on lyte (allyt), d. on dryȝe (adreȝ)** hold back, *Cl* 71, 599, *G* 1031, 1463
draȝt *n.* drawbridge, *G* 817; *pl.* **draȝtes** characters, marks, *Cl* 1557
draueled *pa.t.* muttered
draw(e)(n) *see* **draȝe**
drechch *n.* delay
dred(e) *n.* dread, fear; **wythouten d.** without doubt; **dredles** *adj.* fearless
drede *v.* (**dred** *pa.t.*) fear, be afraid
dreȝ(e)(d), dreȝly *see* **dryȝ(e)**, *adj. & v.*
drem(e) *n.* dream(ing); vision, *Pe* 790
drepe *v.* slay, kill, destroy
dres(se) *v.* arrange, assign, position, place; serve, *Cl* 1518; ordain, *Pe* 495; derive, *Pe* 860; direct, *G* 445; proceed, *G* 474 (*reflex.*), 1415; get up, *G* 566, 2009; **vpon grounde hym dresses** takes his stand, *G* 417
dreue *v.* make one's way, *Pe* 323, 980
drink(ez) *see* **drynk**
driuen, drof *see* **dryue**
droȝ(en) *see* **draȝe**
droȝþe *n.* drought
dronk(k)en *adj.* drunk
drop(p)e *v.* drop; **droppande** *presp.adj.* flowing, *Pat* 383
drounde *see* **drowne**
droupyng, drowping *n.* slumber, heaviness
drouy *adj.* turbid
drowe *see* **draȝe**
drowne *v.* (**drowned, drounde** *pa.t.* **drowned** *pp.*) drown
drowping *see* **droupyng**
drury(e), drwry(e) *n.* love, love-making; love-token, *G* 1805, 2033
druye *see* **drye**
drwry *adj.* cruel, *Pe* 323
drwry(e) *see also* **drury(e)**
drye, druye, dryȝe *adj.* dry, *Cl* 385, 412, 460, 1096; *as n.* (dry) land, *Cl* 472, *Pat* 338
dryed *pp.* dried, *Cl* 496
dryf *see* **dryue**
dryftes *n.* snowdrifts
dryȝ(e), dreȝ *adj. & adv.* heavy, great, *Pe* 823, *Cl* 342; deep, *G* 1750; straight, unmoved, *G* 335; long-suffering, *G* 724; incessant, *G* 1460; **draȝe on d.** detain, *G* 1031; **-ly(ch)** *adv.* angrily, *Cl* 74; solemnly, *Cl* 344; incessantly,

continually, *Pe* 125, *Cl* 476, *G* 1026; relentlessly, *Pat* 235; utterly, *Pe* 223
dryჳ(e), dreჳe *v.* suffer, endure
dryჳe *see also* **drye**
Dryჳt(t)yn *n.* God, the Lord
drynk, drink *n.* drink
drynk *v.* (**drank** *pa.t.*) drink
dryue, dryf *v.* (**drof** *pa.t.*, **driuen, -y-** *pa.t. & pp.*) drive; hurtle, *Cl* 416, *G* 1151, 2263; pour (in), *Pe* 1153, *Pat* 312, *G* 121; fly, *Cl* 472; rise, *Cl* 692; strike, *G* 389; sink, *Pe* 30, 1094; pass (time), *G* 1176, 1468; make, *G* 558, 1020; *pp.* brought, *Pe* 1194; hammered, *Cl* 313; **d. out** proclaim, *Pat* 386; **d. to** press against, *G* 786, 1999; make for, *G* 222; come to, *Cl* 219; strike, *Cl* 1425
dubbed, -et *pp.* dressed, arrayed; adorned, decorated
dubbement(e), dubleres *see* (**a**)**dubbement(e), dobler**
dublet *n.* doublet, jacket
Duches *n.* Duchess
due *adj.* due, *Pe* 894; inevitable, *Pat* 49
duჳty, -o- *adj.* bold, brave; *as n.* *G* 2334
duk, doc *n.* duke, ruler
dulful, delful *adj.* sorrowful, grievous
dumpe *v.* plunge
dungen *see* **dyngez**
dunne *adj.* dun, *Pe* 30
dunt(e) *see* **dynt**
durande *presp.adj.* lasting, *Pe* 336
dure *v.* continue, last; live, survive, *Pat* 488
durst *see* **dar(e)** *v.*[1]
dusched *pa.t.* rushed
dust(e) *n.* dust
dut *n.* merriment, *G* 1020
dutande, duthe *see* **ditte, douþe**
dut(te) *pa.t.* feared
dutte *see also* **ditte**
dwellez *see* **d(o)welle**
dych(e), dich *n.* ditch
dyd, dyჳe(n) *see* **do** *v.*, **deჳe**
dyჳt(e), dyჳttez *see* **diჳt**
dylle *see* **dille**
dymly *adv.* gloomily
dym(me) *adj.* dark; dim, *Pe* 1076
dyn(e) *n.* noise; report, *Cl* 692; tumult, complaining, *Pe* 339, *Cl* 862; sound of revelry, *G* 47
dynge *v.* (**dungen** *pa.t.pl.*) strike
dyngne *adj.* noble, worthy
dyngneté *n.* high office
dynt, dint, dunt(e) *n.* blow
dysche *n.* dish; **disches** *pl.*
dyscouered *see* **disceuer**
dyscreuen *v.* see, discern, *Pe* 68
dysheriete *v.* disinherit
dysplese(s), dyspyt *see* **displese, dispit**
dyssente *v.* descend, *Pe* 627
dys(s)tresse, distres(se) *n.* sorrow, distress; constraint, *Pe* 898; force, violence, *Cl* 1160
dys(s)trye, disstrye *v.* destroy; end, *Pe* 124
dyt *see* **do** *v.*

Ebru *adj.* Hebrew
edé *adj.* (*as n.*) blessed, *Cl* 1717*n*

Effraim *n.* Ephraim
eft(e) *adv.* again, once more; later; back, *Pat* 143; next time, *G* 898, 2388; likewise, *Cl* 562, 1073, *G* 641
eftersones, eftsonez *adv.* again
egge *n.* edge; ridge, *Cl* 451; sword, blade, *Cl* 1104, 1246; blade, weapon, *G* 2392
eggyng *n.* egging, instigation
eke *adv.* also
elde(e) *n.* age; old age, *Cl* 657, *Pat* 125; generation, time, *G* 1520
ellez, elles *adv. & conj.* else; besides; otherwise, *Pe* 32, 724, *G* 1082; provided that, *Cl* 466, 705, *G* 295; *as n.* anything else, *Pat* 2
elnჳerde *n.* measuring-stick of 45 ins. (one ell)
em(e) *n.* uncle
emerad(e) *n.* emerald
emperise *n.* empress, *Pe* 441
emperour *n.* emperor
empyre, empire *n.* empire, imperial rule; control, *Cl* 540
enaumayld(e) *pp.* enamelled
enbaned *pp.adj.* fortified, *Cl* 1459, *G* 790*n*
embelyse *v.* adorn, grace
enbrauded, -aw-, -en *pp.adj.* embroidered
enchace *v.* urge on
enclose *v.* shut in, *Cl* 334; contain, *Pe* 909
enclyin *adj.* lying prostrate, *Pe* 1206
enclyne *v.* bow, *Pe* 236, *G* 340; sink, *Pe* 630; *pp.* inclined, *Cl* 518
encres *v.* increase
encroche *v.* obtain, *Pat* 18; bring, *Pe* 1117
ende *n.* end; **last e.** conclusion, outcome, *Cl* 608; (**vp**)**on e.** upright, *Cl* 423, at last *Cl* 1329, to death, *Pat* 426; **dayes of e.** last days, *Cl* 1032
ende *v.* end, die
endelez, -s *adj. or adv.* endless(ly), perfect(ly)
endent(e) *pp.* inlaid, set, *Pe* 1012; *fig.* *Pe* 629
endentur *n.* jointing
end(e)ure *v.* endure; have power (to), *Pe* 225
endite, endyte *v.* ?accuse, condemn, *G* 1600; utter (in song), *Pe* 1126
endored *pp.adj.* gold-adorned, *Pe* 368
ene *adv.* once; **at e.** at once, *Pe* 291; **mad at e.** settled, made certain, *Pe* 953
enfamined *pa.t.* starved
enforse *v.* drive
enfoubled *pp.adj.* swathed
engendered *pa.t.* begot
Englych *adj.* (*as n.*) the English, *G* 629
enherite *v.* inherit
enker *adj.* pure, intense
enlé *adv.* separately, *Pe* 849
enleuenþe *adj.* eleventh
enmy *n.* (**enmyes, enmies** *pl.*) enemy
Ennias *n.* Æneas
en(n)(o)urned *pp.* adorned; set
enourled *pp.* surrounded
enpoysened *pa.t.* poisoned
enpresses, enprecez *v.* oppresses
enpryse *n.* renown
enprysonment *n.* imprisonment
enquest *n.* question
enquylen *v.* obtain
ensens *n.* incense

entayled *pp.* embroidered
entent *n.* resolution
enterludez *n.* interludes, plays, *G* 472*n*
enurned *see* **en(n)(o)urned**
entre, enter *v.* enter
entré *n.* entry
entyse *v.* provoke, *Cl* 1137, 1808; attract, catch (infection), *G* 2436
er(a)nd(e), ar(e)nde *n.* errand, mission, business
erbes, erbez *n.* herbs, grass, plants
erber *n.*[1] gullet, *G* 1330
erber(e) *n.*[2] (herb) garden, *Pe* 9*n*, 38, 1171
erd(e) *n.* land, region; **on e.** on earth, *Cl* 892; *as intensive:* of old, *Cl* 601, *G* 2416, real-life, *G* 27, truly, *G* 140, the best on earth, *G* 881
ere *n.* ear
er(e) *prep., conj. & adv.* before, until; until then, *Pat* 212; first, *Pe* 319; **e. þis** until (before) now; **e. þenne** before
erigaut *n.* herigaut, cloak
erle *n.* earl
erly *adv.* early; **e. and late** all the time, *Pe* 392
Ermonnes *n.* (*gen.*) Hermon's, *Pat* 463
ermyn *n.* ermine
ernd(e) *see* **er(a)nd(e)**
erne-hwed *pp.adj.* eagle-coloured
ernestly *adv.* gravely, seriously, *Cl* 277; sternly, *Cl* 1240
erraunt *adj.* travelling, questing
Errik *n.* Eric
errour *n.* (in) error, *Pe* 422
erþe, vrþe *n.* earth, ground
erytage *see* **(h)erytage**
eschaped *pa.t.* eluded, *Pe* 187
ese *n.* ease, pleasure
est *n. & adj.* east, eastern
etayn *n.* giant
ete *v.* (**et(t)e** *pa.t.*) eat, dine
eþe *adj.* easy
eþe *v.* entreat
Eue *n.* Eve
euel *adj., adv. & n.* evil; *adv.* ill, *Pe* 310, 930; *as n.* sin, *Cl* 573, unpleasantness, *G* 1552
euen *adj. & adv.* even, quits, *G* 1641; *adv.* directly, exactly, straight, right; actually, *G* 2464
euen *n.* eve (*i.e.* day before), *G* 734, 1669
euen *v.* vie, *Pe* 1073
euenden *adv.* right down, *G* 1345
euentyde, -tide *n.* evening
euer(more) *adv.* (for) ever, always, all the time; *intensive:* **er e.** before ever; **e. þe lenger** the longer, *Pe* 180, by however much, *Pe* 600; **wych ... so e.** whichever
euer-ferne *n.* fern
euervch *adj.* every
euesed *pp.* clipped
euez *n.* edge, border, *G* 1178
eweres *n.* water pitchers
Ewrus *n.* Eurus
exellently *adv.* pre-eminently, *G* 2423
exorsismus *n.pl.* incantation, calling up spirits
expoun, expowne *v.* expound, set forth, explain; describe, *Pe* 37, *G* 209; utter, *G* 1506

expounyng *n.* explanation
expresse *adj. or adv.* explicit(ly), *Pe* 910; *adv.* plainly, clearly, *Cl* 1158

face *n.* face; surface, *G* 524. *See also* **bere**
fade *adj.* bold(?), *G* 149
fader *n.* father
fage *n.* deceit; **no f.** in truth, *G* 531
faȝt *see* **fyȝt**
falce, fals(e) *adj.* false; *as n.*, *Cl* 1168
fale *adj.*[1] brownish, dun, *G* 728
fale *adj.*[2] cheap; **f. of** indifferent about, *Pat* 92
falewed *pa.t.* grew pale
falle *v.* (**fel(le), fellen** *pa.t.*, **fallen** *pp.*) fall, sink; go, rush, *Cl* 399, 837, *G* 1425, 1702; die, perish, *Cl* 725, 1684; befall, happen, come, *Cl* 22, 494, *etc.*, *G* 23, 483, 2378, *etc.*; fall (to someone's lot), *Pat* 178, *G* 2243, 2327; befit, *G* 358, 890, 1303, 1358; **f. fro** spring from, *Cl* 685; **f. in** hit upon, *G* 1699; **is fallen forþwyth my face** has presented itself to me, *Cl* 304
fals(e) *see* **falce**
falssyng *n.* deception, *G* 2378
famacions *n.* defamations
famed *pp.* reputed
fande *see* **fynde**
fange, fonge *v.* (**feng** *pa.t.*, **fonge(d)** *pp.*) take, get, receive; welcome, *G*, 816 *etc.*; **f. in fere** sing together, *Pe* 884
fannand *presp.adj.* spreading out like a fan, *G* 181
fannez *v.* flaps, flutters
fantoum *n.* (**fantummes** *pl.*) illusion
farand(e) *adj.* handsome, *Cl* 607; splendid, *Cl* 1758, *G* 101; wonderful, *Pe* 865
farandely *adv.* pleasantly
fare *n.* journey; fortune; track, *G* 1703; behaviour, *Cl* 861, *G* 1116, 2386; bearing, *Pe* 832; food, *G* 694; celebration, *G* 537
fare *v.* (**ferde(n)** *pa.t.*, **faren** *pp.*) go, travel; behave, bear oneself; pass, *Cl* 403; fare, *Cl* 466; behave, happen, *Cl* 1106
Fasor *n.* Creator, *Pe* 431
fasoun *n.* form, *Pe* 983; manner, *Pe* 1101
faste *adj.* firm, binding, *G* 1636
fast(e), fest *adv.* swiftly, quickly; hard, earnestly, insistently, *Pe* 54, 150, *Cl* 936, *G* 1042, 2403; firmly, *Cl* 1147, *G* 782; fast (deeply), *Pat* 192; closely, *Pat* 290; almost, *Cl* 1194; **a(l)s f.** as quickly as possible, immediately
faste *v.* (*pres.subjunc.*) fast, *Pat* 390
fasten, festen *v.* fasten; establish, confirm, *Cl* 327, *G* 1783, 2329; make fast, *Pat* 273
fasure *n.* form
fat *adj.* fattened, *Cl* 627
fatez *v.* fades, *Pe* 1038
fatte *n.* vat, tub, *Cl* 802
fatted *pp.* fattened
faþmez *v.* gropes, *Pat* 273; **faþmed** *pa.t.* embraced, *Cl* 399
faunt *n.* child
fauo(u)r *n.* grace, noble quality, *Pe* 428; favour, *Pe* 968
faure *see* **fawre**

faurty, fo(u)rty *adj.* forty
faut(e), fawte *n.* fault, misdeed, sin; offence, *G* 1551; sinfulness, *G* 2435
fautles, -z *adj.* (**-lest** *superl.*) faultless, perfect
fauty, fawty *adj.* sinful, guilty
fawne *v.* fondle, *G* 1919
fawre, faure, four(r)e, fowre *adj.* four
fawte, fawty *see* **faut(e), fauty**
fax(e) *n.* hair
fay(e) *n.* faith; **in f.** indeed, truly, *Pe* 263; (**par**) **ma f.** by my faith, (on) my word, *Pe* 489, *G* 1495
fayl(y), fayle *v.* (**faylande** *presp.*) fail, fall short; be missing, lacking, *Cl* 737, 1535, *Pat* 181; miss, lack, *G* 278; sink, *Cl* 1758; finish, end, *Cl* 658; fail to be productive, *Pe* 34; grow pale, *Cl* 1539; wither, *Pe* 270; **f. of** miss, fail to obtain, *Pe* 317, *Cl* 889, *G* 1067
fayn *adj.* (**faynest** *superl.*) glad; **f.** (**of**) pleased to meet, *Cl* 642, *G* 840; *adv.* gladly, dearly, *Cl* 1629; **f. scape wolde** were anxious to escape, *Pat* 155
fayned *pp.adj.* false
fayntyse *n.* fallibility, deceitfulness, *G* 2435
fayr(e) *adj. & adv.* (**fayr(er), feier** *compar.*, **fayrest** *superl.*) *adj.* fair, lovely, fine; courteous, *Cl* 729, *G* 1116; *as n.* **þe fayrer** the upper hand, *G* 99; *adv.* fitly, well; humbly, courteously; precisely, neatly, *Pe* 1024, *Cl* 316, *G* 2309; delightfully, *Pe* 88; reverently, *Cl* 506
fayryȝe *n.* the supernatural, *G* 240
fayth-dedes *n.* deeds of faith
fayth(e), fayþ(e) *n.* belief, religion; (word of) honour, *G* 986, 1783, *etc.*; **in** (**god**) **f.** truly
faythful, fayþful *adj.* faithful, religious, *Cl* 1167; trustworthy, *G* 632, 1679
fayþely *adv.* truly, *G* 1636
feb(e)le *adj.* poor, mean; **feblest** *superl.* weakest, *G* 354
fech(e) *v.* (**feched** *pa.t.*, **fette** *pp.*) fetch, bring, receive; seize, *Cl* 1155; deal (a blow), *Pe* 1158; *reflex.* bring upon oneself, *Pat* 58
fedde *pp.adj.* fed (for killing), *Cl* 56
fede *v.* feed, *G* 1359
fede *adj.* faded, *Pe* 29
fee *n.* fee, payment; *pl.* domain, city, *Cl* 960
fe(e)rsley, ferslych *adv.* fiercely, brightly, *G* 832; proudly, haughtily, *G* 329; spiritedly, *G* 1323; sternly, *Pat* 337
feȝt(yng), feier *see* **fyȝt, fayr(e)**
fel *adv.* cruelly, *Cl* 1040
fel *see also* **falle**
felaȝes *n.* fellows, *G* 1702
felaȝschip, -schyp *n.* brotherly love, *G* 652; company. *Cl* 1764, *G* 2151; intercourse, *Cl* 271
felde *n.* field, country
felde *v.* fold, embrace, *G* 841
felde *see also next*
fele *v.*[1] (**felde** *pa.t.*, *Pe* 1087) feel, perceive; taste, *Cl* 107; smell, *Cl* 1019
fele *v.*[2] conceal; (*pa.subjunc.*) were to conceal, *Cl* 914
felle *adj.* fierce, stern, cruel; daring, *G* 291, 874; deadly, *Pe* 655; *as n.* fierce animal, *G* 1585

felle, fele *adj. & pron.* many; **feler** *comp.* more; **felefolde** many times over, *G* 1545
felle *n.*[1] fell, hill, *G* 723
felle *n.*[2] fur, skin
felle(n) *see* **falle**
felly *adv.* fiercely, cruelly
felonye *n.* crime, sin
feloun *n.* wretch
felt *pp.* matted, *Cl* 1689
femed *pa.t.* foamed, *G* 1572
femmalez *n.*(*gen.*) of a female, *Cl* 696
fende *n.* fiend, devil; (the) Devil; (*pl.*) sinners, *Pat* 82
fende *v.* **f. of** ward off, *Cl* 1191
fenden *adj. or n. g. pl.* fiendish, of fiends
feng *see* **fonge**
fenny *adj.* dirty; *fig.* vile, sinful, *Cl* 1113
Fenyx *n.* Phoenix, *Pe* 430
fer *see* **fer(re)**
ferde *pa.t.* feared, *G* 1588
ferd(e) *pp.* frightened, afraid; **for f.** in fear; *see also next*
ferde *n.* fear
ferde(n) *see also* **fare**
fere *adj.* proud, dignified, *G* 103
fere *n.*[1] (show, array); dignity, reward, *Pe* 616; martial array, *G* 267
fere *n.*[2] (company); **in f.** together
fere *n.*[3] companion; wife, *G* 2411; mistress, *Cl* 1062; equal, *G* 676
fereles *adj.* without equal, unique, *Pe* 431*n*
ferez *v.* conveys, takes, *Pe* 98; **feryed** *pp.* brought, carried
ferk(ke) *v.* go (quickly), ride, pass; **f. vp** jump up; **ferkez hym vp** bestirs himself, *G* 2013
ferly *adj.* wonderful; exceptional, *G* 716 (*or n.*); *n.* marvel; amazement, *Pe* 1086
ferlylé *adj.* marvellous, *Cl* 1460
ferly(ly) *adv.* wonderfully, exceedingly, greatly, terribly
fermysoun *n.* close-season, *G* 1156*n*
fer(re) *adv.* far; **fyr** *adj.* distant, *Cl* 1680; **ferre, fire, fyrre** *compar.* farther (*adj. Pe* 148), further, moreover; **f. þen** in excess of, *Pe* 563
fers, fyrce *adj.* proud, bold; fierce, vehement, *Pe* 54
fersly(ch), feryed *see* **fe(e)rsly, ferez**
fest *see also* **fast(e)**
fest(e) *n.* festival, feast; **ma f.** (*lit.* make a festival) rejoice, *Pe* 283
festen(ez) *see* **fasten**
festival *adj.* befitting a feast, *Cl* 136
festned, -s *see* **fasten**
festres *v.* festers
fet(e) *see* **fot(e)**
fete *n.* (fact); ?deed(s), action(s), *Cl* 1062; **in f.** indeed, *Cl* 1106
feted *pa.t.* behaved, *G* 1282
fetled *see* **fettele**
fetly *adv.* gracefully, neatly
fet(t)e *v.* (**fette** *pp.*) fetch, bring
fette *see also* **fech, fot(e)**
fettele *v.* (**fettled** *pa.t.*, **fet(t)led** *pp.*) prepare; set, fix, *Cl* 585, *G* 656; arrange, *Pat* 38
fetterez, fettres *n.* fetters

fettled *see* **fettele**
fetures, -z *n.* features, parts (of body)
fetys(e) *adj.* well-proportioned, *Cl* 174; **for f.** through skill, *Cl* 1103
fetysely *adv.* skilfully, elegantly
feþer-beddes *n.* feather-beds
fewe *adj.* few; lacking (**of:** in), *Cl* 1735
feye *adj.* doomed, dead
fiften *see* **fyftene**
figure, fygure *n.* figure, form; (written) character, *Cl* 1726; image, *Pe* 1086
fildore, fyldor *n.* gold thread
fire *see* **fer(re), fyr**
fis(s)che(z) *see* **fysch(e)**
flaȝ(e) *see* **fle, flyȝe** *v.*[1]
flaȝt *n.* grass, turf, *Pe* 57
flake *n.* flake, *Cl* 954; blemish, *Pe* 947
flakerande *presp.* fluttering
flambe *v.* shine, *Pe* 769; **flaumb(e)ande** *presp. adj.* flaming, glowing
flat *n.* lowlands, *G* 507
flaumb(e)ande *see* **flambe**
flaunkes *n.* sparks
flauorez *n.* scents, perfumes, *Pe* 87
flawen *see* **fle**
flayed *pp.* terrified, *Cl* 960; *pa.t. Cl* 1723, *Pat* 215
flayn *see* **flyȝe** *v.*[2]
flayr *n.* scent
fle *v.* (**flaȝ(e), fled, flowen** *pa.t.,* **flawen, flowen** *pp.*) flee, *Cl* 377, 914, 945, 975, *Pat* 183, 214, 424, *G* 1628, 2125, 2130, 2272, 2274, 2276(2)*n*; escape, *Pe* 294
fleez *see* **flyȝes**
fleȝe *see* **flyȝe** *v.*[1]
flem *n.* flow
fleme *v.* drive (out), banish; **of f.** banish, *Pe* 358
flesch(e) *n.* flesh, body; living thing, *Cl* 303, 356, *etc.*; **-ly(ch)** *adv.*
flet *see* **flet(te)**
flete *v.* (**flet(t)e, flot(t)(e), fleten** *pa.t.,* **floten** *pp.*) float, drift; fly, *G* 1566; swim, *Cl* 432; flood, fill, *Cl* 685
flet(te) *n.* floor; city, *Pe* 1058; **vpon (on þis, þe) f.** in (this, the) hall
flod(e) *n.* water, *Cl* 531, 538, *etc.*; stream, *G* 2173; river, *Pe* 1058; sea, *Pe* 736, *Pat* 126, *etc.*; flood, *Cl* 369, 397; **f. lotes** the sea's roarings, *Pat* 183; **French f.** English Channel, *G* 13; **flodez fele** (*gen.*) of many waters, *Pe* 874
floȝed *see* **flowed**
flok *n.* (**flokkes, -z** *pl.*) flock, crowd, company
flokked *pa.t.* flocked; **f. in** assembled, *G* 1323
flokkes, flokkez *see* **flok**
flonc *pa.t.* rushed, *Pe* 1165
flone *n.* arrow
flor *n.* floor
flor-de-lys, flores *see* **flo(u)r-de-lys, flo(u)r**
flosche *n.* pool, swamp
flot *n.*[1] scum, *Cl* 1011
flot(e) *n.*[2] host, company
flot(en), flot(t)e *see also* **flete**
floty *adj.* stream-filled, *Pe* 127
flo(u)r, flowr *n.* flower; **vyrgyn f.** virginity, *Pe* 426

flo(u)r-de-lys *n.* fleur-de-lis (water iris), *Pe* 195, 753
floury *adj.* flowery, *Pe* 57
flowed, floȝed *pa.t.* flowed
flowen *see* **fle, flyȝe** *v.*[1]
flowr *see* **flo(u)r**
flowred *pa.t.* flowered
flurted *pp.* figured (with flowers), *Pe* 208
flwe *see next*
flyȝe *v.*[1] (**flaȝ(e), fleȝe, flwe, flowen** *pa.t.*) fly, *Pe* 89, 431, *Cl* 432, 1010, *G* 459, 524, 2276(1)*n*
flyȝe *v.*[2] (**flayn** *pp.*) flay, scourge, *Pe* 809, 813
flyȝes, fleez *n.* butterflies, flying insects, *G* 166, *Cl* 1476
flyȝt *n.* flight
flyt *n.* strife
flyte *v.* strive, wrangle
fnast(ed) *pa.t.* snorted, panted
fo *see* **fo(o)**
foch(che) *v.* take
fode *n.* food; **fodez** *pl.* people, *Cl* 466
fogge *n.* grass (of the second growth), *Cl* 1683
foȝt *see* **fyȝt**
fol *adj.* foolish
fol *see also* **fol(e)** *n.*[2], **ful**
folde *n.* earth; land, ground, *Cl* 477, 1014, *G* 23; **of f.** away, *Pe* 334; **(vp)on f.** on earth, living, *etc.*; **forme vpon f.** very first, *G* 2373
folde *v.* fold; bow, bend, *Pe* 813; pack up, *G* 1363; match, *G* 499; place, lay, *Cl* 1026; assign, *G* 359; enfold, *Pat* 309; **folde(n)** *pp.* wrapped, *G* 959; pledged, *G* 1783; **f. in** plaited, *G* 189; **f. vp** upturned, *Pe* 434
fole *n.*[1] horse; *gen.sg. G* 459; *gen.pl. Cl* 1255
fol(e) *n.*[2] fool
folé, foly *n.* folly
foler *n.* foliage, *Cl* 1410
foles *v.* goes mad, *Cl* 1422
foles *see also* **fole** *n.*[2], **fowle**
folez *see* **fol(e)** *n.*[2]
folȝe *v.* follow, pursue; accompany, *Cl* 677, 974; **f. tylle** serve, *Cl* 1752; **folȝande, fol(e)wande** *presp.* following; matching, *G* 859; in proportion (?) *G* 145*n*; in the order of, *Pe* 1040
folk(e) *n.* folk, people; *as pron.* anyone, *Cl* 1129; **folken** *gen.pl., Cl* 271
folmarde *n.* polecat
folwande, foly *see* **folȝe, folé**
folyly *adv.* foolishly, lewdly, *Cl* 696
foman *n.* foe, *Cl* 1175
fon *see* **fyne**
fonde *v.* try; tempt, *G* 1549; visit, *Pe* 939
fonde(n), fonge *see* **fynde, fange**
font *n.* font, *Cl* 164
fonte *see* **fynde**
foo *adj.* wicked, *G* 1430; *adv.* in hostility, *G* 2326
fo(o) *n.* foe, *G* 716
fooschip *see* **foschip**
for *conj.* (*also* **f. þat**) for, because; but(?), *G* 147*n*
for, fore, four (*Cl* 756) *prep.* for, because of, on account of, through, for the sake of, in exchange for; according to, *Pat* 12; as, *Pe* 830, *etc., Cl* 275, *etc., Pat* 519, *G* 240, *etc.*;

(enough) for, *Pe* 211; to, *Cl* 75, 143, *etc.*; with regard to, *Cl* 740, 867, *Pat* 439; in spite of, *Pe* 890, *Cl* 1332, 1550, *G* 1854, 2132, 2251; for fear of, *Cl* 1143, *G* 1334; before, *G* 965, 1822; **f. to** to; though (I), *Pe* 333; **þe ... f.** for which, *Pe* 734. *See also* **olde, ferde, fetys(e)**
forbe, forbi *prep.* beyond, more than
forbede *v.* (**forboden** *pp.*) forbid
forbi *see* **forbe**
forbrent *pp.* burned up
force, forse *n.* necessity, *G* 1239; strength, *G* 1617
forclemmed *pp.adj.* pinched with hunger
fordez *see* **forþe**
fordidden *pa.t.* destroyed, quelled, *Pe* 124
fordolked *pp.* grievously wounded, *Pe* 11
fore *see* **for** *prep.*
forfare *v.* (**fo(u)rferde** *pa.t.*) kill, destroy; perish, *Cl* 560
forfaren *pp.* headed off, *G* 1895
forferde *see* **forfare**
forfete *v.* forfeit, *Pe* 619, 639; transgress, *G* 2394; lose (their right), *Cl* 743
forgart *pa.t.* (**forgarte** *pp.*) forfeited, lost
forgat *see* **forȝete**
forged *pp.* made, constructed
forgif, forgyue *v.* (**forgef** *pa.t.*) forgive
forgo *v.* lose, give up
forgyue *see* **forgif**
forȝ *n.* furrow, *Cl* 1547; channel, *G* 2173
forȝelde *v.* recompense
forȝete *v.* (**forgat, forȝate, forȝet(e)(n)** *pa.t.*, **forȝeten** *pp.*) forget; forsake, *Cl* 203
forhedez *n.* foreheads, *Pe* 871
forjusted *pp.* overthrown in combat
forknowen *pp.* neglected
forlete *pa.t.* lost, *Pe* 327
forlondez *n.* headlands, *or* low-lying lands near the sea, *G* 699
forlonge *n.* furlong
forlotez *v.* (*imperat.*) omit, overlook, *Cl* 101
forloyne *v.* err, stray; forsake, *Cl* 1165; *pp.adj.* erring, *Cl* 1155
formadde *adj.* stupid
formast *superl. adj.* first (in time), *Cl* 494
forme *adj.* first, *Pe* 639, *Cl* 257, *Pat* 38(2), *G* 2373; *as n.* beginning, *G* 499
forme *v.* form, fashion, make
forme *see also* **fo(u)rme**
forne *adv.* of old, *G* 2422
fornes *n.* furnace, cauldron
forpayned *pp.* afflicted
forray *v.* plunder
forred, furred *adj.* lined (with fur)
forsake *v.* (**forsoke** *pa.t.* **forsaken** *pp.*) renounce; refuse, *Cl* 75, *G* 1826, 1846; deny, *G* 475
forse *see* **force**
forselet *n.* fortress
forser *n.* casket
forsettez *v.* (*imperat.*) beset, surround
forsnes *n.* courage, fortitude
forsoke *see* **forsake**
forsoþe *adv.* indeed, in truth, truly
forst *n.* frost
forth(e), forþ(e) *adv.* forth, forward, on, out;

at f. naȝtes late at night, *Cl* 1764*n*; **f. dayez** well on in the day, *G* 1072
forth *see also* **forþe**
fortune, fortwne *n.* fortune
forty *see* **faurty**
forþe, forth, ford(e) *n.* ford
forþ(e) *see also* **forth(e)**
forþer *v.* (**forþrede** *pa.t.*) carry out
forþering *n.* promoting, advancing
forþi *see* **forþy**
forþikke *adv.* very thickly
forþoȝt *see* **forþynkez**
forþrast *pp.* destroyed
forþwyth *prep.* before, in front of
forþy, forþi *conj.* therefore, and so
forþynkez *v.impers.* (**forþynk** *pres.subjunc.*, **forþoȝt** *pa.t.*) it grieves, displeases
forward(e) *n.* covenant, agreement; *pl.* terms
forwondered *pp.adj.* astonished
forwroȝt *pp.adj.* exhausted with toil
foschip, fooschip *n.* enmity
foster *n.* offspring
fot(e) *n.* (**fet, fet(t)e, fote(z)** *pl.*) foot; *pl.* footsteps, example, *Cl* 1062 (*see also* **fete** *n.*)
fotte *v.* receive, *G* 451
foul *see* **ful**
foule, fouled *see* **fowle, fowled**
founce, founs *n.* bottom
founde *v.* hasten, go, set out. *See also* **fynde**
foundementez, founde(n) *see* **fundament, fynde**
foundered *pp.* engulfed, *Cl* 1014
founs, four *see* **founce, for**
fourchez *n.* legs, haunches
fourferde *see* **forfare**
fo(u)rme *n.* form, shape, figure; pattern, example, *Cl* 3; outward appearance, *G* 145*n*; formula, *Pat* 38; manner, *G* 1295, 2130
four(r)e, fourty *see* **fawre, faurty**
fowle, foule *adj.* foul, dirty, vile; ugly, *G* 717; poor, *G* 1329; *as n.* evil, *G* 2378; *adv.* shamefully
fowle, fo(u)le *n.* bird, fowl
fowled, fouled *pa.t. & pp.* defiled
fowre *see* **fawre**
foyned *pa.t.* struck at
foysoun *n.* abundance; *as adj.* copious, *Pe* 1058
fraunchis, fraunchyse *n.* liberality, generosity
frayes *v.* frightens
frayn *v.* ask; put to test, *G* 489, 1549; wish, *Pe* 129
frayst *v.* (**frayst(ed)** *pp.*) ask (for), seek; try, test, *G* 503, 1679; scrutinize, *Pe* 169
fre *adj.* (**freest** *superl.*) noble, honourable, gracious; liberal, *Pe* 481; *as n.* noble one, *Cl* 929, *G* 1545, *etc.*; *pl.* free men, *Cl* 88
frech, freest *see* **fre(s)ch(e), fre**
frek(e) *n.* warrior, man, knight
frelich, frely(ch) *adj.* noble, glorious; fair, beautiful, *Cl* 173; *as n.* gracious one, *Pe* 1155
frely *adv.* generously, *G* 894; plentifully, abundantly, *Pat* 20, *G* 816; willingly, *Pat* 390; **freloker** *compar.* more nobly, more perfectly, *Cl* 1106

fremedly *adv.* as a stranger, *G* 714
frende *n.* friend
frenges *n.* fringes
frenkysch fare refined manners, *G* 1116
fres *pa.t.* froze, *G* 728
fre(s)ch(e) *adj.* fresh, bright, fair, unsullied, *Pe* 87, *Cl* 173, *G* 2019; *as n.* fair (one), *Pe* 195; **þe f.** fresh food, *G* 122; **freschly** *adv.* eagerly, *G* 1294
frete *v.* (**freten** *pp.*) eat, devour, corrode
frette *v.* (*imperat.*) supply, *Cl* 339; **fretted** *pp.* adorned
fro *conj.* (*also* **f. þat**) after, from the time that
fro *prep. & adv.* from, away from; **f. me warde** away from me, *Pe* 981; *adv.* **to ne f.** neither this way nor that, *Pe* 347
frok(ke) *n.* garment
frote *v.* rub, stroke
froþande *adj.* foaming, defiling, *Cl* 1721
froþe *n.* froth
frounse *v.* crease, pucker
frount *n.* forehead
frunt *pa.t.* struck, kicked, *Pat* 187
frym *adv.* richly, in strength
fryst *v.* delay
fryt(e), fruyt *n.* fruit; fruit tree(?), *Pe* 87
fryth *n.* wood(land), forest
ful, fo(u)l *adv.* fully, entirely, very, quite, most, completely
ful *see also* **ful(le)**
fulfylle *v.* fulfil; complete, *Cl* 1732
fulȝed *pp.* baptized
ful(le) *adj.* full; *as n.* **to þe f.** fully. *See also* **ful** *adv.*
fulsun *v.* help
fundament *n.* foundation; **foundementez** layers of the foundation, *Pe* 993
funde(n), furred, furst *see* **fynde, forred, fyrst(e)**
furþe *adj.* fourth, *Pe* 1005
fust *see* **fyste**
fuyt, fute *n.* trail
fyched *pp. or pa.t.* fixed, established
fyf, fyue *adj. & n.* five
fyft, fyfþe *adj.* fifth
fyftene, fiften *adj.* fifteen
fyfty, fyfté *adj.* fifty
fygure *see* **figure**
fyȝed *pa.t.* joined exactly (to their towers), *G* 796
fyȝt, feȝt (**faȝt, foȝt** *pa.t.*) *v.* fight; contend, *Pe* 54
fyȝt, feȝt(yng) *n.* fighting
fyin *see* **fyn(e)**
fyked *pa.t.* flinched
fykel *adj.* fickle, unreliable
fyldor *see* **fildore**
fyled *pp.*[1] soiled, defiled, *Cl* 136
fyled *pp.*[2] (filed); sharpened, *G* 2225; **f. out** carved out (with a file), *Cl* 1460
fylle *v.* fill; carry out, *G* 1405, 1934
fylor *n.* grindstone
fylsened *pa.t.* aided
fylter *v.* struggle, engage; contend, *G* 986; cling together, *Cl* 224; mix, join together, *Cl* 696; *pp.* tangled, *Cl* 1689

fylþe *n.* filth, defilement, impurity
fylyoles, -z *n.* turrets, pinnacles
fynde *v.* (**fande, fonde, founden** *pa.t.*, **fonde(n), fonte, f(o)unde(n)** *pp.*) find, discover; perceive, notice, *Pe* 170, 871, *Cl* 133; **fonde** *pa.subjunc.* would find, *G* 1875
fyndyng *n.* find, dislodgement (of game)
fyn(e), fyin *adj.* fine, perfect, choice, complete; good, *Cl* 721; pure, *G* 1239; precise, *G* 1636
fyn(e) *adv.* completely, perfectly, *G* 173, 1737; in full, *Pe* 635; **fynly** completely, *G* 1391
fyne *v.* (**fon, fyned** *pa.t.*) end, cease; die, *Pe* 328; come to an end, *Pe* 1030
fynisment *n.* end
fynger *n.* (**fyng(e)res, -z** *pl.*) finger
fynly *see* **fyn(e)** *adv.*
fynne *n.* fin
fyoles *n.* cups
fyr, fyre, fire *n.* fire, sparks; *pl.* inflammations, *Cl* 1095*n*
fyr *see also* **fer(re)**
fyrce *see* **fers**
fyrmament *n.* firmament, heaven
fyrre *see* **fer(re)**
fyrst(e), furst *adj. & adv.* first; at first, *G* 2227; **at þe f.** first, *Pe* 635; **of f.** from the beginning, *Cl* 1714; (**vp)on f.** first, in the beginning; *as n.* first day, *G* 1072
fysch(e), fis(s)che *n.* fish
fyskez *v.* scampers
fyste, fust *n.* fist, hand
fyþel *n.* fiddle
fyþer *n.* feather
fyue *see* **fyf**

gafe *see* **gif**
Galalye *n.* Galilee
galle, gawle *n.*[1] gall, bile, *Cl* 1022; bitterness, *Pe* 463
galle, gaule *n.*[2] flaw, impurity, *Pe* 189, 915, 1060; scum, *Pat* 285; *pl.* wretches, *Cl* 1525
game, gamnez *see* **gomen**
gardyn *n.* garden
garez *v.* (**gart(en)** *pa.t.*, **gart** *pp.*) causes, makes
gargulun *n.* throat
garlande *n.* garland, *Pe* 1186*n*
garnyst *adj.* adorned
gart(en) *see* **garez**
garysoun *n.* treasure; trophy, *G* 1807
garytez *n.* watch-towers
gast *adj.* afraid
gate *n.* way, road; street, *Pe* 1106; **hyȝe g.** highway, *Pe* 395; **bi g.** on the way, *G* 696; **haf þe g.** pass, *G* 1154. *See also* **chose**
Gaua(y)n, Gawa(y)n(e), Gawen, Wawan, Wawen, Wowayn, Wowen *n.* Gawain
gaudi *n.* beadwork(?), dye(?), *G* 167
gaue *see* **gif**
gaule, gawle *see* **galle** *n.*[1] & *n.*[2]
gay(e) *adj.* bright, lovely, beautiful, fine; merry, *Cl* 830; blissful, *Pe* 1186; *as n.* fair lady, fine knight
gay(e), gayly *adv.* finely, splendidly
gayn *adj., adv. & prep.* good, profitable; well-

suited, *G* 178; directly, *G* 1621; *prep.* nearby, *Pe* 138; **at þe gaynest** most directly; **-ly** *adv.* aptly, appropriately, *G* 476; rightly, *G* 1297
gayn(e) *v.* profit, help, serve, benefit; avail, *Cl* 1608
gaynly(ch) *adj.* gracious. *See also* **gayn**
Gaynour, Guenore, Gwenore, Wenore *n.* Guenever
gazafylace *n.* treasury, *Cl* 1283
geder *v.* gather, assemble; lift up, heave up, *G* 421, 2260; pick up (path), *G* 2160; **g. to** spur at, *G* 777, haul on, *Pat* 105
gef *see* **gif**
gele *v.* linger, stroll
gemme *n.* gem, jewel
gendered *pp.* begotten
gendrez *n.* kinds, species
generacyoun *n.* ancestry, *Pe* 827
gent(e) *adj.* noble, fair; courteous, kind, *Pe* 265, 1134
gentryse *n.* nobility
gentyl(e), jentyle *adj.*[1] noble, excellent, fine; reverent, *Cl* 1432; courteous, kindly, *Pe* 278, *etc.*, *G* 774, *etc.*; *as n.* noble man, *G* 542; kindly being, *Pe* 602; *collect.* nobility, *Cl* 1216; *superl.* noblest (ones), *Cl* 1180
gentyl(e), jentyle *adj.*[2] gentile, heathen, pagan, *Cl* 76; **j. prophete** prophet to the gentiles, *Pat* 62
gentylmen *n.* gentlemen
gere, guere *n.* gear, *Pat* 148; armour, *G* 569, 584; clothes, *Cl* 1810; bedclothes, *G* 1470; utensil(s), instrument(s), *Cl* 16, 1505, *G* 2205
gere *v.* dress, clothe, *G* 1872
gered *pp.* arrayed, attired, adorned; made, *G* 1832
geserne *see* **giserne**
gesse *v.* discern, judge, *Pe* 499
gest(e) *n.* guest; visitor, visitant, *Pe* 277
get *n.* winning(s), *G* 1638
gete *v.* (**ȝat, gete(n)** *pa.t.*, **geten** pp.) get, fetch, capture; find, obtain
gettes *n.* fashions
geuen *see* **next**
gif, giue, gyf, gyue, gef, ȝef *v.* (**gef, gafe, gaue** *pa.t.*, **geuen, gyuen** *pp.*) give; allow, *Pe* 270; make known, reveal, *Cl* 1326, 1627; bestow upon, wish, *G* 370, 668, 1029 *etc.*; *reflex.* give in, *G* 1861
gift(e), gyft(e), ȝ- *n.* gift; giving, *Pe* 565; **of my** (*etc.*) **g.** as a gift from me (*etc.*)
gilde, gilt, gyld *pp.* gilded
Gile (Saynt) *n.* St Giles (Aegidius)
giles *n.* gills, *Pat* 269
gilofre *n.* gillyflower, clove-scented pink, *Pe* 43
gilt, girdel *see* **gilde, gordel**
Gilyan (Sayn) *n.* St Julian
giserne, geserne *n.* battle-axe
giue *see* **gif**
glace *v.* glide, *Pe* 171
glad *adj.* happy, merry; **-ly** *adv.* gladly, cheerfully; **-loker** *compar.* with greater pleasure, *G* 1064
glade *v.* (**gladande** *presp.*, **gladed** *pa.t.*) gladden, rejoice
gladnez *n.* gladness(es), joys, *Pe* 136

glam *see* **gla(u)m**
glas(se) *n.* glass
glauer *n.* babble, *G* 1426
glauerez *v.* deceives, *Pe* 688
gla(u)m *n.* din, noise; speech, *Cl* 830; voice, message, *Cl* 499, *Pat* 63
glaym *adj.* slime, *Pat* 269
glayre *n.* egg-white, *Pe* 1026
glayue *n.* spear, *Pe* 654
gle *n.* sound of revelry, music, *Pe* 95, 1123, *G* 46, 1652; joy, *G* 1536
glede *n.*[1] kite, *Cl* 1696
glede(z) *n.*[2] red-hot embers
glem *n.* radiance, brightness, *Cl* 218, *G* 604; beam, ray, *Pe* 79
glemande *presp.* gleaming, shining, *Pe* 70, 990; **glemed** *pa.t. G* 598
glemered *pa.t.* shone, glimmered
glene *v.* glean
glent(e) *n.* beam of light, *Pe* 114; glance, twinkle, *G* 1290; *pl.* glances, *Pe* 1144
glent(e) *pa.t.* shone, sparkled, glinted; sprang, *G* 1652; flinched, *G* 2292; glanced, *G* 476; turned aside (*or* looked?), *Pe* 671
glet(te) *n.* filth, slime
glewed *pa.t.* called, *Pat* 164
glod *see* **glyde**
glode *n.* clear patch of sky, *Pe* 79; bright patch, *G* 2181; **on g.** in a flash, *G* 2266
gloped *pa.t.* was shocked, *Cl* 849
glopnedly *adv.* fearfully, in alarm
glopnyng *n.* shock, terror, *G* 2461
glowed *pa.t.* shone, glowed, *Pe* 114; **glowande** *presp.* shining
glyde *v.* (**glod** *pa.t.*) glide, come, go
glyfte *pa.t.* looked, glanced, *Cl* 849, *G* 2265
glyȝt *pa.t.* looked; glinted, *Pe* 114
glymme *n.* radiance
glysnande *presp.adj.* glistening, shining
glyter *v.* glitter
gnede *adv.* in a niggardly manner
go, goande *see* **go(n)**
gob(e)lotes *n.* goblets
God(d)(e), god(de) *n.* God, god
goddes *n.* goddess, *G* 2452
god(e), godeliest *see* **go(u)d(e), godlych**
god(e)mon, godman, goodmon *n.* householder, landlord, host; sir, *Pat* 524
godhede *n.* divinity, (goodness?), *Pe* 413
godly *see* **go(u)d(e)**
godlych *adj.* (**godeliest** *superl.*) gracious, *Cl* 753, 1608; goodly, fine, *G* 584
godman *see* **god(e)mon**
godnesse *n.* goodness, generosity
gold(e) *n.* gold; **golde-hemmed** *adj.* hemmed with gold
golf *n.* deep source, *Pe* 608
gome *n.* man, knight; servant, *Cl* 77

gomen, game(n) *n.* (**gomnez, -s, gamnez**
pl.) game, pleasure; merriment, *G* 1376,
1933; sport (hunting), *G* 1319, 1894; catch,
G 1635; process, *G* 661; **gomenly** *adv.*
happily, *G* 1079
Gomorre, Gomorra *n.* Gomorrah
go(n) *v.* (**gotz, gos, gon** *pres.*, **goande** *presp.*,
ȝod ȝede(n) *pa.t.*, **gon** *pp.*) go, walk
good *see* **go(u)d(e)**
goodmon *see* **god(e)mon**
gorde, -y- *v.* (**gorde** *pa.t.*) strike; spur, *G* 2062,
2160; rush, *Cl* 911
gorde *see also* **gurde**
gordel, girdel, gurdel *n.* girdle
gore *n.* filth, foulness
gorger *n.* neckerchief, wimple
gorstez *n.* gorse-heaths
gos *see* **go(n)**
gost(e) *n.* spirit, soul; **g. of lyf**, breath of life,
Cl 325
gostly *adj.* spiritual, *Pe* 185, 790
gostlych *adv.* in supernatural manner, *G* 2461
gote *n.* current, stream
gotz *see* **go(n)**
go(u)d(e), go(w)d, good *adj. & n.* good, righ-
teous, worthy; *as n.* good, goodness, good
thing, profit, benefit; *s. or pl.* goods, *Pe* 731,
734, *Cl* 1200, 1282, 1315, *G* 1064, 1944;
go(u)dly *adv.* graciously, generously;
properly, *Pat* 26
gouernour *n.* (**gouernores** *pl.*) master, ruler
goulez, gowlez *n.* gules, heraldic red
goun(e) *v.* gown, robe, vestment
gowdez, gowlez *see* **go(u)d(e), goulez**
grace *n.* grace, mercy, salvation; good fortune,
Pe 194; favour, prayer, *Cl* 1347
gracio(u)s(e) *adj.* gracious; beautiful, pleas-
ing, pleasant; *as adv.* delightfully, *Pe* 260
gracyously, graciously *adv.* pleasingly, *Cl*
488; graciously, kindly, *G* 970
grame *n.* trouble, vexation
grante, grant merci, grattest *see* **gra(u)nte,
gra(u)nt mercy, gret(e)**
grauayl *n.* gravel
grauen *pp.* engraved; buried, *Cl* 1332
graunt *n.* permission, *Pe* 317
gra(u)nte *v.* grant, consent, agree (to); ack-
nowledge, *Pat* 240
gra(u)nt mercy, -i many (*lit.* great) thanks
gray(e) *adj.* grey; (of eyes) blue-grey, *Pe* 254*n*,
G 82; *as n.* greyhounds, *G* 1714
grayes *v.* becomes grey, *G* 527
grayn *n.* spike, *G* 211
graynez *n.* seeds, *Pe* 31
graythly *see* **grayþely**
grayþ(e) *adj.* ready
grayþe *v.* prepare, make ready; adorn, dress, *G*
151, 666, 2014; install, seat, *G* 74, 109; *pa.
subjunc.* would avail, *Pat* 53
grayþely, graythly *adv.* promptly, readily, *Cl*
341, *G* 417, 1683; truly, properly, *Pat* 240,
286, *G* 1006, 1335, 2292; comfortably, *G* 876,
1470; aptly, *Pe* 499
gre *n.* pleasure
grece *n.*[1] steps, *Cl* 1590
grece, gres *n.*[2] fat, flesh; skin, *G* 2313

Grece *n.*[3] Greece
gredirne *n.* gridiron
gref(fe) *n.* suffering, grief
grehoundez *n.* greyhounds
grem(e) *n.* wrath, vexation; resentment, *Pe*
465; injury, *G* 2251
greme *v.* anger; annoy, *Pat* 42; become angry,
Cl 138
grene *adj.* (**grener** *compar.*) green; *as n.* grassy
place, *Cl* 634; vegetation, *Cl* 1028; **þat g.** the
green man, *G* 464
grenne *v.* grin, smile, *G* 464
gres(se) *n.* grass; plant, shoot, *Pe* 31. *See also*
grece *n.*[2]
gret *pa.t.* greeted, *G* 842, 1933
grete *v.* weep, *Pe* 331, *G* 2157
gret(e), grett *adj.* (**grattest** *superl.*) great, big;
exalted, *Pe* 578; magnificent, *G* 2014; boast-
ful, *G* 312, 325; *as n.* noble(s), *Cl* 1363, *G*
2490; **g. cloþ** main sail, *Pat* 105; **grattest of
gres** fattest, *G* 1326; **grattest in grene**
greenest, *G* 207; *adv.* in general, *Pe* 637 (*cf.*
agrete, *Pe* 560)
gretyng *n.* weeping, *Cl* 159
greue *n.*[1] wood, thicket; **Paradys g.** grove of
Paradise, *i.e.* the garden of Eden, *Pe* 321
greuez *n.*[2] greaves (armour), *G* 575
greue(n) *v.* trouble, distress, offend; harm,
punish, *Cl* 138, *Pat* 112, 517; *intrans.* be
troubled
greuing *n.* grieving
grewe(n) *see* **growe**
grome *n.* man, retainer
gromylyoun *n.* gromwell
grone *v.* groan
gronyed *pa.t.* snorted, *G* 1442
gropande *presp.* searching, testing
gropyng *n.* touch, handling
grouelyng *adv.* prostrate, *Pe* 1120
grounde *n.* ground, earth; foundation, basis,
Pe 372, 384 *etc.*, *Cl* 591, 911; field, *G* 508;
land, region, *G* 705; (**vp)on g.** on earth, on
the ground
groundelez *adj.* bottomless
grounde(n) *see* **grynde**
growe *v.* (**grewe, grewen** *pa.t.*) grow,
increase
gruch *v.* (**gruȝt** *pa.t.*) bear ill will, *G* 2251; be
unwilling to grant, refuse, *Cl* 810, 1347
gruchyng *presp.* ill-humouredly, *G* 2126
grwe *n.* grain; **no g.** not a bit, *G* 2251
grychchyng *n.* grumbling
gryed *pa.t.* shuddered, *G* 2370
grymly *adv.* sternly, *Cl* 1534; cruelly, *Pe* 654
grym(me) *adj.* fierce, grim, ugly
grynde *v.* (**grounde(n)** *pp.*) make a grinding
sound, *Pe* 81; *pp.* sharpened, *Pe* 654, *G* 2202*n*
gryndel *adj.* fierce, angry; **-ly** *adv.*
gryndellayk *n.* ferocity
gryndelston *n.* grindstone
Gryngolet *n.* (Gawain's horse)
grypez *v.* (**gripped, gryped, grypte** *pa.t.*)
grips
grysly *adj.* horrible
gryspyng *n.* gnashing
gryste *n.* anger, spite

Guenore *see* **Gaynour**
guere *see* **gere**
guferes *n.* depths
gult(e), gylt *n.* guilt
gulty, gyltyf *adj.* guilty; *as n.* Pe 669, Pat 175
gurde, gorde *pp.* girt
gurdel *see* **gordel**
gut *n.* (**guttez** *pl.*) gut, intestine
Gwenore *see* **Gaynour**
gyde-ropes *n.* guy ropes
gye *v.* rule
gyf, gyft(e), gyld *see* **gif, gift(e), gilde**
gyle *n.* guile, deceit, treachery
gylt(ez), gyltyf *see* **gult(e), gulty**
gyltlez *adj. as n.* guiltless, innocent (one)
gyn *n.* craft
gyng *n.* company
gyngure *n.* ginger
gyrde *see* **gorde**
gyrle *n.* girl
gyse *n.* dress
gyternere *n.* cithern-player
gyue(n) *see* **gif**

ȝare *adv.* soon, G 2410; clearly, Pe 834
ȝark(k)(e) *v.* prepare, make ready, institute, set up; grant, Cl 758; **ȝ. vp** open, G 820
ȝarm *n.* outcry
ȝar(r)ande *presp.adj.* snarling
ȝat *see* **gete**
ȝate *n.* gate, outer door
ȝaule *v.* howl
ȝayned *pp.* greeted
ȝe *adv.* yea, yes, Cl 347, G 813, 1091, *etc.*
ȝe *pron.* (**yow,** *dat. & acc.*) you
ȝede *see* **go(n)**
ȝederly *adv.* promptly, quickly; entirely
ȝedoun *pa.t.* went down, G 1595n
ȝef *see* **gif**
ȝeȝe *v.* cry (out)
ȝelde *v.* (**ȝelde(n),** **ȝolden** *pa.t.,* **ȝolden** *pp.*) yield, give, deliver, (re)pay; restore, Cl 1708; reply, G 1478; *reflex.* yield, surrender, G 1215, 1595
ȝelle *v.* yell
ȝellyng *n.* yelling
ȝelpyng *n.* valiant boasting
ȝeme *v.* govern, rule
ȝemen *n.* labourers, Pe 535
ȝender, ȝonder *adj. & adv.* yonder, that
ȝep(e) *adj.* young, new, G 60; youthful, active, vigorous, Cl 881, G 105, 284, 1510; fresh, blooming, G 951; *as n.* alert man, Cl 796; **-ly** *adv.* promptly, quickly
ȝer(e) *n.* (**ȝer(e)** *pl.*) year; **on ȝ.** a (*i.e.* each) year, Pe 1079; **ȝeres ȝiftes** New Year's gifts, G 67
ȝern(e) *adj. & adv.* quick(ly), eager(ly), G 498, 1478, 1526
ȝerne *v.¹* yearn (for), wish, desire
ȝerne, ȝirne *v.²* (**ȝornen** *pa.t.*) run, pass, Cl 881, G 498, 529
ȝestande *presp.adj.* frothing
ȝet(e), ȝette *adv.* yet, still, even; further, moreover; nevertheless; hitherto, Cl 197, 815, *etc.*, Pat 432; again, Pat 489

ȝet(t)e *v.* grant, allow; **ȝ. out** yield, send out, Cl 842
ȝif, ȝyf, i(i)f *conj.* if, whether; in case, Pat 160, G 1774; *with force of* though, Pe 45, 147, *etc.*, Cl 914, *etc.;* **bot if** unless; **if hit were** for example, G 1799
ȝiftes *see* **ȝer(e), gift(e)**
ȝirne *see* **ȝerne** *v.²*
ȝis(se), ȝise, ȝys *adv.* yes, truly, indeed
ȝisterday *n.* yesterday; *gen.* of yesterday, Cl 463
ȝod *see* **go(n)**
ȝokkez *n.* yokes
ȝol *n.* Yule
ȝolden *see* **ȝelde**
ȝolȝe *adj.* yellow, sallow
ȝolped *pa.t.* shouted
ȝomerly *adj. & adv.* miserable, miserably
ȝon *adj.* yonder, that
ȝonde *adj.* yonder, that
ȝonder *adj.* yonder, that
ȝong(e), ȝonke *adj.* young
ȝore *adv.* long since, a long time, G 2114; **for long ȝ.** for a long time, Pe 586
ȝorefader *n.* ancestor (i.e. Adam), Pe 322
ȝore-whyle *adv.* some time ago, Cl 842
ȝourez, ȝourself, ȝowre *see* **yourez, yourself, yo(u)r(e)**
ȝys *see* **ȝis(se)**

hab(b)es, habbe(z) *see* **haue**
Habraham *see* **Abraham**
hach *n.* hatch, deck; **vnder h.** on board ship, Cl 409; **vnder hachches** below deck, Pat 179
hadet *pp.* beheaded (**wyth:** by), G 681
haf(e) *see* **haue**
hafyng *n.* possession
haȝer *adj.* goodly, noble, G 1738n; *compar.* **-er** more skilful, handy, resourceful, G 352
haȝerly, hagherlych *adv.* fitly, fittingly
haȝþorne *n.* hawthorn
hal *see* **hal(le)**
halawed *see* **halowe**
halce, hals *n.* neck
halche, halse *v.* embrace, salute; enclose, G 185; loop around, G 218; fasten, G 1852, 1613; interlace, G 657
halde, holde *v.* (**helde** *pa.t.,* **halden holden** *pp.*) hold; possess, Cl 35, 652, *etc.,* Pat 14, G 627; keep (to), Cl 244, 335, *etc.,* Pat 333, G 698, 1043, 1090, *etc.; reflex.* keep oneself, remain, Pe 1191, Pat 289; govern, G 53, 904, *etc.;* contain, Pe 1029, Cl 1387, G 124; occupy, Pe 1002; consider, Pe 301, Cl 276, 1062, *etc.,* Pat 522, G 28, 259, *etc.; pp.* bound, G 1040, beholden, G 1828; **h. alofte** keep up, G 1125; **halden her pese** remain quiet, Pat 25; **h. in honde** dispense, G 2056; **h. of** be faithful to, Cl 1162; **h. out** go out, Pat 434; **h. vtter** put outside, Cl 42
hale *v.* (**hal(l)ed** *pa.t.,* **halet** *pp.*) pull, draw, Pat 219, G 1338; shoot (arrow), G 1455; drink, drain, Cl 1520; hasten, rush, Cl 380, G 136, 458; pass, G 1049; sweep, Cl 458, G 788; flow, Pe 125

half, halue *n., adj. & adv.* half; side, *Pe* 230, *Pat* 434, 450, *G* 649, *etc.*; part, *Cl* 719; part, quarter, *Cl* 950; shore, *Cl* 1039; (**vp**)**on Godez h.** for God's sake, in God's name.
halȝed *pa.t.* hallowed, consecrated
halȝez *n.* saints
halidayez *see* **halyday**
halkez *n.* corners, recesses
hal(le) *n.* hall, dining hall, castle
halled *see* **hale**
halme *n.* handle
halowe, -awe *v.* shout (at)
halowing *n.* shouting
hals, halsed *see* **halce, halche**
halt *adj.* lame
halte *n.* stop, stand; **take me h.** offer obstruction to me, *Pe* 1158
halue(s) *see* **half**
halydam *n.* holy object, relic
halyday, -i- *n.* festival, holy day
hame *see* **home**
hamppred *pa.t.* packed
han, hande *see* **haue, hond(e)**
hande-helme *n.* helm, tiller
hanselle *see* **hondeselle**
hapenez *v.impers.* it befalls
hapnest *see* **happen**
hap(pe) *n.* good fortune, happiness, blessing, *Pe* 16, 713, 1195, *Pat* 212, *G* 48; *pl.* blessings, blessed states, beatitudes, *Cl* 24, *Pat* 11, 29
happe *v.* cover, *Cl* 626; imprison, *G* 1224; *pp.* enclosed, *Pat* 450; fastened, *G* 655; wrapped, *G* 864
happen *adj.* (**hapnest** *superl.*) blessed, fortunate
hard(e)(e) *adj. & adv.* hard, difficult, severe; *as n.* what is hard, *Pe* 606, a hard fate (*or adv.* badly), *Cl* 424; *adv.* hard, severely, fiercely; violently, *Cl* 44; firmly, *G* 1783, 655 (*compar.*)
harden *v.* encourage
hardily *adv.* assuredly
hardy *adj.* bold
harez *n.* hares
harled *pp.* entwined
harlot, -lat *n.* villain, beggar
harlottrye *n.* obscenity
harme *n.* harm, injury, offence; evil, wrong, sin, *Pe* 681, *Pat* 17n (*cf. G* 2511); sorrow, *Pe* 388
harme *v.* harm
harmlez *adj.* guiltless, *Pe* 676, 725
harnays *n.* armour, accoutrements
harnayst *pp.* armed, accoutred
harpen *v.* harp
harporez *n.* harpers
hasel *n.* hazel
haspe *n.* hasp, latch, *G* 1233
hasp(p)e *v.* fasten, buckle; clasp, *G* 1388; *pp.* with a clasp, *Pat* 189n
hast(e) *n.* haste, speed; **in** (**with**) **h.** quickly *or* in haste
hasted *pa.t.* urged on, *Cl* 937, pressed hard upon, *G* 1897; hastened, *G* 1165, 1424
hastif, hasty *adj.* hasty, rash, *Pat* 520; urgent, *G* 1051
hasty(f)ly, hastily *adv.* quickly

hastlettez *n.* pig's offal
hat *see* **hat(te)**
hate *n.* hate, hatred
hate *see also* **hot(e)**
hatel *adj.* fierce; cruel, *Pat* 367; bitter, *Pat* 481; vile, *Cl* 227; **for h.** because of anger, *Cl* 200
hater *n.* clothing; *pl.* clothes
hatte *n.* hat; **hard h.** helmet, *Cl* 1209
hat(te) *v.* (**-s** *pres2sg.*, **hyȝt** *pa.t.* (*pres. Pe* 950), **hatte** *pp.*) be called
hatter, hatz *see* **hot(e), haue**
haþel *n.* man; knight; Lord, *G* 2056
hauberghe, hawbergh *n.* tunic of mail
haue, haf(e) *v. & auxil.* (**hab(b)es, habbe(z), hatz, haue(z), hauen, haf, han** *pres.*) have; receive, *Cl* 461, accept, *G* 1980; keep, *Cl* 1140; take, *Cl* 349, 941, *Pat* 336, 460n, *G* 773, 1612, *etc.*; draw, *G* 1051; bring, *Cl* 1443; put, *Cl* 321, *G* 1446; reach, *G* 700; beget, *G* 2466; **h. in honde** control, *Cl* 1704; **haf at þe** take guard, *G* 2288
hauek, hawk *n.* hawk
hauen *n.* haven, harbour, *Cl* 420, *Pat* 108
hauilounez *v.* doubles back
haunte *v.* practise, *Pat* 15
hawbergh *see* **hauberghe**
hawtesse *n.* pride
hay *exclam.* hey!
hay, ay *n.* hay, *Cl* 1684, *Pat* 394, 438
haylse, haylce *v.* greet, salute
hayre *n.* hair shirt, *Pat* 373, 381
hayre *see also* **ayre**
he *pron.* (**him hym** *dat. & acc.*) he
hed(e), heued *n.* head; (of stream), *Pe* 974
hede *v.* observe, *Pe* 1051
hedlez *adj.* headless
hef *see* **heue**
hegge *n.* hedge
heȝe, heȝest *see* **hyȝ(e)** *adj.*
heȝed *pa.t.* vowed, *Cl* 1584n
heȝly *see* **hyȝly**
heȝt, heȝþe *see* **hyȝt**
helde *adv.* readily; **as h.** quite probably, *Pe* 1193; **helder** *compar.: **neuer þe h.** none the more (for that), *G* 376, 430
helde *v.* turn, come, go (*reflex. G* 221); sink, fall, *Cl* 1330, *G* 1321; bow, *G* 972, 1104; fall, become (insane), *Cl* 1681
helde *see also* **halde**
hele *n.*[1] health, healing, *Pe* 713, *Cl* 1099; safety, *Pat* 92, 335; prosperity, *Cl* 920; well-being, *Pe* 16
hele *n.*[2] heel; *pl.* spurs, *G* 777, *etc.*
heled *pa.t.* healed
helle *n.* hell; *gen.* of hell, *Pe* 643. *See also* **hellen**
helle-hole *n.* the pit of hell
hellen *adj.* of hell
helme *n.*[1] helmet
helme *n.*[2] helm, tiller, *Pat* 149
help *n.* help
help(e) *v.* (**help** *pa.t., Cl* 1163) help
hem, him, hom, hym *pron.* (*dat. & acc.*) (to, for) them; themselves (*reflex.*), *Pe* 551, *Cl* 62 *etc., Pat* 216 *etc., G* 1130, *etc.*
hemself, hemseluen, hymseluen *pron.* themselves; (it pleased) them, *G* 976

heme *adj.* neat
hemely *adv.* closely
hemme *n.* hem; (edge); step, *Pe* 1001
hende, hynde *adj.* noble, gracious, courteous; meek, well-behaved, *Pe* 184; *as n.* gracious knight, lady, *Pe* 909, *G* 827, *etc.*; *pl.* gracious things, *Cl* 1083; **-ly** *adv.*
hendelayk *n.* courtesy
hend(e)ly *see* **hende**
heng(e) *v.* hang
henne *adv.* hence
hens, hence *adv.* hence
hent(e) *v.* (**hent** *pa.t. & pp.*) take, receive, seize; find, *Pe* 669; suffer, *Pe* 388, *Cl* 151, *G* 2277
hepe *n.* heap; **on a h., (vp)on hepes, -z** in a heap/crowd
her, hir, hyr *adj.*[1] *& pron.* (*acc. & dat.*) her; *reflex.* herself, *G* 1193, 1735, *etc.*
her, here, hor *adj.*[2] their, *Pe* 92, 93, *etc.*, *Cl* 24, 75, *etc.*, *Pat* 16, 17, *etc.*, *G* 54, 130, *etc.*
herande *see* **here** *v.*
herber *n.* lodging; *v.* lodge
herd(e) *see* **here** *v.*
her(e), heere *adv.* here; in this instance, *Pat* 520; in this respect, *G* 2366; **hereaway** hither, (to) here, *Cl* 647
here *n.*[1] warrior-band, *G* 59; army, *G* 2271; company, *Cl* 409, 902
here *n.*[2] hair, *G* 180, *etc.*
here *v.* (**herande** *presp.*, **herd(e)** *pa.t. & pp.*) hear
here *see also* **ayre**
her(e)after *adv.* hereafter
hered, heyred *pa.t.* worshipped, *Cl* 1086, 1527. *See also* **herȝe**
herebiforne *adv.* before now
heredmen *n.* retainers
her(e)inne *adv.* herein, in this place; ?dressed in this, *Cl* 147; in this matter, *Cl* 1595
herȝe *v.* (**herȝed** *pa.t.*, **herȝed, heyred** *pp.*) ravage, harry, *Cl* 1179, 1294, 1786; **h. out** rout out, *Pat* 178
heritage, (h)erytage *n.* heritage
herk, herk(k)en *v.* listen (to), hear
herle *n.* strand, *G* 190
hernez *n.*[1] eagles, *Cl* 537
hernez *n.*[2] brains, *Pe* 58
herre *see* **hyȝ(e)** *adj.*
hersum *adj.* glorious, festal
hert *see* **hurt**
hert(e), hertte *n.*[1] heart; mind; courage, *G* 2296; purpose, *Cl* 682
herttes, herttez *n.*[2] harts, stags, *Cl* 391, 535, *G* 1154
heruest *n.* harvest, autumn
hes *n.* promise
hest(e) *n.* command, bidding; promise, *Cl* 1636
Hestor *n.* Hector, *G* 2102
hete *n.* heat. *See also* **hetes**
hete *v.* (**hyȝt(e), hettez** *pa.t.*, **hyȝt, hette** *pp.*) promise, assure; command, decree, *Pat* 11, 336. *See also* **heȝed**
heter *adj.* rough
heterly *see* **het(t)erly**

hetes *n.* promises, assurances, *G* 1525
hethe *see* **heþe**
het(t)erly *adv.* bitterly, fiercely; cruelly, *Cl* 1222; suddenly, quickly
hette(z) *see* **hete**
heþe, hethe *n.* heath
heþen *adv.* hence, away; **h. into Grece** from here to Greece, *Pe* 231
heþyng *n.* scorn, contempt, abuse
heué, heuy *adj.* heavy; serious, *G* 496; grievous, *Pe* 1180
heue, hef *v.* (**hef** *pa.t.*, **houen, hofen** *pp.*) lift, raise; rise, *G* 120; mount, *Pat* 477; heave, *Pat* 219; address (words), *Pe* 314; *pp.* raised
heued *see* **hed(e)**
heuen (**heuen(e)z, heuenesse** *pl.*) heaven; *attrib.* of heaven, *Pat* 185, *G* 647; **heuen-glem** light of dawn; **heuen-kyng** king of heaven; **heuen-ryche** (kingdom of) heaven
heuen *v.* raise, exalt; increase, *Pe* 16; extol, *Cl* 24
heuy *see* **heué**
h(e)we, huee *n.* hue, colour, complexion
h(e)we *v.* cut; **hewen** *pp.* made, cut
heyred *see* **hered, herȝe**
hid, hid(d)e *see* **hyde** *v.*
hider(e), hyder *adv.* hither, here
hidor *n.* terror
hiȝe *see* **hyȝ(e)**
hiȝlich *adj.* splendid, *G* 183
hiȝly *see* **hyȝly**
hiȝtly *adv.* fitly; **h. bisemez** is right and proper, *G* 1612
hiled *pp.* covered, *Cl* 1397
hil(le), hyl(le) *n.* hill; (castle-)mound; **on h.** in (any) castle (?), *G* 59 (*but cf. G* 2271)
him, hym *pron.* (*dat. & acc.*) him; them, *Pe* 635, *etc.*, *Cl* 130, *etc.*, *Pat* 213, *etc.*, *G* 49, *etc.* (*also* **hem, hom**)
himself(e), himseluen *see* **hymself**
hir, hindez *see* **her, hyndez**
hirself *pron.* herself
his(e), hys(se) *possess. pron. & adj.* his; its, *G* 447
hisseluen *see* **hymself**
hit, hyt *pron.* (**his, hit** *possess.*) it; **h. ar(n) (wern)** they are (were), *Pe* 895, 1199, *Cl* 171, *etc.*, *Pat* 38, *etc.*, there are, *G* 280, 1251; **his** *possess.* its, *G* 447; **hit** *possess.* *Pe* 108, *etc.*, *Cl* 264, *etc.*, *Pat* 12, *etc.*
hitself, -seluen *pron.* itself
hit(te), -y- *v.* hit, strike; jump, fall, *Pat* 380, *G* 427; come down, *Cl* 479; **h. to** come upon, *Pat* 289; seek, wish, *Pe* 132
ho, a *pron.* (**her, hir, hyr** *dat. & acc.*) she; *unstressed* **a**, *G* 1281
ho-bestez *n.* female animals
hod(e) *n.*[1] hood
hode *n.*[2] order of knighthood, *G* 2297
hodlez *adj.* hoodless
hofen *see* **heue**
hoge, huge *n.* huge, great
hoȝez *n.* hocks, *G* 1357
hokyllen *v. pres.pl.* cut down, *Cl* 1267n
hol *see* **hol(l)(e)**

holde *n.* stronghold, *G* 771; grasp, *G* 1252; dominion, *Cl* 1597

holde(ly) *adv.* carefully, faithfully

holde(n) *see also* **halde**

hole *n.* hole

hole *see also* **hol(l)(e)**

hole-foted *adj.* web-footed

holʒ(e) *adj.* hollow

holkked *pa.t.* dug

hol(l)(e) *adj.* whole, sound; healed, *G* 2484; amended, *G* 2390; total, *Pe* 406; perfect, *Pat* 335; **þi hert h.** all your courage, *G* 2296

hol(l)y *adv.* wholly, completely

holsumly *adv.* restoratively, *G* 1731

holt *n.* wood

holt(e)wodez *n.* woods

holy *adj.* holy. *See also* **hol(l)ly**

holyn *n.* (*attrib.*) holly, *G* 206

hom *see* **hem**

home, hame *n.* home

homered *pa.t.* (hammered), struck, *G* 2311

homly *adj.* humble, obedient (*perh. also* of [God's] household), *Pe* 1211

hommes *n.* backs of the knees

hond(e), hande *n.* hand; **out of h.** at once; **halden in h.** dispense, *G* 2056; **me on h.** to my notice, *Pe* 155; **h. myʒt** power, *Pat* 257

hondel(e) *v.* handle

hondelyng *n.* handling, touch

hondelyngez *adv.* with the hands

hondeselle, hanselle *n.* (*collect.*) New Year's presents, gratuities, *G* 66; omen, present (*iron.*), *G* 491

hondewerk *n.* handiwork, creation

hondewhyle *n.* moment

hondred *see* **hundreth**

hone *n.* delay, *G* 1285

hone *v.* be situated, *Pe* 921

honest(e) *adj.* clean, pure, seemly

honestly *adv.* fittingly, properly

honour *n.* honour, dignity; favour (hospitality), *G* 1963, 2056

honour, honowr *v.* honour, worship; *pp.* celebrated, *G* 593

honysez *v.* condemns, ruins

hoo! *interj.* stop!, *G* 2330

hope *n.* expectation; belief, *Cl* 1653; hope, trust, *Pe* 860

hope *v.* think, suppose, believe; hope, *Cl* 860; **h. of** expect, *G* 2308

hor, horce *see* **her** *adj.*², **hors(s)(e)**

hore *adj.* grey (with frost), *G* 743

hores *n.* hairs, *Cl* 1695

hores *possess. adj.* theirs, *Pat* 14, 28

horne *n.* horn

hors(s)(e), horce *n.* horse; horse's, *G* 180, 1904

hortyng *see* **hurt** *v.*

horwed *adj.* unclean

horyed *pa.t.* hurried

hose *n.* hose, tights, *G* 157

(h)ostel *n.* house; **bone h.** good lodging, *G* 776n

hot(e), hate *adj.* hot; angry, *Cl* 200; biting, *Cl* 1195, 1602, *Pat* 481; grievous, burning, *Pe* 388; *adv.* hotly; **hatter,** *compar. adv.*

houe *v.* pause, tarry; lie, be situated, *Cl* 927; rest, *Cl* 485

houen *see* **heue**

houes *n.* hoofs, *G* 459

houndes, -z, howndes, -z *n.* hounds

(h)oure, howre *n.* hour

hourlande *see* **hurle**

hourle *n.* sea, surge

hous-dore *n.* house-door

hous(e), hows *n.* house, building; hall, castle, church, temple, *etc.*

housholde *n.* household

hov, how(e) *adv.* how; **h. þat** how

howndes, -z *see* **houndes**

howre, hows *see* **(h)oure, hous(e)**

howso, how-se-euer *adv.* however

hue *n.* shout, cry, *Pe* 873

hue(e), huge *see* **h(e)we, hoge**

hult *n.* hilt

hundreth, -eþe, hundred, hondred *n.* hundred

hunt(e) *n.* huntsman

hurkele *v.* (**hurkled** *pa.t.*) cower, crouch, squat

hurle *v.* (**h(o)urlande** *presp.*) rush; *trans.* hurl, fling, *Cl* 44, 223, *Pat* 149; whirl, *Pat* 271

hurrok *n.* rudder-band, *Pat* 185n

hurt *n.* hurt, wound, *G* 2484

hurt *v.* (**hurt, hert** *pa.t.*, **hurt** *pp.*) hurt, pain; harm, injure; **hortyng** *vbl.n. Cl* 740

huyde *see* **hyde**

huyle, hyul, hylle *n.* clump of plants, gravemound, *Pe* 41, 1172, 1205

hwe *see* **h(e)we**

hwed *pp.* coloured, *Cl* 1045

hyde *n.* hide, skin

hyde, huyde *v.* (**hid** *pa.t.*, **hid, hid(d)e** *pp.*) hide; *pp.adj.* hidden; *as n.* secret thing, *Cl* 1628

hyder *see* **hider**

hyghe! *interj.* look out!, *G* 1445

hyʒ(e), hiʒ(e), heʒe *adj.* (**herre** *compar.*, **hyʒest, heʒest** *superl.*) high, tall, lofty, great; noble, excellent, great, supreme, *Pe* 596, 1051, *etc.*, *Cl* 35, 193, *etc.*, *Pat* 257, 412, *etc.*, *G* 5, 57, *etc.*; soemn, important, *Pe* 39 (**h. seysoun:** festival), *Pat* 9 (high mass), *G* 932, *etc.*; vigorous, *Cl* 976; mature, *G* 844 (*cf. Cl* 656 *& see* **out**); loud, *Cl* 1564, *etc.*, *G* 1165; *as n.* high ground, *Cl* 391, *G* 1152, *etc.*; **h. and loʒe** great and small; **on h.** on high, *Cl* 413, *Pat* 463, *G* 1607, 2057; **on (ful) h.** loudly, aloud, *Cl* 67, 307, 468, 1602; **ful h.** highest, supreme, *Pe* 454; **h. gate** highway, *Pe* 395; *adv.* high, loud(ly). *See also* **hyʒly**

hyʒe *n.*¹ servant, *Cl* 67

hyʒe *n.*² haste; **in h.** suddenly, *G* 245

hyʒ(e), hiʒe *v.* hurry, hasten

hyʒly, heʒly, hiʒly *adv.* greatly, generously, solemnly; up on end, *G* 1587

hyʒt, heʒt, heʒþe *n.* height; **(vp)on h.** on high, *Pe* 501, aloft, *Cl* 458, *G* 421, towering, *G* 332, as strongly as possible, *Pat* 219

hyʒt(e) *see also* **hat(te), hete**

hyʒtled *pa.t.* adorned, ornamented

hyl-coppe *n.* hilltop, *Pe* 791

hyl(le) *see* **hil(le), huyle**
hym *see* **him**
hymself, hymselue(n), himself(e), him-
seluen, hisseluen *pron.* (*reflex.* & *emph.*)
himself; him, *Cl* 924 *etc.*, *G* 113 (*i.e.* Bald-
win), 226, *etc. See also* **hemself**
hyndez, hindez *n.* hinds (female deer)
hynde *see also* **hende**
hyne *n.pl.* labourers, *Pe* 505, 632; servants, *Pe*
1211; fellows, *Cl* 822. *Cf. also* **hyȝe** *n.*[1]
hypped *pa.t.* vaulted, *G* 2232; **h. aȝayn**
bounced back, *G* 1459
hyr *see* **her**
hyre, hyure *n.* pay; (terms of) hire, *Pe* 534, *Pat*
56
hyre *v.* hire
hyrne *n.* corner, nook
hys(se) *see* **his**
hyt, hyttez *see* **hit, hit(te)**
hyue *n.* hive
hyul, hyure *see* **huyle, hyre**

I *pron.* (**me** *dat.* & *acc.*, **me** *reflex.*) I
ibrad *pa.t.* spread over
iche, ichose *see* **vch(e), chose**
idolatrye *n.* idolatry
i(i)f *see* **ȝif**
iisseikkles *n.* icicles, *G* 732
iles *n.* islands, *G* 698; regions, *G* 7
ilk(e) *adj.* & *pron.* same, very; **þat i.** the same;
of þat i. to match
ille, ylle *adj.* evil; *as n.* evil, sin; **ta(t)z to non**
i. do not take (it) amiss
ille *adv.* ill, badly, amiss; with ill will, *Cl* 1141;
wrongfully, *Pe* 681
ilych(e) *adv.* alike, in similar manner; equally;
ay i., euer i. all the time, *Cl* 975, *Pat* 369
everywhere, absolutely, *Cl* 1386; **i. ful** kept
up in full, *G* 44
image, ymage *n.* statute, *Cl* 983; image, *G* 649
in, inn(e) *prep.* & *adv.* in; on; into; within; for
(*of time*), *Pe* 416; at, *Cl* 781, *G* 1096, *etc.*
inblande *prep.* among, *Cl* 885
inhelde *pp.* poured in
inlyche *adv.* alike, the same, *Pe* 546, 603
inmong(ez) *prep.* among
inmelle *see* **in(n)melle**
inmyddes, inmyd(d)ez *prep.* amongst, in the
middle (of)
inn(e) *see* **in**
innermore *adv.* farther in, *G* 794
in(n)melle *adv.* & *prep.* in the midst (of them),
G 1451; amongst, *Pe* 1127
innocens *n.* innocence
innocent, innos(s)ent, inoscente *adj.* in-
nocent, *Pe* 672; *as n. Pe* 625 *etc.*
in(n)ogh(e), in(n)oȝ(e), innowe *adj.* & *adv.*
enough, *Pe* 649, 661, *etc.*, *Cl* 669, 808, *etc.*, *G*
404, *etc.*; many, in plenty, *Cl* 116, *Pat* 528, *G*
77, 219, *etc.*; very, *G* 289, 803 (*iron.?*), 888;
very well, *Pe* 637, *Cl* 297
innome, innowe *see* **nym(e), in(n)ogh(e)**
inobedyent *adj.* disobedient
inogh(e), inoȝ(e) *see* **in(n)ogh(e)**
inore *adj.* inner, *G* 649
innos(s)ent, inoscente *see* **innocent**

inspranc *pa.t.* sprang into
insyȝt *n.* opinion
into *prep.* into, to; (from here) to, *Pe* 231, *G*
2023; up to, *Cl* 660
inwyth, inwith *prep.* & *adv.* within
ire, yre *n.* wrath
irked *pa.t.* (*impers.*) it wearied, *G* 1573
Israel, Israyl *n.* Israel
iwys(s)(e), iwyis *adv.* indeed, certainly

jacynght *n.* jacinth
janglande *presp.* grumbling
jape *n.* trick, device; pastime, *Cl* 877; jest, joke,
Cl 864(?), *G* 542, 1957
Japh *n.* Joppa
jasper, jasporye *n.* jasper
jaueles *n.* louts
jeauntez *n.* giants
jentyle *see* **gentyl(e)**
Jerico *n.* Jericho
Jerusalem, Jherusalem *n.* Jerusalem
John, Jon *n.* (**Jonez** *gen.*) John
joly(f), jolef *adj.* noble, worthy, *Cl* 300, 864;
lively, happy, *Pat* 241, *G* 86; lovely, *Pe* 842,
929; *adv.* **jolilé** gallantly, *G* 42
Jonas *n.* Jonah
jopardé, joparde *n.* jeopardy; uncertainty, *Pe*
602
jostyse *n.* judge
journay *n.* day's journey, *Pat* 355
jowked *pa.t.* lay asleep
joy(e) *n.* joy
joyfnes *n.* youth, *G* 86
joyful, joyfol *adj.* joyful
joyles, -z *adj.* joyless
joyne *v.*[1] join, unite, *Cl* 434 (& *cf. next*), *G* 97;
add, *Pe* 1009; **j. to** unite with, share in, *Cl* 726
joyne *v.*[2] enjoin, order, *Cl* 1235; appointed, *Cl*
877, *Pat* 62
joynt *adv.* continuously
joyntes *n.* joints
joyst *adj.* lodged
Juda *n.* Judah
Judé(e) Judy londe *n.* Judea
Jue, Jwe *n.* (**Jues, -z, Juise** *pl.* **Juyne** *gen. pl.*)
Jew
jueler(e), joueler *n.* jeweller
juel(l)(e) *n.* jewel, treasure, *Pe* 23, 249, *etc.*, *Cl*
1441, *etc.*, *Cl* 1856
juelrye *n.* jewellery
jugge *v.* judge; try, *Pe* 804; condemn, *Pat* 224,
245; adjudge, assign, *G* 1856
juggement *n.* judgement
juis(e) *n.* judgement, doom
Juise *see* **Jue**
jumpred *pp. as n.* those jumbled together, *Cl*
491*n*
juste *v.* joust, *G* 42; **justyng** *n.* jousting
justyfyet *pp.* justified
justised *pa.t.* ruled
Juyne *see* **Jue**

kable *n.* cable
kach, kaȝt(en) *see* **cach(ch)(e)**
kakez *n.* cakes
kalle *see* **calle**

kanel *n.* neck
kare *see* **care**
kark *n.* trouble
karle, karp *see* **carle, carp**
kart *n.* cart
kast(e), kastel *see* **cast, castel**
kauelacion, cauelacioun *n.* argument, objection
kay *adj.* left
kayre *v.* lament, grieve, *Cl* 945
kayre *see also* **cayre**
kayser, kende *see* **cayser, kenne**
kene *adj.* (**kennest** *superl.*) bold, brave, great; zealous, *G* 482; bitter, *G* 2406; wise, *Cl* 1575; stout, *Cl* 839; sharp, *Pe* 40, *Cl* 1253, *etc.*; **ken-(e)ly** *adv.* quickly, eagerly, *Cl* 945, *G* 1048; keenly, bitterly, *G* 2001
kenet *n.* small hound
kenne *v.* (**kende, kenned** *pa.t.*) make known, teach, *Pe* 55, *Cl* 697, 865, *G* 1484, 1498; recognize, *Cl* 1702; understand, *Pat* 357; commend, *G* 2067, 2472
kennest *see* **kene**
kepe *v.* keep, hold, possess; obey, *Cl* 979; preserve, *Cl* 1229, *G* 2016, 2298; await, *G* 1312; entertain, *Cl* 89; take notice of, *Cl* 292; attend to, *G* 1688; behave, *Cl* 234; care, *G* 546, 2142; wish (for), *Cl* 508, *Pat* 464; *reflex.* take care, *G* 372
kerchofes *n.* kerchiefs
ker(re) *n.* wooded marsh
kerue, cerue *v.* (**carf, coruen** *pa.t.* **coruen, coruon** *pp.*) cut, carve; fashion, make; tear, rend, *Cl* 1582
kest(e)(n) *see* **cast, cast(e)**
keue *v.* sink, *Pe* 320; **keued** *pa.t. or pp.* fell away, *Pe* 981n
keuer, c- *v.* manage (to); recover, *G* 1755; restore, *Cl* 1605, 1700; find, obtain, *Pat* 223, 485, *G* 1221, 1254; give, *G* 1539; come, *G* 2221; **c. to** reach, *Pe* 319
keyes *n.* keys
klerk *see* **clerk(k)**
klubbe, clobbe *n.* club
klyf(f)e, klymbe *see* **clyff(e), clym**
knaged *pp.* fastened
knape *n.* fellow
knarre *n.* rock, crag
knaue *n.* servant, *Cl* 801; knave, *Cl* 855
knaw(e), know(e), cnawe *v.* (**kn(e)w(e)(n)** *pa.t.*, **knawen, knowen, knauen, cnowen** *pp.*) know, acknowledge; perceive, recognize, *Pe* 66, *etc.*, *Cl* 281, 373, *etc.*, *G* 1272
knawlach *n.* knowledge; **com to k.** recover one's senses, *Cl* 1702
kne, cne *n.* knee
knele *v.* (**knelande** *presp.*, **kneled** *pa.t. & pp.*) kneel
knew(e)(n), knit, knokkes *see* **knaw(e), knyt(ten), cnoke**
knokled *adj.* lumpy, knobbed
knorned *adj.* rugged
knot *n.* knot; group, *Pe* 788; wooded mound, *G* 1431, 1434
know(e)(n), knwe *see* **knaw(e)**
knyf(fe) *n.* knife

knyȝt, -i- *n.* knight
knyȝtly *adv.* in courtly manner, *G* 974
knyȝtly *adj.* courtly, chivalrous, *G* 1511
knyt(ten), knit *pa.t. & pp.* tied, *G* 1331, 1831; established, agreed on, *Cl* 564, *G* 1642; *pp.* woven (*& fig.* bound up), *G* 1849
kok, kort, koste *see* **coke, cort, cost(e)**
kote *n.* cottage, *Cl* 801
kow *n.* (**kuy** *pl.*) cow
kowarde *adj.* cowardly, *G* 2131
kowpes *see* **cuppe**
koynt(yse), (-ise) *see* **coynt, coyntyse**
krakkes, kry(es) *see* **crak, cry(e)**
Kryst(e), Cryst, -i- *n.* Christ; **-mas(se), -enmasse** *n.* Christmas
Krysten, Krystyin *adj.* Christian
kuy, kyd(de) *see* **kow, kyþe**
kylle *v.* (**kylled, kylde** *pp.*) kill; strike, *Cl* 876
kyndam, kyndom *n.* kingdom
kyn *n.* (**kynnes, kyn(n)ez** *g. & pl.*) kind(s) (of); **what k. he be** what he is like, *Pe* 794
kynde *adj.* natural, lawful, *Cl* 697; proper, courtly, *Pe* 276, *G* 473
kynde *n.* nature; true character; quality, kind, *Pe* 74; species, sort, *Cl* 334, 336, *etc.*; race, offspring, *G* 5; **þe worldes k.** mankind, mortal men, *G* 261; **agayn k.** unnaturally, *Cl* 266; **by k.** properly, *G* 1348; **bi lawe of any k.** by any natural law, *Pat* 259
kynd(e)ly, *adv.* properly, fittingly; gently, courteously, *Pe* 369; exactly, *Cl* 319
kyndom *see* **kyndam**
kyng(e) *n.* king
kynnes, -z *see* **kyn**
kynned *pa.t. & pp.* was conceived, *Cl* 1072; engendered, aroused, *Cl* 915
kyppe *v.* seize
kyrf *n.* cut, blow, *G* 372
kyrk(e) *n.* church
kyrtel, kyryous *see* **cortel, curious**
kysse *v.* (**kyssed(es), kyst(en)** *pa.t.*, **kyst** *pp.*) kiss
kyssyng *n.* kissing
kyst(e), chyst *n.* coffer, chest, casket; vessel, ark, *Cl* 346, *etc.*
kyte *n.* (*gen.*) kite's, *Cl* 1697
kyth(e) *n.* country, region; **kythyn** *gen.pl. or adj.* of (all) lands, *Cl* 1366
kyþe *v.* (**kyd(de), kyþed** *pa.t.*, **kyd(de)** *pp.*) show, make known; speak of, declare, *Cl* 23, 851, *Pat* 118; behave (towards), *G* 775, 2340; acknowledge, *Cl* 1368; *pp.adj.* renowned, *G* 51, 263

labor *v.* work (in), *Pe* 504
lace *n.* cord, *G* 217; belt, *G* 1830, *etc.*
lach(ch)e *v.* (**laght, laȝt, leȝten** *pa.t.*, **lach(ch)ed** *pp.*) catch, seize, take; receive, *Cl* 166, 1186, *G* 2499, 2507, *etc.*; conceive, *Pe* 1128; reach, *Pat* 322; **laȝt** *pp.* drawn back, *G* 156; **l. leue** take leave; **þis lote I laȝte** this happened to me, *Pe* 1205n.
lachet *n.* loop
lad *see* **lede**
ladde *n.* fellow
laddeborde *n.* larboard side, port side

laddres *n.* ladders
lad(de) *see* **lede**
lade *pp.* laden, filled, *Pe* 1146
laden, ledden *n.* (*pl.*) voices, sounds, *Pe* 874, 878
lady, ladi, ladé *n.* (**ladi(e)s, ladiez, ladyes, ladyez** *pl.*) lady; **my l.** the Virgin Mary; **ladyly** *adv.* queenly, *Pe* 774
ladyschyp *n.* queenly rank, *Pe* 578
laft(e), laften *see* **leue** *v.²*
lagmon *n. G* 1729*n*
laght *see* **lach(ch)e**
laȝe *v.* (**laȝed, loȝe(n)** *pa.t.*) laugh
laȝt *see* **lach(ch)e**
laȝter *n.* laughter
lake, llak *n.* lake
lake-ryftes *n.* lakeside dens
lakked *pa.t.* sinned against, *Cl* 723; disparaged, *G* 1250; (*impers.*) **yow l.** you fell short, *G* 2366
laled *pa.t.* spoke, said
lamp, laumpe *n.* lamp
langage *n.* language
langour *n.* anguish, *Pe* 357
lante(z) *see* **lene**
lantyrne *n.* lantern, *Pe* 1047
lape *v.* drink, *Cl* 1434
lappe *n.* flap, fold; hanging sleeve, *Pe* 201
lappe *v.* embrace, *G* 973; *pp.* wrapped, *Cl* 175, *G* 217; enclosed, *G* 575
large *adj.* large, great, wide; *as n.* breadth, *Cl* 314
larges(se) *n.* width, *G* 1627; liberality, *G* 2381
lasched *pa.subjunc.* would blaze, burn, *Cl* 707
lasse, les(se) *compar. adj. & adv.* (**lest** *superl.*) smaller; less; lower, *Pe* 491; **þe l. in werke** those who have done less work, *Pe* 599, 600; **bryng . . . lasse of** diminish, *Pe* 853; *adv.* **les** *Pe* 888 (*see also* **neuer, neuerþelese**)
lassen *v.* (**lasned** *pa.t.*) lessen, diminish, *G* 1800; subside, *Cl* 438, 441
last(e) *adj.* last; farthest, *Pat* 320; *as n.* **at, bi þe l., vpon l.** at last, finally
laste *pp.* laden, *Pe* 1146
lastes *n.* sins
last(t)(e) *v.* (**last(e), lasted, lested** *pa.t.*) last, endure; stretch, *Cl* 227
lat(e) *adj. & adv.* late; remiss; tardy
later *compar. adv.* **neuer þe l.** nevertheless
laþe *v.* invite, urge
laþe *see also* **loþe**
lauande *adj.* flowing, *Cl* 366
lauce(n), -us-, -ws- *v.* loosen, break, burst, undo; open, *Cl* 1428; relieve, *Cl* 1589; utter, speak, *Cl* 668, *Pat* 350, 489, *G* 1212, 1766, 2124
laucyng *n. as presp.* undoing, *G* 1334
laue *v.* bale out, *Pat* 154; pour out, *Pe* 607
laue *see also* **law(e)**
laumpe *n.* lamp
launce *n.* lance, spear: *pl.* boughs, *Pe* 978
launce *v.* shoot, gallop
launde *n.* glade, field, grassy plain
laused, lausen *see* **lauce(n)**
law(e), laue *n.¹* law, religion; style, *G* 790; **bi l.** formally, *G* 1643

lawe *n.²* mound, hill
lawles *adj.* lawless
lawsez *see* **lauce(n)**
lay *v.* lay, lay down; abase, lay low, *Cl* 1307, 1650; bestow upon, *G* 1480; assign, set, *Cl* 425; deal out, *Pat* 173; put, *Pat* 106, 174; commit, *Pat* 168; **l. hym bysyde** turn aside, parry, *G* 1777, **l. vp** put away, *G* 1874; **in teme l.** discuss, *Pat* 37
laye *n.* poem, *G* 30*n.*
lay(e) *see also* **ly(ȝ)(e)**
layk *n.* game, sport, fun; holiday, *G* 1023; practice, *Cl* 274, *Pat* 401, *G* 1513; behaviour, *Cl* 1053, 1064
layke *v.* play, amuse oneself, *Cl* 872, *G* 1111, *etc.*
laykyng *n.* playing, *G* 472
layne *v.* conceal; **l. yow (me)** keep your (my) secret
layt *n.* lightning, *G* 199
layt(e) *v.* seek
layth *adj.* foul, *Pat* 401
lazares *n.* leprous beggars
le, leauté *see* **le(e), lewté**
lebardez *n.* leopards
led *n.* lead, *Cl* 1025
ledden *see* **laden**
led(e), leede, leude, lude *n.* man, knight, prince; sir, *Pe* 542, *G* 449, *etc.; collective* people, *Cl* 691, 772, *G* 833, 1113, 1124; **leudlez** *adj.* companionless
lede *v.* (**lad(de)** *pa.t.*, **lad** *pp.*) lead; pursue, *G* 1894; cultivate, *Pat* 428; live, experience, *G* 1927, 2058
leder *n.* leader; **-es** *pl.* leading men, *Cl* 1307
ledisch, ludisch, ludych *adj.* of the people, national, *Cl* 73, 1375, 1556
leede *see* **led(e)**
le(e) *n.* shelter, castle
lef, leef, leue *adj.* (**leuer** *compar.*, **leuest** *superl.*) beloved, dear; delightful, pleasant, *G* 49, 909, 1111; *as n.* dear one, beloved, *Cl* 939, 1066, *Pe* 418; **þat leuer wer** (*impers.*) who would rather, *G* 1251
lef *n.* (**leuez, leues** *pl.*) leaf; *collect.* foliage, *Pe* 77, *Pat* 447; *pl.* leaves of a book, *Pe* 837, *Cl* 966
lefly *adj.* dear, lovely, *Cl* 977
lefsel *n.* bower of leaves, *Pat* 448
leg(g) *n.* leg, *Pe* 459, *G* 575, 2228
leg(g)e *adj.* liege, sovereign, requiring allegiance; *as n.* lord, *Cl* 1368
leghe *see* **ly(ȝ)(e)**
legioun, legyoun *n.* legion
leȝ(en), leȝten, leke *see* **ly(ȝ)(e), lach(ch)e, louke**
leke *see* **lere-leke, louke**
lel(e) *adj.* loyal, faithful, true
lel(l)y *adv.* loyally, faithfully
leme *v.* shine, gleam
lem(m)an *n.* sweetheart, mistress, love, lover
len(c)þe, lenkþe *n.* length, duration (*space or time*); **on l.** along the length (of the table) *Cl* 116, afar, *G* 1231, for a long time, *G* 232
lende *v.* (**lent** *pa.t. & pp.*) remain, stay, dwell, *Cl* 993, *Pat* 260, *G* 1100, 1499, 2440; sit, *G* 1002: come, approach, go, *Pat* 201, *G* 971,

1319; **is lent** is away, *G* 1319; **watz lent** was present, *Cl* 1084

lene *v.* (**lante(z**) *pa.t.*, **lent** *pp.*) grant, give, *Cl* 256, 348, *Pat* 347, *G* 2250

lened *pa.t.* leant, reclined; **he l. with þe nek** he bent his neck, *G* 2255

leng(e) *v.* remain, stay, live; **hym l.** let him stay, *G* 1893; *pp.* persuaded to stay, *G* 1683

lenger, lengest *see* **long(e)**

lenghe *n.* duration, *Pe* 416; **on l.** for a long time, *Pe* 167

lenkþe *see* **len(c)þe**

lent *see* **lende, lene**

Lentoun *n.* Lent

lenþe *see* **len(c)þe**

lepe *v.* (**lep** *pa.t.*, **lopen** *pp.*) leap, run; gallop, *G* 2154 (*reflex.*); burst, *Cl* 966

lepre *adj.* leprous

lere *adj.* worse (?), *G* 1109 (*cf.* **lur**)

lere *n.*[1] ligature, *G* 1334

lere, lyre *n.*[2] cheek, face, *Cl* 1542, 1687, *G* 318, 943, 2228; flesh, *G* 418; coat, *G* 2050; **lere-leke** wimple, *Pe* 210n

lere *v.* teach, *Cl* 843

lerne *v.* learn; teach *G* 1878; *pp.adj.* well-instructed, skilful, *G* 1170, 2447

les *see* **lasse, les(e)**

lesande *presp.* opening, *Pe* 837

les(e) *adj.* false, *Cl* 1719, *Pat* 428, *Pe* 865

lese *v.* (**lest(e)** *pa.t.*, **lorne, lest** *pp.*) lose; destroy, *Cl* 932; fail, *Cl* 887

lesse *see* **lasse**

lest *conj.* lest, in case

lest(e) *see* **lasse, lese**

lested *see* **last(t)(e)**

lesyng *n.* lie, *Pe* 897

let(t)(e) *v.*[1] let, allow; leave, *Cl* 670; utter, speak, *G* 1086, 1206; behave, pretend, *G* 1190, *etc.*; have, cause, *G* 1084; **l. be** stop, *Pe* 715; **l. lyȝt bi, of** care little for, neglect, *Cl* 1174, 1320; **l. se** show, *G* 299, 414

lette *v.*[2] hinder, dissuade, *G* 1672, 2142, 2303; prevent, deprive, *Cl* 1803; obstruct, *Pe* 1050

letter, lettre *n.* letter (of the alphabet); inscription, *Cl* 1580

lettrure *n.* learning, doctrine, *Pe* 751, *G* 1513

leþe *n.* calm, *Pat* 160

leþe *v.* soften, humble, *G* 2438; be merciful (to), *Cl* 752; assuage, be assuaged, *Pe* 377, *Pat* 3; cease, *Cl* 648

leþer *n.* leather, *Cl* 1581; skin, *G* 1360

leude, leudlez *see* **lede**

leue *n.* leave, permission; leave-taking, *G* 1288; **take l.** depart, *Cl* 401

leue *v.*[1] (**laft, lafte(n**) *pa.t.*) leave; leave off, stop, *Cl* 1233, *G* 1502; leave out, *G* 2030; forsake, *Pe* 622; give up, *G* 369; allow, *G* 98

leue(n), *v.*[2] believe, *Pe* 69, 302, *etc.*; *Cl* 608, *etc.*; *Pat* 170, *etc.*; *G* 1784, 2421, *etc.*; **l. on** assent to, *Pat* 405

leue *see also* **lyue**

leued *pp.* leaved, *Pe* 978

leue(r), leuest *see* **lef** *adj.*

leues, leuez *see* **lef** *n.*

lewed *adj.* ignorant, uninstructed

lewté, leauté *n.* loyalty, good faith

leyen, lif, liflode, liȝt(e) *see* **ly(ȝ)(e), lyf, lyflode, lyȝt(e)**

liddez *n.* eyelids, *G* 2007

lik, lyk *v.* lick, *Cl* 1000; sip, drink, *Cl* 1521; taste (*metaph.*), *Cl* 1141, *G* 968

like(s), lis, list(e) *see* **lyke, ly(ȝ)e, lyst(e)**

littel, little *see* **lyt(t)el**

liþernez *n.* viciousness, *G* 1627

liuréz *n.* liveries, garments, *Pe* 1108

llak *see* **lake**

lode *n.* way of life, (?burden), *Pat* 156; **on l., in his l.** under guidance, *Pat* 504, with her (him), *G* 969, 1284

lodesmon, lodezmon *n.* pilot, steersman

lodly(ch), loþelych *adj.* loathsome, horrible; *as n.*, loathsome people, *Cl* 1093; *adv.* with loathing; with a show of repugnance, *G* 1634, 1772

lof *n.* praise, value; **of l.** fine, *Pat* 448

lof(den) *see also* **luf**

lofe *n.* luff, *Pat* 106n

lofly(est) *see* **luflych**

loft(e) *n.* upper room, *G* 1096, 1676; (**vp)on l.** aloft, on high, above, up

log(g)e *n.* small house, arbour

logge *v.* lodge, stay the night

logging *n.* house

loghe *see* **loȝ(e)**

Logres *n.* Britain, *G* 691n, 1055

loȝ(e), loghe, low(e) *adj. & adv.* (**lowest** *superl.*) low; **on l.** down, *G* 1373

loȝ(e), loghe *n.* flood, sea; stream, *Pe* 119

loȝe *see also* **laȝe**

loȝed *pp.* humbled, abased, *Cl* 1650

loȝen *see* **laȝe**

loȝly *adv.* humbly

loke *n.* look, glance, expression, *Pe* 1134, *G* 1480; (act of) looking, *G* 2438

loke *v.* look, watch, see; take care, *Cl* 317, 905, 944, *G* 448; consider, *Pe* 463; watch over, *Pat* 504, *G* 2239

loke(n) *see* **louke**

lokkez *n.* locks, hair

lokyng *n.* gazing, *G* 232; gaze, *Pe* 1049

loltrande *presp.* lounging, *Pat* 458

lombe, lomp(e), loumbe, lamb(e) *n.* lamb; *gen.* of the lamb, *Pe* 1141

lombe-lyȝt *n.* lamplight, *Pe* 1046n

lome *adj.* lame, *Cl* 1094

lome *n.* tool, weapon, *G* 2309; vessel, *Cl* 314, *etc.*, *Pat* 160

lomerande *adj.* stumbling, hobbling, *Cl* 1094

lomp(e) *see* **lombe**

londe, lont *n.* land; world; field, *G* 1561; **in l.** in the land, on earth. *Cf.* **launde**

lone *n.* lane, roadway, *Pe* 1066

long(e) *adj.* (**lenger** *compar.*, **lengest** *superl.*) long (*of space and time*); **vpon l.** at length, *Cl* 1193; *adv.* for a long time

longe *v.* (**longande** *presp.*, *Pe* 462) belong, pertain (to)

longe *v. impers. in* **me longed** I longed, had a longing, *Pe* 144

long(e)yng(e), longing *n.* anxiety; longing, *Pe* 244, 1180

lont, lopen *see* **londe, lepe**

lord(e) *n.* lord; God; landowner, master; husband, *Cl* 656, *G* 1231

lordeschyp, lort- *n.* dominion, command

lore *n.* teaching, *Pat* 350, 428; learning, *Cl* 1556, *G* 665*n*; manner, fashion, *Pe* 236

lorne *see* **lese**

los *n.*[1] renown, *G* 258, 1528

los, losse *n.*[2] loss; losing lot, *Pat* 174; injury, harm, *Cl* 1589, *G* 2507

lose *v.* (**losed, lost(e)** *pp.*) lose, forgo; destroy, end, *Cl* 909, *Pat* 198; perish, *Pe* 908

losyng *n.* perdition

losynger *n.* traitor

lot(e) *n.*[1] speech, word, sound; echoes, *G* 119; noise, clamour, *Pat* 161, *G* 1917; voice, *G* 244, 1623, *Pe* 238; *pl.* manners, *Pat* 47, *G* 1339(?)

lot(e) *n.*[2] lot, *Pat* 194; casting of lots, *Pat* 180; chance, happening, *Pe* 1205; **lay lotes on** cast lots among, *Pat* 173

Loth, Lot, Loot *n.* Lot

loþe *adj.* hateful, *G* 1578

loþe, laþe *n.* injury, *G* 2507; grief, suffering, *Pe* 377; **withouten l.** without offence, ungrudged, *G* 127

loþelych *see* **lodly(ch)**

loud(e), lowde *adj. & adv.* loud(ly)

loue, louue, lovue, lowe *v.* praise, glorify, *Pe* 285, 342, 1124, 1127; *Cl* 497, 925, 987, 1289, 1703, 1719, *G* 1256; be praised, *G* 1399; advise, *Pat* 173

loue *see also* **luf**

loueloker, louelokkest, louely(ch) *see* **lufly(ch)(e)**

louez *n.* palms (of hands), *Cl* 987

louflych *see* **lufly(ch)(e)**

louke, lowke *v.* (**leke, louked** *pa.t.*, **loke(n)** *pp.*) shut, *G* 2007; *intrans.* fasten, *G* 217, 628, *etc.*; shrink, *Cl* 441; *pp.* enclosed, enshrined *or* linked, *G* 35; framed, *G* 765; locked, contained, *Pat* 350

loumbe *see* **lombe**

loupe *n.*[1] loop, *G* 591

loupe *n.*[2] loop-hole, *G* 792

loute *v.* (**lut(te)** *pa.t. & pp.*) bow, bend; come, go, *Pe* 933, *G* 833, 933; defer (to), *G* 248

louue, louy(e) *see* **loue, luf**

louyly *adj.* lawful, *Pe* 565

louyng *n.* praising, *Cl* 1448, *Pat* 237

lovue *see* **loue**

lowande *presp.* shining, brilliant

lowde, lowest, lowke *see* **loud(e), loȝ(e), louke**

low(e) *see* **loȝ(e), loue**

luche *v.* pitch, *Pat* 230

lude *see* **lede**

ludisch, ludych *see* **ledisch**

luf, lof, loue *n* love, affection, friendship; wooing, *G* 1733, 1810, 2497; lover, loved one, *Cl* 401; *collect.* paramours, *Cl* 1419

luf, loue, louy(e) *v.* (**lofden** *pa.t. pl.*) love, like

luf-daungere *n.* aloofness, distance of the beloved, *Pe* 11

luf-lace *n.* (belt as love token), *G* 1874, 2438

luf-laȝyng *n.* flirtatious wit, *G* 1777

luf-longyng *n.* love-longing, *Pe* 1152

luf-lowe *n.* flame of love, *Cl* 707

lufly(ch)(e), louely(ch), louflych, lofly *adj.* (**loueloker** *compar.*, **louelokkest, loflyest** *superl.*) lovely, gracious, courteous, beautiful, comely, *Pe* 693, 962, *Cl* 939, *G* 38, *etc.*; dear, *Cl* 1804; *also iron.*: *G* 433 (precious), *etc.*; **l. loke** look of love, *G* 1480; *adv.* (*also* **luflyly**) courteously, in a friendly manner, *Cl* 81, *G* 369, 595, 981, *etc.*; kindly, *G* 254; gladly, *G* 1606; beautifully, *Pe* 880, 978

lufs(o)um *adj. as n.* lovely (one)

luf-talkyng *n.* conversation about love, *G* 927

luged *pa.t.* moved heavily, laboured, *Cl* 443

lulted *pp.* sounded, *Cl* 1207

luly-whit *adj.* lily-white

lumpen *see* **lymp(e)**

lur *n.* loss; injury, *Pat* 419; penalty, *G* 1284, 1682; *pl.* losses, griefs, *Pe* 339, 358

lurk(k)e *v.* lurk, lie low, *Pat* 277; stay in bed, lie quiet, *G* 1180; *pp.* with eyes closed, *G* 1195; **l. by** pass under, *Pe* 978

lust *see* **lyste**

lusty *adj.* vigorous, *Cl* 981

lut(te) *see* **loute**

luþer, lyþer *adj. & adv.* wicked; vile, *Pat* 156; *as n.* evil, *Pe* 567, *Cl* 1090; *adv.* ill, *Pat* 500

lyf, lif, lyue *n.* life; soul, *Pe* 305, 687; being, person, *Pat* 260, *G* 1780; (**vp)on l.** alive, on earth (*or intensive:* indeed); **l. haue, bere** live *Cl* 308, *etc.*

lyfed *see* **lyue**

lyflode, liflode *n.* means of life, *Cl* 561; food, *G* 133

lyft(e) *adj.* left

lyfte *n.* heaven, sky, *Cl* 212, 366, *etc.*, *G* 1256

lyft(e) *v.* (**lyft(e)** *pa.t. & pp.*) lift, raise; decree, set up, *Cl* 717; **lyftande** *presp.adj.* heaving, *Cl* 443

lygges, lyg(g)ez, lyggede *see* **ly(ȝ)e**

lyȝe *n.* lie, *Pe* 304

ly(ȝ)(e) *v.* (**lyg(g)ez, lys, lis** *pres3sg.*, **lyȝe, lay(e), leȝ(en), leghe, lyggede** *pa.t.*, **leyen** *pp.*) lie; exist, *Pe* 602; be in residence, *G* 37; stay in bed, *G* 88; **l. þeroute** sleep out of doors, *Pe* 930; **l. in hym** be in his power, *Pe* 360

lyȝt *adj.*[1] light (in weight), *Cl* 1026; swift, *Cl* 987, *G* 199; active, energetic, *G* 87, 1119, 1464; joyful, *Pe* 238; **let l. of** care little for, *Cl* 1174, 1320; **set at l.** think lightly of, *G* 1250; **lyȝte** *adv.* lightly, *Pe* 214

lyȝt, lyȝte *adj.*[2] bright, *Pe* 500; pure, unsullied, *Pe* 682

lyȝt *n.* light; first light, dawn, *G* 1675

lyȝt(e), liȝt(e) *v.* (**lyȝt(e)** *pa.t. & pp.*) fall, alight, descend, come down; dismount, *G* 822, *etc.*; stop, *Cl* 800; *pp.* fallen, *Pe* 247

lyȝten *v.* lighten, *Pat* 160

lyȝtloker *compar. adj.* easier, better, *Pat* 47

lyȝtly *adj.* brilliant, dazzling, *G* 608

lyȝtly *adv.* quickly, readily; easily, *Pe* 358, *G* 1299; probably, *Pat* 88

lyk *see* **lik**

lyk(e) *adj.* (**lykker** *compar.*, **lykkest** *superl.*) like, similar (to); *as n.* the same, *G* 498; *conj.* as if, *Cl* 1008, *G* 1281

lyke, like v. like, be pleased, *Cl* 36, 73, *etc.*, *Pat* 47, *G* 694, 893; please, *Cl* 1064, *G* 87, *etc.*; *impers.* it pleases (him, me, *etc.*), *Pe* 566, *Cl* 717, *etc.*, *Pat* 397, *etc.*, *G* 289, *etc.*; **l. oþer greme** whether it please or annoy (anyone), i.e. whether you like it or not, *Pat* 42
lykkerwys *adj.* delicious, *G* 968
lykne v. compare, *Pe* 500; **l. tylle** resemble, *Cl* 1064
lyknyng n. imitation, *Pat* 30
lykores n. liquors, *Cl* 1521
lykyng n. pleasure; inclination, desire, *Cl* 172
lylled *pa.t.* quivered, *Pat* 447
lym, lym(m)e n. limb, member
lymp(e) v. (**lumpen** *pp.*) happen, befall; fall (on), *Pat* 174, 194
lynde n.[1] tree, *Cl* 1485, *G* 526, 2176
lyndes n.[2] loins, *G* 139
lynde-wod n. forest, *G* 1178 (*gen.*)
lyne n.[1] line; course of events, *Pe* 626
lyne, lynne n.[2] & *adj.* linen, *Pe* 731; **vnder l.** in linen, lady, *G* 1814n
lyppe n. lip
lyounez n. lions
lyre, lys *see* **lere, ly(ȝ)(e)**
lysoun n. glimpse, *Cl* 887
lyst n.[1] edge, *Cl* 1761
lyst n.[2] trick, practice, *Cl* 693
lyste, list, lust n.[3] desire, *Pe* 173, *Cl* 843; joy, delight, *Pe* 467, 908, *G* 1719; pleasure, (?lust), *Cl* 1350
lyst(e) *v.impers.* (**lyste, liste** *pa.t.*) it pleases, it pleased; I longed, *Pe* 146, 181; *pa.subjunc.* would see fit, *Pe* 1141
lyste v. hear, *G* 1878
lysten n. sense of hearing, *Cl* 586
lysten v. listen (to), *G* 30; hear, *Pe* 880, *G* 2006
lystyly *adv.* cunningly, cleverly
lyt(e) *adj.* & *adv.* little; *pl.* few, *G* 701
lyte n. *in* **on l., allyt** in delay, in hesitation, *Cl* 599, *G* 1463, 2303
lyth n. limb, *Pe* 398
lyt(t)el, littel, little *adj.* & *adv.* little; small, *Pe* 604; insignificant, *Pe* 574; *as n.* a little; **set at l.** considered of little importance, *Cl* 1710; **wyth l.** in a short time *or* to little effect, *Pe* 575
lyþe v. assuage, *Pe* 357
lyþen v. hear, *G* 1719
lyþer *see* **luþer**
lyþerly *adv.* meanly, wretchedly
lyue, lyuy(e), lyuie, leue (**lyued, lyfed** *pa.t.*) v. live
lyue(s), (-z) *see also* **lyf**
lyued *pp.* given life to, *Cl* 172
lyuer n. liver

ma *see* **make, par**
mace *see* **make**
mach n. mate, *Cl* 695; companion, *Cl* 124
mach(ch) v. equal, match, *G* 282; *reflex.* settle, agree, *Pat* 99; exert oneself, strive, *Cl* 1512
mad *see* **make**
mad(de) *adj.* mad. *See also* **arayde**

madde v. rave, *Pe* 359; behave stupidly, *G* 2414
maddyng n. madness, *Pe* 1154
made(n), maȝt *see* **make, myȝt(e)**
maȝty, myȝty *adj.* mighty, powerful
maȝtyly *adv.* forcefully; fiercely, *Cl* 1267
Mahoun n. Mohammed (*as a heathen deity*)
make n. wife, spouse; mate; equal, *Cl* 248n
make, ma v. (**makes, matz, mas, mace** *pres.3sg.*, **man** *pres.pl.*, **mad(e)(n)** *pa.t.*, **mad(e), maked** *pp.*) make; create; cause, compel, *Pe* 176, *Cl* 1566, *Pat* 54, *G* 1567, *etc.*; do, perform, *Cl* 1238, *G* 43, 1073, *etc.*; tell, *Pe* 304; *see also* **acorde, cher(e), ene, fest(e), paye, rescoghe, somoun, toȝt**
makel(l)ez *adj.* matchless, peerless
male n.[1] male
males, -z n.[2] bags, *G* 1129, 1809
malicious *adj.* wicked, *Pat* 508; severe, *Pat* 522
malscrande *adj.* bewildering
malskred *pp.* dazed
malte v. (**malt(e)** *pa.t.*) melt; condense, trickle, *G* 2080; be resolved, *Cl* 1566; soften (*trans.*), *Cl* 776; dissolve (*trans.*), *Pe* 1154; **m. in** enter into, comprehend, *Pe* 224
malys, malyce n. wickedness, sin; anger, *Cl* 250; malice, resentment, *Pat* 4; severity, *Pat* 523
Mambre n. Mamre
man *see* **make, mon**
manace v. (**mansed** *pa.t.*) threaten
manayre *see* **maner**
mancioun n. dwelling place
Mane n. Mene
maner, manayre n.[1] (manor); house, *Pe* 918; city, *Pe* 1029
maner n.[2] custom; kind, *G* 484; way, *G* 1730; *pl.* manners, *Pe* 382, *G* 924; ways, *Pat* 22
manerly *adj.* polite, dignified, *G* 1656
manerly *adv.* properly, courteously, *Cl* 91
manez *see* **mon**
mangerye, -ie n. banquet, feast
mankyn n. mankind, *Pe* 637
mankynde, monkynde n. mankind
mannez *see* **mon**
mansed *pp.adj.* cursed. *See also* **manace**
mantyle, -ile n. mantle, cloak
marchal, mare *see* **marschal, more**
margyrye, margary, marjory, margerye-perle n. pearl, *Pe* 199, 206, 1037
marie v. (**maryed** *pp.*) marry
marked n. market, *Pe* 513
marre v.[1] destroy, *Cl* 991 (*pp.*), *G* 2262; corrupt, *Cl* 279; disfigure, *Pe* 23; *intrans.* perish, *Pat* 172, 474; suffer, *Pat* 479
marre v.[2] lament, *Pe* 359
marryng n. spoiling
mar(s)chal n. marshal, master of ceremonies
maryag(e) n. marriage
Mary(e) n. (the Virgin) Mary; marry!, *G* 1942, 2140
mas *see* **make**
mase n. confusion, damnation, *Cl* 395n
maskl(l)e, mascle n. spot

maskel(l)ez, -es, mascellez *adj.* spotless, flawless

mas(se), messe *n.* (service of) Mass; gospel read at Mass, *Cl* 51. *See also* **mes(se)**

masseprest *n.* ordained priest

mat(e) *adj.* frightened, subdued, *G* 336; exhausted, *G* 1568; dejected, *Pe* 386

mate *v.* shame, defeat, *Pe* 613

mater *n.* matter, substance; primal matter, *Pat* 503

matz *see* **make**

Maþew, Mathew *n.* (St) Matthew

maugré, maugref, mawgref *prep.* in spite of (**my chekes, his hed,** *etc.* myself, himself, *etc.*). *See Pat* 44*n*

mawe *n.* belly

mawgré *n.* displeasure, *Cl* 250

mawgref *see* **maugré**

may *n.* maiden, *Pe* 435, *etc.*; woman, *G* 1795(2)

mayden(n) *n.* maiden; virgin, *Pe* 869*n*; (the Virgin Mary), *Cl* 248, 1069

may(e) *v.* (**may, moun, mowe** *pres.pl.*, **myȝt(ez), moȝt(e)(n)** *pa.t.*) can, may, will (*fut.*); **quat he m.** (*sc.* **do**) what he would do, *G* 1087

mayn *adj.* great, *G* 94, *etc.*; strong, *G* 497

maynful *adj.* mighty, powerful

maynly *adv.* loudly

maynteine, -tyne, menteene *v.* maintain (in argument), *Pe* 783; support (as lord), *G* 2053; exercise, *Pat* 523

mayntnaunce *n.* maintenance, supporting

mayny *see* **me(y)ny**

mayster *n.* lord, master; **maystres** *pl.* learned men, *Pat* 329

maysterful *adj.* arrogant, *Pe* 401, *Cl* 1328

mayster(r)y *n.* victory, triumph

maystrés *n.* miraculous powers, *G* 2448

maystres *see also* **mayster**

me *pron.* one, *Cl* 553. *See* **mon** *indef.pron.* **me** *see also* **I**

med *see* **mete**

mede *n.* reward; **to m.** as a reward, *Pat* 55

medoes *n.* meadows

megre *adj.* thin

meke *adj.* meek, gentle, submissive; merciful, *Cl* 771; *as n.* humble servant, *Cl* 776

mekely *adv.* meekly

mekenesse, Mekenesse *n.* meekness; Meekness (*personified*), *Pat* 32

mekned *pa.t.* humbled

mele *n.*[1] meal, flour, *Cl* 226, 625

mele *n.*[2] meal, dinner, *G* 999

mel(l)e *v.*[1] speak, say, tell

melle *v.*[2] mingle, flow, *G* 2503

melly *n.* quarrel, *G* 342; battle, *G* 644

membre *n.* limb, member

men *see* **mon**

menddyng *n.* amendment, *Cl* 764; improvement, *Pe* 452

mended *pa.t.* improved, *G* 883

mendez *n.* recompense, *Pe* 351

mene *adj.* poor, *Cl* 1241

mene *v.* mean, signify, *Pe* 293, 951, *G* 233; refer to, *Pe* 937; say, *Cl* 1625

meng(e) *v.* mix, mingle; **menged** *pp.* mingled, *G* 1720

mensclaȝt *n.* manslaughter

mensk *adj.* charming, courteous, *G* 964

mensk(e) *n.* honour, courtesy, grace; **of m.** courteous, *Pe* 162, courteously, *Cl* 646

menske *v.* honour, *Cl* 118, 141; *pp.* adorned, *G* 153

menskful *adj.* fine, noble (*& as n.*)

menskly *adv.* fittingly, with honour

menteene, meny *see* **maynteine, me(y)ny**

menyng *n.* understanding, *G* 924

mercy, merci, Mercy, mersy *n.* mercy; Mercy (*personified*), *Pat* 32. *See also* **gra(u)nt mercy**

mercyable *adj.* merciful

mercyles *adj.* merciless

mere *adj.* noble, *G* 924

mere *n.*[1] sea, *Cl* 991, *Pat* 112; pool, water, *Pe* 140, 158, 1166

mere *n.*[2] boundary, *Cl* 778, *Pat* 320; rendezvous, *G* 1061

meré *see* **myry**

Mergot *n.* Margot, *Pat* 167*n*

merit *n.* reward

merk *adj.* dark, obscure

merk *n.*[1] darkness, *Cl* 894, *Pat* 291

merk *n.*[2] appointed place, rendezvous, *G* 1073

merk(k)e *v.* aim at, *G* 1592; set out, place, *Cl* 558, 637, 1487; write, *Cl* 1617, 1727; *pp.* situated, *Pe* 142

mersy *see* **mercy**

merþe, mirþe, my(e)rþe *n.* joy, pleasure, amusement; merriment, rejoicing; pleasant subjects, *Cl* 132, *G* 541, 1763; harmony, music, *Pe* 92; **make m.** rejoice, make merry. *See also* **myrþe** *v.*

meruayl(e), merwayle *n.* marvel, wonder, amazement; **had m.** wondered, *G* 233; *adj.* marvellous, *Pat* 81

meruelous *adj.* miraculous, *Pe* 1166

mery(ly), mes *see* **myry(ly), mes(se)**

meschaunce *n.* doom, disaster

meschef *n.* misfortune, trouble; plight, guilt, *G* 1774

mese *v.* moderate

message *n.* message; messenger, *Cl* 454

mes(se) *n.* meal, *Pe* 862; 'breakfast' (light meal), *G* 999(1); dish (of food), *Cl* 637, *G* 999(2), 1004. *See also* **mas(se)**

messequyle *n.* time of Mass, *G* 1097

mester *n.* need, *Pat* 342, *Cl* 67

mesurable *adj.* moderate, mild

mesure *n.* moderation; size, *Pe* 224; **on m. hyghe** in height, *G* 137

met *see* **met(e)** *adj.*

metail (metalles *pl.*) *n.* metal

mete, med *adj.* proper, fitting; equal, *Cl* 1662; proportionate, *Cl* 1391*n*; sufficient, *Pat* 420; reaching, *G* 1736; **is ... m.** agrees, *Pe* 833; **-ly** *adv.* properly

mete *n.* food; meal, feast

mete *v.*[1] meet; find, *Pe* 329; greet, *G* 834, 2206*n*, 2235

mete *v.*[2] measure, *G* 2206*n*; **meten** *pp.* measured, *Pe* 1032

meth *see* **meþe**
methles, meþelez *adj.* intemperate, immoderate
mettez *n.* measures
metz *n.* mildness, mercy
meþe, meth *n.* moderation, mildness, mercy
meþelez *see* **methles**
meue, mwe *v.* move, proceed, go; influence, *G* 90; initiate, *G* 985; occur, *Pe* 64; **m. to** portend, *G* 1197, rouse, *G* 1157
me(y)ny, mayny *n.* company, household, retinue; body of workmen, *Pe* 542
miche, mirþe, miry *see* **much(e), merþe, myry**
mislyke, mys- *v.impers.* displease
misschapen *adj.* deformed, evil
mistrauþe *n.* lack of faith
misy *n.* marsh, *G* 749
Mizael *n.* Mishael
mo *compar. adj. & adv.* more (*usu.* in *number*); **þe mo** the greater (benefit), *Pe* 340
mod(e) *n.*[1] anger, temper; mind, mood, *Cl* 713, *G* 1475; message, thought, *Cl* 6135; *fig.* nature, character, *Pe* 738
mode *n.*[2] melody, *Pe* 884
moder *n.* mother
moder-chylde *n.* mother's son
mod(e)y *adj.* proud; brave, *Cl* 1303
moȝt(e)(n), moȝtez *see* **may**
mokke *n.* muck, filth, *Pe* 905
mol *see* **mul**
molaynes *n.* bit-studs, *G* 169
mold(e) *n.* earth; *pl.* clods (*or possess.* of earth), *Pe* 30, *Pat* 494, lands, *Cl* 454
mon, man *n.* man; servant; **vche m.** everyone; **no m.** nobody; *gen.* **man(n)ez, monnez** man's, human; *pl.* **men(ne)** men, people
mon, man, men, me *indef. pron.* one, *Pe* 165, 194, *etc.*, *Cl* 180, 183, *etc.*, *Pat* 43, *G* 565, 1077, *etc.*
mon *v.* must, *G* 1811, 2354
mone *n.*[1] moon; month, *Pe* 1080; **(an)vnder m.** on earth, in existence; completely, *Pe* 923
mon(e), moon *n.*[2] moaning, lamentation, *Cl* 373, *G* 737; grief (*i.e.* loss), *Pe* 374
moni(e), mony(e) *adj. & pron.* many (a); **m. on** many a one, *G* 442
monkynde *see* **mankynde**
mon-sworne *n.* perjury
mony(e) *see* **moni(e)**
monyfolde *adv.* greatly, many times
monyth *n.* month
moon, moote *see* **mon(e)** *n.*[2]. **mot(e)**
more *n.* moor; earth, *Cl* 385
more, mare *compar. adj. & adv.* greater, larger; further, *Cl* 48; moreover, *Pe* 565; **most(e)** *superl. adj.* largest, biggest, greatest; *superl. adv.* most. *Cf.* **much(e), mukel**
Morgne (la Faye) *n.* Morgan le Fay
mornande *presp.* mourning, lamenting
morn(e), moroun *n.* morning; next day
morne *see also* **mo(u)rne**
mornyf *adj.* sorrowful
mornyng, -ing *n.* morning
mornyng *see also* **mo(u)rnyng(e)**

moroun *see* **morn(e)**
morteres *n.* candles
most(e) *see* **more, mot**
mot *auxil.v.* (**most(e)** *pa.t.*) may, must; *pa.t.* must; would have to, *Pat* 55
mot(e) *n.*[1] mote, speck; stain, spot, blemish, *Pe* 726, *etc.*, *Cl* 556; **not a m.** not a jot, *G* 2209
mote *n.*[2] dispute, quarrel, *Pe* 855
mote *n.*[3] moat; castle, *G* 635, *etc.*; court, (walled) city, *Pe* 142, *etc.*, *Pat* 422
mote, motez *n.*[4] notes of the horn
mote *v.* argue, *Pe* 613
moteles, -lez *adj.* spotless
moul *n.* earth, *Pe* 23. *Cf.* **mul**
moun *see* **may**
mountaunce *n.* amount, size
mountaynez *n.* mountains
mount(e) *n.* mountain, hill; **bi m.** among the hills, *G* 718
mounte *v.* amount, *Pat* 332; increase, *Pe* 351
mounture *n.* mount, horse, *G* 1691
mourkene *v.*[1] grow dark, *Cl* 1760
mourkne *v.*[2] rot, *Cl* 407
mo(u)rne *v.* lament, grieve; repent, *Pat* 508
mo(u)rnyng(e) *n.* sorrow; **in m. of** oppressed by, *G* 1751
mouþe, m(o)outh(e), mowþe *n.* mouth; voice
mowe *see* **may(e)**
much(e), miche, mych *adj., adv. & pron.* big, great, large, abundant, strong, *Pe* 604, *etc.*, *Cl* 22, *etc.*, *Pat* 70, *G* 182, *etc.*; a lot (of), much, *Pe* 244, *etc.*, *Cl* 182, *etc.*, *G* 558, *etc.*; **þus m.** as much as this, as follows; **much quat** many things; *adv.* much, greatly, very. *See also* **more, mukel**
muckel *n.* size, *G* 142
mudde *n.* mud
muged *pa.t.* drizzled, lay damp, *G* 2080
mukel *adj.* large, great; *adv.* greatly, *Pat* 324. *See also* **much(e), more**
mul, mol *n.* dust
mulne *n.* mill
mun *n.* mouth
munster, mynster *n.* church, temple
munt *see* **mynt, mynte**
muryly *see* **myryly**
mused *pa.t.* doted, wandered in mind, *G* 2424
mute *n.* pack of hounds; sound (of a hunt), *G* 1915
muth(e), mwe *see* **mouþe, meue**
my, myn(e) *possess. pron. & adj.* my; mine
mych *see* **much(e)**
myddelerde *n.* the earth
myddes, myddez *n.* midst. *Cf.* **inmyddes**
mydmorn *n.* mid-morning, 9 a.m.
mydnyȝt *n.* midnight
myd ouer vnder *n.* well on in the afternoon, *G* 1730*n*
myerþe *see* **merþe**
myȝt(e), maȝt *n.* might, power, strength; **at my m.** to the best of my ability
myȝt(ez) *see also* **may**
myȝty *see* **maȝty**
myke *n.*[1] crutch (forked support for lowered mast), *Cl* 417
mykez *n.*[2] (friends); chosen, *Pe* 572*n*

mylde *adj.* merciful; mild, gentle, *Pe* 961, 1115; *as n.* gentle ones, *Pe* 721
myle *n.* mile
mylke *n.* milk
mylke *v.* milk, *Cl* 1259
mynde *n.* mind, heart, spirit; intention, *Cl* 1502; memory, *G* 1283, 1484; **in m. hade** remembered, *G* 1283; **gotz in m.** is questionable, *G* 1293
myn(e), mynez *see* **my, myn(n)e**
mynge *v.* draw attention to, *G* 1422; think, *Pe* 855
mynne *adj.* less(er), *G* 1881
myn(n)e *v.* remember, think about; remind, declare; *impers.* **me mynez** I think, *Cl* 25
mynster *see* **munster**
mynstra(l)sy(e), -cie *n.* minstrelsy
mynt, -u- *n.* aim; feint, *G* 2345, *etc.*; purpose, intention, *Pe* 1161
mynte *v.* (**mynte, munt** *pa.t.*) aim (a blow), swing, *G* 2262, 2274, 2290; intend, purpose, *Cl* 1628
mynystred *pa.t.* served
myre *n.* mire; swamp
myri, myrþe *see* **myry, merþe**
myrþez *v.trans.* rejoices, gladdens, *Pe* 862
myry, mery, meré, mi(y)ry, myri *adj.* merry, pleasant, good-humoured, bonny, *etc.*; fine, beautiful, handsome, *Pe* 23, 158, *etc.*, *Cl* 417, 783, *etc.*, *G* 142, 153, *etc.*
myryly, meryly, muryly *adv.* happily, cheerfully; playfully, *G* 2345; splendidly, *G* 740
mys *see* **mys(se)**
mysboden *pp.* ill used, mistreated, *G* 2339
mysdede *n.* sin
myself(e), myseluen *pron.* myself; me, *Pe* 414, *Cl* 1572
myserecorde *n.* mercy, *Pe* 366
mysetente *pp.* misunderstood, distorted, *Pe* 257
myslyke *see* **mislyke**
mys(se) *n.* offence, fault; loss, grief, *Pe* 262, 364
mysse *v.* (**myst** *pp.*) lose, lack, miss; fail to obtain, *Cl* 189
myssezeme *v.* neglect, *Pe* 322
mysseleue *n.* misbelief, *Cl* 1230
myssepayed *pp.* displeased
myst, mist *n.* mist
myst *see also* **mysse**
myste *n.* spiritual mysteries, *Pe* 462
mysterys *n.* mysteries, *Pe* 1194
myst-hakel *n.* cape of mist, cap-cloud, *G* 2081n
myte *n.* mite (small coin); **not a m.** not a jot, *Pe* 351
myþe *v.* conceal, *Pe* 359

Nabugo *n.* Nebuchadnezzar
Nabugodenozar, Nabigodenozar *n.* Nebuchadnezzar
Nabuzardan, Nabizardan *n.* Nebuzaradan
naf *v.* have not, *G* 1066; **nade** *pa.t. & pa.subjunc.* had not
nazt(e)(s) *see* **nyzt(e)**

naked *adj.* naked, bare; *as n.* (bare) flesh, *G* 423, 2002
nakerys *n.* drums; **nakryn** *g.pl. or adj.* of drums
name, nome *n.* name
nappe *v.* sleep
nar *v.* are not; **nas** was not; **nere** *pa.subjunc.* were not, *Cl* 21, *Pat* 244
nase *n.* nose
nature, natwre *n.* nature
nauel, naule *n.* (navel); stomach, insides
nauþeles, naw-, nowþelese *adv.* nevertheless, *Pe* 877, *etc.*; *also* **neuerþelese, -ce**, *Pe* 912 *etc.*, *G* 474
nauþer, naw-, nou- *adj., adv. & conj.* neither, either, nor
nawhere *see* **nowhere**
nay *adv.* no, nay
nay(ed) *pa.t.* refused, said no, *Cl* 65, 805, *G* 1836n
naylet *pp.* nailed, studded
naylez *n.* nails
nayte *v.* use; *pp.* **nayted** celebrated, repeated (*a pun*), *G* 65
naytly *adv.* well, properly
ne, nee *adv. & conj.* not; nor; or
nec *see* **nek(ke)**
nece *n.* niece, *Pe* 233
nede *n.* need, *Pe* 1045, *Cl* 1163; *pl.* **nedez** affairs, business, *G* 2216
nede *v.impers.* **in hit nedes** is necessary; (**hem**) **nedde** *pa.t.* was necessary (to them), *Pe* 1044
nede(s), (-z) *adv.* of necessity
nedles, -z *adj.* useless
nee *see* **ne**
nez(e), negh(e) *v.* approach; come to, reach
nez(e), neghe *see also* **nyze**
neked *n.* (a) little
nek(ke), nec *n.* neck
nel, nem(e), nemme *see* **nyl, nym(e), neuen**
nente *adj.* ninth, *Pe* 1012
ner(e) (*orig.compar. of* **nyze**) *adj., adv. & prep.* near(er), nearly; **nerre** *compar.* nearer
nere *see also* **nar**
nesch *adj.* soft; *as n.* what is pleasant, *Pe* 606
neue *n.* fist, hand
neuen, nemme *v.* name, call, mention
neuer *adv.* never; not at all, *Pe* 333, 376, *etc.*, *Cl* 820, 862, *etc.*, *G* 376, 399, *etc.*; **n. bot** only, *G* 547; **n. onez** not one person's, *Pe* 864; **n. so** however, *Pe* 571, *Cl* 1330, *Pat* 156, 391, 420, *G* 2129; **n. þe les(se)** never (not at all) less, undiminished, *Pe* 852, *etc.*, *Cl* 215, nevertheless (*cf.* **nauþeles**) *Pe* 900, *etc.*
neuermore *adv.* never, *Cl* 191
n(e)w(e) *adj.* new, fresh; *adv.* newly, anew; **newes** *gen. sg.* (*as n.*) new thing, *G* 1407; **n. fryt** first fruits, *Pe* 894; **New Zere, Nw(e) Zer(e)** New Year
next(e) *adv. & prep.* next (to), immediately
nice, nys(e) *adj.* foolish; fastidious; wanton
niez *see* **nyze**
niezbor *n.* neighbour
nif, nyf *conj.* if not, unless
nikked, -y- *v.* said no, *G* 706n, 2471

Niniue, Nuniue, Nynyue *n.* Nineveh
nirt *n.* cut, nick
nis, niye, niyȝt *see* **nys, ny(ȝ)e, nyȝt(e)**
no *adj. & adv.* no
nobelay, nobleye, noblé *n.* nobility (of conduct)
noble, nobel(e) *adj.* noble; *and as n.*
nobot *adv.* only
Noe *n.* Noah
noȝt *adv. & pron.* nothing; not (at all); **for n.** in vain. *See also* **bot**
noȝ(t) *see also* **not**
noȝty *adj.* wicked
nok(e) *n.* nook, corner; point, angle, *G* 660
nolde *see* **nyl**
nom(e)(n) *see* **name, nym(e)**
no(n)(e) *adj.* no, any; **non(e)** *pron.* none, nothing, no one
nonez *pron.* **for the n.** indeed
norne, -u- *v.* ask, urge, *Cl* 803, *G* 1771; say, declare, *Cl* 65, 669; propose, *G* 1669*n*; offer, *G* 1823; call, *G* 2443; **n. aȝaynez** refuse, repulse
norture, nurture *n.* nurture, upbringing, good breeding
norþ(e) *adj. & n.* north
norþ-est *n.* northeast
nos *n.* opening
not, noȝ(t) *adv.* not
not *v.* know not, *G* 1053
note *n.*[1] task, activity, business, matter (*sometimes blended with n.*[2]); place, piece of work, *Pe* 922
note *n.*[2] note (musical), tune, *Pe* 879, 883, *Cl* 1413, *G* 514; fame, renown, *Cl* 1651; reputation, custom, *Cl* 727
note(d) *pp./adj.* well-known, famous
notyng *n.* using, partaking of
noþyng *adv.* not at all, *G* 2236
noþyng, noþynk *n.* nothing
noumbles *n.* numbles (offal of deer)
noumbre *n.* number
nouþe, nowþe *adv.* now
nouþer *see* **nauþer**
now(e), nov *adv. & conj.* now; now that, since, *Pe* 283, 377, 389, *G* 2296, 2420; if (now), *Cl* 721; **ryȝt n.** immediately
Nowel *n.* Christmas; the cry 'Nowel'
nowhere, nawhere *adv.* nowhere, anywhere
nowþe, nowþelese *see* **nouþe, nauþeles**
noyce, noyse *n.* noise, sound; music
noye, nye, nwye, nuye *v.* trouble; harass; injure
nummen, Nuniue, nurne(d), nurture *see* **nym(e), Niniue, norne, norture**
nuyez, nuyed *see* **noye**
nw(e) *see* **n(e)w(e)**
nwy(d) *see* **ny(ȝ)e, noye**
ny(ȝ)e, niye, nwy *n.* trouble, difficulty, vexation; bitter cold, *G* 2002
nye(d), nyf *see* **noye, nif**
nyȝe, neȝ(e), nieȝ, neghe *adv. & prep.* nigh, nearly; near. *See also* **ner(e)**
nyȝt(e), naȝt(e), niyȝt *n.* night; **on n., on nyȝtes** at night; **at forþ naȝtes** late at night
nykked *see* **nikked**

nyl, nel, nylt *v.* (**nolde** *pa.t.*) will not
nym(e), nymme, neme *v.* (**nem, nom(e)** *pa.t.*, **nomen, nummen, inome** *pp.*) take, receive; undertake, *G* 91; *pp.* trapped, refuted in argument, *Pe* 703
Nynyue *see* **Niniue**
nys, nis *v.* is not, *Pe* 100, 951, *G* 1266
nys(e) *see* **nice**
nyteled *pa.t.* made a disturbance

o, oo! *interj.* oh!
o *see also* **of**
obes *v.* (**obeched** *pa.t.*) do obeisance (to), *Pe* 886, *Cl* 745
odde *adj.* odd; *as n.* odd one, single one, *Cl* 505
oddely *adv.* singularly, *Cl* 698; entirely, *Cl* 923
odour *n.* fragrance, *Pe* 58
of, o *prep.* of; about, *Pe* 925, *etc.*, *Cl* 26, *etc.*, *G* 94, *etc.*; from, (away) from, out of, *Pe* 31, 334, *etc.*, *Cl* 596, 855, *etc.*, *Pat* 188, 391, *etc.*, *G* 183, 1087, *etc.*; (made) out of, *Pe* 110, *etc.*, *Cl* 1276, *etc.*, *Pat* 438, *etc.*, *G* 121, *etc.*; with, *Pe* 119, *etc.*, *Cl* 1404, *etc.*, *G* 172, *etc.*; because of, through, *Pe* 11, *etc.*, *Cl* 848, *etc.*, *Pat* 443, *etc.*, *G* 86, *etc.*; by (agent), *Pe* 248, *Cl* 243, 1059, *Pat* 386, *G* 64; in respect of, *Pe* 74, *etc.*, *Cl* 92, *etc.*, *Pat* 23, *etc.*, *G* 143, *etc.*; (thank, *etc.*) for, *G* 96, 755, 975, *etc.*
of *adv.* off, *Pe* 237, 358, *Cl* 630, *etc.*, *G* 773, *etc.*
offys *n.* office, position, *Pe* 755
oft(e) *adv.* (**ofter** *compar.*) often, many times
oghe, oȝe, owe *v.* (**aȝt(e), oȝte** *pa.t.*) have, *G* 1941; own, *G* 767, 843, 1775; owe, *Pe* 543; (*pres. & pa.t.*) ought, *Pe* 1139, *Cl* 122, *G* 1526; *impers. Pe* 341, 552
oȝt *n.* anything, something
oke *n.* oak
olde *adj.* (**alder** *compar.*, **aldest** *superl.*) old; long-established, *G* 1124; **for o.** on account of age, *G* 1440
olipraunce *n.* ostentation
olyue *n.* olive
on *prep. & adv.* on, upon; in, *Pe* 97, 425, *etc.*, *Cl* 271, 327, *etc.*, *Pat* 133, *G* 1722, 1730, *etc.*; at, *Pe* 45, 243, *Cl* 578, *G* 47, 479, *etc.*; about, *Cl* 436, 771, *G* 683, 1800, *etc.*; **on a day** a (each) day, *Pe* 510, **on ȝer** a year, *Pe* 1079; **on huntyng**, *etc.* a-hunting, *etc.*, *G* 1102, 1143; **on lyue** alive, on earth (*or intensive:* indeed)
on(e) *adj.*[1] *& pron.* one, (a), *Pe* 9, 551, *etc.*, *Cl* 112, 152, *etc.*, *Pat* 312, 355, *G* 30, 206, *etc.*; one (and the same), *Cl* 716, 718, *Pat* 39; *pron.* one, *Pe* 293, 557, *etc.*, *Cl* 25, 42, *etc.*, *Pat* 34, *G* 137, 223, *etc.*; **þat o.** the one; **at o.** at one, united; *see also* **onez** of one, *Pe* 864
on(e) *adj.*[2] *& adv.* alone; merely, *Pat* 354; single, *Pat* 208, *G* 2249, 2345; **hym (oure**, *etc.*) **o.** (by) himself, ourselves, *etc.*; **myn one** myself, *Pat* 503; **by myn one** by myself, alone, *Pe* 243
onelych, only *adv.* only; alone, *Pe* 779
onende *see* **anende**
ones, -z *adv.* once; **at o.** together, at once; **at þys o.** on this occasion, here and now. *See also* **on(e)** *pron.*

onewe *adv.* anew
onferum *adv.* from a distance
onhede *n.* unity
onhelde *pp.* huddled
onhit *pp.* seized
only *see* **onelych**
onlyue *adj.* alive, *Cl* 356; *cf.* **alyue, lyf**
onstray *adv.* out of course, in a changed direction
onsware, answar *n.* answer
onsware, answ(a)re *v.* answer
on-vnder *see* **an-vnder**
onyȝed *adj.* one-eyed
oo *see* **o**
oquere *adv.* anywhere, *G* 660
or *conj.* or; than, *G* 1543; (*cf.* **oþer** *conj.*)
ordaynt *pp.adj.* ordained
ordenaunce *n.* ordinance, plan
ordure *n.* filth
orenge *n.* orange
ores *n.* oars
organes *n.* wind instruments
orient, oryent(e) the orient, the East, *Pe* 3, 82; *as adj. Pe* 255
orisoun *n.* prayer
oritore *n.* chapel
ornementes, vrnmentes *n.* ornaments
orp(p)edly *adv.* boldly, quickly
oryent(e), oryȝt *see* **orient, aryȝt**
ossed *pa.t.* showed
oste *n.* host
ostel *see* **(h)ostel**
oþer *adj. & pron.* other; second, *Cl* 235, *G* 1020, 2350; another, the other, *Cl* 267, *G* 501, 628; **þat o.** the other, *Pe* 955, *Cl* 299, *etc.*, *Pat* 515, *G* 110, *etc.*; *pl.* others, *Pe* 585, *etc.*, *Cl* 25, *etc.*, *Pat* 176, *etc.*, *G* 64, *etc.*; **an o.** otherwise, a (quite) differing thing, *G* 1268; **non o.** nothing else; **ayþer o., vchon o.** *see* **ayþer, vchon**
oþer, auþer, or *adv. & conj.* or (else); otherwise; **o. . . . o. (or)** either . . . or
oþerquyle, oþerwhyle *adv.* at other times, *G* 722; sometimes, *Pat* 121
oþerwayez *adv.* otherwise
oþez *n.* oaths
ouer *prep. & adv.* over, above, across, upon; too, *Pe* 473
oueral *adv.* all over, *G* 150; in all parts, *G* 630
ouerborde *adv.* overboard
ouerbrawden *adj.* covered over
ouerclambe *pa.t.* climbed over
ouerȝede *pa.t.* passed, went by
ouerloked *pa.t.* looked over their heads, *G* 223
ouerseyed *pp.* passed
ouertake *v.* (**-tok,** *pa.t.,* **-tan,** *pp.*) overtake, *Cl* 1213, *Pat* 127; understand, *G* 2387
ouerte *adj.* plain
ouertorned *pa.t.* passed by
ouerture *n.* neck-opening, *Pe* 218
ouerpwert *adj. & adv.* crosswise, at right angles, *Cl* 316, 1384; *prep.* across, *G* 1438
ouerwaltez *v.* overflows, *Cl* 370; *pp.* **ouerwalt** overthrown, *G* 314
our(e) *possess.adj.* our
oure *see also* **(h)oure**

out *see* **out(e)**
outborst *pa.t.* burst out
outcomlyng *n.* stranger
outdryf *v.* drive out, *Pe* 777
out(e) *adv.* out; whatsoever, in existence, *Cl* 1046; far and wide, *G* 1511; *prep.* **out of** out of, from, *Pe* 3, 1163, *Cl* 287, *etc.*, *Pat* 137, *etc.*, *G* 802, *etc.*; deprived of, away from, *Pe* 642; past, beyond, *Cl* 656 (**hyȝe o. of age** advanced in age); expired, *Cl* 442. *See also* **day(e), dryue**
outfleme *adj.* driven out
outkast *pp.* cast out
outryȝte *adv.* directly out (of), *Pe* 1055
outsprent *pa.t.* gushed out, *Pe* 1137
outtaken *prep.* except
outtrage *adj.* extraordinary
outtulde *pp.* thrown out
ouþer *pron.* either, *Cl* 795
owe *see* **oghe**
owen, owne *see* **aune**
ox(e) *n.* ox

pace *n.* passage, *Pe* 677
pacience, pacyence, Pacyence *n.* patience, long-suffering; Patience (*personified*), *Pat* 33
pacient *adj.* patient, long-suffering
pakke *n.* gathering, company, *Pe* 929
pakked *pa.t.* packed
Palastyn *n.* Palestine
palays, palayce *n.*¹ palace
palays *n.*² fence, palisade, *G* 769
pale *v.* show pale, *Pe* 1004
palle *n.*¹ cloth, robe
palle *n.*² wooden platform, *Cl* 1384*n*
pane *n.* fur facing, edging; side, wall, *Pe* 1034
papejayes, -ez *n.* parrots
paper, papure *n.* paper
par ma fay *see* **fay**
paradys(e), paradis(e) paradise, heaven; the Earthly Paradise, the Garden of Eden, *Pe* 137, 321, *Cl* 238, 1007 (*see also Pe* 9*n*, 65*n*)
parage *n.* lineage
paramorez *n.* lovers, love
parauenture, paraunter, peraunter *adv.* perhaps
parchmen *n.* parchment
pared *pa.t. & pp.* cut, shaped
parformed *pa.t.* performed, brought to pass
parfyt, perfet *adj.* perfect
parget *n.* plaster
parlatyk *adj.* paralytic
part *n.* part, share
part *v.* divide, *Cl* 1107; *intrans.* separate, part, *G* 2473; descend, *Cl* 242
partlez *adj.* deprived, *Pe* 335
partrykez *n.* partridges
passage *n.* passage, journey
passe *v.* (**passed, past(e)** *pa.t. & pp.*) pass, go, travel; finish, end; cross, *Pe* 299, *G* 2071; surpass, *Pe* 428, 753, *Cl* 1389, *G* 1014; go free, *Pe* 707
Pater *n.* Paternoster, Lord's Prayer, *Pe* 485, *G* 757
patrounes *n.* masters

paume *n.* palm, hand; flat antler, *G* 1155
paunce *n.* abdominal armour, *G* 2017
paunch *n.* stomach, *G* 1360
paune *n.pl.* claws, *Cl* 1697
pay(e) *n.* satisfaction, pleasure, *Pe* 1, 1164, *etc.*;
　pay(ment), *Pat* 99, *G* 2247; **makes her
　paye** pays their fee
pay(e) *v.* please, satisfy, pay
payne *n.* penalty, punishment, *Pe* 664, *Cl* 46,
　etc.; pain, hardship, sorrow, *Pe* 124, 954, *Cl*
　190, *Pat* 525, *etc.*, *G* 733
payne *v.reflex.* take pains, endeavour, *G* 1042
paynted, -t *pa.t. & pp.* painted, *Pe* 750, *G* 800;
　portrayed, *G* 611
payre *n.* pair
payre *v.* be blunted, deteriorate; *pp.* wasted, *Pe*
　246
payttrure *n.* breast-harness
pechche *n.* fault
pece *see* **p(y)ece**
pelure *n.* fur
penaunce, Penaunce *n.* penance; Penance
　(*personified*), *Pat* 31
pendaunt, -d *n.* pendant
penez *n.* pens (of animals), *Cl* 322
pené, peny *n.* (**penies, penyes** *pl.*) penny; *pl.*
　money
penitotes *n.* peridots, chrysolites (green gems)
penne *n.* (writing) pen, *Cl* 1546, 1724
penned *pp.* imprisoned, confined, *Pe* 53*n*
penne-fed *adj.* fed in a pen
pensyf *adj.* sorrowful
penta(u)ngel pentangle (*see G* 625*n*)
pented *pa.t.* belonged, pertained
peple *n.* people; *pl.* peoples, races, *Cl* 242
peraunter *see* **parauenture**
Perce *n.* Persia
per(e) *n.* peer, equal, *Pe* 4, *Cl* 1214, 1336, *G*
　873
perelous *adj.* perilous
perez *n.* pear trees, *Pe* 104
perfet *see* **parfyt**
peril(e), peryl(e) *n.* peril, danger; doubt, *Pe*
　695; **at alle peryles** whatever the con-
　sequences, *Pat* 85
perle *n.* pearl
perré *n.* jewellery, precious stones
Perses *n.* Persians
persoun *n.* person
pertermynable *adj.* supreme in judgement,
　Pe 596*n*
pertly *adv.* plainly, openly, publicly
peruing *n.* periwinkles, *G* 611*n*
peryl(e) *see* **peril(e)**
pese *n.*[1] pea, *G* 2364
pes(e), Pes *n.*[2] peace; Peace (*personified*), *Pat*
　33
peté *see* **pité**
Phares *n.* Peres
pich *n.* pitch, *Cl* 1008
piched *see* **pyche**
pike, pyke *v.* gather, get, *Pe* 573; crop, *Pat*
　393; peck, *Cl* 1466; *pp.* polished, cleansed, *G*
　2017, adorned, *Pe* 1036. *See also* **pyked** *adj.*
pinacle, pine *see* **pynakle, pyne** *n.*
pipe *v.* pipe (*of birds*), *G* 747

pipes, pypes *n.* pipes
pité, peté, Pitée, pyté, pyty *n.* pity; compas-
　sion *or* piety, *G* 654*n*; sorrow, *Pe* 1206; Pity
　(*personified*), *Pat* 31
pito(u)sly, pytosly *adv.* piteously; compas-
　sionately
place *n.* place; house, dwelling, city, domain,
　Pe 405, 679, *etc.*, *Cl* 72, 146, *etc.*, *Pat* 68, 349,
　etc., *G* 252, 398, *etc.*; space, room, *G* 123
planed *adj.* planed, smoothed
planetez *n.* planets
plant(t)ed *pa.t.* established
plat *adj.* flat; *adv.* absolutely, *Cl* 83
plat *pa.t.* struck
plate *n.* (metal) plate; piece of armour
plater *n.* platter
plattyng *n.* striking
play *n.* play, sport, enjoyment
play *v.* play, amuse oneself (*also reflex.*); rejoice,
　be happy, *Pe* 261
playferes *n.* playmates, companions
playn *adj.* smooth; bare, *Pat* 439; *adv.* plainly,
　clearly, *Pe* 689
playn *n.* plain, meadow, field
playned, playnez *see* **pleny**
pleny, playne *v.* lament, mourn; complain, *Pe*
　549, *Pat* 376 (**on:** against)
playnt *n.* complaint, *Pe* 815
plede *v.* plead
plek *n.* piece of ground
plesaunce *n.* pleasure, pleasing, *G* 1247
plesaunt *adj.* courteous, obliging, *G* 808;
　pleasing, lovely, *Pe* 1
plese *inf.* please; **plesed** *pa.t.subjunc.* would
　please, *Pat* 376
plete *v.* claim, *Pe* 563
pleyned *see* **pleny**
plonttez *n.* newly-planted shrubs or trees, *Pe*
　104
plow *n.* plough
plyande *presp.adj.* waving
plye *v.* incline, tend, *Cl* 196; join, be attached,
　Pe 1039; be contained, enclosed, *Cl* 1385
plyt *n.* situation, condition, *Pe* 1015, *Cl* 111,
　1494, *Pat* 114, *G* 733; array, grouping, *Pe*
　1114; predicament, *Pe* 647
plyȝt *n.* condition, *Pe* 1075; danger, *G* 266;
　guilt, *G* 2393
pobbel *n.* pebble, *Pe* 117
polaynez *n.* knee pieces (*of armour*)
pole *n.* (pool); water-course, *Pe* 117; *pl.* **pow-
　lez** seas, depths
polle *n.* (hair of) head
polment *n.* pottage, broth
polyce, ice *v.* polish; *fig.* make clean, bright
polyle *n.* poultry
polyst *see* **polyce**
pomgarnades *n.* pomegranates
poplande *adj.* foaming
porchase, -ce *v.* strive (for), *Pe* 439; buy, *Pe*
　744
pore *see* **pouer(e)**
porfyl *n.* embroidered border, *Pe* 216
porpos(e), pur- *n.* purpose, intention, *Pe* 267,
　508, *G* 1734; (aim), quarry, *Pe* 185*n*
porpre, porpor, purpre *n. & adj.* purple

Porros *n.* Porus
port *n.*¹ port, harbour
port *n.*² gate, *Cl* 856
portalez *n.* portals, gateways
portrayed, pourtrayd, purtrayed, *pa.t. & pp.* devised, designed, *Cl* 700; formed, fashioned, *Cl* 1465, 1536; adorned, decorated, *Cl* 1271
poruay v. equip oneself with, *Pat* 36; settle on, *Cl* 1502
postes *n.* pillars
potage *n.* pottage
poudred, powdered *pp.* scattered, *Pe* 44, *G* 800
pouer(e), pore *adj.* poor, wretched; *as n.* the poor, *Cl* 127; poor man, *Cl* 615; *adv.* poorly, *Cl* 146. *See also* **power**
pouert(é), Pouert *n.* poverty; Poverty (*personified*), *Pat* 31
Poule, Saynt *n.* St Paul
poursent, pourtrayd, powdered *see* **pursaunt, portrayed, poudred**
power, pouer *n.* power
powlez *see* **pole**
poyned *n.* wristband, *Pe* 217
poynt(e) *n.* point; point in time, moment, *Cl* 628, *Pat* 68; point of doctrine, *Pe* 594; instance, *Pe* 309; high point, height, *Cl* 1502, 1677; condition, *Pat* 35; good condition, *G* 2049; virtue, *Pat* 1, 531, *G* 654; question, *G* 902; strain (of music), *Pe* 891; **vch a p.** everything, *Cl* 196
poynte v. describe in detail, *G* 1009
poynted *pp.* tipped
poyntel *n.* stylus
poysened *adj.* poisoned
pray *n.* booty, prize
pray(e) v. pray, ask, beseech; invite, *Cl* 72
prayed *pa.t.* plundered, *Cl* 1624
prayer(e) *n.*¹ prayer
prayere *n.*² meadow, *G* 768
prayse v. praise; compliment, *G* 2072; esteem, value, *Cl* 146, *G* 1850; *pp.adj.* valued, prized, *Pe* 1112; **to p.** praiseworthy, estimable, *Pe* 301, *Cl* 189, *G* 356
prec(e), -s *n.* press, crowd; crowding, *Pe* 1114
prece, -s v. hurry, press forward; press, crush, *Cl* 1249
prech(e) v. preach
precio(u)s, presyous *adj.* precious, *Pe* 36, *etc.*, *Cl* 1496; noble, *Pe* 192; rich, *Cl* 1282; in value, *Pe* 4
pref *n.* (test of experience); **is put in p.** is shown to be, *Pe* 272
prelates *n.* prelates, chief priests
pres *see* **prece** *n. & v.*
pres(e) *n.* worth, *Pe* 419; *as adj.* precious, *Pe* 730 (*cf.* **prys**)
presed *see* **prece**
presens(e) *n.* presence
present(e) *n.* presence, *Pe* 389, 1193
presoneres *see* **prisoner(e)s**
prest *adj.* eager, prompt; *adv.* quickly, *Pat* 303
prest(e) *n.* priest
prestly *adv.* promptly, readily
presyous *see* **precious**

preue *adj.* valiant, *G* 262; resolute, steadfast, *Pat* 525
preué, priuy, pryuy *adj.* special, own, *Pe* 12, 24; discreet, *G* 902; **-ly** *adv.* in private, *G* 1877; apart, *Cl* 238; mysteriously, *Cl* 1107; **pryuyest** *superl.* nearest, most confidential, *Cl* 1748
preue, proue v. prove, show, test, demonstrate; discover, *Pe* 4; acknowledge, *Cl* 1748
pride, priyde *see* **pryde**
prik, -y- v. gallop, *G* 2049; incite, *G* 2437
prince *see* **prynce**
pris *see* **prys**
prisoner(e)s, presoneres *n.* prisoners
priuy *see* **preué**
profecie, professye *n.* company of prophets, *Cl* 1308; prophecy, *Pe* 821, *Cl* 1158
proferen v. (**profered, profert** *pa.t.*) offer; propose, *Pe* 1200; address, *Pe* 235; project, *Cl* 1463; *reflex.* present (oneself), *Pat* 41
professye, profete *see* **profecie, prophete**
proper *adj.* noble, fine
property, properté *n.* attribute, *Pe* 446; special virtue, *Pe* 752
prophete, profete *n.* prophet
prosessyoun *n.* procession
proud(e), prowde *adj.* (**pruddest** *superl.*) proud; splendid, *G* 168, 601; high-mettled, *G* 2049; **proudly, prudly** *adv.*
proued *see* **preue**
prouince, prouynce *n.* province
prowes *n.* prowess, valour
pruddest, prudly *see* **proud(e)**
pryce *see* **prys(e)**
pryde, pri(y)de *n.* pride; eminent position, *Cl* 1227
pryk *see* **prik**
prymate *n.* head, chief
pryme *n.* the first canonical hour (6 a.m.); sunrise, *G* 1675
prynce, prince, prynse *n.* prince, nobleman, sovereign, king
prynces *n.* princess, lady, *G* 1770
pryncipal(e) *adj.* princely, royal
pryncipalté *n.* sovereignty
prys(e), pryce, pris *n.*¹ value, *Pe* 193, *G* 79, 1277, 1850; excellence, nobility, *Pe* 419, *G* 912, 1249, 1630; esteem, *Cl* 1124; renown, *G* 1379; **of p.** valuable, *Pe* 272, 746, *G* 615, 2364, excellent, noble, *G* 1770, 2398; *as adj.* excellent, *G* 1945; as excellent, *Cl* 1117; *adj. as n.* chief, *Cl* 1308, 1614; **your p.** your worthy self, *G* 1247
prys *n.*² 'capture' (*call on horn*), *G* 1362, 1601
pryse v. prize, esteem; **to p.** worthy, *Pe* 1131
prysoun *n.*¹ prison, *Pat* 79
prysoun *n.*² prisoner, *G* 1219
pryuély, pryuy(est), pryuyly *see* **preué**
pulle v. (**pullen** *pa.t.*) pull
pure *adj. & adv.* pure, perfect; noble, *Cl* 1570, *G* 262, *etc.*; *adv.* perfectly, *G* 808; **þe p. poplande hourle** the foaming sea itself, *Pat* 319; **pur(e)ly** *adv.* completely, entirely, fully, perfectly; clearly, *Pe* 1004
pure v. purify

pured *pp. & adj.* refined, *G* 633, 912; purified, *G* 2393; trimmed (to one colour), *G* 154, 1737

pur(e)ly, purpose, purpre *see* **pure, porpos(e), porpre**

pursaunt, poursent *n.* precinct, enclosing wall

pursued *pa.t.* made an attack, *Cl* 1177

purtrayed *see* **portrayed**

puryté *n.* purity

put *v.* put, set, place; **p. to** reduced to, *Pat* 35; **p. in** set on, *Pe* 267; **is p. in pref** is shown to be, *Pe* 272

puttyng *n.* putting

pyche *v.* (**pyȝt(e)** *pa.t. & pp.*, **pyched, piched** *pp.*) set, place, fasten; strike, stick, *G* 1456, 1734; occupy, *Cl* 83; array, dress, decorate, *Pe* 192, 205, *etc.*

p(y)ece *n.* piece; (*of armour*), *G* 2021; being, person, *Pe* 192, 229

pyes *n.* magpies

pyȝt(e) *see* **pyche**

pyked *adj.* spiked, *G* 769

pyke(d) *see also* **pike**

pyle *n.* stronghold, *Pe* 686

pyled *pa.t. & pp.* pillaged

pyleres n. pillars

Pymalyon *n.* Pygmalion

pynakle, pinacle *n.* pinnacle

pynakled *pp.adj.* pinnacled, with pinnacles, *Pe* 207

pyne, pine *n.* pain, suffering, torment, anguish; annoyance, *G* 1812; penance, *Pat* 423; pains, trouble, *Pe* 511, *G* 1985; difficult(y), *G* 123

pyne *v.*[1] confine, *Pat* 79; *pp.* **pyned** fenced in, *G* 769

pyne *v.*[2] *reflex.* take pains

pyned *pp.adj.* wasted, *Cl* 1095

pynkardines *n.* precious stones (?cornelians)

pyonys *n.* peonies, *Pe* 44

pypes *see* **pipes**

pypyng *n.* music of pipes

pysan *n.* gorget, throat-armour, *G* 204

pyté, pyty *see* **pité**

pyth *n.* toughness, *G* 1456

pytosly *see* **pito(u)sly**

quaked *pa.t.* trembled, *G* 1150

quat(so) *see* **what(so)**

quatsoeuer *pron.* whatsoever

quauende *adj.* beating, surging, *Cl* 324

quayle *n.* quail, *Pe* 1085

quaynt(yse) *see* **coynt, coyntyse**

qued *n.* evil

quel *see* **whyl(e)**

queldepoyntes *n.* quilted seats

quelle *v.* kill, put to death, destroy; end, *G* 752

queme *adj.* fine, pleasant

quen, w(h)en *adv. & conj.* when

quenches *v.* quenches, extinguishes

quene, whene (*G* 74, 2492) *n.* queen

quere *v.* discover, *Cl* 1632

quere(so) *see* **wher(e)**

queresoeuer, querfore *see* **w(h)eresoeuer, wherfore**

querré *n.* 'quarry', heap of game, *G* 1324

query *n.* complaint

quest *n.* search for game, *G* 1150, 1421; pursuit, *Pat* 39

quethe *n.* sound, utterance, *G* 1150

quettyng *n.* sharpening, *G* 2220

queþen, queþer(soeuer) *see* **wheþen, wheþer**

quik *see* **quyk**

quikken *pres.subjunc.* form, develop, *Pat* 471

quikly, quil(e) *see* **quyk, whil(e)**

quit-clayme *v.* renounce

quit(e), quo(m) *see* **whyt(e), who**

quos *pron.* whose

quoso *see* **whoso**

quoþ, coþe *pa.t.* said

quoynt, quoyntis, -yse *see* **coynt, coyntyse**

quyk, quik *adj. & adv.* alive, living; lively, restive, *G* 177; lifelike, vivid, *Pe* 1179; *as pl.n.* living creatures, *Cl* 567; *adv.* quickly, *G* 975; **-ly** *adv.* quickly

quy, quyl(e) *see* **why, whil(e)**

quyssewes *n.* cuisses, thigh-pieces, *G* 578

quyte *v.* pay, reward; requite, repay

quyt(e), qwyte *see also* **whyt(e)**

raas *see* **race**

rabel *n.* rabble

rac *see* **rak**

race, raas *n.* headlong course, rush; attack, blow, *G* 2076; **on r.** headlong, *G* 1420; **of r.** in rushing headlong, *Pe* 1167

rach *n.* (**rach(ez), rachchez** *pl.*) hound

rachche *v.* (**raȝt** *pa.t.*) go, *Cl* 619, 766 (*cf.* **reche** *v.*[1], **rayke**)

rad *adj.* frightened, afraid, *Cl* 1543, *G* 251. *See also* **rad(ly)**

radde *see* **red(e)**

rad(ly) *adv.* quickly, promptly, *Cl* 671, 797, *Pat* 65, 89, *etc.*, *G* 367, 862, *etc.*

rafte *see* **reue**

raged *adj.* ragged, trailing, *G* 745

Ragnel *n.* Ragnel (a devil), *Pat* 188

raȝt *see* **rech(e), rachche**

rak, rac *n.* (**rakkes** *pl.*) cloudbank, stormcloud, *Pat* 139, 176, *G* 1695; storm, *Cl* 433

rake *n.* water-course, *G* 2144, 2160

rakel *adj.* hasty

rakentes *n.* chains

rakkes *see* **rak**

ramel *n.* muck, *Pat* 279 (*see* 269n)

ran *see* **ren(n)e**

rande *n.* edge, *G* 1710; bank of stream, *Pe* 105

rank *see* **ronk**

rankor *n.* wrath

rape *n.* blow, *Cl* 233

rape *v.* rush, hurry; *reflex. G* 1309

rapely *adv.* hastily, *G* 2219; quickly, *Pe* 1168; rashly, *Pe* 363

rasch *adj.* rash

rased *pa.t.* snatched, *G* 1907

rasez *v.* charges, *G* 1461

rasores *n. gen.* razor's, *G* 213

rasped *pa.t. & pp.* scratched

rasse *n.*[1] ledge, *Cl* 446
rasse *n.*[2] water-course, channel, *G* 1570
ratted *adj.* ragged
raþeled *pp.* anchored, entwined, *G* 2294
raue *v.*[1] go astray, *Pe* 665
raue *v.*[2] rave, *Pe* 363
rauen *n.* raven
rauthe, rauþe *see* **rawþe**
rauyste *pp.* ravished, enraptured
raw *adj.* raw (*of silk*), *Cl* 790
rawe *n.* row; hedgerow, *Pe* 105, *G* 513
rawþe, rauthe, rauþe *n.* pity, *Cl* 972, *Pat* 21, *etc.*; repentance, *Cl* 233; a grievous thing, *G* 2204
raxled *pa.t.* stretched (myself), *Pe* 1174
ray *n.* ray (of light)
rayke *v.* go, depart; *reflex. G* 1735; **out r.** break cover, *G* 1727; **raykande** *presp.* flowing, sweeping, *Pe* 112, *Cl* 382
rayled *pp.* arrayed, set; spread, *G* 745; *pa.t. G* 952
rayn *n.* rain
rayne *n.* rein, *G* 457, 2177
rayne *v.* (**raynande** *presp.adj.*) rain
rayn-ryfte *n.* break in a rain-cloud
rayse *v.* raise
raysoun, reysoun, resoun, Resoun *n.* (faculty of) reason, *Pe* 52; Reason (*person.*), *Pe* 665; wisdom, *Cl* 328; understanding, sense, *Cl* 1633; reason, cause, *Pe* 268, *Pat* 191; argument, *Cl* 2; words, speech, discourse (*also pl.*), *Pe* 716, *Cl* 184, 194, *G* 227, 392, 443; **bi r.** correctly, *G* 1344, by rights, *G* 1804
re(a)me *n.* realm, kingdom. *Cf.* **ryalme**
rebaudez *n.* dissolute men
rebel *adj.* rebellious, disobedient
rebounde *pa.t.* bounded, leapt, *Cl* 422
recen *see* **rekken**
rechate *v.* sound the recheat (to call the hounds together)
reche *n.* smoke, *Cl* 1009
rech(e) *v.*[1] (**raȝt** *pa.t. & pp.*) reach (out), *G* 432; reach, extend *Cl* 1691, *G* 183; reach, arrive at, *Cl* 890, 906; attain, *G* 1243; obtain, *Cl* 1766; offer, give, *Cl* 561, 1369, 1739, *G* 66, 1804, *etc.*; confer upon, *G* 2297
rech(e) *v.*[2] (**roȝt** *pa.t.*) care, *Pe* 333, *Cl* 465, *Pat* 460
rechles *adj.* carefree, *G* 40
recorde *n.* record, testimony
recorde *v.* record, *Cl* 25; repeat, *G* 1123
recouerer *n.* safety
recreaunt *adj.* cowardly
red(de), redden *see* **red(e)** *v.*
red(e) *adj.* red
redé, redy *adj.* ready; willing, obedient, *Cl* 294; alert(?), *Pe* 591
red(e) *v.* (**radde, redden** *pa.t.*, **red(de)** *pp.*) advise, guide; read, interpret, *Pe* 709, *Cl* 7, 194, *etc.*; direct, decree, *Pat* 406; declare, *G* 443; manage, *G* 373, 2111
redles, rydelles *adj.* without counsel, helpless; *as n. Pat* 502; **for r.** for lack of advice, *Cl* 1595
redly, redy *see* **red(y)ly, redé**

red(y)ly *adv.* quickly, soon; without hesitation, *G* 373, 392
refet *n.* refreshment, *Pe* 1064
refete *v.* nourish, refresh, *Pe* 88; *pp. Pat* 20
reflayr *n.* scent, fragrance, *Cl* 1079
refourme *v.* restate, *G* 378
refrayne *v.* restrain
regioun *n.* region, country
regne *see* **re(n)gne**
regretted *pp.* grieved for, *Pe* 243
reȝtful *adj.* righteous
rehayte *v.* urge on, exhort; cheer, encourage, *Cl* 127
reherse, -c- *v.* repeat, mention
reiatéz *see* **rialté**
reken *adj.* lovely, noble, *Pe* 5, 92, 906, *Cl* 1082; righteous, pious, *Cl* 10 (*or adv.*), 738, 756; **-ly** *adv.* fitly, worthily, *Cl* 1318, *G* 39; politely, courteously, *Cl* 127, *G* 251, 821
rekken, recen *v.* reckon; tell, *Pe* 827; **r. vp** reckon up, go through, *Cl* 2
rele *v.* (**relande** *presp.*) reel, roll, *Pat* 147, 270, *G* 304; swerve, *G* 1728; sway (in combat), *G* 2246; *reflex.* swagger(?) *G* 229
relece *v.* release, deliver
reles *n.* remission, end
releue *v.* succour, *Pat* 323
relusaunt *adj.* shining, gleaming, *Pe* 159
relygioun *n.* the (Jewish) Church, *Cl* 1156; **renkez of r.** men in holy orders, *Cl* 7
relykes *n.* relics, sacred treasures
reme *v.* cry out, lament
reme *see also* **re(a)me**
remembred *pa.t. reflex.* remembered
remen *see* **reme** *v.*
remene *v.* recall, *G* 2483
remnaunt *n.* remainder
remorde *v.* bewail, lament, *G* 2434; *pp.* oppressed, *Pe* 364
remwe *v.* remove, take away; change, *G* 1475; **remued** *pp.* removed; remote, separated, *Cl* 1673
Renaud(e), Reniarde, Reynarde the fox, *G* 1728*n, etc.*
renay *v.* refuse; renounce, *Pat* 344
renden *v.* (**rended, rent** *pp.*) rend, tear
re(n)gne *n.* kingdom
rengne *v.* reign, rule
Reniarde, renischche *see* **Renaud(e), runisch**
renk, ring (*Cl* 592), **rynk** *n.*[1] (**renk(k)ez, -es** *pl.*) man, knight
renk *n.*[2] field of combat; **?me r. to mete** to challenge me to a duel, *G* 2206*n*
ren(n)e *v.* (**ran, runnen** *pa.t.*, **runne(n)** *pp.*) run, flow; continue, *Cl* 527; be current, *G* 310, 2458; operate, *Pat* 511; **be runne** may have mounted up, *Pe* 523
renoun *n.* renown, fame, honour
renowle *v.* renew
rent, renyschly *see* **renden, runisch**
reparde *pp.* withheld, *Pe* 611
repayre *v.* be present, *Pe* 1028, *G* 1017
repente *v.impers. in* **ȝif hym repente** if it should grieve him, i.e. if he repents, *Pe* 662
reprené *v.* reproach

repreued *pa.t.* reproved, rebuked, *G* 2269
request *n.* request; **make r.** ask, *Pe* 281
require *v.* ask, *G* 1056
rere *v.* (**rer(e)d** *pa.t.*, **rered, rert** *pp.*) rise; raise, *Cl* 873, *G* 353; rouse, *Pat* 188; *pp.* supreme, *Pe* 591
res, resse *n.* rush; torrent, *Pe* 874
resayt *n. collect.* receiving stations, *G* 1168
resayue *v.* receive
rescoghe, rescowe *n.* rescue, *G* 2308; **matz r.** rescues, *Pe* 610
reset(te) *n.* refuge, shelter; habitation, *G* 2164
resonabele, resounable *adj.* reasonable, sensible
resoun *see* **raysoun**
respecte *n.* comparison (**of**: with), *Pe* 84
respite, respyt *n.* respite, delay, *G* 297; relief, reprieve, *Pe* 644
resse *see* **res**
restay, restey *v.* hold back, restrain, *Pe* 716, 1168; turn back, *G* 1153; persuade, *G* 1672; *intrans.* pause, *Pe* 437
rest(e) *n.* rest, repose; **withouten r.** endlessly, *Pe* 858
restlez *adj.* unceasing
restore *v.* restore, return; replace, *G* 2283
rest(t)(e) *v.* (**rest(ed)** *pa.t.*, **restted** *pp.*) rest; stand, *Cl* 738
retrete *v.* reproduce, *Pe* 92
reue *n.* reeve, bailiff
reue *v.* (**rafte** *pa.t. & pp.*) rob, take away
reuel *n.* revelry, revelling
reuel *v.* revel
reuer *n.* river, *Pe* 1055; river bank, meadow, *Pe* 105
reuerence, reuerens *n.* reverence, honour
reuerence *v.* greet, salute
reward(e) *n.* recompense, return; desert, *Pe* 604
rewfully *adv.* ruefully, sorrowfully
rewled, Reynarde *see* **rule** *v.*, **Renaud(e)**
reynyez *n.* loins, *Cl* 592
reysoun, rial *see* **raysoun, ryal**
rialté, rialty, reiaté *n.* royalty; *pl.* royal dignities, *Pe* 770
riboudrye *n.* debauchery
rich(ch)e, -y-, -u- *v.* prepare; deck out (*infl. by* **rich** *adj.*); proceed, move forward, *G* 8, 367, 1898; direct, *G* 1223; decide(?) *G* 360n; turn, *G* 303
rich(e), rych(e) *adj.* fine, noble, costly, splendid, glorious, *etc.*; wealthy; precious, *Pe* 646; *as n.* great man, *Cl* 1321, nobles, *Cl* 1208, *G* 66, *etc.*, noble steed, *G* 2177; *adv.* richly, splendidly, *Cl* 1411; **-ly** *adv.* richly, brightly, *Cl* 1045, plentifully, *G* 163, nobly, *G* 931, pompously, arrogantly, *G* 308
ridlande, rydelande *presp. & adj.* sifting, sprinkling, winnowing, *Cl* 953, *Pat* 254n
riftes *n.* fissures, clefts
rigge, riʒt *see* **rygge, ryʒt(e)**
rimed hym *pa.t.* cleared his throat(?), drew himself up(?), *G* 308
ring *see* **renk**
ripe, rype *adj.* ripe; mature, *Cl* 869
ris(e) *see* **rys(e)**

robbed *pa.t. & pp.* robbed; *pp.* stolen, *Cl* 1142
robbors *n.* robbers
roborrye *n.* robbery
roché *adj.* rocky, *G* 2294
roche *n.* rock
rocher *n.* rocky bank
rode *n.*[1] rood, cross
rode *n.*[2] road, *Pat* 270
rod(e) *see also* **ryde**
roffe *n.* (**rouez** *pl.*) roof
rof-sore *n.* cut, gash, *G* 2346
rogh(e), roʒ(e), ruʒe *adj.* rough; cruel, *Pe* 646; **for r.** because of the turbulence, *Pat* 144
roghlych *adj.* rough, harsh
roʒly *adj.* fortunate(?), *Cl* 433n
roʒt *see* **reche** *v.*[2]
rok *n.* (**rokkes, -z** *pl.*) rock; castle, *Cl* 1514
rokked *pp.* rocked, *G* 2018n
rollande *presp.adj.* wavy
rol(l)ed *pa.t.* rolled; sagged, flapped, *G* 953
rome *v.* wind one's way, *G* 2198
romye *v.* cry out, *Cl* 1543
ronez *n.* bushes, thickets, *G* 1466
ronge *pa.t.* (**r(o)ungen** *pa.t.pl.*) rang
ronk, rank *adj.* proud, haughty; violent, *Cl* 233; impetuous, *Pe* 1167; full-grown, *Cl* 869; luxuriant, *Pe* 844, *G* 513; wanton, *Cl* 760; *as n.* pride, *Pat* 298
ronkled *pp.* wrinkled, *G* 953
ronkly *adv.* proudly
rop *n.*[1] rope, *Pat* 105, 150; cord, *G* 857
rop *n.*[2] gut, intestine, *Pat* 270
rore *v.* roar
ros *see* **rys(e)**
rose *n.* rose, *Pe* 269, 906; *gen. or adj.* of the rose, *Cl* 1079; **Rose** *Roman de la Rose, Cl* 1057
rose *v.* praise, *Cl* 1371
rost(t)ed *pp.* roasted
rote *n.*[1] root, *Pe* 420, *Cl* 619, *Pat* 467, *G* 2294
rot(e) *n.*[2] rot, decay, *Pe* 26, *Cl* 1079
rote *n.*[3] custom; **bi r.** with ceremony, *G* 2207
rote *n.*[4] stringed musical instrument, kind of violin *Cl* 1082
rote *v.* rot, decay, *Pe* 958, *G* 528
ropeled[1] *pp.* cooked, *Cl* 59
ropeled[2] *pa.t.* hurried, *Cl* 890
roper *n.* rudder
ropun *n.* redness
roue, rouez *see* **ryue** *v.*, **roffe**
roum *n.* room
roun *n.* secret, mystery; **in r.** inscrutably, *Pat* 511
roun, rowne *v.* speak privately, whisper, *Pat* 64, *G* 362; **rownande** *presp.adj.* whispering, *Pe* 112
roun *see also* **roun(de)**
rouncé *n.* horse
roun(de) *adj.* round; **on r.** around, *Cl* 423, *Pat* 147
roungen *see* **ronge**
r(o)urd(e) *n.* noise, sound; voice, *G* 2337; clamour, cry, *Cl* 390
rous *n.* praise, fame, *G* 310
roust *n.* rust, *G* 2018
rout *n.* jerk, *G* 457

route *n.* company, *Pe* 926
routes *v.* snores, *Pat* 186
rowe, rowwe *v.* row
rownande, rowned *see* **roun** *v.*
rowtande *adj.* rushing
rowtes *n.* bands, crowds
ruch(ch)e *see* **rich(ch)(e)**
ruddon *n.* redness
rudede *pp.* reddened, reflected red, *G* 1695
rudelez *n.* (window?) curtains, *G* 857
rudnyng *n.* reddening, redness
rueled *pa.t.* poured
ruful *adj.* piteous, *Pe* 916; terrible, *G* 2076; *adv.*
  rewfully, sorrowfully
rugh(e), ru3e *see* **rogh(e)**
rule *n.* rule, law
rule *v.* (**rewled** *pa.t.*) rule, control; **rewled**
  hym conducted himself, *Cl* 294
rungen *see* **ronge**
runisch, renischche *adj.* strange, outlandish,
  Cl 96, 1545; rough, wild, *G* 457; **-ly** *adv.*
  roughly, violently; **renyschly** strangely, in
  outlandish words, *Cl* 1724
runne(n), rurd *see* **ren(n)e, r(o)urd(e)**
rusched *pa.t.*[1] rushed, poured, *Cl* 368
rusched *pa.t.*[2] swished, *G* 2204, 2219
ruþen *v.* arouse, *Cl* 895, 1208; *reflex.* bestir
  oneself, *G* 1558
ruyt *v.* hasten
rwe *v.* pity; **r. on** take pity on; *impers.* repent,
  Cl 290, 561
rwly *adv.* pitifully
ryal(le), rial, ryol *adj.* royal; splendid, glor-
  ious; *adv. or adj. Cl* 1082; **-ly** *adv.* royally,
  splendidly
ryalme *n.* realm, kingdom
rybaudes *n.* villains
rybbe *n.* rib
rybé *n.* (**rubies** *pl.*) ruby
ryche *n.* kingdom, *Pe* 601, 722, 919
rych(e) *see also* **rich(e), rich(ch)(e)**
rychely *see* **rich(e)**
rychez *n.* wealth, *Pe* 26
ryd(d)(e) *v.* take away (from), *G* 364; part, *G*
  2246; **r. of** clean off, *G* 1344
ryde, ride *v.* (**rod(e)** *pa.t.*) ride
rydelande, rydelles *see* **ridlande, redles**
rydyng *n.* riding
ryf *adj.* plentiful, abundant
ryg(e) *n.* storm, tempest, *Cl* 354, 382
rygge, rigge *n.* back(bone), *Pat* 379, *G* 1344,
  1608
ry3t *adv.* right, just; exactly; properly; cor-
  rectly, *Cl* 1346, *G* 373; duly, *Pat* 326; **r. no3t**
  anything at all, *Pe* 520; **r. non** none at all, *G*
  1790
ry3te *adj.* right, just; right (*as opposed to* left),
  Pat 511; justified (by grace), *Pe* 672
ry3t(e), ri3t, Ry3t *n.* justice (just judgement),
  Pe 591, 665, 721n (*person.*), *Pat* 19, 323, 493,
  G 2346; right (conduct), *Pe* 496, 622, *Pat*
  431; righteousness, morality, *Cl* 194; justice,
  right, (entitlement), *Pe* 580, 703, 708, 1196,
  Cl 2; obligation, *G* 1041; claim, *G* 2342; pre-
  rogative, *G* 274; right (justification by

grace), *Pe* 684, 696, 720; **by r.** correctly, *Cl*
  1633; **r. hade** was right (to do), *Cl* 1318; **on**
  r. (*cf.* **ary3t**) indeed, truly, *Cl* 1513
ry3tez *adv.* precisely, *Cl* 427
ry3t hym *pa.t.reflex.* proceeded, *G* 308
ry3twys *adj.* righteous, just; *as n. Pe* 689; **-ly**
  adv. rightly, *Pe* 709
rymez *n.* membranes, *G* 1343
ryne *v.* touch, *G* 2290
ryng *n.* (**rynk,** *G* 1817, 1827) ring
ryngande, rynkande *adj.* ringing, resound-
  ing, *Cl* 1082, *G* 2337
rynging *n.* ringing
rynk *see* **renk, ryng**
rynkande, ryol *see* **ryngande, ryal**
rypande *presp.* examining, *Cl* 592
rype *see* **ripe**
rypez *v.* ripens
rys *n.* twig; **bi r.** in the wood, *G* 1698
rys(e), ris(e) *v.* (**ros, rysed** *pa.t.*) rise; grow,
  G 528; rise, come into view, *Pe* 103; **r. vp**
  stand up, *Pe* 191, 437
ryth *n.* ox
rytte *pa.t.* cut, *G* 1332
ryue *adv.* abundantly, *G* 2046 (*cf.* **ryf**)
ryue *v.* (**roue** *pa.t.*) cut

sabatounz *n.* steel shoes
sacrafyce, sacrafyse, sacrefyce, sakerfyse
  n. sacrifice
sad(d)(e) *adj.* long, *Cl* 1286; great, advanced,
  Cl 657; grave, dignified, *Pe* 211, 887, *Cl* 640;
  solemn, *Cl* 595; gloomy, *Cl* 525
sade *see* **say**
sadel *n. & v.* saddle
sadly *adv.* firmly, *G* 437, 1593; heavily, *Pat*
  442; deliberately, *G* 437; long enough, *G*
  2409
saf, saue *adj.* safe, *Pat* 334; redeemed, *Pe* 672,
  etc.; **sauer** *compar.adj.* safer, *G* 1202. *See also*
  vouche
saf, saue *prep. & conj.* except (for), except that
saffer *n.* (**safyres** *pl.*) sapphire, *Pe* 118, 1002
sage *adj.* wise
saghe, sa3e(s), -z *see* **sawe**
sa3 *see* **se(ne)**
sa3t(e) *adj.* at peace; *in* **set(t)e s.** reconcile, be
  reconciled, *Pe* 1201, would have reconciled,
  Pe 52
sa3tlyng *n.* reconciliation
sa3ttel *v.* (**sa3tled** *pa.t. & pp.*) become recon-
  ciled; become calm, *Pat* 232; settle, *Cl* 445
sake *n.*[1] charge; fault, *Pat* 84, 172; **s. of**
  felonye criminal charge, *Pe* 800
sake *n.*[2] sake
sakerfyse *see* **sacrafyce**
saklez *adj.* guiltless
sakred *pp.* consecrated
Salamon, Salomon *n.* Solomon
sale *n.* hall
salue *v.* greet, *G* 1473
salure *n.* salt-cellar
Samarye *n.* Samaria
same *adj. & pron.* same; **of þe s.** in the same
  way, to match

same(n) *adv.* together, *Cl* 400, *etc.*, *Pat* 46, *G* 50, *etc.*; **al(le) s.** with one accord, *Pe* 518, *G* 363, 673

samen, samne *v.* (**samned** *pa.t. & pp.*) assemble, bring (be brought) together

samen-feres *n.* fellow-travellers

samne(d) *see* **samen** *v.*

sample *n.* example, *exemplum*, *Cl* 1326; parable, *Pe* 499

sanap *n.* napkin, overlay

sancta sanctorum *n.* holy of holies

sange, -o- *n.* song

sant *see* **Sayn(t)** *n.*[1]

sapyence *n.* wisdom

sardiners *n.* cornelians

sardonyse *n.* sardonyx

Saré *n.* Sarah

sarre(st) *see* **sore**

Satanas *n.* Satan

sat(e) *see* **sitte**

sathrapas *n.* satraps, governors

satteled *pa.t.* settled, descended

satz *see* **say(e)**

sauce, sawse *n.* sauce

saudan *n.* sultan

saue *v.* save, spare

saue *see also* **saf**

sauement *n.* safety

saueour, sauer *see* **sauio(u)r, saf**

sauere, sau(y)our *v.* apprehend, know, *Cl* 581; smell, *Pat* 275; season, *Cl* 825; *pp.* flavoured, *G* 892

sauerly *adv.* feelingly, *G* 1937; in comfort, *G* 2048; *adj.* adequate, satisfactory, *Pe* 226n

sauez *see* **sawe**

sauio(u)r, saueour, sauyour *n.* saviour. *See also* **sauere**

saule *see* **sawle**

saundyuer *n.* sandiver, glass-gall

sauo(u)r *n.* smell, *Cl* 510, 1447; taste, *Cl* 995

sauoured *see* **sauere**

sauter *n.* psalter

sauteray *n.* psaltery (stringed instrument)

sauyour *see* **sauio(u)r, sauere**

sauyté *n.* safety

sawe, saȝe, saghe *n.* (**saȝez, -s, sauez, sawez, -s** *pl.*) speech, statement, saying; words; (spoken) prayer, *G* 1202

sawle, saule, sawele *n.* soul

sawse *see* **sauce**

sayl *n.* sail

sayled *pa.t.* sailed, floated

saym *n.* grease

sayned *pa.t. & pp.* blessed, *Cl* 746, 986; *reflex.* cross oneself, *G* 761, 763, 1202

Sayn(t), Sant *n.*[1] Saint, St

sayn(t) *n.*[2] girdle, *G* 589, 2431

say(e) *v.* (**seggez, says, say(e)z, sa(y)tz** *pres.*, **sayd(e)(n), sade** *pa.t.*, **sayd** *pp.*) say, tell, declare; proclaim (*of a book, with suggestion of* read aloud), *Pe* 593, *G* 690

say(t)z *see* **say(e)**

scale *n.* surface, *Pe* 1005

scape *v.* escape

scarre *v.* frighten, terrify, alarm; be provoked, react fiercely, *Cl* 598

scaþe, schaþe, skaþe *n.* harm, injury, *Cl* 151, *G* 2353; punishment, *Cl* 600; evil, sin, *Cl* 21, 196, *etc.*; a pity, *G* 674

scaþel *adj.* harmful

scayled *pa.t.* scaled, climbed

scelt, schad(d)(e) *see* **skelt(en), schede**

schade *n.* shade

schaded *pa.t.* cast shadow

schadow *n.* shadow

schadowed *pa.t.* cast shadows, *Pe* 42

schafte *n.* shaft; ray, beam (of light); spear, *G* 205

schafted *pa.t.* shone low, set, *G* 1467

schaȝe *n.* thicket

schal(e) *v.* (**schalt** *pres2sg.*, **schal, schul, schyn, schin** *prespl.*) shall, will, must; **schuld(e)(n)** *pa.t.* would, ought to, had to; was about to, *Pe* 1162

schalk(e) *n.* (**schalk(k)ez** *pl.*) man

scham(e), schome *n.* shame

schame *v.* be ashamed, embarrassed

schankes, schonkes, -z *n.* legs

schap *n.* (**schappes** *pl.*) shape

schape *v.* (**schop, schaped** *pa.t.*, **schapen, schaped** *pp.*) fashion, make, *G* 213, 662, 1210; recount, *G* 1626; ordain, *Cl* 742, *Pat* 247, *G* 2138, *etc.*; endeavour, *Cl* 762; befall, *Pat* 160

schaped *pp.* (= **chaped**) mounted (with), *G* 1832

scharp(e) *adj. & adv.* sharp, keen; swift, *Cl* 475; intense, *Cl* 1310; *as n.* blade, *G* 424, 1593, *etc.*; *adv.* loudly, *Pe* 877

schaterande *presp.* dashing, breaking

schaþe *see* **scaþe**

schaued *pa.t.* scraped; **schauen** *pp.* scraped, shaven (smooth)

schawe *see* **schewe**

schede *v.* (**schad(d)(e)** *pa.t.*) sever, *G* 425; fall, be shed, *Pe* 411, *G* 506, 727, 956; shed, *Pe* 741; fall, extend, *Cl* 1690

(s)chelde *n.* shield; shoulder (of boar), *G* 1456; slab (of meat), *Cl* 58, *G* 1611, 1626

schende *v.* (**schended, schent(e)** *pp.*) destroy; disgrace, punish, *Pe* 668, *Cl* 47, 580; batter, *Pat* 246

schene *adj.* lovely, beautiful, bright; *as n.* brightness, sun, *Pat* 440, bright weapon, *G* 2268, fair maiden, *Pe* 166, 965

schent(e) *see* **schende**

schep *n.* sheep

schepon *n.* shippen, cattle-shed

schere *n. see* **cher(e)**

schere *v.*[1] (**scher** *pa.t.*, **schorne** *pp.*) cut

schere *v.*[2] meander, *Pe* 107

schere-wykes *n.* groin

schet *pp.* enclosed

schewe, scheue, schawe *v.* show, reveal, display, set forth; produce, offer, *G* 315, 619, 2061; utter, *Cl* 662, 840; *intrans.* (*also reflex.*) show, appear, *Cl* 170, 553, *G* 420, *etc.*; **to s.** in appearance, *G* 2036

schin *see* **schal(e)**

schinande *presp.adj.* shining

schirly *adv.* completely (*cf.* **clanly**), *G* 1880

scho *pron.* she

scholes *adj.* shoeless
schome *see* **scham(e)**
schomely *adv.* shamefully
schyne *v.* (**schinande** *presp.*, **schon, schynde, schyned** *pa.t.*) shine
schon *see* **schyne**
schonied *pa.t.* shunned, avoided
schonkes, -z, schop *see* **schankes, schape**
schor *n.* (**schowrez** *pl.*) shower, *Cl* 227, *G* 506
schore *n.* bank (of stream); cliff, rock, *Pe* 166, *G* 2161
schorne *see* **schere**
schort *adj.* short
schortly *adv.* hastily, suddenly
schote *v.* (**schot(e), schotten** *pa.t.*) shoot; shoot, rush, spring, *Pe* 58, *Cl* 850, *G* 317, *etc.*; jerk, *G* 2318
schout *n.* shout
schowen, schowrez *see* **schow(u)e, schor**
schowted *pa.t.* roared, rang out, *Pe* 877
schow(u)e, schwue *v.* (**schowen** *pa.t.*, **schowued** *pa.t. & pp.*) push, press, thrust; **s. to** push forward, *G* 1454; **of mensk s.** driven from honour, *Cl* 1740
schrank(e) *pa.t.* shrank, winced, *Cl* 850, *G* 2267, 2372; sank, *G* 425, 2313
schrewe *n.* villain
schrewedschyp *n.* wickedness
schrof *pa.t.* confessed
schroude-hous *n.* ?place of shelter, *Cl* 1076
schrowde *n.* garment, clothing
schryfte *n.* confession
schrylle *adj.* shrill
schrylle *adv.* sharply, brightly, *Pe* 80
schul, schuld(e)(n) *see* **schal(e)**
schulder *n.* (**schulderez, -s, schylderez** *pl.*) shoulder
schunt *n.* sudden deflection, *G* 2268
schunt *pa.t. & pp.* moved aside, *Cl* 605; started aside, flinched, *G* 1902, 2280
schwue, schyire *see* **schow(u)e, schyr(e)(e)**
schylde *v.* shield, protect, *Pat* 440; prevent, *Pe* 965, *G* 1776
schylderez *see* **schulder**
schym *adj.* bright, *Pe* 1077
schymeryng *n.* shimmering, *Pe* 80
schyn *see* **schal(e)**
schynder *v.* sunder, break (apart)
schyp, schip *n.* ship
schyr(e)(e), schyire *adj. & adv.* (**schyrrer** *compar.*) bright, shining, white, fair; *as n.* white flesh, *G* 1331, 2256
sckete *see* **skete**
s(c)lade *n.* valley
s(c)laʒt *n.* slaughter, *Pe* 801, *Cl* 56n; *pl.* strokes, *Pat* 192
scole *n.* cup, *Cl* 1145
scoleres *n.* scholars
scomfyted *pa.t.* (**scoumfit** *pp.*) discomfited, disconcerted
scopen *pa.t.* scooped, *Pat* 155
scowtes *n.* jutting rocks, *G* 2167
scowte-wach *n.* guard, watchman
scoymus, skoymos *adj.* scrupulous; **is s. of** feels repugnance at
scrof *adj.* rough, *Cl* 1546

scrypture *n.* inscription, written characters
scue, scurtez *see* **skwe, skyrtez**
scylful *adj.* righteous, *Cl* 1148
scylle *see* **skyl(le)**
se, see *n.* sea
se, see *v. see*, **se(ne)**
seche *pron.* such, *G* 1543
sech(e) *v.* (**soʒt(e), soʒtten** *pa.t.*, **soʒt** *pp.*) seek, look for, make for; come, go, *Cl* 29, 510, *etc.*, *Pat* 116, *G* 685, 1052, *etc.*; attempt, move, *Cl* 201; try, strive, *Cl* 1286, *Pat* 197; invite, *Pat* 53; **s. fro** leave, *Pat* 116, *G* 685, 1440; **þe water soʒte** was going into the water, *Pat* 249
secounde *adj.* second
sed(e) *n.* seed; offspring, *Cl* 660
seele, seet, seete *see* **sele, sitte, sete**
seg(g)e *n.¹* seat, *Pat* 93; siege, *Cl* 1185, *G* 1, 2525
segg(e) *n.²* man, knight, person; sir, *G* 394; *pl.* men, people; **vche (a) s.** everyone; **alle seggez** everyone
seggez *see also* **say(e)**
segh(e) *see* **se(ne)**
Segor *n.* Zoar
seʒ(e)(n) *see* **se(ne), seye**
seker *see* **siker**
sekke *n.* sackcloth
seknesse *n.* sickness
selcouth *n.* marvel, wonder
selden *adv.* seldom
sele, seele *n.* good fortune, happiness
self, seluen *adj.* same, very, *Pe* 203, *G* 751; **þe s. sunne** the sun itself, *Pe* 1076, **þe S. God** God Himself, *Pe* 1046; *as n.* self, himself, *Pe* 1054, *Cl* 243, 786, *etc.*, *G* 51, 1616, *etc.*; yourself, *Pat* 413; oneself, *Cl* 579
sellen *v.* sell
selly *adj.* (**sellokest** *superl.*) marvellous, *Pat* 353, *G* 1439, 1962; strange, *G* 2170; *as n.* (a) wonder, marvel, *Pat* 140, *G* 28, 239, 475; **selly(ly)** *adv.* exceedingly, *G* 963, 1194, 1803
seluen *see* **self**
selure *n.* canopy, *G* 76
sely *adj.* innocent, blessed
Sem *n.* Shem
sem *see* **sem(e)**
semb(e)launt *n.* appearance, *G* 148; face, *Pe* 211; sign, expression, *G* 468; demonstration (of regard), *G* 1658; friendly welcome, *Cl* 131; demeanour, *Pe* 1143, *Cl* 640, *G* 1273; kindness, *G* 1843
semblé *n.* assembly, throng
sembled *pp.* assembled
seme *adj.* seemly, *Pe* 1115, *Cl* 549, 1810, *G* 1085; *adv.* becomingly, *Pe* 190; *cf.* **semly(ch)**
sem(e) *n.* ornamental strip of material inserted in, or laid over, a seam; border, *Pe* 838; blemish, flaw, *Cl* 555
seme *v.* seem, appear; *impers.* be fitting *or* proper, become, suit, *Cl* 117, 793, *G* 73, 679 (*sc.* to be), 848, 1005, 1929
semly(ch), semely *adj. & adv.* (**semloker** *compar.*) seemly, fitting, *G* 348, 1198; fine, handsome, fair, lovely, *Pe* 34, 45, 789, *Cl*

209, 262, *etc.*, *G* 672, 685; *compar.* more beautiful, *Cl* 868, *G* 83 (*sc.* gem); *as n.* **þat S.** that fair (Lord), *Cl* 1055, the handsome (knight), *G* 672, those lovely (ladies), *Cl* 870; *adv.* becomingly, in a seemly manner, *Cl* 1442, *G* 622 (**semlyly**), 865, *etc.*; sweetly, *G* 1658, 1796

sen *see* **se(ne)**

sendal *n.* silk

sende *v.* (**sende** *pa.t.*, **sendez** *pa.t.2s.*, **sende** *pp.*) send

sene *adj.* visible, *Pe* 1143; outward, *G* 148; plain, *G* 341; *see also* **se(ne)** *v.*

se(ne), **se(e)** *v.* (**segh(e)**, **seȝ(e)(n)**, **saȝ**, **syȝ(e)** *pa.t.* **sen(e)** *pp.*) see; **on to s.** to look upon (at), *Pe* 45; *see also* **sene** *adj.*

sengel *adj.* alone, *G* 1531; **-ey** *adv.* apart, *Pe* 8

serched *pa.t.* examined, *G* 1328

ser(e) *adj.* various; different, *G* 2417; diverse, *Pat* 12; several, *G* 822; single, separate, particular, *Cl* 507, *G* 761, 1985; *adv.* severally, *G* 632; **sere twyes** on two different occasions, *G* 1522

serelych, **serly** *adv.* severally, individually

sergauntez, **serjauntes** *n.* servants, *Cl* 109; officers, *Pat* 385

serges *n.* candles

serjauntes *see* **sergauntez**

serlepes, **serlypez** *adv.* in turn, *G* 501; *as adj.* single, *Pe* 994

serly *see* **serelych**

sermoun *n.* speech; account, *Pe* 1185

sertayn *adv.* certainly, for sure

seruage *n.* servitude, bondage

serua(u)nt *n.* servant

serue(n) *v.*[1] serve; suffice, *Cl* 750; avail, be of use, *Pe* 331

serue *v.*[2] deserve, *Pe* 553, *G* 1380

seruyse, **-ce**, **-ise** *n.* service; (*in church*), *G* 751, 940(*and cf.Cl* 1152); (*of a meal*),*Cl* 1401, *G* 130

sese *v.*[1] cease, stop; fail, *Cl* 523

sese *v.*[2] seize, snatch, take possession (of); touch, take, *G* 1825; put in possession, *in pp.* **sesed in** made possessor of, *Pe* 417

sesoun(ez) *see* **se(y)soun**

set *adj.* set, appointed, *Cl* 1364

sete *adj.* excellent, *G* 889

sete, **seete** *n.* seat, throne; sitting, *Cl* 59*n*; **wenten to s.** took their places, *G* 72, 493

sete(n) *see* **sitte**

set(t)e *v.* (**set(te)(n)** *pa.t.*, **set(te)** *pp.*) set, put, place; sit, seat (*pass. & reflex.*), *Cl* 1401, *G* 437, 1083, *etc.*; strike (blow, *etc.*), *G* 372, ?*Cl* 1225; prepare, *Pat* 193, ?*Cl* 1225; lay the table, *G* 1651; make, put, *G* 1883; establish, found, build, *Pe* 1062, *Cl* 673, 1015, *G* 14; invent, *G* 625; *reflex.* endeavour, devote (oneself), *Cl* 1453, *G* 1246; achieve, *Pat* 58; esteem, value, *Pe* 8, 307, 811, *Cl* 1710, *G* 1250; *pp.* (had) arrived, *Cl* 986, ingrained, *G* 148, determined, *Pat* 487, beset (by), *Pat* 46; **s. at liȝt, lyttel** make light of, disregard, *Cl* 1710, *G* 1250; **s. hym on** *reflex.* charge at, *G* 1589; **s. in asente** agree, *Pat* 177; **s. on** choose, *Cl* 469; **s. on his hede** call down on him, *G* 1721; **s. saȝt(e)** reconcile, be recon-

ciled, *Pe* 1201, (*pa.t.subjunc.*) would have reconciled, *Pe* 52; **s. solace** find pleasure, *G* 1318; **s. syȝt toward** turn toward, *Cl* 672. *See also* **set**

settel *n.* seat

seþe *v.* (**soþen** *pp.*) boil

seue, **seve**, **sewe** *n.* broth, pottage

seuen *adj.* seven

seuentenþe *adj.* seventeenth

seuenþe *adj.* seventh

seuer *v.* separate, part, depart

seve *see* **seue**

sewe *v.* sew

sewe *see also* **seue**

sewer *n.* servant waiting at table, *Cl* 639*n*

sewrté *n.* security

sex(te) *adj.* six(th)

seye *v.* (**seyed** *pa.t.*, **seȝen** *pp.*) go, come, pass

se(y)soun *n.* season; time, *G* 1958, 2085; **hyȝ s.** festival, *Pe* 39

sidbordez, **sidebordez** *n.* side-tables, lower tables

side, **siȝt** *see* **syde**, **syȝt(e)**

siker, **seker**, **syker** *adj.* true, firm, *G* 403; trustworthy, *G* 96, 111, 115, 2048, 2493; sure, *G* 265; *adv.* surely, *G* 1637

siker *v.* promise, pledge

silk(e) *see* **sylk(e)**

sille *n.* floor; **on s.** in the hall, *G* 55

sister-sunes *n.* nephews, sister's sons

sitte, **-y-** *v.* (**sat(e)**, **seet**, **sete(n)** *pa.t.*, **seten** *pp.*) sit

siþen *see* **syþen**

siue *n.* sieve, *Cl* 226

skarmoch *n.* skirmish

skaþe *see* **scaþe**

skayned *pp.* grazed

skeles *n.* dishes, *Cl* 1405

skelten, **scelt** *pa.t.* (**skelt** *pp.*) launch, *Cl* 1186, 1206; revile, *Cl* 827; hasten, *Cl* 1554

skere *adj.* innocent, pure, *G* 1261

skete, **sckete** *adv.* quickly, sharply

skewe *see* **skwe**

skowtez *v.* scouts, searches, *Cl* 483

skoymos *see* **scoymus**

skwe, **scue**, **skewe** *n.* sky, cloud

skyfte *v.* apportion, *Pe* 569; *pp.* changed, *Cl* 709, alternated, *G* 19

skyg *adj.* fastidious

skyl(le), **scylle**, **skyly** *n.* reason, (faculty of) judgement, *Pe* 312, *Cl* 151; mind, attitude, *Cl* 827; reason, argument, *Pe* 674, *Cl* 823, *G* 1296, 1509; meaning, *Cl* 1554; excuse, *Cl* 62; judgement, decree, *Cl* 569, 709

skylly *adj.* wise, *Cl* 529

skyre *adj.* bright, clear

skyrmez *v.* darts about

skyrtez, **scurtez** *n.* skirts, lower parts of a saddle or garment

skyualde *n.* division, separation, *Cl* 529

slade, **slaȝt(es)** *see* **s(c)lade**, **s(c)laȝt**

slake, **sloke** *v.* come to an end, stop, *Pe* 942; die away, *G* 244; **slokes** *see* *G* 412*n*

slauþe *n.* sloth

slayn(e) *see* **slow(e)**

sleȝe *adj.* intricate, subtle; **-ly** *adv.* *G* 1182*n*

sleȝt *see* **slyȝt**
sleke *v.* quench
slente *n.* slope, hill; **by s. oþer slade** somewhere or other, *Pe* 141
slepe *n.* sleep; (**vp**)**on s.** asleep
slepe *v.* (**slepande** *presp.,* **sleped, slepte** *pa.t.,* **slepe** (*G* 1991) *pa.t.subjunc.*) sleep
slepyng-slaȝte sudden heavy sleep, *Pe* 59*n*
sloberande *presp.* slobbering
slode *see* **slyde**
slokes *v. see G* 412*n*
slot *n.* hollow at base of throat
slouen *see* **slow(e)**
sloumbe-s(e)lep(e) *n.* heavy sleep
slow, slowen, slouen *pa.t.* (**slayn(e)** *pp.*) slew, killed
sluchched *adj.* soiled
slyde *v.* (**slode** *pa.t.*) slide, slip
slyȝt *adj.* slim, slender, *Pe* 190
slyȝt, sleȝt *n.* skill; stratagem, device, *Pat* 130, *G* 1854, 1858; skilled demonstration, *G* 916
slyp *n.* blow, *Cl* 1264
slyppe *v.* (**slypped, slypte** *pa.t.,* **slypped** *pp.*) slip; escape, *Cl* 1785, *G* 1858; slip, fall, *Pat* 186, *G* 244
smach *n.* flavour, taste, aroma
smachande *presp.* smelling
smal(e) *adj.* small, *Pe* 90; slender, slim, *Pe* 6, 190, *G* 144, 1207; fine, *Cl* 226, *G* 76
smart *adj.* sharp, bitter
smartly *adv.* sharply, *Cl* 711; promptly, *G* 407
smelle *n.* smell
smeten *see* **smyte**
smeþely *adv.* gently, *G* 1789
smod *n.* filth
smolderande *adj.* stifling
smolt *adj.* gentle, *G* 1763
smolt *v.* go, set off, *Cl* 461; escape, *Cl* 732
smoþe *adj.* smooth, *Pe* 6, 190; pleasant, friendly, *G* 1763; **smoþely** *adv.* easily, *Cl* 732, deftly, *G* 407
smylt *adj.* sieved, sifted, fine
smyte *v.* (**smeten** *pa.t.pl.,* **smyten** *pp.*) smite, strike; fall, *G* 1763
snart *adv.* swiftly, sharply, *G* 2003
snaw(e) *n.* snow
snayped *pa.t.* cut, stung, *G* 2003
snitered *pa.t.* showered, *G* 2003
snyrt *pa.t.* snicked, touched, *G* 2312
so *adv. & conj.* so, thus, in this way; such (a); *with indef.pron.* so ever, *Cl* 100, 422, *etc., G* 384, 1107, *etc.*; then, *Pe* 1187, *G* 218; *conj.* as; **sone s.** as soon as
soberly *adv.* reverently, solemnly, gravely
sobre *adj.* sober, serious, *Pe* 391, 532
Sodamas, Sodomas *n.* Sodom
sodanly, sodenly *adv.* suddenly
soffer(ed), soffraunce *see* **suffer, suffraunce**
soft(e) *adj.* soft, gentle, mild; *adv.* softly, quietly, comfortably
soft(e)ly, softly *adv.* softly, quietly; meekly, *Pat* 529
soghe *v.*[1] sow, spread, *Pat* 67
soghe *v.*[2] *impers.* (it may) hurt, *Pat* 391

soȝt(e), soȝtten *see* **seche**
sojorne *n.* sojourn, stay
sojo(u)rne *v.* stay; *pp.* lodged, *G* 2048
sok *n.* sucking
sokored *pp.* succoured
solace *n.* pleasure, joy; entertainment, *G* 1985
solased *pa.t.* entertained
solde *pa.t.* sold
solem(p)ne *adj.* solemn, dignified
solempnely *adv.* ceremoniously, solemnly
solem(p)neté *n.* solemnity, dignity; high position, *Cl* 1678; festival, *Cl* 1757
solie, soly *n.* throne
somer *n.* summer, spring
somones, som(m)oun *n.* summons; **mad s.** summoned, *Pe* 539
sonde *n.*[1] embassy, sending, command, *Pe* 943; message, *Cl* 781*n*; message, messenger, *Cl* 53
sonde *n.*[2] shore, *Pat* 341
sondezmon *n.* messenger
sone *adv.* immediately, quickly, soon; **s. so** as soon as
sonet *n.* music
sonetez *n.* sennets, fanfares
songe, sange *n.* song
songe(n), sonkken, sonne *see* **syng(e), synk, sunne**
sop(e) *n.* mouthful, morsel
soper *n.* supper
sore *adj.* (**sarrest** *superl.*) painful, grievous; diseased, afflicted, *Cl* 1111; *adv.* (**sarre** *compar.*) sorely, grievously; hard, *Pe* 550
soré *adj.* sorry, *G* 1826, 1987
sor(e) *n.* pain, sorrow
sorȝ(e), sorewe *n.*[1] sorrow, misery: imprecation, *G* 1721; contrition, *Pe* 663
sorȝe *n.*[2] filth, *Cl* 846, *Pat* 275
sorquydryȝe *see* **sourquydry**
sorsers *n.* sorcerers
sorsory *n.* sorcery
sortes *n.* lots
soth(e), soþ(e) *adj. & adv.* true; *adv.* truly, in truth, indeed; for a fact, *G* 348; **-ly** *adv.* truly (*see also* **soþly** *adv.*[2])
soth(e), soþ(e) *n.* truth
sothfol *adj.* true
sotte *n.* fool
sotyle *adj.* fine, transparent, *Pe* 1050
soþ(e) *see* **soth(e)**
soþefast *adj.* true
soþ(e)ly, sothely *adv.*[1] truly
soþen *see* **seþe**
soþly, sothly *adv.*[2] softly, *Cl* 654*n*, *G* 673*n*
souerayn *n.* lord; *as adj.* sovereign
soufre *n.* sulphur
souȝed, swe(y) *pa.t.* soughed, moaned, *Cl* 956, *Pat* 140; sounded, *Pat* 429
soumme, sowme *n.* number, quantity
soun *n.* sound, noise; voice, *Pe* 532, *Pat* 429; report, *Cl* 689; *see also* **sun**
sounande *presp.adj.* sonorous, *Pe* 883
sounde *adj.* sound, safe, well; undamaged, *Cl* 1795; *as n.* safety, *G* 2489
sounder *n.* herd (of wild pig), *G* 1440
souned *pa.t.* sounded

souped *pp.* supped, eaten supper, *Cl* 833
sour(e) *adj.* bitter; disagreeable, disgusting, *Cl* 192, *G* 963; *as n.* leaven, *Cl* 820
sourquydry, surquidré, sorquydryȝe *n.* pride
sowlé, sovly *adj.* unclean
sowme *see* **soumme**
soyle *n.* soil, ground
space *n.* time; distance, *Pe* 1030; respite, delay, *Cl* 755; opportunity, *Cl* 1774; **in s.** soon, in due course; **in þat s.** there and then
spak *adv.* readily, *Pat* 104
spakest *superl.adj. as n.* sharpest, wisest, *Pat* 169
spakk *see* **speke**
spakly *adv.* quickly
spare *adj.* spare, reserve, *Pat* 104; bare, *Pat* 338; restrained, tactful, *G* 901
spare *v.* spare; *intrans.* hold back, *Cl* 755, 1245
sparlyr *n.* calf (of leg)
sparred *pa.t.* sprang, rushed
sparþe *n.* battle-axe
spec *n.* speck
spece *see* **spyce**
spech(e) *n.* speech, conversation, discourse, words; *pl.* expressions, *G* 1261, 1778
special, specyal *adj.* special, specially chosen, *Cl* 1492; precious, *Pe* 235, 938
specialté *n.* partiality, affection, *G* 1778
sped(e) *n.* aid, *Cl* 1607; success, *G* 918; speed, *G* 1444; **a s. whyle** a short time, *Cl* 1285
spede *v.* (make) prosper, bless, quicken, further; cause, *Cl* 551; succeed, *Cl* 1058, *G* 410; *reflex.* hasten, *G* 979
spedly *adv.* happily, *G* 1935; quickly, *Cl* 1729
speke *v.* (**speked, spakk, speke, speken** *pa.t.*, **spoken** *pp.*) speak, say, declare
spelle *n.* speech, words, discourse
spelle *v.* tell, say, *Pe* 793. *G* 2140
spende, spenet *pa.t.* (**spend** *pp.*) fastened, *Pat* 104*n*; clasped, *Pe* 49; *intrans.* clung, *G* 158; *pp.* fastened, *G* 587
spende *v.* (**spent** *pp.*) spend; utter, *G* 410; **of speche s.** speech uttered about (*i.e.* tell of), *Pe* 1132
spenné *n.* ?fence, thorn hedge. *Possibly same as next*
spenne *n.* piece of land; **in s.** there, *G* 1074
spenne-fote *adv.* with feet together, *G* 2316*n*
spere *n.* spear
sperre *v.* strike, spur, *G* 670
spied *see* **spye**
spitous, spetos *adj.* abominable, *Cl* 845; cruel, *G* 209
spitously *adv.* contemptuously, maliciously
sponne *pa.t.subjunc.* would shoot up, *Pe* 35
sprez, spures, -z *n.* spurs
spornande *presp.* stumbling, *Pe* 363 (*fig.*)
spot(t)(e) *n.* spot, blemish, *Pe* 12, *etc.*, *Cl* 551; place, location, *Pe* 13, *etc.*; (*these senses perhaps combined in* **wythouten s.** *Pe* 12*n*, 24, *etc.*); **-lez** spotless, *Pe* 856; **-ty** spotty, *Pe* 1070
spoyle *v.* plunder, *Cl* 1774; seize, *Cl* 1285
sprad(de), sprang(e) *see* **sprede, spryng**
sprawlyng *n.* struggling

sprede *v.* (**sprad(de)** *pa.t.*) spread, extend; be overspread, *Pe* 25
sprenged *pa.t.* (dawn) broke, *G* 1415
sprent *pa.t.* leapt, *G* 1896
sprete *n.* bowsprit
sprit *pa.t.* jumped, *G* 2316
spryng *v.* (**sprang(e)** *pa.t.*) spring, leap (forth), shoot up; spread, *Cl* 1362; leap, rise, ascend, *Pe* 61; grow, *Pe* 453*n*; jump, fall, *Pe* 13
spryngande *presp.adj.* flourishing, *Pe* 35
spumande *presp.adj.* foaming
spured *pa.t.* (**spur(y)ed** *pp.*) asked
sput *v.* (*pres.subjunc.*) spit, *Pat* 338
sputen *pa.t.* uttered, *Cl* 845
spyce, spyse, spece *n.* creature, being, *Pe* 235*n*, 938; spice, *G* 892; spice-bearing plant, *Pe* 25, 35, (*collect.*) 104; spiced cakes, *G* 979
spye, -i- *v.* inquire, investigate, discover; look for, *G* 1896
spylle *v.* (**spylled, spylt** *pa.t.*) destroy, kill; scatter, spill, *Cl* 1248
spyrakle *n.* breath
spyryt *n.* spirit
spyse *see* **spyce**
spyserez *n.* spice sellers
spyt *n.* anger, *Cl* 755; (doing) injury, *G* 1444; evil deed, *Pe* 1138
stabeled *pa.t.* stabled, *G* 823
stable *adj.* steadfast, *Pe* 597
stable *v.* set, place, *Pe* 683; establish, *Cl* 1334, 1652, 1667, *G* 1060
stablye *n.* ring of beaters, *G* 1153
stac *see* **steke**
stad(de) *pp.* placed, fixed; set down, *G* 33; provided, armed, *G* 2137; **watz (wern) s.** found himself (themselves), *Cl* 806, *G* 644
staf *see* **staue**
staf-ful *adj.* cram-full, *G* 494*n*
stage *n.* degree, *Pe* 410
stal(e) *n.*[1] place, *Pe* 1002, *Cl* 1506
stalked *pa.t.* walked (warily), *Pe* 152, *G* 237; strode, *G* 2230
stal(l)e *n.*[2] standing position; **in s.** erect, *G* 104, 107
stalle *v.*[1] check, stop, *Cl* 1184; bring to a stand, *Pe* 188
stalle *v.*[2] (**stalled** *pp.*) install, *Cl* 1334; situate, *Cl* 1378
stalworth *adj.* (**stalworþest** *superl.*) strong, mighty; immovable, *Cl* 983; *as n.* bold knight, *G* 1659
stamyn *n.* prow
stanc *n.* (**stangez** *pl.*) pool, *Cl* 439, 1018
standen, standez, standes *see* **stonde**
stange *n.* pole, *G* 1614
stangez, stank *see* **stanc, stynke**
stape *adj.* advanced, *Pat* 122
stare *n.* power of sight, *Cl* 583
stare *v.* stare, *Pe* 149, *Cl* 389, 787; shine, glitter, *Pe* 116, *Cl* 1506; **starande** *presp.adj.* glittering, *G* 1818
start(e) *v.* start, jump, leap
statut *n.* agreement
staue, staf *n.* staff; club, *G* 2137
staue, stawe, stowe *v.* stow, place, lodge

stayned *pp.* stained, coloured
stayre *adj.* steep, *Pe* 1022
stayre *n.* rung (of a ladder), *Pat* 510*n*
stayred *adj.* arranged as steps, *Cl* 1396
sted(de), stud *n.* place; high place, *Cl* 389; **in s.** there, *G* 439
sted(e) *n.* steed, horse
steke *v.* (**stac, stek(en), stoken** *pa.t.*, **stoken** *pp.*) shut (up), enclose; cling (to), *G* 152; restrain, *Cl* 754; fasten, lock, *Cl* 884; *pp.* fixed, fastened, locked, *Pe* 1065, *Cl* 1524, *G* 33, 782; crammed (**of**: with), *G* 494; imposed on, *G* 2194. *Cf.* **stik**
stel *see* **stele** *v.*.
stel-bawe *n.* stirrup
stel(e) *n.*[1] steel; armour, *G* 570
stele *n.*[2] handle, *G* 214, 2230; upright (of a ladder), *Pat* 510*n*
stele *v.* (**stel(en)** *pa.t.*) steal, creep; take by surprise, *Cl* 1778; **stollen** *pp.adj.* secret, *Cl* 706, surreptitious, *G* 1659
stel-gere *n.* armour
stem(m)e *v.* stop, delay, pause
stepe *n.* step, *Cl* 905; footstep, foot, *Pe* 683
stepe *see also* **step(p)e**
step(p)e *adj.* bright, brilliant, *Pe* 113, *Cl* 583
steppe *v.* (**stepe, stepped** *pa.t.*) step, walk; ascend, *Cl* 1396
stere *v.* guide, control, govern; restrain, *Pe* 1159
sterne *n.*[1] rudder, *Pat* 149
sternes, -z *n.*[2] stars, *Pe* 115, *Pat* 207
sterop, stirop *n.* stirrup
sterrez *n.* stars
steuen *n.*[1] voice, *Cl* 770, *Pat* 73, 307, *G* 242, 2336; sound, noise, *Pe* 1125, *Cl* 1203, 1402, 1524, 1778
steuen *n.*[2] time, time of meeting, appointment, *Cl* 706, *G* 1060, 2008, 2194, 2213, 2238; **at s.** for a meeting, *Pe* 188
steuen *n.*[3] command, *Cl* 360, 463
stif(fe), styf(fe) *adj.* (**stifest, styf(f)est** *superl.*) bold, brave, *G* 34, 260, *etc.*; rigid, *Cl* 983; firm, *Pe* 779, *G* 431, 846; unflinching, *G* 294; strong, *Cl* 255, *Pat* 234, 322, *etc.*; powerful, *G* 176, 1364; vigorous, *G* 104
stifly, styfly *adv.* firmly, *Cl* 157, 352, 1652, *G* 606; boldly, *G* 287, 1716
stiʒtel, styʒtel *v.* rule, be in command, *G* 104, 2213; master, *G* 2137; direct, ordain, *Pat* 402; **s. þe vpon** limit yourself to, *G* 2252; *pp.* directed (**with**: by), *Cl* 90
stik *v.* (**stykked** *pa.t.*) put, fasten, *Cl* 157, 583. *Cf.* **steke**
stille, stylle *adj. & adv.* (**stiller** *compar.*) still; quiet(ly); silent(ly); motionless; silent, dumb, *Cl* 1523; private, secret(ive), *Cl* 589, 706, *G* 1659; in peace and quiet, *G* 1367, *etc.*; in private, *G* 1085, 2385; at rest, *Pe* 683
stilly, stylly *adv.* quietly; stealthily, *Cl* 1778
stirop, stod(e)(n) *see* **sterop, stonde**
stoffed *pp.* filled, *Cl* 1184, lined, padded, *G* 606
stoken *see* **steke**
stokkes, stok(k)ez *n.* (punishment) stocks, *Cl*

46, 157, *Pat* 79; blocks of wood, *Cl* 1343, 1523, *etc.*; *sg.* tree stump, *Pe* 380*n*
stollen *see* **stele** *v.*
stomak *n.* stomach
ston *see* **ston(e)**
stonde, stande *v.* (**stod(e)(n)** *pa.t.* **standen** *pp.*) stand; be present; remain, *Pe* 597; put up with (from), take (from), *G* 294, 2286; shine, *Pe* 113; **s. alofte** stand out, *G* 1818
stonde *see also* **sto(u)nd(e)**
ston(e) *n.* stone, jewel; rock, *Pe* 822, *G* 2166, 2230, *etc.*; pavement, *G* 2063; **by stok oþer s.** anywhere at all, *Pe* 380
stonen *adj.* (made of) stone, *Cl* 995
ston-fyr *n.* flint-sparks
stonge *pa.t.* stung, struck, *Pe* 179
ston-harde *adv.* firmly
ston-stil *adj.* stone-still
stonye *see* **stoune**
stoped *pa.t.* closed up
stor(e) *adj.* powerful, *G* 1923; stern, harsh, *G* 1291
store *n.* supply, number, *Pe* 847
stote *v.* halt, stop, *Pe* 149
sto(u)nd(e) *n.* time; hour, time of hardship, torment, *Cl* 1603; blow, *Cl* 1540; **bi stoundes** at times
stoundez *v.* stupefies, *Pat* 317*n*
stoune, stowne, stonye *v.* astound, stun
stout(e) *adj.* strong, bold, mighty
stoutly *adv.* strongly, loudly; securely, *G* 1614
stowed, stowned *see* **staue, stoune**
strake *v.* (**strakande** *presp.*) sound (on horn)
stratez *see* **stre(e)te**
stra(u)nge, stronge (*Cl* 1494, *G* 1028) *adj.* strange; unnatural; foreign; visiting
stray *adj. or adv.* distracted, in bewilderment, *Pe* 179
stray *v.* stray; slip away, *Pe* 1173
strayn(e), streny *v.* strain; control, *G* 176; constrain, *Pe* 128, *Pat* 234; lead, make go, *Pe* 691; *reflex.* exert oneself, *Pe* 551
strayt *adj.* close-fitting, *G* 152
strayt *adv.* closely, severely, *Cl* 880, 1199
streche *v.* go, make one's way; **on s.** touch, cling to, *Pe* 843
stre(e)te *n.* (**stre(e)tez, stratez** *pl.*) street; highway, *Cl* 77
streʒt *adj.* (stretched); smooth, *G* 152; constricting, *Pat* 234; narrow, *Pe* 691
strem *n.* stream current
stremande *presp.adj.* streaming (with light), *Pe* 115
strenkle *v.* dispel
strenþe, strenkþe, strenghþe *n.* strength, power, intensity; force, *Cl* 880
streny *see* **strayn(e)**
stresse *n.* affliction, anguish, *Pe* 124
stretez, strike *see* **stre(e)te, stryke**
strok(e) *n.* stroke
strok(e) *see also* **stryke**
stronde *n.* shore; bank of stream, *Pe* 152
strong(e) *adj.* (**stronger** *compar.*) strong, powerful; steadfast, *Pe* 476; great, *Pat* 305; severe, *Cl* 1227, 1540. *See also* **stra(u)nge**
strot *n.* wrangling

strothe *n*. wooded marsh (*attrib*.), *G* 1710
stroþe-men *n*. fen-dwellers, men of earth, *Pe* 115*n*
strye *v*. destroy
stryf *n*. strife, contention; struggle, *Pe* 776; resistance, *G* 2323
stryke, strike *v*. (**strok(e)** *pa.t.*) strike; pierce, *Pe* 1125; come, go, *Pe* 570, 1186*n*; fly, *G* 671
stryndez *n*. currents
stryþ(þ)e *n*. stance
stryue *v*. (**stryuande** *presp*.) strive, contend
stubbe *n*. tree stump, *G* 2293
stud *see* **sted(de)**
studie *v*. gaze (to see), ponder
study *n*. thought
sturez *see* **styry**
sturn(e) *adj*. grim, formidable, *G* 334, 494, *etc*.; massive, *G* 143, 846, *etc*.; loud, *Cl* 1402; *as n*. redoubtable knight, *G* 214; **-ly** *adv*. fiercely
styf(est), styffe, styffest *see* **stif(fe)**
styfly *see* **stifly**
styȝe *n*. path, *Pat* 402
styȝe *pa.t.* climbed, *Cl* 389
styȝtel, stykked, stylle, stylly *see* **stiȝtel, stik, stille, stilly**
styngande *presp.adj*. stinging
stynke, stynkke *v*. (**stank** *pa.t.* **stynkande** *presp*.) stink
stynt *v*. (**stynt** *pp*.) cease, stop (**of:** from, *Pe* 353)
styry, sture *v*. (**styryed** *pa.t.*) stir; *trans*. brandish, *G* 331
styþly *adv*. strongly, *G* 431
such(e), seche (*G* 1543) *adj. & pron*. such
sue, sve, sw(y)e *v*. follow, pursue; proceed, go, *Cl* 87
suffer, soffer *v*. suffer, endure; allow, *G* 1967
suffraunce, soffraunce *n*. sufferance, patience
suffyse *v*. be adequate, *Pe* 135
sulp(en) *v*. (**sulpande** *presp*., **sulped** *pp*.) defile, pollute
sum *n*. total; **of al and s.** in full, *Pe* 584
sumkyn *adj*. some (kind of), *Pe* 619
sum(me) *adj. & pron*. some; *adv*. partly, *G* 247 (*contr*. **al** wholly, *G* 246)
sum(m)oun *see* **somones**
sumned *pp*. summoned, *G* 1052
sumquat *adv*. somewhat, a little, *G* 86
sumquat *n*. something, *Cl* 627*n*, *G* 1799
sumquyle, -whyle *adv*. formerly, once (upon a time); sometimes, *G* 720, 721
sumtyme *adv*. formerly, once, at one time; at some time, *Pe* 760; sometime; *Cl* 582
sun, son, soun, sun(n)e *n*. son
sunderlupes *adv*. severally
sunkken *see* **synk**
sunne, sonne *n*. sun; **s. bemez** beams of the sun, *Pe* 83
suppe *v*. sup, drink
supplantorez *n*. usurpers
sure *adj. & adv*. sure, *Pat* 117; firm, *Pe* 1089; reliable, *G* 588; *adv*. firmly, *Pe* 222
surely *adv*. surely, firmly; reliably, *G* 1883
surfet *n*. transgression

surkot *n*. surcoat, gown
surquidré *see* **sourquydrye**
sustnaunce *n*. sustenance
sute, swete *n*. kind, suit; **of (a) s., of self s., of folȝande s., in s.** to match (in colour or pattern), *Pe* 203, 1108, *Cl* 1457, *G* 191, 859, 2518; **of his hors s.** matching that of his horse, *G* 180
sve, swalt(e) *see* **sue, swelt**
swanez *n*. swans
swange *n*. middle, hips
swange *pa.t.* worked, toiled, *Pe* 586
swange *see also* **swynge**
swangeande *presp*. swirling, *Pe* 111
swap *n*. blow, *Cl* 222
swap *v*. strike a bargain, exchange (?), *G* 1108
sware *adj*. square; squarely built, *G* 138
sware *v*. answer
swarmez *v*. swarms
swart *adj*. black
swat *pa.t.* sweated, laboured, *Pe* 586
swayf *n*. swinging blow
swaynes *n*. servants
swayues *n*. sweeps
swe *see* **souȝed, sue**
sweande *presp.adj*. driving, propelling, *Cl* 420 (*cf*. **sweȝe**)
sweft(e) *see* **swyft(e)**
sweȝe, swey *v*. (**sweȝe(d)**, **sweyed** *pa.t.*) go, *Pat* 72; come, *Cl* 788; swing, *G* 1429; drop, *Pat* 151, *G* 1796; *trans*. bring, *Pat* 236
swelme *n*. heat (of suffering), *Pat* 3
swelt *v*. (**swalt(e)** *pa.t.*) perish, die, *Pat* 427, *Pe* 816, 1160; *trans*. destroy, *Cl* 332
swemande *adj*. grievous
sweng *n*. labour, *Pe* 575
swenge *v*. (**swenged** *pa.t.*) swing; rush, hasten, *Cl* 109, 667, *G* 1439, 1615; start, *G* 1756
swepe *v*. hurry, rush, *Cl* 1509; sweep, drift, *Pat* 341; sweep by, flow, *Pe* 111; *trans*. swoop on, catch, *Pat* 250
swere *v*. (**swer(e)** *pa.t.*) swear
swete *adj. & adv*. (**swetter** *compar*., **swettest** *superl*.) sweet, lovely, fair; pure, unsoiled, *Cl* 1810; kind, courteous, *Cl* 640, *Pat* 280; delicious, *Cl* 1521; *as n*. sweet lady, *Pe* 240, *G* 1222; dear (one), *Pe* 325, 763, 829; dear (sir), *G* 1108, 2237; *adv*. sweetly, pleasantly; kindly, graciously, *Pe* 717; *compar*. gentler (one), *Pat* 236; **me were swetter to** I would rather, *Pat* 427*n*
swete *n*. life-blood, *Pat* 364
swete *see also* **sute**
swetely *adv*. kindly, graciously, *Pe* 717; happily, *G* 2034
swetnesse *n*. sweetness
swetter, swettest *see* **swete**
sweþled *pa.t. or pp*. wrapped, *G* 2034
sweued *pa.t.* whirled, swept
sweuen *n*. sleep, dream, *Pe* 62; *pl*. *G* 1756
swey *see* **souȝed, sweȝe**
sweyed *see* **sweȝe**
swoghe *adj*. deathly, *G* 243
swolȝ *n*. throat, *Pat* 250
swolȝed *pa.t. & pp*. swallowed, *Pat* 363; killed, *Cl* 1268

swone *n.* swoon
swowed *pa.t.* fell asleep, *Pat* 442
swyed *see* **sue**
swyerez *n.* squires, young knights
swyft(e), sweft(e), *adj. & adv.* swift(ly)
swyftly *adv.* swiftly
swymme *v.* (**swymmed** *pa.t.*) swim
swyn *n.* swine, boar
swynge *v.* (**swange** *pa.t.*) rush, *Pe* 1059, *G* 1562
swypped *pa.t.* escaped
swyre *n.* neck
swype(e), -ly *adv.* quickly, swiftly; very, *Cl* 816, 1283, *etc.*; greatly, *Cl* 354, 1176, *etc.*; strongly, earnestly, very much, *G* 1479, 1860, 1866, 2034; **as s.** at once
swypez *v.* burns, *Pat* 478
Syboym *n.* Zeboim
syde *adj.* wide, large, *Pat* 353; long, *G* 2431
syde, side *n.* side; direction, *G* 659, 2170; *pl.* surroundings, regions, *Cl* 956, 968
syence, cience *n.* learning; *pl.* different kinds of knowledge, *Cl* 1289
syfle *v.* blow; *reflex. G* 517
syȝ(e) *see* **se(ne)**
syȝt(e), siȝt *n.* sight, vision; look, glance, *Cl* 672, 1005; appearance, *Cl* 1406; **in s.** plainly, *Pat* 530, *G* 28; **se(e) wyth (in) s.** see (with one's own eyes), set eyes on
syked *pa.t.* (**sykande, sykyng** *presp.*) sighed
syker *see* **siker**
sykerly *adv.* securely, *Pat* 301
sykyng *n.* sigh, sighing, *G* 1982; *as presp. Pe* 1175, *G* 753
syled *pa.t.* passed, went
sylk(e), silk(e) *n.* silk; piece of silk, *G* 1846
syluer *n.* silver
syluerin, -en *adj.* silver, of silver; *as n.* **þe s.** the silver (dishes), *G* 124
symbales *n.* cymbals
sympelnesse *n.* sincerity, *Pe* 909
symple *adj.* (**symplest** *superl.*) meek, humble; guileless, *Cl* 746; plain, *G* 503, 1847
syn *see* **sypen**
synful *adj.* sinful; *as n. Cl* 716
syng(e) *v.* (**songe(n)** *pa.t.*) sing; sing the service, *Cl* 7
synglerty *n.* uniqueness, *Pe* 429
synglure *n.* uniqueness, *Pe* 8
syngne *n.* sign
syngnettez *n.* seals, *Pe* 838
synk *v.* (**synkande** *presp.,* **sunkken** *pa.t.,* **sonkken** *pp.*) sink; penetrate, *Cl* 689, *Pat* 507
synne *adv.* since, after, then, *Pat* 229, *G* 19
synne *n.* sin
synne *v.* sin
Syon *n.* Zion
syre, Syre *n.* lord; my Lord, *Pat* 413
syt(e) *n.* grief, sorrow; misfortune, *Pat* 517
sytole-stryng *n.* string of the cithern (type of guitar), *Pe* 91
sytte(n), (-s), (-z) *see* **sitte**
sype *n.*¹ scythe, *G* 2202
sype *n.*² (**sype(s), -z** *pl.*) time, period; *pl.* times, occasions; periods of time, *Cl* 1686; groups (of five), *G* 656

sypen, sipen, syn *adv. & conj.* after, afterwards, next, then, since; because

ta *see* **ta(ke)**
tabarde *n.* jerkin
tabelment *n.* tier (of foundation), *Pe* 994
table *n.* table; tier (of foundation), *Pe* 1004; cornice, *G* 789; **þe Rounde T.** the court of Arthur
tabornes *n.* tabours, small drums
tach(ch)e, tacche *v.* fasten, attach; *pp.* (*fig.*) implanted, *Pe* 464
taȝt *see* **tech(e)**
ta(ke) *v.* (**takes, -z, totz** *pres3s.,* **take(z), tatz** *imperat.,* **tok, toke(n)** *pa.t.,* **take(n), tan, tone** *pp.*) take; seize, capture, catch, *Cl* 836, 943, *etc., Pat* 78, 229, *G* 1210; acquire, receive, get, *Pe* 539, 552, *etc., G* 1396, 2243, 2448; give, offer, *Pe* 1158, *G* 1966; commit, *G* 2159; go, *Pe* 513; discover, find, *Cl* 763, *G* 2488, 2509; *pp.* situated, found, *G* 1811; **a counsayl hym takes** makes a plan, *Cl* 1201; **t. for** recognize as, *Pe* 830; **in theme t.** give an account of, *Pe* 944; **t. in vayne** spend in folly, *Pe* 687; **t. on honde** undertake, *G* 490; **t. to** take upon, *G* 350, 1540; *see also* **ille**
takel *n.* tackle, *Pat* 233; **takles** *pl.* gear, *G* 1129
tale, talle *n.* tale, story; account, statement; words, speech, conversation; message, *Pat* 75
talent *n.* wish, purpose
talentlyf *adj.* desirous
talk(e) *n.* speech, *Cl* 735, *G* 1486
talke *v.* talk, speak, say
talkyng *n.* conversation, *G* 917, 977
talle *see* **tale**
tame *adj.* tame; *as n.* tame animals
tan *see* **ta(ke)**
tapit *n.* tapestry, *G* 77, 858; carpet, *G* 568
tap(p)e *n.* tap, blow
Tarce *n.* Tarshish
tars *n.* rich fabric (*from Tharsia*)
tary *v.* tarry, linger; *trans.* delay, *G* 624
tatz *see* **ta(ke)**
tayl *n.*¹ tail
tayles *n.*² numbers (tallies), *G* 1377*n*
taysed *pp.* driven, *G* 1169
tayt *adj.* merry, *G* 988; attractive, *Cl* 871; well-grown, *G* 1377
tayt *n.* pleasure, *Cl* 889; sport, folly, *Cl* 935
teccheles *adj.* faultless, *G* 917
Techal *n.* Tekel
tech(e) *n.* sign, *Cl* 1049; spot, stain, *Pe* 845, *G* 2436, 2488; defilement, *Cl* 943; sin, *Cl* 1230
tech(e) *v.* (**taȝt** *pa.t.*) teach; direct, show, *Pe* 936, *Cl* 676, *G* 401, 1069, *etc.*
tede *see* **tyȝed**
tee *v.* (**towen** *pp.*) go, proceed, *Cl* 9, 1262, *Pat* 87, 416; *pp.* come, *G* 1093; **towen in twynne** severed (from each other), *Pe* 251
tel *see* **tyl(le)**
telde *n.* house, dwelling
telde *v.* raise, set up; **t. vp** build up, increase, *Cl* 1808

telle *v.* (**tolde** *pa.t.*) tell, speak, say; relate, describe, *Pe* 134; express, utter, *Pe* 815, *Pat* 358; recite, *G* 2188

teme, theme *n.* subject; **in t. layde** discussed, *Pat* 37; **in t. con take** described, *Pe* 944

teme *v.*[1] conceive, *Cl* 655

teme *v.*[2] **t. to** belong to, *Pe* 460, *Cl* 9, *Pat* 316

temple, tempple *n.* temple

tempre *v.* temper, moderate

temptande *presp.adj.* afflicting, *Cl* 283

tempte *v.* test

tender *adj.* tender, *Pe* 412, *Cl* 630; susceptible, liable, *G* 2436

tene *adj.* troublesome, *G* 1707; perilous, *G* 2075; angry, *Cl* 1808

tene *n.* anger, vexation, trouble, pain, grief, *Pe* 332, *G* 547, 1008; harm (inflicted), *Cl* 1232, *G* 22

tene *v.* torment, harass; punish, *Cl* 759; *intrans.* suffer torment, *G* 2501

tenfully *adv.* sorrowfully, bitterly

tenor *n.* purport

tent *v.* attend to; attend on, accompany, *Cl* 676; tend, *Pat* 498

tent(e) *n.* care, notice, *Pe* 387; **in t.** in a mind, *G* 624

tenoun *n.* joint, joinery; **of riche t.** admirably joined, *Pe* 993

tenþe *adj.* tenth

teres *n.* tears

terme *n.* limit, border, *Pat* 61; beginning, *Pe* 503; appointed time, *Cl* 1393; appointment, *G* 1671; trysting place, *G* 1069; period, *Cl* 239, 568; duration, *Pat* 505; word, expression, *Cl* 1733, *G* 917; **in termez** expressly, plainly, *Pe* 1053

terne *n.* lake

teþe *see* tothe

teueled *pa.t.* contended, *Cl* 1189

teuelyng *n.* striving, endeavour, *G* 1514

th- *see also* **þ-**

thaȝ *see* **þaȝ**

Thanes *n. see Cl* 448n

that, thay *see* **þat, þay**

the *see* **þe, þou**

theme, then(ne), ther(e), these, thik *see* **teme, þen(e), þer(e), þis, þik(ke)**

this, thow *see* **þis, þou**

t(h)rone *n.* throne

thus, thys, tid, til(le), tit(e) *see* **þus, þis, tyd, tyl(le), tyd**

titleres *n.* hounds (*specif.* those kept in reserve at a relay), *G* 1726

to *adv.* to, up, there; too, *Pe* 481, 492, *etc.*, *Cl* 22, 182, *etc.*, *Pat* 128, 425, *G* 165, 719, *etc.*

to *prep.* to, into, towards, at; against, *Cl* 1230; in, *Pat* 58; from, *Cl* 1586; for, *Pe* 507, 508, *etc.*, *Cl* 204, 309, *etc.*, *Pat* 98, *G* 420, *etc.*; as, *Pe* 759; as regards, *Cl* 174, 315, *etc.*; according to, *Cl* 1604; until, *Cl* 1032, *Pat* 317, *etc.*, *G* 71, *etc.*; in order to, *Pe* 507, *etc.*, *Cl* 107, *etc.*, *Pat* 97, *etc.*, *G* 43, *etc.*; as to, *G* 291; **to mede** as a reward, *Pat* 55; **to meruayle** (as) a marvel, amazing, *G* 1197; **for to** in order to; **gripped to, laȝt to,** *etc.* took hold of, *G* 421, 433, *etc.*

to *n.* toe, *Cl* 1691, *Pat* 229

tocleue *v.* cleave asunder

toclose *adv.* together, *Cl* 1541n

tocoruen *see* **tokerue**

todrawe *v.* dispel, *Pe* 280

tofylched *pa.t.* pulled down

togeder(e) *adv.* together

toȝe *adj.* tough, *Cl* 630

to-ȝere *adv.* this year, *Pe* 588n

toȝt *adj.* hardy, *G* 1869; **made hit t.** made it firm, made an agreement of it, *Pe* 522

tohewe *v.* cut down

tok(e)(n) *see* **ta(ke)**

token *n.* token; **in t. of** as a symbol of, *Pe* 742

tokened *pa.t.* signified, *Cl* 1557

tokenyng *n.* sign; **in t.** to signify, as a sign, *G* 2488

tokerue *v.* (**tocoruen** *pa.t.*) divide, *Cl* 1700; cut to pieces, *Cl* 1250

tolde, tole(s), tolk(e) *see* **telle, tool, tulk**

tolouse, tulé, tuly *n.* rich red fabric (from Toulouse), *G* 77, 568, 858

Tolowse *n.* Toulouse, *Cl* 1108n

tom *n.* leisure, time; opportunity, *Cl* 1153; interval, *Pat* 135

tomarred *pp.* spoiled, disfigured, *Cl* 1114n; (*cf.* **marre** *v.*[1])

tomorn(e) *adv.* tomorrow (morning)

tomurte *pa.t.* broke

tone *see* **ta(ke)**

tong(e) *n.* tongue

tool, tole *n.* (cutting) tool; weapon

top *n.* hair of the head, *Pat* 229

topasye, topace *n.* topaz; *pl. Cl* 1469

toppyng *n.* forelock, *G* 191

topreue *v.* prove conclusively, *Pat* 530

tor *n.* (**torres, -z, toures, towres** *pl.*) tower, stronghold; towering cloud, *Pe* 875n, *Cl* 951

tor *see also* **tor(e)**

toraced *pp.* pulled down, *G* 1168

tor(e) *adj.* difficult

torent(e) *pa.t. & pp.* tore (torn) apart

toret *pp.* (*for* **toret-ed**) with embroidered hem, *G* 960

toriuen *see* **torof**

Torkye *n.* Turkey

tormenttourez *n.* torturers

tornayeez *see* **to(u)rnaye**

torne *pp. & adj.* torn, *Cl* 1234, *Pat* 233, *G* 1579

torne *see also* **t(o)urne**

torof *pa.t.* (**toriuen** *pp.*) *intrans.* tore asunder, *Cl* 964; *trans.* tore, *Pat* 379; *pp.* shattered, *Pe* 1197

torres *see* **tor**

tortors *n.* turtle-doves, *G* 612

toruayle *n.* task, trouble

tote *v.* peep, *G* 1476

totez *n.* points (toes) of the shoes

totered *pa.t.* tottered

tothe *n.* (**teþe** *pl.*) tooth

totorne *pp. adj.* torn, ragged

totz, touch *see* **ta(ke), towche**

toun(e) *n.* town, city; court, *G* 31, 614; homestead, *Cl* 64; **out of t.** away, *G* 1049

tour *n.* entourage, *Cl* 216

toures *see* **tor**

to(u)rnaye *v.* double back, *G* 1707; joust, tourney, *G* 41

t(o)urne, torne *v.* turn; repent, *Pat* 506, 518; return, *G* 1099; go, make one's way, *Cl* 64, *G* 2075; **t. to hele** become sound, *Cl* 1099; *pp.* changing, turbulent, *G* 22

tournez *n.* deeds, acts, *Cl* 192

tow *see* **tweyne**

towalten *pa.t.* overflowed, burst forth, *Cl* 428

toward(e) *prep.* toward(s); *also* **to ... warde** *Pe* 820, *G* 1200, *and cf.* **fro me warde,** *Pe* 981

towch(e), tuch *n.* touch, *Pat* 252; deed, action, *Cl* 48; covenant, *G* 1677; tone, strain, *G* 120; hint, *G* 1301

towche, touch *v.* touch; taste, *Cl* 245; reach, *Cl* 1393; tell, relate, *Cl* 1437, *G* 1541

towe *v.* take, *Pat* 100

towen *see* **tee**

towrast *adj.* awry, *G* 1663

towres *see* **tor**

tramme *n.* gear, tackle, *Pat* 101; device, plot, *G* 3

tramountayne *n.* north

trante *v.* twist, dodge, *G* 1707

tras *n.* course, way; **trone a t.** made (their) way, *Pe* 1113

traschez *n.* rags, ragged clothes, *Cl* 40

trased *pp.* set, *G* 1739

trauayl(e) *n.* labour, *Pe* 1087, *Pat* 505; journey, *G* 2241

trauayle *v.* labour, work, *Pe* 550, *Pat* 498; *pp.* had a hard journey, *G* 1093

traunt *n.* cunning practice, *G* 1700

trauthe, trauþe *see* **trawþe**

traw(e), trave, trow, trow(e) *v.* believe, think, be sure; trust, *G* 2238; hope, *Cl* 388

trawþe, traweþ, trauthe, -þe *n.* (word of) honour, *Cl* 63, 667, *Pat* 336, *G* 394, 403, *etc.*; pledge, loyalty, integrity, *Cl* 236, *G* 626, 2470; righteousness, *Cl* 723; truth, *Pe* 495, *Cl* 1490, 1736, *G* 1050; **in t., with t.** truly, *Cl* 1703, *G* 1057, 1108

trayle *v.* trail, follow a trail, *G* 1700

trayled *pp.adj.* ornamented (with a pattern of trailing foliage), *Cl* 1473

traysoun, tresoun *n.* treason

trayst *adj.* sure

trayto(u)r *n.* traitor; *gen.pl. Cl* 1041

trayþ(e)ly *adv.* ?ferociously, grievously, *Cl* 907, 1137

tre *n.* tree; wood, *Cl* 1342; *pl.* trees, *Pe* 1077, *Cl* 1041; planks, *Cl* 310, *Pat* 101 (**on þo tres** on board)

trede *v.* walk

treleted *pp.* with (lace) lattice work, *G* 960

trendeled *pa.t. reflex.* rolled, *Pe* 41

tres *see* **tre**

tresor(e) *n.* treasure, *Pe* 331, *Cl* 866; price, value, *Pe* 237

tresorye *n.* treasury, *Cl* 1317

tresoun *see* **traysoun**

tresour *n.* treasurer, *Cl* 1437

trespas *v.* (**trespast** *pp.*) sin, transgress

tressour *n.* hair-fret, *G* 1739

trestes, -z *n.* trestles

trewest *see* **trwe**

trichcherye, tricherie, trecherye *n.* treachery

tried, trifel *see* **tryȝe, tryfle**

troched, trochet *pp.adj.* crocketed

tron(e) *see* **t(h)rone, trynande**

trot *n.* trot, run

trow, trowe(e) *see* **traw(e)**

Troye *n.* Troy

true *n.* truce, *G* 1210

true *see also* **trwe**

trulofez, truly *see* **trw(e)luf, trw(e)ly**

trumpen, -s, -z *n.* trumpets

trusse *v.* pack (up), stow away

trwe, true *adj.* (**trewest** *superl.*) true, correct, right; faithful, virtuous, trustworthy; firm (*fig.*), *Pe* 822; *as n. Cl* 702, *G* 2354; *adv.* firmly, truly, *Pe* 460

trw(e)luf *n.* true love; **trulofez** *pl.* true-love flowers, *G* 612

trw(e)ly, truly, *adv.* truly, faithfully

tryed *see* **tryȝe**

tryfle, trifel *n.*[1] trifle, pleasantry, *G* 108, 1301; idle talk, *G* 547; detail, *G* 165, ?960 (*see next*)

tryfle *n.*[2] trefoil, ?*G* 960 (*cf. n.*[1])

tryfled *adj.* ornamented with trefoils, *Cl* 1473

tryȝe *v.* (**tryed, tried** *pp.*) test, *Pe* 311n; *pp.* tried judicially, *Pe* 707, *G* 4; *adj.* chosen, choice, fine, distinguished

trylle *v.* quiver, *Pe* 78

trynande *presp.* going, *Cl* 976; **tron(e)** *pa.t.* went, *Pe* 1113, *Cl* 132, *Pat* 101

tryst(e) *v.* believe, depend (**þerto:** upon that), *G* 2325; rely on, *G* 380; **mukel to t.** greatly to be depended on, very trustworthy, *Pat* 324

tryste *adv.* faithfully, *Pe* 460

trystor, -er *n.* hunting station

trysty *adj.* faithful, *Cl* 763

trystyly *adv.* faithfully, *G* 2348

tuch *see* **towch(e)**

tulé, tuly *see* **tolouse**

tulk, tolk(e) *n.* (**tulk(k)es** *pl.*) man, knight

tulket *pa.t.* sounded, *Cl* 1414

tult, turne(d) *see* **tylte, t(o)urne**

tuschez *n.* tusks

Tuskan *n.* Tuscany

twayne *see* **tweyne**

twayned *pp.* separated, parted, *Pe* 251

twelfþe *adj.* twelfth

twelmonyth *n. & adv.* twelvemonth, year; *adv.* a year hence, ago

twelue *adj.* twelve

twenty-folde *adv.* twenty times

tweyne, twayne, two, tow *adj.* two

twiges *n.* twigs, branches

twyez, twy(e)s *adv.* twice

twynande *presp.* entwining; **twynnen** *pp.* plaited, *G* 191

twynne *adj. as n.* two; **in t., on t.** in two, apart

twynne *v.* part, be separated, *Cl* 402, *G* 2512

twynne-hew *adj.* two-coloured

twynne, twys *see* **twynande, twyez**

tyd, tyt, tid, tit(e) *adv.* quickly, at once; **a(l)s, also t.** as quickly as possible, very quickly, immediately; **tytter** *compar.* sooner, *Pat* 231

tyde *n.* time, occasion; time of year, season, *G* 585, 2086; **hyȝe t.** festival
tydez *v.* befalls, is due to, *G* 1396
tyffe *v.* prepare, *G* 1129
tyȝed, tyȝt, tede *pp.* joined together; fixed, fastened, *Pe* 464, 1013
tyȝt *v.* (**tyȝt(e)** *pa.t.* **tyȝt** *pp.*) intend, *G* 2483; manage, succeed, *Cl* 1108; grant, appoint, *Cl* 1153; set forth, *Pe* 1053; spread, *G* 568, 858; come, *Pe* 503, 718; *reflex.* go on one's way, *Cl* 889
tykle *adj. as n.* uncertain, *Cl* 655
tyl(le), til(le), tel *conj. & prep.* until; **t. . . . þat** until; *prep.* to, *Pe* 676, *Cl* 882, 1174; *G* 673, 1979; **lykne t.** resemble, *Cl* 1064; **folȝe t.** serve, *Cl* 1752
tylte *v.* (**tult** *pa.t.*, **tylt** *pp.*) tumble; knock, *Cl* 1213; lean, *Cl* 832
tymbres *n.* timbrels, tambourines, *Cl* 1414
tyme *n.* time, period, occasion; **by tymez** on occasions, *G* 41
tymed *pp.* timed
tynde *n.* branch, *Pe* 78
tyne *n.* moment, *Pat* 59
tyne *v.* (**tynt** *pa.t.*) destroy, finish, *Cl* 775, 907; lose, *Pe* 332, *Cl* 216, *Pat* 500, 505
tyned *pa.t.* shut, enclosed, *Cl* 498
Tyntagelle *n.* Tintagel
type *v.* throw; **t. down** overthrow, *Pat* 506
typped *adj.* consummate, extreme, *Pat* 77n
tyrauntez *n.* evil men, *Cl* 943
tyrauntyré *n.* tyranny
tyrue *v.*[1] strip (**of:** off), *Cl* 630, *G* 1921
tyrue *v.*[2] overturn, *Cl* 1234
tyt *see also* **tyd**
tytel, tytle *n.* right, *G* 480, 626
tytelet *pp.* inscribed as a title, *G* 1515
tytter *see* **tyd**
type *adj.* tenth
typyng, typynges, -ez *n.* tidings, information
tyxt(e) *n.* text; (actual) words, *Cl* 1634; passage, *Pat* 37; heading, rubric, *G* 1515; **temez of t.** subject matter, *G* 1541

þ' *see* **þe**
þad *see* **þat** *demonstr.*
þaȝ, thaȝ *conj.* though; even though; even if; if, *Pe* 368, *Cl* 743, *G* 496, 2282, 2307, 2427
þanne *see* **þen(n)(e)**
þar *v.* need, *G* 2355
þare, þore *adv.* there, then, on that occasion; in that respect, *G* 2356
þat *conj.* that, so that; *see also* **bi, for, with**
þat, that, þad (*G* 686) *demonstr.adj. & pron.* (**þo, þos(e)** *pl.*) that, the; *pl.* those, the; **þat ilk(e)** the same; **þat on, þat oþer** the one, the other. *See also* **þo, þos(e)**
þat *rel.pron.* who(m), which, that; what, that which, *Pe* 327, 521, *etc.*, *Cl* 652, 898, *etc.*, *Pat* 178, 336, *G* 291, 391, *etc.*
þay, thay *pron.* (**hem, him, hom, hym** *acc. & dat.*) they
þayr *possess.adj.* their
þayres *pron.(possess.)* theirs
þe, þ', the *def.art.* the
þe, the *adv.w.compar.* (so much) the (farther,

etc.), *Pe* 127, *etc.*, *Cl* 296, *Pat* 6, 34, *etc.*, *G* 87, *etc.*
þe *relat. pron.* who, *Pat* 56
þe *see also* **þou**
þede *n.* land, country, *Pe* 483, *G* 1499
þeder *see* **þider**
þef *n.* thief, *Pe* 273, *G* 1725
þefte *n.* theft
þen(e), þenn(e), then(ne), þanne *adv. & conj.* then, *Pe* 155, 277, *etc.*, *Cl* 15, 53, *etc.*, *Pat* 7, 33, *etc.*, *G* 116, 301, *etc.*; than, *Pe* 134, 555, *etc.*, *Cl* 76, 168, *etc.*, *Pat* 8, 48, *etc.*, *G* 24, 236, *etc. See also* **er(e)**
þenk(ke), þynke (*Cl* 749) *v.* (**þoȝt(en)** *pa.t.*, **þoȝt** *pp.*) think, consider, remember; intend, *Pe* 1151, *Cl* 304, 711, *etc.*, *G* 331, 1023; decide, *Cl* 138; **þ.** (**vp**)**on** bear in mind, *Pe* 370, *Cl* 819, *Pat* 294, *G* 2052, 2397. *See also* **þynk(k)(e)**
þenne *adv.* thence, *Cl* 1089
þerabof *adv.* above (it), *Cl* 1481, *Pat* 382
þeraboute *adv.* (working) at it, *G* 613; thereabouts, *Cl* 1796, *G* 705; round it, *G* 2485
þerafter *adv.* after(wards), behind, *G* 671; again, *G* 2418
þeralofte *adv.* on it, *G* 569
þeramongez *adv.* with it, *G* 1361
þeranvnder *adv.* underneath, *Cl* 1012
þeras *see* **þer(e)as**
þerat(t)e *adv.* at that, at it, to it, there
þerby, þerbi *adv.* near there, around it, *Cl* 1034; on them (the trumpets), *Cl* 1404, *G* 117
þerbyside, -syde *adv.* beside it, *G* 1925; near by, *Cl* 673
þer(e), ther(e) *adv. & conj.* there; then, on that occasion, *Cl* 203, 216, *Pat* 135, *etc.*; *conj.* where, when, as, *Pe* 26, 30, *etc.*, *Cl* 158, 238, *etc.*, *Pat* 37, *etc.*, *G* 195, 334, *etc. See also* **þare**
þer(e)as *conj.* where; in which, *Cl* 24; as, *Pe* 129
þerfor(e), þerforne *adv.* therefore, for that reason; for it, *G* 1107
þerin(ne), þerine *adv.* therein, in it, in them, there, in that place; in that (course), *Pe* 1168; *relat.* in which, *G* 17
þerof *adv.* thereof, of it; from it, from them, from there, *Pe* 1069, *Cl* 1499, 1507; because of that, *Cl* 972
þeron *adv.* on there, on that, on it; in them, *Cl* 1719; for it, *Pe* 645; of it, *Pe* 387
þerouer *adv.* above
þeroute *adv.* out, out of it (them); outside; out of doors, *Pe* 930, *Cl* 807, *G* 2000, 2481; overboard, *Pat* 153, *etc.*
þerto *adv.* at it, there, to it (them), *Pe* 664, *Cl* 1394, *G* 219, *etc.*; with these, *Pe* 833; to (do) that, *Pe* 172; for that, *Pe* 1140; for that purpose, *Cl* 701; accordingly, *G* 757
þertylle *adv.* to it, to that place, there
þerþurȝe *adv.* through it, *Pat* 354
þerue *adj.* unleavened, *Cl* 635
þervnder *adv.* underneath (it)
þervpone *adv.* upon it, *Cl* 1665
þerwyth, þerwith *adv.* with (by) it, with them; at this, about this, *Cl* 138, 1501, *G* 1509; through it, by means of it, *Pat* 60; thereupon, *Cl* 528, *Pat* 232, *G* 121

þes(e) *see* þis
þester *n.* darkness
þewed *pp.* endowed with virtue, *Cl* 733
þewes, -z *n.*[1] noble qualities, virtues; courteous manners
þewes *n.*[2] thieves, *Cl* 1142
þi *see* þy
þider, þeder, þyder *adv.* thither, to it, there
þiderwarde *adv.* in that direction
þik(ke), þike, þyk(ke), thik *adj. & adv.* (þik(k)er *compar.adv.*) thick(ly), close(ly), dense(ly); burly, thick-set, *G* 138, 175; frequent, *Cl* 952; hard, fast, *G* 1702; with (such) clatter, *Cl* 1416; insistently, *G* 1770; *compar.* more closely, *Cl* 1384, more intensely, *Pat* 6
þing(es), þingez, þink(ez) *see* þyng(e)
þink(kez) *see also* þynk(k)(e)
þirled, þurled *pa.t.* pierced, *Cl* 952, *G* 1356
þis, þise, þys(e), þysse, this, thys *adj. & pron.* (þis(e), þes(e), þyse, these *pl.*) this; the (usual), *Pe* 42, 505, *Cl* 428, *G* 1139*n*, *etc.*; = þis is *G* 2398
þiself *see* þyself
þo *adj. & pron.* those, the; *pron.* them, *Pe* 557; (five) such, *Pe* 451*n*
þof, þoȝ *conj.* though
þoȝt(e) *n.* thought
þoȝt(en) *v. see* þenk(ke), þynk(k)(e)
þole *v.* endure; allow, *G* 1859
þonk(e), þonc *n.* thank(s)
þonk(ke) *v.* thank
þoo *adv.* then, *Pe* 873
þore, þorȝ *see* þare, þurȝ(e)
þorne *n.* (þornez *pl.*) thorn(s), *G* 2529; thorn bush, *G* 1419
þorpes *n.* villages
þos(e) *adj. & pron.* those; them, *Pe* 515
þou, þow, thow *pron.* thou; þe, the *acc. & dat.* thee
þowsande(z), þousandez *n.* thousands
þrad *pp.* punished, *Cl* 751
þral *n.* serf, fellow, *Cl* 135
þrange *adv.* grievously, *Pe* 17
þrast *n.* thrust, onslaught, *G* 1443
þrat(ten) *see* þret(e)
þrawen, þrawez *see* þrow(e)
þre *adj.* three
þred *n.* thread; limit, *G* 1771
þrefte *adj.* unleavened, *Cl* 819
þrenge *see* þrynge
þrep(e) *n.* contradiction, dispute, *Cl* 350; contest, *G* 2397; insistence, *G* 1859
þrepe *v.* contend, *G* 504
þrepyng *n.* strife, quarrelling
þresch *v.* (thresh, thrash); strike, *G* 2300
þret(e), þrat *n.* compulsion, force, *Pat* 55, 267, *G* 1499
þrete *v.* (þrat(en) *pa.t.* þreted *pp.*) urge, *G* 1980; urge on, *Cl* 937; threaten, *Cl* 680, *G* 1725, 2300; attack, *G* 1713; rebuke, *Cl* 1728; wrangle, *Pe* 561
þretty, þretté *adj.* thirty
þreuenest *see* þryuen
þrich *n.* rush, *G* 1713
þrid *see* þryd(de)

þro *adj.* eager, earnest, *G* 645, 1751; fierce, *G* 1713 (*as n.*), 2300, proud, noble, *Pe* 868; stubborn, impatient, *Pe* 344; packed, hectic, *G* 1021
þro *adv.* eagerly, earnestly, *G* 1867, 1946; thoroughly, fully, *Cl* 1805; violently, *Cl* 220; quickly, *Cl* 590
þro *n.* anger, resentment, *Cl* 754, *Pat* 6, 8
þrobled *pa.t.* (þrublande *presp.*) crowded
þroly *adv.* violently, quickly; earnestly, *G* 939
þrong(e) *n.* throng, crowd
þrong(en) *see also* þrynge
þrote *n.* throat
þrow(e), þraw *v.* (þrwe(n) *pa.t.* þrawen, þrowen *pp.*) throw; rush, fly, *Cl* 590, *Pat* 267; fall violently, *Cl* 220; crowd, *Cl* 879; roll, *Pe* 875; þ. forth give vent to, *Pat* 8; þrawen, þrowen *pp. & adj.* laid, *G* 1740; twisted, drawn up, *G* 194; turned, *Cl* 516; crowded, packed, *Cl* 504, 1384; dense, *Cl* 1775; muscular, *G* 579
þrowe *n.* time, while, *G* 2219
þrublande (þrobled *pa.t.*) crowding, jostling
þrwe(n) *see* þrow(e)
þrych *v.* (þryȝt *pa.t. & pp.*) oppress, *Pe* 17; push down, flatten, *G* 1443; crowd, *Cl* 1687; *pp.* pushed, brought (with difficulty), *Pe* 670; pierced, *Pe* 706; imprinted on, *G* 1946; packed, in a throng, *Pe* 926; crowded, iammed, *Cl* 135
þryd(de), þryde, þrid *adj. & pron.* third
þrye(s), þryse, þryez *adv.* thrice, three times
þryf *see* þryue
þryftyly *adv.* in a seemly manner, *Cl* 635
þryȝt *see* þrych
þrynge, þrenge *v.* (þronge, þrong(en) *pa.t.*) press, crowd; go, pass, hasten; rush, *Cl* 180; þ. after follow, serve, belong to, *Cl* 930, 1639
þrynne *adj.* three; in þ. in three words, *Cl* 1727
þryuande *presp.adj.* worthy, *Cl* 751; hearty, *G* 1980; -ly *adv.* heartily, abundantly, *G* 1080, 1380
þryue, þryf *v.* (þryued *pa.t.subjunc.*, *Pat* 521) thrive, flourish; so mot I þ. as as I hope to prosper, upon my soul, *G* 387
þryuen *pp.adj.* (þreuenest, þryuenest *superl.*) fine, noble; fair, lovely
þuȝt *see* þynk(k)(e)
þulged *pa.t.* indulged, bore (with), *G* 1859
þunder *n.* thunder
þunder-þrast *n.* thunderbolt
þurȝ(e), þorȝ *prep. & adv.* through, throughout; because of, by, by means of, through, *Pe* 413, 640, *etc.*, *Cl* 236, 241, *etc.*, *Pat* 257, 284, *etc.*, *G* 91, 998, *etc.*; beyond, *G* 645, 1080; *adv.* through, *G* 1356
þurȝout *adv.* throughout, everywhere
þurȝoutly *adv.* completely, *Pe* 859
þurled *see* þirled
þus, thus *adv.* thus
þwarle *adj.* intricate, *G* 194
þwong *n.* thong, lace
þy, þyn, þi(n) *possess.adj. & pron.* thy, thine
þyder *see* þider
þyȝez *n.* thighs

þyk(ke), þyn *see* **þik(ke), þy**
þyng(e), þing, þink, þynk *n.* thing, matter, something; person, *Pe* 771, *G* 1526
þynk(k)(e), þink *v.impers.* (**þoȝt, þuȝt** *pa.t.*) (**me**) **þynk**, (**me**) **þynkkez,** *etc.* it seems (to me, *etc.*); *sometimes crossed with* **þenk(ke)**, *esp. in pa.t.*; seem good (to you), *G* 1502
þynke *see also* **þenk(ke)**
þys(e) *see* **þis**
þyself, þiself, þyseluen *pron.* thyself
þysse *see* **þis**

uengaunce, uenged, ueray, uerayly, uesture, uisage, uoched *see* **vengaunce, venge, ver(r)ay, verayly, vesture, vysayge, vouche**
uyage *n.* journey, *G* 535
uyne *see* **vyne**

valay *n.* valley
vale *n.* valley
vanist *pa.t.* vanished
vanyté *n.* vanity, folly
vayl *v.* (**vayled** *pa.t.*) be effective, *Pe* 912; be of service, be used, *Cl* 1151; be of value, *Cl* 1311
vayles *n.* veils, *G* 958
vayn(e) *adj.* vain, useless; **in v.** in folly, *Pe* 687; at nought, *Pe* 811
vayned *see* **wayne**
vayneglorie *n.* pride
vayres *n.* truth, *G* 1015
vch(e), vuche, iche *adj.* each, every, (all); *also* **vch(e) a; v. wy, haþel, lede,** *etc.* everyone
vch(e)on(e) *pron.* each one, every one; **v. . . . oþerez** each one . . . the other's
veluet *n.* velvet
vengaunce, uengaunce, vengiaunce *n.* vengeance, retribution
venge, weng *v.* (**uenged, venged, wenged** *pa.t.*) take vengeance, punish; avenge; *reflex. Pat* 71
ven(k)quyst *pa.t.* (**venkkyst** *pp.*) overcame
venture *n.* hazard, peril, *G* 2482
venym *n.* venom, poison
venysoun *n.* venison
ver *n.* spring, *G* 866n
veray *see* **ver(r)ay**
verayly, uerayly *adv.* truly
verce *n.* verse
verdure *n.* green(ness)
vere *v.* turn, *Pe* 177, 254
vergyn, vyrgyn *n.* virgin; **v. flour** virginity, *Pe* 426
vergyn(y)té *n.* virginity
Vernagu *n.* Vernagu, *Pat* 165n
ver(r)ay, ueray *adj.* true; *as adv.* truly, faithfully, *Pat* 333
vertu(e) *n.* virtue; power, *Pat* 284
vertu(o)us *adj.* potent, *Cl* 1280, *G* 2027n
vessel, vessayl *n.* vessel; vessels (*collective*)
vesselment *n.* vessels (*collective*)
vesture, u- *n.* clothing; *pl.* vestments, *Cl* 1288
veued *see* **wayue**
vewters *n.* keepers of hounds, *G* 1146
vgly *adj.* (**vglokest** *superl.*) ugly, gruesome, *Cl*

892, *G* 441; threatening, *G* 2079; oppressive, *G* 2190
vȝten *n.* early morning
vice, vyse *n.* vice
vilanous *adj.* ill-bred, *G* 1497
vilanye, vyla(y)ny(e) *n.* ill-breeding, discourtesy, *Cl* 863, *G* 345; *shifting towards* degeneracy, villainy, wickedness, sin, evil, *Cl* 544, 574, *Pat* 71, *G* 634, 2375
vilté *n.* vileness, *Cl* 199
vmbe *adv. & prep.* (a)round, about
vmbebrayde *pa.t.* greeted, accosted, *Cl* 1622
vmbeclypped *pa.t.* encircled, ringed, *G* 616
vmbefolde *v.* envelop, *G* 181
vmbegon *pp.* encompassing, *Pe* 210
vmbegrouen *adj.* covered, grown over
vmbekeste *v.* (**vmbekesten** *pa.t.pl.*) cast about, search around, *Cl* 478, *G* 1434
vmbelappe *v.* interlace, *G* 628
vmbelyȝe *v.* surround, *Cl* 836
vmbepyȝte *pp.* arrayed about, *Pe* 204, 1052
vmbeschon *pa.t.* shone around, *Pat* 455
vmbestounde(s) *adv.* sometimes; some time (or other), *Pat* 122
vmbesweyed *adj.* surrounded, *Cl* 1380
vmbeteȝe *pa.t.* enclosed, *G* 770
vmbetorne *adv.* round, *G* 184
vmbeþour *adv.* around the outside, *Cl* 1384
vmbewalt *pa.t.* surrounded, *Cl* 1181
vmbeweued *v.* enveloped, *G* 581
vmbre *n.* shadow
vnavysed *pp.adj.* thoughtless, *Pe* 292
vnbarred *pp.* unbarred
vnbene *adj.* cheerless, *G* 710
vnblemyst *pp.adj.* unblemished
vnblyþe *adj.* unhappy, *G* 746; dismal, *Cl* 1017
vnbrosten *adj.* unbroken
vnbynde *v.* separate, divide, *G* 1352
vncely *adj.* ill-fated, hapless, *G* 1562
vncheryst *pp.* uncared for
vnclannes(se) *n.* uncleanness, impurity
vnclene *adj.* unclean, impure
vncler *adj.* indistinct
vnclose *v.* disclose, *Cl* 26; open, *Cl* 1438, *G* 1140
vncortayse *adj.* discourteous
vncoupled *pa.t.* uncoupled
vncowþe, vncouþe *adj.* unknown, strange
vndefylde *pp.adj.* undefiled
vnder *adv.* below, underneath, *G* 158, 742, 868; down, *G* 2318n
vnder *n.* the third hour (9 a.m.), *Pe* 513; **myd ouer vnder** well on in the afternoon, *G* 1730n
vnder *prep.* under; dressed in, *G* 260; **v. God, v. heuen, v. mone,** *etc.*, on earth
vnderȝede *pa.t.* understood, *Cl* 796
vndernomen *pa.t.* understood, *Pat* 213
vnderstonde *v.* understand; **to v.** that is to say, *Pe* 941
vndertake *v.* discern, understand, *G* 1483
vndo *v.* (**vndyd** *pa.t.*) cut open, *G* 1327; destroy, *Cl* 562
vneþe *adv.* hardly, scarcely
vnfayre *adj. or adv.* horrible, hideous(ly), *Cl* 1801, *G* 1572

vnfolde *v.* open, *Cl* 962; disclose, *Cl* 1563
vnfre *adj.* ignoble, *Cl* 1129
vngarnyst *adj.* not properly dressed, *Cl* 137
vnglad *adj.* unhappy
vngoderly *adj.* base, vile
vnhap *n.* misfortune
vnhap *v.* unfasten, *G* 2511
vnhappen *adj.* ill-fated, accursed
vnhardeled *pa.t.* unleashed, *G* 1697
vnhaspe *v.* disclose, *Cl* 688
vnhole *adj.* unsound, insane, *Cl* 1681
vnhonest *adj.* impure, *Cl* 579
vnhuled *see* **vnhyle**
vnhyde *v.* reveal, *Pe* 973
vnhyle *v.* (**vnhuled** *pp.*) uncover
vnknawen *adj.* unknown, unexplored, *Cl* 1679
vnkyndely *adv.* unnaturally, discourteously, *Cl* 208
vnlace *v.* cut up, *G* 1606
vnlapped *adj.* unbound, *Pe* 214
vnleuté *n.* faithlessness, *G* 2499
vnlouked *pa.t.* opened, *G* 1201
vnlyke *adj.* different, *G* 950
vnmanerly *adv.* discourteously
vnmard *adj.* undefiled, *Cl* 867
vnmete *adj.* monstrous, *G* 208; unfitting, *Pe* 759
vnneuened *pp.adj.* not mentioned, *Cl* 727
vnnynges *n.* signs, *Pat* 213
vnpynne *v.* unbolt, open, *Pe* 728
vnresounable *adj.* unreasonable
vnrydely *adv.* confusedly, *G* 1432
vnryȝt *n.* wrong, crime, *Cl* 1142
vnsaueré *adj.* disagreeable, *Cl* 822
vnslayn *pp.adj.* not killed
vnslyȝe *adj.* incautious, *G* 1209
vnsmyten *adj.* unharmed, unpunished
vnsounde *adj.* diseased, corrupt, *Cl* 575; ragged (clothes), *Pat* 527
vnsounde *n.* misfortune, trouble, *Pat* 58;
vnsoundely, vnsoundyly *adv.* mortally, harshly, *Cl* 201; menacingly, *G* 1438
vnsparely *adv.* in plenty, *G* 979
vnspurd *pp.* (he being) unasked, *i.e.* without asking him, *G* 918
vnstered *adj.* undisturbed, *Cl* 706
vnstrayned *pp.adj.* untroubled (**of**: by), *Pe* 248
vnswolȝed *pp.adj.* unconsumed, *Cl* 1253
vnto, vnte *prep.* to; as, *Pe* 772
vntrawþe *n.* perfidy, dishonesty (*see* **trawþe**), *G* 2383, 2509
vntrwe *adj.* untrue, false; unfaithful
vntwyne *v.* destroy, *Cl* 757
vntyȝtel *see* **dele**
vnþewez *n.* faults, vices
vnþonk *n.* disfavour, displeasure
vnþryfte *n.* wickedness
vnþryftyly *adv.* wickedly, improperly
vnþryuande *presp.adj.* unworthy, ignoble, *G* 1499
vnþryuandely *adv.* meanly, *Cl* 135
vnwar *adj.* ignorant, foolish
vnwaschen *adj.* unwashed
vnwelcum *adj.* unwelcome
vnworþelych *adj.* shameful, *Cl* 305

vnworþi, -y *adj.* unworthy, *G* 1244; of little worth, *G* 1835
vnwyse *adj.* foolish
vnwytté *adj.* ignorant
vouche, uoche, wowche *v.* summon, *Pe* 1121; make, affirm, *Pat* 165; give, hold, *Cl* 1358; **w. ... saf** bestow, *G* 1391
vowes *n.* vows
voyde *v.* leave, *G* 345; clear, rid, *G* 1342, 1518; disappear, *Cl* 1548; annihilate, destroy, *Cl* 1013, *Pat* 370; **v. away** put aside, *Cl* 744; *pp. adj.* **voyded** (**of**) free (from), *G* 634
vp, vp(p)e *adv.* up; open, *Cl* 1263, *G* 820, 1192, *etc.*; away, *G* 1874; aroused, *Cl* 834
vpbrayde *v.* (**vpbrayde** *pp.*) upbraid, reproach, *Pat* 430; throw up, raise, *Cl* 848, *G* 781
vpcaste *pp.* proclaimed, *Cl* 1574
vpe, vpen *see* **vp, vpon** *adj.*
vpfolden *adj.* extended, *Cl* 643 (*cf.* **folde vp** *Pe* 434)
vphalde *v.* hold up, *G* 2442
vphalt *pp.adj.* drawn up, high, *G* 2079
vplyfte *v.* lift, *G* 505; *pp.adj.* raised, *Cl* 987
vpon, vpen, open *adj.* open, *Pe* 183, 198, 1066, *Cl* 453, 501, 882, *G* 2070
vpon *adv.* on, *Cl* 141, 1427, *G* 2021; in, *Cl* 1049; on it, on them, *Pe* 208, *Cl* 1276, *G* 1649
vpon(e) *prep.* on, upon; at, *Cl* 893, *G* 9, 37, *etc.*; by, *Cl* 578, *G* 47; in, *Pe* 545, *Cl* 902, *Pat* 12; into, *Pe* 59, *G* 244; of, *Pe* 370; *for phrases see also* **ende, hyȝ(e), longe, stiȝtel, wyse,** *etc.*
vpon, open *v.* open, *Cl* 1600, *G* 1183
vponande *presp.adj.* opening, *Cl* 318
vppe *see* **vp**
vprerde *pa.t.* raised up
vpryse *v.* (**vpros, vprysen** *pa.t.*) rise, get up
vpset *pp.* raised up, *Pat* 239
vp-so-down *adv.* upside-down
vpwafte *pa.t.* flew up, *Cl* 949
vpynyoun *n.* opinion
vrnmentes, vrþe *see* **ornementes, erþe**
vrþ(e)ly *adj.* earthly
Vryn *n.* (*gen.*) (of) Urien, *G* 113
vrysoun *n.* band of silk, *G* 608n
vsage *n.* custom
vse *v.* practise; use, *Cl* 11; spend, *Cl* 295; have relations with, *G* 2426; *reflex.* have sexual relations, *Cl* 267
vsellez *see* **vsle**
vsle *n.* (**vsellez** *pl.*) ash
Vter *n.* Uther (Pendragon), *G* 2465
vtter *adv.* outside, out
vtwyth *adv.* outwardly, on (from) the outside
vuche, vus *see* **vch(e), we**
vycios *adj.* vicious, depraved
vyf, vyuez *see* **wyf**
vygour *n.* power, *Pe* 971
vyl *adj.* vile, repugnant, *Cl* 744
vyla(y)ny(e) *see* **vilanye**
vyle *v.* disgrace, *Cl* 863
vyne, uyne *n.* vineyard
vyolence *n.* violation, *Cl* 1071
vyoles *n.* incense dishes, *Cl* 1280
vyrgyn *see* **vergyn**

vysayge, uisage *n.* face, *Pe* 178; appearance, *G* 866

vys(e) *n.* face, *Pe* 254, 750

vyse *see also* **vice**

wace *see* **be(ne)**

wach(e) *n.* vigil, state of wakefulness, *Cl* 1003; sentry, *Cl* 1205

wade *v.* (**wod** *pa.t.*) wade, *Pe* 143, 1151, *G* 2231; go (down in), *G* 787

waft(e) *see* **wayue**

wage *n.* pledge, foretaste, *G* 533; *pl.* wages, payment, *G* 396

wage *v.* ?continue, ?bring reward, *Pe* 416

waged *pp.* fluttered

waȝez *see* **wawez**

wake *v.* (**wok(e), waked** *pa.t.*, **waked** *pp.*) stay awake, watch, *Pat* 130; stay up late revelling, *G* 1025; *trans.* guard, *Cl* 85

waken *v.* (**wak(e)ned(e)** *pa.t.* & *pp.*) waken, arouse; *intrans.* waken, wake up, arise; shine, blaze, *G* 1650; *subjunc.* would wake up, *G* 1194

wakker *compar.adj.* weaker, *Cl* 835

wakkest *superl.adj.* weakest, *G* 354

wal *see* **wal(le)**

wale *v.* (**waled, walt** *pp.*) choose, *Cl* 921, *G* 1276; look for, *G* 398; distinguish, *Pat* 514; perceive, *Pe* 1000, 1007; take, *G* 1238; *pp.* chosen, *Cl* 1734

wale, walle *adj.* choice, noble, excellent, delightful, *Cl* 1716, 1734, *G* 1010, 1403, 1712; **w. chere** urbane manner, *G* 1759

walk(e) *v.* (**welke** *pa.t.*) walk; *reflex. Pe* 711; travel, *G* 1521

walkyries *n.* sorceresses, *Cl* 1577

wallande *presp.adj.* welling, surging

wal(le) *n.* wall. *See also* **wale** *adj.*

walle-heued *n.* (**welle-hedez** *pl.*) fountain, spring

walled *pp.* walled, *Cl* 1390

walour *n.* valour

walt *pa.t.* (**walte** *pp.*) (cast); tossed, *G* 1336; threw, *Cl* 501; *pp.* taken, removed, *Pe* 1156. *See also* **wale, welde** & *cf.* **walte** *v.*

walte *v.* flow, *Cl* 1037; pour, *Cl* 364

walter *v.* roll; pour, flow, *Cl* 1027, *G* 684

walterande *presp.adj.* rolling, wallowing

wamel *v.* feel sick

wan *see* **wynne** *v.*

wande *n.* staff, *G* 215; bough(s), *G* 1161

wane *adj.* lacking, *G* 493

waning *n.* reduction, *Pe* 558 (*cf.* **woned** *pp.*)

wanlez *adj.* without hope

wap *n.* blow; **at a w.** at a stroke, in one moment, *Pat* 499

wappe *v.* strike, swish, *G* 1161, 2004; **w. vpon** fling open, *Cl* 882

war *v. reflex.* beware, see to it

war *see also* **war(e)**

warde *see* **toward(e)**

warded *pp.* guarded

war(e) *adj.* aware, wary, cautious, alert; ware! (*hunter's cry*), *G* 1158; **be by hem w.** take warning from them, *Cl* 712; **be w. of** be

aware of, perceive; **-ly** *adv.*; **warloker** *compar.adv.* more cautiously, *G* 677

ware *v.* spend, use, *G* 402, 1235; pay back, *G* 2344

ware *see also* **be(ne)**

warisch *v.* (**waryst** *pp.*) protect, *Cl* 921; *pp.* recovered, *G* 1094

warlaȝes *n.* wizards, *Cl* 1560; **warlowes** *gen. sg.* the Devil's, *Pat* 258n

warlok *n.* fetter, *Pat* 80

warloker, warly *see* **war(e)**

warlowes *see* **warlaȝes**

warm(e) *adj.* & *adv.* warm; *adj. or adv. Pat* 470

warne *v.* warn, order

warnyng *n.* warning

warp(e)(n) *v.* (**warp(ped), werp** *pa.t.*) (cast); toss, *Cl* 444; put, *G* 2025; utter, say, *Pe* 879, *Cl* 152, 213, 284, *Pat* 356, *G* 224, 1423, 2253

warþe *n.* shore, *Pat* 339; ford, *G* 715

wary *v.* condemn, curse

waryed *pp.adj.* cursed

waryst *see* **warisch**

wasch(e) *v.* (**wesch(e)** *pa.t.*, **waschen(e)** *pp.*) wash

wassayl *interj.* good health!

was(se) *see* **be(ne)**

wast *n.* waist, *G* 144

waste *n.* wasteland, *G* 2098

wast(e) *v.* (**wast** *pa.t.* **wasted** *pp.*) destroy, *Cl* 326, 431, 1178, *Pat* 475; waste, *Cl* 1489

wasturne *n.* wilderness

wate, waþe *see* **wyt** *v.*[1], **woþe**

wat(t)er *n.* (**watt(e)rez, -s, wateres** *pl.*) water; flood(s), *Cl* 323, *etc.*; stream, *Pe* 107, 230, *etc.*, *Cl* 1380, 1776, *G* 715, 1595, *etc.*; tears, *G* 684

Wawan, Wawen *see* **Gaua(y)n**

wawez, waȝez *n.* waves; *fig.* water, *Pe* 287

wax *n.* wax, *Cl* 1487

wax *v.* (**wax(ed), wex(en)** *pa.t.*, **waxen** *pp.*) become, grow; grow (*of a plant*), *Pat* 499, *G* 518; increase, *Cl* 375, 397, *etc.*, *G* 997; stream, pour, *Pe* 649

waxen *adj.* of wax, *G* 1650

waxlokes *n.* lumps of wax, *Cl* 1037

way *adv.* away; **do w.** stop, *Pe* 718, *G* 1492

way(e) *n.* way, path; **by þe w. of** according to, *Pe* 580

wayferande *adj.* wayfaring

wayke *adj.* weak, feeble, *G* 282. *Cf. also* **wakker, wakkest**

waykned *pa.t.* weakened, grew feeble, *Cl* 1422

waymot *adj.* peevish

wayne *v.* (**vayned** *pp.*) bring, *Pe* 249, *Cl* 1616, *G* 264, 1032; send, *Pe* 131, *Cl* 1504, *Pat* 467, *G* 2456, 2459; restore, *Cl* 1701; direct, *G* 984. *Cf.* **wayue, weue** *v.*[1]

wayte *v.* watch, look; take care, make sure, *Cl* 292; search, *Cl* 99; study, *Cl* 1552; **w. after** watch over, *Pat* 86

wayth *n.* catch, game, *G* 1381

wayue *v.* (**wayued, waft(e)** *pa.t.*) wave, *G* 306, make to wave, *Pat* 454; flow to and fro, *Cl* 422; pull, close, *Cl* 857; **w. vp, w. vpon** push open, *Cl* 453, *G* 1743. *Cf.* **wayne, weue** *v.*[1]

we (**loo**) *interj.* alas!

we *pron.* (**vus** *acc. & dat.*) we

webbez *n.* tapestries, *Pe* 71

wed *pa.t.* went mad, *Cl* 1585

wedde *v.* wed, marry

wedded *pp.adj.* wedded, *Cl* 330

weddyng *n.* wedding, marriage-ceremony

wede *n.* garment, clothing; *pl.* clothes; **heȝe w., bryȝt w.** armour

weder *n.* weather, storm; fine weather, *G* 504*n*; air, sky, *Cl* 475, 847, 1760; *pl.* storms, *Cl* 948

weete *see* **wete**

weȝe, weye *v.* weigh, *Cl* 719; weigh (anchor). *Pat* 103; (carry), bring, *Cl* 1420, 1508, *G* 1403

weȝtes *n.* scales

wekked *see* **wykked**

wel *adv.* (**better** *compar.*, **best** *superl.*) well, certainly; much, *Pe* 145, *Pat* 114, 132, *G* 1276, *etc.*; very, *Pe* 537, *Pat* 169, *G* 179, 684; admittedly, *G* 1847; generously, *G* 1267; *as n.* good fortune, happiness, *Pe* 239, 1187, *G* 2127 (*cf.* **wele**); **w. nere** very nearly, *Pat* 169

wela *adv.* very

welawynnely *adv.* very joyfully, *Cl* 831 (*cf.* **wela, wynne**)

welcom, welcum *adj.* (**welcomest** *superl.*) welcome

welcume *v.* welcome, greet

welde *v.* (**walt** *pa.t.*) rule, govern; enjoy, use, possess, have, *Cl* 644, 705, 835, *Pat* 16, 464, *G* 231, 835, 837, 1064, 1528, *etc.*; pass (time). *G* 485

welder *n.* ruler

wele *n.* happiness, good fortune, prosperity; wealth, costliness; *as n.* precious one, *Pe* 14; *pl.* delights, *Pe* 154

welgest *superl.adj.* strongest, *Cf.* **wylger**

wel-haled *adj.* well pulled-up, *G* 157

welke *see* **walk(e)**

welkyn *n.* (the) sky

welle *n.* spring, fountain

welle-hedez *see* **walle-heued**

welnygh, welneȝ(e) *adv.* almost; **w. now** (*lit.* almost now) just now, *Pe* 581

welt *pa.t.* revolved, *Pat* 115

welwed *pp.adj.* withered

wely *adj.* blissful, *Pe* 101; *see also* **wyse**

wemlez *adj.* flawless, *Pe* 737

wemme *n.* flaw, blemish, *Pe* 221, 1003

wen *see* **quen**

wench *n.* girl; concubine, *Cl* 1423, 1716

wende *n.* turning, *G* 1161

wende *v.* (**wende, went(e), wenten** *pa.t.* went *pp.*) go; turn, *Pat* 403 (**of**: from), *G* 2152; **watz went** had come, *G* 1712

wene *v.* (**wende, went** *pa.t. Pe* 1148, *G* 669, 1711) suppose, think, believe; know; doubt, *Pe* 1141

wener *compar.adj.* lovelier, *G* 945

weng(ed) *see* **venge**

Wenore *n.* Guenevere, *G* 945

went(e), wenten *see* **wende, wene**

wenyng *n.* hope

wepe *v.* (**wepande** *presp.*, **weped** *pa.t.*) weep; *trans.* weep, lament, *Pat* 384

weppen *n.* weapon

werbeland *presp.adj.* shrill, whistling, *G* 2004

werbles *n.* trills, *G* 119

were *n.* defence, *G* 1628. *See also* **werre**

were *v.*[1] (**wer(e)(d)** *pa.t.*) wear, *Pe* 205, *Cl* 287, *G* 1928, 2037, 2358

were *v.*[2] (**wer(ed)** *pa.t.*) defend, *G* 2041; protect, shelter, *Pat* 486; keep out, *G* 2015; *reflex.* excuse oneself, *Cl* 69

wer(e)(n) *see* **be(ne)**

werk(e) *n.* (**werk(k)es, -z** *pl.*) work, labour, activity; creation, *Cl* 198, *Pat* 501; deed, practice, *Cl* 305; conduct, *Cl* 589; workmanship, *G* 2367; construction, *Cl* 1390; ado, *Cl* 1725; *pl.* structure, *Cl* 1480; labour(s), *Cl* 136, 1258; deeds, *G* 1515, 2026(?); ornamentation, *G* 216, 1817, 2432; embroidery, *G* 164, 2026(?)

werkmen *n.* workmen, labourers, *Pe* 507

werle *n.* circlet, *Pe* 209*n*

wern *see* **be(ne)**

werne *v.* refuse, *G* 1494, 1495, 1824

wernyng *n.* refusal, resistance, *G* 2253

werp *see* **warp(e)(n)**

werre, were *n.* war, fighting. *See also* **were**

werre *v.* fight, *G* 720

wers, worre, wors(e) *compar.adj.* (**werst, worst** *superl.*) worse; (socially) inferior; *as n. Cl* 80; **þe w.** the worst (of it), *G* 1588, 1591

wertes *see* **wort**

wery *adj.* weary

weryng *n.* wearing; **in w.** through being worn, *Cl* 1123

wesaunt *n.* gullet, *G* 1336

wesch(e) *see* **wasch(e)**

west(e) *n.* west; west wind, *Pat* 469

westernays *adj.* reversed, awry, *Pe* 307*n*

wete, weete *adj.* wet

wete *v.* wet, *Cl* 1027

weterly *adv.* clearly, truly, *G* 1706

weþer *see* **w(h)eþer**

weue, veue *v.*[1] proffer, give, *G* 1976, 2359; pass, *Pe* 318; *pp.* brought, *Pe* 976. *Cf.* **wayue, wayne**

weue *v.*[2] (**weuen** *Pe* 71, *pa.t.pl.* or *pres.pl.*, **wouen** *pp.*) weave

wex(en), weye *see* **wax, weȝe**

whal *n.* (**whallez** *gen.sg.*) whale

whallez bon *n.* ivory (from walrus), *Pe* 212

wham *see* **who**

wharred *pa.t.* whirred, *G* 2203

what, whatt, quat *interrog. & indef. pron. & adj.* what; why, *Pe* 1072, *Pat* 197, *G* 563; *interj.* why!, oh!, *etc.*, *Cl* 487, 845, *etc.*, *G* 1163, 2201*n*; *indef.* whatever, *Pe* 523, *G* 1073

whatkyn *adj.* whatever kind of, *Cl* 100

whatso, qu- *pron.* (*also* **w(h)at, qu- ... so**) whatever; what, *Pat* 243, *G* 255

whatt *see* **what**

whederwarde *adv.* in what(ever) direction

wheder, whyder *adv.* whither, where, *Cl* 917, *Pat* 200. *See also* **wheþer**

when, whene *see* **quen, quene**

whenso *adv.* whenever

wher(e), qu- *adv. & conj.* where; wherever, *Cl* 444, *G* 100; **whereso, quer(e)so** wherever. *See also* **wheþer**

wherfore, querfore *adv.* for which reason; *interrog.* why?

w(h)eresoeuer, queresoeuer *adv.* wherever

whete *n.* wheat, *Pe* 32

whette *v.* (**whette** *pa.t.*) sharpen, whet; grind

wheþen, qu- *adv.* whence (ever)

wheþer, wheder *adv.* yet, nevertheless, *Pe* 581, 826, *Cl* 570, *G* 203

w(h)eþer, qu-, where (*Pe* 617) *interrog.adv. introd. direct qu.*, *Pe* 565, **w. wystez þou euer** did you ever know?, *Pe* 617, **w. þis be** is this?, *G* 2186; *pron. & conj.* whichever, *shifting to* whether, *Pe* 130, 604, *Cl* 113; whether, *Cl* 583, etc.; **q. ... so** *adj.* (to) whichever (man), *G* 1109; **queþersoeuer** *pron.* whichever, *Pe* 606

whichche *n.* chest (*i.e.* ark), *Cl* 362

whiderwarde-soeuer *adv.* to whatever place, *G* 2478

whil(e), whit *see* **whyl(e), whyt(e)**

who, quo *interrog. & indef. pron.* (**quom, wham** *dat.* (*rel.*)) who, whoever; you who, *Pe* 344; **as q. says** like one who says, *Pe* 693

whoso, quoso *pron.* whoever, if anyone

why, wy, quy *adv.* why; *interj.* why!, oh!

whyder *see* **wheder**

whyle *adv.* once, formerly, *Pe* 15

whyle, quyle, quile *n.* time, while; moment; **þe w.** *adv.* for the time, *conj.* while; **þe ... q., þat ... w.** during, *G* 940, 985

whyl(e), wyl(e), whil(e), quyl(e), quel *prep. & conj.* while, as long as; until, *Pe* 528, *Cl* 1686, *G* 536, 1072, 1180, *etc.*

whyssynes *n.* cushions, *G* 877

whyt(e), whit, quit(e), quyt(e), qwyte *adj. & n.* white

wich, wych *pron. & adj.* what, of what sort, *Cl* 169, 1060, 1074, *G* 918; **w. ... so euer** whichever, *Pat* 280

wiȝt *see* **wyȝt(e)**

wil, wyl(le), wol *v.* (**wolde(z), woled** *pa.t.*) will, be willing, wish (for), desire, intend; **wolde** *pa.t.* was about to, *Pat* 424; would say, meant, *Cl* 1552; *in pres. sense* would, wish(es) to, *Cl* 1140, *etc.*

wit *see* **wyt**

with, wyth *prep.* (together) with; among, *G* 49; against; towards, *Cl* 849, *G* 1926, 2220; for, *Cl* 56; in comparison with, *Pat* 300; in respect of, *G* 418; by, through (*agent or instr.*), *Pe* 806, etc., *Cl* 90, 91, 111, 1142, 1178, etc., *Pat* 2, etc., *G* 314, 384, 681, 949, 1119, 1153, 1229, etc.; (tired, afraid) of, *G* 1573, 2301 (*or* within); **w. hymseluen** with him, *G* 113, inwardly, *G* 1660; **w. þis, w. þat** thereupon; *see also* **lyt(t)el**

withinne, wythinne *adv. & prep.* within, inside, inwardly, among

withnay *v.* refuse, reject, *Pe* 916

withoute(n), wythoute(n) *adv. & prep.* without; outside

wittnesse, wyttenesse *n.* witness; evidence, testimony, *Cl* 1050

wlate *v. impers.* (disgust); be disgusted, feel loathing, *Cl* 305, 1501

wlatsum *adj.* loathsome, disgusting

wlonk, wlonc *adj.* fine, handsome, splendid, lovely; cordial, *Cl* 831; *as n.* **þat, þe w.** purity, pure conduct, *Cl* 1052, noble man, *G* 1988; *predic. adj. or adv.* proud(ly), presumptuous(ly), *Pe* 903, splendid(ly), *G* 2022

wo *n.* woe, misery, suffering; (fear of) harm, *Pe* 154; *adj.* sorrowful, *Cl* 284

wod *see* **wade, wod(e)**

wodbynde *n.* woodbine (climbing plant), *Pat* 446, *etc. See also* **bynde**

wod(e) *adj. & adv.* (**wodder** *compar.*) mad; angry, furious, *Cl* 204; (of waves, *etc.*) furious, raging, *Cl* 364, *Pat* 162; *adv.* fiercely, *Pat* 142

wod(e) *n.* wood, forest

wodcraftez *n.* woodcraft, hunting skills, *G* 1605

wod-schawez *n.* groves

wodschip *n.* fury

wodwos *n.* men of the woods, satyrs, *G* 721

woȝe, woghe *n.*[1] wrong, harm, *Pe* 622, *G* 1550

woȝe, wowe *n.*[2] wall, *Pe* 1049, *Cl* 832, 839, *etc.*, *G* 858, 1180, 1650

wok *see* **wake**

wolde *n.* possession, *Pe* 812

wolde(z), wol(ed) *see* **wil**

wolen *adj.* woollen, *Pe* 731

wolfes, wolues *n.* wolves

wolle *n.* wool, fleece, *Pe* 844

wombe *n.* belly, stomach

wommon *see* **wymmen**

won *n.* custom, *Cl* 720

won, wony(e) *v.* (**wonez, won(ie)s, wony(e)s** *pres.*, **wonyande** *presp.*, **wonde, won(y)ed** *pa.t.*, **wonde, wonyd, wont(e)** *pp.*) live, dwell; remain, *Cl* 362, *G* 50, 257, 814; **wont(e)** *pp.adj.* accustomed, *Pe* 15, 172, *Cl* 1489

won *see also* **won(e)**

wonde *v.* shrink, hesitate

wonde, woned *see* **won**

wonder *adj.* wonderful; *adv.* amazingly, wonderfully, exceedingly

wonder, wunder *n.* wonder, amazement; marvel, *Cl* 584, *Pat* 244, 256, *G* 29, 147, *etc.*; ?disaster, *G* 16; *collect.* marvels, *Cl* 1390; **haue w.** be amazed, be surprised

wonderly *adv.* amazingly, greatly; in an awesome manner *Cl* 570

won(e) *n.* dwelling, house; town, city, *Pe* 1049, *Cl* 891, 928, *Pat* 69, 436; (animal's) stall, *Cl* 311; pleasure, *G* 1238; multitude, company, *G* 1269; *pl. as collect.* abode, *Pe* 917, *etc.*, *Cl* 779; *G* 685, 1051, *etc.*; lands, *Cl* 841; **to w. wonne** brought in, harvested, *Pe* 32

woned *pp.* decreased, subsided, *Cl* 496

wonen *see* **wynne**

wonez, wonies *see* **won**

wonne *adj.* dark, *Pat* 141

wonne(n) *see also* **wynne**

wonnyng *n.* dwelling, *Cl* 921

wons *see* **won**

wont *n.* lack, *G* 131

wont *v.impers.* lack, be wanting
wont(e) *pp. see* **won**
wonyande, wony(e)(s), wony(e)d *see* **won**
worch(e) *see* **wyrk(k)(e)**
Worcher *n.* Creator
worchyp, worchip *v.* worship, *Pat* 206; honour, *G* 1227. *See also* **wor(s)chyp**
word(e) *n.* word, speech; *pl.* words, statement(s); command, *Cl* 348; fame, *G* 1521
worded *pp.* spoken, *Pat* 421
wordlych *adj.* earthly, *Cl* 49
wore, work *see* **be(ne), wyrk(k)(e)**
world(e) *n.* world, earth; nature, *G* 504, 530, 2000; prosperity, *Cl* 1298; **no worldez goud** no goodness in the world (at all), *Cl* 1048; **worldez kynde** mankind, mortal men, *G* 261; **w. wythouten ende** for ever; **in þis (of þe) world,** *etc.,* on earth (*intensive*), *Pat* 202, *G* 238, 871, *etc.,* at all, *Pe* 65*n*, 293
worme *n.* worm, *Pat* 467; snake, *Cl* 533; dragon, *G* 720
worre *see* **wers**
wor(s)chyp, wor(s)chip, wourchyp *n.* honour, dignity; reverence, *Cl* 1592; value, (honour of) possession, *G* 984, 2432
wors(e), worst *see* **wers**
wort *n.* (**wortes, wertes** *pl.*) plant, *Pe* 42, *Pat* 478, *G* 518
worth(e), -þe *v.* become; be; happen, befall (to); **is worþen to** has become (one of), *Pe* 394; **to noȝt w.** be destroyed, *Pat* 360; **worþe** *pres.subjunc.* let it (there, *etc.*) be, *Pe* 362, *G* 727, 925, *G* 1302, *etc.*
worþe, -th *adj.* worth, *Pe* 451, *Cl* 1244, *G* 1269, 1820
worþely(ch), worþilych, worþ(y)ly, worthyly *adj.* (**worþloker** *compar.*) noble, honoured; splendid, fine; glorious, *Pe* 1073; *as n.* precious one, *Pe* 47
worþly *see also* **worþyly**
worþy, worþé, worthé *adj. & adv.* noble (*& as n.*); worthy, *Pe* 616, *Cl* 84; virtuous, *Cl* 718; able, *Pe* 100; fitting, *G* 819; of value, valuable, *G* 559, 1848; *adv.* courteously, *G* 1477
worþyly, -ily, -th-, worþly (*Pe* 1133) *adv.* fittingly, becomingly, *Pe* 1133, *G* 72, 144; courteously, *G* 1759; honourably, *G* 1386, 1988
wost(e), wot(e) *see* **wyt** *v.*[1]
woþe, waþe *n.* danger
wounde *n.* wound
wouen, wounden, wourchyp *see* **weue** *v.*[2], **wynde, wor(s)chyp**
Wowayn, Wowen *see* **Gaua(y)n**
wowche, wowe, wrache *see* **vouche, woȝe, wrake**
wraȝte *pa.t.* suffered, was tormented, *Pe* 56
wrak, wrek *pa.t.* (**wroken** *pp.*) took vengeance; *pp.* driven out, removed, *Pe* 375
wrake, wrache *n.* vengeance, retribution
wrakful *adj.* vengeful, bitter
wrang(e), wrank, wronge *adj., adv. & n.* twisted, awry, *Cl* 891*n*; perverted, *Cl* 268; evil, *Pat* 384; (put in the) wrong, *G* 1494; *adv.* unjustly, wrongly, *Pe* 488, 614; amiss,

badly, *Pe* 631; *n.* wickedness, misdeed, *Cl* 76, *Pat* 376
wrappez *v.* (**wrapped** *pp.*) wrap, envelop; *reflex.* (*pres2sg.*) wrap (dress) yourself, *Cl* 169
wrast *adj.* loud, *G* 1423
wrast *v.* (**wrast(en)** *pa.t.,* **wrast** *pp.*) (wrest); pluck, *Pat* 80; force, *Cl* 1166; resound, *Cl* 1403; *pp.* turned, disposed, *G* 1482; **w. out** thrust out, *Cl* 1802
wrastel *v.* (**wrastled** *pa.t.*) wrestle, struggle
wrath(þe) *n.* wrath, anger; (cause for anger), offence, *Pe* 362
wrath *v.* (**wrathed** *pa.t. & pp.*) become angry, *Cl* 230, 690, *etc., Pat* 74, 431, *etc., G* 1509; *trans.* anger, *Cl* 719, 828; trouble, *G* 726, 2420
wrech(che) *n.* wretch
wrech(ed) *adj.* wretched, *Pe* 56, *Pat* 258
wreȝande *presp.* denouncing, vilifying, *G* 1706
wrek *see* **wrak**
wrenchez *n.* deceits, *Cl* 292
writ *see* **wryt**
wro *n.* nook, *G* 2222; passage, *Pe* 866
wroȝt(e)(z), wroȝten *see* **wyrk(k)(e)**
wroken, wronge *see* **wrak, wrang(e)**
wrot *pa.t.* dug, *Pat* 467
wroth(e), wroþe *adj.* (**wroþer** *compar.*) angry; fierce, *Cl* 1676, *G* 1706, 1905; at variance, enemies, *Pe* 379 (*cf. Pat* 48)
wroth *see also* **wryþe**
wroþ(e)ly *adv.* (**wroþeloker** *compar.*) angrily, fiercely; (more) harshly, *G* 2344
wrux(e)led *adj.* adorned, arrayed, *Cl* 1381, *G* 2191
wryste *n.* wrist
wryt, writ *n.* writing; scripture, *Pe* 997, *Cl* 657; **holy w.** the Bible
wryte *v.* (**wryten** *pp.*) write; *reflex. Pe* 1033
wryþe *v.* (**wroth** *pa.t.*) writhe; wriggle, *Cl* 533, *G* 1200; labour, toil, *Pe* 511; turn aside, *Pe* 350; **w. so wrange away** blunder so badly, *Pe* 488; *trans.* twist, torture, *Pat* 80; turn, *Cl* 821
wunder, wunnen, wy, wych *see* **wonder, wynne** *v.,* **why, wich**
wychecraft *n.* witchcraft
wychez *n.* wizards, *Cl* 1577
wyd(e) *adj. & adv.* wide, broad; **on w.** round about, *Cl* 1423
wyddered *pp.adj.* withered, *Pat* 468
wydoez *n.* widows, *Cl* 185
wyf, vyf *n.* (**wyuez** *gen.sg.,* **wyues, -z, vyuez** *pl.*) woman, lady, wife
wyȝ(e) *n.* being, person, man, knight, servant, sir, *Pat* 492, *G* 252, *etc.*; **vch w.** everyone; **no w.** no one
wyȝt(e) *n.* creature; person, *G* 1792; maiden, *Pe* 338, 494
wyȝt(e), wiȝt *adj.* strong, *G* 261, 1762; valiant, *Pe* 694; piercing, *G* 119; **þe wyȝtest** the strongest current, *G* 1591; *adv.* quickly, *Cl* 617, *Pat* 103; **wyȝtly** swiftly
wyket *see* **wyk(k)et**
wykez *n.* corners, *G* 1572
wyk(ke) *adj.* bad, wickd; disagreeable, difficult, *Cl* 1063*n*
wykked, wekked *adj.* wicked

wyk(k)et *n.* door
wyl *see* **wil, wyl(le)**
wylde *adj.* wild; *as n.* wild animal(s)
wyldren *n.* wild places, *Pat* 297
wyldrenesse *n.* wild country, *G* 701
wyle, wylé *see* **whil(e), wyly**
wylfulnes *n.* wilfulness, obstinacy
wylger *compar.|adj.* stronger. *Cf.* **welgest**
wyl(le) *adj.* wild, wandering, *Pat* 473, *G* 2084
wylle *n.*[1] will, mind, temper, *Pe* 56, *Cl* 200, 232, *etc.*, *Pat* 298, *G* 57, 352; will, wish, desire, pleasure, *Pe* 131, *Cl* 309, *etc.*, *Pat* 16, *etc.*, *G* 255, *etc.*; **at w.** abundant(ly), *G* 1371; **bi ȝoure w.** if you please, *G* 1065; **with (a) god w.** willingly, gladly, *G* 1387, *etc.*
wylle *n.*[2] error, perversity, *Cl* 76
wylle *v. see* **wil**
wylne *v.* wish, *Pe* 318
wylnyng *n.* wish, *G* 1546
wylsfully *adv.* perversely, ?lustfully, *Cl* 268
wylsum *adj.* out-of-the-way, *G* 689
wylt *pp.* escaped, *G* 1711
wyly, wylé *adj.* wily; *as n.* this wily one, *G* 1905; *adv.* cunningly, cleverly, *Cl* 1452
wylyde *adj.* skilful, *G* 2367
wymmen *n.pl.* women; **wommon** *gen.pl.* of women, womanly, *Pe* 236
wyn, wyne *n.* wine
wyndas *n.* windlass
wynd(e) *n.* wind; speech, message, *Pat* 345
wynde *v.* (**wounden** *pp.*) turn, *Cl* 534; come round, *G* 530; *pp.* bound, *G* 215
wyndow(e) *n.* window
wyndowande *presp.adj.* scattering in the wind
wyne *see* **wyn**
wynge *n.* wing
wynne *adj.* delightful, lovely; precious, *Pe* 647
wynne *n.*[1] joy, *G* 15, 1765
wynne *n.*[2] gain, advantage, *G* 2420
wynne *v.* (**wan, wonnen** *pa.t.*, **won(n)en, wonne, wunnen** *pp.*) win, obtain, gain, get; beget, *Cl* 112, 650; bring, *Pe* 32, *Cl* 617, *G* 831, *etc.*; win over, persuade, *Cl* 1616, *G* 1550; reach (*also reflex.*) *Pat* 237, *G* 402, 1569, 2231; *intrans.* win, *G* 70; go, come, *Pe* 107, 517, *Cl* 140, 882, *etc.*, *G* 461, 1365, *etc.*
wynnelych *adj.* gracious, *Cl* 1807; pleasant, *G* 980
wynter *n.* winter
wynt-hole *n.* windpipe
wypped[1] *pp.* wiped, polished, *G* 2022
wypped[2] *pa.t.* whipped, slashed, *G* 2249
Wyrale *n.* Wirral (in Cheshire)
wyrde *n.* fate, destiny; Providence
wyrk(k)(e), work, worch(e) *v.* (**wroȝt-(e)(z), -en** *pa.t.*, **wroȝt** *pp.*) do, act, perform; commit, *Pe* 622, *etc.*, *Cl* 171, *etc.*, *Pat* 513, *etc.*; bring about, accomplish, *Cl* 663, *etc.*, *G* 22, *etc.*; make, create, *Pe* 638, *etc.*, *Cl* 5 *etc.*, *Pat* 206, *G* 399, *etc.*; work, labour, *Pe* 511, 525, *etc.*, *Cl* 1287
wyrled *pa.t.* whirled, circled, *Cl* 475
wyschande *presp.* longing for, *Pe* 14; **wysched** *pa.t.* wished, *Pat* 462
wys(e) *adj.* wise, clever; skilful, *Pe* 748, *G* 1605; *as n. Cl* 1319, 1741

wyse *n.* manner, way, state; array, *Pe* 133, *G* 2456; **in feȝtyng w.** in battle array, *G* 267; **in wely w.** blissfully, in a blissful state, *Pe* 101; **on basteles w.** in the manner of a tower on wheels, *Cl* 1187n; **on a wonder w.** miraculously, *Pe* 1095; **vpon a grett w.** magnificently, *G* 2014; **vpon a ser w.** diversely, individually, *Pat* 12; **vpon spare w.** discreetly, *G* 901
wyse *v.* (**wysed** *pa.t.*) show, be visible, *Pe* 1135; send, *Cl* 453
wysse *v.* guide, *G* 549, 739; instruct, enlighten, *Cl* 1564, *Pat* 60
wyst(e)(n), wystez *see* **wyt**
wysty *adj.* desolate, *G* 2189
wyt, wytte, wyte *n.* mind, reason, intelligence, understanding, wisdom; meaning, *Cl* 1630; sense, *G* 677; *pl.* senses, *Cl* 515, *G* 640, *etc.*
wyt, wyte, wit *v.*[1] (**wot(e), wate, wost(e)** *pres.*, **wost(e) wystez, wyst(e)(n)** *pa.t.*) know, understand, be sure; perceive, learn
wyte *v.*[2] blame, *Pat* 501; **to w.** blameworthy, *Cl* 76
wyte *v.*[3] look, *G* 2050
wyter *adv.* clearly, *Cl* 1552
wytered *pp.* informed, *Cl* 1587
wyterly *adv.* clearly, surely
wyth *see* **with**
wythal *adv.* in addition, *Cl* 636
wythdroȝ *pa.t.* removed, *Pe* 658
wythhalde *v.* (**withhelde, wythhylde** *pa.t.*) withhold, restrain, check
wythinne, wythoute(n) *see* **withinne, withoute(n)**
wytles *adj.* foolish, *Pat* 113; distracted, *Cl* 1585
wytte, wyttenesse *see* **wyt, wittnesse**
wyþe *adj.* mild, *Pat* 454
wyþer *adj.* opposite, *Pe* 230
wyþer *v.* **w. wyth** oppose, resist, *Pat* 48
wyþerly *adv.* rebelliously, *Pat* 74; fiercely, implacably, *Cl* 198
wyues, wyuez *see* **wyf**

ydropike *adj.* dropsical, *Cl* 1096
yȝe *n.* (**yȝen** *pl.*) eye
yle, ymage *see* **ille, image**
Ynde *n.* India; **ble of Y.** dark blue, indigo, *Pe* 76
ynde *adj.* dark blue, indigo, *Cl* 1411, *Pe* 1016
yot *pa.t.* ran, fell (like a tear), *Pe* 10
yo(u)r(e), yowre, ȝowre *possess.adj.* your
yourez, yowrez, ȝourez *pron.* yours
yourself, yow-, yowre-, ȝour-, yo(u)r-seluen *pron.* (you) yourself
yow *see* **ȝe**
yre, ire *n.* ire, anger
yrn(e) *n.* iron, *G* 215; weapon, *G* 2267; pl. armour, *G* 729
Ysaye *n.* Isaiah
yuore *n.* ivory, *Pe* 178
yþez *n.* waves
Ywan, Aywan *n.* Iwain

Zedechyas *n.* Zedekiah
Zeferus *n.* Zephyrus, the West Wind

Appendix

Passages from the Vulgate used as source material in the poems.

1 *Pearl*

St Matthew 20:1-16

20

Simile est regnum cœlorum homini patrifamilias, qui exiit primo mane conducere operarios in vineam suam.

2 Conventione autem facta cum operariis ex denario diurno misit eos in vineam suam.

3 Et egressus circa horam tertiam, vidit alios stantes in foro otiosos.

4 Et dixit illis: Ite et vos in vineam meam, et quod justum fuerit dabo vobis.

5 Illi autem abierunt. Iterum autem exiit circa sextam et nonam horam; et fecit similiter.

6 Circa undecimam vero exiit, et invenit alios stantes, et dicit illis: Quid hic statis tota die otiosi?

7 Dicunt ei: Quia nemo nos conduxit. Dicit illis: Ite et vos in vineam meam.

8 Cum sero autem factum esset, dicit dominus vineæ procuratori suo: Voca operarios, et redde illis mercedem incipiens a novissimis usque ad primos

9 Cum venissent ergo qui circa undecimam horam venerant, acceperunt singulos denarios.

10 Venientes autem et primi, arbitrati sunt quod plus essent accepturi: acceperunt autem et ipsi singulos denarios.

11 Et accipientes murmurabant adversus patremfamilias,

12 Dicentes: Hi novissimi una hora fecerunt, et pares illos nobis fecisti, qui portavimus pondus diei, et æstus.

13 At ille respondens uni eorum, dixit: Amice non facio tibi injuriam: nonne ex denario convenisti mecum?

14 Tolle quod tuum est, et vade: volo autem et huic novissimo dare sicut et tibi.

15 Aut non licet mihi quod volo facere? an oculus tuus nequam est, quia ego bonus sum?

16 Sic erunt novissimi primi, et primi novissimi: multi enim sunt vocati, pauci vero electi.

Revelation 5:1-14, 7:9-14, 14:1-5, 19:7-8, 21:1-27, 22:1-5.

5

1 Et vidi in dextera sedentis supra thronum, librum scriptum intus et foris, signatum sigillis septem.

2 Et vidi Angelum fortem, prædicantem voce magna: Quis est dignus aperire librum, et solvere signacula ejus?

3 Et nemo poterat neque in cœlo, neque in terra, neque subtus terram, aperire librum, neque respicere illum.

4 Et ego flebam multum, quoniam nemo dignus inventus est aperire librum, nec videre eum.

5 Et unus de senioribus dixit mihi: Ne fleveris: ecce vicit leo de tribu Juda, radix David, aperire librum, et solvere septem signacula ejus.

6 Et vidi: et ecce in medio throni et quattuor animalium, et in medio seniorum, agnum stantem tamquam occisum, habentem cornua septem, et oculos septem: qui sunt septem, spiritus Dei, missi in omnem terram.

7 Et venit: et accepit de dextera se dentis in throno librum.

8 Et cum aperuisset librum, quattuor animalia, et vigintiquattuor seniores ceciderunt coram agno, habentes singuli citharas, et phialas aureas plenas odoramentorum, quæ sunt orationes sanctorum:

9 Et cantabant canticum novum, dicentes: Dignus es, Domine, accipere librum, et aperire signacula ejus: quoniam occisus es, et redemisti nos Deo in sanguine tuo ex omni tribu, et lingua et populo, et natione:

10 Et fecisti nos Deo nostro regnum, et sacerdotes: et regnabimus super terram.

11 Et vidi, et audivi vocem angelorum multorum in circuitu throni, et animalium, et seniorum: et erat numerus eorum millia millium.

12 Dicentium voce magna: Dignus est Agnus, qui occisus est, accipere virtutem, et divinitatem, et sapientiam, et fortitudinem, et honorem, et gloriam, et benedictionem.

13 Et omnem creaturam, quæ in cœlo est, et super terram, et sub terra, et quæ sunt in mari, et quæ in eo: omnes audivi dicentes: Sedenti in

throno, et Agno, benedictio, et honor, et gloria, et potestas, in sæcula sæculorum.

14 Et quattuor animalia dicebant: Amen. Et viginti quattuor seniores ceciderunt in facie suas: et adoraverunt viventem in sæcula sæculorum.

7

9 Post hæc vidi turbam magnam, quam dinumerare nemo poterat ex omnibus centibus, et tribubus, et populis, et linguis: stantes ante thronum, et in conspectu Agni, amicti stolis albis, et palmæ in manibus eorum:

10 Et clamabant voce magna dicentes Salus Deo nostro, qui sedet super thronem et Agno.

11 Et omnes Angeli stabant in circuitu throni, et seniorum, et quattuor animalium: et ceciderunt in conspectu throni in facies suas, et adoraverunt Deum,

12 Dicentes, Amen. Benedictio, et claritas, et sapientia, et gratiarum actio, honor, et virtus, et fortitudo, Deo nostro in sæcula sæculorum, Amen.

13 Et respondit unus de senioribus, et dixit mihi: Hi, qui amicti sunt stolis albis, qui sunt? et unde venerunt?

14 Et dixi illi: Domine mi, tu scis. Et dixit mihi: Hi sunt, qui venerunt de tribulatione magna, et laverunt stolas suas, et dealbaverunt eas in sanguine Agni.

14

1 Et vidi: et ecce Agnus stabat supra montem Sion, et cum eo centum quadraginta quattuor millia habentes nomen ejus, et nomen Patris ejus scriptum in frontibus suis.

2 Et audivi vocem de cœlo, tamquam vocem aquarum multarum, et tamquam vocem tonitrui magni: et vocem, quam audivi, sicut citharœdorum citharizantium in citharis suis.

3 Et cantabant quasi canticum novum ante sedem, et ante quattuor animalia, et seniores: et nemo poterat dicere canticum, nisi illa centum quadraginta quattuor millia, qui empti sunt de terra.

4 Hi sunt, qui cum mulieribus non sunt coinquinati: Virgines enim sunt. Hi sequuntur Agnum quocumque ierit Hi empti sunt ex hominibus primitiæ Deo, et Agno.

5 Et in ore eorum non est inventum mendacium: sine macula enim sunt ante thronum Dei.

19

7 Gaudeamus, et exultemus: et demus gloriam ei: quia venerunt nuptiæ Agni, et uxor ejus præparavit se.

8 Et datum est illi ut cooperiat se byssino splendenti et candido. Byssinum enim justificationes sunt Sanctorum.

21

1 Et vidi cœlum novum, et terram novam. Primum enim cœlum, et prima terra abiit, et mare jam non est.

2 Et ego Joannes vidi sanctam civitatem Jerusalem novam descendentem de cœlo a Deo, paratam, sicut sponsam ornatam viro suo.

3 Et audivi vocem magnam de throno dicentem: Ecce tabernaculum Dei cum hominibus, et habitabit cum eis. Et ipsi populus ejus erunt, et ipse Deus cum eis erit eorum Deus:

4 Et absterget Deus omnem lacrymam ab oculis eorum: et mors ultra non erit, neque luctus, neque clamor, neque dolor erit ultra, quia prima abierunt.

5 Et dixit qui sedebat in throno: Ecce nova facio omnia. Et dixit mihi: Scribe, quia hæc verba fidelissima sunt, et vera.

6 Et dixit mihi: Factum est: ego sum ᴪ, et ω: initium, et finis. Ego sitienti dabo de fonte aquæ vitæ gratis.

7 Qui vicerit, possidebit hæc, et ero illi Deus, et ille erit mihi filius.

8 Timidis autem, et incredulis, et execratis, et homicidis, et fornicatoribus, et beneficis, et idololatris, et omnibus mendacibus, pars illorum erit in stagno ardenti igne, et sulphure: quod est mors secunda.

9 Et venit unus de septem Angelis habentibus phialas plenas septem plagis novissimis, et locutus est mecum, dicens: Veni, et ostendam tibi sponsam, uxorem Agni.

10 Et sustulit me in spiritu in montem magnum, et altum, et ostendit mihi civitatem sanctam Jerusalem descendentem de cœlo a Deo,

11 Habentem claritatem Dei: et lumen ejus simile lapidi pretioso tamquam lapidi jaspidis, sicut crystallum.

12 Et habebat murum magnum, et altum, habentem portas duodecim: et in portis Angelos duodecim, et nomina inscripta, quæ sunt nomina duodecim tribuum filiorum Israel.

13 Ab Oriente portæ tres: et ab Aquilone portæ tres: et ab Austro portæ tres: et ab Occasu portæ tres.

14 Et mures civitatis habens fundamenta duodecim, et in ipsis duodecim nomina duodecim Apostolorum Agni.

15 Et qui loquebatur mecum, habebat mensuram arundineam auream, ut metiretur civitatem, et portas ejus, et murum.

16 Et civitas in quadro posita est, et longitudo ejus tanta est quanta et latitudo: et mensus est civitatem de arundine aurea per stadia duodecim millia: et longitudo, et altitudo, et latitudo ejus æqualia sunt.

17 Et mensus est murum ejus centum quadraginta quattuor cubitorum, mensura hominis, quæ est angeli.

18 Et erat structura muri ejus ex lapide jaspide: ipsa vero civitas aurum mundum simile vitro mundo.

19 Et fundamenta muri civitatis omni lapide pretioso ornata. Fundamentum primum, jaspis: secundum sapphirus: tertium calcedonius: quartum, smaragdus:

20 Quintum, sardonyx: sextum, sardius: septimum, chrysolithus: octavum, beryllus: nonum, topazius: decimum, chrysoprasus:

undecimum, hyacinthus: duodecimum, amethystus.

21 Et duodecim portæ, duodecim margaritæ sunt, per singulas: et singulæ portæ erant ex singulis margaritis: et platea civitatis aurum mundum, tamquam vitrum perlucidum.

22 Et templum non vidi in ea. Dominus enim Deus omnipotens templum illius est, et Agnus.

23 Et civitas non eget sole neque luna, ut luceant in ea: nam claritas Dei illuminavit eam, et lucerna ejus est Agnus.

24 Et ambulabunt gentes in lumine ejus: et reges terræ afferent gloriam suam et honorem in illam.

25 Et portæ ejus non claudentur per diem: nox enim non erit iliic.

26 Et afferent gloriam et honorem gentium in illam.

27 Non intrabit in eam aliquod coinquin-

atum, aut abominationem faciens, et mendacium, nisi qui scripti sunt in libro vitæ Agni.

22

1 Et ostendit mihi fluvium aquæ vitæ, splendidum tamquam crystallum, procedentem de sede Dei et Agni.

2 In medio plateæ ejus, et ex utraque parte fluminis lignum vitæ, afferens fructus duodecim, per menses singulos reddens fructum suum, et folia ligni ad sanitatem Gentium.

3 Et omne maledictum non erit amplius: sed sedes Dei et Agni in illa erunt et servi ejus servient illi.

4 Et videbunt faciem ejus: et nomen ejus in frontibus eorum.

5 Et nox ultra non erit: et non egebunt lumine lucernæ, neque lumine solis, quoniam Dominus Deus illuminabit illos, et regnabunt in sæcula sæculorum.

2 *Cleanness*

Genesis 6 : 1–9 : 1

6

1 Cumque cœpissent homines multiplicari super terram, et filias procreassent,

2 Videntes filii Dei filias hominum quod essent pulchræ, acceperunt sibi uxores ex omnibus, quas elegerant.

3 Dixitque Deus: Non permanebit spiritus meus in homine in æternum, quia caro est: eruntque dies illius centum viginti annorum.

4 Gigantes autem erant super terram in diebus illis. Postquam enim ingressi sunt filii Dei ad filias hominum, illæque genuerunt, isti sunt potentes a sæculo viri famosi.

5 Videns autem Deus quod multa malitia hominum esset in terra, et cuncta cogitatio cordis intenta esset ad malum omni tempore,

6 Pœnituit eum quod hominem fecisset in terra. Et tactus dolore cordis intrinsecus,

7 Delebo, inquit, hominem, quem creavi, a facie terræ, ab homine usque ad animantia, a reptili usque ad volucres cœli: pœnitet enim me fecisse eos.

8 Noe vero invenit gratiam coram Domino.

9 Hæ sunt generationes Noe: Noe vir justus atque perfectus fuit in generationibus suis, cum Deo ambulavit.

10 Et genuit tres filios, Sem, Cham, et Japheth.

11 Corrupta est autem terra coram Deo, et repleta est iniquitate.

12 Cumque vidisset Deus terram esse corruptam, (omnis quippe caro corruperat viam suam super terram.)

13 Dixit ad Noe: Finis universæ carnis venit coram me: repleta est terra iniquitate a facie eorum, et ego disperdam eos cum terra.

14 Fac tibi arcam de lignis lævigatis: mansiunculas in arca facies, et bitumine linies intrinsecus et extrinsecus.

15 Et sic facies eam: Trecentorum cubitorum erit longitudo arcæ, quinquaginta cubitorum latitudo, et triginta cubitorum altitudo illius.

16 Fenestram in arca facies, et in cubito consummabis summitatem ejus; ostium autem arcæ pones ex latere: deorsum, cœnacula, et tristega facies in ea.

17 Ecce ego adducam aquas diluvii super terram, ut interficiam omnem carnem, in qua spiritus vitæ est subter cœlum: Universa quæ in terra sunt, consumentur.

18 Ponamque fœdus meum tecum: et ingredieris arcam tu et filii tui, uxor tua, et uxores filiorum tuorum, tecum.

19 Et ex cunctis animantibus universæ carnis bina induces in arcam, ut vivant tecum: masculini sexus et feminini.

20 De volucribus juxta genus suum, et de jumentis in genere suo, et ex omni reptili terræ secundum genus suum: bina de omnibus ingredientur tecum, ut possint vivere.

21 Tolles igitur tecum ex omnibus escis, quæ mandi possunt, et comportabis apud te: et erunt tam tibi quam illis in cibum.

22 Fecit igitur Noe omnia, quæ præceperat illi Deus.

7

1 Dixitque Dominus ad eum: Ingredere tu, et omnis domus tua, in arcam: te enim vidi justum coram me in generatione hac.

2 Ex omnibus animantibus mundis tolle septena et septena, masculum et feminam: de animantibus vero immundis duo et duo, masculum et feminam.

3 Sed et de volatilibus cœli septena et septena, masculum et feminam: ut salvetur semen super faciem universæ terræ.

4 Adhuc enim, et post dies septem ego pluam super terram quadraginta diebus et quadraginta noctibus: et delebo omnem substantiam, quam feci, de superficie terræ.

5 Fecit ergo Noe omnia, quæ manda verat ei Dominus.

6 Eratque sexcentorum annorum quando diluvii aquæ inundaverunt super terram.

7 Et ingressus est Noe, et filii ejus, uxor ejus et uxores filiorum ejus cum eo, in arcam propter aquas diluvii.

8 De animantibus quoque mundis et immundis, et de volucribus, et ex omni, quod movetur super terram.

9 Duo et duo ingressa sunt ad Noe in arcam, masculus et femina, sicut præceperat Dominus Noe.

10 Cumque transissent septem dies, aquæ diluvii inundaverunt super terram.

11 Anno sexcentesimo vitæ Noe, mense secundo, septimodecimo die mensis, rupti sunt omnes fontes abyssi magnæ, et cataractæ cœli apertæ sunt:

12 Et facta est pluvia super terram quadraginta diebus et quadraginta noctibus.

13 In articulo diei illius ingressus est Noe, et Sem, et Cham, et Japheth, filii ejus, uxor illius, et tres uxores filiorum ejus cum eis, in arcam:

14 Ipsi et omne animal secundum genus suum, universaque jumenta in genere suo, et omne quod movetur super terram in genere suo, cunctum que volatile secundum genus suum, universæ aves, omnesque volucres.

15 Ingressæ sunt ad Noe in arcam, bina et bina ex omni carne, in qua erat spiritus vitæ.

16 Et quæ ingressa sunt, masculus et femina ex omni carne introierunt, sicut præceperat ei Deus: et inclusit eum Dominus deforis.

17 Factumque est diluvium quadraginta diebus super terram: et multiplicatæ sunt aquæ, et elevaverunt arcam in sublime a terra.

18 Vehementer enim inundaverunt: et omnia repleverunt in superficie terræ: porro arca ferebatur super aquas.

19 Et aquæ prævaluerunt nimis super terram: opertique sunt omnes montes excelsi sub universo cœlo.

20 Quindecim cubitis altior fuit aqua super montes, quos operuerat.

21 Consumptaque est omnis caro quæ movebatur super terram, volucrum, animantium, bestiarum, omniumque reptilium, quæ reptant super terram, universi homines,

22 Et cuncta, in quibus spiraculum vitæ est in terra, mortua sunt.

23 Et delevit omnem substantiam, quæ erat super terram, ab homine usque ad pecus, tam reptile quam volucres cœli: et deleta sunt de terra: remansit autem solus Noe, et qui cum eo erant in arca.

24 Obtinueruntque aquæ terram centum quinquaginta diebus.

8

1 Recordatus autem Deus Noe, cunctor-

umque animantium, et omnium jumentorum, quæ erant cum eo in arca, adduxit spiritum super terram, et imminutæ sunt aquæ,

2 Et clausi sunt fontes abyssi, et cataractæ cœli: et prohibitæ sunt pluviæ de cœlo

3 Reversæque sunt aquæ de terra euntes et redeuntes: et cœperunt minui post centum quinquaginta dies.

4 Requievitque arca mense septimo, vigesimo septimo die mensis super montes Armeniæ.

5 At vero aquæ ibant et decrescebant usque ad decimum mensem: decimo enim mense, prima die mensis, apparuerunt cacumina montium.

6 Cumque transissent quadraginta dies, aperiens Noe fenestram arcæ, quam fecerat, dimisit corvum:

7 Qui egrediebatur, et non revertebatur, donec siccarentur aquæ super terram.

8 Emisit quoque columbam post eum, ut videret si jam cessassent aquæ super faciem terræ.

9 Quæ cum non invenisset ubi requiesceret pes ejus, reversa est ad eum in arcam: aquæ enim erant super universam terram: extenditque manum, et apprehensam intulit in arcam.

10 Expectatis autem ultra septem diebus aliis, rursum dimisit columbam ex arca.

11 At illa venit ad eum ad vesperam, portans ramum olivæ virentibus foliis in ore suo: intellexit ergo Noe quod cessassent aquæ super terram.

12 Expectavitque nihilominus septem alios dies: et emisit columbam, quæ non est reversa ultra ad eum.

13 Igitur sexcentesimo primo anno, primo mense, prima die mensis imminutæ sunt aquæ super terram: et aperiens Noe tectum arcæ, aspexit, viditque quod exsiccata esset superficies terræ.

14 Mense secundo, septimo et vigesimo die mensis arefacta est terra.

15 Locutus est autem Deus ad Noe, dicens:

16 Egredere de arca, tu et uxor tua, filii tui, et uxores filiorum tuorum tecum.

17 Cuncta animantia, quæ sunt apud te, ex omni carne, tam in volatilibus quam in bestiis et universis reptilibus, quæ reptant super terram, educ tecum, et ingredimini super terram: crescite et multiplicamini super eam.

18 Egressus est ergo Noe, et filii ejus, uxor illius, et uxores filiorum ejus cum eo.

19 Sed et omnia animantia, jumenta, et reptilia quæ reptant super terram secundum genus suum, egressa sunt de arca.

20 Ædificavit autem Noe altare Domino: et tollens de cunctis pecoribus et volucribus mundis, obtulit holocausta super altare.

24 Odoratusque est Dominus odorem suavitatis, et ait: Nequaquam ultra maledicam terræ propter homines: sensus enim et cogitatio humani cordis in malum prona sunt ab adolescentia sua: non igitur ultra percutiam omnem animam viventem sicut feci.

22 Cunctis diebus terræ, sementis et messis, frigus et æstus, æstas et hiems, nox et dies non requiescent.

9

Benedixitque Deus Noe et filiis ejus. Et dixit ad eos: Crescite, et multiplicamini, et replete terram.

Genesis 18:1–19:28

18

1 Apparuit autem ei Dominus in convalle Mambre sedenti in ostio tabernaculi sui in ipso fervore diei.

2 Cumque elevasset oculos, apparuerunt ei tres viri stantes prope eum: quos cum vidisset, cucurrit in occursum eorum de ostio tabernaculi, et adoravit in terram.

3 Et dixit: Domine, si inveni gratiam in oculis tuis, ne transeas servum tuum:

4 Sed afferam pauxillum aquæ, et lavate pedes vestros, et requiescite sub arbore.

5 Ponamque buccellam panis, et confortate cor vestrum, postea transibitis: idcirco enim declinastis ad servum vestrum. Qui dixerunt: Fac ut locutus es.

6 Festinavit Abraham in tabernaculum ad Saram, dixitque ei: Accelera, tria sata similæ commisce, et fac subcinericios panes.

7 Ipse vero ad armentum cucurrit, et tulit inde vitulum tenerrimum et optimum, deditque puero: qui festinavit et coxit illum.

8 Tulit quoque butyrum et lac, et vitulum quem coxerat, et posuit coram eis: ipse vero stabat juxta eos sub arbore.

9 Cumque comedissent, dixerunt ad eum: Ubi est Sara uxor tua? ille respondit: Ecce in tabernaculo est.

10 Cui dixit: Revertens veniam ad te tempore isto, vita comite, et habebit filium Sara uxor tua. Quo audito, Sara risit post ostium tabernaculi

11 Erant autem ambo senes, provectæque ætatis, et desierant Saræ fieri muliebria.

12 Quæ risit occulte, dicens: Postquain consenui, et dominus meus vetulus est, voluptati operam dabo?

13 Dixit autem Dominus ad Abraham: Quare risit Sara, dicens: Num vere paritura sum anus?

14 Numquid Deo quidquam est difficile? juxta condictum revertar ad te hoc eodem tempore, vita comite, et habebit Sara filium.

15 Negavit Sara, dicens, Non risi: timore perterrita. Dominus autem: Non est, inquit, ita: sed risisti.

16 Cum ergo surrexissent inde viri, direxerunt oculos contra Sodomam: et Abraham simul gradiebatur, deducens eos.

17 Dixitque Dominus: Num celare potero Abraham quæ gesturus sum:

18 Cum futurus sit in gentem magnam ac robustissimam, et BENEDICENDÆ sint in illo omnes nationes terræ?

19 Scio enim quod præcepturus sit filiis suis, et domui suæ post se, ut custodiant viam Domini, et faciant judicium et justitiam: ut adducat Dominus propter Abraham omnia quæ locutus est ad eum.

20 Dixit itaque Dominus: Clamor Sodomorum et Gomorrhæ multiplicatus est, et peccatum eorum aggravatum est nimis.

21 Descendam et videbo, utrum clamorem, qui venit ad me, opere compleverint: an non est ita, ut sciam.

22 Converteruntque se inde, et abierunt Sodomam: Abraham vero adhuc stabat coram Domino.

23 Et appropinquans ait: Numquid perdes justum cum impio?

24 Si fuerint quinquaginta justi in civitate, peribunt simul? et non parces loco illi propter quinquaginta justos, si fuerint in eo?

25 Absit a te, ut rem hanc facias, et occidas justum cum impio, fiatque justus sicut impius, non est hoc tuum: qui judicas omnem terram, nequaquam facies judicium hoc.

26 Dixitque Dominus ad eum: Si invenero Sodomis, quinquaginta justos in medio civitatis, dimittam omni loco propter eos.

27 Respondensque Abraham, ait: Quia semel cœpi, loquar ad Dominum meum, cum sim pulvis et cinis.

28 Quid si minus quinquaginta justis quinque fuerint? delebis, propter quadraginta quinque, universam urbem? Et ait: Non delebo, si invenero ibi quadraginta quinque.

29 Rursumque locutus est ad eum: Sin autem quadraginta ibi inventi fuerint, quid facies? Ait: Non percutiam propter quadraginta.

30 Ne quæso, inquit, indigneris, Domine, si loquar: Quid si ibi inventi fuerint trginta? Respondit: Non faciam, si invenero ibi triginta.

31 Quia semel, ait, cœpi, loquar ad Dominum meum: Quid si ibi inventi fuerint viginti? Ait: Non interficiam propter viginti.

32 Obsecro, inquit, ne irascaris, Domine, si loquar adhuc semel: Quid si inventi fuerint ibi decem? Et dixit, Non delebo propter decem.

33 Abiitque Dominus, postquam cessavit loqui ad Abraham: et ille reversus est in locum suum.

19

1 Veneruntque duo Angeli Sodomam vespere, et sedente Lot in foribus civitatis. Qui cum vidisset eos, surrexit, et ivit obviam eis: adoravitque pronus in terram,

2 Et dixit: Obsecro, domimi, declinate in domum pueri vestri, et manete ibi: lavate pedes vestrols, et mane proficiscemini in viam

vestram. Qui dixerunt: Minime, sed in platea manebimus.

3 Compulit illos oppido ut diverterent and eum: ingressisque domum illius fecit convivium, et coxit azyma; et comederunt.

4 Prius autem quam irent cubitum, viri civitatis vallaverunt domum a puero usque ad senem, omnis populus simul.

5 Vocaveruntque Lot, et dixerunt ei: Ubi sunt viri qui introierunt ad te nocte? educ illos huc, ut cognoscamus eos.

6 Egressus ad eos Lot, post tergum occludens ostium, ait:

7 Nolite, quæso, fratres mei, nolite malum hoc facere.

8 Habeo duas filias, quæ necdum cognoverunt virum: educam eas ad vos, et abutimini eis sicut vobis placuerit, dummodo viris istis nihil mali faciatis, quia ingressi sunt sub umbra culminis mei.

9 At illi dixerunt: Recede illuc. Et rursus: Ingressus es, inquiunt, ut advena; numquid ut judices? te ergo ipsum magis quam hos affligemus. Vimque faciebant Lot vehementissime: jamque prope erat ut effringerent fores.

10 Et ecce miserunt manum viri, et introduxerunt ad se Lot, clauseruntque ostium:

11 Et eos, qui foris erant, percusserunt cæcitate a minimo usque ad maximum, ita ut ostium invenire non possent.

12 Dixerunt autem ad Lot: Habes hic quempiam tuorum? generum, aut filios, aut filias, omnes, qui tui sunt, educ de urbe hac:

13 Delebimus enim locum istum, eo quod increverit clamor eorum coram Domino, qui misit nos, ut perdamus illos.

14 Egressus itaque Lot, locutus est ad generos suos qui accepturi erant filias ejus, et dixit: Surgite, egredimini de loco isto; quia delebit Dominus civitatem hanc. Et visus est eis quasi ludens loqui.

15 Cumque esset mane, cogebant eum

angeli, dicentes: Surge, tolle uxorem tuam, et duas filias quas habes: ne et tu pariter pereas in scelere civitatis.

16 Dissimulante illo, apprehenderunt manum ejus, et manum uxoris, ac duarum filiarum ejus, eo quod parceret Dominus illi.

17 Eduxeruntque eum, et posuerunt extra civitatem: ibique locuti sunt ad eum, dicentes: Salva animam tuam: noli respicere post tergum, nec stes in omni circa regione: sed in monte sal vum te fac, ne et tu simul pereas.

18 Dixitque Lot ad eos: Quæso, Domine mi,

19 Quia invenit servus tuus gratiam coram te, et magnificasti misericordiam tuam quam fecisti mecum, ut salvares animam meam, nec possum in monte salvari, ne forte apprehendat me malum, et moriar;

20 Est civitas hæc juxta, ad quam possum fugere, parva, et salvabor in ea: numquid non modica est, et vivet anima mea?

21 Dixitque ad eum: Ecce etiam in hoc suscepi preces tuas, ut non subvertam urbem pro qua locutus es.

22 Festina et salvare ibi: quia non potero facere quidquam donec ingrediaris illuc. Idcirco vocatum est nomen urbis illius Segor.

23 Sol egressus est super terram, et Lot ingressus est Segor.

24 Igitur Dominus pluit super Sodomam et Gomorrham sulphur et ignem a Domino de cœlo:

25 Et subvertit civitates has, et omnem circa regionem, universos habitatores urbium, et cuncta terræ virentia.

26 Respiciensque uxor ejus post se, versa est in statuam salis.

27 Abraham autem consurgens mane, ubi steterat prius cum Domino,

28 Intuitus est Sodomam et Gomorrham, et universam terram regionis illius: viditque ascendentem favillam de terra quasi fornacis fumum.

Exodus 25:31–7

31 Facies et candelabrum ductile de auro mundissimo, hastile ejus, et calamos, scyphos, et sphærulas, ac lilia ex ipso procedentia.

32 Sex calami egredientur de lateribus, tres ex uno latere, et tres ex altero.

33 Tres scyphi quasi in nucis modum per calamos singulos, sphærulaque simul et lilium: et tres similiter scyphi instar nucis in calamo altero, sphærulaque simul et lilium: hoc erit opus sex calamorum, qui producendi sunt de hastili:

34 In ipso autem candelabro erunt quatuor scyphi in nucis modum, sphærulaque per singulos, et lilia.

35 Sphærulæ sub duobus calamis per tria loca, qui simul sex fiunt, procedentes de hastili uno.

36 Et sphærulæ igitur et calami ex ipso erunt, universa ductilia de auro purissimo.

37 Facies et lucernas septem, et pones eas super candelabrum, ut luceant ex adverso.

2 Chronicles 36:11–21

11 Viginti et unius anni erat Sedecias cum regnare cœpisset, et undecim annis regnavit in Jerusalem:

12 Fecitque malum in oculis Domini Dei sui, nec erubuit faciem Jeremiæ prophetæ, loquentis ad se ex ore Domini.

13 A rege quoque Nabuchodonosor recessit, qui adjuraverat eum per Deum: et induravit cervicem suam et cor, ut non reverteretur ad Dominum Deum Israel.

14 Sed et universi principes sacerdotum, et populus, prævaricati sunt inique juxta universas abominationes Gentium, et polluerunt domum Domini, quam sanctificaverat sibi in Jerusalem.

15 Mittebat autem Dominus Deus patrum suorum ad illos per manum nunciorum suorum de nocte consurgens, et quotidie commonens: eo quod parceret populo et habitaculo suo.

16 At illi subsannabant nuncios Dei, et parvipendebant sermones ejus, illudebantque prophetis, donec ascenderet furor Domini in populum ejus, et esset nulla curatio.

17 Adduxit enim super eos regem Chaldæorum, et interfecit juvenes eorum gladio in domo sanctuarii sui, non est misertus adolescentis, et virginis, et senis, nec decrepiti quidem, sed omnes tradidit in manibus ejus.

18 Universaque vasa domus Domini tam majora, quam minora, et thesauros templi, et regis, et principum, transtulit in Babylonem.

19 Incenderunt hostes domum Dei, destruxeruntque murum Jerusalem, universas turres combusserunt, et quidquid pretiosum fuerat, demoliti sunt.

20 Siquis evaserat gladium, ductus in Babylonem servivit regi et filiis ejus, donec imperaret rex Persarum,

21 Et compleretur sermo Domini ex ore Jeremiæ, et celebraret terra sabbata sua: cunctis enim diebus desolationis egit sabbatum usque dum complerentur septuaginta anni.

Jeremiah 52:1-26

1 Filius viginti et unius anni erat Sedecias cum regnare cœpisset: et undecim annis regnavit in Jerusalem, et nomen matris ejus Amital, filia Jeremiæ de Lobna.

2 Et fecit malum in oculis Domini, juxta omnia quæ fecerat Joakim.

3 Quoniam furor Domini erat in Jerusalem et in Juda usquequo projiceret eos a facie sua: et recessit Sedecias a rege Babylonis.

4 Factum est autem in anno nono regni ejus, in mense decimo, decima mensis: venit Nabuchodonosor rex Babylonis, ipse, et omnis exercitus ejus adversus Jerusalem, et obsederunt eam, et ædificaverunt contra eam munitiones in circuitu.

5 Et fuit civitas obsessa usque ad undecimum annum regis Sedeciæ.

6 Mense autem quarto, nona mensis, obtinuit fames civitatem: et non erant alimenta populo terræ.

7 Et dirupta est civitas, et omnes viri bellatores ejus fugerunt, exieruntque de civitate nocte per viam portæ, quæ est inter duos muros, et ducit ad hortum regis (Chaldæis obsidentibus urbem in gyro) et abierunt per viam, quæ ducit in eremum.

8 Persecutus est autem Chaldæorum exercitus regem: et apprehenderunt Sedeciam in deserto, quod est juxta Jericho: et omnis comitatus ejus diffugit ab eo.

9 Cumque comprehendissent regem, adduxerunt eum ad regem Babylonis in Reblatha, quæ est in terra Emath: et locutus est ad eum judicia.

10 Et jugulavit rex Babylonis filios Sedeciæ in oculis ejus: sed et omnes principes Juda occidit in Reblatha.

11 Et oculis Sedeciæ eruit, et vinxit eum compedibus, et adduxit eum rex Babylonis in Babylonem, et posuit eum in domo carceris usque ad diem mortis ejus.

12 In mense autem quinto, decima mensis, ipse est annus nonusdecimus Nabuchodonosor regis Babylonis: venit Nabuzardan princeps militiæ qui stabat coram rege Babylonis in Jerusalem:

13 Et incendit domum Domini, et domum regis, et omnes domos Jerusalem, et omnem domum magnam igni combussit.

14 Et totum murum Jerusalem per circuitum destruxit, cunctus exercitus Chaldæorum, qui erat cum magistro militiæ.

15 De pauperibus autem populi, et de reliquo vulgo, quod remanserat in civitate, et de perfugis, qui transfugerant ad regem Babylonis, et ceteros de multitudine, transtulit Nabuzardan princeps militiæ.

16 De pauperibus vero terræ reliquit Nabuzardan princeps militiæ vinitores, et agricolas.

17 Columnas quoque æreas, quæ erant in domo Domini, et bases, et mare æneum, quod erat in domo Domini, confregerunt Chaldæi, et tulerunt omne æs eorum in Babylonem.

18 Et lebetes, et creagras, et psalteria, et phialas, et mortariola, et omnia vasa ærea, quæ in ministerio fuerant, tulerunt:

19 Et hydrias, et thymiamateria, et urceos, et pelves, et candelabra, et mortaria, et cyathos: quotquot aurea, aurea: et quotquot argentea, argentea, tulit magister militiæ:

20 Et columnas duas, et mare unum, et vitulos duodecim æreos, qui erant sub basibus, quas fecerat rex Salomon in domo Domini: non erat pondus æris omnium horum vasorum.

21 De columnis autem, decem et octo cubiti altitudinis erant in columna una, et funiculus duodecim cubitorum circuibat eam: porro grossitudo ejus, quattuor digitorum, et intrinsecus cava erat.

22 Et capitella super utramque ærea: altitudo capitelli unius quinque cubitorum: et

retiacula, et malogranata super coronam in cir-
cuitu, omnia ærea. Similiter columnæ secundæ,
et malogranata.

23 Et fuerunt malogranata nonagintasex
dependentia: et omnia malogranata centum,
retiaculis circumdabantur.

24 Et tulit magister militiæ Saraiam sacer-
dotem primum, et Sophoniam sacerdotem
secundum: et tres custodes vestibuli.

25 Et de civitate tulit eunuchum unum, qui

erat præpositus super viros bellatores: et septem
viros de his, qui videbant faciem regis, qui
inventi sunt in civitate: et scribam principem
militum, qui probabat tyrones: et sexaginta
viros de populo terræ, qui inventi sunt in medio
civitatis.

26 Tulit autem eos Nabuzardan magister
militiæ, et duxit eos ad regem Babylonis in
Reblatha.

Daniel 4:27–5:31

27 Responditque rex, et ait: Nonne hæc est
Babylon magna, quam ego ædificavi in domum
regni, in robore fortitu dinis meæ, et in gloria
decoris mei?

28 Cumque sermo adhuc esset in ore regis,
vox de cœlo ruit: Tibi dicitur,
Nabuchodonosor rex: Regnum tuum transibit
a te,

29 Et ab hominibus ejicient te, et cum
bestiis et feris erit habitatio tua: fœnum quasi
bos comedes, et septem tempora mutabuntur
super te, donec scias quod dominetur Excelsus
in regno hominum, et cuicumque voluerit, det
illud.

30 Eadem hora sermo completus est super
Nabuchodonosor, et ex hominibus abjectus est,
et fœnum ut bos comedit, et rore cœli corpus
ejus infectum est: donec capilli ejus in
similitudinem aquilarum crescerent, et ungues
ejus quasi avium.

31 Igitur post finem dierum ego
Nabuchodonosor oculos meos ad cœlum levavi,
et sensus meus redditus est mihi: et Altissimo
benedixi, et viventem in sempiternum laudavi,
et glorificavi: quia potestas ejus potestas sem-
piterna, et regnum ejus in generationem et
generationem.

32 Et omnes habitatores terræ apud eum in
nihilum reputati sunt: juxta voluntatem enim
suam facit tam in virtutibus cœli quam in hab-
itatoribus terræ: et non est qui resistat manui
ejus, et dicat ei: Quare fecisti?

33 In ipso tempore sensus meus reversus est
ad me, et ad honorem regni mei, decoremque
perveni: et figura mea reversa est ad me: et
optimates mei, et magistratus mei requisierunt
me, et in regno meo restitutus sum: et magnifi-
centia amplior addita est mihi.

34 Nunc igitur ego Nabuchodonosor laudo,
et magnifico, et glorifico regem cœli: quia
omnia opera ejus vera, et viæ ejus judicia, et
gradientes in superbia potest humiliare.

5

1 Baltassar rex fecit grande convivium
optimatibus suis mille: et unusquisque secun-
dum suam bibebat ætatem.

2 Præcepit ergo jam temulentus ut afferren-
tur vasa aurea et argentea, quæ asportaverat
Nabuchodonosor pater ejus de templo, quod

fuit in Jerusalem, ut biberent in eis rex, et
optimates ejus, uxoresque ejus, et concubinæ.

3 Tunc allata sunt vasa aurea, et argentea,
quæ asportaverat de templo, quod fuerat in
Jerusalem: et biberunt in eis rex, et optimates
ejus, uxores et concubinæ illius.

4 Bibebant vinum, et laudabant deos suos
aureos, et argenteos, æreos, ferreos, ligneosque
et lapideos.

5 In eadem hora apparuerunt digiti, quasi
manus hominis scribentis contra candelabrum
in superficie parietis aulæ regiæ: et rex
aspiciebat articulos manus scribentis.

6 Tunc facies regis commutata est, et
cogitationes ejus conturbabant eum: et com-
pages renum ejus solvebantur, et genua ejus ad
se invicem collidebantur.

7 Exclamavit itaque rex fortiter ut
introducerent magos, Chaldæos, et aruspices.
Et proloquens rex ait sapientibus Babylonis:
Quicumque legerit scripturam hanc, et inter-
pretationem ejus manifestam mihi fecerit, pur-
pura vestietur, et torquem auream habebit in
collo, et tertius in regno meo erit.

8 Tunc ingressi omnes sapientes regis non
potuerunt nec scripturam legere, nec inter-
pretationem indicare regi.

9 Unde rex Baltassar satis conturbatus est,
et vultus illius immutatus est, sed et optimates
ejus turbabantur.

10 Regina autem pro re, quæ acciderat regi,
et optimatibus ejus, domum convivii ingressa
est: et proloquens ait: Rex, in æternum vive:
non te conturbent cogitationes tuæ, neque
facies tua immutetur.

11 Est vir in regno tuo, qui spiritum deorum
sanctorum habet in se: et in diebus patris tui
scientia et sapientia inventæ sunt in eo: nam et
rex Nabuchodonosor pater tuus principem
magorum, incantatorum, Chaldæorum, et aru-
spicum constituit eum, pater, inquam, tuus, o
rex·

12 Quia spiritus amplior, et prudentia,
intelligentiaque et interpretatio somniorum, et
ostensio secretorum, ac solutio ligatorum
inventæ sunt in eo, hoc est in Daniele: cui rex
posuit nomen Baltassar: nunc itaque Daniel
vocetur, et interpretationem narrabit.

13 Igitur introductus est Daniel coram rege.
Ad quem præfatus rex ait: Tu es Daniel de filiis

captivitatis Judæ, quem adduxit pater meus rex de Judæa?

14 Audivi de te quoniam spiritum deorum habeas: et scientia, intelligentiaque, ac sapientia, ampliores inventæ sunt in te.

15 Et nunc introgressi sunt in conspectu meo sapientes magi, ut scripturam hanc legerent, et interpretationem ejus indicarent mihi: et nequiverunt sensum hujus sermonis edicere.

16 Porro ego audivi de te, quod possis obscura interpretari, et ligata dissolvere: si ergo vales scripturam legere, et interpretationem ejus indicare mihi, purpura vestieris, et torquem auream circa collum tuum habebis, et tertius in regno meo princeps eris.

17 Ad quæ respondens Daniel, ait coram rege: Munera tua sint tibi, et dona domus tuæ alteri da: scripturam autem legam tibi, rex, et interpretationem ejus ostendam tibi.

18 O rex, Deus altissimus regnum, et magnificentiam, gloriam, et honorem dedit Nabuchodonosor patri tuo.

19 Et propter magnificentiam, quam dederat ei, universi populi, tribus, et linguæ tremebant, et metuebant eum: quos volebat, interficiebat: et quos volebat, percutiebat: et quos volebat, exaltabat: et quos volebat, humiliabat.

20 Quando autem elevatum est cor ejus, et spiritus illius obfirmatus est ad superbiam, depositus est de solio regni sui, et gloria ejus ablata est:

21 Et a filiis hominum ejectus est, sed et cor ejus cum bestiis positum est, et cum onagris erat habitatio ejus: fœnum quoque ut bos comedebat, et rore cœli corpus ejus infectum est donec cognosceret quòd potestatem haberet Altissimus in regno hominum: et quemcumque voluerit, suscitabit super illud.

22 Tu quoque filius ejus Baltassar, non humiliasti cor tuum, cum scires hæc omnia:

23 Sed adversum Dominatorem cœli elevatus es: et vasa domus ejus allata sunt coram te: et tu, et optimates tui, et uxores tuæ, et concubinæ tuæ vinum bibistis in eis: deos quoque argenteos, et aureos, et æreos, ferreos, ligneosque et lapideos, qui non vident, neque audiunt, neque sentiunt, laudasti: porro Deum, qui habet flatum tuum in manu sua, et omnes vias tuas, non glorificasti.

24 Idcirco ab eo missus est articulus manus, quæ scripsit hoc, quod exaratum est.

25 Hæc est autem scriptura, quæ digesta est: MANE, THECEL, PHARES.

26 Et hæc est interpretatio sermonis: MANE: numeravit Deus regnum tuum, et complevit illud.

27 THECEL: appensus es in statera, et inventus es minus habens.

28 PHARES: divisum est regnum tuum, et datum est Medis, et Persis.

29 Tunc jubente rege indutus est Daniel purpura, et circumdata est torques aurea collo ejus: et prædicatum est de eo quod haberet potestatem tertius in regno suo.

30 Eadem nocte interfectus est Baltassar rex Chaldæus.

31 Et Darius Medus successit in regnum annos natus sexagintaduos.

St Matthew 22:1–14

1 Et respondens Jesus, dixit iterum in parabolis eis, dicens:

2 Simile factum est regnum cœlorum homini regi, qui fecit nuptias filio suo.

3 Et misit servos suos vocare invitatos ad nuptias, et nolebant venire.

4 Iterum misit alios servos, dicens: Dicite invitatis: Ecce prandium meum paravi, tauri mei et altilia occisa sunt, et omnia parata: venite ad nuptias.

5 Illi autem neglexerunt: et abierunt, alius in villam suam, alius vero ad negotiationem suam:

6 Reliqui vero tenuerunt servos ejus, et contumeliis affectos occiderunt.

7 Rex autem cum audisset, iratus est: et missis exercitibus suis, perdidit homicidas illos, et civitatem illorum succendit.

8 Tunc ait servis suis: Nuptiæ quidem paratæ sunt, sed qui invitati erant, non fuerunt digni.

9 Ite ergo ad exitus viarum, et quoscumque inveneritis, vocate ad nuptias.

10 Et egressi servi ejus in vias, congregaverunt omnes, quos invenerunt, malos et bonos: et impletæ sunt nuptiæ discumbentium.

11 Intravit autem rex ut videret discumbentes, et vidit ibi hominem non vestitum veste nuptiali.

12 Et ai illi: Amice, quomodo huc intrasti non habens vestem nuptialem? At ille obmutuit.

13 Tunc dixit rex ministris: Ligatis manibus et pedibus ejus, mittite eum in tenebras exteriores: ibi erit fletus, et stridor dentium.

14 Multi enim sunt vocati, pauci vero electi.

St Luke 14:16–24

16 At ipse dixit ei: Homo quidam fecit cœnam magnam, et vocavit multos.

17 Et misit servum suum hora cœnæ dicere invitatis ut venirent, quia jam parata sunt omnia.

18 Et cœperunt simul omnes excusare.

Primus dixit ei: Villam emi, et necesse habeo exire, et videre illam: rogo te habe me excusatum.

19 Et alter dixit: Juga boum emi quinque, et eo probare illa: rogo te habe me excusatum.

20 Et alius dixit: Uxorem duxi et ideo non possum venire.

21 Et reversus servus nunciavit hæc domino suo. Tunc iratus paterfamilias, dixit servo suo: Exi cito in plateas et vicos civitatis: et

pauperes, ac debiles, et cæcos, et claudos introduc huc.

22 Et ait servus: Domine, factum est ut imperasti, et adhuc locus est.

23 Et ait dominus servo: Exi in vias, et sepes: et compelle intrare, ut impleatur domus mea.

24 Dico autem vobis quod nemo virorum illorum, qui vocati sunt, gustabit cœnam meam.

3 *Patience*

Jonah: complete

I

1 Et factum est verbum Domini ad Jonam filium Amathi, dicens:

2 Surge, et vade in Niniven civitatem grandem, et prædica in ea; quia ascendit malitia ejus coram me.

3 Et surrexit Jonas, ut fugeret in Tharsis a facie Domini, et descendit in Joppen, et invenit navem euntem in Tharsis: et dedit naulum ejus, et descendit in eam ut iret cum eis in Tharsis a facie Domini.

4 Dominus autem misit ventum magnum in mare: et facta est tempestas magna in mari, et navis periclitabatur conteri.

5 Et timuerunt nautæ, et clamaverunt viri ad deum suum: et miserunt vasa, quæ erant in navi, in mare, ut alleviaretur ab eis: et Jonas descendit ad interiora navis, et dormiebat sopore gravi.

6 Et accessit ad eum gubernator, et dixit ei: Quid tu sopore deprimeris? surge, invoca Deum tuum, si forte recogitet Deus de nobis, et non pereamus.

7 Et dixit vir ad collegam suum: Venite, et mittamus sortes, et sciamus quare hoc malum sit nobis. Et miserunt sortes: et cecidit sors super Jonam.

8 Et dixerunt ad eum: Indica nobis cujus causa malum istud sit nobis: quod est opus tuum? quæ terra tua? et quo vadis? vel ex quo populo es tu?

9 Et dixit ad eos: Hebræus ego sum et Dominum Deum cœli ego timeo, qui fecit mare et aridam.

10 Et timuerunt viri timore magno, et dixerunt ad eum: Quid hoc fecisti? (Cognoverunt enim viri quod a facie Domini fugeret, quia indicaverat eis.)

11 Et dixerunt ad eum: Quid faciemus tibi, et cessabit mare a nobis? quia mare ibat, et intumescebat.

12 Et dixit ad eos: Tollite me, et mittite in mare, et cessabit mare a vobis: scio enim ego quoniam propter me tempestas hæc grandis venit super vos.

13 Et remigabant viri ut reverterentur ad aridam, et non valebant: quia mare ibat, et intumescebat super eos.

14 Et clamaverunt ad Dominum, et dixer-

unt: Quæsumus, Domine, ne pereamus in anima viri istius, et ne des super nos sanguinem innocentem: quia tu, Domine, sicut voluisti, fecisti.

15 Et tulerunt Jonam, et miserunt in mare: et stetit mare a fervore suo.

16 Et timuerunt viri timore magno Dominum, et immolaverunt hostias Domino, et voverunt vota.

2

1 Et præparavit Dominus piscem grandem ut deglutiret Jonam: et erat Jonas in ventre piscis tribus diebus, et tribus noctibus.

2 Et oravit Jonas ad Dominum Deum suum de ventre piscis.

3 Et dixit: Clamavi de tribulatione mea ad Dominum, et exaudivit me: de ventre interi clamavi, et exaudisti vocem meam.

4 Et projecisti me in profundum in corde maris, et flumen circumdedit me: omnes gurgites tui, et fluctus tui super me transierunt.

5 Et ego dixi: Abjectus sum a conspectu oculorum tuorum: verumtamen rursus videbo templum sanctum tuum.

6 Circumdederunt me aquæ usque ad animam: abyssus vallavit me, pelagus operuit caput meum.

7 Ad extrema montium descendi: terræ vectes concluserunt me in æternum: et sublevabis de corruptione vitam meam, Domine, Deus meus.

8 Cum angustiaretur in me anima mea, Domini recordatus sum: ut veniat ad te oratio mea ad templum sanctum tuum.

9 Qui custodiunt vanitates frustra, misericordiam suam derelinquunt.

10 Ego autem in voce laudis immolabo tibi: quæcumque vovi, reddam pro salute Domino.

11 Et dixit Dominus pisci: et evomuit Jonam in aridam.

3

1 Et factum est verbum Domini ad Jonam secundo, dicens:

2 Surge, et vade in Niniven civitatem magnam: et prædica in ea prædicationem, quam ego loquor ad te.

3 Et surrexit Jonas, et abiit in Niniven juxta

verbum Domini: et Ninive erat civitas magna itinere trium dierum.

4 Et cœpit Jonas introire in civitatem itinere diei unius: et clamavit, et dixit: Adhuc quadraginta dies, et Ninive subvertetur.

5 Et crediderunt viri Ninivitæ in Deum: et prædicaverunt jejunium, et vestiti sunt saccis a majore usque ad minorem.

6 Et pervenit verbum ad regem Ninive: et surrexit de solio suo, et abjecit vestimentum suum a se, et indutus est sacco, et sedit in cinere.

7 Et clamavit, et dixit in Ninive ex ore regis et principum ejus, dicens: Homines, et jumenta, et boves, et pecora non gustent quidquam: nec pascantur, et aquam non bibant.

8 Et operiantur saccis homines, et jumenta, et clament ad Dominum in fortitudine, et convertatur vir a via sua mala, et ab iniquitate, quæ est in manibus eorum.

9 Quis scit si convertatur, et ignoscat Deus: et revertatur a furore iræ suæ, et non peribimus?

10 Et vidit Deus opera eorum, quia conversi sunt de via sua mala: et misertus est Deus super malitiam, quam locutus fuerat ut faceret eis, et non fecit.

4

1 Et afflictus est Jonas afflictione magna, et iratus est:

2 Et oravit ad Dominum, et dixit: Obsecro, Domine, numquid non hoc est verbum meum, cum adhuc essem in terra mea? propter hoc præoccupavi ut fugerem in Tharsis: scio enim quia tu Deus clemens, et misericors es, patiens, et multæ miserationis, et ignoscens super malitia.

3 Et nunc, Domine, tolle quæso animam meam a me: quia melior est mihi mors quam vita.

4 Et dixit Dominus: Putasne bene irasceris tu?

5 Et egressus est Jonas de civitate, et sedit contra Orientem civitatis: et fecit sibimet umbraculum ibi, et sedebat subter illud in umbra, donec videret quid accideret civitati.

6 Et præparavit Dominus Deus hederam, et ascendit super caput Jonæ, ut esset umbra super caput ejus, et protegeret eum: laboraverat enim: et lætatus est Jonas super hedera, lætitia magna.

7 Et paravit Deus vermem ascensu diluculi in crastinum: et percussit hederam, et exaruit.

8 Et cum ortus fuisset sol, præcepit Dominus vento calido, et urenti: et percussit sol super caput Jonæ, et æstuabat: et petivit animæ suæ ut moreretur, et dixit: Melius est mihi mori, quam vivere.

9 Et dixit Dominus ad Jonam: Putasne bene irasceris tu super hedera? Et dixit: Bene irascor ego usque ad mortem.

10 Et dixit Dominus: Tu doles super hederam, in qua non laborasti, neque fecisti ut cresceret: quæ sub una nocte nata est, et sub una nocte periit.

11 Et ego non parcam Ninive civitati magnæ, in qua sunt plusquam centum viginti millia hominum, qui nesciunt quid sit inter dexteram et sinistram suam, et jumenta multa?

St Matthew 5:1–10

1 Videns autem Jesus turbas, ascendit in montem, et cum sedisset, accesserunt ad eum discipuli ejus:

2 Et aperiens os suum docebat eos, dicens:

3 Beati pauperes spiritu: quoniam ipsorum est regnum cœlorum.

4 Beati mites: quoniam ipsi possidebunt terram.

5 Beati, qui lugent: quoniam ipsi consolabuntur.

6 Beati, qui esuriunt et sitiunt justitiam: quoniam ipsi saturabuntur.

7 Beati misericordes: quoniam ipsi misericordiam consequentur.

8 Beati mundo corde: quoniam ipsi Deum videbunt.

9 Beati pacifici: quoniam filii Dei vocabuntur.

10 Beati, qui persecutionem patiuntur propter justitiam: quoniam ipsorum est regnum cœlorum:

Additional Notes

The following are some of the more significant differences in treatment or interpretation of the text between the present edition and *Cleanness* edited by J. J. Anderson (Manchester and New York, 1977).

15–16. Anderson keeps MS *sulped*, understanding *ar* again from the previous clause (subject *Boþe God and His gere*); this seems unlikely in view of the difficulty it creates in understanding *þay* as subject for *cachen*.

28. We have followed Gollancz and Menner in reading the MS *bone*, which we emend to *leue*. A reads *loue* (the 'biting' form of *bo* is very similar to *lo*) which he takes as a rare spelling for *lowe*.

40. *clutte traschez:* A cites the evidence of modern dialects in support of the sense 'old shoes' for *traschez* (as suggested by the *OED* s.v. *Trash* sb.). Note, however, that 'patched old shoes' would be out of order at this point (*cf. totez oute*, 41).

48. *in talle ne in tuch:* A ingeniously suggests that *talle* is from OF *ta(i)lle* 'bodily appearance, shape' and that *tuch* means here 'small part' (*cf. G* 120, 1301, 1677). Thus he translates the phrase 'in general appearance or in detail of dress'. This may well have been the poet's intention (it continues the dress-metaphor), though, in view of his predilection for puns, the more obvious 'in word or in deed' (Skeat's interpretation, followed by Menner and Gollancz) is not necessarily ruled out. It is worth noting that *talle* 'tale, account' is so spelt in *Pe* 865 (*tale* in catchwords at foot of previous page).

73. *ludych:* A suggests the meaning 'princely, noble', both here and in 1375 (deriving it from OE *leod* m. 'prince' rather than *leod* f. 'people').

78–9. Using different punctuation, A takes *þe wayferande frekez* as direct object of *forsettez*, and *on vche a syde þe cete aboute* as an adverbial phrase.

110. *þat demed as he deuised hade:* A convincingly construes this as a relative clause qualifying *sergauntez* 109: 'making proclamation (*lit.* those who made proclamation) as he had ordained'; there is thus no need to emend.

172. *lyued:* We have taken this as an instance of *OED live v²* 'give life to'. A's reading *lyned* (*u* and *n* are written identically in the MS) is quite possible in view of the sustained clothing metaphor of this passage; *lykyng*, however, would still be the neutral 'inclination, desire', rather than A's 'good disposition', since both good and bad deeds are in question.

215. Deriving the noun *metz* from OF *mes* 'proper distance or range for shooting' (here with the extended sense 'blow'), A renders the line 'Nevertheless, His blow was in keeping with the moderation of His nature'.

307. *I schal strenkle my distresse* is rendered by A 'I shall put forth my power'—a possible interpretation, with *strenkle* 'scatter' in the extended sense 'put forth' and *distresse* meaning 'force, power', as in 1160.

385. *dryȝe:* A relates this to OIcel *drjúgr* (see Glossary, *dryȝ(e)*, *dreȝ*), interpreting as 'secure'.

433. *roȝly:* Arguing that the MS form *roȝ* always represents 'rough', OE *rūh*, A suggests that here it occurs in a sense borrowed from OE *hrēoh* 'troubled' and is used substantivally to mean 'the troubled thing' (i.e. the ark). The line would then read: 'All that remained was that troubled vessel that the storm drives'.

473. *bot:* Following Thomas (*MLR*, 17 [1922], 65), A understands 'boat, the Ark'.

544. *þewez:* A translates 'good nature'.

863. *hit is your vylaynye:* A translates 'it is to your disgrace'.

891. *al wrank:* A reads *awrank*, arguing that the *l* has been deleted. This is a debatable point.

1057–64. A observes that the passage from *Le Roman de la Rose* used here is the same as that alluded to in *Pat* 30.

1076. *schroude-hous:* A provides the convincing gloss 'vestry, sacristy', comparing OE *scrūdelhūs*.

1107. A suggests that *Displayed* is pa.t. 'fell apart, was broken', and that *pryuyly* is used in a developed sense such as 'delicately, clearly'.

1287. *clene to wyrke:* A glosses 'in fine workmanship', *lit.* 'in working excellently', making the phrase directly dependent on *coyntyse*.

1383–4. A provides a useful note, complete with drawing, to explain the architectural references. However, his understanding of 1384 is: 'and horizontal paling set round about at closer intervals'.

1391. *med:* A suggests that this is derived from OE *gemede* 'agreeable, appropriate (to)'.

1396. A treats *Stepe* as an adv. 'brightly', *stayred* as pa.t. 'shone', and *stones* as 'gems'.

1402. A takes *strake* as a noun 'blast', and *trumpen* as a g.pl. used adjectivally, translating the line as an absolute construction: '(There was) a loud blast of trumpets, clamour in the hall'.

1405–12 (and **1441–88**). A provides an instructive note on the traditions of decorative art alluded to in the descriptions of the serving dishes and the Temple vessels.

1413. *nakeryn:* A follows Huntsman (*MP*, 73 [1975–6], 278) in taking 'nakers' to be horns rather than drums, both here and in *G* (118, 1016).

1459. A provides another good illustrated note (*cf.* 1383–4 above) on the architectural features.

1470. *Alabaundarynes:* A *alabaundeirynes*. The MS is indistinct and it is difficult to decide which reading is correct.

1478. *bi a cost:* A reads *bi acost* and glosses 'alongside', comparing OF *par a cost* with the same meaning. The vagueness of the noun *cost* makes this an attractive solution, though the adverbial phrase does not appear to be exactly paralleled elsewhere in ME.

1520. A translates: 'As each man was aged, (so) he drank from the cup', suggesting that the line renders the Vulgate Dan. 5:1 (*unusquisque secundum suam bibebat aetatem* 'everyone drank according to his age'). It is doubtful, however, whether the ME idiom supports this interpretation.

1542. *dispyses:* A retains MS *displayes*, glossing 'tears (open)' and comparing OF *despleier* ('tear to pieces' in Anglo-Norman).

1586. *chambre:* A glosses 'officers of the chamber', comparing Vulgate *optimatibus* 'nobles' (Dan. 5:10), and making reference to *OED chamber*, sense 4(b), and *MED chaumbre*, sense 5(b). However, although *chide to* is sparsely attested in the sense 'rail against, scold (somebody)', we feel that *to þe chambre* is idiomatically more likely to mean 'as far as the bedroom' (*cf.* Chaucer, *The House of Fame* 1927–30, and *OED to* prep., conj., adv., sense 3), and this interpretation is supported by the poet's account of the queen's movements in 1587–90.

1622. *vmbebrayde:* A is undoubtedly right in seeing the literal sense of this verb as 'embraced'. In view of the two senses of the analogous verb *halche, halse*, however, 'embrace' or 'salute, greet', it is possible that the latter is the meaning in this context.

1762–4. A is probably right in reading these lines as referring to ordinary townsfolk rather than Belshazzar's guests.